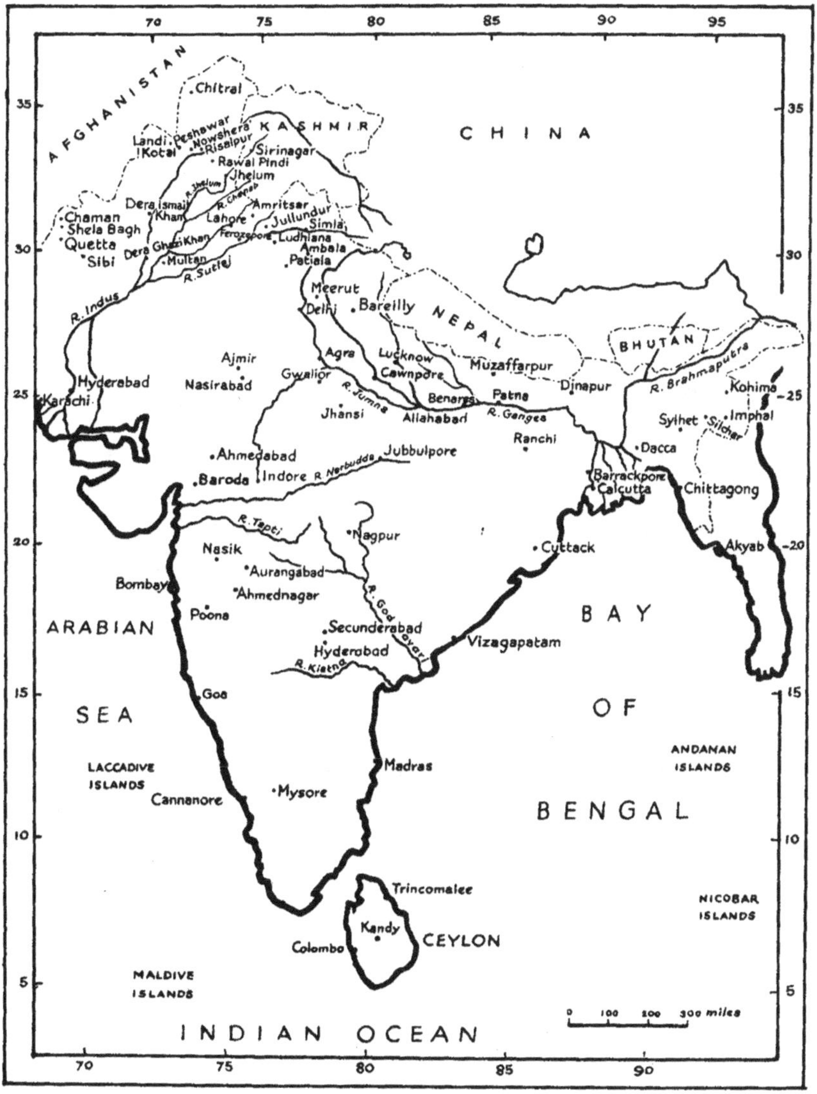

INDIA BEFORE SEPARATION — showing as far as possible places at which battalions of the 11th Sikh Regiment were from time to time stationed during the Second World War · 1939 to 1945 · and immediately before and after.

The SIKH Regiment in the Second World War

★

Colonel F. T. Birdwood
OBE

The Naval & Military Press Ltd

Published by
The Naval & Military Press Ltd
5 Riverside, Brambleside, Bellbrook
Industrial Estate, Uckfield, East Sussex,
TN22 1QQ England
Tel: +44 (0) 1825 749494
Fax: +44 (0) 1825 765701
www.naval-military-press.com
www.military-genealogy.com

In reprinting in facsimile from the original, any imperfections are inevitably reproduced and the quality may fall short of modern type and cartographic standards.

DEDICATION

For India, 1947 was a year of destiny. It marked the transition from dependency to responsible self-rule. It marked, too, an abrupt and violent change in the political pattern. A second new Dominion was born. Pakistan emerged to take its part, with a re-adjusted India, in the new order of Eastern nations.

So much could not happen without much individual change. Time-honoured relationships were severed—in especial in the organization and manning of the army. Regiments and corps with a tradition of service to the Crown, had to be separated out between India and Pakistan, and the British connection, in which so many diverse soldiers from east and west had found their life's work and pride in common loyalty to the united India of pre-separation days, had necessarily to be ended. There had been a comradeship in arms, in un-selfseeking loyalty and courage, and a fighting spirit above class and creed, which had brought the Indian Army to the height of its fame by the close of the Second World War, of which these pages are in some small part the record. But this chapter in the Indian Army's history had now to close.

So it is in some sense from the shadows that this story of the Sikh Regiment of the old days comes, but it is dedicated to the undying glory of the Sikhs and Punjabi-Mohammedans, the Indian and British officers, that then served it. May their fame live on.

"Their task is done. To us the calling high
To guard the simple things for which men die."

CONTENTS

	page
DEDICATION	iii
FOREWORD by General Sir Frank Messervy, K.C.S.I., K.B.E., C.B., D.S.O.	ix
INTRODUCTION	xi
PROLOGUE	xiii
H.M.S. *Sikh*	xviii

Chapter I. SEPTEMBER 1939 TO FEBRUARY 1940
Backscreen	1
1st Battalion	5
2nd Battalion	6
3rd Battalion	8
4th Battalion	8
5th Battalion	10

Chapter II. MARCH TO AUGUST 1940
Backscreen	11
1st Battalion	18
2nd Battalion	19
3rd Battalion	19
4th Battalion	19
5th Battalion	20
6th Battalion	20
7th Battalion	20

Chapter III. SEPTEMBER 1940 TO FEBRUARY 1941
Backscreen	21
1st Battalion	25
2nd Battalion	26
3rd Battalion	27
4th Battalion	27
5th Battalion	35
6th Battalion	35
7th Battalion	35

Chapter IV. MARCH TO AUGUST 1941   *page*
  Backscreen   39
  1st Battalion   49
  2nd Battalion   50
  3rd Battalion   56
  4th Battalion   59
  5th Battalion   64
  6th Battalion   65
  7th Battalion   65
  8th Battalion   67
  9th Battalion   68
  25th Battalion   68

Chapter V. SEPTEMBER 1941 TO FEBRUARY 1942
  Backscreen   70
  1st Battalion   85
  2nd Battalion   87
  3rd Battalion   90
  4th Battalion   91
  5th Battalion   106
  6th Battalion   146
  7th Battalion   147
  8th Battalion   148
  9th Battalion   151
  M.G. Battalion   152
  25th Battalion   152

Chapter VI. MARCH TO AUGUST 1942
  Backscreen   154
  1st Battalion   169
  2nd Battalion   184
  3rd Battalion   203
  4th Battalion   204
  6th Battalion   215
  7th Battalion   216
  14th Battalion   221
  M.G. Battalion   222
  25th Battalion   222
  26th Battalion   223
  8th Battalion   223
  9th Battalion   225

Chapter VII. SEPTEMBER 1942 TO FEBRUARY 1943	*page*
Backscreen	227
H.M.S. *Sikh*	238
1st Battalion	239
2nd Battalion	240
3rd Battalion	243
4th Battalion	244
6th Battalion	246
7th Battalion	247
14th Battalion	248
M.G. Battalion	248
15th Battalion	249
26th Battalion	249
Chapter VIII. MARCH TO AUGUST 1943	
Backscreen	250
1st Battalion	257
2nd Battalion	257
3rd Battalion	258
4th Battalion	259
6th Battalion	260
7th Battalion	264
14th Battalion	267
M.G. Battalion	268
15th Battalion	269
26th Battalion	269
Chapter IX. SEPTEMBER 1943 TO FEBRUARY 1944	
Backscreen	270
1st Battalion	279
2nd Battalion	284
3rd Battalion	284
4th Battalion	286
6th Battalion	286
7th Battalion	286
M.G. Battalion	289
14th Battalion	289
15th Battalion	290
26th Battalion	290

Chapter X. MARCH TO AUGUST 1944   *page*
  Backscreen   291
  1st Battalion   310
  2nd Battalion   336
  3rd Battalion   342
  4th Battalion   343
  6th Battalion   345
  7th Battalion   346
  M.G. Battalion   348
  14th Battalion   348
  15th Battalion   348
  26th Battalion   349

Chapter XI. SEPTEMBER 1944 TO FEBRUARY 1945
  Backscreen   350
  1st Battalion   364
  2nd Battalion   373
  3rd Battalion   383
  4th Battalion   386
  6th Battalion   390
  7th Battalion   391
  M.G. Battalion   391
  14th Battalion   399
  26th Battalion   399

Chapter XII. MARCH TO AUGUST 1945
  Backscreen   400
  1st Battalion   409
  2nd Battalion   429
  3rd Battalion   430
  4th Battalion   433
  6th Battalion   435
  7th Battalion   436
  M.G. Battalion   438
  26th Battalion   445

EPILOGUE   446
CONCLUSION   461
SUMMARY OF HONOURS AND AWARDS   462

WITH MAPS ILLUSTRATING VARIOUS PHASES OF THE CAMPAIGNS

FOREWORD

By General Sir Frank Messervy

K.C.S.I., K.B.E., C.B., D.S.O.

It is a great honour to me to have been asked to write this foreword to the history of the Sikh Regiment in the Second World War.

As I read the proud story of the exploits of the various battalions, so well presented in this book, many memories arise of those which it was my good fortune to have under my command.

There was the 4th Battalion in Eritrea with Gazelle Force, and again in the Western Desert with the 4th Indian Division—always ready for anything, cheerfully surmounting the greatest difficulties and dangers; companies staunchly lying doggo while German tanks over-ran them, but still there to deal with any infantry that might follow.

Then the 1st Battalion in Burma and Malaya, always magnificent in and out of action, a unit to which one could give the most severe task and know that it would be done. As I recall their many fine actions, that finest of all battle cries "Jo bole, so nihal, sat siri akal", rings in my ears. I remember, too, how the jawans looked upon it as my main duty as divisional commander to give them an extra tot of rum whenever I visited the Battalion.

Except for the Machine Gun Battalion in Burma in 1944, which upheld the high tradition of the Regiment, I did not serve with any of the other ten battalions.

But as one reads, so one is inspired by the great spirit of a great regiment, shining bright and clear in many places, overcoming every doubt, exultant in hard-won victory, undimmed in adversity. In fine achievement and victory, as the 2nd Battalion in Iraq, Persia, the Western Desert, and Italy. In defeat and disaster, as the 5th Battalion in Malaya, yet still fighting undaunted to the end. In the less glorious but essential duty of keeping the peace in Persia and Iraq, yet never losing efficiency, as the 3rd Battalion. In the enthusiastic training of all reinforcements for Burma, as the 14th Battalion. In keeping watch and ward on the frontiers of India, as the 6th, 7th and 15th Battalions. As infantry turned gunners, as the 8th and 9th Battalions. In monotonous but necessary garrison duties, as the 26th Battalion.

Behind the glory and achievements of all battalions lies the steady, solid, vital work of the Regimental Centre, the foundation of efficiency, the guardian of the regimental tradition and spirit.

It is this great spirit, bred of tradition and of firm trust and comradeship between British and Indian officers and Sikh and Mohammedan ranks, which made the Sikh Regiment what it was. Long may the same spirit remain in the Regiment of to-day.

Finally, we that live on, can never forget those comrades who, in giving their lives, gave so much that is great and good to the story of the Sikh Regiment. No living glory can transcend that of their supreme sacrifice. May they rest in peace.

INTRODUCTION

This record of the 11th Sikh Regiment in the Second World War is written in England far from direct sources of information. It is written at a time when the vast preponderance of officers and men who fought with the Regiment in the war have been released from the Service, and scattered to the four quarters of the compass.

India has been divided, and with it the Indian Army we knew. The Punjabi-Mohammedans, who played a gallant part in maintaining the traditions of the Sikh Regiment, have been drafted to Pakistan battalions, or released. The Regimental Centre, the focus of the Regiment's records, moved down at short notice from Nowshera, now in Pakistan, to Ambala; and with the departure from India and Pakistan of so many British officers, threads have been lost and links broken. Re-organization to conform with changed conditions necessarily takes up most of the energies of the officers now charged with this duty, so that gaps in the story have not always been filled—more especially in relation to the war effort of the Training Battalion, later the Regimental Centre, of which regrettably little information has been secured. One must hope that this may be put right when matters settle down.

Despite these difficulties, however, it has been possible to follow the detailed activities of most battalions of the Regiment during the late world war. For this, thanks are due in many cases to officers who filled in their spare time during their last hot weather in India writing up the story of their battalions. Among these may be mentioned the late Maj. D. O. T. Dykes, whose account of the raising of the 14th Battalion was completed only a week or so before his tragic murder at Baramullah in Kashmir. It is not possible to name all those officers who contributed to this record, but it is hoped that if these lines ever meet their eye, they will accept them as conveying the compiler's earnest thanks.

Other parts of the story have been taken from the excellent periodical letters battalions sent out. For the 1st Battalion's record, reliance has been placed on the commemorative history compiled by Lieut.-Col. G. C. Bamford, D.S.O. Our best thanks are due to Lieut.-Col. Bamford and the officers of the 1st K.G.O. Battalion for permission to draw upon this work so extensively. The story of the 5th Battalion's gallant but unavailing efforts in Malaya is taken verbatim from *A Diary of the 5th Battalion (D.C.O.) The Sikh Regiment in the Malaya Campaign—8th December,*

1941, to 15th February, 1942, written by Lieut.-Col. J. H. D. Parkin, D.S.O.

As regards the lay-out of the record, the decision to split it chronologically into six-monthly sections, was taken for a number of reasons. Material available varied as between battalions, while some battalions had a greater share than others in the more spectacular side of the war. Again, good anecdotal background to lighten the duller periods was not always forthcoming in all battalions. Such defects tend to be evened up by the method adopted. More important, however, than these, it seemed essential, if the record was to be a Regimental one, and not a collection of individual battalion stories, that the picture should be displayed as a whole against the common background of military action in all theatres. For this background, recourse has been made to a variety of sources, great and small, but much use has been made of the information given in Gen. J. F. C. Fuller's *The Second World War*, and to the Rt. Hon. Mr. Winston Churchill's work now being published under the same name.

The experiment has accordingly been attempted of dividing the record into fourteen parts, consisting of a prologue, which briefly locates battalions as at the beginning of hostilities, twelve six-monthly periods, carrying the record through from September 1939 to August 1945, and an epilogue to collect the scattered threads, and wind up the story. The six-monthly periods are in each case preceded by a reasonably detailed sketch of contemporary events on the various world fronts, and battalion stories are presented in numerical order against this background. Generally speaking, it will be found that operations on most fronts fit reasonably well into this concept, and that continuity is not seriously prejudiced. Again, as battalion stories come in the same order in each chapter, it will not be difficult for those desiring to follow the history of one particular battalion, to do so.

PROLOGUE

Prior to the outbreak of the Second World War, the 11th Sikh Regiment was composed of five Active Battalions and one Training Battalion. The Training Battalion, stationed permanently in Nowshera, in the North-West Frontier Province, acted generally as a recruit training unit and reservist centre, co-ordinating authority and clearing house, for the active battalions. It was designed to free them in war from as much as possible of administrative responsibility unconnected with operations. In peacetime, it could absorb the limited shocks of frontier campaigns, more especially when battalions involved acted under the "Special Procedure Pamphlet"; but for wars of magnitude, some considerable expansion would obviously be needed.

Training battalions were, then, the pivot on which the fighting efficiency of battalions in the field very much depended. No one could say what the daily impact of casualties, whether from enemy action or climatic stresses and disease might be. Unless reinforcements were trained and built up in advance, operations would be prejudiced and disaster might follow.

When the war broke out in September 1939, no one could doubt the possibility of its spreading, and increasing in violence. The opening moves made this sufficiently clear. The Polish land and air forces were shattered in an eighteen-day campaign, and the methods used, and treatment meted out to civilians, during and after the campaign, revealed a ruthlessness and resolution in keeping with Hitler's belief in "total war". None-the-less, her Western allies, to whom the Poles had looked, remained seemingly complacent, taking little apparent constructive action to force their will on the Nazis; and what came to be called the "phoney" or "twilight" war followed.

India's strategic policy was naturally tied to Britain's, and so long as this curious uncertainty or lethargy prevailed in the West, it was bound to colour the military outlook in India. No doubt the disassociation of Congress from the war effort had some indirect effect. At all events, in spite of the existence on India's north-western frontier of Russia, a power of unknown military capacity but of immense potentialities, whose active competition in the dismemberment of Poland shocked many, and whose official friendship with Germany was an established fact, we find little early evidence that the fighting services as a whole, including their training establishments, were placed on the war footing which the prospects warranted.

Apart from the odd circumstance that training battalions and regimental centres in India were never in fact mobilized throughout the war, one example may perhaps be allowed to show the slow burgeoning of the war effort over the first ten months after the outbreak. Naturally, in peacetime, finance had a controlling influence on the army's costs, and one aspect of this was what was known as the "man-day system".

It will be remembered that training battalions were responsible for watching the strengths of active battalions to ensure that they did not over-recruit and hence incur unnecessary expense. An account was therefore kept of the numbers of personnel in each active battalion, and it was part of the duty of the commandant of the training battalion to supervise this. As some flexibility was needed, active battalions were permitted to adjust their strengths to the changing needs of the day by temporarily going over-strength, provided that they showed a commensurate reduction later on. Such variations were tied rigidly to the financial year, at the close of which battalions were forbidden to show any excess expenditure of the man-days they had been credited when the year opened.

Manifestly, such a nicety of calculation, tied to the calendar, could not possibly work where wastage is unpredictable, but liable to be very heavy and continuous, and where trained drafts must be ready and waiting before the wastage occurred. Yet, the man-day code persisted even after the war had passed its "phoney" stage, and when the map of Europe was being daily re-fashioned by the Nazis. The strain this placed on responsible subordinate officers was great, and where no lead came from higher authority, it is hard to find fault with anyone for taking the initiative in the general interest. In point of fact, the then commandant of the Training Battalion, Lieut.-Col. D. H. Gordon, D.S.O., O.B.E., acted in this way, writing out to the commanders of the Active Battalions of the Regiment, in July 1940, to ignore the terms of the man-day order, and carry on "regardless". The fact that three weeks later, the man-day system was officially abandoned, is not to the point. Col. Gordon had no pre-knowledge of this intention.

That all policy was dealt with in this way is not for a moment to be supposed, but where it directly touched the troops it certainly made small appeal. Too little was known about the changes in Nazi tactics for fresh training policy to be introduced for some time, and when it was, essential equipment was not to be had. The spirit and will were there, as will be plain enough from the record that follows, but the strain on subordinate commanders and the strong feeling of frustration continued for a very long time.

It is as well to remember this when reflecting on the humdrum activities that filled the many months that were to pass before the 11th Sikh Regiment sent its first battalions overseas to the war.

Turning, now, to the individual battalions of the Regiment, a short account will be given of their whereabouts and activities during the immediately preceding years.

The 1st Battalion, 11th Sikh Regiment (King George's Own) (Ferozepur Sikhs)—the old 14th Sikhs—a Sikh class battalion, raised in 1846, and with a long record of service to its name, was stationed in Chittagong, with two companies in Comilla, when war broke out. It had moved east from Jubbulpore in March 1939 on the Bengal reliefs, and was presently mewed up in the sea of mud which invades Bengal in the monsoon. Anyone who has flown over the Sunderbans from Calcutta at that time of the year, or attempted to navigate a road vehicle between the paddy fields in the teeming rain, will understand what it meant to a fine battalion to be booked for a Bengal tour, with an internal security role.

1st Bn.

The men kept keen and cheerful, however, in their bamboo huts through a very severe monsoon, and earned a reputation with the Civil Government, which found expression in a reference by the Commissioner in Chittagong, which will be quoted in the next chapter.

Meanwhile, two unusual and interesting events may be noted. The first was the presentation to the Battalion of one of the Union Jacks which then flew day and night over the Residency at Lucknow from the 1st of January to the 1st of April. When replacements were hoisted, the old flags used to be offered to those with special claims to them. The Battalion's claim lay in its special battle honour: "Lucknow—Defence and Capture".

The other event, about the same time, in June, was the gift by Captain Harpal Singh Gill, on retiring from the Army in India Reserve of Officers. This took the form of a specially fitted shisham-wood box, designed to carry the Granth Sahib, Manjhi, and Channi Chaur on service. The gift was a timely one for the war-clouds were gathering, and, in the event, it enabled the Gurdwara to accompany the Battalion throughout the whole of the war.

The 2nd Royal Battalion, 11th Sikh Regiment (Ludhiana Sikhs) —the old 15th Sikhs—raised in 1846 in the same year as the 14th, and, like it, composed wholly of Sikhs, had moved down to

2nd Bn.

Nowshera from Waziristan, in 1938. It had taken a prominent part in the 1936-37 operations in Waziristan, including the night advance on the Iblanke, which set a new standard of tactical achievement in frontier warfare. It was also present at the operations round Arsal and the Sharawangi Tangi. These places are no more than names on the map since Pakistan withdrew her troops from Waziristan. But they rank high in history and in the traditions of the old Indian Army.

In Nowshera, the Battalion occupied Umbeyla Lines, adjoining those of the Training Battalion, at the extreme eastern end of the cantonment. On 22nd March, 1939, new colours were presented there by His Excellency Sir George Cunningham, the Governor of the North-West Frontier Province, in a colourful and impressive ceremony on the polo ground. The Battalion counted itself fortunate to have the services of Brig. (later Maj.-Gen.) A. E. Barstow, M.C., its Colonel, at that time commanding the Kohat Brigade, to assist in the ceremony, which was attended by a very large number of pensioners.

3rd Bn. *The 3rd Battalion, 11th Sikh Regiment (Rattray's Sikhs)*—formerly the 45th Sikhs—raised in 1856, and with an all-Sikh composition, had spent two good years in Chitral between 1936 and 1938. In a sense, the Battalion created history on the move there, inasmuch as one echelon was carried through from Rawalpindi by air—the first occasion on which troops had been moved by air in India. This makes curious reading in the light of the tremendous advances in air-borne lifts during the years that followed, and it to some extent fixes the standard of military experience in India at that time.

During its stay in Chitral, the Battalion was extensively filmed by a party from the London Film Company for *The Drum*. This took place in June, 1937, and all aspects of individual and collective training were included.

The following November, the troops were well shaken up by an earthquake. Chitral Fort had to be evacuated by the Company located there, until repaired and made safe; but there were no casualties.

In September, 1938, the Battalion left Chitral and went to Allahabad after a very brief halt at Nowshera. In October, most of the men went on five months furlough, and the Battalion was more or less in cadre form until March, 1939. The outbreak of war found it at normal duty in the very new, and very hot and dusty, barracks on the Ganges bank there.

4th Bn. *The 4th Battalion, 11th Sikh Regiment*—the old 36th Sikhs—raised in 1887 in Jullundur on an all-Sikh basis, had had its

composition altered after the First World War, to one of half Sikhs
and half Punjabi-Mohammedans. The Headquarters Company with
its Signals and Support Platoons, and administrative personnel,
etc., were mainly Sikh, but included a proportion of Punjabi
Mohammedans. Among the rifle companies, "A" and "C" Companies were Sikh, and "B" and "D" Companies Punjabi-Mohammedan. A four-year tour in Mardan alongside the Guides Cavalry
had been followed by a further two in the Khyber, and the Battalion
was awaiting move-orders to Delhi when war broke out.

    The *5th Battalion, 11th Sikh Regiment (Duke of Connaught's Own)*—earlier known as the 47th Sikhs—raised in 1901, had begun "indianizing" some years before. Organized on the same lines as the 4th Battalion, it had completed a four-year tour at Aurangabad in the Deccan by early 1939, and had moved up in February of that year to Razmak on the North-West Frontier.   5th Bn.

    It is convenient to mention here a special point of regimental interest concerning our relations with the Royal Navy.   H.M.S. *Sikh*

    During the First World War, one of the "S" class destroyers, built during the emergency war programme, had been named *Sikh*. The ship was not completed until the 29th June, 1918, and the circumstance went unnoticed in the Regiment.

    When, in due course, she was scrapped, her ship's bell was presented as a war souvenir to Rumania.

    Shortly before the Second World War broke out, the 4th Battalion had the happy idea of trying to get the bell back for the Quarter Guard. The British Military Attache in Bucharest took the matter up, and in due course, the bell was received.

    Meanwhile, and at about the same time, a new class of destroyers was being built for the Royal Navy. This, the "Tribal" class, included a new H.M.S. *Sikh*. This time, the opportunity of creating a regimental connection with the ship was not lost, and at the Regimental Conference at Nowshera in 1939 it was decided to make her a presentation of plate. For the silver statuette, intended for the wardroom, Jem. Samund Singh, of the 2nd Battalion, posed in the battledress of a sepoy. A fine silver-mounted challenge shield was also presented. In return, the Ship sent each battalion of the Regiment a ship's badge, which made an unusual and effective souvenir.

    When the war broke out, the plate from H.M.S. *Sikh* was put in store in the Royal Marine Barracks in Chatham for safe custody.

    H.M.S. *Sikh* was sunk off Tobruk in the Mediterranean on the 14th September, 1942. A fuller account of this will be given in a later chapter. Meanwhile, the plate, still held, as at May, 1948, at Chatham, has been preserved for any future ship which might bear the same name.

As an interesting postscript to the above, it remains to add that after the *Sikh* had been sunk, it was felt that something should still be done to perpetuate the memory of a connection in which much pride had been taken. Accordingly, the Regimental Centre sent home for a model of the ship in the middle of 1946. The model was received in July, 1947—an excellently carried-out piece of work, about two feet in length and correct in every detail. This was placed on the mantelpiece of the men's recreation room in Nowshera, just below the framed photograph of the ship—and presumably now stands in a similar place in the new Centre Lines in Ambala.

Chapter I

SEPTEMBER 1939 TO FEBRUARY 1940

Backscreen

Twelve months had passed since Munich, and during that time extraordinary efforts had been made by the statesmen of many countries to avert world-wide war. On 10th August, 1939, British and French missions went to Moscow in pursuance of earlier negotiations, seeking to enlist Russian assistance against the growing pressure of Germany on Poland. But the Poles would not accept Russian help except on their own terms, the passage of Russian troops through Polish territory was firmly resisted, the attitude of Britain and France seemed too indefinite to make much appeal to the realists in Moscow, and, in the upshot, Russia elected on the 19th August to sign a pact with Germany instead. Thus the last obstacle to a new world war was removed, and on the 24th the non-aggression treaty between Russia and Germany was announced with jubilation in both countries.

A week went by—Hitler, it is said, still hoping that Britain would bow before the coming storm, and evade her protective guarantee to Poland. But, as has happened so often before, her attitude stiffened in proportion as the crisis drew nearer. It was too late, however. Hitler decided to force on the attack on Poland and advanced his armies across the frontier into Polish territory as from 4.45 a.m. on the 1st September.

The same night, a British ultimatum was delivered to Germany. Parliament endorsed it the following evening in the most resolute manner, and at 9 a.m. on the 3rd, a second and final ultimatum was delivered. At 11.15 a.m. that Sunday morning, the Prime Minister, Mr. Neville Chamberlain, broadcast the news that the country was at war with Germany, and the French declaration followed a few hours after.

For his campaign against Poland, Hitler held most of the cards. Russia was out of it. The French and British were too far away to exert early influence on the fighting. Poland herself was both strategically and tactically at a disadvantage. With an army and an air force both smaller and less well equipped than the Germans she was attempting to hold an exposed industrial salient with a frontier 1700 miles long, and open to attack from the west, south

Margin notes: Poland · 10 Aug. · 19 Aug. · 24 Aug. · 1 Sept. · 2 Sept. · 3 Sept.

1939

and north. Expecting action on the lines of the First World War, the Polish command was paralysed and overwhelmed by the novelty of the German tactics. Air supremacy passed decisively to the Germans within a matter of hours, air landings and parachute descents in back areas hopelessly dislocated the chain of command and threw mobilization into chaos, and the rapid penetration of German tank formations and their ancillary fighting units, completed the disaster.

A very brief account of the operations is all that is needed here, and they are perhaps best understood by reference to the Vistula. This river pursues a devious course like a capital "S" from Cracow in southern Poland, first east, then north and west through Warsaw. Down-stream of Warsaw it circles back north, entering the Baltic at Danzig. The Germans planned two successive envelopments, the first in the Vistula bend west and south of Warsaw, the second well beyond it to the east in the neighbourhood of Bialystock, Brest Litovsk, and the river Bug. By the 17th September, the Germans had reached the Bug, and what slender hopes the Poles still had were finally dashed by the immediate forward move of the Russians, in line with their secret agreement with the German government, westwards into Poland.

17 Sept.

18 Sept. This last blow had decisive consequences. On the 18th, the Polish government fled into Rumania and the campaign was
27 Sept. virtually over. Warsaw held out till the 27th when an armistice was asked for. The 120,000 troops in the Warsaw garrison marched
30 Sept. out and surrendered their arms on the 30th. The Germans claimed in all 694,000 prisoners against a loss by them of 10,572 killed, 30,322 wounded, and 3,400 missing. There was food for thought in this short, brilliant and decisive campaign.

France

In western Europe, mobilization went on undisturbed. France was being organized as a fortress, with the Maginot Line as its main defence system. The northern extremity of the Maginot Line rested at Montmedy on the river Chiers, east of the Meuse, and almost due west of the point in the frontier where France, Luxembourg, and Germany meet. From Montmedy, a line of frontier defences running north-west, parallel with the Franco-Belgian frontier, was under active preparation to link the Maginot Line with the sea.

The British component to the Allied army in France was established south of Lille, a little over half-way from Montmedy to the sea. French troops were deployed to either flank. The British force by the end of the year comprised five divisions. By the end of February it had increased to eight, and further arrivals were

earmarked. But it was still numerically far inferior to the French
forces deployed up and down the line. Policy was defensive. The
armies were standing fast, improving their positions and state of
training, and awaiting events. Strong as their defences were,
however, they had one fatal defect. There was no provision for
the strong mass of offensive reserves without which no success
was possible.

This was the time of the phoney war, the sitzkrieg, or the
twilight war, as this phase was variously termed. It stood out in
strong contrast against the First World War for its inexpensive-
ness in life and limb. By Christmas 1939, the five British divisions
had suffered a total loss of three men killed. In the incomparably
greater French forces, including in addition their navy and air-
forces, the total casualties at that time amounted to only 1,433.
From this circumstance arose an optimistic belief in many
quarters that the Second World War would be fought throughout
at an unprecedentedly cheap cost in human lives.

All through the winter the troops deployed behind the Belgian
frontier, laboured unceasingly at their defences. The Germans
worked with equal zest at their West Wall, or Siegfried Line as it
was known to us, carrying it northwards from the Moselle.
Optimistic tales circulated about this line. It was liable to
flooding, and it was thought to have been constructed in part, at
least, with poor-quality concrete. But no attempt was made by
either side to test the other's strength, and in the prevailing
political set-up, there was unwillingness to take any offensive
action which might be interpreted by the Germans as directed
against or involving the civilian populations. This despite the
known German ruthlessness towards civilians exhibited in
Poland. Or perhaps, rather, because of it.

All through the winter, thus, digging, training and preparation
went on. The Allied air-forces carried out what were called
"leaflet raids" over Germany, dropping vast quantites of leaflets
designed to try and detach the civilian German population from
the Nazi regime. Propaganda took its place in the strategy of
both sides—but the German article was incomparably more subtle than
the Allied at this time. It was directed principally on the French,
and undoubtedly did much to diminish their army's resistance and
morale against the time when the German armies should be ready
to advance.

Meanwhile, at sea, the *Athenia* was sunk by the German sub- At Sea
marine U30 off the Irish coast the same day that war was declared. 3 Sept.
During September and October, magnetic mines began to take toll

1939
22 Nov.

of our shipping. During the night of the 22nd November, however, a German aircraft was seen dropping a large object on the end of a parachute over the sea near Shoeburyness. Before daylight next morning, experts had discovered the object in the mud 500 yards below high-water mark, and found it to be one of these magnetic mines. An antidote was quickly worked out, and before Christmas 1939, this one of Hitler's secret weapons was under reasonable control.

At Sea
13 Dec.

On the 13th December, 1939, three British cruisers, *Exeter*, *Ajax*, and *Achilles*, fell in with the German pocket-battleship *Graf Spee* off the river Plate, and drove her into Montevideo, where she was blockaded. To avoid internment, the *Graf Spee* was

17 Dec.

taken out to sea on the evening of the 17th December, and blown up by her crew. Her auxiliary, the *Altmark*, however, was still at large, with some 300 British seamen on board, captured from nine merchant ships the *Graf Spee* had sunk. On the 14th February,

14 Feb.

the *Altmark* was sighted in Norwegian territorial waters on her way home to Germany, and was shepherded by British destroyers into Josing Fiord. Here, a Norwegian gunboat certified that she was unarmed and had no British prisoners on board, but H.M.S.

16 Feb.

Cossack being instructed on the 16th to go in and make sure, did so, boarded the *Altmark* in the darkness, and after a sharp hand-to-hand fight, rescued 299 prisoners, as well as establishing that the ship did in fact carry arms—two pom-poms and four machine-guns.

Finland
30 Nov.

Looking east from Germany, a new campaign broke out on the 30th November. Russia invaded Finland. It is permissible to suppose that just as the German army had tried out its organization and fighting efficiency against Poland, Russia now felt impelled to do the same with Finland. The Russians are said to have expected the Finnish workers to rise and overthrow their government. In the event, however, the 33,000-odd men of the Finnish army held off the huge Russian forces mobilized against them for over three months, and did not capitulate till mid-March. Here was a demonstration of Russian military ineffectiveness not likely to have been lost on Hitler. It also had its lesson for the Allies on the unwisdom of relying overmuch on detaching a civil population, or section of it, from the regime.

India

Still farther east, on the 12th February, the better part of two Australian and New Zealand divisions landed in Egypt. Meanwhile in India, as already noted, there was no spectacular rise in military tempo. War was ushered in without to-do or clamour.

1939

Units knew what to do if mobilization were ordered, and business proceeded very much as usual. Those on leave were ordered back to duty, and many old friends, including officers from the Special Unemployed List, in and out of England, began to arrive. Mild festivities were held to welcome them. There was a re-union dinner for example on the 14th October in the Officers' Mess of the 2nd Royal Battalion in Nowshera, when past and present officers, twenty-three strong, sat down to table with the whole of the Training Battalion Officers' Mess from next door. But there was an atmosphere of expectancy over all, which became tinged with some sense of frustration as time passed by without mobilization orders. And over the North-West Frontier hung like a cloud the threat from Russia.

India sent a contribution of muleteers from the Royal Indian Army Service Corps to France, together with what in those days seemed a vast quantity of munitions of war. And so it was, considering the proportion it bore to the total stocks then available in the country.

Time was available for adjustments to training in the light of new lessons from the West. But as already indicated, not much use could be made of it. Little in the way of modern weapons was to be had even for fleeting inspection. General mechanization was still away in the future, and the notion of Frontier operations for example unattended by the faithful and ubiquitous mule was something few could take much joy in. Training was a matter for complicated and ill-understood "conventions", leading to artificial and unsatisfactory situations. Lessons were hence learnt, many of which were to be rudely untaught at the hands of the enemy later. A spate of air defence exercises was solemnly worked through, with set situations conveyed by the umpires—difficult enough for the officers, but often wholly unintelligible to tne men. Humorous consequences sometimes followed, as for example when the men's wives in the family lines in the 2nd Battalion were discovered by the C.O.'s wife cowering in their quarters, expecting instant extinction; or when, in the Afghan Mission Hospital in Peshawar, a patient was wheeled in, suffering, so the umpire's card informed a wonder-struck surgeon, from a fractured abdomen.

The credit of the Regiment stood high. Whether at work or in the field of sports and athletics, it gained a high share of the honours. Let us turn aside then and see what it was doing while the war cranked slowly into action far away to the West.

The 1st Battalion was in Chittagong, with small expectation of relief. Hopes rose in October, when orders to mechanize

1st Bn.
Oct.

5

1939

26 Nov.

1940

29 Feb.

arrived, but fell again somewhat when news came in on the 26th November that the Battalion had been earmarked for a tour with Frontier Defence troops in Kohat. Even this move was subject to long and disappointing delays, and, in the event, the Battalion did not leave Chittagong till the 29th February, 1940.

The troops had made a good name for themselves in Chittagong, and the civil authorities saw them go with regret. In his 1940 Durbar speech, the Divisional Commissioner paid the Battalion a welcome compliment. He said:

"In conclusion, may I take this opportunity of acknowledging on behalf of the whole civil population of this Division the services rendered by the King George the Fifth's Own 11th Sikh Regiment. Not only have they helped to maintain a peaceful and orderly atmosphere in this Division; they have endeared themselves to the whole population by their readiness to go out of the ordinary routine of their military duties in order to help in an emergency, such as flood in the river, or fire in the bazaar. Their orderly behaviour, their martial spirit, and their fine physique remind us constantly of the dignity and might of the Indian Army, of which the whole of India is justly proud. And their cheerful disposition and love of outdoor games are a stimulating example to our own young men. Everywhere the troops go they are welcomed and recognized as friends, and the whole population realizes that they are indeed fortunate to have such stalwart protectors in their midst."

2nd Bn.

The 2nd Battalion, meanwhile, was in Nowshera. What sort of life the troops led during the first six months of the war in a non-operational cantonment in the North-West Frontier Province can be glimpsed from the Battalion half-yearly letter covering the period, and from which some extracts follow:

"Company and Battalion camps were held . . . and the men were satisfactorily hardened up for the strenuous but, to us, dull District Exercise, which preceded Christmas. This exercise was a kind of glorified hike, involving a tramp of 76 miles in four consecutive days (the battalion was not at that time mechanized), and carried us nearly to the Peshawar-Kohat road. The dust was appalling—fine floury stuff, inches deep—the wind was generally a following one—and we were not sorry to be home. The exercise involved our joining the Peshawar Brigade camp for one night, and it is a matter for satisfaction that the manner in which the Battalion marched into and out of that camp was apparently the subject of a good deal of favourable comment in Peshawar.

1940

"The Brigade camp, early in January, took the form of a nine-days Column Exercise in Mountain Warfare in the Attock region. The first night, which was spent in Akora, was bitter, and it was still perishingly cold and freezing hard, when the Column marched off at 8 a.m. for what proved to be a baking hot day in the hills to the South. The camp as a whole was very strenuous, and the Battalion had its full share. Immediately it concluded, the Brigade marched out, after a night in Barracks, on a different role, and took up a defensive position over-night against a mechanized force, on the other side of Nowshera. Some small concessions to modernized warfare were made in the form of dummy tank-mines, but the front of 6 miles allotted to the Battalion even in a supposedly tank-proof locality, was too much for a Column strength of only 500 men. In the upshot, the front proved much more vulnerable than had been supposed, but as all the fun took place on our six-mile front, the jawans had some relief from tedium. Great emphasis was laid on camouflage from the air, and not the least stirring moment on the exercise was a result of this. The mules at Battalion H.Q. had been pecking away at their bhoosa all night, and had spread it well out, and an R.I.A.S.C. driver was deputed at dawn to sweep it up and camouflage it. This he did by thrusting a match into it, and raising a column of smoke which even the Children of Israel would have accepted as a master-piece, just as the first potentially hostile aeroplane sailed into view.

"Marching has been adopted as the special role of troops in these parts this year, and the Battalion has covered a good deal of ground one way and another. Two 18-mile marches, plus one Brigade Column Exercise a month, have kept the men hard. To give an idea of their capabilities at present, the February Brigade Column involved 24 miles cross-country or along country tracks, with, for some of the men, a five-hundred foot climb to piquet positions, and a rear-guard action with plenty of doubling; whilst the March Column, which started at 3.30 a.m. in a blinding thunder- and rain-storm, involved 21 miles mostly cross-country, in almost continuous violent rain. Never have we been wetter, but, as ever, there were no fall-outs.

"One pleasant item of training remains to be recorded. As is generally known, drill has been subject to much alteration lately, and the 15th were given the duty of giving a demonstration of the new drill (in February). The demonstration was staged on the rather barren Brigade Parade Ground, with the spectators high up on the hills running along the south edge. There was very little time to polish the drill up, once its elements had been taught, but

1939

greater precision of movement and smartness of turn-out could not have been found on the peacetime Horse-Guards Parade. The Battalion was, of course, in its Review Order."

Christmas was celebrated in the time-honoured way. The huge, iced Christmas cake was cut ceremoniously with the sword at mid-day, and the British and Viceroy's commissioned officers devoted themselves to its destruction and the salvaging of the silver small change with which it was stuffed. Needless to say, not a crumb remained, an hour later. It was not all training, war or no.

3rd Bn.   *The 3rd Battalion* left Allahabad for Chaman in the middle of October. All along the Frontier at this time, fortifications were being modernized in the light of an unpredictable future, and the Battalion was kept very busy on the construction of defences in the Khojak Pass.

4th Bn.   *The 4th Battalion* had been similarly employed in Landi Kotal, and left its mark on the new defences there. On the 1st October, however, it left Landi Kotal, on normal relief, for Delhi. As regards the relief, details are available in a contemporary Battalion letter, and may be found of interest as illustrating a normal peacetime rail transfer. The arrival in Delhi, and the notes recorded on that city, will revive nostalgic memories in many an old soldier of the time.

Quoting, then, from the letter:

"The Battalion under Mitcheson left Landi Kotal by train on October 1st and were met at Nowshera at 11 p.m. by a number of officers and men who had turned out to see them. A large number of pensioners, among whom were Sub. Chaudri Khan and Hav. Mohd Fazal, were at Jhelum the next morning. While the train was in the station an officers' special with officers recalled from England drew in. Among them were Purves and Rowlandson recalled from leave and Kilroy from the S.U.L. Sub.-Maj. Bahad" Khan met the train at Wazirabad.

"I had asked for a long halt at Amritsar in the hope that a strong contingent would be able to visit the Golden Temple. Unfortunately the train reached Amritsar after dark and, except for Granthi Atma Singh and a party of I.O.s who took a 'rumala' to the Durbar Sahib, the visit was perforce cancelled. Many old pensioners were at Amritsar, including some who had come from beyond Ludhiana. Needless to say all those who could be helped on the return journey, were crowded into the train.

"Among those present were Lieut. Pertab Singh, Lieut. Khem

1939

Singh, Sub. Ralla Singh, Sub. Sant Singh, Sub. Bara Singh, Sub. Ram Singh, Jem. Durga Dass, and Hav. Lahna Singh.

"The train passed through Jullundur at 1 a.m. and Ludhiana an hour later; Jem. Mall Singh (late head clerk), Hav.-Maj. Jowala Singh and Sep. Bachittar Singh turned up. The hour of arrival and the fact that the train was only scheduled to stop for a short while was obviously responsible for such a small attendance.

"The men were not impressed with their first introduction to the Imperial Capital. The Cantonment station and its approaches would not do credit to any way-side halt. The train arrived at 3.30 p.m. The transport allotted for the move of all the kit consisted of 7 civilian lorries one of which broke down after a trip or two. However, the men got down to it in their inimitable way and all the kit was cleared by 10 p.m. I forgot to mention that the lighting arrangements consisted of three oil lamps, two of which were minus their burners. Johnson and Denyer, both of whom had been recalled from leave, had travelled up in the officers' special and had been stopped at Delhi.

"The other units here are the 6th D.C.O. Lancers (old 13th Lancers and 16th Cavalry), and the 2nd Battalion Duke of Wellington's Regiment. There are normally two Indian Battalions but so far we are the only one and there is no prospect at present of another one coming. There is no government transport, mechanical or otherwise. We are finding guards on the Viceroy and Commander-in-Chief. For this we have to keep two companies in the Escort Lines 5 miles away. The accommodation in Escort Lines is admirable, the best that any of us has ever seen, and the lines in Cantonments are good. New Delhi and Cantonments are laid out on a generous scale which is reflected in one's petrol bill. There are many distractions and, in spite of the war, a good deal of entertaining which has its appeal to some of us. Games are a problem. The soil is sandy and the cost of a lipai hockey ground prohibitive."

It is interesting to recall that the band under its veteran bandmaster, Sub. Gulab Singh, broadcast twice monthly on Sundays over All-India Radio, from the 3rd December. The band, together with a guard of honour, had taken part on the 14th November in the unveiling ceremony of the statue of King George V. Apart from two pensioners of the Viceroy's bodyguard, Sub. Gulab Singh was probably the only person at the ceremony who had been present at the Durbar of 1911, when he had been serving as L.-Naik in the band.

The Battalion, meanwhile, had been selected for mechanization, and 3 officers and 94 non-commissioned officers and men went

1939

off to learn to drive and maintain M.T. The establishment of vehicles was to be 48 lorries or trucks of various sizes, 13 motor-cycles, and 31 bicycles.

5th Bn. *The 5th Battalion* added fresh laurels to its record in Waziristan during the current cold weather—particularly during the Shahwali Column in October.

Chapter II

MARCH TO AUGUST 1940

Backscreen

The spring of 1940 saw the abrupt termination of the sitzkrieg. Since as far back as the previous 14th December, Hitler had been devising means for carrying the war into Norway—at that time, and subsequently, a strictly neutral country. The secret of this was well-kept. Though preparations for "Weser Exercise", as this operation was called, went steadily on through the winter, the Allies knew nothing about it.

Absorbed by the Russian attack on Finland, the Allied Supreme War Council was actively discussing the despatch there of important forces, including two British divisions, destined otherwise in February, for France. It was not known whether the Norwegians and Swedes would agree to the passage of these forces through their territory, and in fact, they were never asked to do so. Possibly Norwegian reactions to the *Altmark* affair were too discouraging. In any event, the Finns gave up the struggle on the 12th March—the two British divisions were sent to France—and the British reserves available for emergency employment elsewhere dropped to only eleven battalions.

It is doubtful whether Allied plans to send forces through Scandinavia were kept as close a secret from Hitler as were his plans against Norway and Denmark from us. He at least knew such a move was likely. He knew, too, that if it came, it would prejudice the by now well-advanced plans for carrying the war into France. It would have been an embarrassment to have Allied troops threatening the lightly defended Baltic coast—the flow of Swedish iron ore via Narvik would have been interrupted—and the liberty of action of the German fleet at Wilhelmshaven would have been prejudiced. Weser Exercise was to be the preliminary to the sudden heavy blow in France, and the time to employ it was at hand.

Meanwhile a useful pretext had been provided. The Allied Governments had long been irked by the flow of ore to Germany through Norwegian territorial waters. Diplomatic representations having failed, it had been decided to resort to physical obstacles and, on the night of the 7th-8th April, to mine Norwegian territorial waters. It was suggested later that this arbitrary action against a neutral country was in fact to some extent responsible for

Norway
14 Dec.
1939

1940
12 March

7-8 April

1940

Hitler's immediate counter-move in Scandinavia. Nothing, of course, was further from the fact. The invasion of Denmark and Norway had been long decreed, and troops had been sent, hidden away in the holds of cargo ships sailing up the coast of Norway, before a single Allied mine was laid.

Such grim humour as may be thought to lie in the Teutonic flight of fancy which borrowed inspiration from the Trojan Horse in the despatch of these advanced sea-borne detachments, was very soon dispelled. "To protect their freedom and independence", as the German disclaimer cynically put it, the German assault on

9 April Denmark and Norway on the 9th April was carried out with ruthless efficiency and disregard for neutral privileges. "All resistance," the order went on, "would be broken by every available means by the German armed forces, and would therefore only lead to utterly useless bloodshed." Denmark was overcome almost without a shot. In Norway, the same day, strong German sea- and air-borne forces secured the main ports and air-fields, with the assistance of fifth columnists, and paralysed the means of effective resistance.

The secret had been kept, and surprise was complete. British forces were sent to Norway as quickly as they could be got ready,

14 April but the Germans had time to improve their defences. On the 14th April, the first landings were made, north of Narvik, and at Namsos, which was under 4 feet of snow, some 70 miles north of

17 April Trondheim. On the 17th another landing was made, at Andalsnes, 150 miles by road south of Trondheim. These two latter landings were to cover an assault on Trondheim itself—but the command of the air had passed so decisively to the Germans that the attack was cancelled. Various other landings were, however, made at a variety of points later on, and footholds secured.

In an effort to make the best use of limited resources and maintain an effective footing in Norway till the auspices became more favourable, a small leavening of experienced British officers of the Indian Army was sent back to England at short notice to advise on the mountain warfare aspect of the operations. Maj. J. P. L. Eustace, M.C., from the 2nd Battalion was one of those selected. Not all reached Norway, and Maj. Eustace was one of those who did not. He was, however, retained in the United Kingdom for a considerable time as an instructor at the mountain warfare school opened on the west coast of Scotland.

Meanwhile it became increasingly plain that the troops were operating under crippling difficulties. The situation was also looking increasingly serious in France, and the two circumstances combined to take the heart out of the venture. The most that could be said for it was that it proved once again the unwisdom of attacking a modern enemy with forces insufficiently prepared and not backed up with every available means of support. Lack of air power placed ships and troops at a crushing disadvantage. The greatest courage and spirit was shown by the troops, but the operations gradually contracted, and the troops were withdrawn from their one remaining foothold in Narvik on the 8th June.

1940

8 June

Whatever danger our invasion of Norway had brought to Hitler had vanished by early May, and conditions were ripe for the German invasion of France. On the 10th May, in the early hours of the morning, Dutch air-fields and nodal points were seized by German parachutists followed by air-borne troops. German armoured forces crossed the Maas at Genapp, and at points farther south, and made straight westwards across Holland parallel with the Belgian frontier. Courageous resistance was made at various points, but next day, when heavy bombing attacks reduced the whole Dutch air-force to a total of twelve machines, confusion redoubled.

Holland

10 May

11 May

On the 12th, soon after mid-day, the armoured column from Genapp contacted the air-borne troops south of Rotterdam, near the Dutch west coast. On the 14th, Dutch surrender was demanded, on pain of bombing of Rotterdam and Utrecht. Soon after, and before a reply could be received, Rotterdam was bombed by a force of some fifty German aircraft. Surrender could no longer be deferred.

12 May

14 May

On the 10th, meanwhile, when Holland was attacked, Belgian air-fields were also bombed, together with the suburbs of Brussels, Antwerp and Namur, and the railway junction of Jemelle, 15 miles or so east of the Meuse (or Maas). Parachutists were freely dropped, and carried out the most daring attacks on the bridge at Maastricht, three other bridges over the Albert Canal, and the fortress of Eben-Emael. The latter, esteemed so strong that the Belgians doubted if it would ever be attacked at all, was taken from the air by 120 men in some 10 gliders and completely paralysed.

Belgium

10 May

By next morning, the Germans were across the Albert Canal, running east and west from the Meuse near Eben Emael, to Antwerp. A German armoured division was passed through, moved south-west past Tongres, and manoeuvred the two Belgian divisions holding the canal defences, out of their positions, and back to the Antwerp-Namur line barely covering Brussels. Confusion was complete, but the French commander of the armies of the north-east was already implementing the suicidal plan of quitting his prepared defences, and was moving forward in support of the Belgian armies, paving the way for German victory. The Germans

11 May

1940

were aiming their blow, not round the northern flank in an elaboration of the Schlieffen plan, but through the centre over ground which it was thought was too difficult for large forces to use. This was still unsuspected by the French Higher Command, but it is plain enough, now, that the forward swing of the four Allied armies strung out along the left, played straight into the enemies' hands.

12 May   On the 12th, however, these Allied armies linked up with the Belgian right, about Louvain, and carried the front south to Sedan, not far from Montmedy and the Maginot Line. The British were posted on a 12-mile front between Louvain, and Wavre to the south, and the situation seemed satisfactory enough. Enemy pressure was heavy over the whole front from Louvain to Sedan, but there was nothing to show that the main thrust was coming in the south of this line rather than the north.

France
13 May   On the 13th May, however, von Kleist's group of five Panzer and three motorized divisions broke through at Sedan, employing a combination of dive-bombing with tank action which tried the French very hard. For three hours from mid-day, waves of Stuka dive-bombers attacked French pillbox defences west of the Meuse on a front of only a few miles near Sedan. At 6.30 p.m. German
14 May   troops began crossing the Meuse, and at 1 a.m. on the 14th the river was bridged. The break-through was complete, as were two other crossings the same day, at Monthermé and Houx, farther north.

15 May   On the 15th the armoured forces moved westwards across the Ardennes Canal, where two bridges were found undestroyed. By
16 May   8 p.m. on the 16th they were 27 miles to the west at Rozoy, with other forces approaching Rethel some 20 miles to the south-east. An immense triangle had been driven into the Allied positions—its base stretching from near the British right at Wavre, to Montmedy, at the left of the Maginot Line 90 miles or so to the south, and its apex not so far from St. Quentin, and about 70 miles west of Sedan. The whole of the Allied northern positions were thus turned, and there was no course open but to fall back. This was begun that night, and the troops reached the line of the
18-19 May   Scheldt, 50 miles to the west, on the night of the 18th-19th.

The Germans were fanning out. Armoured forces were moving west towards Amiens to cut the communications between the armies in Belgium and those in France, and south towards Rheims to get across the lines of communication with the Maginot Line.
20 May   On the 19th they were in Amiens, on the 20th in Abbeville
23 May   30 miles farther down the Somme, and on the 23rd they attacked Boulogne and Calais 50 miles or so to the north. The Allies in

1940

the north now found themselves squeezed into a triangle with a 100-mile base, mostly along the Belgium coast, and its apex a little north of Cambrai, 60 miles to the south, and with pressure momentarily strengthening against the Belgians, manning the Scheldt south-west from Antwerp.

This pressure, on the 24th, took the form of furious attacks from the air. On the 25th, the Belgians began to give. There had been hope of a French counter-offensive from the south, but, as this seemed unlikely now to materialize, the British, on the 26th, began falling back towards the coast as the safety of their left flank was being jeopardized by the pressure on the Belgians. While this move was still in progress, in the early hours of the 28th, the Belgian army surrendered. The remaining Allied forces now found themselves compressed into a tiny area, of which the base along the coast only measured 23 miles. 24 May 25 May 26 May 28 May

To save what was possible was now the only course, and the evacuation from Dunkirk began. Different figures are quoted by various authorities for the actual numbers of men taken out, but it was in the general neighbourhood of 337,000. The story of the "little ships" that poured across the Channel to help is well enough known. Very heavy casualties were inflicted on these craft. The evacuation went on at full pressure from the 29th May to the 4th June, with less German interference than might have been expected. Von Rundstedt, who was in command of the German forces, seems to have been nervous of incurring further damage to his armour, and Hitler appears to have concurred. Whatever the cause, German commanders took the view that a great opportunity was lost. 29 May- 4 June

With few exceptions, then, the British Expeditionary Force— with a considerable contingent of French—got away. One of these exceptions was the 52nd Highland Division, most of which was captured at St. Valery at the mouth of the Somme. The G.S.O.1 of this division was Lieut.-Col. H. R. Swinburn, M.C., of the 2nd Battalion of the Regiment, who was taken prisoner at the same time.

The Germans now turned their attention to the French forces farther south. The "Weygand Line" had been organized, running from the mouth of the Somme to the Aisne, and thence to the Maginot Line at Montmedy. This line was attacked on the 5th June between Amiens and Peronne. By the 9th, the attack had extended to the Argonne, and the line had been broken near Rethel, 30 miles south-west of Sedan. Chalons-sur-Marne, 40 miles to the south, fell on the 10th. The Swiss frontier was reached on the 17th, and the whole Maginot Line boxed up. 5 June 9 June 10 June 17 June

15

1940	
10 June	Meanwhile, in the west, Rouen had been occupied on the 10th.
11 June	The Germans crossed the Seine below Paris on the 11th, and the French Government withdrew to Tours and thence to Bordeaux,
14 June	followed by a vast concourse of refugees. On the 14th June, the Germans entered Paris, which had been declared an open city.
16 June	On the 16th, the French Prime-Minister, M. Reynaud, resigned.
17 June	Marshal Pétain took over, and, next day the 17th, asked for an
22 June	armistice. This was agreed upon, and signed on the 22nd, in the Forest of Compiègne, in the same old railway saloon that had been used for the signing of the earlier armistice, when the position was reversed, in 1918.
Italy and N. Africa 10 June	On June the 10th, Italy entered the war on Germany's side, and gave the Axis the command of the Central Mediterranean. There were no immediate consequences of note in Europe, but it brought the Near East at once into the picture. There, in Tripolitania and Cyrenaica, there were some 215,000 Italians under arms. A further 200,000 were disposed in Eritrea, Italian Somaliland, and Abyssinia. Facing them was a weak British force comprising in all some 80,000 men—among them two-thirds of the 4th Indian Division. With his forces spread over a vast area, and including only the armoured division (the 7th) of two partly equipped brigades, General Wavell's position seemed critical. He had a desperately weak air-force, equipped with machines of obsolete types, and he had been prevented from taking any active defence measures prior to Italy's entry into the war, for fear of annoying that government.
	Our communications with Europe via the Mediterrean had been practically blocked. The alternative route, down the Red Sea and round the Cape of Good Hope, was threatened by Italian air and naval forces based in Eritrea and Italian Somaliland. However, with fine audacity, General Wavell, operating from a line running south from Mersa Matruh, set about magnifying his numbers in the enemy's eyes by a policy of tip-and-run attacks and raids, and was so successful that stories went the rounds in the Italian lines that up to five armoured divisions were in action, and that a large-scale British attack was impending. Marshal Balbo drew in his horns and called for reinforcements—but was killed in a British
28 June	air-raid on the 28th June in Tobruk before anything could come of this. His successor, Marshal Graziani, gave the British no immediate cause for alarm, for he had a reputation for slow moving, earned in the Abyssinian campaign. Little, in fact, happened beyond the threat to Khartoum from Kassala, which the Italians occupied, just inside the frontier between Abyssinia and the

	1940

Soudan, and the less satisfactory campaign in British Somaliland, where a force of seventeen battalions of the enemy, with medium and light tanks and armoured cars, crossed the frontier on the 3rd August. The British force of five battalions, including two Indian Army units, put up a stout defence, but were compelled to withdraw about the 16th.   3 Aug.
16 Aug.

Back in the west, the Germans had been marking time. Hitler only announced his intention of invading England on the 16th July—though, even then, it is uncertain whether his object was not, at least partly, to pull wool over Russian eyes, since his troops were already on the move in that direction, if the evidence of the Nuremberg trial is to be believed. On the 19th he told the Reichstag he would offer a negotiated peace to England. If it were to be rejected, he would invade, but if the invasion failed, a prolonged war would have to be faced.   Britain
16 July

19 July

On the 22nd July, the peace offers were emphatically rejected. Britain and the Dominions were ready to carry on the war alone. And there were many who felt relief at this re-statement of our intentions, knowing that the Empire would give a good account of itself, freed from the diversion of effort implicit in the support of weakened allies.   22 July

Of the German invasion plans, nothing eventuated except as affected the German air-force. Between the 8th and 18th of August, attacks were made on convoys and coastal objectives to draw out British fighters and shoot them down. From the 19th August, these attacks were extended to inland fighter air-fields. And there the position stood at the end of this period, except that in the absence of proper landing-craft, the Germans began to accumulate great concentrations of barges and small craft along the Channel ports. In Hitler's great conception of total war, he made insufficient allowance for the English Channel, and those critical miles of water were never to be crossed.   8-18 Aug.

19 Aug.

At sea, as already noted, the Mediterranean route to the East was closed to us by June, and reinforcements in men and stores had to accept the delays implicit in the Cape route. This had the further disadvantage of much lengthening the turn-round of ships, which in turn made shipping, already scarce, still more of a problem.   At Sea

Shipping losses kept fairly constant, but embarrassingly high. Not much short of 1,500,000 tons were sunk in the third quarter of the year.

1940
India

Against this sombre background, what was the position in India? It had already been accepted that India's strategical boundaries lay at a distance from her coasts, and that her adequate defence required an addition of nine new battalions and other arms in proportion. But this bore no relation at all to the world crisis that was impending, and in the early summer of 1940, a more effective expansion was announced. As the Regiment's contribution to this, orders were received by the Training Battalion in May, for the raising, in August, of two new battalions, the 6th and 7th.

To create these new battalions, somewhat elaborate arrangements were made. Each of the pre-war battalions was to provide a trained nucleus of some ninety Indian ranks. This process was known as "milking", but as battalion commanders concerned were made responsible for drafting their best men into the nucleus, while at the same time fully maintaining their former standards of efficiency, more picturesque terms for the process were not infrequently heard.

Over and above the nuclei, each new battalion received a draft of 250 recruits from the Training Battalion, so that evidently the new formations would require a good deal of time before they could be operationally efficient. The need for more forethought in preparing for war expansion was thus driven home—especially as it will be recollected that the deadening man-day system was not to be called off for many weeks after this expansion programme was notified.

While sovereign states were collapsing all over Europe under Hitler's total war, and the Empire itself was in the direst jeopardy, what was the Regiment doing in India? The tempo was rising, and training growing more in line with the times, but in most respects the troops were at their peacetime duties, keeping order on the Frontier, or at garrison duty in cantonments.

1st Bn.
29 Feb.
March

The 1st Battalion had left Chittagong on the 29th February for Kohat. A twelve-hour halt was arranged at Ludhiana, where a Regimental re-union was staged. Somewhere about fifteen hundred pensioners and relatives collected there, including five former Subedar-Majors and eighteen other Viceroy's Commissioned Officers, and a memorable time was had.

Arrived in Kohat, the Battalion was sent up to the Thal Column, which it joined five days later in a perimeter camp at Nawidand. This lies on the border of the Ahmedzai Salient, where there had been a good deal of fighting a few weeks earlier. Although the Battalion moved out into hostile territory on several occasions, there was little opposition, and no large force of tribesmen was encountered.

In May, the Battalion returned to Kohat where, under Brig. A. E. Barstow, M.C., Colonel of the 2nd Battalion, who was commanding the Kohat Brigade, it continued training, and carried out station duties for the next five months, through the stiflingly hot summer and on into October.

The 2nd Battalion in Nowshera had had the pleasure of entertaining His Highness the Maharajah of Patiala, himself an honorary officer of the Battalion, for four days in March. In spite of many and insistent demands on his time from outside sources, His Highness spent most of his time with the Battalion, living with the Commandant, Lieut.-Col. F. T. Birdwood and his wife, and seeing every aspect of the Battalion's daily life. On his last evening he was the guest of honour at a Regimental Guest Night, which the officers of the Training Battalion attended in full force. These latter, it appeared, thanks in part to their emergency commissioned reinforcements, had worked up a slosh team of unsuspected skill, but His Highness was better still, and pulled his Battalion safely through to victory. Later that night, when His Highness left, the troops lined the railway embankment at the back of the lines, and their "fatehs" as the train pulled slowly up the gradient in the dark, could have been heard very nearly in Risalpur.

In mid-August, the Battalion moved at very short notice to Jamrud at the foot of the Khyber, where it was employed on normal garrison duty.

The 3rd Battalion passed an uneventful summer in Chaman, but began mechanizing in August.

The 4th Battalion, in Delhi, had already made some progress in mechanization. What truth there was in the story current at the time that the first news they had of their equipment was an agitated telephone call from the station-master telling them there was a consignment of trucks on the platform addressed to them, and would they please take them away, is not certain. Nor is it known how they managed to drive them up to the lines without accident. Another story that went the rounds at the time, and which is recorded here with the same object as the foregoing—to illustrate the confusion hurried re-equipment created, and the cheerful optimism with which it was overcome—relates to the then Jemadar Quarter-Master—an elderly officer who had not previously experienced the pleasures of piloting a

1940

May

2nd Bn.

August

3rd Bn.

4th Bn.

1940

motor-cycle. The story goes that he let in the clutch, and, his beard streaming over his shoulder, went off with a steadily accelerating pendulum action which made him swerve from side to side of the road with increasing violence. The M.T. Officer, in a state of some panic, bellowing after him—"Jemadar Sahib!—Gas band karo"—the latter finally did so, and came to rest by the side of the road, telling the M.T. Officer, with a delighted smile, when he came up—"Sahib, *bahut* asan hai!"

Towards the end of the hot weather, the Battalion was moved down to Poona and mobilized.

5th Bn.   *The 5th Battalion* earned further laurels in Waziristan, particularly in the Tochi Valley campaign of 1940. The Battalion was to amass during its two years tour in Waziristan a very respectable list of honours, including one Distinguished Service Order, two Military Crosses, two Indian Orders of Merit, and four Indian Distinguished Service Medals. The list says much for the nature of the fighting and for the spirit and courage of the troops.

6th Bn.   *The 6th Battalion* came into being on the 7th August, on a basis of two-thirds Sikh and one-third Punjabi-Mohammedan. It was raised in Nowshera by Lieut.-Col. E. C. Johnson, formerly of the 4th Battalion.

7th Bn.   *The 7th Battalion* was also raised on the 7th August, on the same basis as the 6th, but in Nasirabad, under Lieut.-Col. J. J. P. Connolly of the 5th Battalion.

Chapter III

SEPTEMBER 1940 TO FEBRUARY 1941

Backscreen

The Invasion of Britain still hung fire at the beginning of September. On the 16th July, Hitler had ordered all preparations to be completed by the middle of August. Five days later, the date was put back to the 15th September. Disorganization and losses in the invasion fleet due to British attacks caused a further postponement till the 21st September. On the 11th, it was put back to the 24th. On the 14th, it was put off again, and on the 17th, it was indefinitely postponed, though this was not formally announced till the 12th October. Britain
September

In the air, the battle went on. Up to the 6th September, targets for the German air-force had for some while been mainly fighter air-fields in the south and south-east of England. From the 7th, they switched to attacks on big centres, especially London, to destroy food and similar stocks and try and break down civilian morale. The 15th September was the culminating date. But the British resistance, albeit strained to the last fighter aircraft, was too much for the Luftwaffe, and, as we have seen, on the 17th, Hitler postponed his invasion plans *sine die*. 6 Sept.
7 Sept.
15 Sept.
17 Sept.

If the invasion was off, however, the air battle was not. For fifty-nine consecutive nights, from the 7th September to the 3rd November, London was bombed by an average of 200 enemy aircraft. Thereafter, attacks were spread, and many towns felt the full weight of German air attack. On the 29th December, an all-out incendiary attack was made on the City of London. Nearly 1,500 fires were started, and great damage was done. Some idea of the suffering undergone by the civil population during this phase of the war is revealed by the casualty figures. Between August and December, 22,744 people were killed and 30,498 injured. 7 Sept.-
3 Nov.
29 Dec.

Meanwhile, at sea the German campaign of unrestricted sinkings continued to claim the same high average of British and neutral shipping. Mr. Churchill, however, made history in the House of Commons on the 5th September, describing "the memorable transaction" by which fifty American destroyers were transferred to the British flag to swell our anti-submarine resources, and the United States of America received leases of naval and air bases on British territory in the Western Atlantic. At Sea
5 Sept.

1940	
N. Africa	As early as the 6th September, German troops had been trending eastwards in important numbers—with careful regard to suspicious minds in Moscow. The storm-centre was, however, swinging south of east, to the Mediterranean, where General Wavell was carrying on his lonely campaign against the numerically far stronger Italians.
September	In the Western Desert our patrols were operating from a defence line running south from a point near Mersa Matruh—the dusty seaport where the 2nd Battalion of the Regiment had spent some time during the First World War. The Italians had haltingly crossed the Egyptian frontier in mid-September to a line running south-west from Sidi Barrani—about 75 miles west of Mersa Matruh. During the month, fifty "I" tanks reached General Wavell—a reinforcement of decisive value.
28 Oct.	Despite the discrepancy in strengths, it had been hoped to attack the Italians in Libya in the autumn, but this had to be postponed owing to the confusion created in southern Europe by the outbreak of war on the 28th October, between Italy and Greece. Our mid-eastern forces occupied Crete, and a small air component was sent to Greece. The Italians made no attempt in Libya to exploit this further weakening of the British force. The Italian strength on the spot at that time was about 80,000 men with 120 tanks, and an air-force three times as strong as the British, and it may perhaps have been partly due to this superiority over the 31,000 men opposed to them that they took less care of their security than they should have. At all events, British patrols established that there was an undefended 20-mile gap between Nibeiwa and the two Sofafis in the middle of their line, and that the Italian defended posts were not prepared for all-round defence.
	On a careful re-assessment of the situation in the Middle-East, it was judged possible to stage a limited five-day operation against the Italians in Libya, in spite of commitments in Greece and Crete Administratively as well as otherwise, it called for bold planning and the acceptance of risk. To begin with, supply dumps had first to be sited and stocked 20 to 30 miles ahead of our line, in the wi no-man's-land between the Italians and ourselves. An advance by stages was followed by a night approach and a night advance on successive nights, and the assault was delivered on the morning
9 Dec.	of the 9th December.
	By dawn that day, our forces had swept through the gap between Nibeiwa and the two Sofafi's. Nibeiwa was then carried from the rear, while the Sofafi's, to the south-west, were masked by the 7th Armoured Division's Support Group. Next, Tummar East, 10 miles north-east of Nibeiwa, was carried from the rear. Sidi

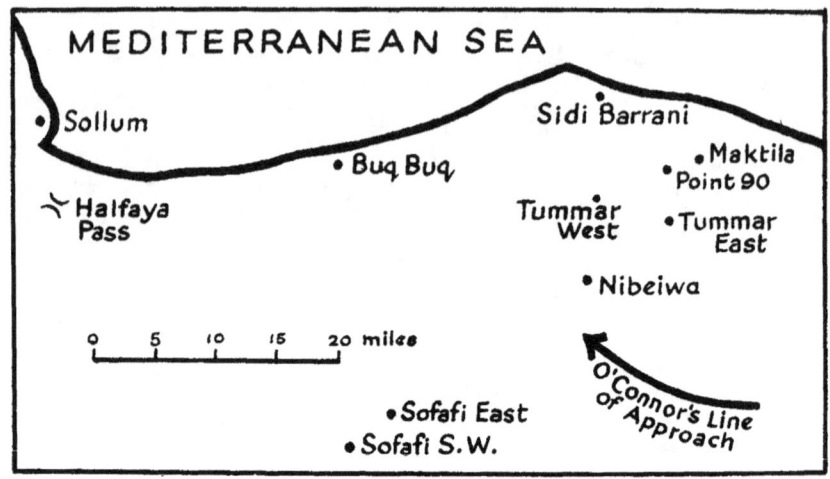

BATTLEFIELD OF SIDI BARRANI   7th – 11th December 1940
(With acknowledgements to "The Second World War" by Major-General J. F. C. Fuller, Page 96)

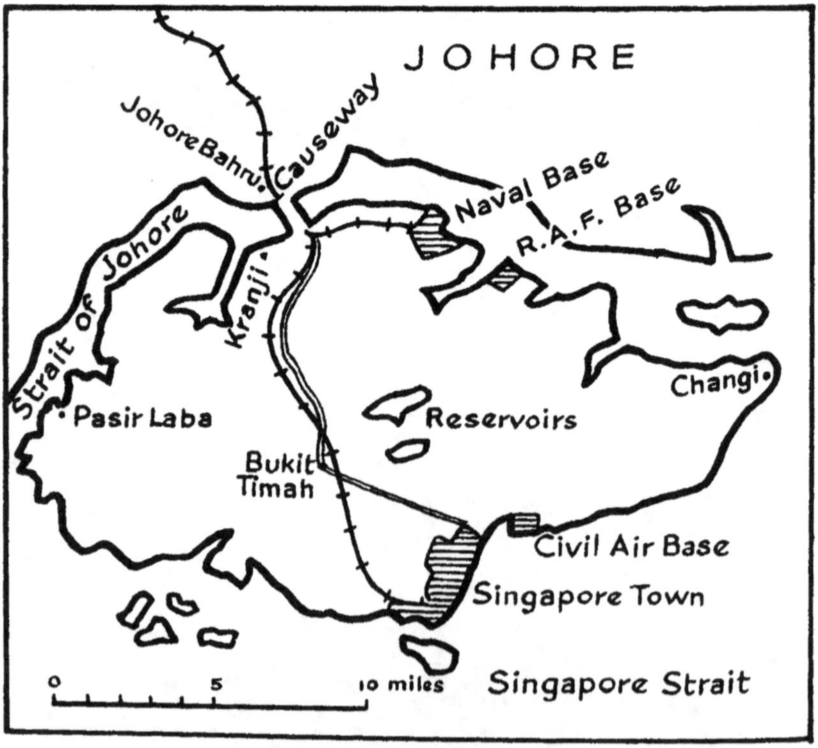

SINGAPORE
(With acknowledgements to "The Second World War" by Major-General J. F. C. Fuller, page 144)

                                                                    1940-41
Barrani's rearward communications were cut by the 4th Indian and
7th Armoured Divisions, and by the following evening, the 10th   10 Dec.
December, Sidi Barrani itself was taken. Next day, the 11th, the   11 Dec.
pursuit was launched down the long road west to Buq Buq and
Sollum, and the total enemy losses brought to the staggering total
of over 38,000 prisoners, 400 guns, and 50 tanks, at a cost to the
British of 133 killed, 387 wounded, and 8 missing. The greater
part of five Italian divisions had been destroyed.

This startling success opened up fresh possibilities, and it was
decided to carry operations westwards as soon as preparations
could be made. Meanwhile, the daring and far-seeing decision was
made to detach the 4th Indian Division from the Libyan front, and
send it immediately to join the 5th Indian Division in Eritrea for
the Abyssinian campaign. This decision, come to on the 12th   12 Dec.
December, the moment victory at Sidi Barrani was certain, led to
the decisive operations 700 miles to the south, to which a further
reference is made below.

Meanwhile, in the north, by the 15th December, all enemy troops   15 Dec.
were back over the Egyptian frontier, and the pursuit was carried
on to the strong posts of Bardia and Tobruk. After methodical
preparation, these were captured on the 5th and 22nd January   5 Jan.
respectively, with a further total of 75,000 prisoners, 698 guns, 22 Jan.
and 99 tanks. Only two worth-while Italian detachments still
remained in Cirenaica. These were held by the 60th Italian
Division, less a brigade, east of Derna, approximately 100 miles
west along the coast from Tobruk, and one brigade, with 160 tanks
at Mekili, 50 miles south of Derna. The Mekili force did not await
attack, but withdraw on the night of the 26-27th January towards   26-27 Jan.
Barce. Barce lies about 80 miles west-north-west of Mekili and not
far from the coast. From the general neighbourhood of Barce, the
coast-line begins its grand southwards bend past Benghazi to
El Agheila, 150 miles farther south. By withdrawing towards
Barce, therefore, the Mekili force ensured that the whole of the
Italian detachments should fall squarely into our hands. The
7th Armoured Division, with its remaining fifty cruiser and ninety-
five light tanks, cut straight across the desert, west-south-west,
to cut the escape-route via the coastal road running south from
Benghazi, while the remainder of the British forces pushed the
enemy back along the coastal road into Benghazi.

The 60th Italian Division began its withdrawal from Derna
towards the Barce detachment on the 30th January. The British   30 Jan.
forces, whose administration was still incomplete, went ahead as
quickly as they could. The 7th Armoured Division cut the coastal
road in two places at Beda Fomm, south of Benghazi, on the

1940-41

5 Feb.	5th February, having covered 147 miles as the crow flies in 29 hours. It bagged a force of 5,000 men the same evening, and caught
6 Feb.	the main body of the 60th Italian Division next day. The enemy
7 Feb.	were fairly trapped, and at dawn on the 7th they surrendered unconditionally, with over 20,000 prisoners, 120 tanks, and 190 guns.

In this startling campaign, there were never more than two full British divisions employed, yet in the two calendar months starting on the 7th December, an Italian army of four corps, comprising nearly ten divisions, was destroyed. The enemy losses amounted to 130,000 prisoners, 400 tanks, and 1,240 guns—at a cost to the British of 500 killed, 1,373 wounded, and 55 missing. Here, however, operations had to cease, for the curtain was being rung up on the full-dress German invasion of Greece, and an armoured brigade and three infantry divisions had to be found to help hold them off.

Eritrea	Meanwhile, the Abyssinian campaign had been taking shape. The Italians had occupied Kassala, just inside the Sudan border
Mid-Jan.	from Eritrea, in July 1940. They moved back into Eritrea in mid-January, 1941, in anticipation of our impending operations.

The Abyssinian campaign was to be a double-headed operation, with Lieut.-Gen. Sir William Platt and the 4th and 5th Indian Divisions moving east from Kassala, while Lieut.-Gen. Sir Alan Cunningham and the 1st South African, and 11th and 12th African Divisions, moved up from Kenya, nearly a thousand miles away in the south.

20 Jan.	The Kassala force crossed the frontier into Eritrea on the 20th January, and caught the Italians up at Agordat about 80
31 Jan.	miles to the east. Here, the enemy were turned out of their position on the 31st, and followed up to Keren, where the Kassala-Asmara road passed through a formidable defile. Severe fighting was necessary before the British forces could break through, and the cost was fairly heavy, with some 3,000 killed and wounded. The
3 March	break-through did not occur till the 3rd March, and the further progress of this campaign, together with the inter-linked movement from Kenya, will be followed in the next chapter.

S. Europe	Meanwhile, events were slowly leading up to climax in southern Europe.
27 Sept.	Germany had strengthened her world position on the 27th September by expanding the Axis into the Three-Power Pact embracing Germany, Italy, and Japan. This pact was aimed mainly at the United States, whose practical aid to the British was the cause of serious misgivings in the Axis.

	1940-41
Germany next occupied Rumania. On the 28th October, Italy declared war on Greece. This latter campaign did not prosper, and the Italians soon found themselves well entangled in Albania, with no prospects of easy victory.	28 Oct.

It is uncertain whether Germany's increasing interest in southeastern Europe was designed in part to throw dust in Russian eyes, and permit of troop movements east without causing unnecessary misgivings in Moscow. At all events, German political pressure was extended to Bulgaria in January. Bulgaria became a party to the Three-Power Pact and was peacefully occupied by Germany on the 1st March. Pressure had by then been worked up against Yugoslavia, and it seemed clear to the Greeks that their turn would come next, and that Hitler would soon be coming to Mussolini's help. They accordingly invoked Britain's guarantee, and asked for assistance; and there matters stood when General Wavell's offensive was called to a halt and reinforcements sent up.

1 March

With the exception of the story of the 4th Battalion, it gives a sense almost of unreality to turn now to the Regiment's mundane doings during this time of stress. With the world as we knew it tumbling about our ears, and civilization descending into chaos, it is odd to reflect on the slow and painful deliberation with which democracy was turning its ploughshares back into swords.

India

Here, however, are the detailed histories of the seven battalions of the Regiment, so far as the records reveal them. It must, however, be added that there was not a man in any of the battalions that would not have gone to any of the fronts with rejoicing in his heart. But they were only small cogs in a huge machine, and for the present the greater part of them had to be content to know that Indian troops had played a large part in General Wavell's Libyan victory, and to know that the war had suddenly become a more heartening and personal matter in India than before.

The 1st Battalion, after the summer in Kohat, moved across in October to join the Bannu Brigade, then commanded by Brig. W. J. Crocker, who had himself previously served in the 1st Battalion.

1st Bn.
October

During the second week in December, trouble broke out in the Razmak direction. One of the regular routine columns from Razmak had met heavy and unexpected opposition from a Mahsud lashkar near Tauda China. The column suffered about a hundred casualties, and was virtually cut off. The Tochi Column was at once called

December

25

1940-41

out in Bannu, and ordered to move up, a few days before Christmas, in support of the Razmak Column.

The 1st Battalion was included in the Tochi Column, and marched up the Tochi Road with it, to Razani. The Razmak Narai 25 Dec. was crossed on Christmas Day, in intense cold, under heavy snow. Though the Narai was partly snowbound, the Column got safely through to Razmak the same evening. A warm and cheerful night 26 Dec. followed, and on Boxing Day, the Column moved on to Tauda China where it was found that the situation had improved, and most of the Mahsud lashkar had dispersed.

For the next few weeks, the Battalion was employed in the same general neighbourhood on road protection duties, the destruction of towers in Makin village, and clearing the countryside of parties of Mahsuds. The country was thickly covered with scrub, and protection duties not easy. The Sikhs had a few brief encounters, but suffered no casualties.

January In the second half of January, the Column started back to Bannu. As always at that time of year, it was intensely cold in those high altitudes, and the troops suffered much hardship. One particular night outside Razmak will live long in their memories, when it snowed all night.

Arrived back in Bannu, the Column was almost immediately called out again. The trouble this time was with the Daurs in the Upper Tochi, where they had been looting civilian lorries and levying subscriptions for the Faqir of Ipi. The Column returned up the Tochi Road, accordingly—not turning off across the river at Tal, on the Razmak Road, but keeping straight on to Miranshah. From Mirenshah, the Battalion took over as advanced guard on the way to Ahmad Khel. Only slight opposition was met that day, but the camp was heavily sniped during the night. The fire was reckoned as being nearly as severe as that in the Tori Khel's attack on Biche Kashkai in 1937. The troops were well dug in, however, and casualties were few.

Operations during the next few days were opposed, but the opposition was brushed aside, and the destruction of towers in Dilpurai and Kharra Kilai was completed to programme. The only sizable operation was when "B" Company, under Lieut. Workman, successfully surrounded a village, killed five wanted men, and captured their arms. The Column marched back to Bannu at the end of January, and remained there undisturbed until the summer.

2nd Bn. *The 2nd Battalion* was left in comparative peace in Jamrud
September during September, to carry on training. It played some part in testing out the vulnerability of the approaches to the Peshawar

1940-41

Plain down the Khyber river from Ali Masjid, and caused much alarm among the local villagers, who had seen no military action in that direction since 1896, and who turned out with rifles to defend their independence, if need be. However, the day ended with a gargantuan feast in the dry river-bed with the local Maliks, and all was well.

On the 8th October, the Battalion left Jamrud for Loralai, where training followed a normal course, and no operational columns were called for. Vacancies were allotted for courses in M.T. driving and maintenance, but the Battalion remained on a mule transport basis. 8 Oct.

The 3rd Battalion marched down from Chaman to Quetta in September, to join the 9th Indian Division, forming under Maj.-Gen. A. E. Barstow, M.C. The Battalion notes that the first Emergency Commissioned Officers arrived on posting to the Battalion at this time, and adds that many changes were taking place in officers, men, equipment and the normal routine life of peacetime. Mobilization orders were received early in February 1941, but the Battalion remained in Quetta for the time being. 3rd Bn. September

February

The 4th Battalion had mobilized and moved to Poona, where intensive training was undertaken, coupled with a good deal of attention to M.T. work. All manner of shifts were employed in bringing drivers up to a good standard on the road, including, it is understood, the daily Poona milk-round. 4th Bn.

Embarkation under sealed orders took place at the end of September, and the battalion found itself on its way to Egypt in the largest convoy (forty-four ships), which had so far passed up the Red Sea. September

The Italians held Eritrea, with a force of destroyers based on Massawa, but they left the convoy alone, otherwise than bombing it on three occasions—ineffectively—from a single aircraft flying at 25,000 feet.

Arrived in Egypt, the Battalion moved, on the 11th October, to Mena Camp, west of Cairo and close to the Pyramids. Here it joined the 7th Indian Infantry Brigade, the other two battalions in which—the 1st Battalion The Royal Sussex Regiment, and the 4th Battalion, 16th Punjab Regiment (the old 9th Bhopals)—were already there. 11 Oct.

Under Brig. H. R. Briggs, late of the 10th Baluch Regiment, training went ahead hard. Special attention was paid to desert movement, dispersion against air attack, and movement in mechanical transport. Meanwhile, the Battalion was brought on to the higher scale of equipment. Vickers-Berthiers were changed

1940-41

for Bren light machine-guns, and Bren carriers were issued, as also 2- and 3-inch mortars, tommy-guns for all section commanders, and 2-pounder guns for the anti-tank platoon. To underline, as it were, the significance of the occasion, an officer from the Public Relations Department spent ten days with the Battalion, and extensively filmed it. These shots were understood to have been shown later in *Drums in the Desert.*

23 Nov.   On the 23rd November, the Battalion moved forward by road and rail to Bagush, a defended locality on the coast some 15 miles west of Mersa Matruh. Work on the defences had to be combined with training, and the days were hardly long enough. Water had to be rationed, but, at one gallon per man per day, it proved ample, as the weather was still warm enough for the excellent sea bathing.

December   Early in December, the Brigade moved up to Bir Raslan, some 60 miles E.S.E. of Sidi Barrani, to take over guard duties on the large ration, ammunition, petrol, and water dumps there. The Royal Sussex was about 15 miles to the south, while the 4/16th and Brigade Headquarters were at Charing Cross, south of Mersa Matruh. The Brigade was now under orders of the 4th Indian Division.

Signs of an impending offensive were now in evidence, and on
8 Dec.   the morning of the 8th December, the Commanding Officer, Lieut.-Col. J. J. Purves, M.C., was told it would start next morning. This was not, however, to be passed on to the men till that evening.

In point of fact, it was that evening, at 8 p.m., that the bombardment of Sidi Barrani from the sea began. It could be heard going
9 Dec.   on all night. The Battalion was not engaged in next day's operations against Nibeiwa, the Tummars, and Sidi Barrani—having the useful, but less spectacular, role of helping with the forwarding of supplies. Daily, from dawn till dark, rations, petrol, and oil were dug up from carefully hidden pits, loaded into lorries, and sent off. In addition, a prisoner-of-war cage had to be built and manned. Though 12,000 prisoners passed through it in five days, the duties involved bore comparatively lightly on the Battalion as compared with the forwarding of supplies. Prisoners were usually brought in after dark, which meant turning out men to marshal them into the cage, and the issue of food and water was a long job. But the prisoners seemed glad to be out of it all, and required little guarding.

A week was spent in Bir Raslan, and dust-storms raged daily from 9 a.m. till 4 p.m. Water was down to only ¾-gallon per man, and it was difficult to keep clean, and have enough water for tea

1940-41

and other drinks. Soda-water could, however, be had from the
Mersa Matruh canteen, and the men found a few wells which, though
not fit for drinking, were a great boon for washing.

Big changes were in prospect, however. The decision to
initiate the drive into Eritrea, taken as soon as the Sidi Barrani
victory was assured, was put into effect without an instant's
delay, and on the 13th December the Battalion moved back to   13 Dec.
Bagush by M.T., on the first stage of its journey to the Sudan.
After two or three not unpleasant days in Bagush, the Battalion
moved on to Amariya, where several days were passed while
transport was loaded into a ship in Alexandria. Finally, on the
23rd December, the Battalion entrained for Port Said, where it   23 Dec.
arrived in the early hours of Christmas Eve. Embarkation on the 24 Dec.
S.S. *Etheopia*, in company with the 4/16th Punjabis, took place
the same evening, and at 9 a.m. on Christmas Day, the ship cast 25 Dec.
off.

An uneventful trip brought the troops to Port Sudan, where they
disembarked and entrained at once for Gebeit, where they arrived
on New Year's Eve. The Brigade was deployed over a vast front,   31 Dec.
stretching from Port Sudan to Khartum—somewhere of the order of
400 miles—with headquarters at Gebeit, and, knowing nothing of
the campaign about to start, the troops looked forward discon-
solately to a long spell of line-of-communication duty. Training
continued accordingly, and the hilly nature of the country enabled
the Battalion to keep up a standard of fitness which proved of
inestimable value later in the Eritrean hills.

At 11 p.m. on the 11th January, 1941, orders came in for the   11 Jan.
battalion to move at 9 o'clock next morning, by M.T. to Aroma,
a small village north of Kassala, the capital of Kassala Province,
and 250 miles east of Khartum. Kassala town was at that time
held by the enemy. A hard two-day cross-country drive, varied by
stretches on roads which would need experiencing to be believed,
brought the Battalion to its destination, where it joined "Gazelle
Force", commanded by Col. Messervy, who was later to command
the 4th Indian Division. "Gazelle Force" comprised a Field
Regiment R.A., Skinner's Horse, the Sikhs (lorry-borne), and an
armoured car and motorized infantry detachment of the Sudan
Defence Force. It was soon to achieve some enviable distinction
for the dash and leadership of its commander and for the speed
of its movement across country.

The first task was to attack Kassala, but the Italians slipped
away beforehand. A rapid pursuit caught them up about 70 miles
to the west, prior to which offensive enemy action had relied
upon fairly severe low-level bombing, and dive machine-gunning

1941

from the air. The Battalion got off lightly, and with no loss in equipment except for two trucks burnt out as a result of machine-gun fire.

The Keru Gorge, however, where the Italians made their first stand, gave a certain amount of trouble. The road, here, passed through a very narrow valley, about a mile-and-a-half long, with high rocky hills to either side. Cavalry advanced troops, in the first instance, reconnoitring the position, reported that a ridge covering the gorge was certainly only very lightly held, if held at all. But when at 1.30 p.m., after an hour-and-three-quarters for prior preparation, the Battalion went in to the attack, in order to hold and occupy this ridge, it was found that there were two ridges, not one, and the enemy was holding them in considerable strength. From the second ridge, which was separated from the first by a narrow valley, heavy fire was suddenly opened, and the Battalion was temporarily held up. Outstanding gallantry won Sub. Fateh Mohammed the Indian Order of Merit. Lieut.-Col. Purves was wounded, command of the Battalion passing to Maj. R. Bampfield, the Second-in-Command.

21 Jan. This attack took place on the 21st January, and the position remained unchanged till dark. The 5th Indian Division, meanwhile, made a threat to the enemy's rear, and the Italians slipped away in something of a hurry, during the night. The Battalion, however,
23 Jan. stayed up on the hills till the evening of the 23rd January, when it came down and bivouacked a few miles short of the gorge.

Transport, as always, was difficult. The Battalion's troop-carrying lorries were now required elsewhere, so the troops continued the advance on foot. They were attached for the time being to the 11th Indian Infantry Brigade commanded by Brig. R. A. Savory, late of the 1st Battalion. The pursuit went on at a fast rate, and during the next two days, the Battalion covered
25 Jan. 42 miles, reaching Biscia on the second afternoon, and halting there for the night.
26 Jan. Next morning, the 26th January, the Battalion moved forward to a defensive position five miles short of Agordat, where the enemy was in position. Some bombing and light shelling of the Battalion caused no loss.
27 Jan. On the 27th, the Battalion suffered yet another change of Higher Command, and came under the orders of the 5th Indian Infantry Brigade. It was ordered forward to a ridge near Laquatat Fort, which formed part of the outer defences of Agordat, and which lay on a hill rising some 500 feet from the plain. Little movement was seen in the fort, and the general opinion was that it was only lightly held, if held at all. The Battalion was

                                                                    1941
accordingly ordered to occupy it at 3 a.m. on the 29th. After a   29 Jan.
night advance under cover of darkness, the troops rested or slept
till 1.30 a.m. The two companies detailed for the attack then
moved off up the hill, but about two-thirds of the way up
pandemonium broke loose. The enemy were holding the fort in
considerable strength. Two platoons of the left company were
held up, but one platoon moved forward with the right company,
which got to within about 40 yards of the main enemy positions,
behind their double apron barbed-wire defences. This wire could
not be penetrated, but the troops gave a good account of themselves with hand grenades, Jem. Nazar Mohammed doing
particularly gallant work. As day came on, however, it became
obvious that their position was quite untenable, and they were
withdrawn to the start-line, where there was some protection. The
withdrawal was conducted most skilfully by Capt. A. McNiven,
who was awarded a well-deserved Military Cross. For the remainder
of the day, the enemy kept up steady light machine-gun and rifle-
fire on the Battalion's position, but achieved no more than making
the day relatively uncomfortable.

Col. Messervy came up during the afternoon and told the Battalion
that it had reverted to his command, and was now back in Gazelle
Force again. He gave orders for the Battalion to pull back about
2 miles, and take up a position on a 3-mile front to cover the left
flank of an attack on Agordat to be made at 6 a.m. on the 31st.   31 Jan.
This attack was to follow the valley through which the Barentu-
Agordat road passed, and it provided a magnificent spectacle for
Battalion Headquarters as the 5th and 11th Indian Infantry Brigades
went forward with a small detachment of five "I" tanks. The fight
was won by 1 p.m.—and was closely followed by a telephone
message to say that the Battalion had reverted to command of the
5th Indian Infantry Brigade, and was to move back at once to a
bivouac area about a mile from Brigade Headquarters, which was
itself about 8 miles away.

The Battalion did not reach its new area till 7 p.m., and was
away again at 8.15 p.m. to cut the road leading out of the far side
of Agordat and prevent as many Italians as possible from escaping.
However, though the troops were in position by 2.30 a.m. on the
1st February, moving with no more reliable assistance than an   1 Feb.
inaccurate map printed on cloth, from which no worth-while bearing
could be taken, the Italians had beaten them to it, and were gone.
The pursuit was carried on by the 11th Indian Infantry Brigade,
leaving the 5th with the unsavoury business of clearing the
battlefield round Agordat, guarding prisoners and protecting the
aerodrome. The town was in a sorry state. In the short interval

1941

between the departure of the Italians and the arrival of our troops, the Italian quarters had been thoroughly looted, and broken household furniture, papers, and equipment littered the streets. Salvage included thirty guns of various sizes, and enormous quantities of rifle, machine-gun and artillery ammunition.

During this enforced halt, the Battalion was glad to be able to pay a visit to Laquatat Fort to recover and bury the men killed there on the 29th of January. The opportunity was also taken to look over the defences and see how the Italians went about these things. The Italians, apparently, were in the habit of choosing a dominating feature and ringing it round, about 40 feet below the crest, with a wide concrete trench, bastioned for machine-gun posts. On the reverse slope there would be a few gun and mortar emplacements. Three or four strongly built dug-outs, supposedly for the higher commanders, were usually included.

Well down the slopes, and dug in under the huge rocks and boulders with which the Eritrean hills are covered, would be positions for snipers and light machine-guns. During artillery bombardments, the occupants of these positions, sheltering under the rocks, suffered few casualties, and the moment the artillery lifted, they would be back in their positions, ready to meet an attack with a hail of small-arms fire.

The stay at Agordat did not last long. The other battalions of the 5th Indian Infantry Brigade soon started moving forward, and 5 Feb. at 10 p.m. on the 5th February, the Sikhs were warned that another battalion was on its way to relieve them, and that they were to be ready to move at midnight after handing over. The Sikhs were well spread out. Some companies were upwards of five miles distant from Battalion Headquarters. The relieving unit arrived a little late, however, after everyone was in, and the Battalion went on as a whole, reaching a point near the Keren hills, 45 miles ahead 6 Feb. from Agordat, at 7 a.m. on the 6th, and bivouacking. At 10 a.m., a Brigade conference was held. Those attending were given the rather damping news that the pass leading up to Keren had been blown up by the Italians and that Gazelle Force and the tanks had failed to get through. The Italians were strongly posted on the hills to the left of the road, and the 11th Indian Infantry Brigade had been held up in the attempt to take them.

It had now been decided to send the 5th Indian Infantry Brigade round along a route lying well to the right. There was known to be a small path there which led to Keren via the Aqua Col, and it was thought that this might be made fit for tanks and light transport.

The Brigade was to move forward at 1 p.m. to a lying-up position

1941

4 miles short of the Aqua Col. Here it would remain till dark, when the advance towards the Col would be continued. When the attack went in, the 4/6th Rajputana Rifles would lead off by advancing against and occupying the Aqua Col, while the remainder of the Brigade stood fast. Half-an-hour after success was signalled, the Sikhs would follow, and assault the ridge overlooking Keren. Another half-hour's pause, and the Royal Fusiliers would go forward and attack Keren itself. To solve the maintenance problem, one company per battalion was to be employed carrying three days water and food. But little time could be allowed for reconnaissance, and all orders had to be given off the map.

When all is said, it is not surprising that the operation failed, in spite of the great gallantry displayed by the leading battalion, in which Sub. Richpal Singh won a posthumous Victoria Cross. The advance to the lying-up position was carried out in full view of the enemy, though he reacted at the time with only light shelling. Later, however, on arrival at the lying-up position, the Royal Fusiliers came under heavy shell-fire. Though all hope of surprise had gone, the attack duly started about 6 p.m., the Rajputana Rifles meeting very strong resistance on their way up, and being unable to get on. As a result, the Sikhs and Fusiliers spent the night where they were. The Rajputana Rifles held the ground they had gained all next day and into the following night, and were then withdrawn under a screen of the Central India Horse and Skinner's   7 Feb.
Horse. The Brigade then pulled back 2 miles to Happy Valley where it spent the next two days. Though, despite its name, the   8 Feb.
valley was overlooked by the enemy, there was little shelling, nor did he show any inclination to send down patrols or put in any other form of offensive action from the hill-tops.

On the 10th, fresh attack orders came in—this time, with proper   10 Feb.
opportunities for prior reconnaissance. This attack was to be directed on the Aqua Col on a two-battalion front. The Sikhs were to attack on the right, with the Rajputana Rifles on the left, and the Royal Fusiliers in reserve to exploit success. The 25-pounders were to put down a support programme of 3,000 rounds in 50 minutes on the Sikh front, and 4,000 in 60 minutes for the Rajputana Rifles.

The same evening, it was decided to postpone the attack for one day to allow the 29th Indian Infantry Brigade to be brought forward next night—the 11th—to exploit success. In the interval, Lieut.-   11 Feb.
Col. Bampfield made good use of the opportunity, and took his company commanders right forward to Rajputana Ridge, which the 4/6th had held so gallantly a few days before, for a detailed reconnaissance of routes and objectives.

1941
12 Feb.   At 5.45 a.m. on the 12th, the attack went in. On the Battalion front "C" Company (Hartley) was on the right, and "A" Company (Sub. Ujagar Singh) on the left. Hill-side and crest had disappeared under a cloud of smoke and dust from the artillery barrage. The advance went well until the troops were within a hundred feet of the top. The artillery then lifted—and a storm of fire burst out from the enemy screen among the rocks and boulders under the crest. This fire, at point-blank range, caused very heavy loss, but two sections of "C" Company reached the top through a shower of hand-grenades, both section commanders scoring several of the enemy to their own individual bayonets. One of them, Gurpal Singh, as good a centre-forward as the Battalion hockey team ever had, was killed. The other, Naik Ujagar Singh, the battalion goalkeeper, moving ahead of his section, attacked a machine-gun post single-handed. He shot down two of the enemy with his rifle, and then, after throwing grenades into the post, rushed the position, bayoneted the remainder of the detachment, and captured the machine-gun and a revolver. In spite of being severely wounded by a grenade immediately after, he held on to the captured position with the three surviving men of his section, till definitely ordered to withdraw and have his wounds dressed. For this outstanding display of gallantry and leadership, he was very properly awarded the Indian Order of Merit. Seventy out of the eighty-seven men of "C" Company that went into action were either killed or wounded, and among those seriously wounded was Sub. Bahadur Singh, whom some will remember as first a bugler and then an intelligent young signaller in the First World War, and as a brilliant athlete between the wars.

Meanwhile, "A" Company on the left had made steady progress, and were nearly at the crest when heavy pressure caused the Rajputana Rifles on their left, to pull back. As a consequence, orders were issued for the Sikhs to establish their line about one-third of the way up the hill, and hold on there till dark. This was accomplished at no great cost, and as darkness fell, both battalions withdrew without interference to Happy Valley. The 29th Indian Infantry Brigade went back at the same time to Tessenei, near Kassala.

The Battalion took up its old bivouac area at Kilo 112, and spent the rest of this six-month period with alternate weeks on the hills around Cameron Ridge or farther north, and back down the valley resting. The British left flank was being continually extended to keep pace with the extension of the Italian right, but there was little hostile activity in the air. Such small air-forces as we had available sufficed to keep the Italians well away from the front line.

	1940-41
The 5th Battalion spent the cold weather in Razmak once more, on the same strenuous routine duties as before.	5th Bn.

The 6th Battalion left Nowshera at short notice in October. 6th Bn.
Joining the Landi Kotal Brigade, it was immediately absorbed into the construction duties of the new Khyber defences, digging trenches and strong-points, and achieving a fine state of physical fitness. It says a good deal for the hard work put in by the officers and Viceroy's commissioned officers that a battalion put together like a jig-saw puzzle only two months before could be judged fit for a tour of duty in the Khyber.

The 7th Battalion had been raised, as already noted, simul- 7th Bn.
taneously with the 6th Battalion, on the 7th August. It may be convenient here to give a detailed account of its start in life and first few months of service, from a record kindly made available by Maj. N. Egar, as this will not only illustrate the start of the 7th Battalion, but give a glimpse of the conditions under which most new battalions came into being.

As already described, the Battalion was to be raised in Nasirabad. Composition, as in the 6th Battalion, was to be two-thirds Jat Sikh and one-third Punjabi-Mohammedan, and the Battalion was to be raised by "milking" the active battalions, and receiving a draft of 250 recruits from the Training Battalion. "The recruiting of the latter started immediately the decision to raise the Battalion was announced, and on the date of raising they had completed about two months training."

On the 7th August, the British officers and advanced parties of 7 Aug.
the drafts from the five active battalions reported their arrival in Nasirabad. "The main bodies of these drafts were not due to arrive for several days, and this period was devoted to preparing for their reception and the organization of the Battalion office. The latter presented a depressing spectacle on the first day, consisting of five completely empty rooms and one in which boxes of type-writers, stationery, etc., were piled high; the task of creating order out of such chaos appeared rather terrifying. For several days each company office consisted of a table, chair, some paper and a pencil. Affairs were gradually straightened, however, and on the 8th August, the first Battalion Order was published." 8 Aug.

Nasirabad was a good station in which to start life. Two other battalions were being raised there at the same time—the 7/8th Punjab Regiment, and the 7/13th Frontier Force Rifles—so there was plenty of company and opportunity to talk problems over. The Sikhs were in the old British infantry lines, with unlimited space and electric light in every barrack-room. The climate was

35

1940

reasonable for the time of year, and the country admirable for mountain warfare training. The hills were only three or four miles to the N.W. of Cantonments—and the absence of cultivation allowed free movement cross-country in almost every direction.

11 Aug. The drafts of trained soldiers came in on the 11th and 12th August, and were immediately posted to companies. There were insufficient Punjabi-Mohammedans among the Viceroy's and non-commissioned officers to form a Punjabi-Mohammedan Company, so all Punjabi-Mohammedans were attached to "A" Company for the first few months. Thereafter there was to be a Punjabi-Mohammedan platoon in each company. This compromise was, of course, due to the circumstance that only the 4th and 5th Battalions had Punjabi-Mohammedans on their establishment.

The first fortnight was spent organizing the new companies, and selecting and training non-commissioned officers as instructors for the recruits. "Training was much handicapped by a lack of equipment"—the common cry. "Rifles and bayonets (imaginary) made it difficult for the men to maintain their original and very marked enthusiasm."

22 Sept. The recruits began arriving on the 22nd September, and all were in by the end of three or four weeks. The thirty best N.C.O.s were put on to training them, with a view to their joining their companies in January 1941. The training of officers and the remaining non-commissioned officers went on during September and October, followed by section and platoon training on a limited scale till the recruits joined their companies.

In games and athletics, the Battalion soon began to make its mark. Hockey went ahead well, but in athletics results were better still. The Battalion easily won the cross-country race, with the first five men home, to its credit, and in the triangular sports meeting, it won every event.

The problem of an officers' mess was taken in hand. The various active battalions had made generous contributions to all Battalion funds, including the mess, but there could naturally be no question of raising anything but a Field Service Mess. The Government grant of 1500 rupees for the purpose was received, and equipment ordered.

Orders had already been received, in September, for the Battalion's move to Bareilly early in February, and thence to Razmak, but these were varied early in October, and Dinapur, in Bihar, substituted for Bareilly. This decision presented the Battalion with a whole crop of new problems connected with its training, and welding into a corporate whole. One company was to be detached to Muzaffarpur, six hours distant by train, and in

1940

Dinapur itself, another company was to live by itself in lines a mile away from the remainder. Battalion training would be a farce—not less so thanks to the cultivation surrounding the cantonment in all directions but one, where there was a small area of waste land, the possibilities of which would soon be exhausted.

On the 14th October, the advance party was despatched to Dinapur. 14 Oct.
On the 20th, "C" Company left for Muzaffarpur. The remainder of 20 Oct.
the Battalion left on the 21st in two trains, linking up in Agra. 21 Oct.
Here, thanks to a twelve-hour halt, parties were able to visit and admire the Taj Mahal.

"C" Company reached Muzaffarpur on the 22nd. The Battalion, 22 Oct.
less "C" Company, reached Dinapur on the morning of the 24th. 24 Oct.
"A", "B" and "H.Q." Companies were located in Victoria Lines, while the recruits and "D" Company went to Arrah Barracks, which had the only respectable parade ground. These barracks, put up by the Dutch, were the oldest occupied barracks in India, but seem to have been in a state of good repair. Their proportions are described as very good, and the setting most impressive. Built of red brick, faced here and there with concrete, they overlooked two sides of a well-grassed square intersected by two fine avenues of trees. Originally, the other two sides of the square comprised the Governor's residence and the officers' quarters, traces of which still remained. The only other comment on Dinapur, other than its poor training facilities, records its possession of three enormous graveyards. One can forgive a somewhat gloomy approach to Dinapur with such embellishments.

Training was pushed on, and early in December, a two-company December scheme was put up for the Army Commander. With Razmak looming closer, however, and complications in training due to companies being under strength, it had been decided to curtail recruit training by one month, and post recruits to companies at the end of November. The signallers and the machine-gun platoon being much under strength, the necessary number of specialist recruits were also transferred to "H.Q." Company. Training was now devoted to three main subjects:

Training of recruit specialists in "H.Q." Company.
Training of one Lewis-gun section per platoon.
Mountain warfare training.

In addition, a sepoy cadre for appointment to Lance Naik was started with twenty-four men in December, and arrangements were made for another thirty in January.

Mountain warfare had perforce to be practised on the flat. But lectures and sand model exercises helped. In addition, a C.O.'s fortnightly parade was held, with either a route march or

37

1941

1 Jan.

a limited exercise, together with a weekly drill parade under the Adjutant. Practice was also put in hand for the Proclamation Day parade on the coming 1st of January, and the Battalion made a very good showing before the Governor of Bihar and a number of visitors from Patna on that occasion, albeit dressed in grey shirts, and lacking puttees.

**11 Jan.-
8 Feb.**

During January, the Battalion went into a mountain warfare camp at Jamalpur, in the standing camp of the East Indian Railway Regiment, Auxiliary Force (India). The camp lasted from the 11th January to the 8th February. "H.Q." Company was out for the whole period, and rifle companies each had a fortnight. "D" Company also relieved "C" Company in Muzaffarpur.

So far as actual mountain warfare training was concerned, this was limited by the rather small scale of the hills, but much could be done by way of sangaring, and the occupation and construction of perimeter camps. Each party concluded its period of training with two Battalion schemes which gave a good picture of column conditions.

Another preoccupation during January was the receipt of news of the prospective raising of the 8th and 9th Battalions of the Regiment, towards whom the 7th Battalion would be expected to contribute its quota of trained men. The sepoy cadre, already referred to, was some set-off against this. Indeed, the cadre had been started very much with this in view. But the prospect of being "milked" of trained non-commissioned officers and men just as the Battalion was preparing to move up to the North-West Frontier and take its share of the burden there, commended itself to none. Numbers to be sent totalled 2 Viceroy's commissioned officers, 40 non-commissioned officers, and 21 sepoys. This included a number of Punjabi-Mohammedan non-commissioned officers whom the Battalion could ill afford to lose, and whose despatch was to postpone still further the formation of a Punjabi-Mohammedan company. However, a little time was given to absorb the shock and make the necessary reorganization—and there matters stood at the end of the period.

Chapter IV

MARCH TO AUGUST 1941

Backscreen

General Wavell's strategy in the Middle East further unfolded during the summer of 1941. General Platt, with the 4th and 5th Indian Divisions, broke through the Keren position on the 27th March. On the 1st April, they were at Asmara, and at Massawa on the 4th.	Abyssinia 27 March 4 April

The other half of the pincer-movement, meanwhile, was making quick progress from the south. Here, the 1st South African Division, and the 11th and 12th African Divisions, from Kenya, under General Cunningham, had moved up north-east on the 24th January, towards the Juba river. On the 18th February, the river was crossed, and at 6 a.m. on the 23rd, a motorized African Brigade Group was sent off, heading for Mogadiscio, on the Indian Ocean, 275 miles away to the north-east. This operation was a complete success—the Italians, surprised, abandoning 350,000 gallons of motor spirit and 80,000 gallons of aviation petrol. This invaluable find enabled the advance to go forward at once without waiting for a supply terminal to be established—whether at Mogadiscio or at Merca, an Italian port some distance down the coast to the south-west.

    24 Jan.
    18 Feb.
    23 Feb.

On the 1st March, the troops moved on in the direction of Giggiga, an Abyssinian township a little east of north from Mogadiscio, from which it was 774 miles distant by road. Apart from slight opposition at Dagabur, on the 10th March, 590 miles from Mogadiscio, there was no sign of the enemy, and the force marched into Giggiga on the 17th.

    1 March

    10 March

    17 March

Meanwhile, one day earlier, on the 16th, a small force from Aden had reoccupied Berbera in British Somaliland. Berbera, lying 204 miles north-east of Giggiga on the Gulf of Aden, provided Gen. Cunningham with a much shortened supply line, and its recapture had the additional happy consequence of causing the Italians to evacuate British Somaliland altogether.

    16 March

From Giggiga, the axis of the advance was changed from north to west, towards Harar, which was occupied on the 25th. Addis Ababa, already abandoned by the Italians, was in our hands by the 4th April. Up to this date, Gen. Cunningham's forces had captured over

    25 March

    4 April

1941

50,000 prisoners and occupied 360,000 square miles of country at a cost of 135 men killed, 310 wounded, 52 missing, and 4 captured.

13 April Pausing till the 13th April, the 1st South African Brigade next led off towards Dessie, 250 miles to the north. Opposition was encountered in the Combolcia Pass, south of Dessie. It took five
18 April days to turn the Italians out; but when the South Africans did so, they captured 8,000 prisoners at a cost, in killed, of 10 men.
20 April Dessie was occupied on the 20th April.

The Duke of Aosta, commanding the Italian forces, had withdrawn to Amba Alagi, a mountain stronghold 140 air-miles north of Dessie. With Gen. Platt attacking him from the north and Gen. Cunningham from the south, he surrendered unconditionally on
18 May the 18th May, but was accorded the honours of war. Other operations followed, more especially at Gondar, before the country was cleared, but it was the fact that in the four months to the beginning of June, the Italian forces numbering about 220,000 men, had been practically eliminated with all their equipment, and nearly a million square miles of land occupied. This success removed a serious embarrassment from the southern flank of the Mid-Eastern front, where an increasingly threatening situation was rapidly taking shape.

S. Europe Before turning to the main front in the Western Desert, however, it is necessary to look farther north to Greece and the Balkans.
March German pressure on Yugoslavia had intensified during March and had brought the country into association with the Three-Power Pact by the 24th. Gen. Simovitch reversed the situation on the
27 March 27th by means of a *coup d'état*; but the end was foregone, and
6 April Germany invaded both Yugoslavia and Greece on the 6th April.

This moment of gloom, however, was briefly lit up by Admiral Cunningham's victory at Matapan, when seven Italian warships were sunk, and the immediate strategical issue in the central Mediterranean to that extent cleared up.

Returning to the land front, the Yugoslavs fell in a sense into the same error as the Poles in 1939. They tried to defend too much with too little. Endeavouring to protect the Croats and Slovenes in the north, they laid both flanks open to attack. They were quickly pushed back to Sarajevo, where twenty-eight divisions
17 April surrendered on the 17th April.

In Greece, similar causes led to similar effects. Political reasons again over-ruled good strategy. The Greeks insisted on holding a very forward line, with serious over-extension, and open to penetration from the direction of Serbia. The Greeks disposed of twenty and a half divisions; the British a little over

three, comprising 57,660 men of the New Zealand Division, the
6th and 7th Australian Divisions, the 1st Armoured Brigade, and
a Polish Brigade, and deployed on a front of about a hundred miles
in the middle of the Greek line.

1941

Opening the invasion on the 6th April with a heavy air attack, the Germans moved in with a number of armoured columns deployed over a wide front. They pinched out Salonika, which they occupied on the 8th April, and simultaneously forced their way through the Monastir Pass from Serbia against the over-extended Allied centre, which they deeply penetrated. The two separated halves were driven apart, and the main Greek armies on the left were cut off in the Epirus, in west central Greece, where they capitulated on the 21st April.

6 April

8 April

21 April

There was no further object in the British forces remaining in Greece which was now irretrievably lost, and a move back to the Peloponnesus in southern Greece was begun; and a very close thing it was. For the Germans, too, had lost no time and, on the 26th April had seized the bridge over the Corinth Canal west of Athens by means of an air-borne landing, and much dislocated our programme. A German motorized division from the Epirus crossed the Gulf of Corinth from Patras, but the retreating forces slipped away, and something under 43,000 of our men were evacuated out of Greece on the nights of the 26th-27th and 27th-28th April. All heavy equipment was lost.

26 April

26-28 April

The weakness and dislocation of our Middle-Eastern forces caused by this excursion into Greece had regrettable consequences in the Western Desert. Gen. Wavell had opened the way to Tripoli but was unable to exploit it. The Axis forces were in no two minds about the opportunity now presented to them, and of the advantage over us they possessed in being so much closer to their home bases. It followed that while our forces were being weakened, theirs were reinforced, by a big diversion of German and Italian formations, including much armour. Gen. Wavell was at a special disadvantage from the despatch of so much of his air strength to Greece, and could not adequately either protect his installations in Cyrenaica from air attack, or keep a good watch on the enemy. The port of Benghazi had been rendered unsafe as a British supply terminal, and our troops were being supplied from large and vulnerable dumps established in the desert. This implied a certain degree of administrative immobility since the dumps could not easily be moved, once established, and the troops were deprived of much liberty of manoeuvre should enemy pressure increase.

N. Africa

1941
March

At the end of March, some two months after Gen. Wavell's winter campaign had been interrupted by the developments in Greece, all we had in the forward areas east of Agheila, 150 miles south of Benghazi, were the 2nd Armoured Division less one brigade, the 9th Australian Division less one brigade, together with one Indian Motor Brigade Group at Mekili, 200 miles away to the north-east and 100 miles east of Barce. The tanks of the 2nd Armoured Division were under establishment, and not all completely battleworthy, and several of its units were not fully trained in desert warfare. Strategical policy at the moment was unavoidably negative, and it was accepted that if hostile pressure developed, our forces might have to move back. Reports of current enemy strengths could not be checked owing to the shortage of reconnaissance aircraft, but it was known that Gen. Rommel had arrived, and that important forces had come with him.

31 March

In point of fact, when Rommel attacked on the 31st March, he had with him one German light armoured division, and two Italian divisions, one armoured and the other motorized. Knowing the British dependence for mobility on their petrol dumps, special emphasis was laid on the destruction of these in the Axis plan, by air bombing.

Rommel used very similar strategy to Wavell in his use of the Benghazi bulge. He aimed in exactly the same way, at pushing our forces northward up the coastal road, while cutting across towards Mekili to block our retreat. In anticipation of this, our 2nd Armoured Division, when pressed back northwards from Agheila,

2 April

took up a position, on the evening of the 2nd April, to the north of Agedabia, from which it could both flank the Benghazi road and block the track running via Msus to Mekili.

What effect these dispositions, if persisted in, would have had on Rommel's plans will never be known, for within a very few

3 April

hours, on the 3rd April, the report of a strong German armoured column approaching Msus caused the detachment there to set fire to the petrol on which the British armoured forces had relied.

Benghazi, meantime, had been abandoned, and the organization of a defensive line between Derna and Mekili had been taken in hand. Enemy pressure in any event made this line untenable, but the situation was not made easier by the inability of the 2nd Armoured Division to co-operate till something was done about its petrol supply—and this in turn was complicated by violent air attacks directed against its wireless vehicles and petrol lorries. The Armoured Division succeeded in getting back to Mekili on the

6 April

evening of the 6th April, but its 3rd Armoured Brigade was captured next day, struggling to get through to Derna in the hunt for petrol, while the remainder of the Division was heavily attacked at Mekili. An attempt was made to get it away, that night, and the 1st Royal Horse Artillery and some Indian troops managed to break through and escape at dawn on the 8th. But the rest of the Division was captured, and hence passes out of our story.

1941
7 April

8 April

In the north, meanwhile, on the 7th, the 9th Australian Division reached Tobruk. Later that day, the 7th Australian Division, with some tanks, arrived by sea to join them. There was no intention of abandoning Tobruk, which was invested by the enemy on the 11th. The main enemy forces then pushed on some 75 miles to Sollum, just inside the Egyptian frontier. An attempt to turn them out of Sollum and Fort Capuzzo failed, and operations then came to a halt.

7 April

11 April

Further causes of embarrassment had been working up in Iraq, where the government was linked to Britain by a treaty of friendship which gave the latter a measure of control, and ensured preferential treatment in certain directions. A political set-up of this kind is never really satisfactory. Interested parties can always make capital out of it under the nationalist ticket, as an infringement of sovereign independence. Under world conditions as disturbed as they were in 1941, it was not difficult for Nazi agents to create an atmosphere very detrimental to Britain, and in Rashid Ali Ghailani, the Prime Minister, the Germans found a tool ready to their hand.

Iraq

Throughout the war, the British Empire was to be continually over-extended, and this time was no exception. To meet the deteriorating position *vis-à-vis* Japan, Maj.-Gen. A. E. Barstow's 9th Indian Division was being gradually shipped across to Malaya, but, in April 1941, certain of its units and formations had still not actually left India. These included its H.Q. Divisional Artillery, the 3rd Field Regiment R.A., the 20th Indian Infantry Brigade, and other units including most of the Divisional M.T., which were embarking in a convoy of ten ships at Karachi preparatory to joining the Division. Though not in any sense distributed according to tactical requirements in their ships, these troops did represent a reserve conveniently sited for diversion to Busra early in April, when the crisis blew up. Though strict secrecy was observed on the diversion of these troops to Iraq, it leaked out, however, and it was learnt later that the news reached both Baghdad and Teheran on the 12th April, actually a few hours before the ships cast off and sailed down the harbour.

12 April

The Commander and the A.A. and Q.M.G. (Col. F. T.

1941

Birdwood, late of the 2nd Battalion) from the 10th Indian Division, joined the convoy, arriving by air from Delhi an hour or two before it sailed. The G.S.O.1 of the Division was to follow by air direct to Busra. With the 20th Indian Infantry Brigade was the 3rd Battalion of the Regiment. Capt. P. J. Mitcheson of the 4th Battalion was Staff Captain of the Brigade—so the Sikh Regiment was well represented.

Sufficient general detail of this expedition will be found in the 3rd Battalion record below, and no further comment is accordingly included here.

Crete

30 April

Looking back towards the Mediterranean, it will be remembered that our forces had evacuated Greece at the end of April. A proportion was diverted to Crete to reinforce the small garrison established there on the 1st November, 1940. Maj.-Gen. Sir Bernard Freyberg, V.C., took over command at Crete on the 30th April, with 27,550 men, of whom many were unarmed and without essential equipment, under his orders.

It had never been possible to find sufficient aircraft for Crete, though there were three aerodromes along the north coast. These aerodromes were at Heraklion, a little east of the centre—at Retimo, farther west—and at Maleme, near the western end of the island. Troops were stationed at these three points, and at Suda Bay, between Maleme and Retimo. Lack of transport kept these detachments from being mutually supporting, though, in any case, the unceasing attacks from the air, gradually built up, would have severely limited movement between them. Crete was well within range of a number of hostile airfields, but outside the range of British fighters based in Egypt.

19 May

20 May

By the 19th May, British aircraft in Crete could no longer maintain themselves in the face of German pressure from the air, and were withdrawn. Next day, the 20th, the enemy attacked.

The attack was heralded at 8 a.m. by the dropping of a cloud of parachutists, under cover of a violent air bombardment, on points at and between Maleme and Suda Bay in the west of the island. A small force of glider-borne troops was landed west of Maleme aerodrome. Other detachments descended on Heraklion and Retimo—bringing the total of enemy troops landed that day to about 7,000. Many were killed by fire from the defence, but the balance held on.

21-22 May

During the next two days, intense bomber and fighter support covered the landing of further strong forces of glider-borne troops at Maleme, where they established themselves in spite of the aerodrome being under British artillery fire. Enemy plans were

1941

somewhat dislocated, however, during the nights of the 21st-22nd and 22nd-23rd May, when sea-borne forces attempted to make the crossing in caiques. Though without air-cover, ships of the Royal Navy decisively checked them, but at a cost of two cruisers and four destroyers lost, and many ships damaged.

Something of a come-back on land was staged on the 26th, when "I" tanks cleared up the situation at Retimo, but some 20,000 Germans were now ashore on the west of the island, while an Italian landing was effected on the 28th at Sitia in the east. The decision had already by then been taken to evacuate the island, and this was begun on the night of the 28th-29th May, from Sphakia in the south, towards the western end of Crete.

26 May

28 May

The Germans lost a little time in following up. They contacted our rearguard on the 30th, but were repulsed. Shipping and naval escorts, taking off men, were meanwhile suffering heavy losses from the air, and it was decided that the evacuation could not be continued after the night of the 31st May-1st June. There had been some 13,000 casualties in killed or captured, but, against this, Gen. Wavell estimated that the enemy had suffered between 12,000 and 15,000, a high proportion killed. The total British strength taken off amounted to 14,580.

30 May

Infiltration, meanwhile, had been going ahead in Syria among the Vichy French. In May, German aircraft appeared on a Syrian landing-ground about the same time that German Messerschmidts made their appearance in Iraq. A short and bitter campaign followed to expel the German element. Operations began on the 8th June, with the 7th Australian Division, less one brigade left in Tobruk, and a Free French formation, from the Middle East, co-operating with other formations which moved over from Iraq. Gen. Dentz, commanding the Vichy French troops, applied for an armistice on the 11th July and Syria came under Allied occupation on the 14th.

Syria
May

8 June

11 July
14 July

On the 18th June, a treaty of mutual assistance was signed between Germany and Turkey at Angora. By now, Hitler presumably thought his southern flank sufficiently protected to cover his forthcoming operations against Russia. He had attempted the previous month to cover his rear as well, but that had failed. On the 10th May, it will be remembered, his deputy, Rudolph Hess, had made a lonely flight across the North Sea, baling out over southern Scotland, in an eleventh-hour effort to detach Great Britain. Success in this would have brought rich rewards, and large forces could have been freed from a passive role in the west. But

Russia
18 June

10 May

1941

he much misjudged the temper and character of the British people if he placed any faith in the success of Hess's mission.

One must suppose that the fast-moving and locally decisive operations in the Mediterranean theatre counted as very little in the main German strategy at the moment. Plans against Russia had long been maturing, and, as already suggested in an earlier chapter, the extension of the war to Greece and the Mediterranean may have partly, at least, originated in the excuse it offered for moving large German armies in good time, towards the east. At what exact moment Hitler abandoned his western strategy and decided to divert his armies to the conquest of Russia can never be known, but it is clear that active preparation to this end began about the middle of December, 1940, and that it was then hoped to launch the attack in the middle of May, 1941. As already shown, the drift eastwards of German forces began very soon after the fall of France. Probably neither of the contracting governments had any illusions about the lasting qualities of the Russo-German non-aggression pact, and a movement towards the west of Russian troops from Siberia had started early in 1941. In the weeks before June warnings from Allied sources gave the Russians some information of the type of attack likely, but how much attention the Russians paid to this is not known. All that seems reasonably certain is that the tactical methods which the Germans used caught the Russians very much by surprise.

The German force allotted to the attack was an impressive one. Beginning with 121 divisions, including 17 armoured and 12 motorized divisions, the all-in strength was rapidly increased to 200 divisions after the initial break-through. Some 3,000 aircraft co-operated.

Of the Russian strength, nothing is known except that, in common with so many other countries which had started in a defensive role, too large a proportion of the available armies was committed in advance to the frontiers, while too little attention was paid to reserves for counter-attack purposes when the German attack should begin to lose momentum. However that may be, simultaneously with violent attacks on Russian air-fields, strong German mechanized forces crossed the Niemen at dawn on the

22 June 22nd June, and within 25 days had forced the Russians in the centre back to the outskirts of Smolensk, 500 miles east of
16 July Warsaw, and only about half that distance from Moscow. The Russians were not broken, however, and were showing much moral resilience. What was more, in place of a fifth-column to help the Germans, partisan opposition of a highly organized and quite ruthless nature came as a serious embarrassment to them.

Armoured forces battled about Smolensk from the 16th July till
the 7th August, when a halt was called on this part of the front.
The German southern group of armies under Field-Marshal von
Rundstedt had moved more slowly at first than Gen. von Bock's
group in the centre. The right wing crossed the river Pruth on the
6th July, and by the end of August was in the neighbourhood of
Zaporozhe on the river Dnieper, where the Russians had blown up
the great Dnepropetrovsk dam on the 24th. The left wing of this
southern group was checked at Kiev some hundreds of miles to the
west-north-west, and operations momentarily paused there.

In the north, the group under Field-Marshal von Leeb pushed
through Estonia and captured Nava and Pskov, within a comparatively short distance of Leningrad, on the 20th August.

The most impressive operation of the campaign, however, was
to be the pinching out of Kiev. For this, troops south of Smolensk
moved south to threaten the rear of those Russian troops which
were covering Kiev from the north-west. Others were moving
north-west from the direction of Dnepropetrovsk, working round in
a vast encirclement a hundred miles and more east of Kiev. The
consummation of this vast plan belongs to the next chapter, and
will be dealt with there.

The Russians had sustained tremendous losses in the two-
and-a-quarter months since the invasion. Their armies had been
out-generalled, and, by all ordinary standards, extremely roughly
handled. Yet, under the surface, trouble was already mounting
against the Germans. The fifth-column they had learnt to expect
from their operations in the west and south, had not materialized,
and information was hence not readily obtainable. Morale in the
Russian reserves remained high in spite of the crippling losses
sustained in the frontier zones. Road communications in Russia
were much below the standard required for maintenance in an
advance of so impressive a weight and speed, and vehicle
casualties mounted. Finally, the systematic and well-organized
armies of partisans brought a new factor into play, of which the
Germans had had small experience, and which had its effect in
intensifying the normal processes of exhaustion. But little of this
was yet apparent to the outside world, and the outlook at this time
from the general Allied viewpoint was even more threatening and
incalculable than it had been when Stalin and Hitler seemed hand-
in-glove.

Enough has been said to show the grave character of the world
scene in this eventful summer of 1941, but there was more yet to

1941

7 Aug.

6 July

24 Aug.

20 Aug.

Far East

1941 come, in the growing, if still unpredictable, signs of friction with Japan. Japan had been involved in war with China virtually since the invasion of Manchuria in 1931, and more directly since the assault on China in 1937. By 1941, these operations had reached a critical stage for the Japanese, and it was clear to them that they never could achieve decisive success unless the Chinese supply-lines were cut—through the ports of Indo-China, and down the Burma Road.

The first of these desiderata was achieved as a consequence of the fall of France. France had little option when faced with a Japanese proposal for their temporary occupation of Indo-China.

21 July This demand was made on the 21st July, 1941, and was rapidly followed by economic sanctions from the United States, Britain and the Netherlands, when Japanese warships appeared off Camranh

24 July Bay on the 24th. But there matters still stood at the end of the period under review.

The second Japanese need—the closing of the Burma Road—seemed unlikely to be effected. Chiang Kai-Shek had appealed for American help in the spring and America had undertaken to reorganize the Burma Road, and help turn it as soon as possible in to an efficient supply route. It is quite true that as an apparent concession to Japanese insistence, the British Government did consent to close the road for a limited period. But this was during the monsoon when movement along the road was precarious, and the flow of supplies very small.

Still, Japanese demands were steadily growing more urgent in character, and were presented with increasing arrogance, so that the outlook was at best unsatisfactory, in view of the already over-extended Allied forces.

Britain Meanwhile the tempo of German bombing raids over England had steadily lessened. Civilian casualties between January and May stood at 19,576 killed and 19,177 injured, and thus showed an average of some 4,000 per month under each head. In June, the figures fell to 399 killed and 461 injured, and thereafter there was relatively small loss except briefly in April and May, 1942.

United States Important events often spring from small beginnings. As no more than the shadow of a shade against the vast background of military operations in the world of 1941, something new in mechanical transport had taken shape in the United States. Known as the "G.P."—a motor-manufacturing classification—the new design quickly achieved world-wide fame as the Jeep, and under that name played no insignificant part in the campaigns to come.

Against this inauspicious background, how did the Regiment fare? — 1941

The 1st Battalion, it will be remembered, had returned to Bannu, and now passed a peaceful spring and early summer at normal duty. June, however, brought a recrudescence of trouble up the Tochi valley, and on the 14th June, the Battalion again led the way in an expedition against its old opponents, the Daurs. The latter had invested the militia posts at Boya and Datta Khel, beyond Miranshah, and, with the assistance of some tribal artillery, were making a thorough nuisance of themselves. — 1st Bn. 14 June

Following the usual daily stages along the Tochi road, the Column reached Boya on the 20th June. There had been no incidents on the way, but the glaring frontier hills can be singularly unpleasant under the scorching June sun, and this was no exception. Camp duties and piquet construction, coupled with the excessive heat of the daily marches, bore very heavily on the troops, and they were glad to be closing with the enemy. — 20 June

From Boya, the Column moved on to Degam, where a fortnight's pause gave time for a second column and a divisional headquarters to arrive. The troops were mainly occupied with road protection duties and reconnaissance during this time, and only one clash occurred with the enemy. This happened on the 23rd June. Normal road protection procedure involved "opening the road", usually every morning, when troops moved out and took up daylight positions and made sure no enemy parties were hanging about to molest those using the road. The Sikhs were employed on this duty in the Boya direction when they encountered an enemy party and suffered a few casualties. What losses they inflicted there was no means of telling, but the enemy made no attempt to repeat it. — 23 June

During the second week in July the advance began towards Datta Khel, but strong opposition was met only 3 miles west of Degam. The advance-guard being held up, the Sikhs were passed through to the attack. This they did with considerable dash, under air, artillery and tank support. The combination worked with marked efficiency, and the enemy were driven out at small cost to our troops. The 5th/8th Punjab Regiment was then passed through the Sikhs, but was not so lucky, and suffered fairly heavily. The whole operation took up a good deal of time, and the Column had to camp for the night 5 miles west of Degam. Datta Khel was reached next day without serious opposition. — July

It was not intended to stay at Datta Khel. Supplies were moved in to the post for the garrison, and the Column then moved back to

1941

Degam. Here it spent some time destroying the towers of tribal leaders known to have been actively involved.

Towards the end of July, the Commander-in-Chief in India, now Gen. Sir Archibald Wavell, visited the Column and inspected the troops. Soon after, its task done, the Column went back to Bannu.

Two honours were awarded the Battalion for gallantry during the operations, Indian Distinguished Service Medals being awarded to Naik Jagir Singh and L.-Naik Katha Singh.

2nd Bn.

It has already been noted that the 3rd Battalion represented the Regiment at the opening of the Iraq operations in April. *The 2nd Battalion,* though not present at the outset, was to follow the 3rd very soon after. Though chronologically the 3rd Battalion's story should come first, as giving the record of the start of this short campaign, it has been thought better to keep to the rule, and continue taking battalions in order. For those who desire to know the conditions in which the campaign, generally, started, a reference to the 3rd Battalion record is invited.

March

The 2nd Battalion, then, was in Loralai under command of Lieut.-Col. A. E. Farwell, O.B.E., who had taken over command from Lieut.-Col. F. T. Birdwood the previous January. At the end of March, the Battalion mobilized and moved down to Ahmednagar to join the 10th Indian Division. It was accommodated there in temporary hutted lines, which were being thrown up as fast as the contractors could put them together, on some unused ground beyond the racecourse.

31 May

At the end of May, the Battalion embarked for Busra. The voyage passed off without incident, and the troops disembarked at Maqil about dusk on the 31st. The weather was extremely close and sticky, and the immediate 20-mile night-march to relieve the 3rd Battalion in the Shaiba-Zobeir-Jabal Sanam line was a most unpleasant introduction to Iraq. The march was excessively hot, and the dust hung round in clouds and coated the men's sweat-drenched bodies. They arrived, though, in good heart, as ever, in the

June early morning next day, and lost no time in organizing the take-over.

2 June Next day, the 2nd June, "A" Company and one section of machine-guns went out to the posts at Jabal Sanam and Safwan. A pioneer battalion was employed in the area quarrying stone, and its protection was one of the detachment's responsibilities. A good deal of traffic normally passed by this route between Iraq and Kowait, and a customs service at the two posts operated when conditions were more normal.

5 June On the 5th June, Battalion Headquarters with the Headquarter Company (less its mortar platoon), and "B" Company,

moved the 4½ miles from Shaiba to Zobeir, and took over local
protection of the 10th Indian Division Headquarters from the
3rd Battalion. A two-company detachment with the mortar
platoon remained at Shaiba.

1941

Thompson sub-machine-guns were issued on the 12th June, and 12 June
on the 16th, six 3-inch mortars arrived. These had no base-plates, 16 June
and there was no ammunition, but the base-plates and thirty
rounds of ammunition per mortar were, fortunately, received on the 21 June
21st, just before the Battalion went forward.

That day, the 21st, the Battalion concentrated in a camp west
of Shaiba, moving forward next day with the 25th Indian Infantry 22 June
Brigade to Ur (117 miles). The move cannot have been a wholly
pleasant one. The Battalion was in the middle of the column of
800 vehicles, and the heat and dust were very trying.

Next day, the 23rd June, the Brigade moved on 121 miles to 23 June
A. D. Diwaniyeh. A culvert broke down on the way, and "D"
Company, bringing up the rear, was much delayed. Ultimately, the
Company was directed to stay the night in Diwaniyeh, and
collect lame ducks among the Column's vehicles. In A. D.
Diwaniyeh, some excitement was caused by rifle thieves, and one
can sympathize with that unfortunate pair of sepoys when their
rifles were suddenly grabbed, and they found themselves being
hauled off by the rifle chains into the bushes. They were lucky in
losing neither their rifles nor their lives.

On the 24th, the brigade covered the remaining 125 miles into 24 June
Baghdad, where they settled in in Taji Camp, 8 miles west of the
town.

Next day, "A" Company crossed the narrow belt of desert to 25 June
the Euphrates to take over guard duties on Faluja bridge. After
the rigours of the desert heat, they settled very readily into the
cool and shady bivouac by the river.

On the 28th June, "B" Company moved to Habbaniya, 55 miles 28 June
north-west of Baghdad. Battalion Headquarters followed them there
next day in M.T., and encamped beside the lake. 29 June

Here, on the 1st July, the mortar platoon was at last able to get 1 July
in a little practice with live ammunition.

On the 10th July, the Battalion followed the 3rd Battalion to 10 July
Haditha (K3) Pumping Station, 95 miles from Habbaniya, and was
employed for a couple of days on improving a stretch of the desert
road towards Tripoli.

Meanwhile, hostilities in Syria were drawing to a close, and on
the 12th July, at 00.01 hours, a standfast took effect pending 12 July
armistice negotiations between the British and Vichy French at
Beirut. These negotiations were satisfactorily concluded a couple 17 July

51

1941

of days later, and on the 17th July, the Battalion moved on 178 miles to Deir Ez Zor, then garrisoned by the 2nd/4th Gurkha Rifles. It was a trying march, with a severe dust-storm blowing most of the time, and it was difficult for the Battalion to keep together in station. However, the troops had the night and the next morning to clean up before taking over the protection of the town from the Gurkhas, and special efforts were made to ensure that the turn-out of the occupation troops should be worthy of their tradition. Protective duties were carried out by deploying two companies with detachments of the Headquarter Company outside the southern and western sides of the town, while a third company looked after the bridge. Battalion Headquarters and the fourth company were billeted in the area of the post office and the "Club des Sous-Officiers".

3 Aug. On the 3rd August, the post was handed over to the 4th/13th Frontier Force Rifles, and the Sikhs moved out to a camp 5 miles from the town. A Divisional sports meeting was held that evening, and the Battalion won every event, except for one in which it was disqualified.

4 Aug. Next day, the Battalion moved back to K3, and on to Habbaniya on the 5th. On the 6th it moved on to Baghdad, where reception arrangements seem to have been on the sketchy side, and the onward move orders equally confused. All ended well, however, and,

8 Aug. on the 8th, leaving the M.T. to follow by road, the Battalion entrained for Busra. Relations with Persia were deteriorating and troops were moving south to deal with them.

9 Aug. In Busra on the 9th, the Battalion was ferried over by steamer to Tanooma on the left bank, where buses were waiting to take the troops to the camp site 4 miles away. The battalion M.T. joined

10 Aug. up next day, the 10th, its only casualties in the 700 miles between Deir Ez Zor and Shaiba being one 15-cwt. truck and one 30-cwt. lorry, both repairable.

13 Aug. On the 13th August, warning orders were received for the Brigade to be ready to move into Persia, and accupy Ahwaz, 80 miles or so across the frontier. Confirmatory orders held fire for some time, but the troops made good use of the interval, and carried out four embussed schemes in conjunction with the 157th Field Regiment R.A. and No. 30 Field Ambulance.

24 Aug. On the 24th, orders at last arrived, and at ten minutes past five
25 Aug. next morning, the Battalion led the advance of the 25th Indian Infantry Brigade towards the frontier, which was crossed without opposition.

At five minutes past seven, however, some 2 miles on, the Battalion closed up on the mobile group, operating ahead, near a

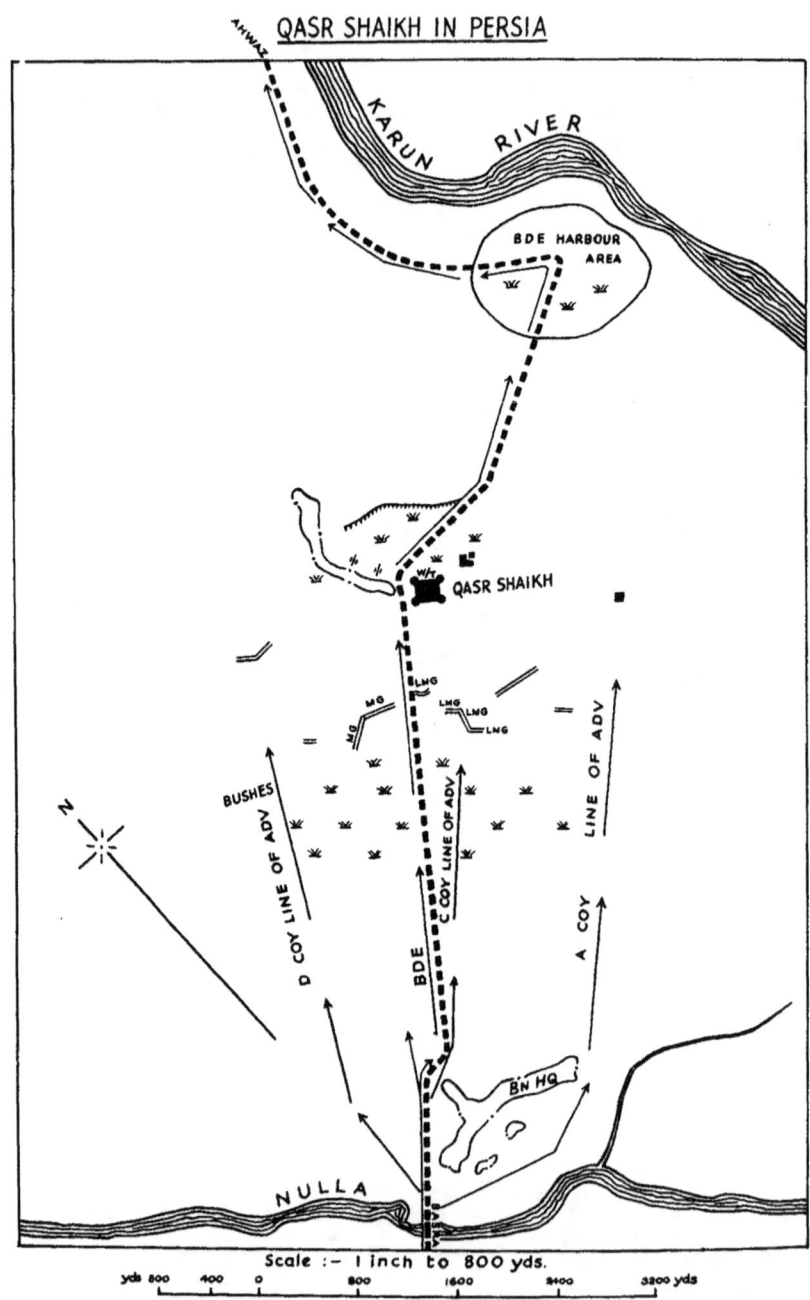

1941

frontier post manned by gendarmerie, and at half-past eight, the leading element of the Battalion advance-guard, consisting of one troop of the 13th Lancers, and "C" Company, under the command of Maj. R. A. d'E. Ashe, came under long-range rifle and automatic fire from the direction of the fort of Qasr Shaikh, just as it was crossing a nala about 4,000 yards west of the fort.

The main body of the Battalion halted about half-a-mile back, while the C.O. and Adjutant went forward with the Brigade reconnaissance group to join Maj. Ashe. "C" Company, meanwhile debussed and took up a position on the high ground to the right.

The Adjutant went back to call up the operation group and Battalion Headquarters, and the C.O. gave orders with a view to the capture of the fort and destruction of the enemy in and in front of it. The advance was to be on a two-company front, with "C" Company (Maj. C. H. McVean) on the right, and "D" Company (2nd/Lieut. J. B. G. Franklin) on the left. "A" Company (Capt. R. B. Penfold) was to the right rear, and "B" Company (2nd/Lieut. D. J. Rimmer) to the left rear. Two detachments of mortars were put under command of the leading companies, and one section of machine-guns was placed on the right flank, where it could cover the advance.

The advance started at 9.30 a.m. Almost immediately, heavy fire was opened on "C" and "D" Companies from some enemy trenches about 1,500 yards away. Armoured cars of the 13th Lancers, with one platoon of "B" Company under command, had been moved round the left flank against the fort, but the enemy did not react to the threat, and bursts of machine-gun fire from well-sited positions across their front, could be seen kicking up the dust amongst "C" and "D" Companies as they advanced.

"D" Company, on the left, was slowed up a little by this, but "C" Company was making good progress. "A" Company was accordingly sent up well round the right to exploit, crossing the starting line at 9.50 a.m.

The artillery, unfortunately, had not been able to give much help. Five rounds only had been fired before they had to stop, to avoid endangering the armoured cars, which were already nearing the fort.

"A" Company's advance soon drew fire, and at 10 a.m. the Company Commander was reported wounded. Machine-gun fire from the enemy in front of "D" Company was catching "A" and "C" Companies in enfilade, as well as sweeping the front of Battalion Headquarters, now sited on the pimples where "C" Company had originally formed up. However, the troops were quite unshaken by all this. A party of signallers, for example, under the signal havildar, came under heavy fire as they took out a wire behind "A" Company, and it was heartening to see No. 15698 Sep. Kesar Singh press his buzzer and call down the telephone "Buzzer and speech O.K." in the correct Signal School manner when he came to the end of a drum of cable.

At 10.10 a.m., Battalion Headquarters moved forward 500 yards. A runner from "C" Company came in and reported that the enemy were holding up the Company from entrenched positions to their left, between "C" and "D" Companies. These positions were in scrub and long grass in the centre of the depression, and were extremely difficult to locate. The runner also reported that his Company Commander had been wounded in the shoulder.

At 10.30 a.m., "B" Company was ordered straight forward down the middle of the depression, to clear the enemy out. Battalion Headquarters accompanied them. Before the Company could make its presence felt, however, No. 16 Platoon of "D" Company, led by the Company Commander, 2nd/Lieut. J. B. G. Franklin, and Sub. Samund Singh (the Viceroy's commissioned officer, it will be remembered, who had posed for the statuette for H.M.S. *Sikh*), assaulted and cleared the trench with Thompson sub-machine gun, bomb and bayonet. 2nd/Lieut. Franklin and Sep. Lall Singh were killed, and three sepoys wounded. No fewer than 38 enemy dead, 4 wounded and 6 prisoners were afterwards collected from this trench. One sepoy—Bachan Singh—had seven enemy to his own bayonet. It was largely due to the gallantry of 'Sonny Jim' Franklin, the son of a former commandant, and of his men that the remainder of the Battalion was able to get on without heavy loss.

The two left platoons of "D" Company were still held up by machine-gun fire, and enemy infantry situated to their front. These were now attacked by two armoured cars, No. 19 Platoon of "D" Company, and "B" Company, who captured the position with ninety prisoners.

At 11.15 a.m., "C" Company, in conjunction with No. 10 Platoon of "B" Company, and the 13th Lancers, captured the fort. "A" Company at the same time captured the two houses 500 yards to its right. "C" Company then consolidated in the neighbourhood of the fort, while "A" Company pushed on. "D" Company came into reserve on relief by "B" Company, after which Battalion Headquarters moved up to the fort, where it arrived at 12.15 p.m.

The enemy fought well, and those in the front-line trenches in front of "D" Company died at their posts. In all, they left 80 dead on the ground; 6 officers and over 300 other ranks were taken prisoner, and of these some 50 were wounded. Equipment captured included 11 machine-guns, 21 light machine-guns, 6 pistols,

262 rifles, and many thousands of rounds of ammunition.
Casualties in the Battalion were: 1 officer and 1 Indian other rank killed; 4 Indian other ranks died of wounds; 2 officers and 12 Indian other ranks wounded.

Among the awards received for this action were an immediate Military Cross for Colin McVean, son of Col. McVean, a former commandant of Rattray's Sikhs, later the 3rd Battalion; and two Indian Distinguished Service medals—one to 9185 Naik Chanan Singh, the grand Battalion sprinter, who was with Franklin, and who, with his section, cleared the trench near which Franklin fell, and the other to 14456 Sep. Bachan Singh of the same platoon, whose bayonet work has already been recorded.

The Brigade, its way clear, now moved forward to the river Karun, leaving the Battalion to clear up the fort area, and follow on later in the afternoon. "D" Company, under Maj. Ashe, was to stay behind for the moment and garrison the fort.

The Battalion duly rejoined the Brigade, and camped on the right bank of the Karun river. Standing patrols were sent across, while a patrol of one company worked southwards to intercept enemy withdrawing before the attacks of the 24th and 18th Indian Infantry Brigades on Kharramshah and Abadan. No enemy, however, were seen, and the locals were friendly.

On the 27th August, the Brigade moved 16 miles upstream along the Karun right bank. The Adjutant and Intelligence Jemadar went ahead with a company of Mahrattas and two troops of armoured cars to reconnoitre enemy positions outside Ahwaz. The reconnaissance was interfered with by hostile tanks, but a sufficiently satisfactory report was submitted for orders to be issued the same night for the further advance to the town. 27 Aug.

This advance took place next day. Hostile tanks were about, and the Sikhs, in rear, were responsible for the anti-tank protection of the column's flanks and rear. None, however, were met. Closing up with the hostile positions, the Mahrattas stormed some of the trenches. The Jats had just received orders to clear a second series when a car was seen approaching with a large white flag on it. It contained a Persian envoy, carrying the Shah's orders to treat for an armistice. That concluded the operations; the column closed and headed for Ahwaz, where the streets were packed with enthusiastic crowds, twelve to fifteen deep. Passing through the town, the troops went into camp on the river bank a little to the north-east. 28 Aug.

Defences over the bridges were hurriedly organized, and next day, the 29th, the Battalion took these over. With this was coupled the additional duty of preventing the movement of arms across to 29 Aug.

1941

30 Aug. the east bank. This was not, however, fated to weigh very heavily on the Battalion, for welcome orders arrived next day for a move away from the trying heat of Ahwaz, where the troops were without tents for shelter, to Haft Khel, 68 miles away, one of the largest centres of the Anglo-Iranian Oil Company, and in a very much pleasanter part of the country.

"B" Company was accordingly relieved on the bridges that day, handing over to the 5th Royal Mahrattas from the 24th Indian Infantry

31 Aug. Brigade. On the 31st, the Battalion moved off.

Haft Khel proved just the change the Battalion wanted. Though located amongst barren hills, it stands 1,000 feet above sea-level, which made all the difference after three hot months in the desert. Hospitality was lavished on the troops by the officials of the Company. The troops had the use of the swimming bath from 10 a.m. to 4 p.m. each day, and new stand-pipes, showers, washing-places and latrines were put up at the Company's expense. The officers were equally kindly dealt with. The direct beneficiaries were Battalion Headquarters, and "A" and "D" Companies. The other two companies, under Maj. Ashe, were at Wais, 10 miles farther up the river, in company with Brigade Headquarters and the Mahrattas—and equally glad of the change from Ahwaz.

3rd Bn. *The 3rd Battalion* had received its mobilization orders in February while still in Quetta. By the beginning of April, the Batta-
6 April lion's war outfit had been received. On the 6th, it entrained for
8 April Karachi, and, two days later, embarked on the H.T. *El Medina*, with a strength of 16 British officers, 22 Viceroy's commissioned officers, 823 Indian other ranks, and 69 followers.

During the next four days, the balance of the 20th Indian Infantry Brigade and a number of the 9th Indian Divisional units
12 April arrived and embarked, and by the 12th April, a convoy of 10 ships was ready to leave. The convoy's destination was not officially known, but it was assumed to be Malaya, where the remainder of the 9th Indian Division, under Maj.-Gen. A. E. Barstow, M.C., had already gone.

About mid-day on the 12th, however, Maj.-Gen. W. A. K. Fraser, commanding the 10th Indian Division, with one Staff Officer, Col. F. T. Birdwood, arrived in Karachi by air to join the convoy, some ships of which had already dropped down the fairway. Under escort of H.M.A.S. *Yarra*—later sunk in the Java Sea action—the convoy put out to sea in the afternoon. The destination—Busra—was not made known till next day.

The convoy had not been tactically loaded, but it was an even chance that it would meet an unfriendly reception. H.M.S. *Emerald* was anchored in the Shatt-el-Arab opposite Busra, and R.A.F. stations at Maqil, Shaiba and Habbaniya had not been molested, but the Iraqi forces were well equipped and were known to have artillery distributed at important points to dispute the passage of ships up the relatively narrow and difficult river passage from Fao. The political position was exceedingly fluid and might flare up at any moment.

Rightly or no, it was supposed at the time that Japanese ships were regularly cruising up and down the Indian coasts, keeping a watch on British shipping. It was said that one of these ships had been hanging about off Karachi while the convoy formed, and shadowed the convoy to the mouth of the Shatt-el-Arab. Only a limited number of pilots were available when the convoy reached the Shatt-el-Arab, owing to a strike of the Arab personnel, and the convoy took the lot. Japan was still a neutral country in those days, and it was not deemed possible to interfere directly.

The voyage through the Arabian Sea and up the Persian Gulf was pleasant and uneventful. Everything possible was done to redistribute the troops the day before crossing the bar, in case of opposition on the way up the river, or at Busra, but meanwhile the situation had momentarily moved in our favour. The Regent of Iraq had fled from Baghdad and taken refuge with the British. In his absence, the British Ambassador in Baghdad had given the prescribed official notice of the impending arrival of our troops to the pro-German Prime Minister Rashid Ali, as *de facto* ruler. This probably did much to pre-dispose Rashid Ali in our favour, particularly in the absence of equally realistic favours from the Axis. Either way, he gave his blessing to the landing. The Iraqi army was less complacent, and its Kurdish commander at first refused to accept the Prime Minister's orders. He announced his intention of disputing the passage of the convoy up-river by every means in his power. These were sufficient at least to cause grave embarrassment, if no more. One ship sunk or disabled by shell-fire might have completely disorganized the whole thing, and led to an infinity of trouble.

Fortunately, the convoy was delayed twenty-four hours in its journey by strong head-winds, and it was during the last few hours of this time that the Iraqi troops were reluctantly withdrawn, and undisputed passage given to the convoy and its somewhat augmented escort. Additionally, a sudden swing-round of the wind to the south had somewhat piled up the river, so that prevailing doubts whether there would be enough water to float the largest ship of the convoy, the *Lancasbire*, over the bar at Mohammerah, many miles up the river, were set at rest. So, under a bright half-

1941

18 April moon in the early hours of the 18th April, the long line of ships passed into the Shatt-el-Arab.

The R.A.F. detachments at Maqil and Shaiba had not been molested, but it was with a good deal of relief that they welcomed the troops, who disembarked uneventfully at Maqil later in the day. Things were not easy, however. The political position almost immediately deteriorated. A strike of port workers caused a good deal of inconvenience, and hostile crowds did some damage to lorries working down towards the landing-stage. Fantastic situations developed from time to time, but for a while fell short of actual hostilities. As for the terrain, this was quite unsuitable for military operations round Busra and Shaiba, a few miles inland, even had sufficient troops been available. The river was high, and seepage had turned the surrounding desert into a slippery quagmire for miles around. It was interesting to note the raised plinths of rest-camp huts of the earlier war standing up in parallel islands in this sea of slippery sand. The great dumps of broken glass between them spoke eloquently of the gallons of Japanese beer that had been drunk there—but it also posed the question how had these innumerable bottles come to be so effectively shattered in a countryside so totally devoid of stones or other natural "hardware"?

Seepage and labour troubles drove the force to dangerous expedients. The generous supply of M.T. was a sore embarrassment in the early stages. It was impossible to disperse it, owing to the state of the desert off the roads, and no cover was to be had. So it was herded together in packed lines on an old disused landing-strip which no raiding aircraft could have missed. Again, on the landing-stage, the broad wooden structure projecting into the river along a considerable stretch of the water front, often piled high over most of its length with combustible stores. A single incendiary, with the wind in the right direction, could have created utter havoc. But the luck held.

At the end of April the mounting tension broke. Iraqi forces invested Habbaniya, where the garrison had been reinforced by a detachment of British troops flown in from Karachi. At the outset the situation was acute, for the defenders could hardly man the perimeter, and they had no artillery at all. They had three trophy 18-pounders there without breech-blocks, and a master-gunner was flown up with the necessary parts to make them work. Some German Messerschmidts were at large at the time, and the strain on R.A.F. crews flying up supplies in unarmed and unescorted D.C.'s must have been great. However, with its three trophy guns, the Habbaniya garrison took the offensive, captured some enemy 3.7 inch howitzers with their ammunition, and drove off the numerically much stronger and better armed besiegers without much difficulty. 1941

The 3rd Battalion remained in the Busra area, where a number of small sticky actions were dealt with during May. Operations were much restricted by floods and by the shortage of troops. It took some days to get matters stabilized. The Battalion's contribution was a small engagement in which an officer and ten other ranks out on patrol, captured a small armoured train from some Iraqi troops. May

By the end of May, the Battalion was deployed on a 25-mile front along the railway from Shaiba Junction Station, through Zobeir to Jabal Sanam. The last-named post lay close to the Kowait border, and derived its special importance from being the sole source of road-metal in the whole of lower Iraq. It was in this line that the 3rd Battalion was relieved by the 2nd in the first week of June. June

The move northwards to Baghdad had already begun, and the 3rd Battalion followed close on the heels of the 20th Indian Infantry Brigade to Ur, where it caught up. Baghdad was reached on the 12th June, and from here the Battalion was sent out on a special mission into Syria, to capture Abu Kemal, then held by a Palestinian rebel leader. This was the first unit of the British forces in Iraq to penetrate into Vichy-held Syria; and the mission landed the Battalion into a wholly isolated position, 250 miles ahead of the nearest reinforcements. 12 June

Hostile air attacks developed over Abu Kemal on the 28th and 29th June, with three bombing and two low-level machine-gun attacks by Vichy-French planes. The second attack on the 28th was a concentrated one, and forty bombs were dropped by six aircraft in the camp area. Thanks to good slit-trench discipline, the total casualties from these attacks only amounted to one man killed and two wounded. 28-29 June

At the end of June, the Battalion moved back to the Haditha (K3) Pumping Station, where the I.P.C.'s pipe-line forks, with branches leading to Tripoli and Haifa respectively. It stayed on here till early August, when it returned to Baghdad. There were two minor skirmishes during this time between detachments and the local Arabs, but without casualties. August

The 4th Battalion, back in its old bivouac area at Kilo 112, after the Aqua Col action on the 12th February, passed alternate weeks in defensive positions in the Cameron Ridge neighbourhood, or north of it, with spells of rest. 4th Bn.

At the beginning of March there were signs of preparation for a large-scale British offensive, and advance parties from the 5th March

1941

Indian Division were seen in the area. A large dumping programme was notified, and six days rations and water, and three lifts of first-line ammunition, were to be placed on the hilltops in rear of Battalion positions. Stores of all sorts, and ammunition, had to be sent up from rail-head at Tessenei, 230 miles away, by lorry convoy. Impressive figures are named: 180,000 rounds of 25-pounder gun ammunition, for example, in a little over two thousand 3-ton lorry loads. Transport demands for other stores were in like proportion. They presented a "Q" problem of great complexity, in which three native transport companies from South Africa did sterling work in support of the R.I.A.S.C.

For distribution to the hilltops, stores mostly came up on the railway line. By day, single wagons were hauled by 15-cwt. trucks running astride the metals. By night, trains of three wagons were drawn by small diesel engines. From the railway up to the hilltops, supplies were carried by mules of the Cypriot Mule company, and by carrying parties from battalions. The trip up the hill from the railway to the 4th Battalion headquarters took an hour and a half, and it was an understandably weary business. However, on

12 March the 12th March the Battalion received a badly needed draft of 272 men from India, so that both the carrying party roster and the prospects for the coming offensive improved. The draft did not arrive a moment too soon. Operation orders for an attack to be mounted at 7 a.m. on the 15th March arrived on the same day as

13 March the draft, and next day, the 13th, the Battalion moved off with the 5th Indian Infantry Brigade to the top of Hill 1702 on the extreme left of the 4th Indian Division.

Opposite Hill 1702, and 300 feet above, across a small valley, lay the Battalion objective. This bore the name of Samana Ridge, and it was heartening to the troops to be reminded of the other Samana Ridge in the Tirah where the Battalion, then the 36th Sikhs, won imperishable fame nearly forty years before.

The Samana Ridge of the Keren Hills was held by Italian Alpine troops and Eritrean native formations. It had three prominent features, known as the Right Bump, the Centre Bump, and the Left Bump. The Battalion plan was to debouch from the narrow valley between Hill 1702 and the enemy, opposite Left Bump, and attack the three bumps in echelon, with one company against each.

14 March The 14th March was spent, comparatively undisturbed except by a few mortar shells, reconnoitring, and making all final preparations.

15 March At 7 a.m. on the 15th, the offensive opened with the crash of 122 guns firing at four rounds a minute. The 4th Indian Division advanced on a 4-mile front from Cameron Ridge to Hill 1702, and caught the enemy completely by surprise. For five or ten minutes,

his guns were silent. When he did open fire, many of the 126 guns he was credited with were soon silenced.

1941

Meanwhile, on the Sikh front, "A" Company, under Capt. Mohd Siddiq, stormed the Left Bump position as the artillery concentration moved off it. Mohd Siddiq was awarded a well-earned Military Cross for his leadership in this action, whilst an Indian Distinguished Service Medal was won by a young soldier, No. 16626 L.-Naik Nasib Singh, who had six Italians to his individual score. Another Indian Distinguished Service Medal went to No. 10228 Naik Daulat Singh, also of "A" Company, for fine and resolute leadership, which enabled the right forward platoon of the company, on his right, which had been held up at the wire, to continue its advance.

Middle Bump was a harder nut to crack. When just short of the top, "B" Company was driven back by automatic weapons and showers of grenades. "C" Company, moving below Middle Bump on its way to attack Right Bump, was directed on to Middle Bump in support of "B" Company—but to no purpose. Attack and counter-attack continued throughout the day, and nightfall found the advance still held up below the crest of Middle Bump. During these attacks, Mohd Siddiq, Weston, Latham and Trestrail were wounded, together with 4 Viceroy's commissioned officers and 180 Indian other ranks. The losses in killed were mercifully light —1 Viceroy's commissioned officer and 15 Indian other ranks.

The Battalion's attention was so concentrated on its own front that little could be spared for the progress of the battle elsewhere. It was noticed, however, that the artillery fire was thickening up at 10 a.m., and this told of the opening of the 5th Indian Division's attack on Fort Dologorodoc, and the hills to the east of it, commanding the entrance to the gorge.

Twelve days of attack and counter-attack were to pass before the block in the Keren Pass was cleared. The Italians finally left their positions during the night of the 26th-27th March, and fled down the road towards Asmara. The Sikhs played no dramatic part in this struggle, but advanced when the time came, mopping up what stragglers remained, and still hardly able to believe that this mountain stronghold had been given up by a force believed to outnumber us by five to one. The 5th Indian Division carried on the pursuit, while the 4th Indian Division stayed in Keren and cleared the battlefield, collecting very large quantities of ammunition and equipment. The Battalion was given charge of the salvage dump, and for the next three weeks had daily working parties collecting stuff and bringing it into the dump where a hundred Italian prisoners were employed sorting and listing it. After the capture of Asmara,

26-27 March

1941

men were sent there on daily leave, and could be seen queueing up outside the many watchmakers' shops which are to be found in this well-planned modern town, anxious to buy watches while the exchange was favourable.

Visits were also paid to Massawa, where the 7th Indian Infantry Brigade was at last contacted again. With Free French troops under command, the Brigade had advanced down the coast and captured Massawa. It had also staged a diversion north of Keren which had drawn off four battalions and some guns. In Massawa, the harbour was a pitiful sight. Some thirty ships had been scuttled at their moorings, and had little more than their masts and upper works showing. Most, however, were later refloated.

Duties at Keren completed, the Battalion was moved back to Kassala. The men were much interested, surveying the barren countryside as they passed, recalling the good and bad times that made them memorable. Arrived in Kassala, the Battalion entrained for Port Sudan, where they were presented with a gift of 1,500 oranges and 10,000 cigarettes from the Indian and Sudanese merchants of the town. A similar presentation was made to every unit of the 4th Indian Division that passed through, in appreciation of the fine work done in Eritrea.

5 May   After a stay of three days, the Battalion left Port Sudan at the end of April on the S.S. *Cap St. Jacques* for Suez. By the 5th May, the Division was back in its old positions at Bagush. Here for two and a half months, the troops dug anti-tank ditches and improved the defences, laid many more minefields, and trained. Weekly leave parties went into Cairo, and a "dilution" party of 4 Viceroy's commissioned officers and 80 Indian other ranks was sent back to India.

June   For the operations in June against Helfaya, Sollum, and Fort Capuzzo, only the carrier and anti-tank platoons were used. The operation was carried out by the 11th Indian Infantry Brigade and tanks, so that the Sikhs, as a battalion, were not involved. A number of trucks, light machine-guns, etc., were, however, handed over to the 11th Indian Infantry Brigade, to complete their outfit. This was the anti-tank platoon's first opportunity for trying out its marksmanship against German tanks, and it did so with considerable success. The one casualty was Hav. Amrik Singh, who was blown up by an anti-tank mine.

August   At the beginning of August, the Battalion, with a battery of field guns, a squadron of the Central India Horse, and a detachment of sappers, under command, moved to Giarabub. This was an interesting place, both from operational and other stand-points. The main claim to fame of this tiny village of about 150 stone huts,

1941

was jointly the Senussi University, and the tomb of Mohd Bin Senussi, the founder of the sect. The Italians had run a 15-feet wide double apron barbed wire fence along their former eastern boundary, all the way from Sollum, 180 miles to the north, to Giarabub, and on for another dozen miles to the south, to a small fort where the Sand Sea starts. They had also embellished Giarabub with a fort, which the Australians had captured after the fall of Benghazi early in 1941—and which was not to be reoccupied after the Sikhs withdrew.

The oasis boasted plentiful water—of a sort. It was most useful for washing, but, being heavily impregnated with magnesium sulphate, was most unpleasant to drink and had a powerful aperient effect. One wonders how the University coped with this undeniable drawback. As for the troops, they had their own methods, which included a daily water convoy, sent out to Siwa, whence unlimited supplies of fresh water could be had. This arrangement was not to last, however, for the small paradise was later invaded by the whole 7th Indian Infantry Brigade Group, together with anti-aircraft artillery and a South African armoured car squadron. There was no longer sufficient transport then for the water convoy, and the troops had to fall back on the local supply. Still, though stomachs rebelled, the troops did get fairly accustomed to the water in time, and when they got to a place where fresh water could be had, the evening gin, they say, seemed to have lost its bite.

Having been first on the ground at Giarabub, the Battalion had had its pick of the accommodation, and had established its headquarters in the fort. From the outside, the fort was in the authentic Beau Geste tradition; but its former owners had not subscribed to the aura of toughness proper to those tales of the desert. The Italians had, in fact, fitted it out with a variety of modern luxuries, including electric light, hot and cold running water, long baths, filter and refrigeration plants, and a very fine mens' recreation room. Most of this had been destroyed when the fort was captured, but one must suppose that a certain vicarious pleasure was to be had from surveying the remnants of what sounds quite a reasonable set-up for The Ritz.

The troops other than those with Headquarters were disposed in defensive positions amongst the sand-hills. This was as well, for the enemy sent over four bombers the day after the Battalion moved in and dropped eighty bombs round the fort. Only six of these bombs fell inside, but they cost the battalion thirty-five casualties, including the Jemadar-Adjutant, Jem. Nazar Mohammed, who died of his wounds. In Nazar Mohammed, the

1941

Battalion not only lost one of its best Viceroy's commissioned officers, but yet another member of its hockey team, for Nazar Mohammed was always a tower of strength at full-back.

Headquarters had learnt its lesson, and it moved out into the sand-hills without more ado. Two days later, four more bombers came over, and again dropped eighty bombs round the fort—but this time without a single hit, though they were flying at 5,000 feet. No damage was done, and the only casualty was an unfortunate sapper who was deafened for the day. Aircraft only came over singly after this. On four occasions, eight to twelve bombs were dropped, but they did no damage.

Apart from the occupation of defensive positions, the main duties at Giarabub comprised patrolling and road construction. Patrols went out two at a time, working north and north-west respectively up to a distance of 70 to 75 miles. A third patrol, manned by South African armoured cars, worked to the north-east. Patrols met daily at pre-arranged rendezvous. It was excellent practice in desert navigation, and interest was kept up by the occasional low-flying attacks of German aircraft. The reason for the road-making was the decision to put in a very large dump of petrol and rations at Giarabub. Long stretches of heavy dust or salt marsh obstructed the existing route, and there was no other means of getting the heavy 10-ton lorries through.

5th Bn. In the late winter, *the 5th Battalion* moved down from Razmak to Baleli, a barren spot a few miles out of Quetta on the Chaman road, well known to students of the Staff College at Quetta. Here, the 22nd Indian Infantry Brigade of the 9th Indian Division was forming.

Mobilization orders reached the Battalion in Baleli, but before mobilization could be completed, it was moved down-country to Secunderabad, where some further items of the war outfit were issued. Still short, the Battalion moved down by rail to Madras, **6 April** and embarked on the 6th April for Malaya.

An uneventful passage ended at Penang, but the Battalion was moved on at once to Ipoh for a month's preliminary training in jungle warfare, and to give the men a chance to shake down and get accustomed to the depressing damp heat of the rubber planta-
May tions. In May, the Battalion moved to its operational station at Kuantan, about one-third of the way up the east coast of Malaya from Singapore.

Communications up the east coast of Malaya were very poor and the complete outfit of mechanical transport with which the Battalion (in command with all other troops), arrived, was not calculated to be of much use outside the immediate neighbourhood of Kuantan. Initially, the Battalion was deployed with a view to the defence of 22 miles of the Kuantan and Belat rivers, which flow in from the north-west and south-west respectively, and unite on the south side of Kuantan, two or three miles from the sea. Additional responsibilities were the local defence of the Kuantan aerodrome, the protection of the Brigade line of communications from air-borne attack, and a counter-attack role in the forward Battalion area on the Kuantan beaches.

The Far-Eastern picture was not a reassuring one at the time. Protest its peaceful intentions as it might, no one could be blind to the determination of the Japanese Government to build up its own *lebensraum* in the western Pacific and northern Indian Ocean. The Japanese knew well enough what forces were piling up against them in Malaya, and notices frequently appeared in the British Press describing the arrival of reinforcements in Singapore. At best, these notices were unconvincing, and calculated neither to impress the Japanese nor boost our own morale. The impression, indeed, on the casual observer, was that we protested too much, and showed our weakness rather than hiding it.

As regards the troops on the spot, the 5th Battalion was probably an excellent sample. Much had been done, when hostilities broke out, in the coming December, to absorb the 480 recruits and the six young emergency commissioned officers with whom the Battalion had embarked, but training had been restricted by the need for putting every available man on defence works. Equipment was still short, and the Battalion was not up to scale till a few days before operations began. But the troops were fit and in excellent heart, and determined to give a good account of themselves. More will be said on this head in the next chapter.

The 6th Battalion during this summer was mainly employed, as before, on constructional work on the Khyber defences.   6th Bn.

The 7th Battalion, in Dinapur, sent off its tactical advance party to Razmak, under Maj. A. E. Belchamber of the 1st Battalion, the Second-in-Command, on the 2nd March. The administrative advance party followed on the 25th. The British officers gave a small party to their friends in Patna and Dinapur a few days before the Battalion left.

7th Bn.

2 March
25 March

The move was memorable in one sense, in that it was the first occasion on which the whole Battalion had ever paraded together. Arrived in Bannu on the 5th April, the 1st Battalion welcomed them in with tea and khana for the men. Next day, the 6th, the Battalion moved on up to Razmak.

5 April
6 April

1941

1941

In Razmak, the Battalion was put into "E" Battalion lines, in the Lower Camp. One piquet had to be found—Naralai, only a short distance outside the perimeter. Otherwise, the usual heavy duties, and training, competed for most of the Battalion's time.

Training during the first month was designed to fit the Battalion to take its place in road protection duties in as short a time as possible. The programme, which had been planned by Brigade Headquarters, included demonstrations by other units for officers and non-commissioned officers, and the sending out of two companies on road protection days to "double-bank" the units responsible. These duties were gradually increased until on the

3 May — 3rd May, the Battalion went out as piqueting troops for the first time. This was no sinecure. Hostiles were active at that time, but, though other road protection troops were sniped a certain amount, the 7th Battalion was not bothered.

16 May — On the 16th May, "A" Company went up to Alexandra Piquet for
19 May — a week, and on the 19th, the Battalion took part in a two-day column which passed off quietly.

22 April — The Battalion had already proved itself, however. On the 22nd April, a party of twelve rifles from "B" Company had been detailed as close escort to the convoy. On the far side of the Narai, two cars containing the District Commander and his staff, were ambushed. One of these had overturned in the ditch, and a private lorry was being looted. The escort was in a lorry two or three hundred yards short of the Narai when they heard the shots of the ambush. They drove forward and debussed and opened fire on the fifty or so raiders, and saw them off in no uncertain manner, with a loss estimated at two killed and four wounded, at no cost to themselves.

2 June — On the 2nd June, the Army Commander inspected the Battalion and expressed himself as well satisfied with what he saw. The Battalion had found its feet.

Games received what attention was possible in the circumstances, and there is a moving account of the making and inauguration of a five-a-side hockey ground, completed after a deal of hard work by the Pioneer Platoon, parties from the companies "and the ever-willing donators of free advice". "The inaugural ceremony," the record goes on, "took the shape of an exceedingly fierce hockey match—B.O.s v. I.O.s. This was played at terrific speed and no little skill. Honours went to the referee, Sub. Lall Khan, for deciding the game a draw at about 10 goals to all".

July — Towards the end of July it is noted that cloth shoulder-badges replaced the old bronze ones, while officers wore cloth badges of rank. Officers' topees were camouflaged.

	1941
Duties continued very heavy all through August. The Battalion had to take its turn in providing a four-platoon garrison for Alexandra Piquet, as well as finding garrison duties. At times it was a struggle to get sufficient men to take out on road protection. The Battalion was still eighty Sikhs under strength, and there was no prospect of receiving a draft owing to the large demands for casualty replacements from battalions overseas. On the 17th August, the Battalion sustained its first casualties, when Seps. Lall Singh and Dewa Singh were killed in a bold ambush at Alexandra Piquet. Briefly, No. 1 Section of No. 13 Platoon was moving down a spur, under cover of two other sections, already in position. When 8 yards from it, a concealed enemy party, twelve or fifteen strong, fired a volley at the approaching section, which consisted of one non-commissioned officer and five sepoys. One sepoy was killed by the fire, and another badly wounded. A knife party rushed in, seized the rifles of the two casualties, and tried to drag the wounded man away. They dragged him about 10 yards before the rapid fire opened by the rest of the section took effect. One of the raiders being then shot and another wounded, they knifed the wounded sepoy. The remaining four men of the section then rushed to their objective, and opened fire on the enemy moving down the slope. One killed and one wounded raider were claimed—the dead Pathan being seen dragged a few yards into the bushes.	August 17 Aug.

Fresh battalions now appeared on the Regiment's lists, in its second wartime expansion.

The 8th Battalion was raised on the 1st May in Umbeyla Lines in Nowshera. Four regular officers were posted—Lieut.-Col. A. R. Walker of the 2nd Battalion (but at that time Second-in-Command of the Training Battalion) as commandant; Maj. C. F. H. Walter of the 3rd Battalion, but then serving with the 6th, as Second-in-Command; Capt. Mohd Hassan of the 5th Battalion as Adjutant; and Capt. T. E. B. Anthony of the 1st Battalion, but serving with the 6th, as one of the company commanders. Four emergency commissioned officers joined shortly after.	8th Bn. 1 May

Four Viceroy's commissioned officers were posted. These were Sub.-Maj. Attar Singh Bahadur from the 5th Battalion; Jem.-Adj. Sarmukh Singh from the 2nd Battalion; Jem.-Q.M. Kartar Singh from the 1st Battalion; and Jem. Head Clerk Khushal Singh from the 3rd Battalion. Trained Indian other ranks were provided from the five regular battalions, and the still very young 6th and 7th Battalions.

During May, two complete divisions of semi-trained recruits

1941

were drafted in from the Training Battalion. Demands from overseas made any better contribution impossible. The two divisions, however, completed their training, and were attested on the 22nd August and the 25th October respectively. As with the 7th Battalion, it may be said that the new battalion, for its first five months, played much the same role as the Training Battalion itself.

22 Aug.
25 Oct.

22 July

Other officers were gradually posted in, and on the 22nd July, the Battalion's officers and Viceroy's commissioned officers were met by the Commander-in-Chief, Gen. Sir Archibald Wavell. Officers' training was being taken very seriously, with a long succession of tactical exercises without troops, which thoroughly rubbed in the geography of the area round Nowshera Thana Station, Khairabad, and Dera Khatti Khel, sand-table exercises, lectures, demonstrations, and weary hours with the munshi. Those who know Nowshera in the summer will sympathize.

There were, however, lighter moments—hockey matches with the Training Battalion and the 9th Battalion, also in its infancy. and inter-company sports meetings, and many of the other advantages of living next-door to the Training Battalion—including the band in mess once a week.

9th Bn.
1 May

The 9th Battalion, like the 8th, was raised in Nowshera on the 1st May, under Lieut.-Col. E. C. Spencer, M.C., of the 1st Battalion, with Maj. H. W. Gayer of the 2nd Battalion as his Second-in-Command. Three other regular officers were also posted —Cap. M. G. Collins of the 1st Battalion, later to lose his life in Burma as a "Chindit", Capt. K. K. Bhandari of the 5th Battalion, and Capt. Gurpartab Singh of the 4th Battalion. Sub.-Maj. Mian Ahmed, I.D.S.M., was posted from the 4th Battalion.

During its early months of training and equipping, the Battalion passed through the same phases as the 8th Battalion, to which detailed reference has already been made.

1 April
25th Bn.

On the 1st April, a new category of unit was raised. It had become evident that too many fighting troops were tied up in India on duties which less-active men could perform. Hence *the 25th Battalion* was now called into being, made up from pensioners, category "B" men, and over-age recruits. The composition was fixed at three-fourths Sikh and one-fourth Punjabi-Mohammedan. British officers were posted from active battalions, and captured Italian rifles were issued as arms.

After a short breathing-space in Nowshera for shaking down, the Battalion, under command of Lieut.-Col. J. V. Gordon, M.C., of

1941
August

the 1st Battalion, moved down to Dehra Dun in August for general duties at Prem Nagar over Italian civilian internees and a number of captured Italian generals. The duties were heavy but the campsite and accommodation generally were sufficiently satisfactory. With its considerable proportion of Viceroy's and non-commissioned officers, and senior sepoys, with a record of long years of colour service in the pre-war battalions of the Regiment, a high standard of smartness and discipline prevailed. Difficulties were experienced due to the unaccustomed "set-up" of these newly established internees and prisoners-of-war camps, but they were met and disposed of with soldierly efficiency.

Chapter V

SEPTEMBER 1941 TO FEBRUARY 1942

Backscreen

General The autumn and winter of 1941 came in on a note of restrained optimism in spite of gathering clouds over the Western Desert. The Germans were held outside Leningrad and Moscow. Better still, the Harriman Mission which was conducting a sort of inquest into the progress of the war for the United States Administration, had encouraging views on the Russian campaign. When they returned home in October, it was with a reasoned conviction that not only could Russia hold out, but that she would probably take the offensive in the not-distant future. The threat to Syria and Iraq had receded, and the Abyssinian campaign had ended in rousing victory. The Battle of the Atlantic still hung in the balance, and the Mediterranean was closed as a shipping route. But the alternative way round the Cape of Good Hope was working reasonably well, and arrangements for co-ordination of supplies from Australia and the Far East were in hand.

In December, this somewhat brighter prospect was to be rudely shattered by the entry into the war on the Axis side, of Japan.

N. Africa Taking events as they occurred, in broader detail, it will be remembered that in the Western Desert, Rommel's counter-offensive
April had stabilized during April, at the Sollum escarpment, with Tobruk, invested, in his rear.

Both armies were busy reorganizing and refitting. For Rommel, this was made very difficult. The offensive character of the Tobruk garrison held back four Italian divisions and three German battalions—double the strength of the forces in Tobruk—and kept them there from April till November. At the same time our naval and
Aug. air forces were very active against Rommel's sea communications; 35 per cent. of his supplies and reinforcements were sunk in
Oct. August, and 63 per cent. in October. By the end of October, the percentage had risen to 75 per cent., and the Germans were driven to divert 25 "U" boats from the Atlantic to the Mediterranean on this account.

Apart from his superiority in the air, the balance lay heavily with the enemy in armour—more so than the bare figure would

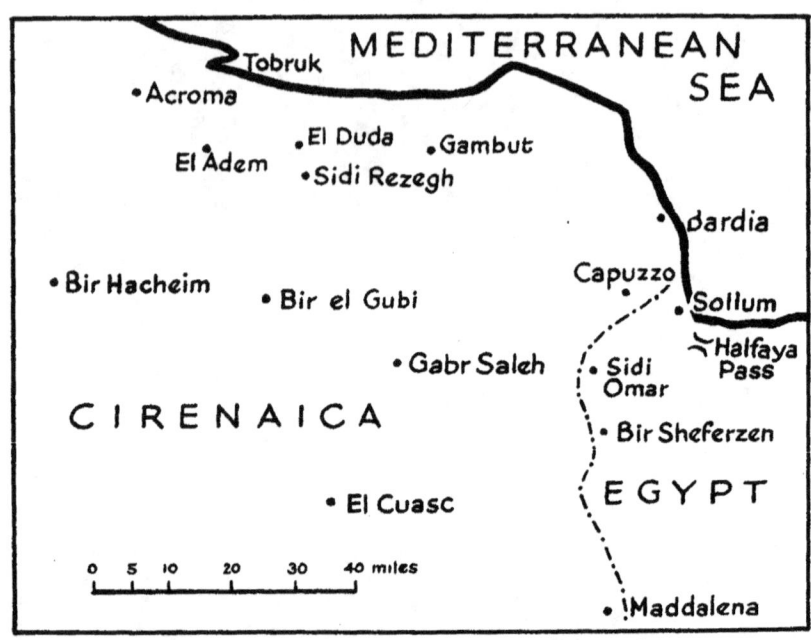

BATTLEFIELD OF SIDI REZEGH
18th November 1941 – 17th January 1942
(With acknowledgements to "The Second World War" by
Major-General J. F. C. Fuller, Page 157)

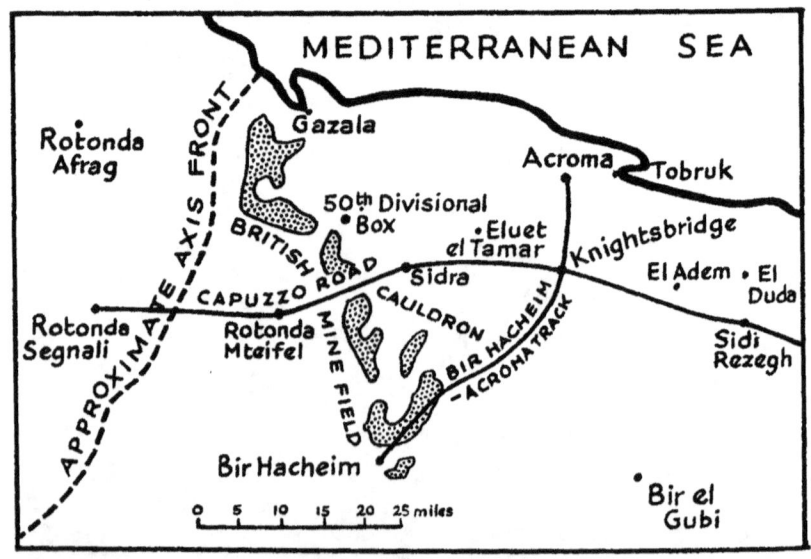

THE BATTLE OF TOBRUK • 27th May – 30th June 1942
(With acknowledgements to "The Second World War" by
Major-General J. F. C. Fuller, page 169.)

1941

suggest. Rommel had only 412 tanks against the 8th Army's 455, but he scored in the far harder hitting-powers of his tank and anti-tank guns. Of the latter weapons, he had, in any case, 194 guns against the British 72.

Both forces were ready to take the offensive by late autumn. Rommel's first task was to liquidate Tobruk, and free himself from an expensive embarrassment to his left flank and rear. Gen. Cunningham, commanding the 8th Army, aimed at the re-conquest of Cirenaica, and, on the 18th November, advanced to the attack. 18 Nov. The grounding of all aircraft by storms which broke over the front the previous night, may have given him some initial advantage, for surprise was complete, and immediate successes were scored.

Our armoured division moved out north-west from about Maddalena. Maddalena stood on the Egyptian frontier, 50 miles south of Sollum and the Mediterranean Sea. The general axis of the armoured division's advance lay via Gabr Saleh, through Sidi Rezegh, to Tobruk. By nightfall on the 18th, its brigades stood as follows—7th Armoured Brigade 10 miles beyond Gabr Saleh—itself 60 or 70 miles north-west of Maddalena; 22nd Armoured Brigade in rear and to the west; 4th Armoured Brigade south-east of the 7th. The 1st South African Division was approaching El Cuasc, 40 miles east-north-east of Maddalena. No enemy had been met or hostile aircraft sighted.

On the 19th November, the 7th Armoured Brigade pushed on some 19 Nov. 20 miles and reached the north of the Sidi Rezegh southern escarpment. The remainder of the Division lagged behind, however, under stress of enemy pressure. The 22nd Armoured Brigade, 20 miles south, had a sharp engagement with the Italian Ariete Division, in a blinding dust-storm, at Bir el Gubi. It was pretty roughly handled in spite of the enemy losses it caused. The 4th Armoured Brigade, east of Gabr Saleh, 30-odd miles from the 22nd Brigade, and still further from the 7th, became involved with a German armoured column. The three brigades were thus well scattered, and in a vulnerable position.

Early on the 20th November, the 4th Armoured Brigade, east of 20 Nov. Gabr Saleh, was attacked by a strong force of German tanks, and the 22nd Brigade, was called in from Bir el Gubi to help. After some fighting, the Germans broke off the fight and made off south, but they then wheeled north-west, and made for Sidi Rezegh where the 7th Armoured Brigade already had its hands full enough with German tanks and infantry.

Developments round Sidi Rezegh, where the position of the 7th 21 Nov. Armoured Brigade became increasingly critical during the 21st, boiled up into a fierce tank battle which raged during the 22nd 22-23 Nov.

and 23rd. The 4th and 22nd Armoured Brigades, which had arrived on the scene late on the 21st November, after some delay over refuelling, were in the thick of the tank battle, but the 7th Support Group, holding the Sidi Rezegh air-field, was forced back on to the southern escarpment, from where it withdrew to Gabr Saleh. The Sidi Rezegh escarpment was lost, despite its easy occupation on the 19th, and the balance of success lay with the enemy, whose tank recovery organization was, besides, in better shape than ours.

Forty miles east of Sidi Rezegh lay Bardia and the Halfaya Pass, and here the enemy were still strongly entrenched, though admittedly the 70th Division from Tobruk threatened the communications of the enemy armour. Rommel took a chance on that, however, and pushed his 15th and 21st Panzer Divisions directly

24 Nov. at the British centre at Bir Sheferzen, on the 24th. Great confusion ensued, but that was the limit of his success. The British stood firm under General Auchinleck's personal orders.

26 Nov. Sidi Rezegh was still the storm-centre, and on the 26th it fell to the New Zealand Division, which, however, was driven out again
27 Nov. next day. After holding its ground with great tenacity for several difficult days, the Division was compelled by exhaustion to with-
1-2 Dec. draw south of the escarpment, on the night of the 1st-2nd December.

Success generally lay with the Axis, but, none-the-less, the enemy was not happily placed between Tobruk and the XXXth Corps. His area of manoeuvre was sadly confined, and he set about expanding it by moving his armoured forces south to Bir el Gubi,
5 Dec. where they were attacked on the 5th December, by the 11th Indian Infantry, and 4th Armoured Brigades. These were later reinforced by the remainder of the 4th Indian Division and the Guards Brigade, and the enemy was forced to withdraw north-west. Rommel was gradually being squeezed out, but much stubborn fighting was yet to come.

9 Dec. On the 9th December, the 7th Indian Infantry Brigade and part of the XIIIth Corps linked up with the 70th Division from Tobruk at El Adem, 10 or 15 miles to the south. Rommel, by now, was on his way back, but delay occurred in organizing the pursuit. The enemy hence withdrew in good order to Agedabia, moving back
7 Jan. from thence to Agheila on the 7th January. Bardia, however, had
2 Jan. been stormed by the 2nd South African Division on the 2nd January,
17 Jan. and Halfaya surrendered on the 17th. Casualties for the whole intricate operation were put at 24,500 killed and wounded and 36,500 prisoners among the enemy. Total British losses were about 18,000. Rommel had lost two-thirds of his army, 386 out of 412 tanks, and 850 out of about 1,000 aircraft—an amazing achievement for the British.

All this time, however, the pendulum was gathering momentum
in the opposite direction. As already noted, measures had been
taken by the enemy to remedy his shipping losses in the Mediterranean, and these proved disastrously effective. The aircraft-carrier *Ark Royal* was sunk. So also were the battleship *Barham*,
the cruisers *Neptune* and *Galatea*, the destroyer *Kandahar*, and the
submarines *Perseus* and *Triumph*. Other ships were damaged, and
on the night of the 18th December, the battleships *Queen Elizabeth*
and *Valiant* were put out of action by "human torpedoes" in
Alexandria harbour. These solid achievements virtually eliminated
our available naval power, which was reduced, in the Central and
Eastern Mediterranean, to three cruisers and a few destroyers.
During January 1942, the Germans lost nothing whatever on the
sea passage across the Mediterranean, and Rommel was able to
complete his preparations for a counter-offensive, untroubled.

1941-2

18 Dec.

Jan.

There were curious resemblances between what now followed,
and what preceded Rommel's previous counter-offensive. The 8th
Army followed up to Agedabia, and there attempted, with inadequate forces, to consolidate its gains. Supply difficulties proved
very great, and troops were hence very thin on the ground. Between Agedabia and Agheila, some 75 miles apart, was one
armoured brigade, deployed over a vast area. Northwards, between
Agedabia and Benghazi—another 100-mile stretch—lay the 7th
Indian Infantry Brigade. From Benghazi to Barce, to its north-east,
was about 50 miles—and between them was the 4th Indian Division,
less the 7th Indian Infantry Brigade. There was little else
immediately available, for the 1st Armoured Division, which had
newly arrived from the United Kingdom in relief of the 7th, had to
be largely discounted at this stage by reason of its inexperience.
The main preoccupation was the building up of supply dumps
in preparation for an advance on Tripoli, and to this end many
of the troops, including the 4th Indian Division, between
Benghazi and Barce, had been temporarily immobilized for lack
of vehicles.

Three enemy armoured columns moved forward with little warning
on the 21st January, took Agedabia easily enough, and moved on
north-east towards Antelat and Msus. From Msus, they turned
north-west towards Benghazi, trapping the 7th Indian Infantry
Brigade to the west. The Brigade, however, broke out, and escaped
eastwards over the desert. The 4th Indian Division fell back on
Derna, 150 miles east-north-east of Benghazi, which the enemy
entered on the 28th January. The 1st Armoured Division lost a
damaging proportion of both its tanks and of its guns, including
anti-tank and anti-aircraft as well as 25-pounders. The enemy

21 Jan.

28 Jan.

1941-2

was not held up till the 7th February, a little east of Gazala, 60 miles or so east of Derna. Our dumps had proved of considerable value to him. The problem of providing mobile installations in keeping with the fluid conditions of war in the Western Desert, had still not been solved.

In the Gazala position, however, operations stabilized for the meanwhile.

Russia
14 Sept. In Russia, the vast encirclement of Kiev was taking shape. On the 14th September, Gen. Guderian's armoured group, by-passing Kiev on the north, joined hands at Lokvitsa, 120 miles east of Kiev, with Gen. Kleist's armoured group from the south. The Germans claimed 665,000 prisoners, and there is no doubt that the Russian losses were of this order. The remnants of Marshal Budyonny's armies withdrew east, followed up by von Runstedt's

October Southern Group. At the end of October, the latter was on the line Khursk-Kharkov-Stalino-Taganrog, a little east of south from Moscow, and with its southern extremity near the eastern end of the Sea of Azov.

2 Oct. A little before this, on the 2nd October, Field-Marshal von Bock's Central Group of armies, stiffened by a further forty-eight infantry and twelve armoured divisions, including those brought back with Gen. Guderian, resumed the advance on Moscow, with in the neighbourhood of one-and-a-half million men.

A great tank battle at Trubehovsk, on the right, a little west of south from Moscow, was followed by a rapid advance on Orel, due south of Moscow and about 200 miles from it. At Bryansk, 100 miles west of Orel, another victory was won. Further advances

15 Oct. were made, and by the 15th October, German armoured divisions were storming Mozhaisk, only 65 miles short of Moscow. This, however, was almost as far as the Central Group got. Winter came down three weeks earlier than usual, before a fresh full-scale advance could be mounted. The Germans did make good a further 30 miles north-east from Mozhaisk, and reached Klin, 35 miles

5 Dec. north-west of Moscow. But here, on the 5th December, the advance finally stopped, the Russians, under Marshal Zhukov, vigorously

6 Dec. counter-attacking on the 6th.

Meanwhile, in the south, Field-Marshal von Mannstein stormed the Isthmus of Perekop, connecting the Crimea with the mainland,

30 Oct. on the 30th October, but was held up before Sevastopol at the southern end of the Crimea. On the 11th November, Gen. von Kleist

11 Nov. occupied Rostov at the eastern tip of the Sea of Azov. In the north, the Northern Group had a measure of success in capturing

Schlusselburg, 30 miles east of Leningrad, which was invested. But it could not capture the city.

And now winter had come.

The German Supreme Command had never been in two minds about the consequences of the weather breaking up before their main objectives were achieved, and they were ready with the announcement issued on the 8th December that "Warfare in the east will henceforth be conditioned by the arrival of the Russian winter". What is less certain is that they had fully appreciated the detailed consequences of a winter campaign. On the 6th December, the temperature on the Moscow front had dropped to 40 degrees below zero—yet the troops had been neither clothed, equipped nor trained for winter warfare. Morale had kept very high with the earlier succession of vast manoeuvres and constant success. But now the bottom had been knocked out of it, the men were cold, and there was no likelihood of a decision for many weary months. Another matter that worried them was the sudden change made in the commanders who had led them to victory so far. Whether or no Hitler's own personal assumption of the chief command was well received, the sudden dismissal, about the 19th December, of the previous Commander-in-Chief, Field-Marshal von Brauschitsch, together with his Chief of Staff, General Halder, and Field-Marshals von Rundstedt, von Leeb, von Bock and List, and Generals Guderian and von Kleist, must have come as a personal shock to many. Meanwhile, thousands of German lorries and hundreds of railway engines were frozen up, and put out of action for many weeks pending repair—and the immediate necessity had to be accepted—if the troops were not to be frozen to death—of getting them under shelter and organizing the forward communications.

Advanced depots on the railways had already been built up, in particular at Staraya Russa, Rzhev, Vyazma, Kaluga, Bryansk, Orel and Kursk and Kharkov. Between these were smaller depots. All were fully stocked, and provided shelter. Fortified areas were now organized round these depots, covering many square miles, and providing all-round defence. They were self-contained, and designed to hold out independently of the situation elsewhere. Known as "Igels" or "hedgehogs", they were linked up by the air services, and, if necessary, were to be supplied by air as well.

On to these hedgehogs, the Germans now withdrew, while fresh advanced depots were built up behind them. The Russians, of course, followed up, and began infiltrating between the hedgehogs. Fighting of an increasingly savage type swelled up as the guerillas, some with the Cossacks, and others well in the German

1941

8 Dec.

6 Dec.

19 Dec.

1941-2

rear, provoked reprisals from the much-tried German troops. Quarter was given by neither side.

Operating with sledge-mounted artillery, ski-troops, and sledge-borne infantry, success followed success for the Russians.

16 Dec. On the 16th December, they retook Kalinin. Extensive pincer movements were developed against Rzhev, Gzhatsk and Vyazma.

30 Dec. Kaluga, one of the principal hedgehogs, was captured on the 30th.

From Kaluga, the Russians advanced north-west to Yukhnov, a hedgehog due east of Smolensk and south-east of Vyazma. At the same time, columns worked round the west of Rzhev towards Vitebsk, and reached Velikiye to the north of it. This brought

20-22 Jan. them within 50 miles of Smolensk. Meanwhile, between the 20th and 22nd January, they occupied Mozhaisk, 65 miles west of Moscow and 40 east of Gzhatsk.

In the north, on the Leningrad front, the Germans fell back from

9 Dec. Tikhvin on the 9th December. They then linked up Schlüsselburg and Novgorod, north of Lake Ilmen, and position warfare set in.

January In January, however, the Russians built a motor road over the ice on Lake Ladoga, regaining contact with Leningrad. Working round south of Lake Ilmen, they cut off a considerable part of the 16th German Army in the Staraya Russa area, and gradually annihilated it.

In the south, the Taganrog, Stalino and Artemovsk hedgehogs were by-passed in order to concentrate all available forces against Kharkov, which, however, stood firm. Losovaya, to the south, was taken, and the advance pushed on to within 30 miles of Poltava.

Massive though the Russian operations were, and of high significance in the general prosecution of the war, they were over-

Japan shadowed in December by the dramatic entry of Japan and the United States into the war.

Pearl The attack on Pearl Harbour and the Hickman and Wheeler air-
Harbour fields, in the island of Oaihu, came in at 7.50 a.m. on the 7th
7 Dec. December, while Mr. Kurusu, the Japanese envoy in Washington, was still engaged in negotiations with the United States Administration for a peaceful settlement of their differences. The Americans paid insufficient attention to such warnings of the attack as reached them, and learnt their lesson at a high cost. Some 350 carrier-borne Japanese aircraft delivered the attack. The first two waves met little opposition. The third wave, at 9.15 a.m., was beaten off. Eight battleships were in port at the time. Of these, the *Arizona* was wrecked, the *Oklahoma* capsized, and three others sank. A total of 19 ships was hit—but fortunately

                                                                1941-2
no aircraft-carriers were in port at the time. Of the 202 navy-type
aircraft the Americans had, only 52 were able to take off. Two
thousand seven hundred and ninety-five officers and men were
killed, 879 wounded and 25 missing. The Japanese lost about 60
planes shot down.
   At the same time, Guam and Wake Islands were attacked, and
eventually captured. Midway Island was attacked, but held out.
   In the south, the same tactics were followed as at Pearl   Philippines
Harbour. Systematic bombing of air-fields and key-points in Luzon
Island, the northernmost of the Philippines, destroyed about half
the available 200-odd American aircraft, on the ground. From
the 10th December, landings followed, first on the north coast of   10 Dec.
Luzon, at Aparri, then at Vigan, Legaspi and other places.
It was impossible to meet these various attacks, so Gen.
Douglas MacArthur, commanding the armed forces there, withdrew
to the Bataan Peninsula. This lies between Subic and Manilla
Bays, the entrance to the latter being guarded by the island fortress
of Corregidor. Here the garrison was closely invested, and from
New Year's Day to the 10th February, was under constant and   1 Jan.
fierce attack. On the 11th January, the garrison was put on half-   11 Jan.
rations, and saw out the balance of the period under review in
conditions of increasing misery, sickness and squalor, but with
spirit and courage of the highest order.

   In Hong Kong, when war broke out with Japan, there was a   Hong Kong
British garrison comprising two British infantry battalions— the
2nd Royal Scots, and the 1st Middlesex Regiment; two Canadian
infantry battalions—the Winnipeg Grenadiers and the Royal Rifles
of Canada; two Indian infantry battalions—the 5th/7th Rajput
Regiment and the 2nd/14th Punjab Regiment; the 5th A.A.
Regiment R.A., the 1st Hong Kong Regiment of the Hong Kong
and Shanghai Artillery, coastal artillery, and the usual services.
   Of this force, three battalions were strung out along the
"Gindrinkers Line", on the mainland, with the 5th/7th Rajputs on
the right, the 2nd/14th Punjab Regiment in the centre, and the
2nd Royal Scots on the left. This line was 10½ miles long, had
little depth, and was held by means of platoon localities. The
gaps were covered with fire by day, and by patrols by night. The
other three battalions of the garrison had roles on the island.
   Equipment was not complete, particularly in mortars. The
3-inch mortars were fired and registered for the first time in their
battle positions, twelve hours before coming into action against
the enemy. There was neither pack-mule nor carrying equipment for

1941

the men, and everything, including ammunition, had to be manhandled. The 2-inch situation was even worse. Without preliminary shooting, or any practise with dummies, ammunition for these mortars was delivered for the first time actually in battle.

The garrison was not caught by surprise. At 4.45 a.m. on the
8 Dec. 8th December, intelligence sources noted from a Tokyo broadcast, code instructions to their nationals that war with Britain and the United States was imminent. Two hours later, the outbreak was officially confirmed.

At 8 a.m., the Kai Tak aerodrome was attacked from the air. Flying very low, the Japanese destroyed and damaged five R.A.F. and eight civil planes. The barracks were also attacked—but the troops were out before, and there were few casualties. Enemy infantry began moving forward on the mainland at the same time, but demolitions delayed them. Their flanking tactics, however, proved hard to withstand. Pressure continued all that night, under a bright moon, and to a lesser degree next day. During the night
9 Dec. of the 9th-10th December, the Japanese penetrated the "Gin-
10 Dec. drinkers Line" on the left, and next day, the 10th, the R.A.F. were ordered to evacuate Kai Tak aerodrome and destroy their obsolete aircraft—of which in any case only one was fit to operate—and equipment.

11 Dec. On the 11th, the Japanese made further progress on the left and it became necessary to order the evacuation of the mainland. Fifth-column activities broke out in Hong Kong, together with rioting and looting, and desertion of civilian employees of the defence services.

Evacuation of the main land took place on the nights of the 11th-12th and 12th-13th December, and the troops were disposed
13 Dec. in the island defences. At 9 a.m. on the 13th, a flag of truce came over from Kowloon with a demand for unconditional surrender. This was refused. Civil disorders became an increasing nuisance.

Extremely accurate Japanese artillery fire caused much damage
17 Dec. to the island defences during the next few days. On the 17th December, surrender was again demanded, under the white flag, and was again rejected.

During the 17th and 18th December, very heavy artillery concentrations were carried out, supplemented with damaging air-
18 Dec. raids. By 10 p.m. on the 18th, the enemy had landed at two points on Hong Kong island against heavy resistance.

Enemy pressure rapidly increased, and, in spite of every effort, the enemy reached the reservoirs and cut the supply by the night
22-23 Dec. of the 22nd-23rd December. At 9 a.m. on Christmas Day, two
25 Dec. prisoners were sent across by the Japanese under the white flag,

78

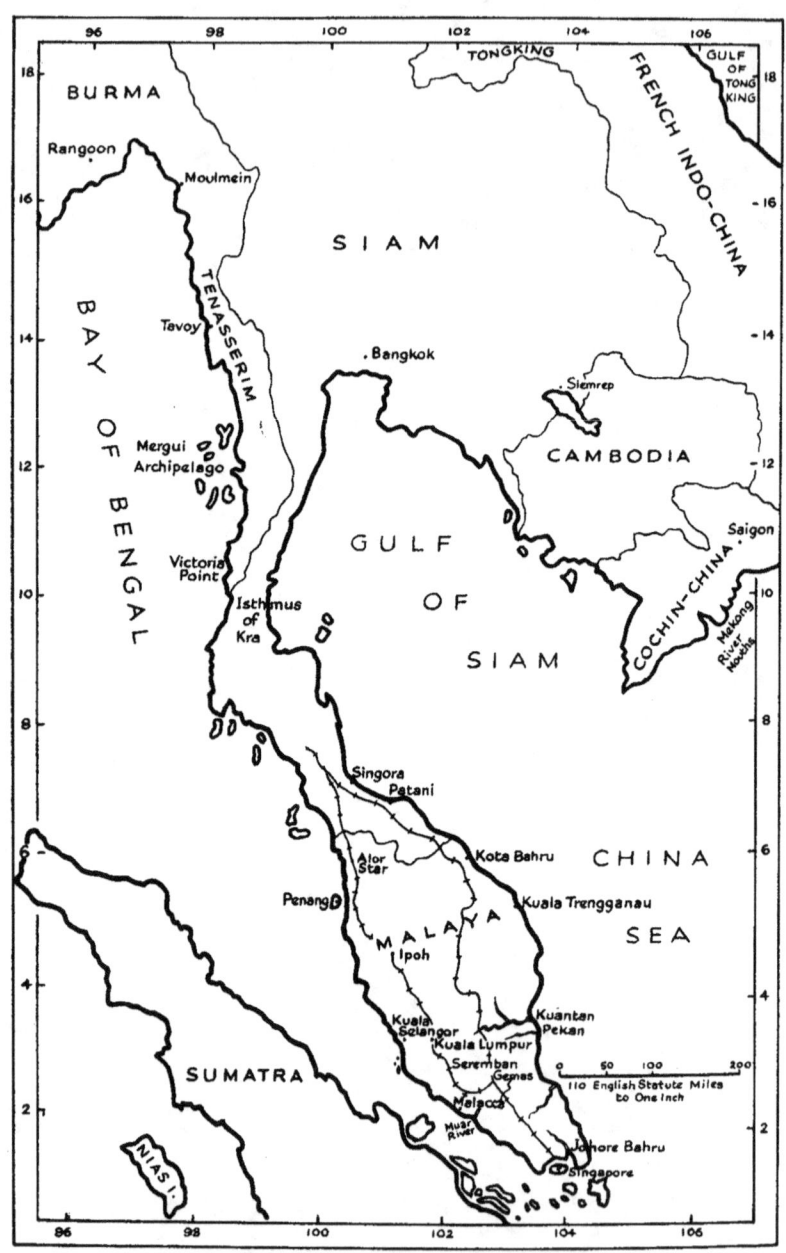

THE MALAYA CAMPAIGN
7 December 1941 to 14 February 1942

                                                                1941
to discuss the situation from the point of view of what they had
seen behind the Japanese lines, but, at a defence meeting, it was
decided not to surrender. However, by 3.15 p.m., a further series
of heavy attacks made it clear that no continued resistance was
possible, and the weary remnants of the garrison were authorized
to capitulate.

    The Japanese operations against Malaya began with an attack   Malaya
on Siam, to the north. They already had the use of several air-fields
in Indo-China. Based on these, they crossed the Indo-Chinese
frontier into Siam near Siemrep on the 7th December, whilst sea-   7 Dec.
borne detachments landed on the east coast of Siam not far north
of the Malaya border, at Singora and Patani, and occupied the
air-fields there.
    At the same time, a Japanese fleet appeared off the mouth of the
Menam river. Troops were landed, and Bangkok was occupied on
the 8th. After a token resistance, the Siamese government, on the   8 Dec.
21st December, signed a treaty of alliance with Japan.   21 Dec.
    Meanwhile, fierce air attacks had been delivered on the northern
air-fields in British Malaya, and many aircraft were destroyed on the
ground. Docks were bombed, especially at Singapore, but bridges
and communications generally were left untouched. Moving by road
and rail, Japanese forces debouched southwards from Kra, Singora
and Patani, and a detachment, moving west, crossed the isthmus,
and seized the air-field at Victoria Point—the stepping stone on the
air-route between Burma and Singapore. The immediate consequence
of this was the denial of fighter reinforcements from India by air.
    Late at night on the 7th December, ships were reported anchor-   7 Dec.
ing off the coast near Kota Bharu, on the east coast, not far from
the Siamese border. Soon after midnight, Japanese troops landed,   8 Dec.
and, twenty-four hours later after fierce resistance, carried the air-
field.
    Next day, the false report of a Japanese landing at Kuantan,   9 Dec.
something under half-way up the east coast from Singapore, drew
the newly-arrived battleships *Repulse* and *Prince of Wales* to
intercept. Themselves intercepted off Kuantan by shore-based
bombers and torpedo-carrying aircraft, both were sunk. With their
sinking, what remaining balance of naval power still belonged to
the Allies in these waters passed to the Japanese.
    On land, after the capture of Kota Bahru, the enemy carried the
axis of their attack over to the west coast, with its easier communication system. The air-field at Alor Star in Kedar was occupied
and the withdrawing British forces pursued towards Penang Island,
a further 50 miles to the south.

1941-2

11-13 Dec.	Penang was savagely bombed on the 11th, 12th and 13th, and indescribable confusion caused. On the 18th, the Japanese occupied the island and pressed on south into Perak. By the 31st December, their east coast troops had reached Kuantan.
18 Dec.	
31 Dec.	

The Japanese had long been preparing for their campaign in Malaya and had been able to concentrate on this one problem. The British, on the other hand, already distracted by the differing demands of several different theatres, were not equipped to make the best of a jungle campaign in Malaya. Weighed down with their heavy loads, and depending on mechanical transport, they were at a heavy disadvantage compared with the Japanese. The latter may have lacked much of the conventional panoply of war with their singlets, shorts and rubber-soled shoes, their fleets of bicycles, their tommy-guns and 2-inch mortars, and their light two-wheeled man-hauled carts. But, living on a ration-scale which would never have been accepted as sufficient for our own troops, the Japanese lived and moved with small restriction, and reaped their reward.

7 Jan. By the 7th January, the British were back in Kuala Lumpur in Selangor, more than half-way to Singapore. The Japanese now pushed through a considerable number of tanks some hours before daybreak, but in bright moonlight, and with disastrous losses to the British. Retreating southwards to Tampin and Gemas, another 50 miles, and to the Endau river on the east, our forces

30 Jan. fell back again till by the 30th January, the Japanese were about Kulai in Johore, less than 20 miles north of Singapore. Next day,

31 Jan. at 8 a.m., the causeway leading across the straits to Singapore Island was blown, and the siege of the island had begun.

There is little to add to the story. All the heart-breaking weariness and courage of the long withdrawal were to end in disaster. Singapore had not been designed for landward defence, and so much of the base installation of the fortress was now facing the Japanese at the north side of the island. Defence, though gallant, was unavoidably embarrassed by the obvious tactical difficulties of the situation.

4 Feb. The Japanese held their hand till the 4th February, bringing up artillery and co-ordinating their plans. That day they opened a

8-9 Feb. bombardment across the Strait of Johore. On the night of the 8th-9th February, they moved their forces across in iron barges specially brought down, and landed on a 10-mile front between Kranji Creek and Pasir Laba.

At first, the situation seemed reasonably well in hand. The Japanese began pressing forward from Kranji Creek and Pasir

9 Feb. Laba in two columns, on the 9th, and the demand for our sur-
11 Feb. render, dropped from the air on the 11th, was ignored. The

                                                                1942
Japanese, however, had been busy repairing the breach in the
causeway. They now passed their tanks across it, and on the 14th   14 Feb.
February, these seized the reservoirs. With the loss of the water
supply, further resistance was impossible, and at 8.30 p.m. next
day, the 15th, the force surrendered.   15 Feb.

In common with most regiments of the Indian Army, the Sikh
Regiment paid its share of the cost of this disaster. Most of the
5th Battalion was captured with the 22nd Indian Infantry Brigade
in the neighbourhood of Johore Bahru in the last days before the
withdrawal to Singapore Island. The Brigade, lying forward in the
Layang Layang area, had lost touch with the 8th Indian Infantry
Brigade, which was supporting it, and enemy troops had penetrated into this gap. Maj.-Gen. Barstow went forward up the
railway to try and contact the 22nd Indian Infantry Brigade. His
trolley was ambushed, and there seems no doubt that the General
was killed. In Gen. Percival's despatch he is referred to as a
gallant and gifted officer whose loss was a severe blow, and all
who knew him will recognize the solid truth of this description.
As to the Brigade, and the 5th Battalion, they endeavoured to
rejoin the Division—the 9th—moving through the jungle west of
the railway. Some parties of the enemy were met and dispersed,
the 5th Battalion, so the despatch reads, again distinguishing
themselves—"but the dense jungle proved too much for the troops
who were hampered by having to carry a number of wounded. In
spite of a continuous march of three days and nights they were
unable to catch up and efforts to locate them by ground and air
patrols failed. The final withdrawal was postponed as long as
possible in an effort to recover this Brigade, but without success,
and arrangements were made to ferry them across the Straits from
a point east of Johore Bahru. Eventually only about 100 were saved
in this way. The remainder were captured in the neighbourhood of
Johore Bahru on the 1st February".

After the withdrawal into Singapore Island, the remnant of the
9th Indian Division was absorbed into the 11th Indian Division,
commanded by Maj.-Gen. B. W. Key. Other officers of the Regiment
included Lieut.-Gen. Sir Lewis Heath, commanding the IIIrd
Corps, also captured in Singapore. There were likewise a number
of individual regimental officers serving with other units, including Maj. F. R. Neep, of the 4th Battalion, Capt. B. Wilson, and
Capt. Robertson, both of the 2nd Battalion.

The successful operations in Malaya opened the way for the   Burma
Japanese to their next objectives—Rangoon and the Burma Road.
For the defence of Burma, the British had two weak divisions

1942

scattered along a 1,600 mile front. The Japanese held command of the air.

The main entrance from Siam into lower Burma was through the Kawkareik Pass, about 60 miles east of Moulmein and the Salween river. On the 21st January, the Japanese brushed aside the defences on the Kawkareik Pass, and, with strong detachments already moving up the Tennaserim coast, advanced on Moulmein. A gallant defence failed to deny them the crossing of the Salween river, and they followed our troops up to the Bilin river, some 30 miles to the west. Fierce fighting here between the 15th and 20th February resulted in a further withdrawal to the river Sittang. This brought the enemy close to Rangoon, and the question of its defence or abandonment became a matter for anxious debate.

21 Jan.

15-20 Feb.

Java

At this time, Gen. Wavell was appointed to supreme command in the south-west Pacific, to direct the operations of all Allied forces in the general area of Burma, Malaya, the Netherlands East Indies and the Philippines. The new Command was designated A.B.D.A., to signify the American, British, Dutch and Australian forces.

10 Jan.
15 Jan.

Headquarters opened at Lembang in Java by the 10th January, and Gen. Wavell assumed direct operational control on the 15th.

The Command had a life of only six weeks. In the first instance, efforts were directed to the maintenance of a line of bases—Port Darwin, Timor, Java, Southern Sumatra, Singapore—on which to build up an air-force strong enough to secure local air superiority, and hence check the southward flow of the Japanese. By the 24th January, however, the enemy's air offensive had reached impressive proportions, and Allied air-fields in Sumatra had been reconnoitred and bombed. Japanese air bases were already being pushed forward on Borneo and Celebes, and a landing had been made on Balikpapan, directly threatening Java, which was everywhere, but especially in the naval base at Sourabaya, very inadequately defended.

24 Jan.

The hope of acquiring a sufficient air-force for the Command was never fulfilled. Only a small proportion of the aircraft promised ever set out for the Netherlands East Indies at all. Of those which did, a high proportion, possibly as high as 40 or 50 per cent., never arrived. The air routes to the Command were long and hazardous, with a high rate of wastage. Sea routes were so long that few crated aircraft arrived before the Command closed down. Some of the United States machines were diverted to Australia for defence of that country. At the same time, air-fields in Southern Sumatra and Java were limited and only partially developed, an

1942

adequate air warning system was out of the question with material available, and very few anti-aircraft guns were to be had for aerodrome protection. For these and other like reasons, wastage of aircraft after arrival in the Netherlands East Indies was very high, and the Allied air-force, instead of increasing in strength and obtaining superiority over the Japanese, wasted with accelerating rapidity till it was finally completely destroyed.

All available land troops were originally earmarked for Singapore, but an important part of them did not arrive in the Command, until not only had Singapore fallen and Sumatra been captured, but Java itself was too closely threatened for large forces to be landed.

The naval situation was that much of the available force was employed escorting convoys into Singapore, and occasionally between Australia and Java. The striking force was therefore small. No air protection could be provided for it except close in to Java, whereas Japanese naval forces or convoys always moved under strong air cover. Naval operational planning hence laboured under a crippling disadvantage and the sole—and successful— case of a planned encounter lies in the five-day naval action about the 23rd January in the Straits of Macassar when several Japanese transports were sunk. This never had a chance to be repeated.

23 Jan.

Five separate Japanese lines of attack were expected. These pointed to:

    Amboina, Timor, and possibly Port Darwin:
    Celebes (Kendari and Macassar):
    Borneo (Balikpapan, Bandjermasin, and Pontianak):
    Johore and Singapore:
    Burma (Moulmein and Rangoon).

In these advances, a regular sequence could be seen. A line of air bases would be secured, and air attacks made from them on the next air bases to the south. When it was judged that the air-forces based on these were sufficiently reduced, a sea-borne expedition would attempt to seize them. And so on. These methods became so stereotyped that it became possible to predict with reasonable accuracy the date of each fresh advance and its objective.

By mid-January, the Japanese had already seized Menado in Celebes, and Tarakan and Kuching in Borneo. They attacked Balikpapan on the 23rd January, Kendari on the 24th, Amboina on the 30th, Macassar on the 9th February, Bandjermasin on the 10th. All were sea-borne expeditions except for Bandjermasin, captured by land columns from Balikpapan.

23-30 Jan.
9-10 Feb.

With the fall of Singapore on the 15th February, Southern

15 Feb.

1942

Sumatra became the last outpost of Java to the west. A convoy of warships and transports had been seen at the Anambas Islands, north-east of Singapore in early February, and it was suspected that its objective was Southern Sumatra. Efforts were made to get available forces to the western end of Java in time to intercept it,
13 Feb. but the Japanese got there first. At dawn on the 13th February,
14 Feb. the convoy began moving south. Early on the 14th February some 700 Japanese parachutists came down on or near Palembang aerodrome and the oil refineries, whilst heavy attacks by bombers and low-flying fighters wrought havoc among the inadequately guarded defending aircraft. The convoy moved in, and on the morning of
15 Feb. the 15th a force of about a division was advancing on Palembang by all possible river approaches. Our naval force was too late to intercept, and though very heavy casualties were inflicted from the air, these were not able to stop the Japanese advance. Clearly, there was little hope of holding Southern Sumatra, and, with the forces available, a successful defence of Java seemed unlikely.
18-19 Feb. On the night of the 18th-19th February, an enemy landing took place at Bali just east of Java. Sea and air reaction inflicted some loss on the enemy. But with aerodromes in enemy hands on three sides—Sumatra in the west, Bali in the east, and Borneo and Celebes to the north—the days of the Allied air-force were numbered, and, with it, the remaining security of Java from invasion. The Command could exercise no further useful functions. Control of the sea, land and air forces in the Netherlands East Indies was transferred to Dutch commanders on the 25th February, and the A.B.D.A. Command was dissolved. The Allied forces left, under the orders of the Combined Chiefs of Staffs to fight alongside the Dutch for the defence of Java, included about 5,500 British troops, mainly anti-aircraft and administrative, but including one squadron, 3rd Hussars; about 6,000 Royal Air Force personnel, mainly unarmed, and without aircraft, for the last machine had
25 Feb. been expended by the 25th February; about 3,000 Australians for aerodrome protection, with some administrative troops; and about 500 United States artillery personnel. Fighter resistance was aimed at by the despatch of some P.40's on the United States seaplane tender *Langley*—which was sunk from the air while approaching the island; and by twenty-seven other P.40's which arrived at Tjilatjap in the *Seawitch*, but which had to be destroyed to prevent their falling into enemy hands.

This short chapter in the history of the Japanese offensive in the south-west Pacific has been given some prominence as showing in some degree the all-over extent of the problem with which the

Allies were now faced, and the appalling difficulties under which
they laboured in stemming the onrush. Everywhere, it was a fight
against odds, and that the fight went everywhere to the Japanese
is no reflection on the endurance and gallantry of the small weak
Allied detachments which, one by one, were overwhelmed.

In India, it was not long before *the 1st Battalion* was drawn
into the vortex. Before taking up that part of the story, however,
it would be as well to consider in what shape the Battalion stood
to engage in operations against a well-prepared and highly trained
enemy, in country almost the exact opposite to that in which
regular Indian battalions were accustomed to serve.

1941

1st Bn.

We have already seen something of the conditions under which
the 5th Battalion had been despatched to Malaya, and we shall
learn in due course how magnificently its men acquitted themselves in the face of great hardship during the few brief weeks
which ended in Singapore, and its neighbourhood.

Since the war began, two years earlier, the 1st Battalion, in
common with most other regular battalions of the Indian Army,
had been drained of good officers, non-commissioned officers and
men to meet the needs of drafts for battalions overseas, and for
new battalions raising within the Regiment. Trained replacements
were not available, other than reservists. Of the reservists, a
high proportion were unfit for active service overseas, and had to
be sent off to sundry static units for garrison duties in India.
Only six days before the Battalion left the frontier to join its
formation for service in Burma, one officer, two Viceroy's commissioned officers and 100 men had been drafted off for the 5th
Battalion in Malaya.

Turning to equipment, none of the more modern weapons needed
had been issued to battalions on the North-West Frontier, and few
of the officers or men had ever seen the 2-inch and 3-inch mortars,
Bren light machine-guns, anti-tank rifles and mines, wireless sets
and armoured carriers with which infantry were then equipped
overseas. That this was the common lot will be evident from
previous references to this subject. The fact is, of course, that
the weapons simply were not available. But that made it no easier
for a commanding officer whose command was suddenly plunged
into an overseas theatre, where performance was calculated on the
basis of such equipment.

It will be remembered that the 1st Battalion had returned to
Bannu from its expedition with the Tochi Column to relieve
Datta Khel. Nothing further happened for some months, but then
movement orders arrived, and, on the 29th December, the Battalion

29 Dec.

1942 left by rail to join the 63rd Indian Infantry Brigade in Jhansi.

The 63rd Indian Infantry Brigade was raising as part of the 23rd Indian Division, commanded by Maj.-Gen. R. A. Savory, D.S.O., M.C., who had been commandant of the Battalion at the outbreak of the war. What the Division's likely role was to be no one had the faintest idea at the time, but the Brigade was told that units would have six months in which to reorganize and train before going on active service. Perhaps in the light of this, it was not so odd that a draft should have been sent to the 5th Battalion, but even at this stage of the war with Japan, it seems obvious enough by now that regular troops were not likely to be given six months more to get themselves ready.

January The Battalion was still under strength, and, by the end of January, had received no new equipment. Consequently, when
1 Feb. orders arrived to mobilize on the 1st February, with the added pious hope that the Brigade would not be sent into action until two months training had been carried out, the news came as something of a jolt.

From this moment, however, events moved with steadily accelerating speed. Mobilization was first carried out on a compromise war establishment, with mixed mule and motor transport. Some 400 recruits arrived from Nowshera to bring the Battalion up to strength, but the majority of these had only five months service and could not be drafted into specialist groups. Trained men were needed for anti-tank, anti-aircraft, mortar and pioneer platoons, for employment as mule leaders and motor transport drivers and for attachment to Brigade Headquarters. When these had been drafted out of their rifle companies, it left the latter with a nucleus of not more than twenty trained men in any one company.

Reorganization on these lines was carried out with all speed.
15 Feb. It was no sooner completed than, in mid-February, just over a fortnight after mobilization orders had been received, and before new arms and equipment had been issued, the Brigade was ordered overseas at the shortest notice to reinforce the troops in Burma.
19 Feb. On the 19th, accordingly, the Battalion entrained for Madras. With them went the 2nd Battalion 13th Frontier Force Rifles, and the 1st Battalion 10th Gurkha Rifles. Reaching Madras on the
24 Feb. 24th, the troops—less the transport personnel and mules which went via Calcutta—embarked immediately. It proved a tiring and arduous day. Most of the new equipment had been sent direct to Madras by ordnance depots, and it had to be unpacked, distributed and taken on charge. This was done—and the ship then pulled out into the harbour where it lay for a further two days, sailing on the
26 Feb. 26th in a four-ship convoy.

1941

The weather was good with a calm sea, and it proved possible to keep the men well-exercised and fit, while the new weapons were looked over. Nothing much was known of their use in many cases, but by trial-and-error it was discovered how they worked, and the men had a chance to fire them over the stern of the ship. This was the only opportunity they had to fire these weapons before going into action.

Meanwhile, the transport personnel were collecting armoured carriers and trucks for delivery to the Battalion in Rangoon.

The 2nd Battalion, at the beginning of September, was at the Anglo-Iranian Oil Company's centre at Haft Khel, in Persia. Two rifle companies were on detachment with Brigade Headquarters 10 miles up-river at Wais. An armistice with Persia had already been signed, and the likelihood of further operations was remote. At the outset, night patrolling was carried out in the factory and bungalow areas, but from the 3rd September, it was discontinued. 2nd Bn.

3 Sept.

Life in Haft Khel was extremely pleasant, but it was not to last very long. On the evening of the 7th September, "B" and "C" companies moved in from Wais to Ahwaz, and went into camp; and on the 8th the remainder of the Battalion joined them there, after relief by a company of the 5th Mahrattas.

7 Sept.

8 Sept.

Two days later, the troops bussed in to Tanooma. Here they found part of a draft of ninety-five men that had been sent them from the Training Battalion; and were not best pleased to find that forty-seven of these men had been detained for routine duties at No. 15 Reinforcement Camp. The matter was taken up at once, and the missing men yielded up, arriving on the 12th, with Sub. Ujagar Singh. It is on the record that these men were soft, and below the standard of drafts received in India before sailing for Iraq. But it is fair to add that the Battalion itself had toughened a good deal since then, too, and possibly set too high a standard. At all events there was no question but that the new arrivals had been well-instructed in field-craft, etc.

10 Sept.

12 Sept.

On the 13th September orders were received to concentrate forward at Habbaniya with the rest of the Brigade. The Battalion would move in two parties—one by road and the other by rail. On the 15th, the move began, under conditions of heat not wholly attributable to the weather. "Staff arrangements", said the Battalion, "could hardly be worse, H.Q. L. of C. for a start failing to ensure that the bridge across the river was closed to east-bound traffic, which resulted in a very bad jam on the island in the middle of the boat bridge. The guides ordered by them to meet the M.T. party at Shaiba never turned up, and finally, when the rail

13 Sept.

15 Sept.

1941

16 Sept. party arrived at Baghdad at 12.00 hours on the 16th, over four hours late, they were not to cook their morning meal. The meal, however, was cooked, and men and baggage were embussed and moved out to Habbaniya where they went into camp beside the lake." Here the M.T. party, moving from Tanooma via Shaiba, Ur,

19 Sept. Diwaniya and Baghdad, joined them on the 19th.

As soon as the M.T. arrived, the Battalion began to shake out into posts, as "Desert Battalion". Desert Battalion Headquarters lay at Haditha (or K3), about 50 miles west of Habbaniya along the pipeline.

20 Sept. The move itself took place on the 20th September. The Battalion, less "B" Company and one platoon of "D" Company, took over at K3, while Capt. Rimmer, with the detachment noted above, moved on to H2, and Rutba. H2 was some 70 miles west of K3, on the southern, or Haifa, branch of the pipeline. Rutba, near the Trans-Jordan frontier with Iraq, was about 35 miles farther on.

21 Sept. On the 21st September, "C" and "D" Companies moved out from K3, and took over four posts from the 4th Battalion, 13th Frontier Force Rifles. These were H1, about mid-way between K3 and H2–T1 about 50 miles north-west of K3 on the northern, or Tripoli, branch of the pipeline—and two other posts—Frontier Pos and Al Qaim—in the same general area.

Life at H1 was marred at the start, when a bomb, thrown in
22 Sept, through a loophole, on the 22nd September, by either a local inhabitant, or possibly by one of the Arab employees of the I.P.C., killed No. 18591 Sep. Gurdev Singh, seriously wounded No. 12686 Naik Bakhshi Singh and three sepoys, and slightly wounded four others. This, fortunately, was the only incident of the kind during the tour.

The Battalion was now responsible for a vast area of desert, and patrolling had to be carried out daily in all directions. Provision of escorts was an additional drain on man-power, and the list of "muafis" had to be severely scrutinized. M.T. drivers, who were normally excused when the Battalion was moving about, were now pulled in on the night-duty roster.

During the ensuing month, reliefs were effected from time to time, and changes in posts took place. Training was worked in
18 Oct. somehow, but life proved uneventful till at 8 p.m. on the 18th October, a patrol from T1 found the pipeline punctured some 30 miles to the west. About thirty 50-gallon drums, filled with oil, and a quantity of camel harness, were discovered stacked nearby. An ambush was set, but to no purpose.

19 Oct. Next night, the pipeline was again punctured—this time 15 miles west of the post. The patrol stayed out on the watch for

36 hours, but saw no one. However, no further cases occurred during
the Battalion's tour of duty.

It is pleasant to read that on the 1st November, the bugles, drums and fifes played at guard-mounting—for the first time for a number of years; and that on the 11th, the massed buglers marked the beginning of the two-minutes Remembrance Day silence, and its ending, with the Last Post and Reveille. Next day, the 12th, the posts at Rutba, H1, H2, and two new posts, H3 and LG5, were taken over by the 3rd Battalion, 9th Jat Regiment. The various garrisons moved direct to Mujahrah on the 13th, and the same day, at K3, the Iraq Petroleum Company gave a farewell dinner party for the officers, and Mr. Duff, the chief engineer, made a speech, to which the C.O., Lieut.-Col. A. E. Farwell, replied. On the 17th November, Battalion Headquarters, with H.Q. Company, and "B" and "D" Companies, moved in to Mujahrah in M.T., and settled into E.P tents.

By the 27th November, however, they were on the move again—this time to Fallujah, 16 miles away on the Euphrates. The move was complicated by the absence of twenty-seven vehicles on various tasks, or under inspection in workshops, but the distance was not too great for reasonable improvization.

Policy in Iraq at this time was defensive. On the 28th, tasks were allotted to the Battalion, accordingly. Work on an anti-tank ditch was to start next day, with the men digging steadily for six hours per day. Work went on till the 20th December, by which time the Fallujah defences were practically complete, but as there was still much to be done at Mujahrah, where the Mahrattas were employed, the Battalion was sent there on the 21st, less "B" Company and the Pioneer Platoon which were left behind to finish off the work at Fallujah.

Early in January, the weather turned very cold, and digging was cut down to five hours a day to allow the men to clean up in reasonable comfort before the sun got too low. Meanwhile, the 3rd/9th Jats having been relieved by a British battalion—the the King's Own Regiment—the Sikhs had been made responsible for finding the entire M.T. personnel of Brigade Headquarters.

On the 23rd January, the Battalion had an unusual but welcome visitor in the person of Sir Sikander Hayat Khan, K.B.E., Premier of the Punjab. He saw the men at their digging and gave them a ten-minute talk.

Something has already been said elsewhere on the periodical levies on battalions for provision of trained men for newly-raising battalions, in India. Orders were now received by the Battalion

1941-2

1 Nov.
11 Nov.
12 Nov.
13 Nov.
17 Nov.
27 Nov.
28 Nov.
29 Nov.
20 Dec.
21 Dec.
January
23 Jan.
28 Jan.

1942

to the effect that 3 per cent. of its strength, in all ranks, and including specialists, were to be sent back to India monthly. These drafts would be given leave in India, and then retained there. Small notice of this was given. The orders arrived on the 28th January, and the first batch was due to leave on the 1st February. Whether or no the order was a good one, it appeared to bear heavily on men whom it was indispensable to have back with the Battalion, since they could evidently never be sent back to India at all. However, meanwhile, a small party of fourteen Indian

29 Jan. other ranks was sent off to India on the 29th for repatriation either on extreme compassionate grounds, or because they were too old to be retained overseas, or were non-commissioned officers, unfit for promotion in the Battalion, but capable of useful service in a static unit in India.

31 Jan. Operational policy now reverted to normal, and on the 31st January, all digging of tank defences was stopped. Training re-
2 Feb. started on the 2nd February.

11 Feb. On the 11th February, a draft of forty Indian other ranks arrived under Jem. Pritam Singh from the Reinforcement Camp at Shaiba. Turning to the record once more, we find this draft referred to with some bitterness. It arrived, the record states "equipped with the '07 pattern of equipment, had only 20 rounds of ammunition instead of the correct scale, and were further deficient of many other items of kit. The same story may be told of every draft which joins the Battalion from this camp. The lack of supervision in this respect is deplorable."

12 Feb. On the 12th February, the forces in Iraq were re-named the Tenth Army.

13 Feb. Next day, the 13th, the Battalion moved off in a dust-storm to a camp west of Habbaniya and about 12 miles distant from Mujahrah. For the rest of the month, training went steadily on, including
28 Feb. movements under a live-shell barrage by artillery. On the last day of February, the Battalion's seven tracked carriers were withdrawn, as being unsuitable for desert work, and, pending arrival of the new wheeled carriers, the support platoon was reformed with Vickers machine-guns, under Sub. Balwant Singh.

3rd Bn. *The 3rd Battalion* had returned to Baghdad from K 3 in early August, and it now moved up the Tigris line to Qaiyara, where it was employed on defensive works in much the same way as the 2nd Battalion on the Euphrates. Extensive defences were being prepared against the possibility of a German thrust through Persia and into Iraq from the Caucasus. From Qaiyara, the Battalion went on to Mosul, and after a brief stay of two months there, moved back down the Tigris to Baiji.

1941

The 4th Battalion stayed on in its oasis at Giarabub till the 2nd November when the 29th Brigade moved in on relief. The 7th Brigade halted for a few days at Kilo 49 on the Mersa Matruh-Sidi Barrani road, on its way up from Giarabub, and then moved on to Kilo 91. Whilst here, the raising of a Brigade machine-gun company began. Eight guns were issued for training and personnel were detailed for the Battalion's quota. A further small drain on the Battalion's man-power was provided by the issue of two Italian Breda anti-tank guns, mounted in 15-cwt trucks, as protection for "B" echelon transport vehicles, since crews had to be trained to handle them.

4th Bn. 2 Nov.

At about this time, during the first half of November, there were rumours of an impending German attack in the Sollum area. Battalion and Company commanders were hurried forward to Sidi Barrani where a Brigade defensive area was being reconnoitred. Perhaps it was as well for the Battalion that it was never called upon to hold the 8,000 yards of front allotted to it. As things turned out, the Brigade left Kilo 91 soon after for the Sofafi area. It was at this stage, on the 10th November, that "left out of battle" personnel, consisting of the second-in-command, two other British officers, three Viceroy's commissioned officers, and forty-five Indian other ranks, were ordered back to Rakham, a short distance west of Mersa Matruh. They did not see the Battalion again till they rejoined it at Derna on the 21st December.

For the move to the Sofafi area, troop-carrying 3-ton lorries reported to the Battalion on the evening of the 10th November; and early on the 11th, the column moved out along the coast road to Sidi Barrani. From here, it struck off south for 12 miles, halting about mid-day with the vehicles widely dispersed. That night, the column was on the move again, to a point a farther 35 miles southwest, at the southern end of a well-mined defensive position stretching down from the coast. The area was known as "Play ground" since, from here, our mobile patrols used to sally forth to keep an eye on the enemy positions 45 miles to the west. The Battalion spent the 12th November reconnoitring its positions here.

10 Nov. 11 Nov.

12 Nov.

Until the 15th November it was thought that the move was a normal routine tour of the forward positions. Then, however, plans for the coming offensive were made known.

15 Nov.

The 7th Indian Infantry Brigade, which later, with reason, came to be called the "Fighting Seventh", was billed to contain hostile forces in the Omar areas, some 40 miles to the west, and, if possible, capture the positions there. Other diversions were to be

1941

staged to the north; and, under cover of these various activities, the armoured forces were to pass through in the south, and defeat the German armour.

The Omar positions were sited on a pair of mounds in the middle of the plain, at the southern end of the enemy line which began by the sea, 22 miles away, at Halfaya Pass. The two fortified areas—Sidi Omar and Libyan Omar—corresponded to our "Play ground". They were well-mined, and strongly garrisoned by a mixed German and Italian force. If it was decided, on arrival in the area, to go on to the capture of these positions, this was to be carried out by the Royal Sussex Regiment, and the 4th Battalion (Bhopal), 16th Punjab Regiment. The Sikhs were to stage a series of demonstrations in the direction of Got Adidira, to prevent any withdrawal from the Omars, and also ensure that no reinforcements reached them from the north-east.

The operations were to be carried out in three phases:

First, the move to an assembly area, 30 miles or so west of "Play ground".

Next, an approach march to the objectives.

Finally, the occupation of the objectives.

16 Nov. The Brigade moved off in three columns. The 4th/16th Punjabis were on the left. In the centre came the Brigade Headquarters group, the Sikh carrier platoon less one section, and the Sikh "C" and "D" Companies. On the right were the Sikhs, less the two companies and carrier platoon. Each column had its allotment of supporting arms, a routine arrangement all learned to appreciate in the coming weeks.

The three columns moved independently to a timed programme. The first two phases involved a couple of very severe night marches over difficult country. It is a tribute to navigators and

18 Nov. drivers that at zero hour on the 18th November, when the invasion of Libya was launched, the three columns were either on, or in the very close vicinity of, their objectives.

The decision was quickly made that the Omars should be attacked—but not immediately. In the meantime, during the next few days, forward patrolling was actively carried out, to draw the enemy's fire and keep him guessing where the attack was to be made. In the event, the Royal Sussex moved round to the northern

22 Nov. side on the 22nd November, and, in the face of tremendous fire, captured Sidi Omar, on the east.

Libyan Omar, on the west, was not to fall so easily. The Punjabis attacked on the evening of the 22nd, but could not win through; and it was not till the 30th November that, with the help of the 3rd 1st Punjab Regiment, they over-ran the garrison of

3,000 men, at a combined cost of 336 casualties. "C" Company of
the 4th/11th Sikh Regiment played a successful part in these
operations, and Jem. Gurbaksh Singh was awarded a posthumous
Indian Order of Merit for outstanding gallantry at the head of
No. 12 platoon. An Indian Distinguished Service Medal was awarded
to No. 12653 Hav. Karam Singh for great personal courage and
leadership in command of No. 15 platoon in the same action.

During these attacks the remainder of the Battalion was actively
employed with patrols, and on the 23rd November a Company
attack was made by "A" Company on Pt. 204 (Haqfet el Qineqina)
over unreconnoitred ground, which proved to include an unsuspected enemy minefield. Heavy artillery, machine-gun and rifle fire
added to the difficulties of the attack, which was carried through
in fine style at the bayonet's point. For his fine and resolute
leadership, coupled with a subsequent display of gallantry at the
Derna Landing Ground on the 1st December, Capt. Mohammed
Siddiq, M.C., was awarded a bar to his Military Cross, while
No. 7654 Naik Chanan Singh who had set a magnificent example
leading his platoon forward at the double across the minefield, but
who lost his life just short of the position, received a posthumous
Mention in Despatches. Another well-earned Mention in Despatches
fell to No. 13690 Hav. Bishan Singh, who, like Naik Chanan
Singh, led his men through the minefield, and then charged in with
grenades against an enemy machine-gun post. Finally, his share
in the attack coupled with his later gallantry on the 1st December
at Derna, won No. 13004 Hav. Kishan Singh the Indian Distinguished Service Medal.

During the patrolling preceding the attack, and in the near
vicinity of Pt. 204, two other well-deserved awards had been
earned. One of these was the Indian Distinguished Service Medal
granted to a young soldier, No. 17413 Sep. Ghazni Khan, who was
on patrol with his platoon near Pt. 204 in the early hours of the
22nd November. Very heavy enemy machine-gun and rifle fire had
been opened on the platoon without warning, from close range,
killing one man, and causing some confusion in the darkness.
Sep. Ghazni Khan, however, without a moment's hesitation, doubled
across to the dead man to recover his light machine-gun and
magazine, which he immediately brought into action against the
enemy, thus giving his platoon sufficient breathing-space to take
up a position without further loss. He then rejoined his platoon and
again brought the gun into action. His subsequent behaviour on the
1st December at Derna Landing Ground fully confirmed the opinion
formed of him, and resulted in the award mentioned.

No. 11859 Naik Ghulam Mohd was involved in a somewhat

1941 different kind of trouble when patrolling on the 21st November. The patrol was moving forward to contact the enemy in the Ghot Addidiba position, east of Sidi Omar Nuovo. The route led past Pt. 204, and here very heavy machine-gun and rifle fire was opened on the patrol, and shortly after, artillery fire was opened as well. Orders had been given for the patrol not to get mixed up in an action, so it was moved back to its trucks with the object of falling back half-a-mile to a previously selected position. All went well up to a point. The men embussed and moved off. But, as Naik Ghulam Mohd's truck started, two men were thrown out of it and fell on to the ground. Although enemy fire was still heavy and accurate, Naik Ghulam Mohd did not hesitate. He jumped out and ran straight to their assistance. He helped them to their feet, and back into the by now halted truck. But his troubles were not over. At this point two enemy tanks approached and opened fire on the patrol. Naik Ghulam Mohd seized a light machine-gun and opened fire on the tanks and on the enemy position. His gallantry and inspiring action undoubtedly enabled the patrol, and with it an anti-tank gun, to withdraw successfully to the rear position. He was subsequently mentioned in Despatches for it.

Another well-merited Mention was awarded a few days later to No. 16872 Sep. Saudagar Singh for most gallantly going out under heavy fire, on the 27th November to the rescue of a badly wounded comrade lying out some 15 to 20 yards ahead, near Sidi Omar. He not only brought him safely back, but saved his life in addition, for the wounded man eventually recovered.

For every act of gallantry that came to notice, how many, one wonders, went unremarked in the heat of action or the dim obscurity of night affrays? Self-sacrifice and devotion were a commonplace then as at all other times of stress, and the Regiment's prestige rose ever higher with the growing record of courageous deeds.

While these events were enacting in the south, the position was growing increasingly critical with furious tank battles raging round Sidi Rezegh, 60 miles to the north-west, and culminating in the violent counter-attack of the 15th and 21st Panzer Divisions on the

24 Nov. 24th, against the Allied centre at Bir Sheferzen just south of the Omars. The Omars, not unnaturally, figured in the German plan of operations, and "A" and "B" Companies found themselves attacked in their newly-won position by a German column which included a force of twenty-five tanks. It was a trying moment, for the men were not properly dug in, and only had slit trenches, but they had a ring-side view of the fine gunnery of the 1st Field Regiment R.A., whose guns were out in the open, but who

destroyed eight tanks in the Battalion's area, and a further eleven near Sidi Omar in the evening.

1941

Enemy columns were moving about in the rear areas for the next few days, but by the 28th November, all enemy forces had withdrawn west of the frontier wire, or been captured. On the 30th, as already noted, Libyan Omar fell, and the same day the Battalion took over Sidi Omar from the Royal Sussex Regiment. "C" and "D" Companies also rejoined—"C" with a loss of seven killed and twenty-nine wounded.

28 Nov.
30 Nov.

Time passed uneventfully enough from now on until the 5th December, when the Brigade made a short move of some 20 miles west, to Bir el Gubi. Efforts were made to reconstruct the operations of the 19th November, when the 22nd Armoured Brigade had had its fierce encounter with the Ariete Division at Bir el Gubi, but with disappointingly small success. Of Bir el Gubi, however, this much is said that it was well ahead of our advanced landing-grounds, and that enemy aircraft were for the first time being seen.

5 Dec.

From Bir el Gubi, the Brigade wheeled north, moving up to El Adem, 10 or 15 miles from Tobruk, where contact was made, on the 9th December, with elements of the 70th Division from Tobruk. The air-field at El Adem was found strewn with wrecked enemy aircraft.

9 Dec.

Just west of El Adem, the Brigade halted briefly, before moving on north-west to Acroma, where the 4th Indian Division was collecting. On the 11th December, the Division set off westwards towards Tmimi. Enemy rearguards were brushed aside without difficulty, and coupled with this came the welcome discovery that a dive-bombing Stuka's bark was much worse than its bite.

11 Dec.

On the 12th, south of Alem Hamza, the Division was held up on a broadish front of 10 to 15 miles, by an enemy rearguard, strong in artillery, difficult to spot, and which created some havoc among the transport. An attack on this position was in process of being mounted next day, the 13th, when a column of 39 Mark III and IV German tanks drove straight in on the Brigade area, under close artillery support. The Battalion was some way ahead of the Brigade, and had to withdraw to its earlier position behind our anti-tank artillery screen. The ensuing hour or so was hectic. The tanks pressed home their attack and over-ran the forward guns. However, the day was saved by the Divisional reserve of eight cruiser tanks, and the 25th Field Regiment R.A., old and trusted friends of the Battalion first in Poona and later in Eritrea; but the Battalion itself could do little but look on.

12 Dec.
13 Dec.

Clinging tenaciously to his positions, the enemy held up the

1941	
17 Dec.	advance for some days. A good deal of fighting took place on various parts of the front, and finally, on the 17th December, the Battalion was on the move again, covering 43 miles of very
18 Dec.	rough country, in a north-westerly direction. On the 18th, moving

up from the south towards Derna, the Battalion was ordered to cut the road which passed some 10 miles to the south of the town. This was done by 11 a.m., several enemy vehicles being captured by the carriers. From the road, one could see black smoke rising in the Derna direction. Numbers of planes could be seen, apparently carrying out a shuttle service from Derna towards the west, and it looked as if the enemy were moving out.

It had been intended to circle east after the road was cut, but this order was cancelled when the state of affairs in Derna was appreciated, and the Battalion was now directed to make for that place as fast as its vehicles would take it. Accepting considerable risk, the Sikhs jerked and jolted along the rutty, broken-up track in single file, and on through a narrow defile where they would have been an admirable target for enemy air attack. There was no opposition or interference, however, and the troops duly burst on to the escarpment above Derna, to see where the air-field lay, about 4 miles away.

From a high point nearby, enemy movement on the air-field could be seen. Companies at once deployed, the gunners went into action, and the Battalion moved off on a broad front to engage.

Enemy mines took toll of three of our carriers when nearing the air-field about 3.45 p.m. Hostile machine-guns opened fire. Simultaneously, ten or twelve large J.U. troop-carrying aircraft came over. Fire was not opened on them in the absence of suitable weapons, and the pilots probably thought that our advanced companies, now almost on the air-field, were their own troops. Either way, all but one aircraft came in to land, and then hell broke loose. Everything opened up in a wild fusillade from field and anti-tank guns, rifles, and actually, it is believed, from an occasional pistol. "A" Company tried to charge in on the Junkers with the bayonet. They were beaten to it by our artillery fire, and had to content themselves with opening up with rifles and light machine-guns. Two aircraft took off again, after being riddled with fire, but one certainly crashed not far away.

While the rest of the force were speeding the two escaping aircraft, "A" and "D" Companies also saw, and intercepted, an enemy motor convoy approaching from Martuba, south-east of Derna. Two tanks escorting the convoy broke through, but the first few lorries were successfully shot up.

One German and fourteen Italian officers fell to the Battalion,

1941

with some 2,000 rank and file, and three heavy lorry-mounted dual-purpose guns. A total of some 183 aircraft was captured or destroyed in the whole operation.

It was fitting that this sensational achievement, which came as the climax to a long series of hard-fought actions, should provide an opportunity of, as it were, taking stock, and surveying the growing list of deeds of gallantry which had gone unrecognized during the preceding weeks. Many names figure in the recommendations accepted for awards and honours, and it is proper that we should pause and consider them, not only for the individual distinction they imply, but also in the clearer light they throw on the strains and stresses borne by the Battalion as a whole in the hard fighting that—momentarily—now took pause.

The general background is perhaps best displayed in the citation covering the award of the Distinguished Service Order to Lieut.-Col. J. J. Purves, M.C., who commanded the Battalion at this time. "Outside Sidi Omar", it reads, "his battalion, which was giving local protection to the 1st Field Regiment R.A., was subjected to heavy tank attack but stood firm while the guns beat off the attack. Again, south-west of Gazala his battalion was moving to attack in lorries when the German Panzer Division launched a counter-attack. When ordered to fall back behind the lines of anti-tank defence, Col. Purves coolly turned his battalion about and withdrew them in perfect order. His battalion was largely responsible for the capture of Derna aerodrome, the destruction of several enemy aeroplanes and subsequently the fall of Derna itself. Throughout the period of these operations this officer has set a high standard of personal example and bravery worthy of the highest traditions."

Coupled with that of Lieut.-Col. Purves comes an impressive list of names. Foremost among them comes that of Capt. Mohammed Siddiq, M.C., the award to whom of a bar to his Military Cross has already been mentioned. Mohammed Siddiq was in command of one of the companies concerned in the interception, south-east of Derna, of a tank-escorted German convoy. If one considers that the convoy, besides its escort of two tanks, included twenty lorries full of troops and three guns, it is clear that excellent leadership was behind the successful attack made on it.

In the same attack No. 13694 Hav. Sadhu Singh, who had long been noted for his soldierly qualities, achieved the award of the Indian Distinguished Service Medal. Hav. Sadhu Singh first came prominently to notice on the 23rd November in the Sidi Omar neighbourhood, where his platoon was involved in an advance over completely open ground, well mined, and swept by artillery,

1941

mortar, and heavy machine-gun fire. Hav. Sadhu Singh was well aware that hesitation would be fatal, and that if momentum were lost, the attack might prove an expensive failure. He instantly dashed forward, shouting encouragement to his men, and over-ran the enemy strong-point under attack, with the capture, at small cost, of thirty prisoners, four heavy machine-guns, several mortars and a Breda infantry gun. Later, he set the seal to this example of leadership and personal fearlessness by the initiative and ability he showed at Derna organizing the ambush which broke up and captured the major part of the enemy convoy.

Elsewhere in the fight for the landing-ground, other decorations were earned. A Military Cross went to Capt. G. F. Colley. During the advance to the landing-ground, his platoon of carriers covered the leading companies with a skill and precision worthy of great praise. Three of his carriers, as already noted, were blown up on the minefield covering the landing-ground, but valuable aid was given them by one of Capt. Colley's subordinates, No. 12276 Naik Raunak Singh. The citation records that "in spite of hostile machine-gun and anti-tank fire which might have halted a less resolute leader, Naik Raunak Singh pushed home the attack, which was a complete success, causing the enemy to withdraw". Before this, Naik Raunak Singh had made a name for himself in the Carrier Platoon in Eritrea, and, later, in the operations about Sidi Omar, when the Germans broke through with tank and other columns, into our rear areas. The award of the Indian Distinguished Service Medal confirmed and underlined these services.

Jem. Kapur Singh was another recipient of the Indian Distinguished Service Medal. Carrying his platoon straight forward on the objective when machine-gun fire had temporarily held up the attack on the landing-ground, he forced his way through, capturing fifty prisoners and much material. No. 17413 Sep. Ghazni Khan was similarly decorated with the Indian Distinguished Service Medal, as was No. 13004 Hav. Kishan Singh, for courage and initiative which set the seal to earlier proofs of devotion already recorded. Finally, No. 17303 Sep. Dalip Singh closes the list with the same award for a piece of peculiarly individual courage, carrying forward a vital warning of enemy attack to one of the leading platoons. Though badly wounded in the arm while on his way, he carried the message through in time for urgent action to be taken, and undoubtedly saved many lives at the risk of his own.

19 Dec. Next morning, the 19th December, the Battalion moved into Derna, and took over local administration of the town, which proved a most friendly one. A welcome change from operational scales was provided in the unlimited supply of fresh water, and plenty of vegetables. Some abandoned Chianti was discovered for the officers, and seven biggish casks of brandy for the Sikh rank-and-file. All ranks had a roof over their head, and the stage seemed set for a good Christmas.

1941

The event proved otherwise, however. At 3 p.m. on Christmas Eve, orders arrived to move on to Barce on Christmas Day, and Benghazi the day after. Never did "God rest ye, merry gentlemen" have less real appeal than at 6 a.m. on Christmas morning when the Battalion moved off in darkness, blinding rain, and a bitter cold wind. That was the worst of it, for by 9 a.m. the sun was out, and, in the end, it was a very pleasant run through delightful country. The only regret was that the route allotted was via the southern road beyond Giovanni Berta, which missed the ruins of the ancient Greek and Roman town of Cyrene. By the time the tail of the column reached Barce, it was raining again, but there were reasonable billets for the men in the aerodrome building and good accommodation for the officers in the fine hotel close by. With the departure of the German and Italian forces, the local Arabs had invaded the fertile Barce plain, dotted with the stereotyped cottages of the Italian colonists, and were shooting up any colonist they could find. When, therefore, the Battalion moved on next day to Benghazi, the carriers and "C" Company under Hartley were left behind to work in conjunction with the local administration in quelling the trouble.

24 Dec.
25 Dec.

26 Dec.

The otherwise uneventful run into Benghazi was enlivened by rough going over a diversion where the enemy had blown the Tocra Pass. Here, on the Pass, close to the road, were four shattered German fighters—three so close together that it looked as if they had flown in formation straight into the hillside. Possibly they had been reconnoitring the 5-mile column of headed-up vehicles, waiting nose-to-tail to get past the diversion—but no air attack was made so far as the Battalion knew.

At 1.30 p.m., the Battalion moved into Benghazi. "B" and "D" Companies were detached to the aerodromes at Berca and Benina respectively, and the remainder of the Battalion settled into billets in houses in the area round a railway station about three-quarters of a mile from the port. The town was not very badly damaged, though most of the houses near the harbour were scarred from bomb splinters. One of the generators in the power station on the Cathedral Mole was undamaged, and electric light was available for the Battalion's billets. The cathedral also was intact except for one hole in the south wall. The aerodromes at Berca and Benina, however, told a different tale, and at Benina there were over a hundred wrecked aircraft, mostly German.

1942

The remainder of the 7th Indian Infantry Brigade had not yet come up, and the Battalion had its hands full keeping order. Arabs were breaking into any house they could in the Italian quarter of Benghazi, and a firm hand was needed. Day and night patrols were organized, and control posts set up at all exits from the town. Vital points such as the power house, bank, etc., required guards. Then a mine-spotting party was sited on the Navy Headquarters tower, and the anti-tank platoon was spread round the harbour on coast defence. "C" Company was moved to Coefea, about 7 miles north of Benghazi as guard over an old German store of aero engines and spare parts.

Ships soon began arriving with urgent military stores, and daily working parties of up to 200 men had to be found to help unload them.

This hectic state of affairs, however, only lasted a few days, and the Battalion was relieved of its duties at Berca and Benina as soon as the Brigade arrived.

The enemy was on his way back to Agheila with our armoured division and support group in contact. Staffs were busy getting out a programme for penetrating the minefields to attack this line, and about three weeks respite was given the troops for training, while the administrative services were bringing forward supplies.

January At the beginning of January, the 7th Indian Infantry Brigade began laying out a defensive line, running from the coast to the Benghazi-Soluch railway, about 15 miles south of Benghazi. Parts of this line had already been mined by the enemy, particularly in the long 9,000 yards of front allotted to the Battalion. Apart from occasional bombing raids, life was peaceful. Maj.-Gen. Tuker, who had just taken over command of the 4th Indian Division, took advantage of the opportunity to present the ribbon of the Military Cross to Capt. G. F. Colley, and of the Indian Distinguished Service Medal to Jem. Kapur Singh, Hav. Karam Singh, and two sepoys as immediate awards for gallantry in action during November and December.

As already described, the Germans had been roughly handled, but they had moved back to El Agheila in good order. Their armour had been reinforced, and their morale was high. Hence it did not wholly come as a surprise when a mechanized column comprising some 3,000 vehicles, debouched from their forward areas on the
21 Jan. 21st January. Intelligence reports had given sufficient prior warning for the 7th Indian Infantry Brigade to be moved out of
20 Jan. Benghazi on the morning of the 20th, and to be deployed in the defensive position already referred to, some 15 miles to the south. Here, it had begun digging in.

1942

From the Battalion record, it does not appear that due confidence was felt in the Higher Command at this stage. Whatever the cause, a feeling of indecision seems to have been in the air, but this in no way detracted from the determination of the troops to do their best. On the 22nd, the Battalion was sent forward to lend extra strength to a small composite force at Macrun, 60 miles to the south. This force, commanded by Col. Goulder, R.A., comprised the 31st Field Regiment R.A., now mustering only seven 25-pounder guns, one squadron of the Central India Horse, and one troop each of anti-aircraft and anti-tank guns, and seems to have had a watching role. The Battalion remained with it for two days only, and then went back to the Brigade.

22 Jan.

24 Jan.

What the enemy was doing was still not clearly known, and it was not till the 25th January that a fresh course of action for the Division was made known. This was to be the harassing of the enemy's communications, so far at least as the 7th Indian Infantry Brigade was concerned. The Brigade was to form three mobile columns, and, in pursuance of this, the Battalion was sent back to Macrun to rejoin "Goldcol", and operate forward with small columns against the Agedabia-Antelat road. However, the tables were neatly turned before this could be done, and a force of about 80 enemy tanks and 2,000 vehicles was reported at Msus. Msus lay some 60 miles south-east of Benghazi, towards which the enemy was making. The Brigade was promptly ordered back to the 4th Indian Division's new position in the Jebel el Akdar, west of Cyrene.

25 Jan.

In the meantime, columns operated south of Macrun, and in one of these, "B" Company was employed as escort to the guns, with one platoon forward on standing patrol. This patrol was engaged in frequent brushes with the enemy. However, there was no prospect of immediate movement, and the order was given at Company Headquarters to start cooking the morning meal.

The meal was ready, and No. 70 Cook Fazal Ahmed was on the point of taking forward its share to the forward platoon, when heavy gunfire was heard from that direction. However, nothing loth, off Fazal Ahmed went, quite regardless of the consequences, and delivered his load. This, coupled with a previous case at Sidi Omar, when Fazal Ahmed, like Water-Carrier Rattan Singh, already mentioned, had kept at his job of preparing his platoon's tea, in the face of an enemy tank attack, earned him a Commendation Card. Just how much the Regiment owes its "followers", to give them their bygone name, in keeping the fighting troops fed and content under every kind of stress of weather or enemy threat, no-one will ever know. But they played their part with devotion and singleness

1942

28 Jan.

of purpose, and their name deserves to be remembered.

Time had passed in the move to Macrun, and the relative clearing up of the situation regarding the enemy, and hence it was not till 2 p.m. on the 28th January that the Battalion moved back from Macrun. Contact had not been made with enemy ground forces, but the men were much cheered at the sight of the anti-aircraft troop shooting down three out of a force of fourteen enemy aircraft returning south-westwards from a raid. This brought the troop's score up to six aircraft shot down in three days. Tails were well up just then.

The 7th Indian Infantry Brigade was to concentrate at a point 5 kilos short of Benghazi. From this point, which would be the Brigade starting-point, the Brigade would move back to its sector in the Divisional line away to the north-east. Meanwhile, the "B" echelon transport, consisting of some 600 vehicles, was to move off back through Benghazi ahead of the troops to its new area behind the divisional line. Command of this column fell to Maj. C. Nash, Second-in-Command of the Battalion.

To enable the "B" echelon transport to clear Benghazi ahead of the troops, a halt was called at a point 22 kilos short of the town. Then, at 7.30 p.m., the troops moved on, reaching the starting-point at Kilo 5, at 8 p.m. Here, in the dark, the Brigade Commander contacted them, and told them that Benghazi was in enemy hands, the road cut at Coefea, and the fate of "B" echelon unknown. He told them that the Brigade would have to fight its way out, and to improve its chances in doing so, he had decided that the three columns into which the Brigade had been formed, should move independently, choosing their own routes, and meeting him at Mechili, 50 miles south of Derna, and about 125 miles east of Benghazi.

Col. Goulder at once called a conference of the commanding officers in his column, to consider the alternatives. The road leading north-east from Benghazi offered no solution, as M.T. could not operate off it in the difficult country of the Jebel el Akdar, which was in any case probably well mined. The three tracks leading up the escarpment running from Tocra, 20 miles up the coast from Benghazi to Antelat in the south, were also heavily mined. So it was decided to move back southwards to Antelat, thence north-east to Msus, and on to Mechili. The boldness of this plan will be the better appreciated when it is remembered that Antelat lies about 75 miles south of Benghazi, and not much under half-way to El Agheila, well within what must now be looked upon as enemy country. However, the decision was made, bearings and distances were calculated off the map, and at 11 p.m., the column wheeled about and started off.

	1942
Moving cross-country, south-south-east, the column had covered about 60 miles by dawn. As day broke, the troops dispersed in the area east of Macrun, and spent the 29th there.	29 Jan.

There was little time for rest, for much had to be done in preparation for the break-through that night. It was essential to see what petrol was available, and to limit vehicles to the numbers which could be fuelled for the coming move. So a petrol census was taken, and numbers checked. No vehicle was to be allowed with the column with less than enough petrol for 200 miles. In consequence, six out of the Battalion's ten carriers were destroyed and left. They were far too heavy on petrol, but it was felt that four should be retained for reconnaissance.

During the day, enemy aircraft frequently flew over the area, but thanks to good ground discipline, they seem to have seen nothing amiss.

That evening at 5 p.m., the column moved on, closing in from desert formation to night dispositions as it grew dusk. The Antelat-Agedabia road was reached and crossed without incident, as was also the track leading east from Antelat. The column then headed away on a bearing for Msus and Mechilli, forging steadily on through the night till 7 a.m. on the 30th January, when an hour's halt was called, some 12 miles south of Msus, to make tea. 30 Jan.
The troops did not, of course, know that there was an enemy laager only a few miles ahead. Soon after the column got on its way, however, at 8 a.m.—having had its tea in comfort—the squadron of the Central India Horse, out ahead, sent back information of the laager, with an estimate of four Italian medium tanks and 800 transport vehicles. Col. Goulder ordered his guns into action, and moved the Battalion with all column vehicles 6 miles south. The bluff worked. The enemy tanks moved out to reconnoitre, but, on being fired at by the guns, withdrew, and the whole enemy column moved off north.

In spite of the care being taken to economize on fuel, the petrol situation was beginning to cause anxiety, and it was with relief that information was received by wireless from Corps Headquarters that our troops held Tengeder, 80 or 90 miles south of Mechili. To head in that direction meant less running and better going, and it was decided to make for Tengeder accordingly. While working out the new course, which led a long way south of the original route, a German reconnaissance plane flew over the column and spent about half-an-hour examining it. It fired one burst at one of the Battalion trucks, but the fire was not returned, and it went off. Then, two Italian fighters came over, and each fired a burst. Again no reply was made, and it was hoped they had

1942

concluded that the column was composed of their own troops in captured transport. When it did get away, the column made good going. Travelling at 15 to 17 miles per hour, the squadron of the Central India Horse contacted two British armoured cars on patrol from Tengeder at 4 p.m., and learnt from them of the existence of a large petrol dump some way ahead. At 5 p.m., when still a little short of the dump, the column halted for the night.

31 Jan. At 7 a.m. next day, the 31st, the force closed up on the petrol dump, which it reached at nine. After a meal, and filling up with fuel, the column moved on, and reached Tengeder about noon. Much time was spent hunting for the local Brigade Headquarters,

1 Feb. and the night eventually had to be spent there. Next day, a clear run through Bir Hacheim brought the column to El Adem, where the headquarters of the 7th Indian Infantry Brigade was found.

The troops now had some breathing-space for running repairs, and checking up. With "B" echelon, the Battalion had lost Maj. Nash, and Price, Kealey and Willis, together with Sub.-Maj. Hardit Singh, Sub. Lachman Singh and eighty-seven other ranks. Among the many vehicles lost were those with the quartermaster's stores, and mess and canteen stores. In the column, a number of vehicles had broken down on the way and been destroyed. These included R.I.A.S.C. 3-tonners carrying troops, and, as a result, the men had ended up travelling as many as forty-five in a lorry, and many springs were broken. In the circumstances, it says much for all concerned that the Battalion got back in such good shape.

With less determination on the part of the troops, there might have been a grimmer ending to the story, but the case of Sub. Mohammed Khan, who received an award of the Indian Distinguished Service Medal for the part he played, throws some light on it. Quoting from his citation, Sub. Mohammed Khan "was 2nd-in-command of his company during the withdrawal from Benghazi. Long periods of driving by day and night and subsequent tiredness of drivers and lack of time for maintenance, led to several breakdowns among his company vehicles. Though he knew that anyone staying behind the convoy was liable to be cut off by the enemy he never failed to stop and, where the vehicle was beyond repair, to ensure that all his men, arms and ammunition, water and food were transferred to another vehicle. Then only did he move on again to catch up the convoy, often many miles ahead." One may pause a moment and picture the scenes these lines call up. Truly men like this deserved well.

Of the missing, confirmation of their safety was later received —except for Willis, who, after covering 250 miles on foot, made his way to the XXXth Corps headquarters at Gazala.

	1942
Leaving El Adem on the 3rd February, the troops reached railhead in two marches, and spent a few days drawing up clothing and blankets for men who had had to abandon them. On the 13th the Brigade moved forward 30 miles, and was employed till the 24th digging a large "box". After this, on relief by the 5th and 11th Indian Infantry Brigades, the Battalion, with the rest, went back to Cairo, where an almost complete new war outfit was drawn, and the unit was brought up to strength.	3 Feb. 13 Feb. 24 Feb.

One pleasant postscript, however, still remains to be recorded before we take leave of the Battalion. Reading through the record of gallantry and devotion displayed by the rank-and-file, one is apt to forget the part played in their humbler sphere by the non-combatants --the cooks, water-carriers and the like--who shared the hardships of campaigning with the troops. The story of No. 95 Water-Carrier Rattan Singh, who was honoured for his devotion to duty in Eritrea and the Western Desert by a Mention in Despatches, is true of so many of his class; and if singled out for special mention here, it is so that some small tribute may be paid to the lesser-privileged to whom so much of the soldiers' comfort and well-being was due.

These men took their full share of the danger and hardship to which their units were exposed, moving about in the forward areas under constant heavy fire and carrying out their often onerous duties uncomplainingly and without question. Rattan Singh might have been seen, one noisy day in Eritrea, when the enemy's guns and mortars were strafing his platoon's position, up in the front line, with more than usual intensity, calmly collecting and shouldering cooked rations and tea, and plodding off through the fire quite unperturbed, delivering his rations, and stumping back again, as if this was quite in the normal run of things.

Again, in the advance through the Western Desert, in November, 1941, when his Company was in position with a battery in the Sidi Omar area, on the Frontier wire, Water-Carrier Rattan Singh was crouched over a fire in a slit-trench, preparing the men's tea. The enemy were lining up with some tanks to throw in an attack, and the Company was ordered to withdraw and clear the ground so as to give our artillery full scope for firing at and dealing with the tanks.

The Company withdrew—but not so Rattan Singh. He clung to his fire and his tea-making, though the tanks advanced to within a very short distance of his trench before being finally driven back with heavy loss by our guns.

The Company was then ordered back to its original positions; and on reaching them, was greeted by a completely unconcerned Rattan Singh and a brew of steaming tea.

The compiler may perhaps be forgiven for seeming to gild the lily

1941

if he recalls a little cameo of a recollection from Mesopotamia when with the same Battalion, during the first world war. Orders had been issued to move off next day at 5 a.m., and the last thing he heard the previous night before dropping off to sleep, was the voice of the company langri cheerfully intoning the next day's programme—"Do baje uthhna; tin baje lakar; char baje chha; panch baje taiyar". And "taiyar" they all were, dead on the minute!

5th Bn. The record of *the 5th Battalion*, during the closing months of this gallant battalion's existence, is contained in *A Diary of the 5th Bn. (D.C.O.), The Sikh Regiment in the Malaya Campaign— 8 Dec. '41 to 15 Feb. '42*. The diary is reproduced in full in the following pages, with full acknowledgments to Lieut.-Col. J. H. D. Parkin, D.S.O., the then commanding officer of the Battalion.

It runs as follows:

"1. *General*

"At the outbreak of the campaign the Army in Malaya consisted of the III Indian Corps (Lt.-Gen. Heath) of 9 and 11 Ind Divs (total five Bdes each of three Bns), two Australian Bdes, and the equivalent of two Bdes, forming command reserve and fortress troops in Singapore. This was approximately half the strength which the Commanders on the spot had appreciated as necessary.

"The Air Force was considerably under the essential minimum including in its strength such out-of-date machines as Wildbeestes while the only fighters were Brewster Buffaloes.

"The lavish programme of aerodrome construction indulged in, where a chain of aerodromes had been constructed close to the Northern Frontier and to both Eastern and Western coasts, compelled a dangerous dispersion of our scanty forces for their protection.

"Complete command of the air was the enemy's from the outset. None of these Northern aerodromes nor the one at Kuantan on the East coast were used as operational bases by our Air Forces after the first few days.

"2. *Outline of Dispositions*

"III Indian Corps was responsible for the defence of the main land north of a line Mersing (east coast) Muar River (west coast).

"A high mountain range, jungle clad and steep, divides central and northern Malaya into two distinct sectors—eastern and western. For approximately 150 miles south from the northern frontier no communications of any kind traverse this barrier. Further south it is traversed by two roads both starting from Kuala Lumpur in the west and joining, the one Bentong-Temerloh and the other Raub and Kuantan in the east.

"11 Div held the western sector; 9 Div (General Barstow—an old friend of ours) consisting of two bdes only, held the eastern. 8 Bde (four Bns) was disposed to the north, holding some 30 miles of coast and covering the aerodromes at Kota Bahru, Gong Kedah and Machang, and the Ry to the South.

"22 Bde (Brig. Painter) consisting of two bns, 5 Sikh and 2/18 RGR, was at Kuantan protecting Kuantan aerodrome and the road to Kuala Lumpur, the only road north of Mersing connecting the east coast with the west.

"3. *Kuantan Topography*

"The beaches from Trengannu in the north to Pekan and beyond in the south were throughout suitable for landing operations and could be used by MT or as a landing ground for aircraft except at high tides.

"For 10 miles to the north of Kuantan was a useful network of good metalled roads. North of this for some 10 miles wheeled traffic could only use the beaches.

"Inland, rubber and primary jungle alternated with large belts of mangrove swamps bordering the rivers, traversed only by jungle trails and forest lines difficult to follow without guides.

"South of Kuantan was only one road, that to Pekan on the Pahang River 22 miles away. This road ran approximately 4 miles inland from and parallel to the coast and was connected to it by various tracks, none of them fit for wheels though capable of being made so with little labour.

"The Sungei (river) Kuantan tidal and navigable by large size launches and barges for about 25 miles was crossed by means of one single ferry only, operated by hand and capable of transporting some ten 15-cwt trucks every 20 minutes.

"4. *Attitude of Local Inhabitants*

"The Malays were apathetic and in some cases inclined to help the enemy. Fifth columnists existed in their ranks. The Chinese on the whole were on our side and often helped considerably. Klings (Malay born Tamils), and Indian labour in the country could not be trusted and helped the enemy on at least one occasion to our knowledge.

"Dungan—a place some 60 miles north of Kuantan—housed a population of about 1,000 Japanese in its ore mines—a Jap concern. Most of these had left before the outbreak of war. Those remaining (some 70 or so) were detained in Trengannu from where unfortunately

1941

they were set free by a Malay police inspector and returning to the area caused us considerable trouble.

"5. *State of Preparedness of the Battalion*

"The Bn arrived in Malaya in April having been thoroughly milked, 450 recruits and 6 B.Os (E.C.Os) unable to speak Urdu, having joined a few weeks prior to embarkation.

"Since arrival in Kuantan in June, the Bn had been kept very hard at work constructing defences. Totally insufficient time being given for training, this was pointed out repeatedly but priority of defences was insisted upon by higher authority. In Oct. we were further milked, 30 picked officers, N.C.Os and men being returned to India to form the new M.G. Bn.

"Arms and equipment were slow to arrive. Carriers were received in July but no L.M.Gs to put in them. 3-in. mortars were received in Sept, (and also some 2-in.) Detachments were trained and later our 3-in. mortars did yeoman service. A few tommy guns were received in Sept, but L.M.Gs were still on the scale of one per pl until just before the outbreak of war when 50 V.Bs were despatched to Kuantan for aerodrome defence. With these, the Bn was armed up to full scale.

"V.C.Os were very good throughout with few weak links. N.C.Os, mostly new, were weak, though all had been through a short cadre since arrival in the country.

"The recruits had come on well and were beginning to look more like men than the children they appeared on arrival in the Bn.

"Training in jungle fighting had been limited by the priority allotted to defence works. Some pl, coy, and three 48 hr bn schemes had been done.

"The Bn was physically fit and had been accustomed to carrying F.S. scale ammunition since arrival in Malaya.

"Our M.T. was complete, drivers were well trained and were with 150% reserve.

"Morale was excellent.

"6. *22 Bde Task and Dispositions*

"The Bde task was to defend Kuantan aerodrome, and to do this bns were disposed as follows:

"2/18 R.G.R. fwd holding the coast from S. Kuantan to S. Balok (10 miles) to prevent enemy landing and obtaining access to good roads leading to the aerodrome.

"5 Sikh back were responsible for:

"(*a*) Defence of the river lines from Kampong Putus in the north on the S. Kuantan to incl Pekan rd bridge on the S. Belat (distance by river 22 miles).

1941

"*(b)* The local defence of the aerodrome (9 miles inland from the coast).

"*(c)* Dealing with parachutists, air borne landings or incursions on the L. of C. from the Pahang river in the South or jungle tracks in the north, as far west as Maran (50 miles).

"*(d)* Counter attacks in fwd Bn's area.

"7. *Defence Works*

"These had been prepared in the Bn area as follows:

"*(a)* The Taj line—named after Captain Taj Mohammed Khanzada, whose Coy. B. of P.Ms built and manned it.

"To stop any enemy adv along the one road leading from the South. A good position both flanks resting on the S. Belat which here makes one of its numerous loops. The position lay astride the Pekan road some 800 yds south of the Belat bridge. Defence consisted of three very stout log blockhouses and two small pill boxes, the whole very well camouflaged and wired and amply covered by shrapnel mines along all approaches. A further defended locality of two pill boxes and a blockhouse on the north bank covered the bridge itself and gave depth.

"*(b)* Observation posts each to hold one section covered possible landing places on the Belat down to its junction with the S. Kuantan.

"*(c)* The river junction was covered by two pill boxes amply wired, each holding 1 sec and with 3 L.M.Gs. The ground here was mangrove swamp and under four feet of water at high tide.

"*(d)* Three pill boxes covered the ferry and Seton Kol crossing immediately north of it.

"*(e)* Two stockades at the next loop.

"*(f)* Ten blockhouses of the coy in the Bukit Rangin area watched the Song Sang and Kampong Putus crossings and provided complete roofed-in cover for a whole coy.

"Except for the concrete pill boxes for which the Bn provided working parties, all construction work incl pile tracks through the swamp was carried out by the Bn without assistance of any kind from the sappers.

"*(g)* One pill box at M.S. 5 covered Paya Besar.

"*(h)* Aerodrome. 5 pill boxes provided defence inwards, numerous A.A. posts were built. Outward defence was provided chiefly by three pl localities and a rd and fence round the whole outer perimeter (4½ miles)—a very good piece of work on D Coy's part, necessitating the construction of many culverts, long lengths of corduroy where the rd crossed the swamp, and much clearing of jungle.

"On orders from corps pill boxes were sited to cover the whole

1941

outer perimeter and were under construction when war broke out. They were never completed nor were there ever any troops available to man them.

"8. *Artillery*

"Up to Dec 6 one sec 3.7-in. how of 21 Mtn Bty—fwd. HQ 5 Fd Regt and 63/81 Bty arrived Dec 6 (4.5-in. hows). 464 Bty of 88 Fd Regt arrived Dec 15 (25-pdrs). Distribution was then:

"One sec 25-pdrs at M.S. 5 primary role fwd, secondary role defensive fire for Taj Line.

"One sec 21 Mtn Bty aerodrome defence. Remainder of artillery was in fwd sector.

"9. *Air*

"On Dec 8 there were 21 aircraft on Kuantan aerodrome, 10 Hudsons, 8 old Blenheims, 2 Swordfish, 1 Wildebeeste, and complete ground staff.

"The aerodrome was well equipped complete with every kind of bomb and armament incl 21 torpedoes.

"There were no fighters.

"10. *Outbreak of War—Bn Dispositions*

"The first week of Dec we passed through varying degrees of readiness following with interest reports of the progress of the Jap convoy which had rounded the southerly tip of French Indo-China and was proceeding on a W.N.W. course.

"On Dec 7 the bn was at war stations as follows:
(unless otherwise stated m.s. refers to rd Kuantan Jerantut).

H.Q. North of the road at 6½ m.s.
H.Q. Coy (less detts) under rubber and in tents.
D Coy (reserve)
B Coy, with mortar and M.G. Detts. Holding Taj Line and Belat Bridge defences.
C Coy H.Q. at m.s. 3½ holding ferry defences incl a very weak pl as bridge-head on east bank, the river junction defences and O.Ps along river Belat.
A Coy with M.G. sec and one 18-pdr (manned by the Coy) and one sec of carriers—local defence of aerodrome.
One M.G. sec—at m.s. 5 in pill box.

"11. *Patrols*

"Intensive and extensive patrolling was carried on at all times.

"(a) Launch patrol of 1 B.O. (Gannon) and 6 I.O.Rs of D Coy with 2 B.O.Rs and W.T. Set at the mouth of the S. Pahang.

110

1941

"*(b)* Fighting patrols from B Coy, patrolling the coast from the S. Kuantan to the vicinity of the S. Pahang.

"*(c)* Launch and sampan patrols from C Coy patrolling the rivers Kuantan and Belat.

"*(d)* Patrols from D Coy in the Bukit Rangin area.

"*(e)* Patrols from A Coy along Batu Sawar track, leading to aerodrome from the north (a track impossible to follow without a guide).

"*(f)* Special patrols—on bicycles with H.Q. at Gambang, watching tracks from S. Lembing (the biggest tin mine of its kind in the world) and Pasir Kemudi in the north and Pula Manis in the south.

"12. Adv Bde H.Q. was fwd. Rear Bde H.Q. on aerodrome at m.s. 9. 22 Fd Coy R.B.S. & M. were distributed throughout both areas working hard on pill boxes, preparation of demolitions, approaches for proposed bridge and on the boom with which they had closed the mouth of the S. Kuantan.

"13. *Diary—Outline of Events*

"*Dec 8.* Early in the morning news was received of an enemy landing near Kota Bahru in Kelantan. A Jap recce plane came over high up. During the morning the remains of the R.A.A.F. squadron of Hudsons returned from bombing the enemy landing. They had lost 5 planes, and 3 of the crews in the remaining planes were wounded.

"*Dec 9.* About 1100 hrs a formation of about 27 enemy bombers flying about 3000 ft bombed the aerodrome catching all our planes (about 16) on the ground. Three were destroyed, five damaged. A bomb store and armament store were hit, and there were many near misses around two of the three pl localities. A Coy fired some 3000 rds S.A.A. and the planes retained their height of 3000 ft. There were practically no casualties.

"As soon as the raid was over most of the Air Force left very hurriedly. A Coy stood their first bombing, a severe one, well. The aerodrome, although undamaged, was not used by our Air Force as an operational base again.

"Its eventual destruction and that of its bomb stores and petrol dumps together with the salving of what could be salved was left to the hard-worked 22 Fd Coy.

"There was the usual heavy rain and during the night heavy firing could be heard in the fwd area.

"*Dec 10.* On this morning we learnt that the enemy had been probing the coastal defences in small boats. Patrols reported a bright blue light in the sky about three miles south of Kuantan over the coast.

"Two large warships were reported that morning east of Kuantan and later sounds of gun-fire were heard. These were the ill-fated Prince of Wales and Repulse, both sunk in an incredibly short time by Japanese aircraft.

"In the first two days of war complete command of air and sea had passed to the enemy.

"From now on until the end of Dec there was no important change in the situation in Kuantan.

"The conditions under which all were living were most trying. At the 6½ m.s. the ground was a morass and all transport was completely bogged until we had made corduroy tracks with timber intended for the construction of R.A.F. quarters. All were under canvas. It rained daily and heavily, mosquitoes were ubiquitous and carnivorous. Most of B Coy's area was under water at high tide. The whole Coy were living either in the blockhouses of the Taj Line or in the trees in machans they had constructed well above the water line.

"C Coy in the O.Ps and pill boxes on the river line lived in a perpetual cloud of mosquitoes, so bad that face masks had to be made for them out of mosquito nets; gloves were also given to them.

"Despite these conditions the sick rate which before the war started caused considerable concern, averaging 25 a day, now dropped to nil and remained so for practically the whole campaign.

"Enemy air came over daily without opposition except from our S.A. fire. There were no A.A. guns.

"Early on they heavily bombed what had been Bn H.Q. in every rehearsal of taking up war stations prior to Dec 7. This was near m.s. 6 and south of the main road, our first indication of the very efficient Jap espionage or fifth column activity; we were to have more before the short campaign was over.

"Despite these daily visitations we suffered practically no damage and thanks to efficient camouflage of the entrances and strict traffic control our new position was never discovered.

"*Dec 13.* On the 13th another formation of 27 planes visited the aerodrome and indulged in some fairly accurate pattern bombing of the control buildings and one of our pl localities.

"They used a number of large bombs some craters being 30 ft across and 8 ft deep.

"A Coy had three casualties only, one of them Hav Bawa Singh who was firing a V.B. at the time from an old A.A. post. A bomb dropped within 2 ft of the post and blew him 25 ft through the air with the gun still in his hand. He was badly concussed but we could find no broken bones. A Coy were quite unperturbed.

"About this time our launch patrol at the mouth of the Pahang found an abandoned ship's boat on the coast. It contained Jap rifles, gas masks and other Jap equipment—confirmation probably of the operations of the night of the 9/10 or else a boat from the Kota Bahru landing.

"Car patrols from 2/18 R.G.R. had been active and had succeeded in rounding up a dozen Japs in Dungun. On the 20th Dec they had a second encounter killing 2 or 3. Two however managed to escape including the 'local gauleiter'.

"*Dec 20.* By now the whole of Kelantan and the N.E. provinces north of Krai had been evacuated by our forces, 8 Bde being successfully withdrawn from Kelantan.

"This made the position at Kuantan more interesting. A landing, an adv down the coastal track using M.T. infiltration through jungle tracks leading to the rear of the position and on to the L. of C., were any or all to be expected now, whilst the enemy's unchallenged command of the sea and air made infomation difficult and usually impossible to obtain.

"Car patrols of the 2/18 R.G.R. watched the coastal rd whilst the forest tracks were watched in a fashion by a hastily improvized organization of Chinese wood-cutters in the Jabor valley area and in the S. Lembang area; closer in our patrols watched the tracks.

"Throughout this period work on defences and patrolling was incessant and the bn waited for the intrusion of the enemy into its area with confidence despite its extensive area.

"As a result of experience gained in the Kelantan operations, 1st and 2nd Line M.T. was drastically cut down. Tents, anti-gas stores, pioneer stores were sent back to Singapore. Officers' and mens' kits were drastically reduced. Reserve S.A.A. and mortar ammunition reserves were also cut down.

"Dispensing with tents necessitated cover of some kind being prepared, and within 48 hrs atap bivouacs had been prepared for everyone at m.s. $6\frac{1}{2}$, the Pioneer pl under Jemadar Sher Khan making a very good mess room with windows and boarded floor.

"This reduction of transport was very welcome, as the few schemes we had been able to carry out as a bn had shown the establishment to be much too large and unwieldy for fighting in a country where it was the exception for wheeled transport to be able to leave the rd.

"*Dec 23.* On Dec 23 news was received through a B.O. (the one survivor of the 2/18 R.G.R. patrol) that the Japs had arrived in Dungun in strength, arriving in M.T. using the coastal track.

"*Dec 24.* Welcome reinforcements arrived for 22 Bde of 3 armd cars (Volunteers) and 2/12 F.F.R., one coy of which was put under command of 2/18 R.G.R. in the fwd sector. This bn, less one coy, took over the protection of the L. of C. from us making their H.Q. at Gambang about m.s. 16.

1941

"Rain, mosquitoes and enemy air were with us always and were a damned nuisance but did no material damage worth mentioning.

"As they did not seem to have found the bn position they were only engaged by A Coy on the aerodrome, and occasionally by the A.A. pl who were sent out to try and intercept them on their lines of approach and withdrawal. We hit two planes during this time, one of which most probably came down in the sea.

"Meanwhile things in the west had been going badly. 11 Div had been decisively defeated with heavy losses at Jitra. Penang had fallen. And by means of pressure on the front and a series of landings on their flank and rear, the shattered 11 Div was being forced to carry out a somewhat hurried and difficult withdrawal.

"*Dec 29*. The ferry was now split into two to lessen the damage should enemy air action against it prove more successful; so far in spite of a number of attempts they had failed to hit it.

"*Dec 30*. The Japs arrived down the coast rd and commenced mortaring the northern pill boxes. Other parties appeared in the Jabor Valley; Baldock, the F.O., and Shepherd, a planter, were reported to have been captured and killed by them. Confused fighting followed, the Japs having the better of it, and by evening the two northern coys of 2/18 R.G.R. had been withdrawn from the coast and a line of some kind formed from Beserah to Song Sang to block the roads from the north. Both reserve coys had been committed and the coy on the central coast sector pulled into reserve.

"The direction of the enemy attack being clear, Bde agreed to evacuation of the Taj line withdrawing north of the Belat river, destroying the bridge, and to the occupation of the Bukit Rangin area by D Coy. B Coy (less one pl) now came into reserve. These moves were all completed by dusk.

"At 1600 hrs the Jap air at last managed to hit the ferry and put it out of action. It was working again by 1830 hrs the second half to the split ferry being ready by 0200 hrs on the night 30/31.

"Civil installations W/T, oil tanks and wharves were destroyed and Bde ordered all guns and transport to move to the west bank of the river.

"Working at speed throughout the night the ferries being worked by men of C Coy, all guns and vehicles were got across the last one crossing at 0510 hrs.

"*Dec 31*. At 0540 hrs just before first light Jem. Ajit Singh, who with some 16 men of 13 pl was holding a weak bridge-head on the east bank saw a large number of figures advancing along the bank from the north with their hands above their heads. They were already past the new section of the ferry and were within some 50 yds of the southern original section. Not knowing whether they were sappers, gunners, Garhwalis, M.T. personnel, or others from the medley of troops who had been clustered round both ferries throughout the night, but being alert, he advanced towards them with his pl Hav Punjab Singh and runner, L/Naik Joginder Singh, and challenged. They replied immediately with a heavy burst of fire killing Hav Punjab Singh and wounding Jogindar Singh.

"Jem. Ajit Singh flung himself under cover of the rd bank and immediately hurled a grenade at the advancing enemy, quickly followed by a second one; this checked them whilst one of the section posts opened fire shortly followed by our defences on the west bank.

"Collecting two grenades from Hav Punjab Singh's haversacks and two from Jogindar Singh's, this gallant Jem. commenced to systematically bomb the enemy, helped considerably by directions shouted to him by Lt Whalley of 22 Fd Coy, who was doing good work with a tommy gun from a building on the south bank of the rd behind the Jemadar.

"This action successfully stopped the attack and the enemy withdrew leaving three corpses behind them only 20 yds from the ferry. This gallant action of Ajit Singh saved the ferry and thus secured the only line of withdrawal now open to the hard-pressed 2/18 R.G.R. whose H.Q. arrived at the ferry just after this attack had been beaten off. (Jemadar (A/Subedar) Ajit Singh was granted an immediate award of the Indian Order of Merit).

"Two further attacks during the day were beaten off without much difficulty.

"Orders for the withdrawal of 2/18 R.G.R. west of the river were issued about midday.

"By 1800 hrs 2/18 R.G.R. and Jem. Ajit Singh's party had been successfully withdrawn to the east bank. 2/18 R.G.R. were less their B Coy and the Coy of the 2/12 F.F.R. Two more of their Coys had suffered fairly heavy casualties.

"When the withdrawal commenced across the river Jem. Ajit Singh whose party was now reduced by casualties to 10 men, requested the C.O. 2/18 R.G.R. to allow him and his party to be rear guard and to be the last to cross over.

"The withdrawal across the river was not seriously interfered with by the enemy; a three-sided barrage put down by the guns made him keep his distance.

"That night and for the next two days our coys on the river line ferried over numbers of stragglers from 2/18 R.G.R., a few sappers and 2 men of 2/12 F.F.R. 2/18 R.G.R. moved back the same night to the aerodrome.

1942

"*Jan 1.* On this day 2/18 R.G.R. took over the aerodrome defence from A Coy, at last giving us a reserve we could do something with. The 2/18 were now about 500 strong.

"To give their men further rest A Coy's standing patrol (Jem. Shingara Singh and 12 I.O.Rs) remained out for a further 24 hrs watching the Batu Sawar track north of the aerodrome.

"2/12 F.F.R. less two coys were moved up from Gambang to the aerodrome on which was now concentrated in a perimeter all of 22 Bde less 5/11 and troop 43/81 Bty. The other troop plus H.Q. 5 Fd Regt were on the aerodrome. The remainder of the artillery withdrew to Jerantut.

"Enemy recce parties were seen on eastern bank of the S. Kuantan and engaged, two enemy parties in sampans attempting to cross the river near the river junction were sunk.

"On information received from stragglers and from escaped prisoners, the arty, before leaving, shelled various places and buildings in Kuantan which the enemy were reported to have occupied. (From reports received long afterwards from Jap sources this shelling caused very heavy casualties).

"*Jan 2.* Enemy air, rain and mosquitoes as usual. At 1030 hrs Jem. Shingara Singh's patrol on the Batu Sawar track reported 50 to 60 enemy advancing south some 2 miles N.W. of the aerodrome. The patrol withdrew after encounter in which they killed four enemy. This was immediately reported to Bde but contact with this force was not regained that day.

"About 1900 hrs orders were received from Bde for a withdrawal the next day, the river line defences to be finally abandoned at 1400 hrs.

"Events in the western sector had been going badly. 11 Div in attempting to stand at Gurun had been badly defeated again. They had withdrawn to Kampar south of Ipoh and there had stood firm inflicting heavy casualties until pressure on the flank from further enemy landings made further withdrawal unavoidable. This meant uncovering the first of the lateral roads to the eastern sector, thus threatening the rear and flank of 9 Div. For this reason the withdrawal of 22 Bde was ordered. The aerodrome, however, was to be denied to the enemy until Jan 5 to prevent it being used by Jap fighters for attacks on a convoy that was due to arrive in Singapore any day. The convoy, having arrived safely, the withdrawal of 22 Bde was ordered for the 3rd Jan.

"*Jan 3.* Not being at all happy about the lack of information of enemy north of the rd, we posted 4 pl picquets north of the rd watching tracks at approximately the 7th, 8th, 10th and 11th m.s. Bn Rear H.Q., Pioneer and M.M.G. pls, followers, mess and all impedimenta were

1942

then sent back under 2nd comd with orders to find and prepare a suitable harbour west of Gambang where a good defensive position existed.

"The withdrawal of the remainder commenced at 1400 hrs. Moving at great speed across difficult country fwd coys withdrew some six to seven miles then embussed inside the picquet line. Rear party cleared m.s. 9 at 1600 hrs, a very good piece of work. There was no enemy interference.

"At dusk, 2/18 R.G.R. passed through us in lorries going straight back to Maran.

"Note: The bn withdrew abandoning NO stores or equipment to the enemy.

"About 2000 hrs Bde H.Q., 5 Fd Regt and Armd Cars arrived. We learnt from them that the Japs had made an encircling attack as the last of 2/18 R.G.R. were leaving. Hand to hand fighting was taking place around the buildings which housed Bde H.Q. when the latter, together with H.Q. and sec 5 Fd Regt got out with difficulty under heavy fire.

"Later Lieut Colonel Cummings, 2/12 F.F.R., arrived in a carrier. He had two bayonet wounds but had killed both his assailants and had gone round in a carrier organizing the defence until he fainted. (Note: Lt Col Cummings was later awarded the Victoria Cross for his gallantry and devotion.)

"Approximately two coys and a portion of H.Q. 2/12, all under command of the Sub. Major, were still on the aerodrome and from all accounts putting up a very good fight. We later learnt from survivors that they beat off the attack and commenced to withdraw towards Gambang but ran into two ambushes on the way. Only 40 all told succeeded in getting through and rejoining at Maran on Jan 5th.

"Orders to the Bde from Div repeatedly stressed the importance of keeping the Bde intact. The Brigadier therefore decided that withdrawal must continue next day.

"One did not like abandoning these coys of the 2/12 but as events turned out the decision was correct.

"*Jan 4.* M.T. moved off at 0400 hrs. 2/12 dets at 16 m.s. and Pula Manis withdrew through us, and Bn and Sec 21 Mtn Bty did rear guard. After withdrawing 7 miles without any sign of enemy, we embussed and proceeded to Maran into a very indifferent position.

"*Jan 5.* Selected and occupied new position. Sapper det now arrived (22 Fd Coy det who were to have carried out demolitions during withdrawal had been killed or captured on the aerodrome). Two bridges were destroyed some 5 or 6 miles back on rd to Kuantan. Some 40 survivors from 2/12 arrived. We sent up a bugler to the furthest demolition to sound the 2/12 regimental call.

1942

"At 1600 hrs orders received to withdraw that night. Bn rear guard. Picked up launch patrol from the mouth of the S. Pahang here, this patrol having withdrawn up the river to Lubok Paku having had no contact with the enemy. Dets 2/12 and 21 Mtn Bty from Lubok Paku also rejoined.

"Bde had demanded the services of our adjutant to recce a harbour near 80 m.s. He proceeded on a motor cycle, crashed and got concussion and had to be evacuated.

"We withdrew during the night, D Coy complicating matters by losing themselves for 2 hrs, an easy thing to do in the thick jungle country we were in. After marching 10 miles we were picked up by M.T. and proceeded 80 m.s. arriving just before dawn.

"*Jan 6.* We spent the day in a tapioca plantation, there was no sign of the enemy. Only one Jap plane came over flying very high. We moved off that night in M.T., Bn rear guard destroying two bridges east of Jerantut ferry. Rear party crossed the ferry at 0200 hrs on Jan 7th. Continued throughout the night and arrived Bentong from 0830 to 1400 hrs, distance of nearly 150 miles from our starting point. This was a terrific strain for our carrier drivers with only side lights over a difficult road congested with traffic and with precipitous sides. We lost one carrier over the khud, the commander Nk Bhag Singh, a very good N.C.O., being killed outright and the remainder of the crew being very seriously injured.

"*Jan 7.* Bentong; constructed and manned a rd block on the rd to Kuala Lumpur and recced position on the Gap. 11 Div had suffered further disaster at Slim river and now consisted of only two very weak and shattered Bdes. The first of the two rds across the barrier was open.

"22 Bde had now split up. 2/12 to Fraser's Hill Gap—2/18 to Raub. 8 Bde were moving back from Lipis and Jerantut.

"*Jan 8.* Orders were received mid-day for Bn to join 11 Div and R.V. in the vicinity of Rawang. We moved off in M.T. at 1630 hrs. The CO went ahead and found 11 Div H.Q. about 2100 hrs near Batu Caves. Here were Div Comd, Paris, and G1, Harrison, both very tired. Information of exact situation was vague. C.O. was told to get in touch with Selby commanding 28 Bde under whose orders we would come and to leave Bn at Rawang.

"C.O. found bn just entering Rawang and directed them to a R.V. just west of the ry and under rubber—then went to look for 28 Bde. He found them about 0400 hrs in Serandah and received order for the bn to move up in the morning and occupy a position covering the northern and western approaches of Serandah. He rejoined the bn in R.V. at 0700 hrs and found H.Q. 15 Bde (Muirhead) alongside.

"*Jan 9.* They informed us that enemy had landed at Kuala Selangor

1942

and had over run the bn watching that flank. They then communicated with 11 Div and Bn was ordered to come under orders of 15 Bde to deal with this new threat.

"Bn moved off at 1000 hrs to a rd junc and river crossing some 6 miles west on the Selangor rd. (No maps of the country were available.) Enemy air was extremely active both before and during the move but we could not wait and came in for a severe dose of dive bombing and machine gunning shortly after starting. Two carriers were hit, the first (Nk Mukhtiar Singh's) was hit almost directly, two of the crew (Nk Mukhtiar Singh and one other) being killed instantly and almost unrecognizably. We replied with rifle and L.M.Gs and pushed on arriving at our destination about midday. Carrier patrols were sent out along the rd to the coast and to watch a ry approach some 5 miles to the south. D Coy occupied a position at the rd junction, covering the river crossing.

"This stream was only 30 feet across but was 10 feet deep at the bridge. The rd patrol was recalled that evening without making contact and the bridge destroyed. We had no news of B Echelon since leaving Bentong.

"Fortunately we had learnt always to keep one large 3 ton lorry with the bn loaded with rations and a minimum scale of cooking pots and followers, and with this we replenished as necessary from dumps.

"It rained as usual most of the afternoon and night which was singularly unpleasant, as there was no cover for anyone. However food forays had been successful, and men and officers had a reasonably hot meal late that night. 2nd in Command and rear echelon Bn H.Q. were left to keep touch with 15 Bde as we had no idea which way we were likely to move next.

"*Jan 10.* F.O.O. arrived with a telephone in the morning. It was a damned bad one but better than nothing. At 1002 hrs orders were received for two coy commanders to report to 2nd-in-Comd at Bde H.Q. to recce position for helping 28 Bde. Lyons (A) and Hutchinson (C) were sent.

"At 1100 hrs Bde ordered two coys to Rawang, M.T. for which was already on the way. Telephone now went dis. We sent off B and C under Taj to R.V. for M.T., but as M.T. did not arrive, they proceeded on foot. Enemy air was most active and annoying. We learnt later they had attacked and dispersed M.T. moving to pick up our coys. On return to H.Q. received by D.R. somewhat lengthy, and as far as bn was concerned, complicated orders for withdrawal that day. Two coys were to use the railway and two the road.

"The acting adjutant was sent in C.O's wagon with instructions not to return until he had communicated these orders to 2nd-in-Comd and B and C Coys. C.O. had now only one officer left. This was

1942

Gurmit Singh with D Coy who were in position covering the river crossing. The mortar pl was in action on a ridge some 600 yds S.E. of the bridge. H.Q. with A Coy were under rubber on a ridge near the rd and about 800 yds east of the bridge.

"Some 15 men (Pathans without arms from a Punjab Regt) arrived. They said they had been near the coast and that the bn had been surrounded and disintegrated. We sent them along to Bde H.Q. About midday transport started moving through us going south, British troops, sappers, gunners, R.I.A.S.C. etc.

"At 1430 hrs Brig Muirhead arrived with rear Bde H.Q. He informed us that all the bde was through, that he had stopped our two Coys (B & C) on the outskirts of Rawang and told them to rejoin and that we could withdraw as soon as we were ready.

"The mortar pl was moved to a R.V. near to the rd and to their trucks and Bn H.Q. and A Coy likewise. As soon as this move was completed heavy L.M.G. fire broke out at the river crossing.

"Here D Coy had laid an excellent ambush. Two enemy appeared on cycles, rode up to the bridge, dismounted and started to inspect it. They were shortly followed by two parties each about 30 strong, coming down the rd in close formation.

"A V.B. immediately east of the rd had been sited and camouflaged to deal with this very situation, and were holding their fire hoping to get the whole lot in enfilade at a range of between 100-200 yds. A sapper lorry chose this moment to come tearing down the rd from Rawang and to stop with a jerk exactly in front of our V.B. and within 150 yds of the enemy. He did not stop long but enough to spoil a really good bag.

"Fire was now opened by both sides and after a short time we estimated the enemy had deployed one coy. The mortar pl was in action again within a minute and, working on directions telephoned through by D Coy Comdr, quickly silenced two enemy L.M.Gs and later two enemy mortars.

"These latter were solemnly mortaring the positions (now empty) which had been occupied by our mortars in the morning and later turned their attention to the ridge which had been occupied by Bn H.Q. This was pretty conclusive evidence of the Tamils' fifth column work. Many Tamils in this area had been found making their way N.W. in the morning and had been turned back by us but we were unable to stop them all. We also found large supplies of petrol and oil which we emptied out.

"Bde H.Q. now decided to go, and when both enemy L.M.Gs and mortars seemed to be temporarily silenced, we rushed them down the road covered by fire from mortars and D Coy with carriers moving ahead and in rear. They all got through without casualties as did our own first line trucks a little later.

"Fire was now opened on Bn H.Q. from a ridge 600 yds away on the east i.e. our side of the river and near the rd to Rawang. The enemy got a rude surprise only just escaping from B and C Coys who arrived down the rd a few minutes after they had opened fire. The bn was now together again.

"C, H.Q. and B Coys withdrew through A and D without difficulty.

"As soon as our mortars came out of action the enemy mortars started again from a position some 600 yds north of their original one and enemy L.M.Gs also started again. The mortar shelled H.Q. positions about 3 minutes after we had left.

"D Coy was withdrawn at dusk the enemy making no attempt to follow up. The carrier patrol from the railway was withdrawn having made no contact, and the bn after a tiring night march of about 8 miles passed through 3/16 Punjab Regt at Kuang and embussed in Australian M.T.

"We arrived at Labu about 0300 hrs failed to contact guides sent on ahead and spent a very weary two hours in the dark trying to find position allotted to bn. Got there eventually just before dawn.

"*Jan 11.* Occupied a position with 3/16 Punjab on our right and British Bn (Leicester Surrey) in reserve. Our indefatigable Q.M. Capt Prithipal Singh found us here and brought a welcome supply of food incl a bottle of beer each for the Sikhs.

"*Jan 12.* No sign of enemy. Withdrew at dusk picking up M.T. some 3 miles East of Labu, passing through Seremban in flames and along very congested roads.

"*Jan 13.* Arrived Jasin 0700 hrs, finding a suitable harbour with difficulty. Found 11 Div H.Q. about 0930 hrs and were ordered to rejoin 22 Bde, 9 Div, at Segamat. M.T. was ordered for 1200 hrs. Capt Russell Roberts was sent off with recce parties. Bn waited for M.T. which arrived 1400 hrs. Meanwhile we contacted our B Echelon again. They were bogged getting out of harbour in Bentong on 8 January and the Sappers blew the rd over the gap before they were through.

"C.O. went on ahead as soon as embussing started. The rd even then was beginning to get congested. By nightfall it was complete chaos. With difficulty we managed to get the men of the bn out of their trucks. The bn arrived from 1930 to 2300 hrs in pouring rain and darkness. The distance from Jasin was only about 40 miles.

"For some reason no enemy air was over that afternoon. They missed a wonderful opportunity. For some 30 miles the rd was tight packed with a mass of motor transport, sometimes there being three vehicles abreast. All M.T. discipline seemed to have gone by the board. Finding it impossible to get our own first line transport out, we instructed them to continue in the column to Segamat and to turn north to Batu Anam,

1942

then south again to the X roads where the bn was getting into position. They did this arriving just before dawn by which time the rd was clear again.

"*Jan 14.* The bn remained in position holding the X roads Batu Anam-Jemantah-Segamat till the 18 Jan. The Loyals arrived on 17 Jan and took over C Coy's position, who were fwd watching the bridge on the Jemantah rd. To the north 27 Australian Bde and 8 Ind Bde were in the area Batu Anam Gemas where a coy of 30 Bn (Aus) brought off a good ambush destroying some seven enemy tanks on 14 Jan.

"The position was strengthened, A/Tank mines laid and intensive patrolling carried out, contact being made daily with Australian patrols some 5 miles to the north.

"*Jan 16.* Enemy air came over in considerable strength and for the first time in the war we heard and saw our A.A. defences in action. They were some Bofors of an Indian A/A Regt and succeeded in shooting down two planes. This had a splendid effect on the men who now grinned broadly whenever these guns with distinctive noise went into action. A further factor in raising everyone's spirits was a visit from General Barstow who told us we were not going to withdraw any more. Food and ammn was dumped in all positions and the coming of the Japs was awaited with confidence and eager anticipation.

"*Jan 17.* Not for long alas!

"*Jan 18.* News came through of successful Jap landings at Muar and of disaster to the newly arrived 45 Ind Bde and once more we received orders to withdraw.

"Loyals came through us that morning, going back to Muar river bridge. Bn less B and D Coys then went through to some 2 miles west of Segamat. B and D remained on X roads to cover through 27 Aust Bde, withdrawing to H.Q. at 1400 hrs on 19th.

"*Jan 19.* After some complicated manoeuvres in which C Coy came in for a lot of unnecessary marching, Bde withdrew at dusk. Segamat was in flames as we passed through due not to the Japs but to the enthusiasm of an Aussie Liaison Officer. It was uncomfortable getting through.

"Crossing the river, the bn came under the orders of 27 (Aus) Bde (Maxwell) and the remainder of 9 Div passed through south.

"We went into position immediately at 2200 hrs as left fwd bn covering rail and road bridges with 2/26 on our right and 2/30 in reserve.

"Demolitions were fairly successful though the bridges were still just passable for infantry with difficulty.

"Our own 25-pdrs shelled us during the night but fortunately there were no casualties.

"*Jan 20.* The Japs appeared next morning as usual taking few precautions. Two of them on bicycles came up the rd to the bridge and

1942

pulling out maps climbed down to inspect the damage. They were followed shortly afterwards by a squad of 14 on bicycles and in close formation. B Coy pl watching this approach could restrain themselves no longer and opened fire knocking over three while the rest scattered.

"West of the railway bridge the country bordering the river was thick jungle and was patrolled by A and C Coys incessantly within a 4 mile radius. Observation of the northern bank could only be obtained by climbing trees.

"About midday a patrol of A Coy under Jemdr. Nagindar Singh reported some 200 enemy in close formation near the western outskirts of the town, and followed shortly afterwards by a report that enemy artillery were digging in.

"There was an Aussie F.O.O. and sergeant at Bn H.Q. but they had no cable back to their guns. The maps we possessed stopped short of the river.

"Jemdr. Nagindar Singh, with his second report sent back his map marked with an X on the margin some ¾ inch above the edge of the map. We drew in the mesh on the margin & gave the gunner the co-ordinates of the X as his target.

"Using our telephone back to reserve bn he opened fire. After a few rounds a runner came in from the patrol, with the message "Right 100-Up 50". We sent the sergeant back with the runner ¼ mile through jungle to observe from patrol's position. He returned after about ½ hr, quite excited, and reported two enemy guns in position abandoned by their crews with our shells dropping all round them. Small parties of enemy were observed on the north bank, but apart from some very feeble shelling and mortaring, he was inactive.

"During the morning the C.O. attended a Bde conference, found Bde H.Q. with difficulty as it had moved a long way back and well clear of the main rd owing to reports of enemy infiltration. Major General Gordon Bennett arrived during the conference and painted a gloomy picture of Muar, made some scathing comments on Indian troops, extolled Australian and departed.

"Bde withdrew that night by route march and M.T. after further scare reports of Jap infiltration. Bn rejoined 22 Bde in position 101-99 m.s. rd Segamat-Labis. 2/12 F.F.R. at m.s. 101. 2/18 R.G.R. at m.s. 100. Bn about m.s. 99½. Bde H.Q. m.s. 99.

"*Jan 21.* Moved into position about 0200 hrs, the position having been reconnoitred by Russell-Roberts who had gone back with coy guides on the 20th. It was similar to many positions in Malaya—suitable for an ambush or two but quite indefensible once the enemy has deployed.

"Bn patrolled wide to both flanks but made no contact. In the afternoon 2/12 F.F.R. brought off a successful ambush catching some

30 enemy in close order and then withdrew. Unfortunately one complete coy was lost when withdrawing through jungle.

"2/18 R.G.R. came through us at dusk.

"Bn withdrew without making contact and on arriving at Labis was informed that coy of 2/12 was missing. We waited two hrs and fired very lights but to no avail. Bde then ordered withdrawal to continue and after a further 11 miles we found M.T. and went through 8 Bde via Yong Peng and Ayer Hitam to Kluang arriving about 0430 hrs on 22 Jan.

"*Jan 22.* Bn rested and C.O. reconnoitred a defensive position covering western approaches to Kluang.

"*Jan 23.* Bde in position, 2/18 R.G.R. at Paloh on ry 15 miles north, 2/12 F.F.R. and Dogras and Bahawalpur Inf. holding the aerodrome and northern approaches, and 5 Sikh western approaches. At Ayer Hitam the Australian Bde and Loyals, 8 Bde, withdrawing from Yong Peng. Further west were the shattered remains of 11 Div plus newly arrived British 53 Bde in approx area Batu Pahat. Night 23/24, 8 Bde came through to Renggam. Rifle coys of 2/18 R.G.R. arrived down the ry reporting considerable enemy in the Paloh area and that H.Q. and H.Q. Coy were lost.

"*Jan 24.* At 1100 hrs C.O. was told to report at Bde H.Q. (some 3 miles away). There he was informed that 22 Bde was to retake Paloh, 8 Bde moving up from Renggam to take their place in Kluang.

"The plan was for the Bde less 5 Sikh to adv up the ry. 5 Sikh, with Bty under comd, was to make a detour and adv. along a rd some five miles west of the ry rejoining the bde at Niyor. No infomation was given as to the whereabouts of the enemy.

"No maps were available for the greater part of the route, but Leslie Davis (A. k. Pekan), liaison officer at Bde, had been over it and came with the bn as guide.

"The bn moved off at 1400 hrs with 73 Bty of 5 Fd Regt (Comdr Major Don, Est 8 guns 4.5 hows). Bn M.T. was cut down to 14 vehicles and there were 24 bty vehicles.

"The first 5 miles of the route was already being patrolled by a sec of our carriers. These we picked up en route.

"The route lay for the most part through rubber with only occasional patches of swamp and jungle, enabling all the marching echelons to move well clear of the rd.

"As the bn left Kluang arty and S.A. fire could be heard from the direction of the aerodrome.

"The order of march of the battalion was as shown diagrammatically on the following page:

1942

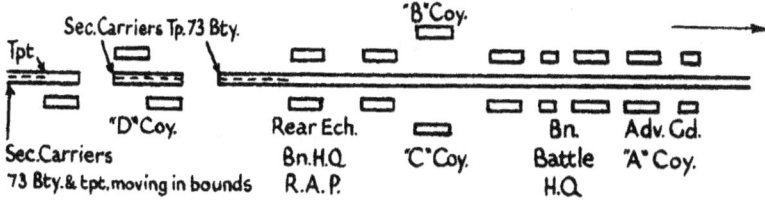

FRONT TO REAR — ONE MILE

"After going three miles west along the rd to Ayer Hitam we swung north through a rubber estate which had a net-work of roads. These we were clear of by 1600 hrs.

"At 1730 hrs when it was estimated that we were within 2½ to 3 miles of Niyor an incomplete message was received by W.T. from Bde ordering us to abandon the original objective and make for m.s. 416 on the ry.

"To move direct on the ry at m.s. 416 would entail either sending guns and Tpt back to Kluang or leaving them on the rd with a considerable portion of the bn as escort and also a night adv by an unreconnoitred route through jungle and swamp. Not having a map showing our exact whereabouts further complicated matters.

"It was decided therefore to continue along the rd we were on to Niyor and then strike South along the ry to m.s. 416.

"By 1800 hrs the Bn had covered some 11 miles and was within about 2 miles of Niyor and just on the map sheet again. It was decided to have a long halt and feed at the first suitable harbour.

"Shortly after, the ground being suitable a halt was about to be ordered when a rd block was seen about 300 yds ahead of Bn Battle H.Q.

"At the same moment enemy L.M.G. and rifle fire opened from front and flanks followed almost immediately by mortar fire, the first shell from which landed among Bn H.Qs, wounding 2/Lt Hutchison, the C.O's orderly (L/Nk Mukarrab) and two others of Bn H.Qs.

"We were advancing through rubber and were in a shallow depression with ridges some 150 yds to right and left of the rd, and with what seemed more open ground beyond them. Beyond the rd block the rd bent slightly to the rt and ascended a small rise. The rd block was made of felled trees with a steep banked nala and then a patch of dense jungle bordering it on the right.

"It was already dusk and would be dark in 20 mins. The C.O. signalled B & C Coys with a wave of the hand to occupy the flanking ridges, which they did immediately. Meanwhile the left fwd platoon of the Adv Gd (Jem Nagindar Singh) had nearly out-flanked the rd block and were busily engaged.

"Jem. Nagindar Singh had a complete grip of the situation and claimed to have dropped 12 of the enemy immediately beyond the rd block and was now engaging other enemy, who were in shallow trenches close to the rd block and on the crest beyond. As he was leading the C.O. to a better view-point Jem. Nagindar Singh (who was awarded the Indian Order of Merit, but who later regrettably died as a Prisoner-of-War) received a burst of enemy L.M.G. fire in his shoulder and his Pl Hav (Hav Dalip Singh) was most unfortunately mortally hit about a minute afterward.

"The C.O. decided to form a perimeter where the Bn was as the light was then fading and sent back a message to the 2nd-in-Comd with Rear Ech. Bn. H.Q. to get Arty and tpt into a harbour in some estate buildings about 1000 yds in rear. D Coy and Carrier pl were to form a perimeter round them.

"A quick walk round the perimeter showed we were in a good position defiladed from both flanks. The immediate seizure of the high ground on the flanks by B & C Coys had fore-stalled the enemy;—a few who were there withdrew and continued to fire ineffectively and spasmodically from the left (Western flank). Enemy fire from the right ceased.

"Strict orders were issued that there was to be no firing during the night, an order which was obeyed except on two occasions when some nervous recruit fired a small burst of L.M.G. at enemy patrols who came up against the position.

"The enemy continued to fire from the front and left flank until about 0030 hrs obviously wanting us to disclose our position. He eventually gave up disappointed and we got some sleep. R.A.P. had been opened in the estate buildings and all the wounded attended to.

"The situation was reported to Bde, but W.T. was working so badly that we never knew if messages had been received or not. Enemy M.T. could be heard arriving during the night including a lot of M.Cs.

"*Jan 25.* At dawn firing commenced again, enemy L.M.G. and rifle fire being soon supplemented by mortars and light artillery.

"As soon as it was light enough to see to move, two fighting patrols were sent out. A pl from C Coy was sent to find out (a) the extent and passability of the patch of jungle bordering the right of the rd near the rd block and if occupied by the enemy, (b) the

1942

position and strength of the enemy on the right of the rd beyond the rd block.

"A pl from B Coy was sent to find out the strength of the enemy on the left rear of our position from whence a certain amount of L.M.G. fire was coming.

"As the light improved two enemy mortar positions and one gun position were spotted on the left front. Here the ground was clear of trees, undulating and covered with scrub, 3 to 4 ft. high, for a distance of some 800 to 1200 yds. Beyond was dense jungle and many very tall trees. Our guns and a sec. of mortars were quickly on to these targets.

"Observation except of our left and left front was very poor, but from two or three positions narrow vistas through the trees could be obtained up to some 500 yds. Looking down one of these the C.O. found himself looking straight at a Japanese Officer doing the same thing at the far end and shortly after saw a mortar detachment going into action.

"From another view-point, a small rise fwd of our right front, a good view was obtained of the rd block and a stretch of ground beyond. Here the C.O. witnessed a spirited action between C Coy's patrol and a body of about 50 enemy.

"The patrol had not gone as wide as they had been ordered and emerging through the patch of jungle close to its near end saw what they afterwards reported as a body of 100 enemy in close formation by the side of the rd. For some reason the Jem. stated afterwards he thought they might have been B Coy (they were wearing tin helmets and the light was bad) and he hailed them as such. The enemy replied in Urdu "B Coy hai. B Coy Extend karo". They were soon recognized and the battle joined before they had opened out. A steep-banked nala some 30 yds across intervened between the two. A sec of C Coy pl descended into the nala and appeared to be attempting to scale the far bank but a shower of grenades with two objects which looked like flame-filled retorts stopped them, killing one (L/Nk Mohindar Singh) and wounding two. The fusilade lasted some 10 mins, the enemy going to ground west of the rd. The patrol then collected their wounded, withdrew a short distance, and crossing the nala, took up a position on a small ridge—a very spirited action in which the enemy came off distinctly the worst.

"Firing on the left flank on B Coy's front increased in intensity and a lively duel was going on between our guns and mortars and those of the enemy on the edge of the jungle some 1000 yds away on the left front. There was also an enemy M.G. well hidden in the scrub on a low ridge some 600 yds to the left front, but we were unable to locate it exactly and failed to silence it. B Coy's patrol returned and reported the jungle to the left rear clear of enemy but they had seen enemy moving in the scrub in small groups all along B Coy's front. A few rifle grenades fired into the scrub proved the correctness of the second part of the report, at least two groups of Japs being flushed by rifle grenades and then dealt with by L.M.Gs. There were a few casualties in B Coy. The enemy was now estimated to be about a Bn in strength, and it was decided to attack with A and C Coys. A Coy to secure the high ground astride the rd some 500 yds ahead. C Coy to carry out a turning movement from the rt with the object of turning the enemy's flank and getting astride the rd behind him.

"Lack of news from Bde was worrying. If as we believed to be the case the Bde had not advanced from Kluang, there was every likelihood of having our communications cut behind us. There were numerous culverts and one large wooden bridge on the rd the demolition of which would mean abandoning guns and transport in the event of withdrawal. The situation was again reported to Bde and this was pointed out

"We now suffered a severe loss the Bty Comdr (Major Don) and the whole of his O.P. were wounded just as they were about to register the new targets given for the attack. This caused a delay in the attack until a new O.P. arrived and could get the targets registered.

"Another two mortars were brought into action although the trees made positions for them most difficult to find. With the arrival of the new O.P. came a mutilated message received over the gunner W.T. the gist of which was orders for us to retire to Kluang as soon as possible and by whatever route we chose.

"It was obvious that unless the enemy could be dissuaded from following up, withdrawal would be a desperate business, and further that if we secured the high ground in front our movements would be screened from observation.

"It was decided to carry out the first phase of the attack (A Coy's) and give the enemy a blow from which he would take some time to recover, and further to make him believe that we intended to continue the adv.

"The attack was ordered to commence at 1045 hrs preceded by three min. arty concentration. The mortars were given targets on the flanks where the enemy M.G. was still in action. All M.T. were ordered to be ready to move back under carrier escort as soon as ordered and a section of guns stepped back. At 1030 hrs heavy small arms fire broke out in the rear where D Coy and the carriers were engaging parties of enemy. At 1040 hrs the F.O.O. stated he could not give the arty fire asked for (there had been an accident at the gun position and a number of casualties including one of D Coy killed, and trees prevented the bty engaging the target from the position they were in).

"All 4 mortars were now turned on the arty task with very good effect and at 1100 hrs A Coy swept fwd, Hav. Lehna Singh's pl well to the fore. They were met by a somewhat ragged fire and some half-dozen men were seen to fall; the rest with loud shouts of "Sat Siri Akal" charged up the crest. The Japs hastily left their positions some of them throwing away their arms in an effort to escape, the rest were bayonetted. From the number of Japs concentrated in a comparatively small space it looked as if he had been about to attack and had been fore-stalled.

"After securing their objective A Coy had a good 15 mins. at tgts from thirty to a hundred yds range as numbers of the enemy attempted to get back to cover in short individual rushes.

"As soon as it was seen that the attack had been successful, preparations for the withdrawal were ordered. At this moment, Hutchison (5 Sikh) B.I.O. arrived in a carrier with written orders from Bde for the withdrawal and with the information that Bde had not been able to adv. at all. This made us anxious to get back before news of our action caused the enemy to move across and cut off our retreat.

"A Coy reported that some 150 M.Cs and 200 bicycles had been abandoned on the rd side on the far side of their objective and that a little further to their left and left front an Inf. gun and two mortars had been abandoned.

"A gallant but unauthorized attempt to bring these in by a pl of B Coy under Jem. Rang Ali caused the pl some 8 or 9 casualties including the Jem. himself. It was unfortunate as it meant delay getting the wounded back. The M.G. which we had been trying, unsuccessfully, to silence most of the morning caused these casualties.

"By 1200 hrs all our casualties now 25 in number had been got back and withdrawal commenced.

"Our arty started shelling both sides of the rd some 200 yds in front of A Coy. A sec of carriers was moved up to near Bn H.Qrs, making a considerable noise. By these measures it was hoped to make the enemy think that we intended a further adv and that he might expect carriers to sweep over the crest as soon as we had removed the rd block.

"Enemy fire from the left flank and from the rear had now ceased. Here D Coy in a skilfully laid trap had killed 10 of a party of 20 enemy, while a carrier had accounted for 3 of another group.

"A Coy withdrew silently through B & C Coys and the latter then were withdrawn without any enemy interference, a little ragged shelling and mortar fire on to the position as we were getting out being the only sign of enemy activity. An annoying delay occurred in our second bound when we found the reserve ammn lorry firmly bogged in the ditch at the side of the rd; it was got out after some 10 mins by two carriers.

"After 4 miles of unmolested withdrawal which was carried out at some speed, all guns and tpt were sent straight back to Kluang under escort of 2 secs of carriers. Up to this time they had been moving in bounds 2 miles ahead of us.

"When we were about 1½ miles from the main Ayer-Hitam-Kluang rd the rear party reported enemy on our right rear—probably enemy from North of Kluang moving across to cut off our withdrawal. They were too late.

"We arrived in harbour 2 miles south of Kluang at 1700 hrs passing through Baluch in our old position. After a short rest and a hot meal the Bn marched again a further 10 miles to a harbour North of Rengam arriving about 0200 hrs damnably tired but in good spirits.

"Since 1400 hrs on the 24 of Jan the Bn had marched over 33 miles and had been in action for 18 hrs.

"Our casualties were 40 including 3 gunners; enemy casualties were conservatively estimated at 150.

"A Coy had brought in a number of trophies including enemy L.M.Gs and rifles and it was a little disappointing that the time factor did not permit of exploitation and bringing back the enemy guns and M.Cs. A Coy had made some effort to destroy these.

"This was a very heartening action. It gave the men confidence, and relieved all pressure on 22 Bde and later on 8 Bde for a full 24 hrs. On the 25th not a shot was fired on their fronts.

"The Bn received congratulatory messages from the Div Comd (Gen Barstow) in person, from Major General Gordon Bennett (A.I.F.) commanding Central Sector, and from General Heath, III Corps Commander. The B.B.C. also gave us a mention a few nights later though we were too busy to hear it at the time.

"Bn H.Q. and H.Q. Coy 2/18 R.G.R. rejoined in Kluang on the afternoon of 25 Jan having been lost in the jungle west of the railway.

"Bde ordered 2nd-in-Command, Major Brown, to proceed to Singapore on 26th Jan to reconnoitre Bde position there.

"It had now been decided to withdraw all forces from the mainland on to Singapore Island.

"9 Div (22 and 8 Bdes) were withdrawing down the ry. Aus. Div & Gordons down the Ayer-Hitam-Johore rd. 11 Div along coast rd from Batu Pahat area.

"*Jan 26*. The Bn marched again at 1000 hrs. Enemy air was extremely active along the roads so the bn moved clear of them—tiring but safe—and arrived some 14 miles south of Rengam at approx 1430 hrs.

"The bn had been allotted a position running from incl the ry on the west to incl the first of a network of roads stretching 4 miles to the east. All these roads converged and joined before entering Layang Layang, a village on the ry some 6 miles to the South. The position was thoroughly bad.

"Flanks were completely in the air, rubber provided good cover and good going for the enemy round either flank and for approach, whilst on the eastern flank he had a choice of roads to use for M.T. To hold it required 3 coys fwd.

"There was no better one however between it and Layang Layang.

"The remainder of Bde and H.Q. were concentrated 2½ to 3 miles to the south in rear and on the ry at m.s. 435.

"We asked that the bn be allotted responsibility for the road approaches and the rest of the Bde for the ry. If echeloned in depth down these we should have been able to delay the enemy for some 10 to 12 hrs at any rate by day. This was not agreed to. Bde agreed that the position was tactically bad but that orders permitted of no alternative as Bde had to keep north of a line East and West through ry m.s. 435 until 1600 hrs on 28 Jan.

"The bn occupied the position by 1630 hrs. Enemy air was particularly active, and much as one wanted to give the men rest we had to spend a lot of the night digging in an effort to make the best of a very bad position.

"Late in the evening a message was received from Bde that everything on wheels had to be clear of m.s. 435 by 1700 hrs next day, 27 Jan, and that 8 Bde would pass through us about that time. 22 Bde itself having got rid of all transport would withdraw down the ry having held their present positions until 1630 hrs on 28 Jan.

"This meant that we were to fight for 24 hrs in a position which was agreed to be tactically unsound, without arty support, without carriers, without mortars, with no reserve ammunition other than dumps, and without any means or even eventual hope of evacuating wounded. Further, no sapper assistance was available for blocking roads which in any case had to be left open until 1630 hrs on 27 Jan to let through transport and carriers of 8 Bde. After this we were to withdraw 10 or 15 miles (the position which 8 Bde was going to occupy was not then nor was it ever known to us) still without any supporting arms or means of evacuating wounded.

"Q.M. was ordered to send up two days cooked rations with extra tins of milk and packets of biscuits, to reach us without fail by 1200 hrs next day, 27th, as we had then with us only rations for the morning meal on the 27th.

"Throughout the afternoon and all next day until 1600 hrs when they had to be sent back in accordance with orders, the carriers patrolled wide to both flanks and reported even more roads and link roads than those shown on the map.

1942

"*Jan 27.* After inspecting coy positions and choosing places for ambushes on two roads, C.O. reconnoitred next morning to 1 mile south of Layang Layang where he found the first reasonable defensive position, and for Malaya it was a good one. Whilst there he met Brig Lay of 8 Bde. He could not say what position his Bde was going to occupy.

"D Coy and one pl of C Coy had prepared two well-laid ambushes. If 8 Bde withdrew not in contact there was every hope of one of them coming off successfully, as when not in contact the Japs seemed to pay little attention to measures for local tactical security.

"The pioneer pl prepared 12 trees for final felling and pulling into position as soon as 8 Bde were through.

"By 1300 hrs, however, the enemy were shelling Layang Layang using heavy stuff. This was the first time in our experience during the campaign that we had encountered enemy medium or heavy arty. Enemy air action was annoying and continuous.

"At 1600 hrs the rearmost troops of 8 Bde (Cookies) withdrew down the ry passing through our left coy (B) with the Japs on their heels.

"Taj, B Coy Comd, had just left Bn H.Q. on his way back to B Coy who reported many enemy advancing astride the ry and that they were being heavily mortared. An arty concentration was put down some 400 yds north along the ry.

"An excited signaller reported that the enemy was on top of them and round their left, and communication was then cut off.

"Some five minutes after this an enemy L.M.G. opened fire on Bn H.Q. from the scrub-covered broken ground on our left, and small groups of A Coy, who were holding the line between the ry and rd with a thin L.M.G. screen were seen withdrawing.

"The only reserve, C Coy less one pl, was sent to clear the broken ground of enemy and to adv to the right sector of B Coy's defences which lay east of the ry. D Coy and the pl of C Coy were then reluctantly called in from their ambush positions on the roads as the enemy seemed to have chosen the ry.

"D Coy reported small parties of enemy on the high ground west of the road some 1000 yds to our front from which position they were inspecting our lay-out and also that many motor cycles could be heard moving on the roads round their right flank.

"At 1630 hrs the F.O.O., Green, said that he had to go as his carrier had to go back. He sent away the carrier and stayed himself, the bty agreeing that he should walk back with us. This gave us another half-hour's arty support.

"The carriers had already gone and all mortars save two 3-in. which the mortar pl said they would carry back. (They later did so for four days and nights without rest or food).

"The arty support in the next half-hour undoubtedly helped in temporarily restoring the situation.

"At 1700 hrs B Coy's telephone came to life and Taj (B Coy Comdr) reported "Situation in hand".

"He had had an exciting trip back to the ry line, being fired at twice by Japs who had infiltrated into the position, and had found his fwd pls had retired some 200 yds. He immediately reformed them, counter-attacked, and re-occupied the position without much difficulty. He reported considerable enemy movement in the rubber round his left flank where a rd ending in a cul de sac overlapped the position. We put a 2 minutes arty concentration down on this spot. He reported more enemy movement immediately east of the ry some 300 yds ahead of his position. C Coy less a pl arrived on his rt having silenced the enemy in the broken ground to our left but without catching or killing them.

"(Individual use of cover by the enemy and also by small groups, both here and at Niyor, was excellent and greatly surpassed anything even our best scouts were capable of).

"The guns left about 1715 hrs.

"The situation was reported to Bde, and permission asked to withdraw gradually after dark down the road to Layang Layang. This was not agreed to, the plan was for us to withdraw slowly down the ry on to Bde during the next day.

"It was then decided that we withdraw to a position some ½-mile south of where we were and from where there was some hope of keeping touch with the Bde. Permission was sought to send a coy to hold Layang Layang, but this was not agreed to.

"We slipped quietly out at 1930 hrs and at 1950 hrs mortar and M.G. fire was opened by the enemy and he attacked finding nothing there. He came in from both flanks missing the rear party by under 100 yds.

"We had settled into our new positions before midnight but had great difficulty in establishing communication with Bde (the only means being by hooking in on the ry telephone wires).

"*Jan 28.* At 0130 hrs enemy M.T. could be heard using the roads to the east. It took ½-hr to get through communication to Bde.

"A fighting patrol C Coy was sent out at 0430 hrs to take offensive action against enemy using the roads, their objective being a road junction nearly a mile to the east. They were given a route from there which would bring them back via Bde H.Q. and told to be back by 1000 hrs.

"At 0800 hrs Bde ordered Bn to withdraw and to join Bde at m.s. (ry) 435. This we were eager to do as rations for two days which should have been delivered at midday had been sent up in charge of a Volunteer Officer. He arrived at Bde H.Q. in his truck at 1630 hrs whilst the battle was going on. Here he was stopped and the rations were dumped, and so for the sake of saving a 15-cwt truck, the Bn had to go hungry. How hungry was even then beginning to worry us.

"The Bn arrived at m.s. 435 at 0930 hrs and found the remainder of the Bde all west of the ry with slight S.A. fire coming from the east.

"Our two days' rations were in a gate-keeper's hut on the ry and under enemy fire. Captain Russell Roberts and two men per coy went up and got them. Unfortunately someone had been at them, the sacks were open, and the floor was covered with chapattis and dal. Instead of two days rations, there was hardly a meal left for the Bn.

"C Coy (Gannon) returned at 1015 hrs. After a difficult march through rubber and swamp and patches of jungle, in pitch darkness, they arrived near the objective given them some half an hr after dawn and shortly spotted a party of 120 Japs seated on the roadside with a small group of officers nearby. They were all eating.

"The Coy crept into position and at a range of 150 yds all L.M.Gs and rifles opened fire on a whistle signal. Gannon himself and his Indian Officers, Subedar Sampuran Singh and Jemdr Ajit Singh, claim to have counted between 70 & 80 Japs hit and lying on the roadside; the remainder bolted into the rubber.

"Finding the route we had given them blocked by more Japs with whom they had a slight brush, the Coy returned to Bn H.Q., and finding it empty, came down west of the ry.

"The Bde plan was to move keeping west of the ry and if possible get astride the ry at Layang Layang. There was no information as to the whereabouts of 8 Bde and communication with no one.

"Bde moved off as soon as C Coy arrived, the Bn doing advanced guard.

"There was no defined route, the ground was undulating and lay for the most part through rubber with patches of swamp and jungle near the ry.

"At 1200 hrs the vanguard, B Coy, came under very heavy fire from the front and left flank. A number of men fell. It was obvious that the enemy was there in some strength and had crossed the ry to dispute our passage.

"Quickly recovering from their surprise, B Coy leading pls with a pl of C Coy (13 pl Jemdr Ajit Singh) on their left, fixed bayonets, and with loud cries of "Ya Ali" and "Sat Siri Akal", charged fwd and were swallowed up in a rather dense patch of jungle and bushes which lay ahead and to the left and which bordered the ry. In the next 30 minutes an incessant rattle of S.A. fire punctuated by yells and war cries, and the explosion of mortar shells resounded around us. It was a grim fight.

"About a quarter right and to the south was a swamp clothed in thick elephant grass rising to twice the height of a man.

"Without landmarks, fixing one's position was extremely difficult; if we were where we thought, the map showed a ridge some 50 ft high immediately south of the swamp, which not only lay across our line of adv but, abutting on to the ry, overlooked that portion on which B and C were engaged.

"B Coy were told not to let any of their men cross the ry and then D Coy (Gurmit) was sent with orders to cross the swamp and secure this ridge.

"B Coy and the one pl of C Coy, after a very severe fight, drove the enemy across the ry (to the east). They were obviously in some strength and had two mortars which were very annoying, again finding Bn H.Q. killing two and wounding another five.

"Further reconnaissance found a rd crossing the swamp, the wooden bridge over the stream in its centre having been demolished.

"B Coy having secured their objective, we began to get the casualties back. These were heavy, and as they had to be carried over ground still swept by enemy fire, from the tops of trees bordering the east of the ry, a number more casualties were suffered in evacuating them. Jemdr Mansabdar Khan made some seven trips carrying back men of his pl over this bullet-swept stretch.

"About 1330 hrs enemy fire slackened appreciably and shortly after a runner returned from D Coy to say they had occupied their objective.

"Throughout this action at very frequent intervals enemy aircraft were over us, flying very low, at times almost skimming the treetops and obviously looking for us. Either the rubber proved too good cover or we were too close to their own troops, as they dropped no bombs.

"A Coy were sent across the swamp by the path to join D Coy. The remainder of the Bde followed without having suffered any casualties and without any interference, enemy fire having now ceased.

"Our casualties in this grim fight were, ten killed and about 35 wounded. Ten of these could walk, for the remainder only fifteen stretchers were available in the whole Bde. We improvised others from ground sheets and sticks cut from the rubber trees.

"The Bn had fulfilled its function as advanced guard but at heavy cost.

"B Coy and 13 pl of C Coy had fought splendidly and with true offensive spirit, and when ordered to withdraw on completion of their task, brought in all their wounded and all arms and equipment of the casualties.

1942

"D Coy had a most difficult passage through the swamp being at times up to their arm-pits, whilst elephant grass and bushes formed a barrier maddening in its delay, and making control most difficult.

"However, they won through, and seizure of the ridge was probably the deciding factor in the fight.

"Many gallant deeds were performed during the fight, two of which can be recorded.

"10231 Sepoy Basta Singh, 13 pl of C Coy, (this sepoy had already displayed marked courage and leadership in the defence of the ferry at Kuantan on 31 Dec). Basta Singh was badly wounded in the knee shortly after the action began and left lying in a position exposed to considerable enemy fire. From this position he observed two enemy in the tops of trees bordering the ry some 200 yds distant.

"He shouted to an L.M.G. gunner 10 yds away to bring him his L.M.G. The latter refused. Thereupon Basta Singh despite his shattered knee crawled over to the L.M.G. and taking possession of it, shot down both enemy from the tree tops.

"Later in the fight when two men had been wounded in an effort to get to him to carry him back, he shouted to his pl commander not to send any one else but to shoot him before they left.

"Jemdr Munsabdar Khan, after leading his pl in a gallant attack and after attaining his objective, carried back seven of his pl who were wounded. He crossed a bullet-swept stretch of open ground on each trip.

"From the absence of any sounds of battle it was clear that 8 Bde was nowhere in the vicinity of Layang Layang. (We learnt later that they had withdrawn 5 to 6 miles south on the previous evening and had blown up the bridges on the ry). The Brig now decided to abandon the original objective of Layang Layang and to make a flank march through the jungle west of the ry hoping to make contact with 8 Bde in the vicinity of Sedenak.

"After proceeding due west for about 1 mile the Bde turned south into the jungle. The Bn was still doing adv gd and the Brig ordered Lt Col Parkin personally to lead the march.

"We found a trail which took us for some ¾-mile on our course, after that a way had to be cut through dense jungle. A pl of 2/18 R.G.R. helped as their kukris were invaluable for this kind of work. The rate of progress was about ¼-mile an hour and often less.

"Darkness fell soon after we entered the jungle. There were three people checking distance but not knowing our exact position when we started made the exact course we were following problematical.

"The suffering of the wounded during this nightmare of a march was unspeakable. Their stoicism and heroism was beyond comment, many of them raised a smile on the few occasions when the C.O. was

1942

able to get back to them to utter a few words of encouragement.
Five of them died during the night.

"*Jan 29.* Dawn found us very weary and hungry about to cross a large swamp. From here Lt Hutchison (5 Sikh), Bde I.O., was sent on ahead with five men of the Bde Int Sec to make contact with 8 Bde and to warn them that we were coming.

"He got through and found them near Kulai (well south of Sedenak, where we hoped they would be), a good bit of work.

"At some period during the previous night, an Indian,—Khan, belonging to the I.M.S., joined the Bde.

"He stated that he had been captured by the Japs just south of Layang Layang at about 1000 hrs on the 28 Jan.

"Later under dire threats he had been sent by the enemy with a letter written in English to be delivered to the Indian troops, telling them that the Japs were friends of Indians and had no wish to fight them but only wished to fight the British. It further enjoined the Indians not to fire on the Japanese but to give themselves up when they would be well treated. He delivered the written message to Bde H.Q.

"The carrying of the wounded through jungle and swamp over great fallen logs, down precipitous slopes and up steep hill-sides, was a heart-breaking business and most tiring. The whole of this burden fell on the Bn who had been fighting and marching incessantly since the 23 Jan.

"As the wounded were obviously delaying the whole Bde the C.O. twice requested the Brig to leave the Bn to get the wounded out and to take the rest of the Bde on. He would not hear of it.

"That night found us in very difficult country—steep jungle-clad hillsides intersected with ravines and steep nalas, heavy rain making foot-holds difficult, and it was realised that we were at least ½-mile north of where we hoped to be. It was a physical impossibility to get the wounded over the hills so we turned south again and, striking the lower contours, at dawn on the 30th reached a wide belt of open country undulating but cleared of trees and all under pineapple and lalang.

"*Jan 30.* Immediately east rose a hill, the last buttress of the range whose lower contours we had been wearily traversing during the night.

"The bn commanders ascended it with difficulty and quickly identified it as Bukit Hantu (the hill of the ghosts).

"The exertion of this climb after two days and a night of incessant labour without sleep and food put a very severe strain on all of us.

"Despite considerable enemy air activity the Bde crossed the open belt in open formation without being seen, and—welcome event —each man was able to collect at least one pineapple.

1942

"Here we were joined by some seven Dogras dressed in mufti and belonging to the Baluch Regiment who informed us that 8 Bde had been driven out of Sedenak two nights previously.

"Leslie Davis now got hold of a Chinese as a guide which certainly saved time but made the checking of our course very difficult.

"About midnight the guide disappeared near a hut which contained two other Chinese who informed us that a force of some 500 Japs were in bivouac some few hundred yards ahead of us (even at that hr sounds of carousing could be heard) but the state of utter exhaustion and weariness of both officers and men precluded any hope of a successful night attack.

"At this check the whole Bde save for a few officers and the van gd pl fell fast asleep.

"One of the Chinese offered to guide us round the enemy forces in the neighbourhood and immediately set forth on a puzzling course and at a very rapid rate. It was some time before we could catch the leading group, halt them and get the rest of the Bde thoroughly woken up.

"After a number of very puzzling changes in direction the guide eventually left us under rubber about 1 mile east of the ry saying that we were now clear of the Japs in the neighbourhood and could go straight ahead.

"A halt was called for the column to close up and to plot a fresh course. On checking the Bn B Coy and the A.A. pl were missing.

"Two volunteers were called for to go back and try to make contact and to lead them round the way we had come. Medhi Khan, mess orderly, and L/Nk Ishaq, signaller, immediately volunteered and went back and the Brig ordered the adv to continue.

"*Jan 31.* The column dragged wearily on, the carrying of the wounded (still only carried by the Bn) trying the men sorely in their exhausted state.

"At 1100 hrs hearing from a Kling (Tamil) that a big coolie settlement equipped with a dispensary lay some ½-mile away, it was decided to leave the wounded in it with a doctor and men to look after them.

"Bde ordered all loads to be lightened and ammunition to be reduced to 5 magazines per V.B. Here we at last abandoned our 3-in. mortars, two of which with 70 rounds of ammunition the mortar pl had carried since the afternoon of the 27th without a word of complaint or any suggestion of leaving them—a very stout effort and probably constituting a record carry for this very useful weapon.

"A Coy were detailed to take over the wounded, see them properly fixed up in the settlement with the doctor, and then proceed independently to the coast east of Johore.

1942

"(All these wounded eventually recovered and are now back in India).

"The Bn, now consisting of C and D Coys and H.Q. were still adv gd. Our course was roughly east of south and about 2½ miles east of the ry. The country was under rubber very undulating and very tiring as we were crossing the grain.

"That evening after protest to Bde about some of their personnel who were crowding on to adv gd H.Q., the S.C. picked up a piece of very dirty cloth which had once been white and tying it to a branch had it carried to denote the foremost limit of Bde H.Q. A most unfortunate occurrence the significance of which failed to penetrate our senses numbed as they were with fatigue, hunger and lack of sleep.

"*Feb 1.* By 0200 hrs everyone in the Bde was exhausted and unable to go further. A halt was called and we slept till dawn. A number of motor cycle patrols were heard moving on estate roads during the night.

"At dawn the adv was continued. During the morning two enemy cycle patrols were seen and about 1100 hrs enemy opened fire on the Bde from the front and rt flank. Sub. Sampuran Singh, C Coy, and some five men of H.Q. & C Coy were hit in the first burst of fire.

"There were probably not more than 60 Japs all told but there was little fight left in the Bde most of whom were in the last stages of exhaustion, all of whom were starving. There was also another demoralizing factor not realized at the time, the sign put up to mark Bde H.Q.

"There was confusion for some minutes, except in the case of the left fwd Van Gd pl (13 pl Jemdr. Ajit Singh C Coy).

"This pl went straight for the enemy nearest them killed 3 and captured the enemy's mortar and its amn which they later brought in.

"Meanwhile with D Coy and 2 pls of C we formed three sides of a square on a slight eminence and the rest of the Bde reformed in the rubber behind us. (Here we were later joined by Gannon C Coy Comdr and Jemdr Ajit Singh and his pl bringing in with them the enemy's mortar and its ammn.)

"It was obvious that most of the tps were incapable of further offensive effort and the Brig decided to extricate the Bde.

"The bn was detailed as rear gd, and the remainder of the Bde withdrew through the rubber. We remained in position for 20 mins. to enable the Bde to get clear (ample time in rubber) and were engaged with enemy to our front and with other parties attempting to work round on our left.

"Then we fixed bayonets formed a square of sorts and started to withdraw slowly through the rubber.

1942

"The enemy made no serious attempt to follow up. (He probably had quite a number of prisoners to look after taken at the beginning of the action and had also learnt to his cost that exhausted as we were there was still a sting or two left in us).

"Although we withdrew slowly as that was all we were capable of doing, the enemy ceased to worry us after the first few hundred yards. The ground now became very broken; this, the trees and the physical condition of the troops played havoc with our formation and the head soon lost direction. The C.O. who possessed one of the few compasses in the bn now moved up from the rear party to lead the adv exhorting the men to keep going for another mile when they could have a long rest.

"(Very soon after the C.O. had left them, the rear party Comdr, Capt Gurmit Singh collapsed and most of his coy remained behind with him).

"Reaching the head at last the C.O. halted them and waited for the rest to close up. During this wait, talking to Sub Major Sucha Singh and Jemdr Ajit Singh, they told him that when on the previous afternoon the tps had seen the dirty piece of rag carried in front of Bde H.Q. most of them had thought that the Bde had decided to surrender.

"It was now well after midday on the 1st Feb. For ten days since the 23 Jan, the Bn had been marching, fighting or digging without rest. They had suffered one hundred casualties killed and wounded and had inflicted more than twice that number on the enemy. For the last five days since the morning of the 27 Jan they had had no food, except for the cold remains of their looted rations picked up on the morning of the 28 Jan.

"Many of them had now reached the limit of their endurance.

"Not many troops in this campaign had endured so much and fought so hard and so successfully.

"After waiting 20 minutes we pushed on 8 officers and V.C.Os and about 30 N.C.Os and men.

"We reached the jungle but finding it too thick for progress turned south where after two miles along a rd under a blazing sun, through acres of open pineapple plantation we heard the noise of approaching M.T. Hastily preparing an ambush we awaited their arrival just below a crest. They turned out to be an Austin 7 and two lorries laden with Chinese and sugar.

"A patrol was sent back a short way to see if any stragglers were in sight, then emptying the transport we turned it about called in the patrol and proceeded in M.T. (a proceeding which thoroughly appealed to the men who raised a slight cheer as we moved off).

"Some three miles on we found the remnants of the Bde. The

1942

place was about 4 miles north of the Tebran river bridge. The Brig told us that he had received information that the bridge had been destroyed. He told us to take the trucks as far as the bridge and then send them back empty to the Bde in its then position.

"We had a break-down on the way and stopping to repair it we were overtaken by Leslie Davis and two Officers in a light truck who had come on after us from Bde. We met them again ½-mile north of the bridge which they reported destroyed and being repaired by Japanese tps and hundreds of local labour.

"We debussed and sent the trucks back with a report to Bde and telling them that we would make for the coast south of Plentong.

"When the trucks arrived back the Bde was not there. (We learnt that night, that a short time after we left they had found a guide who offered to show them a ford over the Tebran river and had moved off).

"Pushing on we shortly stopped another lorry and using estate roads and tracks eventually succeeded in driving on to the beach about one mile east of the Tebran river mouth.

"We found a sampan (canoe) hidden in the village, and Capts Russell Roberts (Actg 2 i/c) Gannon and the Sub Major crossed the strait in it to the Naval Base.

"After dark a patrol boat came across and we boarded it having been joined by Leslie Davis and the party who had gone back with the trucks.

"During the night Lyons (A Coy) who had been sent off with the wounded, arrived with a pl of A Coy. (Finding the village closer than he expected he had sent off two of his pls to catch up the Bde. They had no compass and were naturally soon lost).

"A party of officers from the Bde also arrived stating that owing to the complete exhaustion of the remnants of the Bde it had decided to capitulate.

"All other forces on the mainland had been withdrawn to the Island of Singapore and the causeway blown two days previously.

"SINGAPORE

"*Feb 2.* Hospitals and rest camps were combed for men and all that was left of the Bn concentrated under canvas near Teck Hock village. The total was just over 200 including all M.T. personnel, B Echelon, and one carrier pl under Donaldson complete. These were organized into a very small H.Q., 2 sections of carriers, one Sikh company and one P.M. company less a pl.

"Promotions were made and training of everyone in their new roles carried out. Morale was excellent and we fought hard in the next few days for the retention of the 47th Sikhs as a unit. The C.O. was ordered away to command another Bn, but thanks to the good record

1942

of the Bn during the campaign our appeal to the Corps Commander General Heath, succeeded.

"*Feb 6.* On 6th Feb orders were received for the amalgamation for tactical purposes with 2/12 F.F.R. This Bn was in worse plight than us, their total strength being under 150, largely M.T. and B Echelon personnel. However, some 400 reinforcements of officers and men for the 2/12 were about to be disembarked.

"*Feb 7.* Orders received to join 8 Bde of 11 Div in the Nesoon area on the 8th and advance party sent off that day.

"*Feb 8.* Orders cancelled and later orders received to join 2 Malay Infantry Bde in the Changi area. Very heavy artillery fire was heard throughout the night and we learnt next day that the Japs had landed on the N.W. of the Island on the sector held by the Australian Div. From the date of our arrival on the Island, Singapore and especially the dock area had been bombed daily by Jap planes with very little opposition from our fighters of whom but few remained.

"*Feb 9.* 2/12 F.F.R. reinforcements arrived during the morning. It required the personal intervention of General Heath, Corps Comdr, to get them out of the M.R.C., and during the day the Bn, using its own transport in a shuttle service, moved to its sector on the north coast, holding from incl Serangoon creek to incl Tampines creek.

"The C.O. saw more than half the Bn for the first time after they had moved into position.

"*The Sikh Battalion*

"Designated as above and under the command of Lt Col Parkin, the Bn was organized into a small H.Q. Coy and into five rifle coys.

A Coy	Sikhs of 5/11
B Coy	(Dogras of 2/12
	(P.Ms of 5/11
C Coy	P.Ms of 2/12
D Coy	Sikhs of 2/12
E Coy	Pathans (Territorials from 11/12)

"The fifth coy was formed owing to an almost total lack of specialists for H.Q. Coy. Despite intensive efforts equipment was lacking everywhere. There were insufficient L.M.Gs for even one per pl. 350 men had no bayonets, (the reinforcements arrived without them). There were 5 Tommy guns for the whole Bn. There were no stretchers.

"*Feb 10.* The whole of the night of the 9th and all the 10th was spent in digging defences and wiring. We found to our surprise that no defences of any kind had been prepared on this sector. By evening defences were well forward, all the beach wired and telephone communications established with coys.

1942

"*Feb 11.* At 1030 hrs an officer arrived from Corps H.Q. with orders for Bn to proceed forthwith to Braddell rd N.W. of Singapore coming under orders of "Massey Force".

"That afternoon found the bn holding X rds, Adam and Syme roads, under fairly heavy mortar fire and constant bombing. Our first line transport was caught, reserve ammunition, mortar ammunition and signal trucks being destroyed.

"The remainder was saved by the heroism of our M.T. personnel who drove the trucks out of a small and difficult harbour midst the blaze and crackle of exploding ammunition. Fortunately all that could be saved was got out before the mortar ammunition (450 rounds) went up with a tremendous explosion.

"A small force of details from M.R.Cs was in the neighbourhood and a bn of Suffolk was supposed to be moving through us onto the club buildings on the golf course. However, they went off in the direction of Bt Timah Rd, though we tried to deflect them. Their last coy was stopped by Bde and sent to the right place.

"Late that night orders received from Massey Force for bn to proceed at dawn to west of junction Adam-Bt Timah roads.

"*Feb 12.* Moved at dawn leaving B Coy (Gannon) to hold X roads until relieved by Cambridge.

"The situation was confused. All one could gather was the Japs had landed on the N.W. of the Island on 8/9 Feb. The Australian Div had completely failed to stop them and had withdrawn. The enemy had then advanced to the vicinity of Racecourse Village and were now advancing astride the Bt Timah Rd. A counter-attack by a force called Tom Force consisting of Norfolks, Sherwood Foresters and Recce Bn (without vehicles) had failed to stop them.

"The bn moved to vicinity south of Walten Park and north of Bt Timah Rd arriving about 0800 hrs, the sky being full of enemy aircraft and none of ours in evidence.

"Troops British and Australian were coming back in groups along the Bt Timah Rd; they seemed in poor form.

"A sec of carriers under Donaldson was sent down the rd to find out the situation ahead and we made contact with a bn of Suffolk on our right front. No further orders were received from Massey Force.

"At 0900 hrs Tom Force Comdr came down the rd and told us to cover the occupation of a line he was going to form along Adam and Farrer roads.

"Donaldson returned and reported a small packet of British troops some 800 yds ahead who were withdrawing in contact with the enemy.

"The situation on the flanks was not known.

"By 0930 hrs all our own troops had passed through the bn including the bn of Suffolks on our right.

"We were then subjected to very heavy bombing from the air followed by intensive mortar and artillery fire and suffered a number of casualties.

"The reinforcements stood up to it quite well. About 1200 hrs Lt Col Carpenter (1 Cambridge) arrived and confirmed that there was a large gap on our right between his bn and ours. On the left we failed to make contact with anyone.

"Captain Hawkins, adjutant, now went on a motor-cycle (a) to find Massey Force H.Q. and tell them what we were doing, (b) to find Gannon and his coy who should have rejoined long ago. We did not see Hawkins again until the 14th Feb. He was blown off his cycle by a bomb burst and woke up in hospital.

"At 1230 hrs two enemy tanks appeared down the Bt Timah Rd. They were fired on and withdrew, frightened, probably, by the sight of an A/Tank gun on the side of the rd pointing straight down it. It was not manned.

"At 1300 hrs our own arty (Australian we learnt afterwards) commenced a heavy bombardment of our fwd coys positions.

"Our own F.O.O. had had no communication with his guns since he had joined us. Eventually we sent him back to Tom Force H.Q. to try from there to get this shelling by our own arty stopped.

"At 1330 hrs when fwd coys had reported 24 casualties from our own guns they were withdrawn to an alternative position, previously reconnoitred, some 150 yds back.

"Whilst these coys were being withdrawn to their new position, the F.O.O. returned from Tom Force with orders for the bn to withdraw and rendezvous some hundred yards east of Adam Rd and north of Bukit Timah Rd.

"We withdrew to this point passing through the Recce Bn at about 1430 hrs. There was no enemy pressure or interference during the withdrawal.

"Under orders from Tom Force the Bn now moved into position from exclusive rd junction south along Farrer Rd with Bn H.Q. and reserve coys on Cluny Hill. B Coy now rejoined.

"There was a gap on our left of some 1000 yds beyond which our patrols made contact with a coy of Gordons. Our carriers patrolled the gap continuously by day. Fighting patrols from reserve coys patrolled it by night.

"There was no further enemy pressure on our front that day. A little sniping, mortaring and arty fire and a grenade attack on the carrier patrol, which wounded two men, was all that occurred.

"Feb 13. Brig Backhouse, 54 Bde, 18 Div, arrived to take over the front and some kind of order began to be evident.

"There was considerable increase in enemy mortaring, arty fire

and air bombing, but no infantry attack. Our own arty again shelled
us unmercifully, practically wiping out the whole of our P.M. pl
under Hav Feroze Khan who was badly wounded himself.

"At 1700 hrs the bn was relieved by two bns, Suffolks and Dogras,
and moved into Bde reserve on Raffles Hill.

"Some half-dozen casualties from shelling occurred in the night,
mostly in C Coy.

"*Feb 14.* At 0930 hrs on orders received from Bde the Bn moved
north of the Bt Timah rd to deal with a supposed break-through by
the Japs from the north. This report proved incorrect. Bn was then
ordered to hold a line from Mount Pleasant Rd, along south of Bt
Brown to Kheam Hock Rd, with two coys, the remainder of the bn was
to be the Bde reserve about half way between the Bt Timah Rd and
Bt Brown. There were some Norfolks west of Bn H.Q., and on the
left of the fwd coys, which were facing north. The Foresters were
beyond the Norfolks while details of the Recce Bn and machine
gunners were along the Mt Pleasant Rd.

"The position here was, and remained, nebulous. Patrols were
sent out to clear it up and these suffered casualties but could give
little information of value. (Naik Amar Singh ex-bugler was killed
on one of these patrols) and a few casualties occurred from enemy
arty and mortar fire.

"About 1730 hrs the enemy started a heavy mortar and arty
bombardment which lasted 20 minutes, stopped for 3 minutes and
then commenced again. Suspecting something the reserve coys were
stood to and as they were moving into position fire was opened on
to Bn H.Q. by three small L.M.G. groups very close to.

"We cleared the ridge with A Coy losing unfortunately A/Sub
Ajit Singh and a couple of men who were wounded just as we were
shaking out. The enemy withdrew hurriedly but we came under very
heavy S.A. fire from our own troops in rear.

"A lot of confusion seems to have occurred in this part of the
front and, numbers of troops having withdrawn, the Brig commenced
forming a line along the Mount Pleasant Rd. Some officers had
reported to him that the Sikhs had been cut up and a message from
Bde ordering the taking up of this new line was delivered to the
fwd coys just south of Bt Brown and they withdrew to this new
position.

"At 2100 hrs finding neither enemy nor any of our own troops in
our vicinity an officer (Woodrow) was sent back to report the situation
to Bde. Troops were sent back and the original line reformed by dawn.

"Capt Hawkins rejoined most opportunely about 1800 hrs none
the worse for his bombing. Throughout this day, and the next, enemy
planes were over continuously and flying very low.

1941-2

"*Feb 15.* At about 1200 hrs a car with a white flag passed through along the Bt Timah Rd and we learnt that terms were being sought. Later we were informed that owing to the lack of water (the enemy had cut the supply), very heavy casualties amongst the civilians (the town was burning and under continuous arty fire and (air) bombardment) and lack of ammunition it had been decided to surrender and that fire would cease at 1600 hrs.

"Fire ceased that night at about 1930 hrs.

"The short campaign was over and for causes beyond our control had ended in defeat.

"The Bn when given an objective to take, took it; when given a position to hold, held it; in no instance did the bn withdraw from any position until ordered to.

"They had proved not unworthy of the proud traditions handed on to them by their predecessors.

"*Awards*

"The following immediate awards were granted in 1942—

Lt Col J. H. D. Parkin D.S.O.	Bar to D.S.O.
A/Sub Ajit Singh	I.O.M. 2nd Class
10231 Sep Basta Singh	I.O.M. 2nd Class
Jemdr Nagindar Singh (died as P.O.W.)	I.O.M. 2nd Class
14320 Nk Gurdev Singh	I.D.S.M.
16402 Sep Bhag Singh	I.D.S.M.

"*Periodic Awards*

Capt Taj Mohammad Khanzada M.C.	D.S.O.

"Complete list of honours and awards for the campaign has not yet been published."

So ends the *Diary of the 5th Bn. (D.C.O.), The Sikh Regiment in the Malaya Campaign—8 Dec. '41 to 15 Feb. '42.* It was decided after the war not to re-raise this grand battalion, but its name will live so long as courage, endurance, loyalty and selfless heroism are numbered among the finer virtues of the human race. Throughout its comparatively short life, the 47th Sikhs was known for efficiency, dependability and a standard of behaviour whether in peace or war, second-to-none. It showed these to the full during its many years of active service in France, Mesopotamia and Palestine in the First World War, and no one can read this story of its services in Malaya without again feeling the highest respect for the manliness and spirit that underlined its every action. Long may their memory remain.

6th Bn.   While disaster drew on to its climax in Singapore, *the 6th Battalion* toiled at frontier defences in the Khyber, though the Russian menace had receded and fighting troops were urgently needed elsewhere.

1941-2

    The 7th Battalion, in Razmak, now underwent some reorganization   7th Bn.
to enable it to meet the call for a draft for the newly-raising machine-
gun battalion. Although the Battalion was itself still eighty Sikhs
under-strength, it was obliged to find fifty non-commissioned officers
and men for the machine-gun battalion. The new organization
comprised three Sikh rifle companies, one Punjabi-Mohammedan rifle
company, a Punjabi-Mohammedan mortar platoon on the peace scale,
and details for the first half of the 7th Training Company at the
Training Battalion.

    Early in October, the Battalion received the first of the two
3-in. mortars that arrived during the month. The nucleus of the mortar
platoon had been started, and instructors were trained locally on
Brigade courses. On the 13th, the first draft of thirty-six Indian   13 Oct.
other ranks arrived from the Training Battalion. These were in
replacement of the first party for the 7th Training Company which
left under T/Capt. D. W. Lancaster, with Sub. Atma Singh and
twenty-eight other ranks on the next road-open day. On the 15th,   15 Oct.
the re-organization already referred to, was completed. On the
21st, the first party for the new machine-gun battalion was sent off.   21 Oct.

    Wear-and-tear on boots over the rocky hills soon resulted in a
change-over to chaplis as well, and road-protection duties continued
to be carried out without incident.

    On the 5th November, a draft of fifty-five Sikh other ranks arrived   5 Nov.
from the Training Battalion and soon settled down to their new duties.
On the 7th the remaining men for the machine-gun battalion were   7 Nov.
despatched.

    On the 20th November, "B" Company carried out a demonstration   20 Nov.
of the taking up and evacuating of a position for the benefit of new
battalions arrived in Razmak. On the 22nd, the Remount Officer,   22 Nov.
Northern Command, reporting on the Battalion's mules and chargers,
said: "This is the best turned-out unit I have seen, as yet, in
Northern Command. The greatest attention has been paid to every
detail of animal management and I consider it would be difficult to
find a more thoroughly satisfactory state of affairs."

    Two M.T. training vehicles arrived from Campbellpore on the
12th December, and training was started.   12 Dec.

    A change-over of trained personnel with recruits again took place
this month when a draft of eighty-one other ranks from the Training
Battalion who arrived on the 20th replaced two platoons (sixty other   20 Dec.
ranks), sent back to the Training Battalion on the 22nd for service   22 Dec.
overseas. One complete Sikh and one complete Punjabi-Mohammedan
platoon were sent. Finally, on the 31st, the second half of the   31 Dec.
7th Training Company was sent off.

    The winter had now set in, and some of the worst snowfalls for   January

1941-2

many years took place in the latter part of December, and all through January. Heavy work clearing the road was a natural consequence, between Razmak and m.s. 65, to let the convoys through. Training, such as it was, was mostly in barracks, and, as the Battalion had just received 12 V.Bs, the opportunity was taken to get well acquainted with these.

February   On the 1st February, the troops listened in to a special broadcast on the wireless by Lieut.-Col. J. J. Purves, M.C., and twenty Indian ranks of the 4th Battalion.

25 Feb.   What is described as the longest road-protection day on record marked the 25th February. The Battalion was out from 6 a.m. till 9 p.m. It began snowing early in the day and continued snowing heavily throughout the day and on into the night. The condition of the road, with ice beneath the snow, can be imagined, and lorries had to be manhandled at a graded portion on Razmak Narai. The Brigade Commander congratulated the Battalion on its good work. This pleasant

28 Feb.   appreciation was followed up three days later after the Brigade Commander's administrative inspection, by a similarly appreciative report.

8th Bn.   *The 8th Battalion* had its officer establishment further expanded by the posting of two more officers on the 20th September. Shortly after, it began to emerge from the preliminary training stage, and,

October   during the first week in October, took part in a large-scale air-defence exercise under Northern Command. Apart from local duties, the Battalion provided one rifle company to guard the railway tunnels near Khairabad on the way to Attock, and the week spent under canvas in a perimeter camp of its own making—the first actual duty performed by the Battalion since its raising—was an excellent introduction to life under service conditions on the Frontier.

20 Oct.   Maj. W. R. Lloyd-Jones (formerly Sikh Pioneers, and later 1st Battalion) joined as permanent Second-in-Command on the 20th October. Maj. Walter took over command of "B" Company (Punjabi-Mohammedans).

November   The Battalion received its first allocation of M.T. in November—and learnt that in the wartime army, the term "M.T." covered a good deal, including in this case ten of the most decrepit buses imaginable. It took every trick in the calendar to keep them revving—but it was a move in the right direction; and with 2nd/Lieut. Wattie as M.T. Officer, and one Viceroy's commissioned and six non-commissioned officers who had just completed an instructors' course at Ahmednagar, training of potential drivers began at once. This so-called M.T. remained with the Battalion for six months, and was all that was ever available for training purposes.

1941-2

On the other hand, however, the M.T. personnel must have been without equal for rapid, extemporized running repairs.

The second Recruit Division having been attested, and Battalion training started, more scope was possible. There was a Commanding Officer's parade every Saturday. This, after the inevitable fast cross-country march—traceable perhaps as a legacy from earlier days in the 2nd Battalion—developed into tactical schemes of progressively increasing scope, in the hills around Manki and the area of Walai camp. Although this was the beginning of serious training for active operations, and was accepted as such, those were still the halcyon days when a mess secretary thought in terms of a brace of mules to carry the officers' lunch; and never less than four dozen of the best form of operational nourishment accompanied the Battalion. Needless to add, however much the mules may have grunted on the outward march, they always had an easy journey home.

Shortly before Christmas, 2nd/Lieut. Chittiapa, with one Viceroy's commissioned officer, and thirty other ranks, was detailed, as a complete platoon, as reinforcement for the 5th Battalion in Malaya, and moved over to the Training Battalion to join the other similar reinforcements collecting there. (These reinforcements were eventually detained as a nucleus for the 14th Battalion, as by the time all battalions' parties had reached Nowshera, Singapore had fallen. This does not suggest much urgency in the preparation of the draft. Singapore did not fall until February 15th.) December

About the same time, also, the Battalion was detailed for a tour of duty at Landi Khana, leaving Nowshera on the 30th December. Its task was to assist in the construction of the Khyber defences west of Landi Kotal.

Though ordered to move at "fullest possible strength", the Battalion marched out only 401 strong. This was partly due to the demand for a draft of one Viceroy's commissioned officer and forty-five other ranks for the newly-raising machine-gun battalion just after Christmas. A small depot had also to be left behind in Umbeyla Lines. This was put under Capt. Hassan, who had handed over as adjutant to 2nd/Lieut. Donaldson on the 1st December, and who was now in command of "D" Company.

The march to Landi Khana was carried out in four easy stages. The first night was spent in Pabbi, and the next in Peshawar, where the Battalion spent New Year's Eve. Consequent celebrations in Peshawar Club brought their own reward to some of the officers next day, but the Battalion reached Ali Masjid in good time and spirits. Next day, the 2nd, the Battalion crossed the Kotal, and dropped easily down the steep winding road to Landi Khana, on the Afghan frontier.

30 Dec.
31 Dec.
1 Jan.
2 Jan.

The stay in Landi Khana was a short one, but not lacking in

1942

gaiety. Officially, the troops were categorized as "unskilled labour" assisting the Indian Engineers and Military Engineering Service personnel. Actually, more often than not, they did the skilled work themselves. Defence work undertaken by the Battalion consisted of communication and fire trenches, and platoon positions, mainly in solid rock, for which blasting explosives were required. To enable the troops to cope with the explosives, the sappers gave officers, Viceroy's commissioned officers and non-commissioned officers two days' instruction, and then left them to it, with the strict injunction never to use more than three sticks of gelignite in any one "mine". (These "mines" were holes 3 inches across and 2 to 3 feet deep bored in the rock by hand). They also made it clear that the gelignite should be tamped in with a wooden stick only; and added that the fuse should not be placed till after the gelignite had been secured in the "mine".

These instructions were no doubt admirable, but with the Sikhs in particular, once the novelty wore off, it became an every-day sight to see three or four bearded stalwarts gathered round a mine with a wild glint in their eyes, tamping in anything up to a dozen sticks of gelignite—one of them ready fused—with a steel crowbar. And many were the arguments who had fired the day's biggest mine when the men returned to camp. Strangely enough there were no accidents from this wild mis-use of explosives, though Brigade Headquarters in Landi Kotal were continually sending down urgent enquiries whether the gelignite dump had exploded, on hearing the noise of the latest masterpiece.

It was as well from some viewpoints that the men were kept interested, as the weather throughout the month was bitter. Freezing winds, sleet and rain swept the area. It was a severe winter right along the Frontier, as the 7th Battalion's experiences in Razmak showed. The day's work was an eight-hour day, but the men took well to this new type of soldiering, and by the time they left Landi Khana on the 5th February no less than 9 miles of trenches had been constructed, most of it in solid rock. The 6th Battalion was stationed in Landi Kotal during this time, and despite the long working hours, most of the 8th managed at least one visit, and enjoyed the hospitality of more congenial surroundings. A feature of the officers' mess in camp was the Whisky Mac, to keep out the cold at night, and no doubt comparable arrangements were made for the rank-and-file.

2nd/Lieut. Manico left the Battalion during January on acceptance for the newly-formed Parachute Battalion. But the big news item was that G.H.Q. had selected the 8th Battalion, together with five other Indian Infantry units, including the 9th Battalion of the Regiment,

1941-2

for conversion to a Light Anti-Aircraft role. The Indian Artillery had not hitherto included such troops, and this new decision reflected the march of events on India's eastern frontiers. The date for conversion was fixed for the 1st April, and meanwhile, the Battalion was ordered to pack up in Landi Kotal and move out onto the Khajuri Plain.

On the 5th February, accordingly, the Battalion marched out of Landi Khana. It marched straight up over the Kotal and down to Jamrud—26 miles in seven marching hours. This timing was stated by the Peshawar District staff to be a record for a battalion move through the Khyber with animal transport. Obviously the men felt no ill-effects, for they were away again next morning, to Fort Bara, and Jhansi and Milward Posts—the depot rejoining the Battalion from Nowshera. 5 Feb.

6 Feb.

Here we will leave the 8th Battalion till the next chapter when we shall regretfully wind up the story of the Battalion's stay with the Regiment; but a brief note will be added on its subsequent activities in its new role.

Some administrative details will be found in the 9th Battalion record below.

The 9th Battalion, after organizing and equipping in Nowshera during the hot weather, had been brigaded with the 7th Battalion 15th Punjab Regiment and the 4th Battalion 8th Gurkha Rifles. In October, it moved to Mansar near Attock, and joined the 7th Indian Division. A strenuous but pleasant cold weather followed, including what was significantly called "water training" in the extremely chilly river Indus. 9th Bn.

October

Off parade, the Battalion was finding its feet at hockey; and the basket-ball and volley-ball grounds were kept busy. The Divisional Club provided tennis facilities. Thanks to the six chargers on the establishment, the Commanding Officer, Lieut.-Col. E. C. Spencer, M.C., and two or three others, were able to hunt regularly with Wakely's hounds. Maj.-Gen. Wakely, commanding the 7th Indian Division, ran, at his own expense, a pack each of foxhounds and beagles. The C.O's wife and daughter represented Col. Spencer with the beagles.

As with the 8th Battalion, a surprise packet arrived in January, in a letter from G.H.Q. notifying the impending conversion of the 8th and 9th Battalions into Light Anti-Aircraft Artillery. Commanding Officers of the battalions detailed were to report to the Maj.-Gen., Royal Artillery, in Delhi, and here it was arranged that the 8th Battalion should become the 8th, and the 9th Battalion the 7th Lt. A.A. Regt., Indian Artillery. January

The C.O., having started life in the cavalry, felt he had run the

1942

whole gamut—foot, horse, and guns; and his family suggested he might try the Royal Marines as a logical follow-on. His record, however, could not stand up to John Walker's in the 8th, with a spell of service in the Royal Air Force (or was it the Royal Flying Corps?) All concerned were evidently full of enthusiasm at their new role, and the prospects were bright.

Sepoys were to be re-named Gunners, of course. The Sikh Regimental connection was to be retained through the small quoit which officers were to be allowed to retain as buttons for the chin-strap, and in front of the side-cap. The quoit was also to be worn on the gunner flash on the topi.

The Battalion was to retain all its infantry officers, but thirty Royal Artillery officers were to be posted, bringing the establishment up to forty-one. A complement of British non-commissioned officers and fitters was temporarily posted as instructors until Sikh and P.M. non-commissioned officers were considered competent Detachment Commanders.

Peshawar was selected as the Battalion location for conversion and the troops duly marched there from Mansar, organized as Regimental Headquarters (Sikh), and three batteries (two Sikh and one Punjabi-Mohammedan). As Regimental Headquarters was entirely Sikh, Sub.-Maj. Mian Ahmed I.D.S.M. was transferred in the same capacity to the 15th Battalion, and Sub. Ujager Singh (4th Battalion) became Sub.-Maj.

M.G. Bn.   Meanwhile, towards the end of 1941, G.H.Q., India, had decided on the formation of a *Machine Gun Battalion* in the Regiment, to form on the 15th January, 1942. In point of fact, thanks to co-operation from other battalions of the Regiment, from whom the nucleus of trained personnel was drawn, the Battalion was functioning much before this date. It was established, in the first case, in Cassels Lines, a collection of kutcha barracks on the Manki road in Nowshera.

The training of Viceroy's commissioned and non-commissioned officers was under way, and most had returned from courses, by

January   January, 1942. Four months intensive individual training followed. Simultaneously, M.T. training was carried out with civilian transport,

February   pending receipt of thirty-five vehicles and four motor-cycles in February. Later in the year, the battalion was provided with its full complement of 102 wheeled and eight tracked vehicles.

At the outset, the Battalion was provided with three Regular Indian Army officers, with a large number of emergency commissioned officers fresh from the United Kingdom. In the ranks, apart from the trained nucleus sent by other battalions, the majority of the men came from recruits from the Training Battalion. Composition was half Sikh and half Punjabi-Mohammedan. The first Commanding Officer

1942

was Lieut.-Col. R. Gordon, of the 5th Battalion, posted from
G.H.Q.

The 25th Battalion, in Prem Nagar, remained on general duties 25th Bn.
connected with the internees' and Italian Generals' camps.

Chapter VI

MARCH TO AUGUST 1942

Backscreen

Pacific The summer of 1942 brought no relief to the hard-pressed Allies except in the slowly-won naval command of the Pacific.

In that vast sea area, the Americans were building up a carrier-borne air offensive to cover the consolidation of a supply line to
January Australia. In January, an air station had been established on Johnston Island, and that already on Palmyra Island had been rein-
2 Feb. forced. Troops had then occupied the Fiji Islands. In February, Christmas and Fanning Islands were occupied, and Canton Island taken over. American forces were established in New Caledonia and at Efate in the New Hebrides; and the U.S. naval base in the
28 Mar. Solomons was strengthened. On the 28th March, work was begun on a new base on Espiritu Santo in the New Hebrides.

The Japanese had been equally busy strengthening their own bases in New Guinea, New Britain and the Solomon Islands; and on
3 May the 3rd May, they began to occupy Tulagi on Florida Island in the Solomons. The Americans were thoroughly on the alert, and news of this last enterprise was brought in by an air patrol the same day.

A United States naval force consisting of the carrier *Yorktown*, three cruisers and six destroyers, was cruising in the Coral Sea west of the New Hebrides at the time, and four planes were promptly detached to bomb Tulagi.

Meanwhile, naval reinforcements were on their way, including the carrier *Lexington*, seven heavy cruisers, two light cruisers and nine
5 May destroyers; and two days later, on the 5th May, these were also on the scene.

6 May On the 6th May, the Japanese main naval forces were located in the Bismarck Archipelago, north of New Guinea, and north-west of the more distant New Hebrides.

The centre of gravity was thought to be moving towards Port Moresby on the south coast of Papua, which is itself part of New Guinea, lying at the eastern end of that vast island. It was hence concluded that the Japanese Fleet would be moving in that direction, and would in due course be passing round via Milne Bay at the eastern end of the island. Part of the Allied force was accordingly stationed to intercept, while the rest steamed north on reconnaissance, for the Japanese covering force.

1942

Next day, the 7th, aircraft from the *Lexington* and *Yorktown* discovered and sank the Japanese carrier *Shoho*, at a loss of five aircraft to themselves. On the 8th, two Japanese carriers, four heavy cruisers and several destroyers, were contacted, but again the honours lay with the Allies. Although losses were inflicted on them, including the *Lexington*, which had to be abandoned, the battle altogether cost the Japanese one carrier, three heavy cruisers, one light cruiser, two destroyers and several transports sunk, and more than twenty ships damaged.

7 May

8 May

Significantly, this naval action created history in a new sense, being the first sea engagement on record in which the surface craft involved did not exchange a shot.

This Battle of the Coral Sea was not decisive, and the Japanese were not prepared to let matters stand. Within a month, on the 3rd June, two fresh naval events took place. Far away to the north, an air attack was launched on Dutch Harbour, the American naval base in the Aleutians; and on the same day, American naval aircraft sighted a Japanese Fleet steaming east, 470 miles south-west of Midway Island, in the Central Pacific. U.S. heavy bombers took off that afternoon from Midway Island, and went out to bomb the Japanese Fleet.

3 June

Enemy activity in the Central Pacific following on the Coral Sea action, had been foreseen, and a Central Pacific Fleet was available, consisting of the carriers *Enterprise, Hornet,* and *Yorktown*, seven heavy cruisers, one light cruiser, fourteen destroyers and twenty submarines, supported by a Marine Corps air group on Midway Island.

On the 4th June, a second enemy fleet was located 180 miles north of Midway Island. The appreciation indicated that this great concentration of enemy naval force—the largest yet assembled for Pacific operations—was aimed in the first instance at Midway Island.

4 June

Fierce air fighting developed immediately, every available American land-based or carrier-borne aircraft being engaged. The latter went in without fighter protection and suffered heavily. None-the-less, two enemy carriers were set on fire and a third was sunk. Later, a heavy air attack by thirty-six planes sent up from the Japanese carrier *Hiriyu*, developed over the *Yorktown*, which had to be abandoned—being later sunk, in tow, by an enemy submarine. The *Hiriyu* herself was then set on fire by aircraft from the *Enterprise* and was left in a sinking condition.

Action, however, was not confined to the fleets, and Midway Island itself took a heavy share of the bombing.

By the 5th, the Japanese were in full retreat. Air pursuit took further toll of them, but bad weather then intervened.

5 June

As in the Coral Sea, no surface ships made contact in this decisive

1942

Battle of Midway Island. Casualties were suffered by the Americans; and in the air attacks they had lost 92 officers and 215 men. Japanese losses in ships were estimated at four carriers, two large cruisers, three destroyers, one transport and one auxiliary sunk; and three battleships, three heavy cruisers, one light cruiser, several destroyers and three transports or auxiliaries damaged. More important, this decisive action left the Japanese at a disadvantage in carriers, actual or building, from which they never recovered. Henceforward, the Japanese Navy could only engage American naval forces at night, or under cover of land-based aircraft. The balance of naval power in the Pacific had passed to the Allies, and, though much heavy naval fighting was still to come, the supply line to Australia was secure

Undeterred, however, by these reverses, the Japanese continued to prosecute their plans against Port Moresby, together with the establishment of a powerful air-base to its east, in the Solomon Islands. Selecting a point on the northern coast of Guadalcanal, just **July** south of Florida Island, they started work on an air-field in July. From it, land-based aircraft were to operate against American installations in the New Hebrides and New Caledonia, as well as protecting the sea flank of the projected advance in Papua.

21/22 July The Japanese led off on this latter operation on the 21st and 22nd July with a landing on the north-east coast of New Guinea, at Gona. Forcing their way inland, they presently compelled the Australian militia battalion at Kokoda, midway between Gona and Port Moresby, **August** to withdraw back towards Port Moresby. Early in August, the Japanese occupied Kokoda, and began slowly advancing thence through the thick jungle, southwards.

American forces, meanwhile, landed on Florida and Guadalcanal **7 Aug.** Islands on the 7th August. They met little opposition, surprisingly enough, and occupied the partly finished Japanese air-base, which they named Henderson Field.

The establishment of an American base on Guadalcanal, however, **9 Aug.** necessarily took some time, and on the 9th August, in the early hours of the morning, Japanese naval forces suddenly took a hand. The American Fleet had the worst of it in the action which then developed off Savo Island, lying a little north-west of Guadalcanal and west of Florida Island. Four cruisers were sunk—the Australian *Canberra* and the American *Quincy, Vincennes* and *Astoria*—but the Japanese withdrew that evening, and the landing went ahead.

The Japanese were not prepared to accept this setback in the Solomons, and energetic preparations were put in hand in the Rabaul area, away to the north-west, in New Britain. A large and well-protecte convoy was rapidly organized and despatched, but it was intercepted on the way, and in the Battle of the Eastern Solomons which followed,

1942

between the 23rd and 25th of August, the Japanese were repulsed. 23/25 Aug.
Next day, the 26th, the second phase of the Japanese plan against 26 Aug.
Port Moresby was launched. A force about 2,000 strong was put
ashore north of Milne Bay at the eastern end of New Guinea, with
orders to seize the air-field. It seems they expected little opposition,
or a larger force would have been sent. In the event, however, they
were so roughly handled both on land and from the air, that on the
29th, they abandoned the project and re-embarked, with the loss of 29 Aug.
most of their supplies and with a casualty list which included 700
killed. Clearly, the American attack on Guadalcanal had upset
Japanese calculations, and absorbed all their available reserves. In
consequence, the land-column moving south of Kokoda towards Port
Moresby, was now left to carry on the operation single-handed and
without command of the air.

In the western Pacific, the fall of Malaya freed Japanese reinforcements for the operations in the Philippines, and the remaining Philippines
hopes of the beleaguered Americans in Bataan flickered out in an
eight-day Japanese offensive which began on the 1st April. Corregidor, 1 April
blocking the entrance to Manila Bay, fell on the 5th May, ringing 5 May
down the curtain on organized resistance in these islands.

An extension of Japanese activity south-westwards into the Indian Madagascar
Ocean also followed the fall of Malaya. Reinforcements of men and
stores on their way east to India from the United Kingdom were
accordingly diverted to Madagascar which it was feared might fall
into Japanese hands, and some sticky operations with the French
garrison there, followed. No Japanese attempt on the island was,
however, made.

In Burma, the confused situation at Pegu, where the garrison was Burma
cut off, and the steady infiltration of Japanese troops west and south-
west towards the communications up-country from Rangoon, led to
the abandonment of Rangoon on the 7th March, and a withdrawal 7 Mar.
northwards. The troops left Rangoon not a moment too soon—and it
was an open question when they reached a point 21 miles north of
Rangoon whether they would ever get through at all. However, after
hard fighting the road-blocks were cleared, and in the welcome pause
that followed, the 17th Indian Division fell gradually back towards
Prome on the Irrawaddy, whilst the 1st Burma Division fought a
delaying action up the Sittang to Toungoo, covering the concentration
of the Chinese Fifth and Sixth Armies. These armies were each
numerically something under the strength of a British division.
On the night of the 21st/22nd March, the 1st Burma Division began 21/22 Mar.

157

1942

to move across from Toungoo to the Irrawaddy on relief by the Chinese, to form, with the 17th Indian Division, the 1st Burma Corps. About the same time, the Royal Air Force suffered a locally decisive reverse at Magwe, 20 miles south of Yenangyaung, in the oil-fields, and were forced to withdraw to Loiwing, 400 miles to the north.

26 Mar. On the 26th, Japanese pressure began to increase against the positions round Prome. The 17th Indian Division put up a resilient
2 Apr. defence. Fierce fighting went on for some days, but on the 2nd April, the division was forced to withdraw north and north-east of Prome.
3 Apr. The withdrawal was continued next day through the 1st Burma
4/5 Apr. Division. By the night of the 4th/5th April, the force was back on a line 40 miles in extent, between Minhla and Taungdwingyi, where it remained some days.

10 Apr. On the 10th April, Japanese columns were reported moving north on tracks north-west of Taungdwingyi, and bitter fighting developed.
13/14 Apr. Pressure during the 13th and 14th on the 1st Burma Division south of Magwe, drove a wide gap between the two divisions, and the enemy pushed through, threatening the Yenangyaung oil-fields. Orders for the destruction of the oil-fields were issued on the night of the
16 Apr. 14th, and were successfully carried out by the evening of the 16th.
17/20 Apr. Between the 17th and 20th April, the 1st Burma Division, less its 2nd Brigade, west of the Irrawaddy, was cut off just north of Yenangyaung, and only succeeded in breaking out with the loss of most of its M.T., and with serious casualties in personnel and equipment.

In the eastern sector, the Chinese had withdrawn from Toungoo, opening the way for the Japanese into the southern Shan States, and round the exposed flank on that side. Bad enough as it was, the situation became infinitely worse when the Chinese 55th Division
21 Apr. was scattered on the 21st April. On the 22nd, Japanese armoured
22 Apr. units and motorized infantry were reported moving north on the open eastern flank towards Hsipaw and Lashio, which both lie on the road and railway running eastwards from Mandalay. On the night of
25/26 Apr. the 25th/26th April, evacuation of units and installations from Maymyo, 40 miles east of Mandalay on the Mandalay-Lashio line, was begun, and a withdrawal of the main forces in the Irrawaddy area, to some point northwards from Mandalay came under serious considera

Arrangements were made for stocking-up the road from Ye-U back to Kalewa on the Chindwin, for the withdrawal of the Burma Corps to India, and all unessential kit was abandoned to make lorries available for the purpose. Meanwhile, a force of two brigades was moved up astride the Chindwin towards Kalewa and Kalemyo. The balance of the Corps, less a strong detachment in the Myittha valley, would withdraw on Kalewa via Ye-U.

	1942

On the 29th April, it was accepted that the Chinese Fifth Army would withdraw up the Irrawaddy when Mandalay was given up. The 17th Indian Division, meanwhile, with the 7th Armoured Brigade under command, had been fighting a rearguard action on the axis Meiktila-Mandalay, with the Japanese 55th Division in close pursuit. A number of successful actions was fought between the 26th and 30th April, on which date the rearguard crossed the Ava Bridge to the Irrawaddy north bank and withdrew to its positions west of the river Mu. The Ava Bridge was blown at 11.50 p.m. that night.   29 Apr.

26/30 Apr.

This same day, the 30th, the Japanese were reported in Lashio, from whence they could directly threaten Bhamo and Myitkyina on the upper Irrawaddy. Other enemy forces were reported at Hsipaw and Maymyo. Precautions had to be taken in view of the consequent threat to the river line north of Mandalay, where casualties and evacuees were on their way by river to Katha, for evacuation by rail to Myitkyina and thence by air to India. Measures had also to be taken for the defence and evacuation of Katha, Bhamo and Myitkyina in consonance with these commitments.

On the 30th, the Japanese suddenly increased their pressure up the Chindwin, attacking and occupying Monywa where the troops were taken by surprise. This caused much embarrassment, though the situation was temporarily rectified next morning. Confused fighting followed, however, while the withdrawing troops made a safe getaway past Monywa. The 63rd Indian Infantry Brigade, which included the 1st Battalion of the Regiment, played some part in this difficult operation, which defeated the first Japanese attempt to get across the line of withdrawal.   30 Apr.

1 May

The route the troops were following was no first-class motor road. It was a sandy track over which rapid motion was not possible. Passing from Ye-U and via Kaduma, Pyingyaing and Thetkegyin, it ended at Shwegyin, 8 miles south of Kalewa. To reach Kalewa itself involved crossing a complicated 12-mile stretch of rocky country, which boasted no more than a footpath. It may be added here that it was due to this stretch of unmotorable country that most of the M.T. and all the tanks had later to be abandoned. Both the road-head at Shwegyin, and the path-head from Thetkegyin, lay on the east bank of the Chindwin. Kalewa lay opposite the footpath-head, on the western bank.

Over the whole route from Ye-U westwards, there were innumerable chaungs, or nalas, some dry and sandy, others wet; and there was a hill section between Pyingyaing and Thetkegyin with many rickety bridges constructed of brushwood or bamboo. Bad as the track was, traffic over it was still further complicated by the need to send back

1942

empty lorries to ferry forward more troops and wounded. This should be borne in mind when reading the 1st Battalion record below.

While infantry and mules could follow the footpath from Thetkegyin and be ferried across to Kalewa in country boats, everything else had to move via Shwegyin, and travel thence up to Kalewa by steamer. There were six steamers, each of which could take six to seven hundred men but not more than two lorries and two jeeps. A special vehicle flat was constructed, but embarkation from the beach at Shwegyin was difficult, and full use of this means of transportation could not be made. Consequently, on reaching Kalewa, the force was so deficient in transport that there was barely enough for the most essential loads. Fortunately, staging camps had been stocked up, and troops did not need to carry rations.

Northwards, after passing Kalemyo, the road to Tamu was a dirt-track through the jungle, and would become impassable when the approaching rains set in about the 15th May. There was therefore a race with the weather to be faced, as well as with the Japanese.

Over this road, from Ye-U, the withdrawal slowly passed, not closely followed up after a brush between the 7th Armoured Brigade and some enemy tanks on the 5th May north of Budalin. Various expedients were adopted for relieving the transport problem. These included the despatch of the left flank-guard of one infantry brigade via Pantha instead of Shwegyin; and of the rearguard, the 48th Indian Brigade, by steamer from Shwegyin to Sittaung, to relieve pressure on the Kalewa-Tamu section of the road.

5 May

On the 10th May, the covering force at Shwegyin was attacked by a Japanese battalion and mortars which had come upstream in landing-craft and disembarked a little below. Ferrying continued, and in the evening a Brigade counter-attack drove the enemy off. It was decided, however, that further ferrying from Shwegyin must cease, and that all remaining guns, tanks and motor vehicles on the right bank should be destroyed. From this point, however, the withdrawal continued unmolested. By the 17th, all troops were concentrated in the Tamu area, and shortly after, as the monsoon broke, arrived safely in their new locations.

10 May

17 May

The Chinese Fifth Army had meanwhile moved to Indaw on the railway something over half-way from Mandalay to Myitkyina. By that time, the Japanese were in Bhamo, 50 miles farther up the Irrawaddy, and directly threatening Myitkyina. It therefore abandoned hope of retaining touch with China, turned off west-north-west to Homalin, and over the Chin Hills to Imphal, where it arrived minus its transport on the 20th May.

20 May

The Japanese did not follow up, and a welcome breathing-space was gained during the long monsoon rains.

                                                                1942
 In the Western Desert, the Allies, by the beginning of February,   N. Africa
had been run back as far as Gazala. Between that point and Bir Hacheim,
40 miles south, a series of "boxes" was being organized, each
a mile or two square, and prepared for all-round defence. In front,
extensive unmanned minefields were planted.
 The four principal boxes were: firstly, Gazala, held by the 1st South
African Division; next, the 50th Divisional box some 15 miles to the
south-south-east; after that came Knightsbridge and the Guards
Brigade box where the Bir Hacheim-Acroma track crossed the Capuzzo
road; and finally the Bir Hacheim box held by a Free French brigade.
Between, and in rear of these four main positions, were other boxes,
and the fortified area of Tobruk. Defensive positions to lend added
depth were under preparation on the frontier.
 At this time, in the late spring, the Allies mustered in the Gazala
position the 1st and 2nd South African Divisions, the 50th Infantry
Division, the 1st Army Tank Brigade and the 9th Indian Infantry
Brigade in the XIIIth Corps; and the 1st and 7th Armoured Divisions
with four armoured brigades between them, the 201st Guards Brigade
Group, the 3rd Indian Motor Brigade Group, the 29th Indian Infantry
Brigade, and a Free French Brigade in the XXXth Corps. Other
formations joined seriatim after the impending battle began.
 Opposed to these were six Italian infantry divisions; the XXth
Italian Mobile Corps (made up of one armoured division—the Ariete—, and
one motorized division—the Trieste), the Afrika Corps (the 15th
and 21st Panzer Divisions), and the German 90th Light Division.
 Tank strengths were reckoned at 631 Allied, including 150 infantry
tanks and 160 Grants—the latter mounting 75-mm. guns—and an
improved establishment of anti-tank artillery, now including some
6-pounders, and additional tank transporters for recovery. The Axis
was credited with 550 tanks and some 90 self-propelled guns.
 Both sides were anxious to take the offensive, but Rommel was
ready first. On the afternoon of the 26th May, his armoured forces   26 May
moved southwards. Effective secrecy had been preserved, and it was
not until early next morning when some 200 tanks were reported south 27 May
of Bir Hacheim, that the move was discovered.
 The enemy armour now wheeled north in three columns, with the
Ariete Division on the left, the 21st Panzer Division in the centre,
and the 15th Panzer Division on the right. At 7.30 a.m. the 3rd Indian
Motor Brigade Group was over-run, and soon after the 4th Armoured
Brigade was driven back. The headquarters of the 7th Armoured
Division was surprised, and the attack moved on to Knightsbridge
where the 1st Armoured Division was engaged. By the evening, the
advanced screen had reached Acroma, El Duda and Sidi Rezegh, and
one small column had reached the coastal road. Most of these columns

1942	
28/31 May	were driven back, and Bir Hacheim stood firm under heavy attack. During the next four days the battle raged far and wide, but most fiercely west of the Knightsbridge box.
	Meanwhile the enemy had cleared a lane through the minefield on the Capuzzo road, and had started on another one 10 miles south. Between these points lay the British 150th Brigade box. On the 31st, Rommel's forces fell back on these two lanes, using the minefields
1 June	to protect their flanks; and, next day, under cover of a screen of anti-tank guns, they attacked the 150th Brigade box, over-ran it, and captured over 3,000 prisoners.
2 June	Next day, the 2nd, some mobile operations were undertaken against German communications from the south, but otherwise conditions
4 June	remained fairly stable. On the 4th, the 10th Indian Infantry Brigade which had now entered the battle, was moved up from the south by night against the flank of Rommel's box, in the "Lanes". Unfortunately however, the 22nd Armoured Brigade, and the 32nd Army Tank Brigade,
5 June	which were to have co-operated in this action on the 5th, both failed to make their objectives, with disastrous consequences to the Indian Brigade, which was over-run.
	Enemy pressure was now built up against Bir Hacheim. By the
10 June	10th, lack of ammunition and water made the post untenable. Most of the garrison got away, but the enemy was now free to act against the Knightsbridge box, and against El Adem, 15 miles east. Contact was made with the 2nd and 4th Armoured Brigades in that area on the
12 June	12th, with serious loss to the British, whose strength in armour was
13 June	now down to some 170 tanks. A last effort was made on the 13th to relieve pressure on Knightsbridge, but when this failed, there seemed no alternative but to get the garrison away while the opportunity
14 June	was there. This was done next morning—uncovering the Gazala and 50th Divisional boxes, whose garrisons were similarly withdrawn. The 50th Division was already cut off, with enemy astride its normal line of withdrawal, but by breaking away south-east through country over which enemy columns were freely moving, it made its get-away
15 June	safely. By midnight on the 15th June, most of the Division was at the Egyptian frontier. The 1st South African Division at Gazala had a more conventional withdrawal, covered by the Royal Air Force and by the 1st Armoured Division, which was kept busy heading off the enemy columns on the southern flank. Despite innumerable traffic jams in rear, the Division cleared Tobruk safely on the 15th also.
	Tobruk was surrounded and contained by an enemy force on the
17 June	17th June, while the main body continued the pursuit east, ambushing the 20th Indian Infantry Brigade at Gambut, about midway between
18 June	Tobruk and the Egyptian frontier, on the 18th. With his armour east of

Tobruk, Rommel was now well placed to turn and attack it on its weakest (eastern) face.

The defensive perimeter at Tobruk measured some 25 miles in length, and was nowhere in a good state of repair at this time. The garrison—for which there was no fighter cover—comprised the 2nd South African Division, less one brigade, the 32nd Army Tank Brigade, with some fifty infantry tanks, the 201st Guards Brigade, the 11th Indian Infantry Brigade, the 4th A.A. Brigade less eighteen guns, and a large number of details. The 11th Indian Infantry Brigade held the weak sector facing El Duda on the east.

Italian infantry advanced against the eastern sector, covering the concentration, behind them, of the Afrika Corps, the XXth Mobile Corps and the 90th Light Division. The rear of this formidable concentration was covered by anti-tank artillery and one tank battalion against armoured interference from outside. All available Stuka aircraft were collected on the El Adem and Gazala air-fields.

At dawn on the 20th, first the fortress and then the minefields were heavily bombed. Sappers then moved in to clear unexploded mines. Under an artillery box-barrage, tanks forced a way through for the hostile infantry. Counter-attacking British tanks were destroyed. By mid-day, the enemy was well within the defences. 20 June

Headquarters in Tobruk had been sorely embarrassed from the start by bombing. Communications broke down, and command was paralysed. Groups of men resisted with the utmost gallantry, and some broke out. But the end was foredoomed, and by dawn on the 21st, Tobruk, with 30,000 prisoners, was, as a whole, in the enemy's hands. 21 June

Rommel lost no time. On the 24th, his columns crossed the Egyptian frontier between Maddalena and Sidi Omar. The Eighth Army began falling back on a line southwards from Mersa Matruh which was being organized by the Xth Corps from Syria. The 10th Indian Division had arrived from that front a few days before and had been sent up to Sollum, being pulled back on the 23rd to avoid the risk of being cut off. It was now employed, jointly with the 151st Infantry Brigade, in the Matruh defences, and further details of this phase will be found in the 2nd Battalion record. The XXXth Corps was organizing the defence of El Alamein. 24 June

By the 25th June, the situation had become so serious that Gen. Sir Claude Auchinleck, commanding-in-chief the Middle East forces, took over direct personal control of the Eighth Army from Gen. Ritchie. 25 June

In view of the part played by the Regiment in the Matruh and El Alamein operations, a more detailed description of these positions may be of value.

At Matruh, a fortified perimeter ran round the town, with a covering position out to the west. Southwards, 20 miles distant, was a new

1942

strong-point on the high ground near Minqar Sidi Hamza el Gharbi.

There were three minefields. The northern ran round the covering position from the coast to Charing Cross, and then turned east. Southwards from this minefield came a 6-mile gap, which the 29th Indian Infantry Brigade was deputed to close. Southwards again from the gap came two more minefields, terminating about the high ground near Minqar Sidi Hamza el Gharbi.

Strong as the position should have been, the minefields could not be properly watched. The southern flank was open, and the enemy were coming up too fast for the defence to be properly organized.

26 June On the 26th evening, enemy tanks broke through the gap in the minefields south of Charing Cross, and pushed the detachment of the
27 June 29th Indian Infantry Brigade back. Next morning, these tanks engaged the 1st Armoured Division and the New Zealand Division. The XIIIth Corps were kept busy at the southern end of the line at Sidi Hamza while the Xth Corps engaged enemy forces which had passed through the minefield and were moving north-eastwards. By evening, the enemy had penetrated between the Xth and XIIIth Corps, and the latter withdrew towards Fuka.

The Xth Corps was ordered to conform, but had been too heavily milked of transport to make other formations mobile, to comply immediately. The enemy worked round behind the Corps, and cut the road 20 miles to the east. The 50th Division and the 10th Indian
28 June Division fought their way out on the night of the 28th. The 29th Indian Infantry Brigade, from the XIIIth Corps, was to have co-operated
29 June but was overwhelmed just before dark on the 29th. The Xth Corps withdrawal had to be altered to a southerly course, covered by the 7th Motor Brigade attacking northwards against the enemy right flank. However, a great part of the two divisions made a safe getaway, after which they were withdrawn to the Delta to re-organize and re-fit.

Falling slowly back, the XIIIth Corps took over the southern half
30 June of the El Alamein position on the 30th, with the remnants of the New Zealand and 5th Indian Divisions. The XXXth Corps, in the north, with the 1st South African Division and some of the 50th Division,
1 July were about El Alamein. On the 1st July, the enemy attacked the 1st South African Division at El Alamein without success. An infantry attack at the same time against the 18th Indian Infantry Brigade Group at Deir ez Shein was also beaten off. Later in the afternoon, a second attack was put in against Deir ez Shein strongly supported by tanks. An unlucky dust-storm favoured the attack, and the position was over-run. A more detailed account will be found in the 4th Battalion story

At this time, the only strong fortifications in the whole line were at El Alamein itself. Positions generally were weak, disconnected,

                                                                      1942
and lacking depth. There was little in the way of a reserve, and
what remained of the armour was committed to support of the
forward positions. To regain the tactical initiative was essential,
and this was begun on the afternoon of the 2nd July by a northward   2 July
wheel by the New Zealand and 5th Indian Divisions and 7th Motor
Brigade, from the south. This operation, lasting over till the 5th,   5 July
did much to sweeten the tactical atmosphere. Other similar operations
were undertaken from time to time by either army in the effort to
improve their positions; but by the end of July, the situation was
more or less stabilized, and remained so till the autumn.

    Malta had long been a thorn in the Axis side, and belated efforts   Mediterranean
were now being made to soften up its defences prior to an assault.
A savage air offensive was opened up, rising to a climax in April   April
with a total of 5,715 sorties made on the island, which lacked underground hangars for aircraft, and depended mainly on anti-aircraft
artillery for its defence.

    In February, it had been estimated that even on siege rations,
supplies generally would last only till June. Diesel oil stocks for
submarines would give out by April. Yet the despatch of convoys
with supplies was becoming increasingly costly. Three ships were
sent out from Alexandria on the 12th February, and none arrived.
Part of a second convoy, sailing in the moonless period in mid-March,
got through, but the surviving ships were heavily bombed as they
were unloading, and out of the 30,000 tons of supplies despatched,
only 5,000 were received.

    It had been hoped to secure air cover for the convoys on the
journey and while unloading by means of an offensive in the Western
Desert, and the recapture of at least the western Cyrenaican
airfields; but as has been shown, Rommel anticipated us and drove
us back east instead. Convoys from the west were not possible at
all at that time. In May, however, Spitfires were flown off the American   May
carrier *Wasp*, and accounted for a large number of German dive-
bombers.

    Between the 14th and 16th June, supplies were at last run in, in a   14/16 June
double-convoy operation coming from the east and west simultaneously.
The eastern convoy, from Alexandria, had to turn back. But the
western fleet, from Gibraltar, got through. It was a costly business,
involving the loss of one cruiser, six destroyers, two escort vessels,
and twelve merchantmen sunk, apart from the many ships damaged.
The safety of Malta ranked as of the highest priority in the War
Cabinet, and there can be no doubt that we were extremely fortunate
to be able to hold it. It had been the Axis intention to capture Malta
in mid-June, but the 40,000 tons of fuel oil Mussolini required from

1942

Hitler for the operation was still not forthcoming at the end of June, and at the beginning of July, Hitler, under the spell of Rommel's successes, and without consulting either the Italians or his own naval staff, summarily postponed the operation until after the conquest of Egypt—which of course never came.

Another island—Cyprus—comes more directly into the Regimental picture, as the 2nd Battalion's story will show in due course. In his appreciation of the 1st July, 1942, the Commander-in-Chief, Middle-East forces, gave it as his opinion that the enemy would be unable to launch a large-scale air- and sea-borne attack on Cyprus without prior control in Southern Anatolia. Failing this, the enemy would have no fighter cover on the way to the island, or during the landing and subsequent operations. Naturally, these considerations could not rule out the possibility of small-scale raids by parachutists or landing parties.

1 July

The military object of holding Cyprus was to secure to secure airbases for ourselves and deny them to the enemy. It was accordingly proposed to organize the garrison for mobile and aggressive defence based on a system of keeps and prepared positions astride the main lines of approach inland from the coast.

The necessary garrison was estimated at one infantry division with a proportion of armour and artillery, and six additional infantry battalions. Policy was to stock the island with all requirements for these numbers, but—anticipating some three weeks warning before an attack came in—it was proposed to reduce infantry and artillery personnel to about one-third.

Early in July, the 4th Indian Division under Maj.-Gen. F. I. S. Tuker, took over the island's defence.

W. Europe

The Battle of the Atlantic raged on, with heavy losses, barely made good, and continuing anxiety as to its outcome. On the continent of Europe, in the west, the British raid on the docks at St. Nazaire on the 28th March, put paid to port facilities on which the Germans had counted for heavy-ship operations against our convoys; and on the 19th August came the big cross-Channel raid on Dieppe.

28 Mar.

19 Aug.

In England, the German "Baedeker" raids in April and May, on Exeter, Bath, Norwich, Canterbury and York, marked enemy disapproval of British raids on Lubeck, Rostock, etc.

Russia
April

Coming back full circle eastwards, the Russian winter campaign had heavily scarred the German "hedgehog" defences. In April, however, the thaw set in. Operations came to a standstill except in the Crimea, where the Germans made some progress in their attempted re-occupation of Kerch.

1942

In 1941, the Germans had aimed at annihilation of the Russian armies—evidently without success. The objective for 1942 was accordingly changed, and the economic power on which Russia depended for her fighting strength, was substituted. Three widespread and important areas, conveniently sited north of the Black Sea and west of the Caspian, suggested themselves. These were the Donetz industrial area, the Kuban cornfields and the Caucasian oil-wells.

To deal with these, the Germans planned first to advance to the Volga on two parallel lines. The northern attack would pass via Kursk to Saratov. The southern would be directed through Taganrog to Stalingrad, which lay some 250 miles downstream of Saratov. Under cover of this huge quadrilateral of captured country, a third force would be directed south-east through Caucasia to Baku. The defect of this plant, it has been held, is that it failed to include the capture or neutralization of Moscow. With Moscow in their hands, the Russian northern armies would retain possession of all the necessary means of rail movement to enable them to concentrate against the northern face of the quadrilateral; and this exposed the Germans to much enhanced danger of defeat in detail.

At this time, there were in Russia 225 German and 43 satellite divisions, including 50 which were either armoured or motorized. The Russian strength is not certainly known, but is thought to have been a little over 300 divisions. The fire-power of the German divisions had been increased, and the armoured divisions made more manoeuvrable by the substitution of 250 improved tanks for the former 400. New tank tactics had been evolved. These were in a way a throw-back to the old "square" of 50 years ago. Unarmoured fighting and maintenance units in the division were to be grouped inside an outer frame of tanks and anti-tank artillery.

Prior to the opening of the summer campaign, there was some large-scale fighting as the German formations jockeyed for a place. Between the 8th and 13th May, Field-Marshal von Mannstein, commanding the German Twelfth Army in the Crimea, attacked and carried Kerch. The day before Kerch fell, Marshal Timoshenko made an eleventh-hour attempt to lessen the pressure there by opening a violent offensive south of Kharkov, some distance away to the north. Capturing Krasnograd, 50 miles south of Kharkov, on the 16th, and breaking through the outer defences of the great Kharkov hedgehog, the Russians two days later were fighting in the suburbs of Kharkov itself. Violent German reaction starting on the 19th gradually pushed the Russians back out of Krasnograd, with the loss of many prisoners; and on the 1st June, the Germans proclaimed complete victory in that sector.

On the 5th June, von Mannstein opened the bombardment of Sevastopol,

8/13 May

12 May

16 May

18 May
19 May

1 June

5 June

1942

1 July — which boasted a 20-mile outer perimeter, and an 8-mile inner defence line. By the 1st July, its garrison of 75,000 men had been liquidated, and the whole of the Crimea was in German hands.

Meanwhile a massive concentration of force had been built up west of the Oskol river on the general line Kursk-Byelgorod-Kharkov. Some 40 German infantry divisions, 16 to 18 Panzer divisions, and 15 to 20 Hungarian, Italian and Rumanian divisions had collected there by mid-June. Suspecting the German intention to move forward on to the line of the Volga between Saratov and Stalingrad, the Russians massed strong forces north of Voronezh on the northern flank of the advance, beside fortifying Voronezh itself. They also fortified Rostov on the southern flank, at the eastern end of the Sea of Azov, and the semi-circular line of the Donetz river in the southern half of the front.

22 June — A sudden three-day German offensive opening on the 22nd June about the centre of the line, produced rapid successes, and distracted attention from the northern sector where the main offensive was

28 June — launched east of Kursk on the 28th, with a large measure of success.

2 July — On the 2nd July, a heavy attack was made in the centre between

5 July — Byelgorod and Kharkov. On the 5th, in the north, the Germans reached the western outskirts of Voronezh, and, in the south, the line Svatovo-Lisichensk—another substantial advance.

Voronezh, in a sense, marked the high tide of the whole German operation, inasmuch as although great and far-reaching successes were scored in the south, it was on this northern flank that the keystone of Russian active resistance lay. For ten days Voronezh was the scene of desperate fighting, but failed to fall. And this, it is thought, coupled with the spectacular advances farther south, persuaded Hitler to modify his wide objective on the Volga, and, while masking Voronezh, content himself with the capture of Stalingrad alone. If so, it was an appalling risk to take, for it left the Russian armies with their former freedom of manoeuvre in the north, and it substituted a rapidly narrowing triangle for the flank protection of the move through the Caucasus, in place of the sturdy quadrilateral planned.

General von Weich's northern group of armies accordingly formed a defensive flank about Voronezh, and a fresh northern flank-guard for General von Hoth's centre group was provided from Hungarian, Italian and Rumanian divisions organized for the purpose. In the south, the advance swept forward across the lower Don and on towards the north Caucasian steppes.

During the last week in July and the first week in August, von Hoth moved east-south-east down the Don, and attacked Kletskaya and Kalash, west of Stalingrad, where the Don bends south. The

1942

Kalash crossing was won on the 15th August—that at Kletskaya on the 25th. Capture of these bridgeheads freed the Germans farther south, to continue their advance.

15 Aug.
25 Aug.

Still farther to the south, von Kleist's southern group had fanned out at speed over the north Caucasian plain. Voroshilovsk, something over half-way between the Sea of Azov and the Caspian, was taken on the 4th August. On the 8th, the Russians wrecked and abandoned the Maikop oil-fields to the south-west. On the 20th, Krasnodar fell— mid-way between Maikop and Kerch. On the 25th, the Germans were at Mozdok on the middle Terek, far to the east, and only a hundred miles from the Caspian Sea, and with the Russians still falling back before them. Except for the abandonment of the Saratov offensive in the north, everything was going to plan, and the Allies had as little apparent cause for self-congratulation in this theatre as in any other.

4 Aug.
8 Aug.
20 Aug.
25 Aug.

Meanwhile in India full preparations were made for defence against Japanese air-raids, and the black-out descended over vast areas of the country.

India

Against this anxious background, the Regiment played its varying part.

The 1st Battalion disembarked in Rangoon on the 3rd March to find a critical situation in Lower Burma. Our troops were on their way back from the Sittang river, withdrawing on Pegu.

1st Bn.
3 Mar.

Pegu lies about 55 miles north-north-east of Rangoon, and is an important centre of road and rail communications. It is the junction for the main lines of road and railway joining Rangoon and Upper Burma, with those running east and south to Moulmein and the Tennaserim coast. It was along these latter that our troops were now falling back. Obviously if Pegu fell, forces left in Rangoon would be in a critical position.

For a withdrawal from Rangoon, there was however an alternative route, via Prome about 150 miles north-north-west of Rangoon, on the Irrawaddy. From rail-head at Prome, onward communication was mainly by river, north, but a rather roundabout road system also existed via Thayetmyo, Magwe, and Yenangyaung, to Mandalay. With the Pegu route already virtually blocked, the Prome route would be available just so long as the Japanese were prevented from crossing the jungle-clad hill system called the Pegu Yomas, to attack it.

These considerations had not escaped the civilian population of Rangoon, and the severe air-raids of a few days before the Battalion's arrival, had sent most of them scuttling. The port had been deserted

1942 by its normal labour force, and only a few troops were there to do what they could to keep the port working. So, as the ship drew in with the Battalion on board, not a sound came from the quay, till one or two officers standing there shouted up disembarkation orders. The derricks were being worked by an officer of the Royal Burma Navy. Eerie.

A baggage party was detailed under the quartermaster. Within half-an-hour, the Battalion was off the ship, and away on its march through Rangoon. Rangoon, before the war, was a bustling cheerful place, full of colour and movement and chattering people. Now, it was silent. There was no sound—no people. Here and there lay an unattended corpse. There were bombed and blasted buildings to mark the course of the air-raids. Everywhere was the smell of death.

The Battalion marched to the racecourse, near the railway, and waited. The situation was obscure, and the enemy's whereabouts uncertain. A train was supposed to be picking the Battalion up and taking it to Hlawga, 20 miles up the Prome Road. But time passed with no sign of the train, so the Battalion dug slit-trenches, posted air sentries, and waited. Evening came. There was no food. The air turned cold, and the troops in shirts and shorts, and without their cardigans, sat and shivered. About midnight, the train arrived and the troops scrambled in—and woke later, in the dawn, to find they had left the nightmare world behind, and returned to a normal, orderly world, with the Brigade Staff to meet them, and their baggage, which 4 Mar. had come ahead by lorry, waiting in the camp area for them. There was no news of fighting, and attention was focussed on talks about the training to be done.

5 Mar. However, that did not last long. About noon on the 5th, 36 hours after reaching Hlawga, warning orders were received to the effect that the 63rd Indian Infantry Brigade would be attached to the 17th Indian Division, with the presumptive role of re-inforcing the hard-pressed garrison of Pegu. Lieut.-Col. J. A. McLaren, commanding the Battalion, and accompanied by a small reconnaissance party, went forward in the afternoon, with other Brigade representatives; and Battalion headquarters, with "A" Company and part of "B" Company, in lorries, followed at 5 p.m. Transport for the remainder of the Battalion did not report till midnight, and their move was postponed till the morning.

6 Mar. Early that day, the 6th March, the Battalion concentrated at a cross-roads 4 miles south of Pegu, and debussed. Information about the fighting was still very vague, but it was learned that the Japanese had worked round the Pegu positions and established a road-block on the Rangoon side of the town.

The intention was for the Pegu garrison to break back through this

1942

road-block, and withdraw towards Taukkyan on the Rangoon-Prome road. The 63rd Indian Infantry Brigade was ordered to secure the cross-roads where the troops now were, and hold it at all costs. The Brigade accordingly deployed with the Sikhs on the right, the Gurkhas on the left, and the Frontier Force Rifles in reserve with a troop of tanks in support. During the deployment, in the Sikh sector, "C" Company, which was moving forward with a covering role, encountered some opposition. There were no casualties amongst our men, but there was much firing, and some consequent strain on already taxed nerves.

About mid-day, three friendly tanks appeared down the Pegu road, and brought bad news. The Brigade reconnaissance party had tried to break through the road-block in carriers escorted by tanks. Lieut.-Col. McLaren and the commanding officer of the Frontier Force Rifles had been killed. The Brigadier and the commanding officer of the Gurkhas had been severely wounded. Maj. W. A. Windsor-Aubrey, the Battalion second-in-command, took over command of the Sikhs.

Night drew on, and passed without incident, but early in the morning, considerable firing broke out on "D" Company's front, spreading to both "C" Company and "Headquarter" Company. The situation was very confused. Fifth-columnists were active in the area, and, as we have already seen, the troops had been pitchforked into battle without knowing what they were up against or what the situation was, and incompletely prepared by prior training. Just what happened in front was never rightly known, but two Viceroy's commissioned officers and twenty-eight men from the mortar and signal platoons fell into Japanese hands, and "D" Company and part of "Headquarter" Company began to fall back. The situation was got in hand at once, and the position held. The Pegu garrison then fought its way back through the road-block, passed safely through the 63rd Brigade position, and withdrew to Taukkyan. But the Battalion was unsettled by this upsetting start, and it is to everyone's credit that it made so outstanding a recovery in the appalling conditions which lay ahead. 7 Mar.

About 5 p.m., the Brigade began to fall back on Taukkyan. After marching part of the way, the Battalion was ferried back in lorries, and the rear element reached the neighbourhood of the town about midnight.

What the ration position had been during the past two days is not wholly clear, but it seems certain that the troops had been more or less unfed for most of the time. There had been no proper opportunity for rest or sleep, and when the Battalion closed up and halted by the roadside at Taukkyan, most of the men, filthy, hungry, weary, and

1942

with little notion of how they stood, just dropped asleep where they lay. They would probably have done the same even if they had known how desperate the situation really was. The Japanese had beaten us to it, and had cut the Prome road 4 miles to the north. Unless the block was cleared, Army Headquarters, and the whole of the Rangoon garrison would be killed or captured—and the only available fresh troops to effect the necessary break-through were the Sikhs and Gurkhas of the 63rd Indian Infantry Brigade.

8 Mar.   Lieut.-Col. Windsor-Aubrey was called to a conference at Brigade Headquarters while the troops were settling down. He was back again soon after, and at once roused the Battalion. At 1 a.m. they moved off, in two columns each of two companies, with Battalion Headquarters in the centre. The Battalion only owned one map, and this was entrusted to Naiks Indar Singh and Pritam Singh of the Intelligence Section, who led the Battalion straight to the forming-up area, which they reached just before 6 a.m. It was still dark, so the men lay down and rested till dawn, just after 7 o'clock. As the light came up, and the surroundings came into view, it was seen that the Battalion was spread out over flat, open rice-fields. There was a 6-feet high oil pipeline on the left, between the troops and the road, which lay about a thousand yards to the west. Beyond the road, the 1st/10th Gurkha Rifles were to form up. The enemy appeared to be in a strip of jungle covering the road-block some 500 yards away.

The Brigade plan was to attack the road-block with these two battalions, while the Frontier Force Rifles held a position astride the road some way to the south. At 8.45 a.m., a battery of field artillery was to put down a concentration and the two forward battalions were then to attack.

Simple as the plan sounds, it was not mounted in the most encouraging possible circumstances. No detailed prior reconnaissance was possible during the short hour-and-a-half between first light and the time for the attack, and the troops were definitely not in the fresh well-organized condition necessary for an operation of this sort against the Japanese. Again, as will be seen, any hope of effecting surprise was soon lost, and other unforeseen circumstances were to arise before 8.45 a.m. to make the prospects still more unencouraging.

The Battalion plan was for "B" and "C" Companies to capture the objective. "D" Company would then pass through and exploit. "A" Company would stay in reserve with Battalion Headquarters near the pipeline. There was no cover at all, nor had the men tools for digging any. But there was an early morning mist, and, under this, the forward companies moved out and deployed, and waited lying in the open.

Quite possibly the Japanese had seen enough through the mist to arouse their suspicions. At all events, two enemy horsemen appeared out of the jungle ahead at this moment, and most unfortunately drew "A" Company's fire. They at once withdrew.

About half-an-hour later, seventeen Japanese aircraft appeared and circled over the enemy position. Then they made straight for the Battalion. They dive-bombed and machine-gunned the waiting troops in run after run, while a field gun and some machine-guns opened up from the jungle. The fields became an inferno. Bombs, shells and machine-gun fire plastered the whole Battalion area, throwing up earth and splinters in all directions, and inflicting heavy casualties. Some of the men moved back to the pipe line, hoping for cover, but found they were a better target there than lying in the open. But the Battalion as a whole lay still and took its punishment, while the time dragged on to zero hour.

It must be said that the account of the action that follows does not altogether tally with the official despatch. On the other hand, as will have been obvious enough, the times were not propitious for accurate documenting, and the detailed nature of the Battalion record entitles it to serious consideration, at a time when the normal official channels for the passing of information were not able to function too well.

8.45 a.m. came—but no guns opened. Capt. E.E. Spink, who was taking the leading companies forward, moved off with "B" Company to the attack. And then the astonishing thing happened. As soon as "B" Company moved forward, the other companies, entirely spontaneously, and without orders, jumped up and followed them. In two minutes, some 600 Sikhs, with bayonets fixed, were charging across the rice-fields. This was more than the Japanese had bargained for, and they abandoned the road-block and fled.

The road was clear, but the Battalion was completely out of hand. Only "B" Company had managed to maintain any organized control, and it was difficult to cope with the remainder who were all mixed up, and ignorant of what they had to do on reaching the objective. A large number followed on ahead into the jungle, and were later collected by Brigade Headquarters farther down the road. Captains Spink, Hodges, and Sampuran Singh collected as many men as possible and patrolled up the road to some high ground at a road-junction without incident. Deciding to hold this high ground, Capt. Spink took up a position there. Just sufficient breathing-space followed for the men to calm down, when a counter-attack was put in by about fifty Japanese infantry, supported by four aircraft which straddled the position with twelve bombs. One section post was over-run, but the position was restored and the Japanese withdrew.

Meanwhile there was no sign of Battalion Headquarters, which

1942

was to have moved forward as soon as the road-block was captured. Capt. Spink accordingly took over command of the troops on the spot. There was equally no sign of the Gurkhas, who had apparently lost their way moving to the forming-up point, and had not carried out the attack. There was no further enemy interference, however, and traffic started moving north up the road. It must have been an astonishing sight. Every conceivable type of transport, loaded to capacity, and apparently moving quite independently, appeared up the road. The whole of the transport of the Rangoon garrison and headquarters streamed through the Battalion position, and was clear soon after mid-day. The Battalion then spent a quiet afternoon waiting for the fighting troops to break contact at Taukkyan, and withdraw northwards.

At 4.30 p.m., the first of the withdrawing troops appeared. They looked tired and dirty, but were marching well. Just after 6 p.m., the last troops passed through, and the Battalion was ordered to withdraw and take over as rearguard.

The Battalion marched back 5 miles along the road, before being held up by the transport, which completely blocked the road. A very tiring 10-mile march followed across the rice-fields, as it had been decided to take the division off the road, and leave the latter free for the transport. There were interminable halts, and at each of these, the men dropped where they stood and slept the sleep of sheer exhaustion till awakened and pulled to their feet to march on. There

9 Mar. was a rest for about an hour at dawn, and the Battalion slept till 8.30 a.m. when the march continued. Prior to moving on, a check-up showed the current strength of the Battalion as 350. Nothing was known about the rest.

The transport had moved ahead while the Battalion slept, and the Division got back to the road, with the Battalion still as rearguard. About 11.30 a.m., an hour's halt in a copse gave the men an opportunity to do justice to a small but welcome meal which the staff-captain and the quartermaster between them had arranged. The enemy, however, were not far behind. As the two other battalions of the Brigade moved on, under cover of the Sikhs, Japanese artillery opened up, and enemy infantry were seen advancing across the rice-fields about a mile away. However, the Battalion slipped away without interference, and the march went on till about 2 p.m., when a column of M.T. arrived to ferry the Brigade on ahead.

There was some initial delay in the Brigade while lorry-loads were being organized and embussed, and this nearly gave the enemy their chance. The Battalion was covering the embussment, and advance elements of the Japanese caught up and attacked "C" Company, which was in position astride the road. They were

1942

successfully held, however, and the troops embussed and withdrew without incident to the railway station at Tykohi, about 10 miles on. The remainder of the Brigade was at Tykohi resting, and with them were the Battalion's very welcome first reinforcements. bringing the strength up to 420 men.

From Tykohi, the Brigade moved on in two trains to Thonze. The first train, with the Frontier Force Rifles and Gurkhas, left at 8 p.m., but the second train, with the Sikhs, did not get away till 4 a.m. on the 10th. 10 Mar.

After a halt of a few hours at Thonze, the march was resumed to Tharawaddy, about a third of the way from Rangoon to Prome. At Tharawaddy the Battalion was deployed in a defensive position on the right flank of the Brigade. About 180 stragglers rejoined, bringing the strength up to 600.

The troops dug in, and then, hungry, dirty and very tired, lay down and slept. They had been at it, as the story shows, for four days and nights with almost no food or sleep, and they had undergone strains of a serious nature. But they now had three days in which to sit back and take stock, while re-organization was carried out, and elementary training begun. Under this, the men were quickly back in their true form. The bitter lessons of the past days had sunk in, but they had come through them in fine style, and they never looked back after this.

There was no sign of the Japanese at Tharawaddy, but on the 13th, 13 Mar. the withdrawal was resumed. An 8-mile march brought the Battalion to the railway, where a baggage train lifted the Brigade back to Okpo.

At Okpo, Lieut.-Col. Windsor-Aubrey rejoined, together with the balance of Battalion Headquarters. The party had withdrawn north up the Irrawaddy after losing touch at the road-block on the 8th. In the appalling confusion of that morning's attack, it had become separated from the Brigade, and was lucky to have got away.

The Battalion deployed astride the road at Okpo, and was paid visits both by Gen. Alexander, commanding the forces in Burma, and by Maj.-Gen. Cowan, commanding the 17th Indian Division. The position was held till the 19th March, and no contact was made with any formed body of Japanese, although a patrol under Capt. Grant engaged an enemy patrol some miles in front of the Battalion.

Withdrawing on the 19th, the Battalion moved cross-country for 19 Mar. some miles, and then entrained for Putsu. At Putsu, the Brigade was told that there would be no further withdrawal, and that the town would be held at all costs. This was welcome news for the troops who were growing very restive at the continual falling back not under enemy pressure. But it was to turn out otherwise.

The Battalion quickly had the position organized, and by evening

1942 it was wired. Orders then arrived to continue the withdrawal to Prome. It was a bitter disappointment, as the men were full of confidence, and only asking for an opportunity to hit back at the Japanese.

26 Mar. The move to Prome was effected by rail. The Battalion arrived there on the 26th March to find the town in flames from an enemy air-raid. The defensive position to be occupied was a strong one, astride the main road about 3 miles south of the town, and in line with a boom which had been placed across the Irrawaddy. The other two battalions of the Brigade were in Prome, but other troops were deployed to the south.

At this time, the Japanese were moving up into Central Burma via both the Sittang Valley and the Irrawaddy. In the Sittang Valley they had been delayed by the 1st Burma Division, which had moved down from the Shan States when Pegu was threatened. Chinese forces, however, had relieved the 1st Burma Division on the Sittang front, and had been subsequently pushed out of Toungoo. In the Irrawaddy Valley, there was only the 17th Indian Division at Prome to oppose the Japanese pending the concentration on the Irrawaddy front of the 1st Burma Division.

The main object of the force at this moment was to organize the defence of the Yenangyaung oil-fields, for which much depended on the provision of a Chinese division at Taungdwingyi on the eastern flank. In the upshot, however, this division never arrived.

27 Mar. On the 27th March, there was some confused fighting at Paungde, 30 miles south-east of Prome. A battalion of the Gloucestershire Regiment was surrounded, but cut its way out with the help of the Cameronians. The two battalions withdrew through the Sikh position at mid-day.

29 Mar. Two days later, on the 29th, a force went out and re-took Paungde, but the Sikhs were not involved. They had been withdrawn to positions north of Prome on the 27th, in the afternoon. The forces that had recaptured Paungde soon found themselves in difficulties with Japanese road-blocks between themselves and Prome, and they had to turn about and cut their way out. The 17th Indian Division then withdrew to the Prome area, where it was assembled by the evening of the 30th. During this withdrawal, No. 13079 Signal Hav. Gurnam Singh won a well-earned Indian Distinguished Service Medal by returning alone under heavy fire to secure a F.S.6 wireless set which Brigade Headquarters had left behind. Japanese forces were moving up the far (west) bank of the Irrawaddy, with the intention, it was supposed, of crossing the river farther north, to strike at the Division's rear.

30 Mar. About 7 p.m. on the 30th, the Japanese attacked Prome from the south, and quickly over-ran the forward positions, held by the

5th/17th Dogra Regiment, the Burma Frontier Force, and a company
of the 2nd/13th Frontier Force Rifles. All headquarters in the forward
area were simultaneously accurately mortared. Fifth-column activities
were suspected—reasonably enough.

1942

The 63rd Indian Infantry Brigade had hardly been engaged, but,
about 11 p.m. an immediate withdrawal was ordered. The Sikhs took
up a covering position through which the rest of the Brigade withdrew. The Japanese did not follow up, and the Battalion remained
in its positions till 6 o'clock the following morning, the 31st March,
when it was ordered back. It passed through the 48th Indian Infantry
Brigade, which was holding a covering position a few miles farther
north, and pressed on after a short halt for food. The Japanese were
now following up in trucks, and it was reported that an enemy
column was attempting to outflank the Division and place a roadblock in its rear.

31 Mar.

To make the flanks more secure, it was decided to piquet the
road with platoon posts to either flank. This was to be most exhausting
work, involving a good deal of movement at the double and beyond
the powers of the by now over-tired British and Gurkha troops.
The task thus devolved on the three Indian Infantry battalions—the
1st/11th Sikhs, the 4th/12th Frontier Force Regiment, and the
2nd/13th Frontier Force Rifles. The Division marched 29 miles,
and was provided the whole way with flank protection by these battalions.
The weather was overpoweringly hot, the roads were hard and dusty,
and there was no water. Enemy aircraft were much in evidence, and
about 4 p.m. they bombed the Division with considerable effect.
Seldom has a division marched harder or faster under such trying
conditions. The Sikhs had the distinction of being singled out by
both the Corps and Divisional Commander, and complimented on the
excellence of their march discipline.

Next morning, the 1st April, the Division set off again at dawn
with the prospect of another 25 miles to cover. However, at the end
of some 10 miles, lorries arrived, and the troops were ferried back
in turn. The 63rd Indian Infantry Brigade took up a position at
Kyaukpadaung, while the other two brigades held Allanmyo, about
10 miles to the west.

1 Apr.

These positions were held over the 2nd April, but next evening,
a start was made for Taungdwingyi, 60 miles north. The Battalion
took over left flank protection for the Division, being allotted a
rough track running for 50 miles through the jungle on the east of
the road. The Battalion marched off up this track about 6 p.m., but
found great difficulty in moving along it in the dark, it was so
extremely rough. However, they toiled along, not halting till
1.30 p.m. the next afternoon, by which time both men and animals

2 Apr.

3 Apr.

4 Apr.

177

1942

were exhausted. A halt was called for the remainder of the day, and the torrid hours were spent resting, bathing, and cooking meals.

5 Apr.   At dusk the Battalion moved on. The going was much easier the second night, and good progress was made. Still, by noon next day, the 5th, the main road was still at some distance, and it was decided to rest again during the heat of the day, and continue the march in the evening. The main road was reached about 8 p.m., but it took another two hours marching to catch up. The main body had settled down for the night behind an outpost screen from the 16th Indian Infantry Brigade, with the 4th/12th Frontier Force Regiment in the forward positions. When the Sikhs arrived, the outposts took them at first for forward elements of the Japanese, and opened fire. However, the quartermaster very pluckily galloped straight ahead up the road on his horse through a hail of bullets, and managed to stop the fire before any damage was done. Only one man was wounded. After this inhospitable welcome, the Battalion passed through the 4th/12th for a rest.

The rest was well-earned. The Battalion had covered 62 miles in 52 hours over appalling tracks and difficult country, and in stifling weather. With the exception of the unfortunate mule-leaders, who had to march, the Battalion was now ferried back in lorries to Taungdwingyi, at the eastern end of the defensive position along which the Burma Corps was now deploying.

The 1st Burma Division was holding Yenangyaung and Magwe, the 17th Indian Division was in Taungdwingyi, and the 48th Brigade and 7th Armoured Brigade filled the gap between the two divisions. A strong defensive position was dug and wired.

Heavy and generally successful fighting took place to the south of the 17th Division sector, and also on the east bank of the Irrawaddy. The 17th Division was not involved, and to that extent the Battalion had a quiet time. The story was rather different in the air, however, for by this time most of the available Allied aircraft had been destroyed, and enemy bombers came over and attacked the Allied positions at their leisure. The officers' mess was bombed on

17 Apr. the 17th April, and Lieut. Shivdarshan Singh was killed and eleven men wounded.

The situation was not a satisfactory one. The Japanese were pushing at the weakly-held centre of the Corps, as well as round the flanks, and threatening to drive a deep wedge between the two divisions. The failure of the Chinese division, promised earlier, to take over the Taungdwingyi sector meant that the Corps had no reserve. It soon became apparent that the position could not be held, and that the oil-fields would have to go. Key installations

	1942
were destroyed between the 14th and 16th April, and the Corps again fell back. It was a close thing. The 1st Burma Division was cut off before it could get away, and only cut its way out after several days of savage fighting. The Chinese 113th Regiment was sent down from Kyaukpadaung to assist, and played a gallant part in the operation.	14/16 Apr.

There was a fresh outbreak of savage fighting when the Japanese worked in behind the 48th Brigade and attacked them from the rear. They got into the transport lines, and though they were driven back, practically the whole Sikh transport platoon, which was attached to that brigade, was wiped out. This was a sad blow to the Battalion. The platoon had marched the whole way from Rangoon, getting no lifts when the others were lorried. The men throughout had been noted for their cheerful acceptance of adversity. They had never complained, nor let the Battalion down in any way. The mules were sorely missed.

The 63rd Indian Infantry Brigade withdrew without interference and moved back some 50 or 60 miles northwards to a position about 20 miles west of Meiktila. The troops were embussed the first night, but marched the following two. They were long tiring marches along tracks deep in dust, but they were carried through without incident. The Brigade remained in this position till the rest of the Corps had withdrawn. This was completed by the 23rd April, on which day the Battalion set out again on the way to Wunwin, about 20 miles north of Meiktila. While resting in a small copse next morning, it was bombed and machine-gunned by Japanese aircraft, but fortunately suffered no casualties. That afternoon, it reached Wunwin and took up a rearguard position under the command of the 7th Armoured Brigade to cover the withdrawal of the Chinese forces out of the Sittang Valley. At dawn on the 25th, the tanks moved out and fought a hard, day-long battle, assisting the Chinese back through the Brigade position. Enemy aircraft bombed and straffed the Brigade all day, and the Battalion was again fortunate in having no casualties.	23 Apr. 24 Apr. 25 Apr.
At 4 p.m. the Battalion was ordered to withdraw to the Myitnge river. There was no interference by the enemy, and the troops duly passed through the 48th Brigade at Kyaukse, 35 miles south of Mandalay. The latter part of the march to the Myitnge river was done in lorries, the Battalion reaching its positions about dawn on the 26th, and deploying on the north bank of the river to cover the 48th Brigade through from its current position, 17 miles to the south. This, however, took time, for the 48th Brigade were attacked next day at Kyaukse, and a battalion of Gurkhas had to put in a counter-attack, which threw the Japanese back with heavy loss. The Brigade	26 Apr. 27 Apr.

1942

28 Apr. slipped back in the lull which followed, and passed through the Sikh position during the night. As soon as the Brigade was clear, the bridge was blown, and the Sikhs pulled back, leaving a platoon under Lieut. Sheehan on the bridge to prevent the Japanese from carrying out repairs undisturbed. As it turned out, four enemy tanks appeared on the opposite bank of the river about 4 p.m. on the 28th, and the crews dismounted and crowded down to look at the damage. Sheehan's platoon opened fire. Two Japanese were killed, while the remainder dashed back to their tanks and made off. The platoon then withdrew, and rejoined the Battalion.

By this time, the 63rd Brigade was on the Irrawaddy, where the Battalion was posted in a bridgehead on the southern approaches of the Ava Bridge near Mandalay.

The strategic position meanwhile had been developing fast. The enemy offensive on the Chinese left flank in the Shan States was making rapid progress. The Chinese Sixth Army had been surprised and scattered, and the enemy were in Lashio at the western end of the Burma Road to China, the rail-head from Mandalay. Chinese withdrawal eastwards into China was threatened, and at the same time, the Japanese were favourably situated to move down on Mandalay, and thence across to the Chindwin to cut off the British troops' communications with India. Not a promising situation.

A further general withdrawal had accordingly been decided on. The 63rd Indian Infantry Brigade was in a good position to cover the movement of forces back from the east bank of the Irrawaddy, but the operation passed off without Japanese interference. The
30 Apr. Ava Bridge was blown just before midnight on the 30th. All Allied troops were safely across, but it seems that the Japanese did not enter Mandalay, which had been garrisoned by the Chinese, till the
2 May 2nd May. By that time, Mandalay was a deserted city—devastated by the fires which had raged there since the withdrawal started; and it must have been a prize of small value to the Japanese.

30 Apr. The Battalion withdrew during the 30th to a railway station a few miles along the line, and here the Brigade waited all day for a train. The Gurkhas and Frontier Force Rifles entrained in the evening, and
1 May the Sikhs followed at midnight. A short journey brought the Battalion to Chaungu in the early hours of the morning, and here it was met by a staff officer with urgent information and orders.

The Japanese, he said, had moved round the Corps right flank on the Chindwin river, in boats, and had captured Monywa, 60 miles due west of Mandalay, after over-running the headquarters of the 1st Burma Division. The 63rd Indian Infantry Brigade, less the Sikhs, had moved ahead to engage the Japanese, and the Battalion was to follow.

1942

After a quick meal, the Battalion set off to Mau, 12 miles to the north. Arrived there, about noon, it was found that the other two battalions of the Brigade had pushed the Japanese back about 2 miles beyond the old Divisional Headquarters. Moving on behind them, the Sikhs passed through the Divisional Headquarters, which was littered with the bodies of the unfortunate prisoners whom the Japanese had bayoneted and left, before withdrawing.

By this time, the Frontier Force Rifles had been held up by a party of Japanese on their flank, and "A" Company of the Battalion was sent up to drive them out, which they did, inflicting some casualties. Enemy resistance was stiffening, however. The Frontier Force Rifles, who were a few hundred yards ahead, were being badly mortared and machine-gunned, and the Sikhs were hurriedly ordered to take up a position astride the road. The Frontier Force Rifles were compelled to pull back, and later, the Gurkhas withdrew through the Sikhs, who were ordered to hold their positions at all costs while the other two battalions re-deployed farther back.

It was a trying night. The Battalion had no tools, and so no positions could be dug. On the other hand, the Japanese, who were actively patrolling all night in an endeavour to fix the Sikh positions, had little success. The troops lay in silence and waited, with bayonets fixed, and gave the enemy no indication of their whereabouts. The Frontier Force Rifles were less fortunate. The enemy penetrated their defences, and it cost them some loss in casualties to drive the enemy out.

Monywa still lay ahead, and at dawn next day, the 2nd May, operations were resumed. The 13th Brigade was to attack Monywa, while the 1st Brigade was to pass through the Sikhs and attack down the road. The 1st Brigade was delayed, and by 8.30 a.m. had still not appeared, and the 63rd Brigade was therefore sent forward with orders to push back the advanced elements of the Japanese as soon as possible.

2 May

The Brigade plan was for the Sikhs to move astride the road, with the Gurkhas on their right, and the Frontier Force Rifles in reserve. The Battalion deployed with two companies forward—"B" on the left and "C" on the right. The Japanese fell back in front of them for about 3 miles, without offering resistance, but they turned and stood at the outskirts of Monywa, and both Sikh forward companies were held up. When the scrub jungle on "C" Company's front was set on fire, however, and "D" Company was despatched round "C" Company's right, the enemy fell back another quarter-mile into open country where the Battalion was at a disadvantage, and came under heavy and accurate mortar and machine-gun fire. "B", "C", and "D" Companies were all pinned, and an attempted move by "A" Company

1942

round the left flank proved ineffective. Stalemate ensued.

Maj. Spink now took a section of mortars forward to help get the companies moving again. It was a gallant conception, gallantly carried out. "B", "C" and "D" Companies started moving on, but the mortars were put out of action by a direct hit after only three rounds had been fired, Lieut. Brough and most of the detachment were wounded. "C" and "D" Companies were immediately held up again, when our mortars were silenced, and Capt. Satinder Singh was wounded. "B" Company, however, under the inspired leadership of Capt. Hodges, did a gallant charge which carried them right up to the enemy trenches. They met a withering fire from machine-guns, grenades and mortars as they tried to cross the wire, and frantic hand-to-hand fighting occurred as the Japanese put in a savage counter-attack. The Company was forced back a short way by sheer weight of numbers, and Capt. Hodges was severely wounded. He refused to hand over his command, however, but stayed on with his company, which was in a very exposed position and suffering heavy casualties. Capt. Hodges then gave orders for the survivors to fall back, waiting himself till the last man went. He was again hit in the chest. Hav. Kartar Singh turned back to bring him in, but was himself wounded, and Capt. Hodges died from his wounds.

The 13th Brigade had been fighting all day without success, but the 1st Burma Division had been enabled to by-pass Monywa, and withdraw to the Ye-U road, south of Budalin, along which the rest of the force was withdrawing. The action in which the Battalion was engaged, was accordingly broken off at 8 p.m. when the Sikhs moved back towards the Chindwin. It had been both a disappointment and a triumph. Tired and hungry as the men were after continual marches with little food or sleep, they had attacked with extreme gallantry and resolution, and endured many hours in exposed positions under heavy fire. Casualties numbered 120 in killed and wounded—but the Japanese had been so roughly handled themselves that they withdrew from the town and across the river just as the Battalion fell back.

3 May

The Battalion marched doggedly back through the night to Alon which it reached as dawn was breaking on the 3rd May. The Brigade deployed in a rearguard position, with the Sikhs forward astride the road. While the other two brigades and transport passed through the position, the Sikhs, in the forward localities, had a brush with the Japanese, but these were driven off with the help of a troop of tanks. In the evening, the Battalion withdrew to Ye-U, 50 miles north of Monywa and 65 miles north-west of Mandalay, arriving at

4 May

dawn on the 4th, without hostile interference.

5/6 May

That night, the Battalion moved back in motor transport to Kaduma, 20 miles to the north-west, and to Tawgwe and Pyingaing the following

two nights. At Pyingaing, it held a rearguard position during the
7th and 8th, and then moved back to Shwegyin on the Chindwin,
which it reached late in the evening on the 9th.

1942

7/8 May
9 May

At Shwegyin, all equipment, vehicles, tanks and guns which
could not be ferried up to Kalewa, on the far bank of the Chindwin
and 8 miles farther up, from Shwegyin, were dumped and destroyed.
The same night, the Battalion was embarked, and ferried up. At
Kalewa the 63rd Indian Infantry Brigade was deployed along the
river line to cover the withdrawal along the road to Tamu, as the
Japanese, attacking the 48th Brigade at Shwegyin, had captured the
hills overlooking the river.

On the 13th May, the last troops crossed the Chindwin and
withdrew from Kalewa, with the Battalion as rearguard. A series of
long and tiring marches followed up the dusty track to Tamu, which
was reached on the 16th. Next day, the whole of the 17th Indian
Division set out at dawn from Tamu, following the bridle-path across
the hills to Lockchao, where the Battalion remained for five days
to cover the last troops back into India. The monsoon broke during
this halt, and it rained incessantly. There was no change of clothes
and no ground-sheets—but morale was high and the men took it as
cheerfully as they had the many hardships that preceded it. Maj. Spink
recorded of them that "no men ever fell out. We had no stragglers,
and although our clothes were tattered and torn, they were well
worn, beards neatly rolled, safas neatly tied and every man had his
arms and equipment."

13 May

16 May
17 May

Moving back again, after their halt at Lockchao, the Battalion
reached Imphal on the 22nd May, where the troops had another brief
rest. They then moved north with the 63rd Indian Infantry Brigade
up the road to Kohima, where they arrived on the 6th June. The
Battalion went into camp about 6 miles from Kohima, whilst the
remainder of the Brigade settled down in Kohima itself.

22 May

6 June

Although the Japanese had not advanced beyond the Chindwin,
and were unlikely to invade Assam during the monsoon, the Battalion
was detailed to cover the tracks converging on Kohima from the
south to give warning of attempted Japanese raids. A detachment
under Lieut. Sheehan was employed on long-range patrols on the
tracks towards Ukrul and the Chindwin. No enemy were seen, but
the duty was arduous, carried out in appalling weather at the height
of the monsoon.

Sickness levied some toll on the Battalion. Many men had contracted
malaria and diarrhoea during the latter stage of the campaign.
Most of these were now sent into hospital, while as many men as
possible were sent on leave. The strength of the Battalion thus
dropped temporarily to about 300. Individual training was carried

1942

out, and cadres held for young non-commissioned officers, but training was hampered a good deal by the monsoon, for it rained almost the whole time.

Leaving this fine battalion to see the summer out in Kohima, we must turn westwards to follow the doings of the 2nd Battalion during these tragic months in Burma.

2nd Bn.
9 Mar. *The 2nd Battalion* was still under training at Habaniya at the beginning of the period. On the 9th March, Gen. Sir Claude Auchinleck, the commander-in-chief Middle East, met all the officers and Viceroy's commissioned officers of the Brigade at Mujara. He promised to send over a party from the 4th Battalion to liaise, and give practical information about the operations in the Western Desert.

15 Mar. On the 15th March, the new divisional commander, Maj.-Gen. Rees, also paid a visit.

Training was severe, and made more so by the dust. Great distances were covered and a high standard achieved. As an example of the kind of work done, it may be of interest to give details of a Brigade exercise carried out about this time.

In this instance, the Brigade moved off in desert formations on

16 Mar. the 16th March, covering 37 miles, and then deploying in a defensive
17 Mar. position south of Hit. From here, on the 17th, the Brigade advanced 63 miles to K3, moving in column of route owing to the nature of the country, but with Battalion groups tactically organized. Next

18 Mar. day, the 18th, the column was away again in desert formation en route to T1. The 74-mile run had added training value from the unpleasant circumstance of a dust-storm and consequent poor—and sometimes

19 Mar. non-existent—visibility. The trip to Haffa, the next port of call, 30 miles away, was done in column of route, and this was followed

23-24 Mar. by a two-day reconnaissance of a defensive position, facing the Syrian border. Digging began on the 23rd, and on the 24th the divisional commander inspected the work. There were no casualties of any sort in the Battalion M.T. during this exercise, and it will be agreed that this argued well for the efficiency of those concerned.

26 Mar.-
1 Apr. The digging, however, was no pretence, but part of the defensive plan, and the Brigade continued work on the position for some time. During this period, the usual incidents occurred. A draft of eighteen Indian other ranks and one British officer—Capt. R. J. Henderson—went back to India on the 3 per cent combined leave and milking scheme on the 26th March, Capt. R. B. Penfold taking over as adjutant. On the 28th March, it is on record that the first mail arrived for fourteen days, "the arrangements for mail during a move being very bad"; and on the 1st April, a draft apparently arrived from the Battalion's old sparring-partner, No. 15 Reinforcement Camp,

including men who had been in Shaiba for five months, and several who were without arms.

1942

Some light was shed on the curious delays at the Reinforcement Camp by the arrival on the 16th April of another small draft of three non-commissioned officers and seven other ranks. Some of these, also, had spent five months in Shaiba. On enquiry, it emerged that several of these men, being cross-country runners, had been kept back to compete in inter-unit sports. A week later, yet another small draft was squeezed out of Shaiba. Of the six men who came up with 2nd/Lieut. Amar Singh, one had been in the Reinforcement Camp six months working as an office orderly.

16-30 Apr.

The remaining small-change of Battalion life during April can be compressed into small enough space. Training competed with digging, though the latter was much held up in mid-April by rock and shortage of explosives. On the 10th April, the Battalion school was re-opened. On the 16th, an officers' week was started. For this, each afternoon a cloth-model exercise was run by a selected officer, assisted by a Viceroy's commissioned officer; and next morning a five-hour tactical exercise without troops on the same subject, followed. On the 18th, there was a lecture by the Divisional commander on the fighting in Libya and Eritrea—and the General followed this up—pleasantly enough—by dining in the Battalion mess. On the 22nd, the Battalion practised the laying and removing of a minefield in the defensive position. Each company had to lay and fuse 500 mines, and then remove them again. Apparently no one was blown up, and the exercise was voted a success.

Hony. Lieut. and Sub.-Maj. Partap Singh, Sardar Bahadur, O.B.I., left on pension during April, after thirty-two years service. His farewell was attended by the Brigade commander and all commanding officers and adjutants in the Brigade. His successor, Sub. Karam Singh, Bahadur, O.B.I., was well qualified to take his place.

Life continued on placid lines, with little variation in the monotony and heat till the 6th May, when the Brigade was put on a week's notice to move. Time passed, however, till the 18th May, when the notice was narrowed down to twelve hours. Digging ceased, and training was stepped up, till the 22nd May, when the Battalion left Safra in M.T. for K3, shaking out from column of route at T1, and travelling thence on a broad front. The distance that day was 83 miles.

6 May

18 May

22 May

On the 23rd, a further 96 miles, via Hit, brought the troops to Mujarah. Here a three-days halt was called. Certain preparations were necessary before the column could undertake the onward journey to Mafraq on the other side of the desert, including issue of an assortment of pool transport—Bedfords, Morrises, Albions, Fordsons,

23 May

185

1942

27 May	Fords and others—most of which were entirely new to all but a few of the drivers—and all of which were apparently minus their tools. The march was resumed on the 27th May, when the Battalion moved to L5, 130 miles away, where three trucks were abandoned.
28 May	On the 28th, the column reached H3, 92 miles ahead. Next day, a
29 May	further 122 miles brought it to H4. On the 30th, an additional
30 May	122 miles saw it in Mafraq.
31 May	Orders received at Mafraq indicated Ismailia on the Suez Canal as the Battalion's immediate destination. Pushing on accordingly on the 31st, the column arrived in Haifa at the end of a 114-mile stage.

In Haifa, the Battalion was accommodated in a staging camp under Mount Carmel. A one-day halt for maintenance was scheduled; and on the 1st June, with the help of Australian and British workshop units, everything possible was done to knock the transport into shape. For lack of spares, however, much had to remain undone.

2 June On the 2nd, the Battalion drove on south 160 miles to Asluj. An accident en route resulted in two men going to hospital, but all vehicles reached their destination safely, including the lame ducks, which were still being set to rights in Haifa when the Battalion moved out.

3 June On the 3rd came the longest stretch to date—170 miles to Ismailia. Greater distances lay ahead, but there had been remarkably little trouble, and it will be conceded that the Battalion had done well. On this last run, however, the previous days' strains did take some toll, for there were several accidents, though one man only needed hospital treatment. All vehicles arrived safely, and here again workshop establishments were of great service.

Information was now received that the Battalion was to be used in the Western Desert, where events were moving fast. The battle was raging west of Knightsbridge—the enemy were successfully clearing lanes through the minefields on the Capuzzo road, and had already over-run the 150th Infantry Brigade.

4 June In Ismailia, no time was lost, and on the 4th the troops carried out an exceptionally long and tiring march of 209 miles, which included driving through Cairo. Anyone who has experienced movement in hot and crowded lorries over dusty country, with the exhaust gases and powdery dust blowing endlessly in over the back, will understand what this meant to the troops. However, everyone arrived safely in Amariyeh, where the only accident of the day occurred, though a number of vehicles did arrive in tow as a result of mechanical failures.

Heavy baggage was dumped at Amariyeh under Naik Sham Singh
5 June and three other ranks; and on the 5th the troops moved on 190 miles

to Mersa Matruh in the wake of the Brigade reconnaissance group, which Maj. Ashe accompanied. At Mersa Matruh, first-reinforcements, consisting of Jem. Gulzara Singh and fifty-one other ranks, stayed behind, for despatch back to Mena.

On the 6th, a march of 155 miles brought the troops to Capuzzo, just across the Egyptian frontier and about 10 miles west of Sollum. From here, the Battalion went back to a defensive position some 5 miles east, at Point 206. The position was occupied by 4 p.m., and reconnaissances were then sent out to learn the lie of the land and the minefields. Capt. Macdwyer went off with a platoon to the frontier post of Fort Maddelina, 45 miles to the south, on aeroplane guard duty, returning on the 10th.

On the 8th, Capt. J. M. S. Smith took up an outpost position at Hamra with "C" Company; and on the 10th, Capt. J. W. Anson was sent off with "D" Company for aerodrome guard duty at Sidi Aseiz, 12 miles south of Capuzzo. This was the day the enemy took Bir Hacheim at the south end of the Gazala line, 90 miles away to the west.

The stay at Point 206 was a short one. On the 13th June, a Brigade reconnaissance, which included the commanding officer and the adjutant, looked over the Sollum box. Next day, the Battalion carried out the first leg of its move there by occupying Halfaya Pass, about 5 miles south-south-east of Sollum.

Proceedings in the Western Desert at this time did not encourage over-confidence, and Maj. Ashe and Capt. Macdwyer were sent out for a few days to Gaps "F" and "H" on the frontier, with traffic control posts, to help watch for fifth-columnists and assist in guiding the withdrawing forces.

On the 15th—while the 1st South African Division and the 50th Division were falling back on the Egyptian frontier—"D" Company rejoined from Sidi Aseiz. Later in the evening "C" Company returned from the Hamra box, after handing over there to elements of the 5th Indian Division.

Next day, the Battalion moved from Halfaya Pass to the Sollum box, and took over the centre of the 25th Indian Infantry Brigade position.

The position was a hard one to prepare. In some cases, preparations had been started, but the sub-soil 2 feet down was rock, and gun positions naturally had priority for explosives. So the work progressed slowly. During the commanding officer's reconnaissance, the Battalion had, for a time, been on one hour's notice to move up the line, but this had been cancelled later.

"D" Company returned to Sidi Aseiz to cover a further evacuation of R.A.F. from the aerodrome, and Maj. Ashe and Capt. Macdwyer

1942

6 June

8 June
10 June

13 June
14 June

15 June

16 June

1942

came in with their traffic posts. The latter had had a very busy day and night controlling the withdrawing troops. 2nd/Lieut. Key, Gen. Key's only son, who had joined the Battalion, was sent out with a fighting patrol, and a traffic-control post, to Gap "D".

17 June Next day, the 17th, formation of a Battalion anti-tank platoon was at last ordered, with an initial strength of one British officer, two Viceroy's commissioned officers, and thirty-two other ranks. It was ultimately to be raised to a strength of seventy-three other ranks. It was formally named No. 7 Platoon. It will be conceded that in view of the enemy's preponderance in armour, anti-tank protection for the Battalion was overdue.

At the same time, three more guns were received, with portees. All had been in action before, and some had suffered, but the Battalion was glad of the addition they made to its fighting strength.

Late that night, orders came in to send another company to help "D" Company at Sidi Aseiz, and Capt. J. M. S. Smith with "C" Company

18 June went off at dawn, taking three anti-tank guns with him. No opposition was encountered, however. "C" and "D" Companies returned in due course, and reported the aerodrome evacuated and necessary measures of destruction carried out.

The Battalion position was still being dug. Another minefield had been laid and reserve positions wired. The Battalion record comments—a little unfairly?—"The news that 'C' and 'D' Companies had cleared for action, and that the enemy was now only 25 miles away, is slowly convincing the Battalion of the necessity for concentrated digging".

The Capuzzo area was again bombed during the night, but the only Brigade casualty seems to have been one man wounded, in the King's Own Regiment, on the Battalion's left.

19 June Next day, the Battalion transport, together with an escort, was taken by Brigade to help in the evacuation of rations and ammunition from Capuzzo railhead. Enemy forward elements had entered Bardia, 15 miles north up the coast from Sollum, and were approaching Sidi Aseiz. Digging in the defensive position went on with steady intensity.

20 June Climax was approaching. On the 20th, the enemy advance-guard, which was reported to muster three battalions of infantry, one battery of artillery, and two squadrons of tanks, reached Capuzzo, 6 miles away. Our defences were still incomplete. The record tells how a man of "A" Company was injured in the hand when some enemy ammunition, evidently abandoned there during earlier operations, exploded during the digging.

A hostile air reconnaissance came over in the evening.

21 June The 21st opened unexpectedly with the arrival of two Free French

1942

stragglers from Gambut, 40 miles to the west. "B" Company found them—one was wounded—outside the wire, and very thankful they must have been to find themselves with friends. Meanwhile, Tobruk had fallen, and the future was full of uncertainty. On the Battalion front the enemy had paused, and patrols from the forward companies failed to contact them.

It was essential to find out what the enemy meant to do. During the morning, "D" Company, under Capt. Anson, moved out with guns on a "Jock" column. At the outset, the column ran into trouble not of the enemy's making, when Sub. Ujagar Singh's truck ran into one of our own minefields, and blew up. The truck was completely destroyed, but all arms and ammunition were saved, and there were no casualties, the subedar only receiving a few cuts.

While the column was away, No. 12 Platoon of "B" Company was shelled accurately, but fortunately, ineffectively. At 11.30 a.m., the column returned. The enemy had been encountered on the Bardia road, and it had looked as if an attack was developing against the Mahrattas on the Battalion's right. There had been no casualties.

At 2.30 p.m., the 8th Royal Tank Regiment moved out from Gap "B" to make a sweep round behind Capuzzo and the railhead. An action blew up under cover of an artillery barrage, but the progress of the battle could not be observed, and when Jem. Naginder Singh came back from Gap "B" with No. 7 Platoon, he had nothing of interest to report.

During the evening, the Royal Air Force carried out a heavy bombing attack on Capuzzo. Later, during the night, "A" and "B" Companies assisted South African sappers in thickening up the existing minefields. Enemy patrols were active on "B" Company's front.

The enemy were clearly jockeying for position before putting in an attack. "Left out of battle" personnel were accordingly sent back. 2nd/Lieut. Harwant Singh had already taken one party back on the evening of the 20th June. Next evening, Capt. Anson followed, en route to Sidi ben Galad, with details of "D" Company, including Sub. Ujagar Singh and Jem. Nagindar Singh. Though the preparation of the position was by no means complete, everything possible had been, or was being done to hold the enemy back.

During the morning and early afternoon of the 22nd, there was no change in the Battalion's position. It was a relatively quiet morning, though "B" Company was again shelled by German artillery—again without loss. The King's Own on the left had slight casualties from bombing, and the Battalion's advanced Intelligence O.P. came under small-arms fire from long range. The enemy were engaged by

22 June

1942

our fighters and bombers during the day, and active work continued on the preparation of the defences.

The position, however, was not to be held, and at 3 p.m., to the general surprise, orders were received to withdraw the same night. As events proved, the orders came not a moment too soon. Meanwhile, at 7 p.m., "A" Company engaged three enemy tanks with small-arms and mortar fire. The artillery lent a hand, and the tanks withdrew under a cloud of smoke and dust which prevented observation of fire-effect.

There was a half-moon that night, and at 10 p.m. the Battalion started its withdrawal. The Mahrattas were to co-operate. By 10.30 p.m. they had taken over "A" Company's position, and "C", "D" and "H.Q." Companies were clear of the Sollum box. Three-quarters of an hour later, "A" and "B" Companies, with a troop of No. 515 Field Battery R.A., were also clear. The enemy were making free use of flares, but were evidently not ready to assault. Only a few shells were coming over.

After shaking free the Battalion drove 50 miles through the night without incident except for the overturning of one lorry, and

23 June halted in dispersed positions at 6.30 a.m., 3 miles west of Sidi Barrani, for the day.

The rear of the Brigade was machine-gunned from the air in the evening, but the Battalion spent a quiet day. At 9 p.m., the Brigade was on the move again for Mersa Matruh, 75 miles along the coast to the east. The march was a lively one, for the Battalion was bombed and machine-gunned twice from the air. There were no casualties, but two vehicles were hit by machine-gun fire. During the second attack the men opened up with their Brens, and—whether or not on this account—there was no further trouble, and the Battalion

24 June arrived in Mersa Matruh at 7.30 a.m. next morning.

The commanding officer and adjutant went off on a reconnaissance of a new defensive position, while the men rested. During the night Mersa Matruh was bombed, though without casualties to the Battalion;

25 June and at 6 a.m. on the 25th June, the Brigade moved out of Mersa Matruh to occupy an outpost line some 9 miles south-west. The remainder of the Division was in the Matruh box, with the 21st Indian Infantry Brigade to the north-east, and the 5th Indian Infantry Brigade filling the gap between the 21st and 25th Brigades, some 6 miles behind and to the east of the latter brigade.

At first sight, the outpost position gave an impression of great strength. With the Mahrattas on the right and the King's Own on the left, the Battalion held a front of some 6,000 yards in the centre. On the Battalion front, "A" Company under Capt. Macdwyer held the right sector, "B" Company under Sub.-Maj. Karam Singh the centre, and "C" Company under Capt. J. M. S. Smith the left.

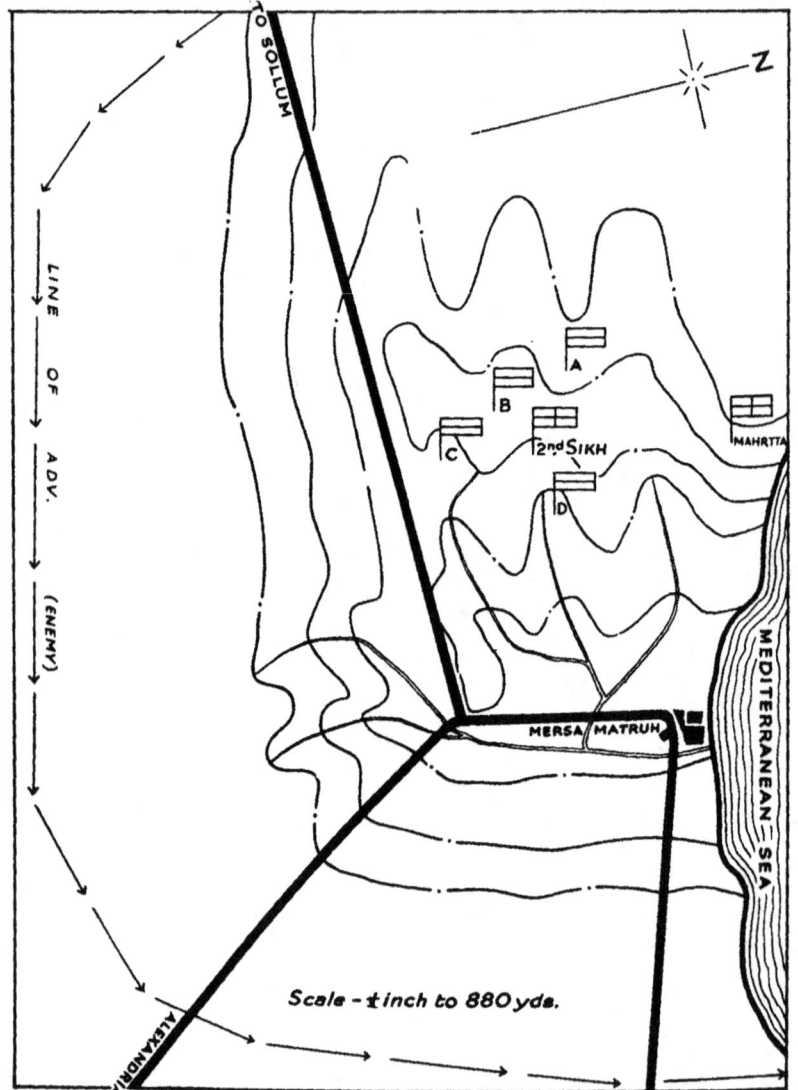

1942

"D" Company under Sub. Balwant Singh was in reserve in an area behind the minefield, between "A" and "B" Companies' sectors. Advanced Battalion Headquarters was 400 yards behind "A" Company, with a rear echelon in a nala behind "B" Company. All vehicles, with the exception of two trucks per company, were dispersed, some 2 miles behind Battalion Headquarters.

The minefield on which the position depended, was of impressive proportions. With an overall length of 16 miles, it was about 1 mile deep. It was intersected by lanes leading to platoon and section posts, and platoon positions themselves were in cleared areas in the minefield. There, however, its defensive value ended. Apart from the circumstance that the position was unwired and only half-dug, it was later learnt that the mines in the minefield had been laid 50 yards apart, and that all anti-personnel mines had been removed some time before. Thus, the main protective system to the position was little more than a myth.

Companies took some time getting into their areas. A South African corporal had been detailed as a guide, but Company areas proved hard to locate, whilst the narrowness of the lanes through the minefield caused congestion and delay. However, by 3 p.m., all troops were in position, telephone lines had been laid to all companies, including the most forward "A" Company platoon, and to rear headquarters, and communications had been established with Brigade Headquarters.

In the evening there was momentary excitement when three German fighters fled by about 20 feet above Battalion Headquarters, closely followed by six R.A.F. Hurricanes. No one saw how the chase ended, but a Mahratta Jemadar was killed by cannon-fire, and his driver wounded.

News came in from Brigade about 10 p.m. that the Germans were about 18 miles away and moving along the coast. Our mobile troops were still active ahead of the Brigade position, and a platoon of "D" Company under Jem. Pritam Singh was promptly sent out to guard one of their petrol dumps off the Siwa road, which ran roughly south-south-west in front of the King's Own position, to the Siwa Oasis, 175 miles away.

At midnight 25th/26th June, a second platoon was ordered out— 26 June this time to patrol the Sidi Barrani road, and contact the enemy. Jem. Ujagar Singh's platoon from "A" Company was detailed for this, and moved out at 3 a.m. The Sidi Barrani road, however, had been mined by the King's Own, and the platoon could not get down it till the mines had been lifted. This took till 7 a.m.—but the platoon was not inactive meanwhile, for it captured a German truck with two prisoners on the Siwa road. The truck was taken over by

1942

the 12th Lancers who were operating to the south of the Sidi Barrani road. It may be added here that when Jem. Ujagar Singh's platoon got back on relief at 2 p.m., it had added two more prisoners to the bag at a cost of two men slightly wounded.

Brigade Headquarters meanwhile moved to a new site behind the King's Own on the main Sidi Barrani road during the morning, and lines were relaid.

At 9 a.m., the Battalion was ordered to send out a small column consisting of one infantry platoon (from "D" Company, under Sub. Balwant Singh), one troop of 25-pounders from No. 515 Field Battery R.A., one platoon of anti-tank guns under Sub. Samund Singh, and the carrier platoon. 2nd/Lieut. Wilson was to command. The purpose of the column was to relieve Jem. Ujagar Singh and his platoon and to find out what it could about the enemy on the Sidi Barrani road, without getting involved.

The column went off at mid-day, returning at 6 p.m. with sixteen prisoners, including an Italian infantry major, and with valuable information about the enemy for Brigade Headquarters. This excellent little operation cost us no casualties, though the carriers had contacted and caused loss to enemy lorried infantry. Enemy tanks later came on the scene, when the column wisely withdrew.

Gunfire had been steadily growing in intensity down the Sidi Barrani road. Everything was quiet on the immediate Battalion front, but it seemed unlikely to remain so much longer. About 2.30 p.m. Battalion Headquarters moved back to the rear headquarter site, in the nala, and telephone lines were changed over. About this time an enemy plane was shot down in flames over "C" Company by one of our fighters, crashing somewhere in the King's Own area.

There was a good deal of air activity going on overhead, and about 5 p.m. R.A.F. fighters shot down an enemy fighter which had been machine-gunning the position. The aircraft crashed in flames in the minefield between "B" and "C" Companies—the pilot baling out and landing in front of "B". "B" Company promptly sent out a section to capture him, but while still about 500 yards from him, the section was stopped by machine-gun fire from an enemy tank, which dashed up and rescued their man.

At 7 p.m. "A" Company reported considerable M.T. activity on their front. Later, at 9.30 p.m., a second report came in to say that sixteen tanks had been seen approaching the Company position. Brigade Headquarters expressed doubts of the correctness of this report—though there were subsequent grounds for supposing it to have been at least partially correct. It was suggested that the reported tanks were probably lorries mistaken for tanks in the dim light, and patrols were ordered out to confirm.

1942

Hav. Bhag Singh accordingly took out an "A" Company patrol through the only gap on the Battalion front—which was in his company's sector—at midnight. It remained out till 3.30 a.m. on the 27th June, when it returned with a report of four tanks seen halted in a hollow some 1,500 yards to "A" Company's front. Beyond them was an enemy M.T. column moving towards the sea. The Company asked permission to stalk these tanks.

27 June

However, the chance was lost. The adjutant, worn out, had fallen asleep after prolonged efforts to improve communications with Brigade Headquarters. Line communication had given out altogether, thanks to a faulty Brigade exchange, and two hours on the W/T 101 set produced no results. The intelligence officer, who would normally have taken duty turn-and-turn-about with the adjutant was away on a course; and Jem. Amar Singh, the only remaining relief, had too limited English to be able to function adequately at the telephone. Whether a Company stalk would have produced satisfactory results cannot of course be known, but at all events permission was not forthcoming.

The disturbing breakdown of communications with Brigade Headquarters was temporarily rectified at 5 a.m., and the opportunity was taken to make an earnest plea for what one would suppose to have been already made available—maps.

By first light, it was clear that a busy day lay ahead. At 6 a.m., "B" Company came under machine-gun fire from enemy armour firing from the neighbourhood of the crashed fighter. Soon after, the Company reported about 150 motor vehicles 2,500 yards south-west. At 7 a.m., enemy, estimated at 800, were seen debussing from these vehicles, and starting to dig in.

During this time, communications with Brigade Headquarters had again been lost, and re-established—and an O.P. was now asked for to engage this excellent target with artillery fire. Meanwhile, at 7.30 a.m., "A" Company reported a large concentration of M.T. halting and dispersing about 2,000 yards to its front. This was taken to be the transport which had brought up the force now digging in opposite "B" Company. Brigade Headquarters were informed. This report must have been forwarded on through Divisional Headquarters, for, although no reaction occurred for four hours, a strong force of Boston bombers then arrived and effectively bombed the area, while escorting fighters shot it up.

The enemy mounted their attack methodically enough. First, a battery was seen coming into action about 3,000 yards to "B" Company's front. But it could not be engaged at this vulnerable moment for lack of the hoped-for artillery O.P. Direct communication was, however, established with Lieut.-Col. Andrey, R.A., commanding the Field Regiment R.A., and an O.P. for "B" Company was promised.

At 12.45 p.m., the enemy battery opened fire and began dropping shells among "D" Company and on the Mahrattas, to its right. It was quickly picked up by our artillery, and the 25-pounders opened counter-battery fire on it with effect.

At half-past one "B" Company reported an estimated 200 infantry advancing on its front, and Brigade Headquarters was informed. The enemy were not moving very fast, however. It took them an hour to reach the edge of the minefield, which was well out of effective small-arms range. They then began lifting the mines. The minefield was no great shakes at the best, whatever it looked like on the map. To have sited it so that part at least was beyond the possibility of effective cover by the forward troops was a waste of good mines—and so the troops no doubt thought them.

Maj. R. A. d'E. Ashe was now sent forward to assist in the "B" Company sector, and at 3 p.m., the long-awaited artillery O.P. arrived in that Company area.

Fifteen minutes earlier, the headquarter nala came under accurate artillery fire, which went on for some two-and-a-half hours. "B" Company was also heavily shelled, and the attack on their position developed rapidly in strength and determination. However, the arrival of the gunner O.P. strengthened the defence.

By 5 p.m., Maj. Ashe reported that the situation was growing serious on "B" Company front. The enemy were infiltrating through the defences, and lifting mines as they advanced.

Thanks to the heavy enemy shelling, effective command of the Battalion had been made quite impossible from the rear headquarters nala. Forward headquarters accordingly moved up to its original position behind "A" Company. This meant a complete change-over in communications, but these were working normally again by 6 p.m., when "A" Company reported an enemy attack developing on its front.

Soon after this, the new Battalion Headquarters position was heavily shelled, but the Battalion was by now drawing useful dividends from the gunner O.P. with "B" Company. The 25-pounders were giving a good account of themselves, and the headquarter shelling was promptly returned. "A" Company targets were likewise telephoned through to Maj. Ashe to pass on to the gunner, and the latter wirelessed them back to his battery. Fire effect was observed in the same way.

At 7 p.m., an enemy aircraft flew down the ridge at a height of about 20 feet, dropped a bomb about 50 yards from Battalion Headquarters, and vanished. This bomb was evidently a marker for

enemy artillery, which sprayed a very accurate salvo over the
Battalion Headquarter command-post about ten minutes later.
  The enemy were held for that day, and the Battalion gave
generous credit for this to the excellent work of No. 470 Field
Battery, R.A. Little damage had been done by the enemy in spite of
nine hours fairly continuous shelling, and only four men were wounded.
Material losses included the office truck, which was hit by splinters
and lost three tyres, while the ambulance was knocked out by
shell-fire. Telephone lines came in for their quota of damage, but the
signallers did fine work during the very trying move of Battalion
Headquarters, and were frequently out repairing the line all through
the afternoon.
  The night provided some breathing-space for strengthening the
defences, but there was little sleep for the men.
  As a start, 150 sappers from No. 61 Field Company came up at
8 p.m. from the Brigade reserve, under a major, to help lay anti-
personnel mines, and erect some wire, in "B" Company's area.
While the work was proceeding, "B" Company was reinforced with
two platoons from "D" Company, while a further platoon of that
company went to "A".
  The sappers found difficulty in getting away when their jobs
were done. They came under enemy fire, to which "B" Company
replied, while the sappers spread and went to ground. Cautiously
crawling back by twos and threes, in the dark, they were taken for
infiltrating enemy, but were mercifully recognized before any harm
could be done. They all got back safely, and the major then reported
having come across an Italian soldier in the minefield, suggesting
the probability of an Italian formation being on the Battalion front.
  The remainder of the night was quiet, except for one bombing
attack.
  At 5.30 a.m. on the 28th June, the guns opened up on both sides,
and by 6 a.m., the enemy, about a battalion strong, were again
pressing forward on the "A" Company front. The situation opposite
"B" Company was quiet. By 7.15 a.m., the enemy were advancing
steadily through the minefield towards "A", and at 7.30 a.m., they
rushed the Company's left forward platoon, and over-ran the forward
section post. The post commander, No. 13638 Naik Zora Singh was
captured, together with the whole of his section and a 2-pounder
anti-tank gun.
  No. 470 Field Battery, R.A., opened fire in "A" Company's
support at 8 a.m., and the situation eased a little. Enemy shelling
throughout had been heavy over both "A" Company and the headquarters areas, and the telephone lines had already been cut and
repaired several times. The Battalion signallers were doing fine

1942

28 June

work, but communication with Brigade Headquarters had become so precarious as to be almost worthless.

After a brief pause, enemy pressure against "A" Company was renewed about 9.30 a.m., and a party of enemy, numbering about 120 men, worked their way round into the nala separating "A" Company from the Mahrattas on its right. This move, however, had been temporarily checked by mortar and light machine-gun fire by about half-past ten.

Half-an-hour later, enemy columns were seen moving along the Sidi Barrani road. Shortly after, the commanding officer, Lieut.-Col. A. E. Farwell, was called in to Brigade Headquarters—the message, as a matter of interest, being passed by wireless in the vernacular.

Meanwhile no one was very happy about the situation in the nala on "A" Company's right, so, while the commanding officer was away, a platoon of "D" Company under Sub. Balwant Singh, was sent up to "A" to strengthen the threatened flank. At the same time, the reserve mortars came into action behind Battalion Headquarters. However, the enemy managed to make some progress down the nala soon after with the help of some heavy shelling put down over the whole area, but they were again checked by mortar fire.

Locally the situation could be described as reasonably satisfactory at the moment, but matters were less promising elsewhere, and the Brigade position was being rapidly made untenable by enemy successes on other parts of the front. Hence, when the commanding officer, Lieut.-Col. Farwell, came back at 1 p.m., he brought with him orders for a withdrawal at 9.30 p.m. that night, through Mersa Matruh, and along the coast road.

Meanwhile, the afternoon saw an attack boil up on "B" Company's front, and, still later, another against "C", enemy troops being pushed in in strength on a narrow front as had happened against "A". The forward companies were shelled pretty heavily throughout these attacks, but by evening the situation had eased and the attacks had been stopped. There was a little enemy air activity, including bombing and machine-gunning attacks.

Preparations for the withdrawal were well in hand long before sun-down. By 6 p.m., elements of Headquarters Company were back in "B" Echelon area, preparatory to the move back, and all companies had their detailed plans.

At 7 p.m., however, the commanding officer was again called to Brigade Headquarters, and came back at 8 p.m. with a new set of orders. The enemy had succeeded in cutting in behind, and had reached the sea, so that it was no longer possible to withdraw along the coast.

The situation was not unlike the position in which the 4th Battalion

1942

had found itself earlier on at Benghazi, and troops were to cut their way out as best they could. Battalion groups were to be formed, and would head south, bearing away east later on, and making for a rallying point 10 miles south of Fuqa, 45 miles away from the outpost position, on the coast road.

To help the Mahrattas on the right pull out, it was agreed that the Sikhs should hold their positions for an extra 15 minutes. "B" Echelon transport, acting on the earlier orders, had already left for Mersa Matruh, but no serious anxiety was felt about them, as it was understood that they had been warned about the changed situation, and would be coming under the wing of the 21st Indian Infantry Brigade.

Companies began pulling back as quietly as possible, forming up as they arrived, in the "B" Echelon area. Battalion Headquarters moved back to the "B" Echelon area at 9 p.m.

At 9.30 p.m., "B" Echelon area was machine-gunned from the air, though without material effect. A graver omen was the simultaneous blowing up of installations in Mersa Matruh. The flames from the town were an impressive sight, but it was feared they might give the game away and put the enemy on the alert, and so jeopardize the success of the break-out—particularly after the two visits already paid by enemy aircraft.

Nothing, however, happened on the Battalion front, and everything went to plan. The only recorded loss of arms was one anti-tank gun which had to be left in "A" Company position, and which was destroyed before leaving.

By 10.45 p.m., the last personnel of all companies were out of the line, and embussing. By midnight, the Battalion was on the march south down the Siwa road. In spite of two days of almost continuous shelling, losses from that cause had been very slight. Six men had been wounded by shell-splinters—none seriously—and some vehicles had been knocked about. The Battalion had its tail well up.

The Battalion moved first to Kilo 12, led by the station wagon, carrying Lieut.-Col. Farwell, Maj. Ashe, and the adjutant. Two troops of 25-pounders—from Nos. 470 and 515 Field Batteries—were picked up on the way. At Kilo 12, an officer of the King's Own met the Battalion and guided it off the road and round the eastern corner of the minefield, before leaving to rejoin his own unit, which was to be the last one out. The minefield was cleared, and the open desert reached by the head of the column, at about 1 a.m. on the 29th. 29 June

The enemy soon discovered the column, and, looking back, tracer fire from harassing aircraft and answering fire from the moving column made an impressive sight—in spite of a full moon—against

1942

the backscreen of flames in Mersa Matruh. This harassing fire from the air was kept up for the first 9 miles of the move through the desert, when the first leg of the break-out was to end, and the column was to turn east from its previous bearing. The wheel, however, was deferred and the Battalion taken farther south as it was felt they were not sufficiently clear. For some while a good deal of firing had been heard and tracer seen on the left, or eastern flank, and this was judged as being the 21st Indian Infantry Brigade in contact with the enemy some 3 miles east. The position must have been very puzzling and obscure; and this was not lessened by sighting another southward-bound column on the Battalion's right. The last lorry in this column was seen to bear the Battalion's number, so it was supposed that this was a "B" Echelon lorry moving with elements of the 21st Brigade.

Moving on south, the Battalion climbed the escarpment, and, topping it—ran straight into an enemy laager.

There was nothing to be done but go on, and this the Battalion did, passing several section posts without drawing fire. It then wheeled east, and the four lines of vehicles headed by the station wagon, drove on sedately at 15 miles per hour through the laager. After traversing about a mile of it, the enemy smelt a rat, and section posts began opening fire with machine-guns. Surprise being now out of the question, the formation broke up, each part trying to find its own way out. Soon after, the station wagon ran into a slit-trench and the leading elements of the column came under anti-tank gun and small-arms fire. Lieut. Reed, commanding the anti-tank troop, R.A., with commendable calm, towed a portee which had caught fire, out of danger; and at least another mile of enemy camp was crossed with comparatively little incident. By that time, the now dispersed column was more or less out of danger, having bluffed its way through with most admirable spirit and coolness.

By 6.15 a.m., it was judged that the column had moved far enough east, and a halt was called for the Battalion to re-organize and check up. At this time, there were only seven other vehicles present with the station wagon—and none of these belonged to the Battalion. However, early tea was brewed—though its consumption was disturbed by a German reconnaissance car which came up to within 300 yards. There is no record what happened to the intruder, but the little column moved on, and by 7 a.m. had contacted elements of the 5th Indian Infantry Brigade. A quarter of an hour later, the whole party came under the welcome protection of the 1st Armoured Division, deployed ready for battle. It was from these good judges that they learned that they had passed within a few thousand yards of an enemy armoured division, drawn up approximately where the 10th

1942

Indian Division had been ordered to rally. Fuqa was in enemy hands, and, in fact, had been since before the break-out from Mersa Matruh.

Bits and pieces of the Battalion soon began to arrive. The party moved on to a rallying-point near the El Alamein line, and encamped for the night next to the 21st Indian Infantry Brigade. A calling of the roll then produced a total of three British officers (the original occupants of the station wagon), five Viceroy's commissioned officers, and 158 other ranks.

Tired as they were, they had an unrestful night, for the camp was bombed, but next morning, the 30th, the Battalion moved back, in company with the rest of the Brigade, passing, en route, through the 18th Brigade box, where the 4th Battalion of the Regiment then was. 30 June

By 10.30 p.m., the Battalion was encamped at Ibayid Station, some 15 miles behind the El Alamein line. The following morning was spent collecting odd trucks and parties of men who had come in. Capt. Macdwyer and 2nd/Lieut. Wilson arrived with Sub.-Maj. Karam Singh, seventy men and three prisoners. Left-out-of-battle personnel and first reinforcements arrived about lunch-time from Amariyeh under Capt. Anson and 2nd/Lieut. Harwant Singh; and it was learnt from these that other details from the break-out had arrived in Amariyeh. 1 July

That night, the Battalion moved back to Amariyeh, and settled into a standing camp, with the added luxury, not enjoyed for many days, of a plentiful supply of water, and the men revelled in their first wash-down for ten days or a fortnight. During the night, Capt. Smith and 2nd/Lieut. Key reported back with thirty-eight more men.

Summed up, losses in the break-out totalled 1 British officer, five Viceroy's commissioned officers, about 200 other ranks and 32 followers, including the mess, with some of the records, and nearly all "B" Echelon. Missing M.T. comprised 2 motor-cycles, 20 15-cwt. trucks, 11 30-cwt. lorries, 2 water tanks, 9 carriers and 2 portees. Compared with the rest of the Brigade, the Battalion came out of it extraordinarily well, but the losses incurred by the Division as a whole in getting away through the four Axis divisions which stood between them and safety, were in any case not unduly high considering the hazards involved. It is pleasant to know that of the Indian other ranks captured in the withdrawal, 77, comprising 4 havildars, 5 naiks, 8 L/Naiks, 60 sepoys, and an additional 5 followers, were recovered in December, during the Alamein offensive, having spent most of their time in Mersa Matruh and Tobruk. The mess havildar, Hassan Khan, and a sergeant had got away two or three days before, and were half-way over to the British lines before they were picked up.

On the 4th July, the Battalion, with the further addition of two men of "A" Company, who had found their way back, moved back 4 July

1942

100 miles to Mena, and were settled in to a standing camp by 4 p.m. The re-forming of the Battalion began at once, and a complete mortar detachment of one havildar and eight men, with truck and weapons complete, arrived the same evening. The transport drivers, as usual, had little breathing-space, for all transport, with drivers, was taken away at 11 p.m. to lift the 5th Indian Infantry Brigade up to Amariyeh.

For the next few days there were normal (mainly drill) parades. The men were undergoing some reaction from the strain they had been through, and smartening-up was the tonic needed. Men and arms kept arriving in a steady stream, including a large batch of
10 July men sent back from courses, who came in on the 10th. Included among them were Capt. Assa Singh from a field works course, and 2nd/Lieut. Carleton from a signals course. These additions brought the strength of the Battalion up to 10 British officers, 1 medical officer, 17 Viceroy's commissioned officers, 629 other ranks, and 31 followers. Much cross-posting within the Battalion was necessary, including a complete change-over in Company appointments, but the Battalion was in being.

11 July On the 11th July news came in that the Brigade would move, on the 13th, to Kilo 110 on the Alexandria road, and this caused some head-scratching in the M.T. officer's department. Most Battalion vehicles were still in the workshops under second-line repair, and there were only 13 15-cwt. trucks, 2 30-cwt. lorries, 11 3-tonners and 3 portees on the road. As this would have meant a complicated ferrying programme, it was probably some relief when orders were changed at 2 p.m., and a new deployment ordered.

It was now proposed that the Battalion should provide a battle-group, made up of two rifle companies, a skeleton Battalion Headquarters, the carriers, mortars and the anti-tank platoon. This was to be commanded by Maj. Ashe, who would take his orders as required from the Guides Cavalry. After some changes in timing, Maj. Ashe
12 July and his men moved out of Mena at 8 a.m. on the 12th, en route to a rendezvous with the Guides Cavalry at Kilo 40.

The group must be admitted to have been a somewhat nondescript affair. "B" Company, under Capt. Assa Singh, and "D" Company under Capt. Anson, had been made up to strength in both men and weapons from "A" and "C", and the other sub-units had been completed with old lorries, mortars and anti-tank guns from all units in the Brigade. Unfortunately there is no record of the column's activities, but it may be presumed that no special excitements came its way before it rejoined the Battalion, in good order, on the 20th.

Meanwhile, the remainder of the Battalion, under Capt. R. B. Penfold,
14 July moved off at 9 a.m. on the 14th, in R.A.S.C. transport, to a new

camp at Kilo 106 on the Alexandria-Cairo road. The move was completed without incident, though much difficulty was experienced with the transport, from sand. 1942

Two days later, Company commanders went out and made a detailed reconnaissance of a three-battalion defended area about Kilo 110. This position was to be dug by the Battalion and the King's Own, and work was duly started on the 18th, after artillery sitings had been fixed. "B" and "D" Companies were allotted the No. 3 Battalion position, and settled down in camp there on their return from column on the 20th. 16 July

18 July

20 July

Work on the position went steadily on till the end of the month. The mine-laying was at first slow as the mines were the S.P. Mark V type, which were new to the men. The new Divisional commander visited the position on the 25th, and approved it. On the same day, classes in signals, 3-inch mortar, M.T. driving, and 2-pounder gun work, were started. 25 July

On the 1st August, the new Brigade commander visited the Battalion, saw the men at work, and afterwards met the Viceroy's commissioned officers in their mess. 1 Aug.

On the 4th, the Battalion was warned for a move next day, but the order was cancelled an hour later. 4 Aug.

On the 8th August, the Brigade marched back to Mena, but left the Battalion behind. The Battalion was now posted to the 18th Indian Infantry Brigade of the 5th Indian Division, in succession to the 4th Battalion, which was now in Cairo, preparatory to moving up to Haifa. This (temporary) posting away from the 10th Indian Division removed the last of its original members from that formation. 8 Aug.

However complete the Battalion may have looked on paper, it was by now very short of experienced men for non-commissioned rank. Men originally passed over were sorted out again, and a number tested to see whether they could now function in charge of a guard and of a section-post, and in drilling a section, weapon-training, bayonet-fighting and verbal orders. Similar tests were to be applied to all non-commissioned officers who had been promoted without first passing a cadre.

No one familiar with the Sikh need be told what followed. Not much warning had been given, and preparations began among the candidates with tremendous enthusiasm. Digging on the defensive position was billed to end on the 15th August, and next day the test was held. Out of 60 men previously passed over, 25 got through, while of 65 who had been promoted without passing a cadre, 40 were successful. 16 Aug.

Next day, the 17th, the Battalion's nine-day period with the 18th Indian Infantry Brigade came to a close, and orders were received to 17 Aug.

201

1942

18 Aug.	move to Khatatba, and thence to a destination to be disclosed later. The move was to be on the lightest possible scale—remaining stores and all vehicles being handed over to 18th Brigade Headquarters. "B" and "D" Companies left next day under Maj. Assa Singh. With them went advance parties from the remaining companies.
19 Aug.	"A", "C" and "H.Q." Companies followed on the 19th, leaving the M.T. officer and the quartermaster to hand over vehicles and stores.
21 Aug.	At Khatatba on the 21st, orders came in for a rail move up to Haifa, and Maj. Assa Singh's party, now under Maj. Ashe, left at
22 Aug.	4 p.m. on the 22nd. The Battalion dump meanwhile was collected from Cowley Camp at Mena, and with it a draft consisting of 2nd/Lieut. King and twenty other ranks, from No. 11 Reinforcement Camp.
23 Aug.	At 1.30 p.m. on the 23rd August, the second half of the Battalion, under the commanding officer, left Khatatba Station. Arrived in
24 Aug.	Haifa, they spent the night of the 24th August at At Rirah Camp, getting their orders for embarkation for Cyprus next day.
25 Aug.	On the 25th, on the quayside, things went with a swing. Sixty men of the first party had been left behind, but there was the entire Battalion heavy kit to deal with. It took just three-quarters of an hour to get the whole lot on board, and the ship sailed at 11.30 a.m.

By a happy circumstance, H.M.S. *Sikh* escorted the ship. A signal was made to her and a reply received that she was glad to have been of use to the Battalion, and would effect a meeting if circumstances allowed. A few days later, in Cyprus, the opportunity was made, but her regretted sinking not long after off Tobruk ended this pleasant acquaintanceship.

The trip itself to Cyprus was a short one, and without incident. The Battalion reached Famagusta at 11.30 p.m. the same night, and was met by Maj. Ashe with transport to take it to Malounda, on the

26 Aug.	north-east end of the island. Here, next day, the troops took over from the 4th/13th Frontier Force Rifles, Keep "E", which straddles the Malounda Pass, and settled down to work.
27 Aug.	Cadres and classes were started, and companies spent a couple of days reconnoitring their positions. These were all on the tops of the hills covering the pass, and were difficult to pick up. There was little transport to get about in, so everyone had plenty of much-needed exercise. After reconnoitring one position, companies moved on in rotation to the next to acquire as complete a knowledge of the Battalion lay-out as possible.
28 Aug.	Next day, transport was taken over, with other stores, from the 1 P.C.L.H. The transport consisted of 4 8-cwt. vans, 37 15-cwt. trucks, 9 3-ton lorries, 26 carriers, 6 quads, 39 motor-cycles and a station wagon. An impressive parade they would have made if all had not been in extremely bad condition, with nearly half off the road.

A further issue included 4 25-pounders and 19 Spiggot mortars. With
these to contend with, we must now go east again and follow the
fortunes of the 3rd Battalion, in Iraq.

The 3rd Battalion had spent part of the winter at Baiji on the Tigris, about 130 miles downstream from Mosul. In April, it moved on again, down-river to Busra. Here the Battalion was inspected by H.R.H. The Duke of Gloucester, and Gen. Sir Claude Auchinleck, and received their congratulations on the fine appearance and arms drill of the men. Soon after this a detachment was ordered down to Bahrein Island—a circumstance which was to have over-riding consequences in the future employment of the Battalion. But this could not be foreseen at the time.

The Bahrein detachment consisted of "D" Company, the carrier platoon, one section of the mortar platoon, and a troop of the anti-tank platoon, armed with two captured Persian "75's", which were later replaced by 3.7-in. hows. Capt. "Bruce" Burridge was in command, with Lieut. G. H. Blatchford as his second. The precise threat at that moment to Bahrein is not mentioned in the record, nor the reason for so much of the Battalion's fire-power being sent, but the oil installations were of the first importance, and in the confused strategical lay-out of the moment, precautions had to be taken. It may be remarked in parenthesis that this threat was not judged to have passed till March 1943, when the detachment rejoined. Meanwhile, in spite of the extreme humidity of the July climate, the high temperatures, and the incessant sandstorms, which were a severe test at the start, efficiency and morale both remained high.

On the 24th July, the Battalion, less its detachment, moved down-river from Busra, to take over from a Baluch battalion the protection of Abadan, with its big oil refinery. The tour of duty there was expected to be a temporary one, lasting two weeks. By an unfortunate conjunction of circumstances, however, the Battalion was doomed to linger there without relief for seven long months.

Iraq was at this time under command of G.H.Q., Middle East, and the Battalion was expecting a move to the Western Desert theatre in August in the ordinary course of reliefs. Whether or no it would so have gone is uncertain, for it so happened that shipping was not immediately available to bring the Bahrein detachment back, and the Battalion could hardly have gone to an operational theatre without it. But it would have gone in the end. Unfortunately for the Battalion, however, the Prime Minister, Mr. Churchill, paid his first visit to Teheran about this time, and accepted certain proposals for re-organization of the area covering the strategically vital oil resources of Persia and Iraq, and the trans-Persian line of communications with Russia.

1942

The upshot was the creation of a new command—the Persia and Iraq Force, more commonly "Paiforce". Those troops present in the area were naturally earmarked for the new command, and though an exception might possibly have been made for the 3rd Battalion if it had been already under orders for the Western Desert, this was not the case, and there was nothing more to be said. It was a sore disappointment for the Battalion, and with nothing good to set against it—only the never-ending monotony of life in Abadan, with constant duties, nights-in-bed down to one-and-a-half, and few opportunities for training or contact with other troops. None-the-less the men kept cheerful, and with efficiency unimpaired.

4th Bn. *The 4th Battalion* had returned to Cairo at the end of February after the withdrawal from Benghazi. Measures were now taken to establish relations with H.M.S. *Sikh*. Lieut.-Col. R. Bampfield, who was in officiating command of the Battalion, paid a visit to Royal Naval headquarters in Cairo to see if it would be possible to contact the ship, and—a fortnight later—was told that a favourable opportunity had come. Naval headquarters wired ahead to announce the visit,

24 Mar. and on the 24th March, a small party comprising Bampfield, Colley, the Sub.-Maj., the senior Sikh Viceroy's commissioned officer, Sub. Mit Singh, and eight other ranks, left Cairo for Alexandria. The two British officers contacted the ship that evening, and at 10 next

25 Mar. morning, they all went aboard—the first Battalion party from the Regiment to meet the ship. With them, they took a small frame enclosing the badge, a button and a shoulder-title of the Regiment, while Sub. Mit Singh made a further presentation of a picture of Guru Gobind Singh, from the Gurdwara. Both these were hung up in the ward-room.

After handing over these tokens, the visitors were divided into three parties and shown all over the ship. By all accounts, no corner was missed. It was, all-in-all, a memorable occasion—to be happily revived over a period of weeks that August.

The threat to the Middle-East had by now reached a pitch that transcended local resources in troops. Iraq was still under Middle-East headquarters, and the troops there had to be made ready for short-notice service in the Western Desert. Each brigade in the 4th and 5th Indian Divisions accordingly now sent one Battalion to Iraq to give training in desert warfare. The 4th Battalion of the Regiment was one of those selected.

At the end of March, the remaining M.T. was handed in, and the Battalion entrained for Haifa. After one night there, spent in At Rirah camp, it was provided with troop-carrying transport, and moved off at 7 a.m. one morning, on the six-day journey to Baghdad via Rutbah Wells and Habbaniya. Apart from the first day, when the

1942

convoy traversed the Plain of Esdraelon and Vale of Jezreel, through a profusion of wild flowers, the journey was dull in the extreme. Arrived in Baghdad, the Battalion war outfit was completed, but Lieut.-Col. J. J. Purves, who had rejoined from India just before the move, was now appointed to command the 21st Indian Infantry Brigade, and Bampfield succeeded him in command.

In Baghdad, Lieut.-Col. Bampfield took the opportunity to visit the memorial church, and saw the window presented by the Battalion in memory of those who had fallen in the First World War. It had been faithfully rendered, and looked dignified and effective. All the chairs in the church had been presented by relatives of those who served in Mesopotamia, and the names of the officers of the Battalion who had fallen there were seen, inscribed on the backs of several chairs.

The stay in Baghdad was a short one, and on the 9th April, the M.T. was sent off by road to Erbil. The troops followed next day, travelling by rail as far as Kirkuk, where there was a pleasant little function when representatives of the 2nd/3rd Gurkha Rifles, who were permanent honorary members of the mess, met the Battalion at the station and provided the troops with a welcome mug of tea. The stage was set for the picking-up of many old threads, for the commander of the 18th Indian Infantry Brigade, in which Sikhs and Gurkhas were to serve side-by-side, was Brig. Lochner, who had been a good friend of the Battalion's in the Khyber in 1938, when commanding a battalion of the South Wales Borderers. The third member of the Brigade was a Territorial battalion of the Essex Regiment.

9 Apr.
10 Apr.

Moving on after their welcome cup of tea at Kirkuk, the Battalion travelled by road to Erbil, where it settled down to intensive training. Among its visitors were Maj.-Gen. C. O. Harvey (late Central India Horse), Brig. C. W. W. Ford, late commandant of the 5th Battalion, and Colin McVean of the 3rd. But events were moving too fast in the west for a prolonged stay in Iraq, and after not very many weeks, orders came in for the Brigade to cross the desert to Haifa and come into G.H.Q. reserve.

The return journey was more interesting than the earlier one. Prospects of action perhaps coloured the scene a little, but the records speak of the interest taken in the scenes of the fighting in the Syrian campaign, the story of which was still fresh in every memory, though few, if any, had taken part in it. The route lay through Mosul, Deir ez Zor, Palmyra, and Damascus, at each of which points a night was spent. The final destination was Lejeun, the site of an old Roman camp at the northern end of the Musmus Pass. Here, one of the few roads across the extension of the Carmel Range debouches into the Plain of Esdraelon. It was an important strategical pivot in ancient times, and its name Lejeun was

205

said to date back to the Roman Legio that had occupied it.

1942

The Battalion had a week to study the historical and other amenities of Lejeun, and then, at twelve hours notice, moved off back to the Western Desert.

21 June

As so often in war, move orders came in with a touch of the dramatic. On the evening of the 21st June, the commanding officer was called over to Brigade Headquarters, some 25 miles away, in connection with an important reconnaissance due to start next day at 6 a.m. It was midnight before he got back. He warned company commanders, and they duly appeared at the appointed rendezvous at

22 June

6 o'clock. They were no sooner there than they were told the reconnaissance was cancelled, and that the Brigade was moving with all speed to the Cairo area in G.H.Q. reserve. The situation in the desert was critical, and brooked no delay. (Tobruk had, in fact, fallen twenty-four hours before, though this was not made known to the troops at the time.)

Not a moment was lost. The M.T. was loaded up, and started for

23 June

Cairo at 5 o'clock next morning in the wake of a small advance party that had left the previous night. The commanding officer had been in to Haifa on the 22nd with the adjutant to fix up transport to take the Battalion to the station next day, and after some confusion and counter-ordering, this was done. The Battalion was very short of senior officers at the time, for three of the regular company commanders were away in Busra—two on a reconnaissance, and the third doing duty with a big reinforcement camp. Strenuous efforts were made to secure their return, but the Battalion left without news of them.

Piling into their lorries at 5 a.m., the troops drove down to the station. The train steamed out at 10 a.m., and brought them to Kantara

24 June

by 2 a.m. on the 24th. Here, hot water was provided for the men to make tea, together with an issue of hard-boiled eggs. The officers had an excellent breakfast in the NAAFI restaurant. Then came the ferry over the Suez Canal. On its way to Iraq, the Battalion had suffered from bad organization. This time, it saw that matters were arranged more sensibly, and all spare kit was loaded in goods wagons and sent across on the wagon ferry. The men, meantime, each with a small hand-load, crossed separately, and completed the crossing in a time which beat all previous records by about an hour.

On the other side of the canal, the train was ready waiting in the station, but its destination was not now Cairo, but Semilla, a small junction about 10 to 15 miles east of Mersa Matruh. It was reckoned from this that things were not going too well—and in point of fact, the enemy had crossed the Egyptian frontier, and were already on their way to Mersa Matruh. Crossing the Delta, the train arrived at

Amariyeh at 2.30 p.m., and stopped for two hours to let the men cook. Then, moving on, it ran through Daba next morning, about 80 miles short of Mersa Matruh. Anti-climax here intervened, however, for the train had gone little farther when the engine ran out of water, and the Battalion had to wait for several hours before it could be brought up. Then it pushed on once more, and, just after dark, halted at a small station called Galal. The Essex Regiment, whose train had passed on ahead while the Sikhs were waiting for water, was in the station, and the Sikh train was halted about half-a-mile outside. The halt was expected to be a long one, but the troops were to be ready to move at short notice.

1942

25 June

In view of the air risk, Lieut.-Col. Bampfield at once ordered the Battalion to de-train and disperse, but before this could be done, enemy aircraft flew over, dropped flares, and followed this up by bombing the Battalion as well as the Essex. A truck in the Essex train was hit by a bomb in the first stick, and went up in flames, and this much helped the enemy in dropping his subsequent sticks. Only one stick dropped near the Sikhs, but that straddled the train and caused casualties of seven killed and eighteen wounded. Of the wounded, two later died in hospital. In the dark it was difficult to deal with the casualties, but the doctor, despite an injured foot, did sterling work, and by three in the morning all the wounded had been attended to and made as comfortable as possible. The dead were decently buried. It was not a propitious return to the Western Desert, but the men took it in good heart, and their spirits remained high.

26 June

At 7 a.m., a trolley-car came down the railway. The officer in it brought orders for the troops to return to Daba. The train moved off half-an-hour later, and got into Daba about half-past nine. Here, the Battalion found a harassed R.T.O., but no orders. Some quick work on the telephone, however, brought results, and the Battalion was ordered to move on back to El Alamein station, de-train, and wait for orders.

The run to El Alamein seems to have had a nightmare quality of frustrated good intentions. All the world was on its way back, and Daba station was crowded with personnel waiting for transport and eager to jump the Sikhs' train. Nothing could be done, though. The train was already jammed full, and they had to be turned away. Farther on along the line, at each of the frequent halts in the long, slow journey, parties of Bedouins, making their way back with everything they could carry, kept trying to board the train, and had to be kept at bay. However, all things have their endings, and in due time the Battalion arrived, and went into as dispersed a position, alongside the Gurkhas, who were already there, as the nature of the

1942

ground would allow. The M.T. also rejoined after having been turned back on the road to Daba—and the Battalion was again complete, except for its advance party under Morrison.

Meanwhile, there was no sign of Brigade Headquarters, which had gone on ahead. The brigadier had gone down with pneumonia at Haifa, and Lieut.-Col. Grey of the Gurkhas had taken over officiating command.

The night was quiet. Only one stick of bombs was dropped—and this fell about three-quarters of a mile away, near the main road.

27 June At 9.30 a.m. on the 27th June, the commanding officer was sent for by Lieut.-Col. May of the Essex, who was acting as brigadier in Lieut.-Col. Grey's absence, and told that the Brigade was to move to the Deir ez Shein area, about 11 miles south of El Alamein. Here, it was to prepare a Brigade defensive position. Lieut.-Col. Bampfield left with a reconnaissance party at 11 o'clock, and was shortly followed by Company commanders. The troops were ferried down in the Battalion transport, the last party arriving about 8.30 p.m. Lieut.-Col. Grey got back the same night, as did the advance party, which had had a bewildering time in some respects. It had been up as far as Mersa Matruh, where, as Morrison said, orders for position after position had been given him. Each was cancelled almost as soon as issued, and he was eventually told to come back. Advancing German columns were already filtering in behind, and it was only by taking a circuitous route through the desert that he got through. The 2nd Battalion, it will be remembered, was at this time standing up manfully against attack in the covering position west of Mersa Matruh, with no thought of withdrawal or of enemy in their rear, and were not to fall back for another twenty-four hours yet.

Work was started immediately the men arrived on the position at Deir ez Shein, and continued without pause till 1 a.m. next morning. Wire had not come up, so work started with weapon pits. The ground was very rocky, but the Battalion was fortunate in being able to get, for a short time, some compressor drills from the 1st South African Division, under whose command it had now come.

Work on the defences re-started after a short rest, and went on
28 June all day on the 28th. By this time there was some wire, and a fair supply of mines. Knox, the son of Col. E. F. Knox, D.S.O., who had commanded the Battalion—then the 36th Sikhs—in the second half of the First World War, went out on a reconnaissance about 20 miles ahead, and brought back most valuable information of what was going on. He had also been able to help one or two parties from other units which were out in the desert on the same mission. Meanwhile, in the Battalion, there were serious problems to solve. One was water. The nearest water-point was 40 miles away, but the Battalion

had only one 220-gallon water-vehicle for the 800-odd men. Worse— the water-point was being used by so many units that there was a queue of twenty or thirty vehicles waiting to fill up. This meant that the most it was reasonable to expect was one journey a day. However, by loading up a 30-cwt. lorry with pakhals, and sending that as well, it was just possible to ration the men at half-a-gallon a day.

The other worry was artillery support. The Field Regiment usually in support had parted company with the Brigade at Haifa. It had gone on ahead, and nothing had been heard of it since. It was assumed that the normal scale of artillery would sooner or later be allotted to the Brigade, but in the meantime something had to be done to ensure that when the guns did come, there would be no avoidable delay in getting them into action. At the moment all the Battalion had was two 2-pounder anti-tank guns, which it had borrowed from a unit going down the line.

Enquiry confirmed that guns would be allotted in due course, but there was nothing to show how many. So, anti-tank gun positions were prepared on the Battalion front on the assumption that a full quota would be sent. It was an anxious time, as may be supposed, and not made easier by the lack of definite information, whether of the enemy troops or our own. The varying distances of our air bombing provided the only indication of the enemy's progress.

Thanks to a full moon, it was possible to put in work at full pressure by night as well as by day, and the Battalion was averaging a little over twenty hours a day on digging, mining, and wiring. Previous service in the desert was a tremendous asset, for most of the men were able, with only the minimum of help, to lay the three different types of mine supplied. The minefield grew at a great pace, as also did the defensive wire, especially the Dannert concertina type. Both the Essex and the Gurkhas were helped by the two or three non-commissioned officers the Battalion sent over to show them the way of it.

Work thus continued full out on the defences on the 29th and 30th June, and resulted in a position of some strength. Apart from one raid on the night of the 29th/30th, there were no air attacks, and there were no casualties. The Royal Air Force, however, were much in evidence, and this heartened everyone. A regular service of bombers used to go over well escorted by fighters. The same number used to return with cheering regularity. It was these raids, and the relative noise of the bomb-bursts, as heard in the position, that gave the Battalion its clue to the enemy's progress, which, by that test, was coming ominously close. Though they were not to know it, it was one of the key battles of the whole World War that was about to break over these devoted men, and it seems in a way rather odd that

1942

their feverish preparations should be justified by so very little in the way of official advance information.

As already recorded, the 2nd Battalion passed through the position on the 30th June, after its break-out from Mersa Matruh, and no doubt, the 4th Battalion welcomed the information it brought.

Not only the 2nd Battalion, but many others withdrew through the position during the day. By evening, all our forward troops were through, and it is time to give some fuller description of what were now the forward defensive localities. Ten miles or so to the north lay the 1st South African Division in a box astride the road and railway. The same distance to the south were the New Zealanders. To watch these two long gaps, there was in each a "Jock" Column of an infantry company and a few guns.

The 18th Brigade box, midway between the South Africans and the New Zealanders as we have seen, was slightly irregular in shape. The west face was held by the Sikhs, the sappers, and medium machine-guns. The Essex manned the faces on the north-east and north. The Gurkhas were on the south-east and south, with, in their area, part of the now famous Ruwaisat ridge. Artillery requirements had at last been met, and the Brigade was better off in this respect than had been thought likely. But the guns had come up so late that there had been no time to get them properly dug in. In addition to ten field-guns, a number of 2-pounder and 6-pounder anti-tank guns had been sent, and a further reinforcement comprised seven Mathilda tanks, and four medium machine-guns of the Cheshire Regiment.

Morale was high, and the Battalion records with appreciation the two visits paid it by Maj.-Gen. "Dan" Peinaar, commander of the 1st South African Division, while constructing the position. The record pays him fine tribute in saying that "there can have been few more inspiring and understanding commanders", and adds "in the short time that we knew him, we felt that we had made a real and life-long friend".

As the afternoon of the 30th June passed by, clouds of dust were seen moving eastwards, away to the north-west. Soon after, sounds of gunfire were heard. This was a German attack on the South African position astride the road. It was beaten off. Divisional Headquarters sent out a warning that attack was to be expected shortly. Nothing came of it, however, and the night was undisturbed.

1 July Early next morning, firing broke out again to the north. Soon after a Guides Cavalry patrol reported enemy movement, with infantry and tanks, towards the 18th Brigade box.

About 9 a.m., two shells fell in the southern part of the position, and for an hour thereafter, the enemy carried out systematic ranging with air-bursts and contact H.E. There must have been observation posts well forward, but none could be seen. It was discovered later that one was in a derelict truck which had been blown up in the minefield.

Between nine and ten there was a short interlude when the Germans sent in a message by two captured British officers under a flag of truce, to say that unless the position surrendered at once, it would be attacked. After getting some useful information from the unfortunate envoys, they were sent back with a flat refusal.

At 10 a.m., the enemy artillery opened on the Essex. They were heavily shelled, but escaped fairly lightly. From 11 a.m., the enemy extended his concentrations to include Brigade Headquarters, and began a general search of the area. The Sikh "B" Echelon transport suffered rather heavily, and two ammunition trucks were hit and burnt out. While this shelling was going on, Battalion telephone lines to companies were frequently cut, and the signallers had much difficulty in repairing them.

A small infantry formation, probably Italian, assisted by guns, now made a half-hearted attack on the south face, but was easily repulsed by the Gurkhas.

Shelling went on throughout the morning in various degrees of intensity, but progress was made none-the-less in digging in the 2-pounder anti-tank guns which had arrived the previous evening. If only there had been time enough to complete this properly, the artillery would have been saved many unnecessary casualties this day.

At 1 o'clock, under cover of a dust-storm, which was further thickened by the dust thrown up by his own shelling, the enemy managed to clear a lane in the minefield on the north-east face of the perimeter between the Essex and the Gurkhas, and to pass through some infantry and machine-guns. The infantry were quickly ejected by mortar fire, but the machine-guns got into broken ground and established themselves.

Under cover of the machine-guns, a force of tanks now moved up and opened fire on everything that offered. Our guns engaged them and knocked out two, but thanks to their lack of protection, were themselves soon put out of action.

It was difficult to see. Visibility was poor owing to the dust, and the artillery and machine-gun fire discouraged over-much personal exposure. There appeared, however, to be some thirty or forty tanks inside the box. Guns, or heavy tanks, sited some way to the north, seemed to be shelling the Essex and Brigade Head-quarter trenches, while the tanks inside the box moved round the rear of the Essex. Most of these tanks moved in on the Essex, while two parties turned towards the Sikh "B" Echelon and forward companies respectively.

The Essex were forced to surrender. The tanks then all moved in on the rear of the Sikh forward companies. The 2-pounders scored two hits before being silenced. In "A" Company area, tanks were engaged by a troop of 25-pounders close to Sikh Battalion Headquarters, and two were hit, though not seriously. The supporting tanks opened fire, and with two salvos of one shot per tank, knocked out all four guns. This gallant action by our gunners lasted a bare minute-and-a-half.

The tanks now closed in on all the now defenceless Sikh companies. It was 5 o'clock and the battle was over, but there was no unnecessary surrender. Orders had been got through for the men to break away to the south if they could, and it was known that some had done so. Some of the transport had also been got away under orders from Brigade Headquarters. Lieut.-Col. Bampfield decided that he would lie up in his battle headquarters slit-trench with his adjutant and the small Battalion Headquarter party. With luck they might remain unobserved, and be able to get away after dark.

Meanwhile, it was an exasperating position. With one anti-tank weapon, much damage might have been done, for there were five German tanks 150 yards away, their crews drinking beer in the Sikh mess and sending off to the rear the other drinks and food they found there. One can sympathize with the onlookers, hot, thirsty and tired, grimed with sweat and dust, and unable to do anything but wait.

All this time, Battalion Headquarters was in touch with the Brigade, as the exchange operator, before he was captured, had plugged the Battalion through. This soon ended, however. Having had their fill of beer, the tanks moved ahead, passing each side of the Sikh slit-trench, and descended on Brigade Headquarters, supported by a very heavy artillery concentration. It was quickly over.

Time dragged on till 7.45 p.m., when the Battalion Headquarter party crept out of its slit-trench. It met a number of enemy vehicles while negotiating its way through the box, so divided up its fourteen members into four small groups. Three were led by Viceroy's commissioned officers. In the fourth were the commanding officer, the adjutant (Trestrail) and one sepoy. There were sufficient compasses for each party, so, after fixing the others' bearings, and issuing general instructions, the commanding officer wished them all good luck, and they parted company.

As to the commanding officer's little party, it got across the box without trouble beyond an occasional lie-up, as enemy vehicles crossed its path, moving into laager. Emerging from the box, a cross-country course was set, and after 2 miles, the party came across a Mathilda tank, whose crew had been killed or captured without the tank being put out of action. This was just what the party wanted. The engine was running, so jumping in, they started off, and with

1942

Trestrail at the controls, though he had never been in a tank before, drove east across the desert at a steady 12 miles per hour. Ultimately an armoured formation was met, and the tank handed over. Trestrail was subsequently awarded the Military Cross.

The party then made its way to Hammam station where it was joined by Wimbush who had come out via the south face of the box, and about thirty-five men.

Next day, all were delighted to see the medical officer, Siqueira, walk in. He had got away, with casualties, in the transport that had been sent out, and had then laid low till dark, when he started to walk. The casualties had presumably gone on ahead. On his way, Siqueira was stopped by an Italian sentry, and some back-chat ensued. The sentry's viewpoint was that the doctor was his prisoner, but the doctor argued that he ought not to take a medical officer prisoner. The sentry, however, was resolute; but not so careful but that he rested the butt of his rifle on the ground during the discussion. Siqueira, then, to use his own words, caught him a right to the jaw and felled him, banged his head against a stone twice to make sure that he was really right out, and then legged it as hard as he could go. He covered the 15 miles to our forward troops, and re-joined. This combined with his sterling work on the night of the 25th/26th June, resulted in a recommendation for the award of the Military Cross.

Battalion Headquarters spent a day or two at Hammam collecting more men as they came in. Quite a number had escaped as they were being marched away in the dark, and others had lain low while the position was being over-run. Lieut.-Col. Bampfield took a trip to Corps Headquarters and met Lieut.-Gen. Sir W. Norrie, commanding the XXXth Corps. He was kind enough to emphasize that the stand that had been made in the 18th Brigade box had materially helped—giving that much extra time to rush reinforcements forward. It marked the limit of the German advance until their ejection in the big Alamein offensive in November.

From Hammam, the Battalion was ordered back to Cairo, with a short halt at Amariyeh on the way. Its losses had been heavy, including seven British officers, nine Viceroy's commissioned officers and about 500 other ranks. Most of these were taken prisoner, but there were a number of whom nothing was ever heard again.

The Battalion spent about a month in Cairo getting new equipment, and collecting all the extra-regimentally employed men to try and make up a good nucleus for the re-forming of the Battalion. After a succession of orders and counter-orders, it left by road for Haifa on the 12th August. The first stage lay across the Delta, highly cultivated, and with much of interest to see. The night was passed

12 Aug.

1942
13 Aug. on the east bank of the Suez Canal. Next day, the column was off at 6 a.m. on a long monotonous drive over the new tarmac road across the Sinai Desert. Here, lorries could only pull off at definitely appointed places owing to the softness of the sand at each side.
14 Aug. The last day was perhaps the most interesting, thanks chiefly to a missed turning, at Beer Sheba, where the previous night had been spent. Instead of taking the coast road, the column moved up by Bethlehem and Jerusalem. The length of the journey was much the same, but both scenery and historical interest were incomparably greater.

Arrived in Haifa, the Battalion settled into the same rest camp it had occupied earlier in the year on the way to Iraq, and began taking over the general guard and protective duties from the 2nd Lancers (Gardiner's Horse). The take-over was completed in two days. General guard duties were assumed as well as the protection of various installations, and the responsibilities included the command of the northern sector of the Haifa defences, with about 4,000 men under command, and a large area of base installations. The Battalion had to be split, and a second officers' mess opened. Much time was spent on reconnaissances and getting to know people. It proved a busy life, and everyone had a job—which was as well.

The Battalion was much under strength, and it was hard to meet its commitments. However, ways and means were found, and a comprehensive programme of individual training was worked in as well. Furthermore, the Battalion now renewed its acquaintance with H.M.S. *Sik* and a lively friendship sprang up with her officers and ratings over the four weeks they were in contact. A memorable occasion was when a party of thirty officers and men of the Battalion went to sea in the ship and spent an interesting day watching target practice. It had been arranged for the ship's officers and a large party of men to attend the Saragarhi Day sports meeting on the 12th September, but unfortunately the ship sailed on what was to be her last mission in the early hours of that day. She had a magnificent ship's company—and it is satisfactory to know that after the gallant action which led to her sinking—a fuller account of which is given in its proper place in the next chapter—the survivors, who were fairly numerous, were in many cases sent to the same prisoners-of-war camp in Italy in which men of the Battalion were then living.

As a small, but dramatic, post-script to the Battalion's operations in the Western Desert—in the latter half of August, No. 10088 Hav. Dhirta Singh and three sepoys of the Battalion, escaped from the prisoners-of-war cage at Tobruk, and reported back to duty in the Battalion, after covering nearly 400 miles in twenty days.

The story behind this dramatic venture is well worth the telling.

1942

When taken prisoner at Deir ez Shein on the 1st July, he was taken back by lorry to Tobruk along the coastal road which he already knew pretty well. During the journey, he made mental notes of enemy activities such as petrol and ration dumping, use of landing grounds and movement of coastal shipping. Then, while employed at the docks in Tobruk, and on the railway extension from El Adem, he was able to note the numbers of lorries carrying German and Italian dead to the neighbouring big war cemetery. He had, at the same time, every intention of escaping, and was able to collect a sandbag half full of biscuits, a two-gallon tin of water, and three trustworthy companions.

On the night of the 17th/18th August, the small party successfully broke out.

Realizing that the coastal road, railway, and plain would be the main area of enemy movement, it had been decided to move due south for some 70 miles, keeping to the west of the El Adem aerodrome. They would then strike east. Though the party had neither map nor compass, it made its way via El Gubi to Sofafi. Here it lost its way, and wandered off to Sidi Omar, which, however, Hav. Dhirta Singh knew and recognized. Turning eastwards again, they were picked up by the 10th Armoured Division in the Southern Sector on the 7th September. During this part of the journey considerable enemy activity had been encountered, and several wide detours had to be made. At one time, the party lay up a whole day watching the enemy forming a ration dump, their lorries at times passing within a few yards only. All these things Hav. Dhirta Singh carefully noted; and when he eventually reached our lines, his information was considered of such value that he was sent back by air to Alexandria for interrogation by senior officers of the Royal Navy and Royal Air Force.

Such an example of coolness and devotion to duty was clearly deserving some special form of recognition; and in addition to the Indian Distinguished Service Medal granted for the military aspects of his exploit, he was further awarded the Mcgregor Memorial Medal for the value of his information and the skilful conduct of his long and difficult journey.

Meanwhile, seven more officers joined from the Training Battalion and completed the officer establishment.

Looking back to India, we have seen the threat that developed with the invasion of Burma. *The 6th Battalion* was to play its part in this, and in February was moved down from the Khyber to join the 4th Indian Infantry Brigade in Jhelum.

6th Bn.
February

After a short stay in Jhelum, the brigade was hurried off to Bengal, to that isolated and unenticing spot Jhikargacha Ghat, some 60 miles

1942

north-east of Calcutta. The threat to India had taken shape too fast for much to be done to meet it; and troops hence found themselves in little-organized areas, completing their training under conditions which had all the discomfort and none of the stimulus of active service. Administrative problems were continuous and acute, and the bad sanitation and excessive humidity accentuated them. Summer begins very early in the year in that part of India; and once the sun gains power, the humid, steamy air has a blanketing effect on the over-clad military body that altogether defies adequate description. None-the-less, morale stayed high, and the men faced up to the new conditions wonderfully fast.

Training in mechanized warfare on the higher scale of transport became the order of the day—and here, during and after the monsoon, the discomfort of living day and night in permanently sopping, warm and clinging clothing, in the constant irk of prickly heat, much tried all ranks. Of the lighter side of this heavy training period, there is unfortunately no record. The spontaneous, domestic small-change of battalion life rarely fits into the written chronicle, but certainly in the Battalions of the Sikh Regiment, it is a rare day when nothing happens to raise a laugh.

7th Bn. Elsewhere in India, troubles on the North-West Frontier, which had been boiling up for some little time, came to a head, and *the 7th Battalion* was to see its share of them.

15 Mar. Meanwhile, on the 15th March, the Army Commander, Lieut.-Gen. C. D. Noyes, inspected the Battalion, and met the officers.

23 Mar. It is on record that summer wear was adopted from the 23rd March, and serge battle-dress cleaned and handed back into store. Camouflage nets for safas were also taken into wear for parades outside the perimeter and for operations. A sort of conditional mobilization order was also received about this time. To quote the record: "orders were received to place the unit in such a position to be prepared for mobilization on receipt of further orders. This was done and the battalion was put on to the new organization. The battalion was re-organized as far as equipment and personnel permitted. This really entailed the ear-marking of personnel in 'HQ' Company and from Rifle Companies for 'HQ' Company platoons. Owing to lack of equipment the A/A Platoon (No 2 Platoon) was only ear-marked, and training was carried out in the afternoon in the handling of the V.B. No 4 Platoon was divided into the proposed carrier Platoon and the Infantry Gun section for training, though they remained intact for operations. The Pioneer Platoon was formed on a one-third P.M., two-third Sikh basis and training commenced forthwith with the help of the Faridkot Sappers and Miners".

1942

A new feature of Indian Army life which had been the subject of much heart-searching and discussion, was introduced at this time, and the 7th Battalion notes that Religious Holidays were now cut down to ten per year. This restriction of holidays, which was thoroughly justified from every point of view, led to amusing anomalies. In the Training Battalion, half-holidays were instituted as a means of attaining the desired object, but the method of notifying them sometimes led to redundancies, as when Routine Orders notified that Sunday would be observed as a half-holiday on one or other account.

The state of efficiency in the Battalion was a continual source of anxiety to the Commanding Officer. As he says, promotions to complete to new War Establishment were made during March, entailing promotion of 11 Paid Acting Naiks to Paid Acting Havildar, 42 Paid Acting Lance-Naiks to Paid Acting Naik, and 47 Sepoys to Paid Acting Lance-Naik—and this, with all the promotions that had taken place in the past quarter, meant a lowered standard of non-commissioned officer, and reduction of old sepoys serving in companies. Sepoys earmarked for specialist employment in the "H.Q." Company platoons had to be among the most efficient, and this could be ensured only at the expense of rifle companies. The final item to cause anxiety was that the Battalion was some 130 men below the strength of the new establishment, and there seemed to be small likelihood of the Training Battalion being able to complete them.

29 Apr. On the 29th April, Lieut.-Col. J. J. P. Conolly left the Battalion to take over as Brigade Commander, Madras Defended Port Area. He was succeeded by Lieut.-Col. A. E. Belchamber of the 1st Battalion, at the moment at the Senior Officers' School, Poona.

2 May Mobilization preparations went slowly along their appointed course, and on the 2nd May, Pay Books 64 M, were issued to all ranks, together with orders for their safe custody. The mortar detachments also made history this day. The two Punjabi-Mohammedan sections of the Mortar Platoon fired their first fifteen rounds of live ammunition. Speed was sacrificed for accuracy, and the results were good.

28 July On the 28th July, the Razmak Column moved out, including the King's Own Scottish Borderers and the 3rd/1st Gurkha Rifles, in addition to the 7th Battalion. Subsequently, the 1st/16th Punjab Regiment also joined the column.

The first day's march to the old permanent camp site in Razani was carried through without incident, but a certain amount of sniping came over in the evening, costing the King's Own Scottish Borderers one officer killed. The local Maliks were promptly warned, and artillery fixed lines laid on their houses—and the sniping ceased.

The hostile lashkar had apparently prepared a position astride the Mami Rogha Algad, relying on some local artillery and light

1942

machine-guns, to help in denying our forces access to Mami Rogha village, Lwargi Narai and Datta Khel.

29 July   A second column, called Garcol, supported by scouts on its right flank, advanced up to Mami Rogha Algad under a strong concentration of Medium and Mountain Artillery. Meantime, the Razmak Column moved from Razani to Gardai without incident.

Razcol then followed Garcol up the Mami Rogha Algad. Garcol made good its objectives with few casualties, and Razcol then, with the Sikhs as "spear head", passed through, and made good the Mami Rogha camp site. The operation was carried out according to plan—and by 2 p.m. all the high ground, including Mami Rogha, was in our possession. "B" Company, on the left, had encountered some opposition, but advanced steadily, and attained their objective. On the right flank, likely enemy positions were engaged by the supporting battery, and the advance of the forward troops, and "A" Company was not held up.

Construction of camp piquets was begun shortly after—the Battalion being allotted four of these. The work was hotly disputed by the enemy. Sniping, for about an hour, was heavy, but work went on well supported by the mountain battery and the Battalion 3-inch mortars, which came into action against an enemy for the first time. Royal Air Force Lysanders backed the Battalion up well with some spectacular dive attacks. Of the two Battalion casualties, one died of wounds, the other recovered. The piquets were constructed and wired in good time.

That evening, there was fairly heavy rifle and light machine-gun sniping, but the Battalion suffered no casualties. Towards dark the sniping died away. Garcol was in an adjoining perimeter camp, and the night passed quietly for both. The lashkar seems to have concluded that it was up against something too strong for a pitched battle, and subsequent action was on a very limited scale, and confined to a few gangs only.

30 July   The two columns opened the road to Lwargi Narai next day, against only slight opposition, reaching the Narai at 5.30 p.m. The 33rd Indian Infantry Brigade took over the camp site at Lwargi, and the two columns returned to their not very attractive camp site at Mami Rogha.

31 July   On the 31st, the two columns and the 33rd Indian Infantry Brigade moved through the Lwargi Narai to Datta Khel. There was a good deal of sniping on the way down to Tut Narai, but no casualties in the Battalion—which was the first unit in, and hence had the privilege of technically raising the siege of the post. One sepoy of "A" Company was badly injured when the trail of a 6-inch gun ran over his ankle.

1 Aug.   The 1st August was a rest-day, and the men took the opportunity to get cleaned up, and had arms and ammunition checked. The change

1942

from the Razmak heights to the Datta Khel plain was not a pleasant
one climatically, and it is not surprising that water discipline
needed taking in hand. However, action was taken, and matters were
set right. The camp was a comfortable one, and all ranks were glad
of the chance to relax.

On the 2nd August, the Battalion together with the King's Own   2 Aug.
Scottish Borderers, opened up the Tochi road to enable road repairs
to be put in hand, as far as the village of Kani Rogha. The Battalion
was advance guard, and piquetted some very difficult country. Apart
from some sniping at "Windy Corner" (Drewasta), where the Razmak
Column suffered fourteen casualties the year before, there was no
difficulty. The Tochi Scouts piquetted some of the big features on
either side of the valley. The Tochi river itself was very low. A
spate of sore backs and girth galls proved an unwelcome text on
which to stress the need of proper mule-loading.

On the 3rd, the Battalion rested again, and cleaned up, and worked   3 Aug.
on the perimeter defences. A fair amount of air activity was noted.

Razmak Column, less the King's Own Scottish Borderers, turned
out on the 4th August, and piquetted the route from Tut Narai up   4 Aug.
the Tut Narai Shaga—the Tochi Scouts assisting. Under this protection,
the Battalion and the sappers and miners repaired the road between
Datta Khel, Tut Narai, and Degam, thus preparing an alternative
route to the Tochi road. The excellent Battalion contribution to the
work was commemorated in "Sikh Corner", at the beginning of the
road, and for which the services of a "Monster" road constructor
were utilized.

The 5th August was again spent in camp, but on the 6th, Maj.   5 Aug.
Walker went out on a Razcol reconnaissance in preparation for a
night operation the same night, in which, however, the 7th Battalion   6 Aug.
was not to take part. Instead, the protection of the camp was handed
over to it, and it remained responsible for about twenty-four hours.
How the column operation went off is not stated, but it was sufficiently
effective to persuade the Faqir of Ipi's men to bring up their artillery   7 Aug.
after the column was back, and try to shell the camp. The fact
that the record thought it worth while noting that one unexploded
shell landed 300 yards from one of the Battalion perimeter posts,
gives a clue to the standard of Ipi's artillery.

Road protection filled the next few days with what may be called
strenuous monotony. Very long hours were worked, as for example
on the 9th August, when the battalion went out at 5.30 a.m., and did   9 Aug.
not get back till 7 p.m. Some of the piquets were in position for
twelve hours. On the 11th, however, something more stimulating was   11 Aug.
laid on. The Razmak Column, consisting of the Sikhs, the 3rd/1st
Gurkha Rifles, and the 1st/16th Punjab Regiment, tackled the

1942

2,000-foot Spera Ghar. Garcol co-operated by taking up positions on the lower features on the camp side of the Tochi Valley, while the Tochi Scouts secured the left flank. The Battalion was sent straight up the forward face, which from the bottom looked very difficult going. In the event, when the troops reached the final jumping-off place, they found it still worse than it looked. However, "A" and "D" Companies had a race for the top, which "D" Company won, by virtue of getting one of its platoons up first. There was no opposition; but just before withdrawal, "B" Company was startled by an explosion about fifty yards from one of its platoons. This was apparently the Ipi artillery, which had at last succeeded in getting a near miss.

Later, the men were congratulated by the District Commander on their good day's work.

12 Aug. The 12th was a rest day, but the record throws some light on these days in camp. "The flies", it says, "are almost unbearable. The whole place is getting pretty lousy!" This trouble, however, 13 Aug. was not confined only to the camp. Thus, on the 13th, when on road protection duty up the Tut Narai road, and shaley nalas made heavy going of otherwise easy piquet positions, the comment follows: 14 Aug. "Flies everywhere". And again next day, when out again: "Very hot—and flies and still more flies".

However, information came in that the force was about to disperse. The 1st/16th Punjab Regiment joined Garcol, in exchange for the 7th/1st Punjab Regiment, which joined the Razmak Column. Kit 15 Aug. was back-loaded on the 14th evening to Gardai, and the 15th was spent packing up and getting ready to leave next day. The record devotes one last comment to the local pests: "Either the flies or ourselves will have to go, and it's going to be us".

16 Aug. On the 16th, the column moved to Mami Rogha without incident. The pull up from Tut Narai to Lwargi Pass proved a strenuous one. The 33rd Indian Infantry Brigade were in position on the Pass. Arrived in Mami Rogha New Camp, the Battalion was given three piquets of one non-commissioned officer and twelve men each to man. Water was scarce, and when it did come to hand, it was foul, and full of chlorine (naturally).

17 Aug. The 17th August was spent in Mami Rogha. The Battalion stayed in camp as stand-by battalion, while the column saw the 33rd Indian Infantry Brigade through. There was sniping most of the day from the King's Own Scottish Borderers camp piquet area. It rained heavily during the night.

18 Aug. Next day, the column moved on to Gardai without incident. The camp there sounds very uncomfortable—crowded, and flooded with further torrential rain in the afternoon. Still everyone was very cheerful.

                                                                1942
On the 19th, the Battalion did rear-guard for the column on the   19 Aug.
last leg back to Razmak. The Battalion was sniped as it started
the pull up from Razani. However, there was no further trouble, and
the troops were in by 2 p.m., again in a deluge of rain.

There was some natural reaction in the way of sickness after the
column broke up, mostly cases of malaria. However, the Battalion
showed up well in this respect, against other battalions, and the
trouble was soon over, and the men back at duty. The Commander-
in-Chief, on the 2nd September, 1942, published an order congratulating
the troops on their work, and awarded Mentions in Despatches to
A.I. 636 Maj. J. W. P. Baxter, and to Jem. Bachan Singh, and No. 13167
Hav. Nand Singh.

Meanwhile, *the 14th Battalion* had been raised, from a draft of   14th Bn.
400 men, plus a proportion of British officers, Viceroy's commissioned
officers and non-commissioned officers, which had been assembled
just too late to reinforce the 5th Battalion before the fall of
Singapore.

The draft itself was composed of two composite platoons, each,
from the 1st, 6th, and 7th Battalions, and a further one each from
the 8th and 9th Battalions. To these were added 160 recently attested
sepoys from the Training Battalion—the total strength on the
26th December, 1941, standing at 4 British officers, 5 Viceroy's   26 Dec.
commissioned officers, and 400 other ranks, all under command of
Capt. D. O. T. Dykes.

The draft assembled at Nowshera on the date shown above, and   31 Dec.
was first scheduled to leave for Bombay on the 31st December. This
date was put back three times; and on the 14th January, 1942, Lieut.-Col.   14 Jan.
F. D. S. Field, commanding the Training Battalion, was told that
its departure date was indefinitely postponed. On this, he asked for,
and obtained, permission for all men to go off on 15 days leave to
their homes. They departed the same day, and the following morning,   15 Jan.
for the Punjab.

On the evening after they had gone, Training Battalion headquarters
received a cypher message to say that the draft would now leave
Nowshera on the 17th January. This was out of the question, so the
situation was explained to G.H.Q. over the telephone, and the draft
was ordered to stand down till further orders. Thanks to this, needless
to add, much suffering and loss of life were saved. The draft, whose
arrival could have made no difference to the situation in Singapore,
was now to be too late, in any case, to get there.

Meanwhile, however, it remained in being; and in February, Capt.
V. R. Khanolkar, of the 5th Battalion, was detailed to take command.
Orders for departure on the 17th February were received, but these

1942

16 Feb. were cancelled on the 16th, when Singapore had fallen. A few days later, it was decided to use the draft as a nucleus for the 14th Battalion, and orders were issued for it to be raised under Lieut.-Col. T. M. Ker of the 2nd Battalion, on the 15th March.

15 Mar. On the 15th March, accordingly, it was raised in Umbeyla Lines, Nowshera, on a basis of two-thirds Sikhs and one-third Punjabi-Mohammedans. Officers were posted, and the Battalion initially organized on a three-company basis. Active battalions were asked to produce further quotas, especially in Viceroy's commissioned officers and non-commissioned officers, and small parties of men began trickling in daily from various directions.

1 Apr. On the 1st April, the Battalion moved over to Auchinleck Lines, a collection of katcha buildings on the Manki road. Next door, in Cassels Lines, was the Machine-Gun Battalion, raised a couple of months before.

Sub.-Maj. Mian Ahmed, I.D.S.M., arrived in April, as first Subedar-Major. The Battalion settled down to a long and strenuous hot weather. The usual teething troubles were met—due mainly to the shortage of Viceroy's commissioned officers, non-commissioned officers, and senior sepoys. Of British officers, there was no shortage, though few, of course, had much seniority. Under a new G.H.Q. scheme substantial numbers of officers were being posted to the Indian army for a period of attachment, from British service, and the Battalion had its full quota of these. Individual training began, together with preliminary instruction in mountain warfare, and non-commissioned officers' and umedwars' cadres were added.

1 May On the 1st May, Lieut.-Col. Ker left on transfer to the Sikh Light Infantry. He was succeeded by Lieut.-Col. J. P. L. Eustace, M.C., formerly of the 2nd Battalion, but more recently second-in-command of the 6th Battalion.

June During May, the fourth rifle company was formed; and in June, the arrival of a draft of eighty Punjabi-Mohammedans enabled the organization of "H.Q." Company to be taken in hand. Formation of this company

1 July was effected on the 1st July, although the Battalion was still nearly 200 men under strength. This was partly met during the month by a draft of eighty Sikhs.

Training and organization now proceeded apace. By the end of
August August, the Battalion was reported ready to assume a mountain warfare
2 Sept. role, and orders were issued for it to move on the 2nd September, to take over the defences on the Malakand Pass.

MG Bn. *The Machine Gun Battalion* continued training in Nowshera.

25th Bn. In March, *the 25th Battalion* moved down from Dehra Dun to Alipur,
March in Calcutta, for aerodrome defence duties, there and at Dum Dum.

Alipur aerodrome at this time was used mainly for fighter aircraft, 1942
while transport and heavy aircraft generally, operated from Dum Dum.
The Battalion continued to set a fine example of reliability and
smartness; and in August it was raised to the status of an active August
battalion, and renumbered the 15th. For the time being, however, it
remained in its existing role as an aerodrome defence battalion.

A further expansion of the Regiment took place on the 1st March, 1 Mar.
with the raising of *the 26th Battalion* of the Regiment, as a Garrison 26th Bn.
Battalion. Lieut.-Col. G. W. Tanner, M.C., was drafted across from
the 8th Punjab Regiment to take command, and a few experienced and
senior non-commissioned officers and sepoys were provided by the
25th Battalion as a nucleus for training recruits.

Early in May, with a strength of only 150 or so all ranks, the Battalion May
took over garrison duties in Mardan. In July, it moved to Bangalore July
as Escort Battalion to the newly constructed prisoners-of-war camps.
Every effort was made to increase the strength of the Battalion, and
one officer was kept continually out on recruiting duty. Considerable
success was achieved, and by the time the Battalion was established in
Bangalore in July, the number of men on the rolls stood at between
500 and 600.

About this time, *the Training Battalion* was re-organized on a T.B.
considerably higher scale in view of its much enhanced responsibilities,
and was constituted a Regimental Centre, with an officer of full
colonel's rank in command.

It remains to add a post-script on the later fortunes of *the 8th and 9th* 8th &
Battalions, whose official ties were severed with the Regiment on 9th Bns.
the 31st March.

By the kindness of Maj. A. N. Donaldson of the 8th Battalion, and
Lieut.-Col. E. C. Spencer, O.B.E., M.C., of the 9th Battalion, an
account of the activities of these two units, after conversion to a Light
Anti-Aircraft artillery role, is available, and will be found of much
interest.

Omitting, therefore, the earlier data from which the previous story
of these Battalions has been drawn, the records prepared by these
two officers is appended in full below.

It will be remembered that *the 8th Battalion* had left Landi Khana for 8th Bn.
the Khajuri Plain in February, after the decision to convert the Battalion
had been announced. "Five very pleasant weeks were spent on the
Khajuri, training and sports replacing the previous month's work;
and, as a result of a conference in Delhi attended by the C.O., a certain
amount of preliminary reorganization for the forthcoming conversion
to A.A. was possible—this entailed the posting of men from five infantry

1942 companies to three artillery batteries (2 Sikh and 1 P.M.) and the selection of suitable instructors to go to Karachi immediately to do a gunnery course. The number of I.O.R.s under training as drivers was also greatly increased—the ultimate object being to have at least one man in five qualified in M.T.

"The 2/2 Punjabis took over the three posts on March 13th and the Bn. marched back to Lockhart Lines in Nowshera on March 14th. Almost immediately, the new equipment began to arrive—40 m.m. Bofors, Predictors and vehicles, closely followed by a large number of R.A. officers new from England; final drafts of I.O.R.s to bring the Bn. to full War Establishment were also received from the T.B. Lieut.-Col. Walker was selected to command the Regiment in its new role, but the remaining regular officers of the Bn.—Majors Lloyd-Jones and Walter, and Captains Hassan and Anthony—were posted to the T.B. This left only nine of the original officers of the Bn. of whom four were in Karachi, and consequently the remaining five had the entire burden of conversion to deal with—the newly arrived R.A. officers knowing neither the men nor the language. The conversion, however,

31 Mar. was duly completed and at midnight on March 31st 1942, the 8th Bn.—only eleven months old—passed into history, to be re-born the
1 Apr. following morning as '8 Sikh Light Anti-Aircraft Regiment, Indian Artillery'.

"Thus the 8th Bn. was officially severed from the 11th Sikh Regiment and became part of the Indian Artillery, who were henceforth responsible for its administration, reinforcements, etc., but the old ties remained, and still do, and the original officers, V.C.O.s and men have always felt with pride that their fine Artillery Regiment had its origins in the 11th Sikh Regiment. Many outward signs also remained—the retention, by G.H.Q. authority, of the title 'SIKH'; and, by a fortunate coincidence, of the number '8'; permission was also granted for the wearing of a small silver Chakri in the centre of the Indian Artillery flash, and the use, by officers, of 'SIKH' buttons on uniform. There can be no doubt that, immediately prior to its conversion, the 8th Bn. was already prepared, in efficiency and contentment, to live up to and even enhance the war record of the 11th Sikh Regiment; and surely it was the remembrance of their true heritage which enabled them likewise—as an Artillery Regiment—to earn a reputation second to none as A.A. gunners on active service.

"Despite early 'teething' troubles after the conversion, the keen spirit of the men was such that within five months of the Bn. becoming an A.A. Regiment, they left for Eastern Army and active service.
Sept. From September 1942 the Regiment was continually on field service in Eastern Bengal, Assam, and Burma, and only left XIVth Army in 1945 when they were withdrawn to Poona in readiness for the initial assault

1942

on Malaya—the assault which was rendered unnecessary by the sudden end of the war in the Far East. Two I.O.R.s were awarded the I.D.S.M. for bravery when 25 Battery (Sikh) was heavily bombed in Assam, and a number of officers, V.C.O.s, and I.O.R.s were mentioned in despatches in 1945.

"The Regiment was selected for retention in the post war army and lives on, upholding the old traditions as '30 Sikh Light Anti-Aircraft Regiment, Royal Indian Artillery': the class composition has, since the war ended, become 100 per cent Sikh, the P.M.s having been transferred to other units of the R.I.A. As Honorary Members of the Sikh Brigade a close liaison still exists with the Bns. of the Sikh Regiment, a most generous gesture on the part of the latter being the gift, in 1947, of a number of pieces of plate to the Officers' Mess of what used to be the 8/11th".

The 9th Battalion had been with the 7th Indian Division when news of the conversion was announced. Reorganizing as a Regimental Headquarters (Sikh), and three Batteries, (two Sikh and one P.M.), the Battalion marched in from Mansar to Peshawar, to start its new career in the Indian Artillery.

9th Bn.

"I was allowed to retain all my infantry officers, and in addition 30 R.A. officers were posted bringing our estab of officers up to 41. In addition we received a complement of British N.C.O.s and fitters who acted as instrs, and stayed with us until our own Sikh N.C.O.s were competent to be Dett Comds. Each Battery had 18 40 m.m. Bofors guns, and was organized into 3 Troops, a Dett consisted of 1 gun with a crew of 10.

"I am happy to relate that relations between the British N.C.O.s and the 'Jawans' was excellent, and we were particularly fortunate to have as our B.R.A. Brig. Farfan, C.B., D.S.O., O.B.E., who had spent practically all his regtl service with Indian Gunners.

"We received generous vacancies for officers and N.C.O.s at the Artillery schools at Deolali and Karachi, and I was amazed at how quickly the Regt. took to A.A. gunnery. At the C.O.'s course at Deolali, the M.G.R.A., in his opening address, said: 'We are glad to welcome the C.O.s of so many distinguished inf bns as Gunners, the only fly in the ointment is, the gaff is blown, they will now discover there is no "jadhu" in gunnery'.

"By July '42 we were considered fit to take up an operational role and the Regt. was deployed as follows:

July

"H.Q. and 22 Bty at Vizagapatam, 23 Bty at Madras, 24 Bty at Bombay.

"When I went round the Regt. I covered 2,000 miles. Guns were manned from dawn—dusk and the first shot had to be in the sky 6 secs

1942

after the 'spotter' had identified a plane as hostile. Unfortunately there were no Jap planes to shoot at, and, particularly in Bombay, the jawans were apt to look at one somewhat pityingly when, on visits to gun sites, we reminded them of the necessity for alertness.

"We kept them busy digging and camouflaging alternative and dummy sites, fighting the monsoon, and, as we were permitted 25 per cent guns out of action, by carrying out 'schemes'. We were fully mobile, carried 20 per cent armour-piercing shell, and were looking forward to a more active role as Div Lt A.A. Regt during the advance **Aug.** into Burma. However, this was not to be as in August 1942 I and the Subedar-Major were summoned to Delhi to G.H.Q., where the M.G.R.A. spoke most highly of the Regt, but said that owing to the fact that it was now known the Japs had so few planes, and inf required trained **30 Sept.** reinforcements, it had been decided to disband the Regt by 30 Sep '42. 22 Bty (Sikh) was, however, to be transferred en bloc to 9th Rajputana Lt A.A. Regt, and this Regt was to be commanded by Tim Gayer, everyone was pleased.

"Needless to say, when 22 Bty left, it took with it the best of everything in the Regt, and was really marvellously equipped."

Chapter VII

SEPTEMBER 1942 TO FEBRUARY 1943

Backscreen
Oddly enough, although the world situation this winter remained tense and threatening, the Regiment played a hum-drum part.

Strategy in the Pacific was swinging in the Allies' favour, but bitter fighting was the rule. In Papua—the eastern part of New Guinea—the Japanese move against Port Moresby, as we saw in Chapter VI, misfired. The enemy land-force moving south from Kokoda, had by the 15th September, reached a point a bare 30 miles north of its objective, but it was too weak, both in numbers and physically, thanks to its privations, to achieve more. Finding the Australians strongly posted and full of fight, the column fell right back to Nauro, 10 miles north of the main ridge of the Owen Stanley Range, enabling the Australians to re-enter Kokoda on the 3rd November.

Pacific (South)

15 Sept.

3 Nov.

It was a harsh and inhospitable country to fight in. Razor-backed mountain ridges alternated with deep and tortuous valleys. The road was no more than a narrow winding trail creeping through the thick tropical jungle that covered everything like a blanket. A precarious system of air-supply, operating over little patches of open jungle grass, like tiny margs, on the sides of the forest-clad mountains, which served as dropping points, kept the Australians supplied with the barest essentials. Unarmed transport aircraft, bringing up supplies under a canopy of fighters, had to thread their way as best they could up the winding valleys. Parachutes were in desperately short supply, and in any case four-fifths of the supplies landed in the jungle and could not be recovered. But it sufficed.

At Nauro, the Japanese had hoped to hold the Australians till reinforcements arrived, but by a brilliant manoeuvre, the American air force flew in a complete striking force, landing 3,600 troops in Port Moresby, and moving 15,000 thence over the Owen Stanley Range to Buna, on the north coast, a matter of about 40 air-miles from Nauro. The Japanese reacted to this threat at once. They fell back, followed by the Australians from the Kokoda front, and were hemmed in at a number of points on the coast. Of these detached parties, those at Gona had been eliminated by the 9th December. Buna was cleared by the 3rd January, and Sananda by the 19th. In every case the Japanese fought to the death.

9 Dec.
3-19 Jan.

1942-43

Just as the unexpected Guadalcanal operations in early August had attracted Japanese reinforcements probably earmarked for the Papua campaign, so now, in January, Japanese reverses in Papua and North-East New Guinea attracted reinforcements earmarked for Guadalcanal. These reinforcements were not brought into Papua, but were landed to the north-west of the Papua border, in north-east New Guinea, at Finschhafen, Lae, and Salamaua. The Allies still had a precarious hold on an air-base at Wau, about 40 miles south of Salamaua in the gold-field area of north-east New Guinea, with a garrison of some 300 Australian commandos. The Japanese moved in on it and a difficult situation developed. At the very eleventh hour,

29 Jan. on the 29th January, air-borne reinforcements, including some 25-pounders, checked the Japanese and drove them back.

The final blow to Japanese dreams of the offensive in this theatre
3-4 Mar. was given on the 3rd and 4th of March. In this action, known as the Battle of the Bismarck Sea, a Japanese convoy bound for Lae from Rabaul, came under air attack. The known Japanese loss amounted to 61 aircraft and 22 ships, with the estimated loss of an entire division of 15,000 men. Allied losses totalled 1 bomber, 3 fighters and 13 men.

Parallel with the operations in Papua, and New Guinea generally, there had been much heavy fighting farther east in the Guadalcanal area. Here, the Japanese had been repulsed in the naval battle of
23-25 Aug. the East Solomons between the 23rd and 25th of August, 1942. On the
11-12 Oct. night of the 11th/12th October, however, they fought a more successful naval action off Cape Esperance, and followed this up on the 16th
16 Oct. October by landing important reinforcements on Guadalcanal. The confused jungle fighting on the island intensified in bitterness, with results disquietingly in favour of the enemy. So much so in fact that an
26 Oct. attack on Henderson Field on the 26th trembled in the balance for some time. The same day, in a naval action off the Santa Cruz Islands, four or five hundred miles east of the Solomons, the United States carrier *Hornet* was lost, and another carrier, the *Enterprise*, severely damaged.

United States forces, however, still had possession of Guadalcanal. In Henderson Field, they had an air-base from which air reconnaissance and attacks could be freely launched. The Japanese largely lacked these facilities, but none-the-less contrived to give a very good account of themselves in the ding-dong naval battles that marked
13-14 Nov. the Guadalcanal campaign. On the night of the 13th/14th November, a furious sea battle boiled up off Guadalcanal, and two Japanese
30 Nov. battleships were sunk. Yet, just over a fortnight later, on the 30th Nov. in another naval battle off Tassafaronga on Guadalcanal, the Americans narrowly escaped defeat. Of the five American cruisers engaged, only one escaped damage. The American hold was a precarious one, and

Japanese reinforcements then assembling in Rabaul might well have ejected them from Guadalcanal if the critical situation in Papua had not diverted them. The upshot was that on the night of the 7th/8th February, 1943, the remains of the Japanese garrison was withdrawn from Guadalcanal, leaving behind it some 10,000 killed, and a further 10,000 dead of starvation and disease.

1943

7-8 Feb.

During these months of savage fighting in the South Pacific, a new instrument of naval warfare was being built up to extend the war to the Central Pacific westwards between Wake Island and the Gilberts. The problem was one of bases. Land-bases were not readily available as they were in the South Pacific, so a floating base, complete with fleet, air force, and army, had to be designed. The successful implementation of this idea has been described as probably the greatest organizational feat in naval history.

Central Pacific

The Battle of Midway Island was fought in the first week of June, 1942. By the autumn of the following year, 1943, an American fleet had been built up, strong in carriers, and more powerful than anything the Japanese could bring against it; 800 carrier-borne aircraft were available, and these were stepped up to 1,000 two months later. A repair organization was attached—each class of warship having its own special type of repair and supply craft—and with floating workshops with foundries, capable of most heavy repairs, including under-water welding. Coupled with these came the "Seabees"— the United States Navy Construction Battalions—which moved in on the heels of the landing forces to build wharves, barracks, roads, hospitals; to build and repair landing-grounds; and establish radio communication. Landing-forces themselves were found from formations of soldiers and marines, trained in jungle and island warfare, and carried with the fleet.

This is all to anticipate, but it is as well to remember that during these critical months, plans were going forward, and thanks to the sacrifices made by the American and Australian forces in the south, effective intervention later in the Central Pacific was made possible.

Northwards, the temporary stalemate in the Aleutians was broken in January 1943 when an unopposed American landing was made on Amchitka Island, 70 miles east of Japanese occupied Kiska Island, and an advanced air-base established there.

North Pacific

Jan.

In the general Burma theatre, the Japanese had occupied the Andaman and Nicobar Islands to protect their sea communications between Burma and Singapore, but they only exercised a nominal command of the Bay of Bengal.

Burma

1942-43

On land, in the north, the American General Stilwell had initiated plans for what became known as the "Hump Route" over the Himalayas to China. The load-carrying aircraft operating this route had to climb to 23,000 feet to cross the mountains. But despite the often appalling weather conditions during the monsoon, a steadily increasing tonnage of supplies was flown in to China by this means.

Oct-Dec. In the reverse direction, 13,000 Chinese troops were brought in to India by air between October and December, 1942, to make the Chinese forces in India up to a strength of two divisions.

In December, the 14th Indian Division started a campaign south through the Arakan, on the east side of the Bay of Bengal, but it failed in its objectives thanks to difficulties of organization and terrain. The operations continued, however, throughout the cold weather and on into April.

More fruitful was the first long-range jungle penetration carried out by the 77th Indian Infantry Brigade under Brigadier O. C. Wingate, and which crossed the Chindwin into Japanese-occupied Burma in

Feb. February. It operated in several columns, without transport, and was dependent on air-supply. Supply was not always easy, and the brigade suffered a good deal of privation. However, during the three months it was out, it definitely placed long-range penetration on the map.

N. Africa In Egypt, an uneasy stability had been achieved on the El Alamein position, with its two unassailable flanks—the Mediterranean on the north, and the Qattara Depression, which was impassable by either wheels or tracks, in the south.

Though the line as a whole ran north and south over its 40-mile length, it conformed to the accidents of the ground. About 15 miles south from the coast, lies the Ruweisat Ridge. This ridge runs back east for some 10 miles from the British front. Then, echeloned back from the Ruweisat Ridge, and about 7 miles to its south, is the Alam el Halfa Ridge, with its western end due south of the eastern end of the Ruweisat Ridge, and about 12 miles east of the British front.

The bulk of the Eighth Army was distributed between the coast and the western end of the Ruweisat Ridge. From there, it followed the ridge, and down to the Alem el Halfa Ridge. Troops located along the ridges thus flanked the relatively weakly-held southern half of the position.

Aug. The Eighth Army was being built up as fast as possible; and by the end of August, it was markedly superior to the Axis forces, particularly in tanks. The Eighth Army had 390 tanks, (of which 140 were Grants), against Rommel's 230.

Rather than wait and let the disparity become greater, Rommel decided

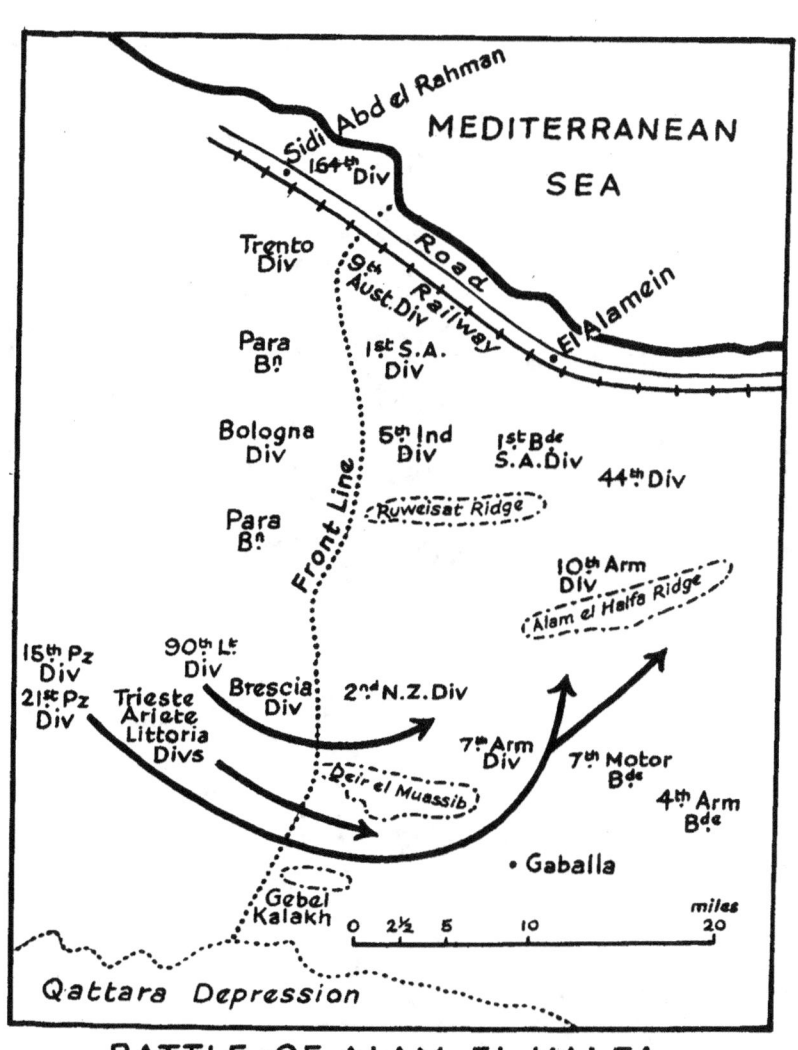

BATTLE OF ALAM EL HALFA
31st August – 6th September 1942
(With acknowledgements to "The Second World War"
by Major-General J. F. C. Fuller, page 233)

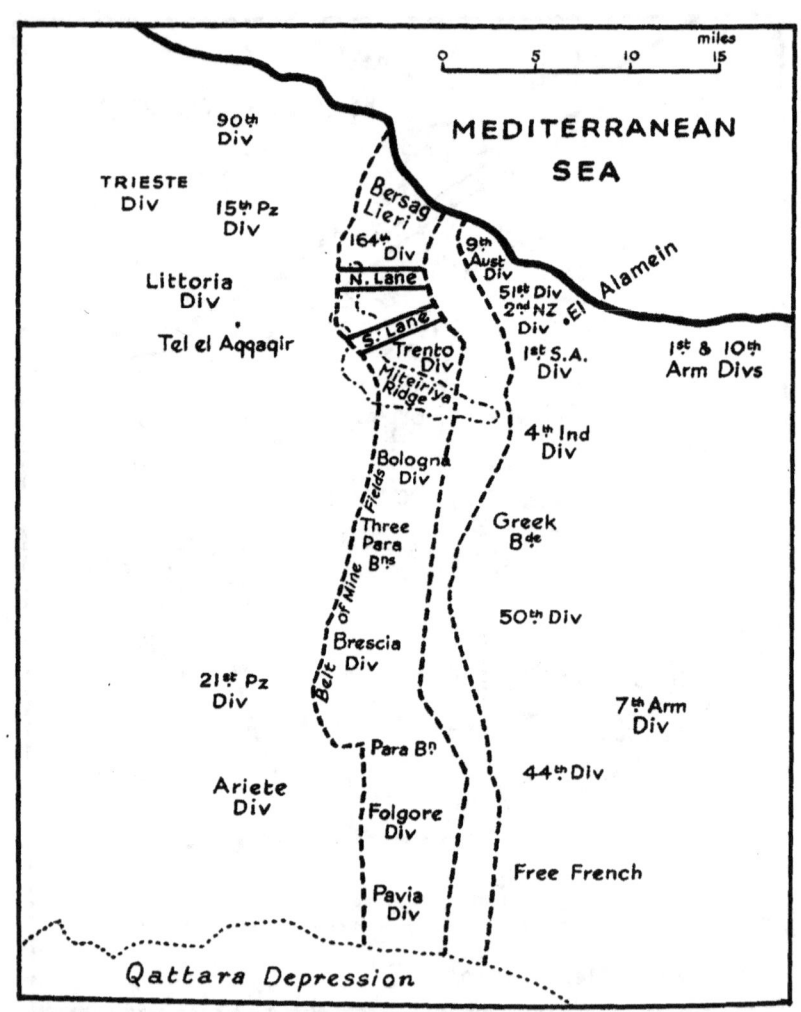

BATTLE OF EL ALAMEIN · 23rd Oct.- 4th Nov. 1942.
(With acknowledgements to "The Second World War" by Major-General J. F. C. Fuller, page 236.)

to attack and make a bid for Egypt while he could. The operation started soon after midnight on the 30th/31st August, with a feint attack in the north and a holding attack in the centre. The decisive assault was entrusted to the Afrika Corps (15th and 21st Panzer Divisions and the 90th Light Division) and the Italian XXth Corps (the Ariete and Littorio Armoured Divisions). These attacked in the south, passing through the minefields on the north of the Qattara Depression. They then swung north towards the flanking defences of the Alam el Halfa Ridge to try and break their way through and take the strong northern defences in rear. By the 3rd September, the attack had failed, and on the 4th, 5th, and 6th heavy counter-attacks harassed the enemy withdrawal. On the 7th September the battle was broken off, and the Eighth Army sat back to bide its time till re-organization and re-equipment were complete.

1942
30-31 Aug.

3 Sept.
4-6 Sept.
7 Sept.

In October, the scales lay heavily against the Axis. Rommel's army of 8 infantry and 4 armoured divisions mustered about 96,000 men, of whom rather over half were Germans. Of his five to six hundred tanks, the Italians had just over half. Montgomery's three Corps—the Xth, XIIIth, and XXXth—disposed of 7 infantry and 3 armoured divisions, with 7 additional armoured brigades—giving a total of about 150,000 men and 1,114 tanks, (of which 128 were Grants and 267 Shermans).

Oct.

The difference between the two armies was not confined only to numbers. The Axis also had a less satisfactory line. The Eighth Army made use of the tactical features already described, to ease its deployment problem. The Axis had no such help. Whether Rommel would have accepted the situation if he had been there cannot be known.

He had been evacuated, sick, to Germany at the end of September after organizing his position and handing it over to General Stumme. His armour had been split up and distributed over the front to try and stiffen up the Italian divisions. The resulting lack of resilience in the defence had been apparently accepted; but in any case he was too weak in motorized troops to contemplate open desert operations at this stage.

The initial Eighth Army plan was to cut off the enemy's centre and right from the coastal road, which was his sole means of communication westwards. Preparatory air action started on the 9th October and lasted with great intensity till the 23rd. Supply bases and ports in Italy were attacked from England, whilst the more immediate targets such as minefields, anti-tank batteries, air-fields, dumps, transport columns and depots in Egypt were dealt with locally. 700 bombers were used. The Axis air-forces in North Africa had been grounded by the 23rd October.

9 Oct.

23 Oct.

231

1942

At 9.40 p.m. that night, the tactical ground offensive opened. The main stroke was to be made against the enemy's left, a few miles south of the coast. A thousand guns opened fire on a 6-mile front, and at 10 p.m. infantry and sappers of the XIIIth and XXXth Corps moved forward and began clearing lanes through the main minefield. The XIIIth Corps attack—in the south—failed, but in the north, the

24 Oct. XXXth Corps had cut two lanes by 5.30 a.m. on the 24th, and was proceeding to occupy its objectives. For the remainder of the day it consolidated.

The battle, however, was by no means won, and anti-tank fire, in which the Axis excelled, held up exploitation for a number of days.

25 Oct. Meanwhile, on the 25th, General von Stumme died, apparently from
26 Oct. heart failure, and on the 26th, Rommel, though still sick, returned and re-assumed command.

27 Oct. Rommel soon made his presence felt. On the 27th October, a series of violent counter-attacks with armour was made against the Xth and XXXth Corps, but without success. However, the British salient in the Axis defences was not considered satisfactory, and the XXXth Corps was detailed to mount a fresh infantry attack to deepen it.

28 Oct. Before the XXXth Corps could complete its plans, Rommel again attacked, and heavy fighting continued till the 1st November, by
1 Nov. which time the XXXth Corps plans were complete.
2 Nov. These plans came to fruition next day, the 2nd November. At 1 a.m. an attack was put in on a 4,000 yard front. A heavy bill had to be paid in Cruiser tanks, but the final minefield was pierced. Rommel reacted with his usual despatch, and by 9 a.m. the 15th and 21st Panzer Divisions came in to the attack. Our 1st and 10th Armoured Divisions from the Xth Corps came up and a violent armoured battle raged round and about Tel el Aqqaqir, which lies some 12 to 13 miles from the coast. The fighting went on all day and into the night, when the German armour had to admit defeat. Rommel began to pull out, with the loss of most of his right wing, and Mersa Matruh was once more in our hands on the 7th/8th November.

This ended the Battle of El Alamein which cost the Axis 59,000 killed, wounded and captured—24,000 being Germans—together with 500 tanks, 400 guns and thousands of vehicles. The British casualty list comprised about 13,500 killed, wounded and missing, and 432 tanks.

Though El Alamein was one of the decisive actions of the war, there was neither a headlong retreat by the enemy nor a whirlwind pursuit by the Allies. Rommel gained strength as he fell back, and there was little fighting on the 1,400-mile road back to Tripoli.

13-20 Nov. The Allies entered Tobruk on the 13th November, Gazala on the 14th,

Benghazi on the 20th, Sirte on the 25th December, and Tripoli on
the 23rd January. On the 13th February, advanced troops of the
Eighth Army came up with the enemy's rearguard at Ben Gardane,
covering Rommel's withdrawal to the Mareth Line, about 175 miles
south down the coast from Tunis.

1942-43
25 Dec.-13 Feb.

The invasion of North-West Africa should have preceded the
Battle of El Alamein, but was held up by lack of landing-craft.
These becoming available in early November, the joint Anglo-
American invasion was fixed to take place on the 8th November.
    Landings were to be made at three points—Casablanca on the
Atlantic coast of Morocco, and Oran and Algiers in the Mediterranean.
The first was to be entrusted to an American force under Maj.-Gen.
George S. Patton, sailing direct from the United States. The second
and third were to be jointly commanded by Lieut.-Gen. K. A. N.
Anderson. Oran was to be invaded by American troops under Maj.-Gen.
Lloyd Fredenhall, whilst British troops under Lieut.-Gen. Anderson
came ashore at Algiers. Troops employed against Oran and Algiers
were organized into the First Army, which sailed from Great Britain
for Gibraltar on the 25th October.
    Over and above these general arrangements, an American air-borne
force was to be flown the 1,500 miles from England, to help in the
capture of the Oran air-fields.
    Supreme command was given to Gen. Dwight D. Eisenhower, who
opened his headquarters at Gibraltar on the 5th November.
    A German look-out post was on duty at La Linea, a few miles
north of Gibraltar. On the 7th November, the post reported that a
large convoy was in view, heading for the Mediterranean. In point
of fact, somewhere about 350 naval craft and 500 transports were
required for the three forces, and most of these would have been
heading east into the Mediterranean. The landings on the 8th, however,
came as a complete surprise to the Germans.
    One of the imponderables facing the planners of the invasion had
been the likely scale of resistance. There were no Axis troops in
Morocco, Algeria, or Tunisia, but there was no means of knowing
what the French there would do. In the event, all the landings were
opposed to some degree; but on the 11th November, Admiral Jean
Darlan, Marshal Petain's successor-designate, who was on a visit to
Algiers when the invasion was launched, suddenly ordered the cease-
fire. This disposed of matters in Algeria, and at once presented the
Allies with the problem of transferring their sphere of operations to
Tunisia. Tunis lies some 375 miles east of Algiers.
    Hitler had not been idle. The day following the Allied landings,
his first echelon of air-borne troops from Europe, touched down at

N.-W. Africa
Nov.

25 Oct.

5 Nov.

7 Nov.

8 Nov.

11 Nov.

9 Nov.

233

1942-43

the el Aouana air-port at Tunis. Subsequent re-inforcements were quickly stepped up to about a thousand a day.

The First Army shipping had been tactically loaded—for operations, not for a long and methodical advance immediately the troops were ashore. Delay naturally followed on the sudden change of role. However, the leading troops of the First Army were hurriedly re-embarked at Algiers, and re-landed at Bougie, 100 miles east. From here,

12 Nov. they set out for Bone—an additional 150 miles to the east—Bone itself having been occupied on the 12th by a sea-borne commando and two companies of parachutists. On the 15th, further parachutists

15 Nov. were dropped near Tebessa, 100 miles south of Bone, to seize an air-
16 Nov. field. On the 16th, another parachutist party was dropped at Souk el Arba, midway between Bone and Tebessa, to cover the advance.

The advance was led by two infantry brigades of the 78th Division of the First Army with what transport was available. Contact was made with German patrols on the 15th, but the two brigades pushed steadily eastwards till they reached Medjez el Bab, 30 miles south-

25 Nov. west of Tunis, on the 25th. On the 28th, American parachutists
28 Nov. reached the Sbeitla-Gafsa area, roughly 120 miles south of Tunis, and 80 west-north-west of the Mareth Line.

Hitler had not confined his reactions to the establishment of strong German forces in Tunisia. He had also occupied Vichy France, and thus indirectly effected the scuttling of the French fleet in

27 Nov. Toulon Harbour on the 27th. He had initiated violent air attacks on Allied shipping, and he was now helped by the elements, with torrential rain turning the three hundred and more miles between Algiers and Medjez el Bab into a sea of mud. The Germans still held the best air-fields, and they continued to pour troops into Tunisia. However, the First Army succeeded in holding on to most of what they had—an unfortunate exception being the high ground north of Medjez el Bab, and in particular Jebel el Ahmera (Longstop Hill), which they lost. Southwards, the line extended in a series of posts to Fondouk, a little over 60 miles south of Medjez el Bab.

Rommel, meanwhile, falling back on to the Mareth Line, saw his communications thence to Tunis, not very far to his north, directly threatened by the American 1st and 34th Divisions in the Sbeitla-Gafsar area, south-south-east of Fondouk. The Eighth Army was not yet ready to advance, and Rommel decided to break up the American

14 Feb. divisions while he could. This he did on the 14th February, moving on and forcing the Kasserine Pass about 90 miles north-west of the
20 Feb. Mareth Line, on the 20th. From this point he divided his forces. Part was directed on Thala, about 30 miles north-north-west of Kasserine, to strike at the communications of the First Army. The rest aimed at Tebessa, 35 miles west-north-west of Kasserine, as

this seemed a likely point of future junction between the First and
Eighth Armies. Opposition was too much for him, however, and he
was forced to withdraw on the 23rd. However, he was still full of
fight, and on the 6th March, attacked the Eighth Army at Medenine,
a few miles east of the Mareth Line. Here he was roundly repulsed,
however, mainly by anti-tank fire, despite the absence of Eighth
Army tanks from the action.

 Meanwhile, in January, the Casablanca Conference was held, and
the policy of unconditional enemy surrender formulated.

 In Russia, opposition at Voronezh on the left, and rapid success
towards the Caucasus on his right, had led Hitler to abandon the
advance of his left to Saratov, 250 miles as the crow flies, upstream
of Stalingrad on the Volga. Saratov was a centre of great strategic
value to the Russians inasmuch as the flow of men, munitions and
supplies from all parts of Russia came this way to the threatened
front. Rail communications thence ran southwards parallel with the
front, behind Stalingrad, to Astrakhan on the Caspian at the mouth
of the Volga, and on down the Persian "pipe-line" to the Allied
ports in the Persian Gulf. These substantial Russian assets were
no longer to be attacked at their nodal point in Saratov.

 The German Sixth Army of 22 divisions, and some 300,000 men,
was at this time—early November—concentrated in a relatively small
area west of Stalingrad. Gen. von Hoth had been succeeded in
command by Gen. Friedrich von Paulus. Away to the north-west, the
defences of the Don were held for some 350 miles from Stalingrad,
by Roumanian and Italian forces. To the south, about 25 miles
from the town of Stalingrad, the 50-mile length of the Ergeni Hills
was held by Rumanian troops, whose flank was in the air, with
no Axis support before the German post at Elista, 80 miles south.
From Elista, the front was weakly held for another 180 miles, as
far south as Mozdok. German operations here, in the south, were
being conducted in a long and very narrow salient, marked by
Rostov, Mozdok and Novorossisk, and their safety depended directly
on the Stalingrad salient holding firm.

 For the Russians then, the immediate objective was the penetration
of the Stalingrad salient, and subsequent elimination of the much-
extended Caucasian salient farther south. Operations to this end
began on the 19th November, when German attention was distracted
by the disturbing threat to Tunisia, and the whole Axis lay-out in
North Africa.

 Of the railway communications centring in Stalingrad, one line
runs back west to Stalino, and another south-west to Novorossisk
on the north coast of the Black Sea. In the Russian plan, the first

Margin notes: 1942-43; 23 Feb.; 6 Mar.; Jan.; Russia; Nov.; 19 Nov.

of these railways was to be cut firstly at Kalash about 40 miles west of Stalingrad, and then at Likhaya, nearly 160 further miles to the west. Gen. Rokossovsky would move down with an army group from the north, cross the river Don at the Russian bridgehead of Serafimovich, 100 miles or so north-west of Stalingrad, and move southwards against Kalash. Other forces under Gen. Vatutin would operate on Rokossovsky's right against Likhaya.

South of Stalingrad, the Rumanians were to be driven off the Ergeni Hills, and operations directed to the capture of Abganerovo, a station on the Novorossisk railway about 50 miles south-southwest of Stalingrad.

By these means, it was hoped to manoeuvre the German Sixth Army out of Stalingrad, and force it to retire.

The operation was a success; and in the south Gen. Yeremenko's army group not only reached Abganerovo, but forced its way up north behind the German Sixth Army, as far as Lyapichevo, only 20 miles from the northern pincer at Kalash.

Hitler, it is said, was very sensitive to his military prestige just then, and not prepared to bow to the storm. The Sixth Army was ordered to stand firm, and await relief. The Sixth Army itself carried out vigorous but unsuccessful operations to relieve

28 Nov. Russian pressure, but further embarrassment followed on the 28th November when von Paulus's land communications were finally cut, and he was compelled to rely on air supply at a time when available aircraft were needed to fly reinforcements into Tunisia. In any case what aircraft he had were subject to heavy casualties from Russian air action. Fifty load-carrying

30 Nov. aircraft were shot down on the 30th November; and the total casualty
10 Jan. list from the 19th November to the 10th January is given as 600 machines.

Relief measures for the Sixth Army were disorganized from the
25 Nov. start by a Russian holding attack on the 25th November, many hundreds of miles away to the north-west on the Velikye Luki-Rzhev front, between Moscow and Riga. Presently, however, Field-Marshal van Mannstein began moving up the Novorossisk line with a force
12 Dec. of about 150,000 men. On the 12th December, he broke through the Russians between Tsimlyansk and Kotelinikovo, about 100 miles south-west of Stalingrad, and captured the latter town. His success was short-lived, for a heavy threat to his left and left-rear developed
16 Dec. on the 16th December, over-running the Italian Eighth Army. This led to the diversion of von Mannstein's much-needed reinforcements to Millerovo about 175 miles west of Stalingrad on the vital Voronezh-Rostov railway, running north and south behind the German front.
27 Dec. Soon after, on the 27th December, von Mannstein's right flank was

driven back by armoured formations under Gen. Malinovsky. Kotelinikovo was lost, and the operation had to be written off as a failure.

The immediate consequence was the withdrawal of the Caucasus armies under von Kleist. Leaving Mozdok on the 2nd January, these armies fell back on the Tamask Peninsula opposite Kerch in the Crimea, with a temporary northern flank-guard east of Rostov at the eastern tip of the Sea of Azov.

The position of the German Sixth Army was an unenviable one. Once again, the men were short of winter clothing. Ammunition and supplies were naturally very short, and disease was rife. On the 8th January, von Paulus rejected a demand for his surrender. On the 31st, having meanwhile received the barren honour of Field-Marshal's rank, he was taken prisoner, with eight of his generals. On the 2nd February, the remaining 22,500 of his men out of the original 300,000 surrendered. These disastrous losses in man-power were balanced by corresponding losses in vehicles, guns, tanks and aircraft. One other consequence was the temporary disappearance of Hitler from chief command.

Meanwhile, north, south and west of Stalingrad, the Russians had not been idle. About the beginning of February, Russian forces were already seeping up the Donetz, north-westwards from Likhaya, and by the 10th February, had reached Chuguyev on that river, only a few miles south-east of Kharkov. On the west and south Gen. Yeremenko captured Voroshilovgrad and Rostov.

Farther afield, on the 22nd January the Second German-Hungarian Army sustained a reverse near Voronezh, 200 miles north-west of Kharkov. On the 26th, it was almost wiped out at Kastornaya. On the 7th February, 150 miles north of Kharkov, the Kursk hedgehog fell to the Russians. On the 9th, the Russians were in Byelgorod only 60 miles north of Kharkov; and on the 16th the super-hedgehog of Kharkov itself fell.

Field-Marshal von Mannstein, with Gen. Halder as his chief assistant, was temporarily in command of the German forces in Russia at this time. In an effort to shorten the over-extended German line, he abandoned the Rzhev-Gzhatsh-Vyazma salient just west of Moscow during the first half of February. About the same time the Russians in the north re-took Schlüsselburg, and raised the siege of Leningrad.

Russian momentum, however, was about exhausted from the effects of an unusually early thaw, and von Mannstein was ready with what in some ways was a remarkable counter-stroke, which extended well on into March, and which will be briefly described in the next chapter.

1942

H.M.S. *Sikh* — An event of more immediate personal concern to the Regiment darkened the early part of this period. This was the sinking of H.M.S. *Sikh*, and the breaking up of the short-lived but happy intimacy with her gallant ship's company.

August — As we have read, H.M.S. *Sikh* escorted the 2nd Battalion to Cyprus at the end of August. After a few days spent in Famagusta,

3 Sept. — she returned on the 3rd September to Haifa, where the 4th Battalion welcomed her back.

12 Sept. — She remained in Haifa till the 12th, but left that morning on an operational mission in the Tobruk area, from which she did not return.

By the courtesy of the Lords Commissioners of the Admiralty, details have been made available for the operation in which she was lost.

13-14 Sept. — It appears that on the night of the 13th/14th September, 1942, combined operations had been planned to take place simultaneously against the ports of Tobruk and Benghazi. The object was to hold both ports for twelve hours, destroy shipping, harbour facilities, petrol and stores, in order to interrupt traffic for a short period at a critical stage in the enemy's supply problem.

The Benghazi operation was made by a military force of 200 from Kufra, with diversionary air-bombing, and no naval units were concerned.

The Tobruk operation involved, among other items, the landing of troops by eighteen torpedo boats south of Tobruk, and of Royal Marines by the destroyers *Sikh* and *Zulu* north of that town. The submarine *Taku*, stationed at Mreipa Inlet, north of Tobruk, reported at 0134C on 14th September that the weather was suitable for assault craft in the inlet but that the beach was unmarked.

The destroyers disembarked their marines two miles, instead of three, from the beach, apparently unobserved. Owing to the swell, the disembarkation journey took forty minutes instead of the estimated twenty. The first flight of 150 marines encountered heavy resistance, but a proportion got ashore.

Coming in again to land the second flight, the destroyers were picked up by searchlights and heavily attacked. The *Sikh* was hit aft at 0526, and her steering gear and one engine were disabled. The *Zulu* took her in tow, but at 0635 enemy fire parted the towing wire, and both ships were frequently hit. The Captain (D) 22nd Flotilla Capt. St. J. A. Micklethwait, in the *Sikh*, ordered the *Zulu* away to avoid further damage. (She was, however, sunk later in the day by air attack). When the *Sikh* was last seen she was circling at ten knots close inshore, heavily on fire and being repeatedly hit by the shore batteries but was still firing her guns.

Casualties in the *Sikh* were 2 officers and 21 ratings killed; 223 officers and ratings became prisoners of war.

	1942
The 1st Battalion had spent the summer at Kohima in Assam	1st Bn.
after the withdrawal from Burma. On the 5th September, it left Kohima	5 Sept.
and moved to Ranchi in Bihar. It was a long move, and took a week.	
Arrived in Ranchi on the 12th, it joined a special training brigade,	12 Sept.

The 1st Battalion had spent the summer at Kohima in Assam after the withdrawal from Burma. On the 5th September, it left Kohima and moved to Ranchi in Bihar. It was a long move, and took a week. Arrived in Ranchi on the 12th, it joined a special training brigade, with a view to future employment as a brigade reconnaissance battalion in the 17th Indian Division. For this role it was to re-organize on a basis of two mounted infantry companies and two jeep-borne companies. The four reconnaissance battalions in the two light divisions under preparation, re-organizing for the future fighting in Burma, were concentrated in Ranchi under command of Brig. A. C. Curtis, late of the 3rd Battalion and subsequently in command of the 4th.

During October, ponies, mules and jeeps arrived, and all ranks were soon hard at it learning to ride or drive—some both. An awkward problem soon cropped up, however. During and after the exhausting Burma campaign, many men had stayed at duty long after they should, strictly speaking, have been in medical hands, and the Battalion had by no means fully recovered. Though many men had been ultimately evacuated sick from Burma and Assam, the majority were very debilitated, and they did not pick up as quickly as hoped.

The situation was a serious one, for the Battalion was due to re-join the 17th Indian Division early in December. It soon became clear that owing to its low strength, and the non-arrival of reinforcements, it could not be ready in time. The Battalion was hence transferred to the 39th Indian Division which was not due to become operational till March.

In pursuance of this decision, the Battalion moved to a camp on the outskirts of Lohadaga about 12 miles from Ranchi.

The Battalion's role was still that of a brigade reconnaissance battalion; but what this role involved seemed still something of a mystery—to higher authority as well as to the Battalion staff. Guidance was not forthcoming in sufficient detail, and tactical training was consequently weak. However, the strength problem began to be solved by the arrival of reinforcements towards the end of the year, and by Christmas the greater part of the men had received some instruction in riding and motor-driving.

Just before this Maj. Vaughan took over officiating command from Lieut.-Col. Windsor-Aubrey.

The Battalion was doing its best to complete its training by the scheduled date, but it proved difficult to practise companies effectively in their new roles while the men themselves were still not fully proficient in riding and driving. However, much can be done where the will exists, and by the end of this current period, the Battalion was preparing to join the 108th Indian Infantry Brigade of the 39th Indian Division,

1942   prior to a spell of advanced training before the move back into an operational theatre.

2nd Bn.   Of *the 2nd Battalion*, the record is almost equally one of concern for the present and preparation for the future.

It will be remembered that the Battalion had taken over the Keep E defences on the Malounda Pass at the north-east end of Cyprus, and had been fitted out with an impressive quota of extremely part-worn mechanical transport, together with four 25-pounders and 3 Sept.   nineteen Spiggot mortars. On the 3rd September, the commanding officer, second-in-command, and adjutant went aboard H.M.S. *Sikh* in Famagusta Harbour for tea; but the stay had to be a very short one, as the ship was sailing the same evening.

That the Keep defences were not as good as they might have been was well enough shown by a divisional scheme worked out on 7-8 Sept.   the night of the 7th/8th September. Judging by the Battalion record, the scheme had its weak points too. The results were hard to weigh up owing to the shortage of umpires and what is cheerfully described as their general ignorance of the scheme.

For the scheme, the Battalion spent the night deployed in the position and was attacked by a company of the Jaipur Infantry, representing a battalion of the enemy which had landed on the north coast. In the upshot, it was finally agreed that the Keep and Harbour defences, as sited, could not be held by the troops available, and that adjustments must be made.

11 Sept.   On the 11th, the Battalion had a small domestic set-back. The provost personnel serving with the 10th Indian Division had been returned before the Battalion left Egypt. They were now ordered back again, though the Battalion was still much under strength. One Viceroy's commissioned officer, two havildars, four naiks, thirty L.-Naiks and four sepoys had to be sent; and another battalion 14 Sept.   cadre had to be started forthwith on the 14th to train fresh non-commissioned officers to take their place.

Hockey and sports were held on the 26th, 27th, and 28th; and on 30 Sept.   the 30th another, but smaller, scheme was held within the Battalion to test the south-east defences of the harbour area. The results were judged to endorse the current lay-out.

Hutted accommodation had been slowly taking shape, but the work was very slow—partly for lack of transport to carry building materials. Additional delays resulted from lack of definite policy for camouflage. The intention had been to site the buildings in the shape of local villages, farm-yards, and monasteries, but this was later cancelled.

14 Oct.   On the 14th October, a draft of twenty-one men arrived from India. Their standard was reckoned much above normal, though the record

adds somewhat grudgingly that their education was of a low standard.

On the 20th October, a platoon of "B" Company took over Keep D, and on the 21st, the detachment with the A.M.E.S.—the Air Ministry Experimental Station—at Ayios Epiktitos was relieved by another "B" Company platoon. A Battalion scheme was then held in which all positions were manned, and digging started on the new harbour defences.

On the 22nd, one Viceroy's commissioned officer, three havildars, two naiks and eighteen sepoys were sent back to India on repatriation, under the 2 per cent dilution scheme.

On the 27th October, an all-island scheme was held with the principal object of testing Crusader Force, but the Keeps were also ordered to be manned. The Battalion stood-to in the Keeps from 7.15 a.m. on the 27th till 8 p.m. on the 28th. The time was not wholly wasted even though the exercise did not concern Keeps, for the surprising discovery was made that when divisional headquarters was on the move, nothing whatsoever came through on the Battalion wireless. Line communication was erratic, line parties being out for most of the scheme, while L/S was impossible owing to the weather. It is to be supposed that energetic action was taken to remedy these defects.

Exercises continued with little intermission, and on the 30th October the Battalion took part in a Crusader Force field-firing demonstration, staged for the benefit of the Ninth Army staff. Crusaders and Valentines were used, with two batteries of artillery. The pace was a little too fast at one time. The Valentines' 2-pounders, growing very erratic under smoke, sent some of their shells extremely close to Battalion Headquarters and the forward companies.

October went out in anti-climax and floods of rain, which spread havoc among the half-built huts, several walls collapsing. Completion of the huts had been guaranteed by the end of six weeks, but fulfilment now seemed remote, especially as the labourers refused to work in bad weather. Trouble also sprang up among the mess servants—the locally-employed men leaving in a body, complaining bitterly of the allegedly long hours and poor pay. Truth to say, the mess saw them go without much regret, and were glad to be quit of them.

As a small set-off against these domestic troubles, the Battalion got its platoon back from duty at the A.M.E.S. at Ayios Epiktitos, for training.

On the 3rd November the Battalion went off, on light scale, towards the Karpas Peninsular for a six-day Battalion camp. Some weakness in night work came to light, and this was remedied. On the 9th November, a field-firing exercise was carried out at Lapathos

1942

20-21 Oct.

22 Oct.

27 Oct.

28 Oct.

30 Oct.

31 Oct.

3 Nov.

9 Nov.

1942

10 Nov.	in conjunction with No. 118 Field Battery and some Crusader tanks; and on the 10th an amusing "free-for-all" exercise was started under Corps arrangements.

The exercise required each battalion to provide ten platoons to be out for four days, following pre-arranged routes. All other platoons were to be treated as enemy. Platoon commanders became wholly responsible for everything—tactics, administration, and everything else.

10-11 Nov.   The first five platoons left after midnight on the night of the 10th/11th November. They returned between 4 p.m. and midnight
14 Nov.   on the 14th. Umpire reports on these platoons were extremely good, and those of Jem. Amar Singh and Hav. Gurdial Singh came in for special mention.

The remaining five platoons went out in the very small hours of
17 Nov.   the 17th and did equally well. Here again, two platoon commanders were singled out for special mention by the umpires—viz. Jem. Bakhtawar Singh and Hav. Jagir Singh.

13 Nov.   Meanwhile, on the 13th the Drums were re-started by the expedient of transferring Hav. Mohan Singh to the command of No. 2 Platoon, and filling it up with old drummers and buglers. It was twelve months since the Drums had last played, and they formally celebrated their
22 Nov.   re-birth by playing on Guru Nanak's birthday on the 22nd when Lieut.-Gen. Blaxland and Brig. Arderne attended as guests of honour at a drink party in the V.C.O.s' mess.

Training was not a wholly solemn pastime, and the officers took
24 Nov.   the stage in an amusing demonstration on the 24th. This was set up on the assault course by Capt. J. M. S. Smith, assisted by 2nd/Lieuts. Farr, Harwant Singh, and King, and was intended to show one way of getting across a barbed wire entanglement. Lieut.-Col. Farwell provided covering fire with a Bren-gun, whilst Farr and King, throwing themselves flat on to the wire, made a bridge for Smith and Harwant Singh to pass over.

Not to be outdone, the Viceroy's commissioned officers then made up a team, and did the course too—led by the divisional commander with his revolver. Comparisons are as odious in these as all other cases, but the Battalion record felt it necessary to observe that it was "apparent that they did not have as much confidence in each others' ability to shoot straight as did the British officers!"

There was less cause for hilarity, however, later that night, when a fire broke out in the forest bungalow, and severely burnt the forest officer, a forest guard, and mess cook No. 202 Hira Lal. It was the old story of a hurricane lamp overturning—though there was less excuse for its being close enough to a tin of petrol to set the latter alight. The fire was put out without damage to the double-storey

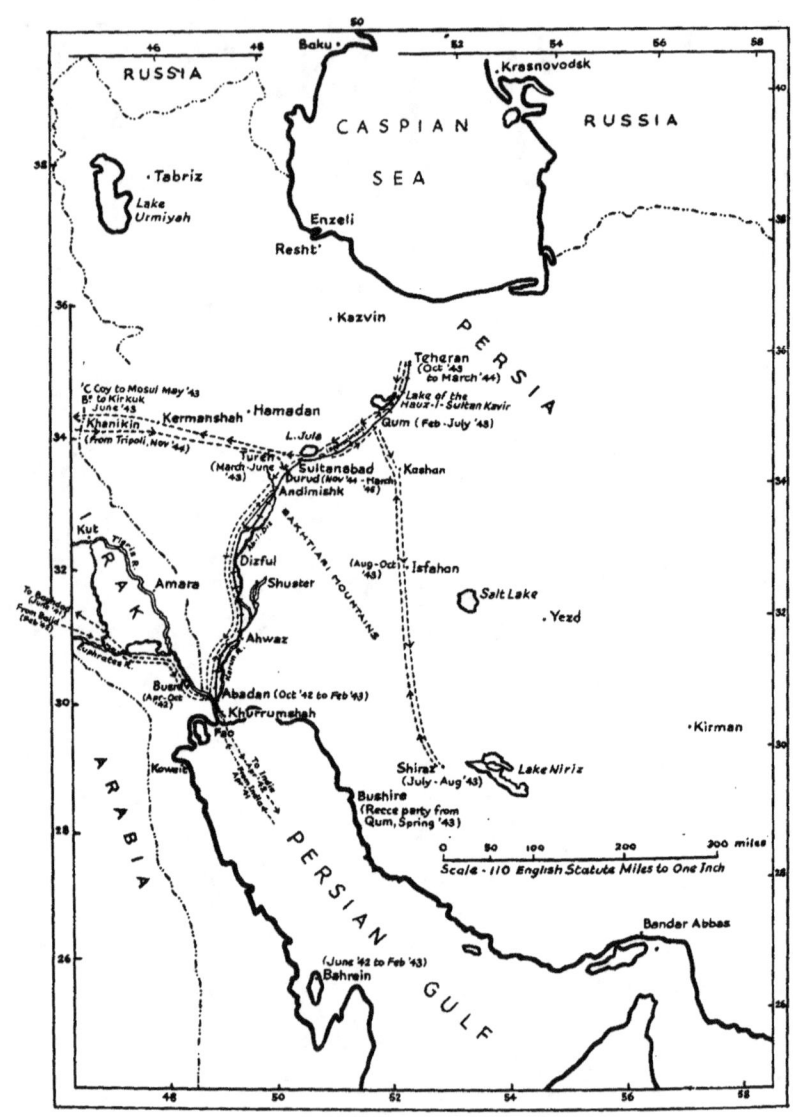

WESTERN PERSIA
— to illustrate the movements of the 3rd Bn, 11th Sikh Regiment between 1942 and 1944 in Persia (----→)

portion or to the kitchen—but it cost poor Hira Lal his life for he died of his burns two days after.

Exercises followed one another in bewildering succession. There was a divisional signal exercise at Lefkoniko on the 26th November. Then, on the 3rd December, the Battalion marched in to Famagusta, 24 miles in seven hours, to take part in a 7th Division exercise designed to test the Famagusta defences.

In this case, the 1st King's Own defended the town against the Sikhs who were to attack. The attack was put in under cover of a diversion on the north-west side of the town. While the diversion was confusing the defence, the main Sikh attack, supplemented by two commando parties, made for the Fort (the old walled town) which dominated the harbour.

From the Sikh view-point the results were entirely satisfactory. The two commando parties worked their way in via drains, unseen and unheard, and the main body were on their way in through the main gate before the headquarters of the defence even knew that the assault had begun.

On the 10th, a divisional camouflage competition produced another pleasing variation on training. For this, each battalion had to provide types of camouflage suits which could be easily made and could be carried in the platoon truck. The Sikhs carried off both the 1st and 2nd prizes, though the record unfortunately makes no mention of the winning suits.

The Battalion was very much on its toes again by now. In athletics it carried off an area cross-country race in fine style on the 17th December. Three teams each of 15 men were entered—the first 12 home in each team, counting. Out of the total of 240 runners from different units, the 45 battalion runners were all home among the first 75 in, and the three teams were placed first, second, and fourth. Two days later, on the 19th, the Battalion played in the finals of the Island hockey tournament, only losing to the Nabha Akal team 1-2. Again, on Boxing Day, the hockey team was presented with the cup for the Eastern Area tournament, together with medals for the Island tournament.

New Year's Eve provided a less welcome Service record. On this day it appears no fewer than seventy-four official letters were delivered, handsomely beating the previous record of fifty-two. No wonder the detailed Battalion story ends, for another ten months, here.

The 3rd Battalion was still in Abadan, some way down-stream from Busra on the Shatt el Arab. Living conditions corresponded closely with the climate. As the relevant *News Letter* puts it—"The ground was below flood level. In wet weather, tents were islands

1942

26 Nov.
3 Dec.

10 Dec.

17 Dec.

19 Dec.

26 Dec.

31 Dec.

3rd Bn.

1942-43
Feb.

surrounded by dykes and connected by slippery and narrow causeways." Spirits, however, rose in February when the news came through that the Battalion was to join the 2nd Indian Infantry Brigade of the 8th Indian Division, in Syria. But this was not to be. At the last moment orders were changed, and the Battalion allocated to the 10th Indian Motor Brigade at Qum in Persia. This seemed to hold prospects of worth-while service, but in fact, the Germans were by now on the move back from the Caucasus, and the Tenth Army role had lapsed. The 10th Indian Motor Brigade, which was to have been the spear-head of the Tenth Army, became instead the 60th Indian Infantry Brigade, and came under Paiforce command.

However, it was something to have a change of role and scene. It was something, too, to be on the move, and along a route which had some claims to interest. The route lay via Khorram Shah, Ahwaz, Andimishk, and Sultanabad, and thence to Qum, where the IIrd Corps of the Tenth Army was concentrated. A strong note of relief is apparent in the Battalion *News Letter*, at being once more members of an operational brigade, and away from the eternal guards and duties of Abadan. With the break-up of the Tenth Army, both army and divisional organizations broke up too, and the brigade role became all-important. Duties naturally were dull. They were of a garrison and internal security nature, but they had a touch of novelty too, as affecting the "Aid-to-Russia" route. Qum, itself, however, came in for the faintest of faint praise. "Here," says the letter, "we took over from a British regiment. We had a very widely-dispersed camp. The continual sand-storms were unpleasant. Moreover, the water was so salt that we all suffered considerable discomfort. In fact, later in the year, at another camp, the M.O. running out of 'saline', sent 160 miles for a pakhal of Qum water, which is a really efficient substitute for the most efficacious of liver salts."

So no wonder the troops appreciated some aspects of the change.

4th Bn.
12 Sept.

The 4th Battalion had taken over general duties in Haifa; and on the 12th September, celebrated Saragarhi Day in traditional style. It had been hoped that a large contingent of officers and ratings from H.M.S. *Sikh* would attend, but the ship sailed on her last voyage that morning. However, a pleasant feature of the day was receipt of news of a number of awards for the Western Desert operations. A Distinguished Service Order was awarded to Brig. J. J. Purves, M.C., a bar to the Military Cross to Capt. Mohd Siddiq, M.C., a posthumous Indian Order of Merit to the late Jem. Gurbaksh Singh, and Indian Distinguished Service Medals to Hav. Kishan Singh and Sep. Ghazni Khan.

1942

Though well away from the operational area, the Battalion continued to see something of the enemy. A number of enemy reconnaissance aircraft came over at different times during the month, though bombs were only once dropped. That particular raid did no very great harm. Most of the bombs fell into the sea, and those that fell on land were well clear of their targets. Total casualties were one donkey and one cow killed.

At the end of the month, the battalion being well settled in and acquainted with the ins and outs of its new role, weekly leave parties of Punjabi-Mohammedans were sent in to Jerusalem where there was an excellent hostel for them, and arrangements for guides to take them round to see places of religious interest to them. One way and another, while the Battalion was in Haifa, every Punjabi-Mohammedan had the opportunity of paying at least one visit to the city.

During October, educational training was stepped up. Tours were undertaken to the various factories and installations in the area. Furthermore, eight non-commissioned officers and men attended regular classes in Arabic under area headquarter arrangements, and made excellent progress. Then a field-firing competition was held in the Nazareth area, with a forced march preceding a company attack. A demonstration followed the competition, to show the best way of carrying out the final attack, and this was attended by a number of officers and men of the Palestine Police, with whom the Battalion had already established a close and friendly liaison. This liaison had a happy consequence at the end of November. The Battalion ran a tactical course for twenty officers and men of the Police, and this in turn did a lot to help in the training of the Battalion's own young officers since they had to come forward in turn to stage the necessary demonstrations.

Oct.

Nov.

Welcome news was received about this time, of the safe return to our own lines of No. 16614 L.-Naik Sohan Singh, who had fallen into German hands at Deir ez Shein on the 1st July. His adventures recall those of Hav. Dhirta Singh, already recorded, and won him recognition similarly, by the award of the Indian Distinguished Service Medal.

Dec.

Briefly, L.-Naik Sohan Singh had been moved back by stages, after capture, first to Mersa Matruh, then to Tobruk, where he must have been in touch with Hav. Dhirta Singh, and finally to Benghazi. With other prisoners, he worked long hours at loading and unloading ships at all these places in addition to other routine fatigues.

Sohan Singh was not ignorant of the countryside. He had been with the Battalion when it broke out from the Benghazi neighbourhood that January, and he was determined to get away. He made his

1943

escape, alone, on the 5th October, and set out on the long road home which the Battalion had followed before.

He seems to have travelled alone for the first eight days, but he then fell in with a havildar and four other ranks from different Indian units. He joined this party, and successfully guided them till they met our own advancing forces on the 14th November some 35 miles west of Tobruk.

Throughout this month of walking across the desert, L.-Naik Sohan Singh was active in making reconnaissances of Libyan villages and camps, and in obtaining food and water from the inhabitants for the party as a whole, and it was largely due to his initiative, endurance and courage that the party came through. There can be no doubt of the welcome he received.

Just before Christmas a large draft from India brought the Battalion up to 75 per cent of full strength. It is, however, a point worth pondering on that it had taken nearly six months to make the Battalion's losses even so far good. However, by New Year's Day, the Battalion was once again properly re-organized by companies. Specialists had been selected, all authorized promotions made, and the stage set for organized constructive training.

1 Jan.

As a preliminary, two courses each of a fortnight were held during the second half of January and early February, for the tactical training of selected officers and men of the various non-operational units in the area. This test of the Battalion's own tactical soundness was underlined by the complimentary letters subsequently received from the commanding officers of units concerned.

Feb.

February, however, brought shocking weather, and it was only with great difficulty that companies were fitted into fresh camp sites not completely flooded out, or inches deep in mud. The rain practically put paid to field-training for a while, as cross-country movement was not possible.

21 Feb. On the 21st February, two companies and six carriers were made available to take part in a garrison parade to celebrate the 25th anniversary of the Russian Red Army. This occasion—which may read curiously in the ears of a later generation—took the shape of a parade through the main thoroughfares of the town, and a march-past, when the District Commissioner took the salute. All services were represented, and the strength involved reached the respectable total of some 3,500 men.

With the long-faded echo of this celebration ringing faintly in our ears, we may take leave of the 4th Battalion, and return to the Eastern borders of India.

6th Bn. In *the 6th Battalion* in Jhikergacha, the tempo rose steadily

1942-43

throughout this period. At this time of year, the Bengal climate reaches its best, and the aftermath of the rains was soon forgotten in a resurgence of energetic training. The rumour was abroad that the division was booked for the Middle East. This lent added zest, particularly to training in the use of M.T., with which the Battalion was now equipped on the full "higher" scale. There was nothing academic or unreal about this aspect of training; and we have it on the commanding officer's authority—Lieut.-Col. E. C. Johnson—that the almost complete absence of roads other than the one main road, and the impossibility of getting off the main road except to be bogged in paddy-fields, brought grey hairs to the M.T.O.s and "Q" staff officers of the formation.

Apart from the rumours of a move, the war made little direct impact on the Battalion. A partial exception was the Japanese air-raids on Calcutta 60 miles to the west, in December 1942, and on the 15th and 19th January, 1943. These raids did almost no material damage at all, and caused negligible casualties; but they had all the consequences of a major "blitz" in the many hundreds of thousands of all classes of citizens who surged out of Calcutta by rail and road in search of safety. It was a pathetic spectacle, with vast numbers of these refugees in a state of practical destitution, clothed in rags, and with a dirty bundle or two on their heads. Many travelled in goods trains to Asansol, where they were bundled out—131 miles from Calcutta up the Grand Trunk Road. Others streamed up the Grand Trunk Road itself, in lumbering convoys of over-loaded bullock carts. A privileged few sped past in taxis liberally topped up with black market petrol. But all this took place miles to the west, and the only direct inconvenience suffered by the Battalion lay in the unstaffed condition of the Calcutta hotels and clubs.

Dec.
Jan.

The 7th Battalion was just back from the operations round Datta Khel to a normal routine life in Razmak. Training of all sorts alternated with the staging of demonstrations to troops of the garrison. Duties were stepped up in November when the 3rd/1st Gurkha Rifles left Razmak for Damdil, without relief. However, a large composite draft of 240 Sikhs and Punjabi-Mohammedans arrived on the 21st November, and brought the Battalion temporarily over strength. The draft did not come from the Training Battalion. It was found from the Training Battalions of the 1st, 8th, and 16th Punjab Regiments, and the 13th Frontier Force Rifles. Some care had to be taken in absorbing so large a body of—comparative—strangers, and by early December they were beginning to take their share of normal duties. No snow-clearing had come the Battalion's way by the end of the year—to the general relief.

7th Bn.

21 Nov.

247

1942-43

Feb.
February brought bracing news. To quote the record once more: "Orders have now been received that we are moving to Baluchistan at the end of next month.

"In the Bn. efforts had been made to keep the move Secret for the time being, but in Bannu and Mari-Indus, security precautions had not been well observed, and news of the move quickly 'leaked out' to men returning from leave and courses.

"After two years in Waziristan, all ranks are glad to have a move, though many had hoped that our next role would be more exciting than Frontier Defence. Still, to be able to get away from barbed wire and do training 'ad lib' in the open country will be a very welcome change.

"The two years in Razmak have done the Bn. a power of good—we arrived very young—less than one year old. Column, other Operations, and Training, have meant hard work under 'semi-active service conditions' and toughened all ranks considerably—we certainly look 100 per cent fitter than when we arrived. Duties have been very heavy with a Bn. short in the Bde, and leave has not been possible on a generous scale, but all ranks have shown a spirit worthy of the Sikh Regiment."

14th Bn.
2 Sept.
The 14th Battalion moved up from Nowshera to the Malakand on the 2nd September, and took over the forts at Malakand, Dargai, and Chakdara. It acted as Reserve Battalion during the final withdrawal of Indian Army troops from Chitral, and supplied the necessary escorts to convoys from Dir.

In February, 1943, the Battalion was moved at twelve hours' notice to Landi Kotal, owing to an outbreak of trouble during the Khyber reliefs. However, the Battalion had no very strenuous role to fill, and it spent two very pleasant and useful months training in the Landi Kotal area. The District and Brigade Commanders set the training exercises during this period, and both expressed themselves most satisfied with the standard the Battalion had reached. On conclusion of this interlude—at the end of March—the Battalion returned to the Malakand.

MG Bn.
Nov.-Dec.
The Machine Gun Battalion had been quietly plugging away at training in Nowshera, and by early autumn was equipped with one company in tracked vehicles, and three others in trucks. During November and December, it was attached to the 7th Indian Division for divisional training about Nowshera and Attock.

Jan.
In January, 1943, the Battalion, which had now been posted as an integral part of the 7th Indian Division, moved down to Chindwara in the Central Provinces, for jungle training.

                                                                    1942
The 15th Battalion—known till August as the 25th Battalion—   15th Bn.
moved from Alipur to Dum Dum in December, remaining there in its
previous role of aerodrome defence.

The 26th Battalion remained uneventfully in Bangalore.   26th Bn.

Chapter VIII

MARCH TO AUGUST 1943

Backscreen

South Pacific

In the South Pacific, the naval success in the Bismarck Sea heralded a period of Allied reorganization and mopping-up. Reinforcements were brought in, and a total of six Australian and four American divisions concentrated in Papua at the eastern end of New Guinea. With this force it was proposed to tackle the big Japanese base at Rabaul, lying at the northern tip of the island of New Britain, 700 miles west-north-west of Guadalcanal, and 400 miles north-east of Salamaua and the Huon Peninsula.

This important operation started with a series of cautious advances. First, Woodlark and Kiriwina Islands in the Trobrian group were occupied on the 22nd and 23rd of June. These islands lie north of the eastern end of New Guinea, and between it and new Britain, and they flanked the proposed operation against New Britain from the east. From them, fighters could operate towards both Dutch New Guinea—which adjoins Papua on the west—and Guadalcanal.

22-23 June

The Solomon Islands provide a series of stepping-stones running north-west towards Rabaul. On the 30th June, the American XIVth Corps from Guadalcanal began moving up them, and occupied Rendova Island about 200 miles north-westwards from Guadalcanal. With artillery assistance from here, New Georgia, immediately to the north, was invaded; and on the 5th August the Munda air-field was captured, though the whole island did not pass into Allied hands till the 25th of that month.

30 June

5 Aug.

25 Aug.

Simultaneously with these operations in the Solomons, forces in New Guinea were sapping north towards the Huon Peninsula, as a base for the operation against New Britain.

29-30 June

As a start, troops were landed on the 29th and 30th of June, at Nassau Bay, 11 miles south of Salamaua. Closing in on Salamaua from that side, the force consolidated while preparations for the methodical reduction of the well-fortified Japanese positions there were put in hand.

These were not completed till early September, and the operation will hence be dealt with in the next chapter.

Central Pacific

In the Central Pacific, operations opened on the 24th and 27th of July with carrier-borne air attacks on Wake Island. Wake Island lies

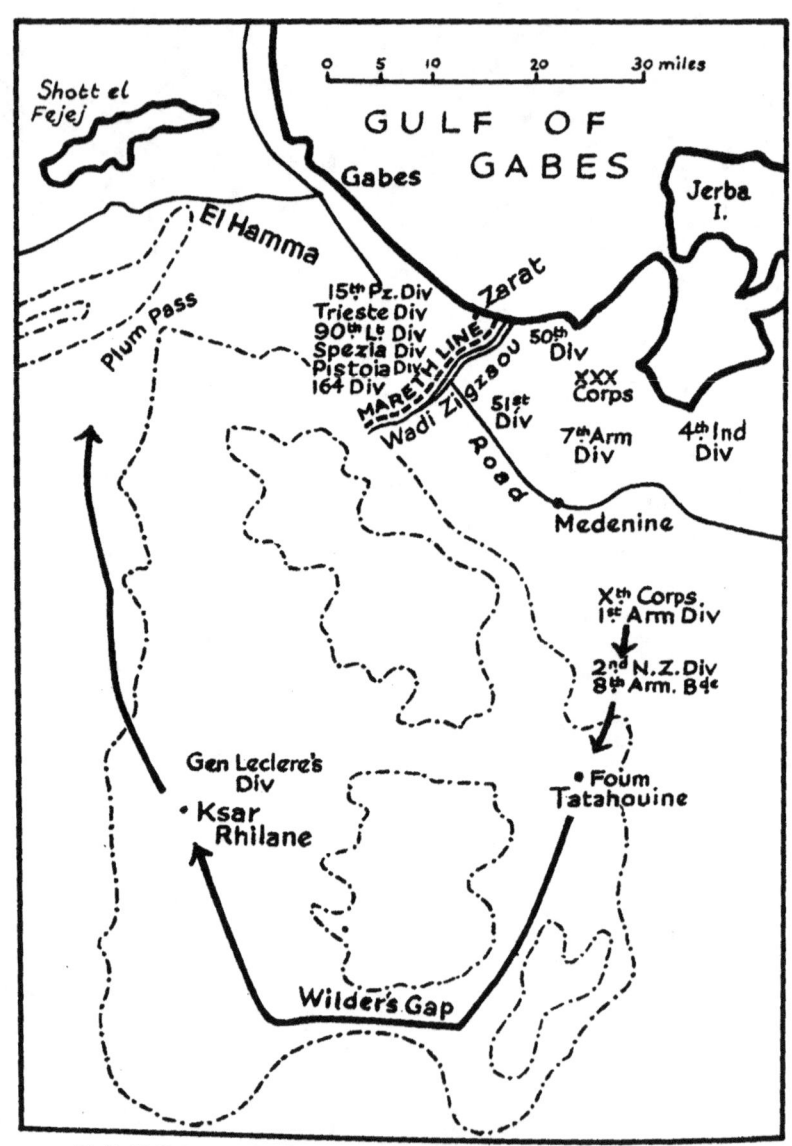

BATTLE OF THE MARETH LINE
20th – 27th March 1943
(With acknowledgements to "The Second World War"
by Major-General J. F. C. Fuller, page 245)

2,000 miles to the north of the Solomon Islands, and about half-way, on an east-west line, between Pearl Harbour and the Philippines.

On the 31st August, a raid was made on Marcus Island, 1,000 miles west-north-west of Wake Island, and half-way between that island and Japan. Marcus Island was an important Japanese air-base and relay-point.

Key islands in the Marshalls which lie between Wake Island and New Britain were raided at the same time.

In the Aleutians, operations re-opened on the 11th May when an American force by-passed Kiska and occupied Attu Island, wiping out the garrison of 2,350 Japanese. The Japanese found themselves unable to maintain their forces in the Aleutians after this, and abandoned the islands altogether on the 15th August. The Americans at once built a number of air-bases on the western islands from which to bomb the Kuriles, away to the south-west, and in particular the important Japanese base of Paramushiro.

In Burma, the first long-range jungle penetration operations by Brig. Wingate's force have been referred to in the preceding chapter. The columns made their way back across the Chindwin in May, bringing with them not only invaluable information but a heightened morale untouched by the, in many cases, severe privations they had suffered. Little else occurred in Burma during the summer of 1943, but events in China were shaping badly, and the Quebec Conference in August saw a series of major decisions which were to step up the war in the Burma theatre on that account to new heights in the coming year.

The position in Tunisia at the beginning of March was roughly as follows: The First Army lay west and south of Tunis, with elements echeloned farther south to give some protection to its exposed rear areas and westward communications, from Rommel's very active forces in the Mareth Line.

The Mareth Line, some 175 miles south of Tunis, stood with its eastern flank on the sea at Zarat. For 20 miles inland from Zarat, it followed the broad, steep-sided Wadi Zigzaou. At its western end, it rested on the Matmata Hills, across which wheels could not pass.

Rommel had not been unduly pressed by the Eighth Army on his withdrawal from El Alamein, and, after his operations against the First Army in the second half of February, fell upon the Eighth Army at Medenine, a few miles short of the Mareth Line, on the 6th March, but was repulsed. However, so long as the First Army screen which

251

1943
24-27 July

31 Aug.

North
Pacific
11 May

15 Aug.

Burma

May

Aug.

N. Africa

6 Mar.

1943

flanked his lines of communication with Tunis was in its currently disorganized condition, he felt secure enough.

The western flank, on the Matmata Hills, however, was not secure in the sense that the Allied flank had been secured by the Qattara Depression at El Alamein, for it was possible to make a detour round it. This detour, 150 miles in length, followed three sides of a square. It ran first southwards through Medenine to the Foum Tatahouine Pass, 40 miles away. Wilder's Gap lay a further 30 miles to the south, and from here the track wheeled west. Twenty miles on, it wheeled north, and a 60-mile run brought one past Kasar Rhilane to the Plum Pass. The Plum Pass itself lay only about 40 miles as the crow flies from the middle of the Mareth Line.

Between Wilder's Gap and the Plum Pass lay a small French force under General Leclerc, which had recently arrived from Lake Chad.

An Eighth Army attempt to make this detour was to be co-ordinated with a frontal attack on the Mareth Line. This attack was launched 20 Mar. at 10.30 p.m. on the 20th March by the 50th Division of the XXXth Corps, assisted by Indian sappers of the 4th Indian Division. Positions were gained on the far side of the Wadi Zigzaou, but the 15th Panzer and 90th Light Divisions drove the defenders out and restored the 22 Mar. situation on the 22nd March.

The 2nd New Zealand Division and the 8th Armoured Brigade, with the 4th Indian Division organizing the supply-line, were moving round by the Foum Tatahouine Pass during this operation. All went well till the force reached the Plum Pass, which was a formidable 23 Mar. obstacle about 3½ miles wide. After dark on the 23rd March, by which time it was clear the pass could not be carried without assistance, Xth Corps Headquarters and the 1st Armoured Division were sent up, while preparations were made for the XXXth Corps to open a new attack with fresh troops against the enemy's centre in the Mareth Line.

26 Mar. Climax came on the 26th March, when the Xth Corps attack on the Plum Pass went in under a tremendous air and ground bombardment which carried all before it. The advance went on by moonlight till only a few miles short of El Hamma, 30 miles north-west of the Mareth Line, and narrowly flanking the communications thence to Tunis. However, the enemy dealt with the situation with their usual skill. They successfully pulled out of the Mareth Line on the night 27-28 Mar. of the 27th/28th March, and occupied defensive positions on the Wadi Akarit north of El Hamma, with a loss of 2,500 men only, taken prisoner. Rommel had by now handed over to the Italian General Messe, and gone to Germany.

The Akarit position much resembled the Mareth Line in its natural

strength, and the enemy held it till the 6th April. They were turned out of it then in a gallant operation in which the 4th Indian Division played a prominent part, and withdrew to Enfidaville, 100 miles to the north.	6 Apr.
On the 7th April the First and Eighth Armies joined hands at Gafsa.	7 Apr.
Just before this, on the 5th, a violent offensive was opened against enemy sea and air communications between North Africa and Europe. By the 19th, this offensive had borne fruit to the extent of 147 troop-carrying and transport aircraft shot down, and thirty-one vessels sunk.	5 Apr. 19 Apr.
On the 20th April, the Eighth Army captured Enfidaville after furious hand-to-hand fighting in which the 4th Indian Division again displayed great gallantry at Djebel Garel. On the 24th, on the First Army front, an assault was made on Longstop Hill south of Tunis, and two days of heavy fighting saw its capture.	20 Apr. 24 Apr. 26 Apr.
On the 30th April, the 4th Indian Division with the 7th Armoured Division and the 201st Guards Brigade, moved off at four hours notice to cross the mountains and join the First Army for the final assault on Tunis. Meanwhile, on the 3rd May, the 1st American Armoured Division captured Mateur 20 miles south-south-west of Bizerta and 25 west of Tunis. The whole extent of perimeter held by the enemy round Tunis now amounted to about 130 miles.	30 Apr. 3 May
Early on the 6th May the battle for Tunis opened, with intense bombing of the enemy's front and rear and a vast programme of artillery support. Pressure was applied all along the enemy front, while the 4th British and 4th Indian Divisions—now part of the newly-organized IXth Corps—moved up behind the parties of sappers which had gone forward at 3.30 a.m. to lift mines and cut gaps in the wire. The enemy outpost position was broken through on a 3,000-yard front before light. By dawn, Allied troops had reached the main positions, and by 11 a.m. these had been penetrated at small cost. The 6th and 7th Armoured Divisions then passed ahead. Fighting their way doggedly on, the tanks were in the suburbs of Tunis by 2.30 p.m. the next afternoon and were in Tunis itself before dark. At the same time, the American IInd Corps on the left took Ferryville and Bizerta.	6 May 7 May

The Axis forces were not yet broken. They were still in being, and were making away north and east towards the Cape Bon Peninsula which runs out in a 50-mile wedge north-east from Tunis. The peninsula is ideally sited for defence, with two lines of hills running from sea to sea across its base.

These lines of hills, however, had two weak points. On the left or north-western flank, there was an opening in the hills at Hamman Lif. On the opposite flank came another gap, called Hammamet. If

1943

8 May   one or both of these could be seized before the enemy had time to organize his defence lines, prolonged and expensive operations would be avoided.

8 May   No time, accordingly, was lost. The 6th Armoured Division was directed against Hamman Lif at nightfall on the 8th May, with the object of breaking through, wheeling south-east behind the hills down the Hammamet road, and capturing the Hammamet gap as well. This it did the same night at moonrise, completing the operation in the course of the next ten hours, and spreading havoc and panic

9 May   throughout the Axis forces, which turned and fled up the Cape Bon roads looking for boats—of which there were none.

Confusion reached its climax by the 12th May, when 252,415 Germans and Italians surrendered, and victory in Africa finally came to the Allies. As a fitting postscript to a story of which the Indian Army is the leading theme, General von Arnim, the Supreme Commander of the Axis forces in Africa, was captured by the 4th Indian Division,— the 1st Royal Sussex Regiment and the 1st/2nd Gurkha Rifles, both of the 7th Indian Infantry Brigade, including him in the many thousands of prisoners collected by them.

Sicily   The Allied forces did not rest long on their laurels, but Sicily, which lay not far across the Mediterranean to the north, could not be immediately attacked for lack of landing-craft.

West and south-west of Sicily, however, lie Pantellaria and Lampedusa Islands. Pantellaria, again, lies 150 miles north-west of Malta, and Lampedusa 100 miles west of that island. Pantellaria had a fighter air-field and a garrison of 11,000 second-line troops.

18 May-
11 June   Between the 18th May and the 11th June, both islands were subjected to saturation bombing—Pantellaria receiving 6,570 tons of bombs alone. However, it is said that the effects of the bombing were a good deal less than might have been thought. Casualties among personnel were small. Underground aircraft hangars were little damaged, and aircraft found in them were not in some cases damaged at all. Out of fifty-four shore batteries, only two were completely knocked out, though presumably others were damaged.

On the 11th June, a naval force approached the island, and the garrison surrendered.

Meanwhile, landing-craft were being collected for the invasion of Sicily. Sicily at the time was garrisoned by five Italian infantry divisions and five coastal divisions. In the western part of the island lay a reserve of two German divisions—the 15th Panzer Grenadier, and the Herman Goering. The German Field-Marshal Albert Kesselring was in command.

From about the last week in May, a six-weeks preliminary bombing

programme was carried through against various enemy targets. This
culminated on the 9th July when 400 Allied transport aircraft and
137 gliders took off from Kairouan in Tunisia, under cover of fighters
and bombers of the Tactical Air Force. The British and American
troops in them had the duty of covering the arrival of a sea-borne
force which was on its way to Sicily. Though they were not in all
cases able to carry out this role, thanks to wind and other causes,
which resulted in some of the gliders coming down in the sea and
parachutists missing their objectives, the sea-borne landing was
made at 2.45 a.m. next morning at small cost.

The landing operation was carried out under command of Gen.
Alexander. Troops involved included four-and-a-half divisions of the
Eighth Army under Gen. Montgomery and two-and-a-half divisions of
the American Seventh Army under Gen. Patton.

Taking the latter first—the Seventh Army contingent landed a little
north-west of the southern tip of Sicily, between Licata and
Scoglitti, with the role of advancing north-west to Palermo on the
north coast of the island near its western end. Arrived at Palermo,
Gen. Patton was to wheel eastwards and follow the coast to Messina
at the eastern end of Sicily. This programme the Seventh Army
completed by the 16th August.

The Eighth Army also came ashore at the southern end of Sicily,
but at the opposite side from the Americans—between Syracuse and
Cape Passaro. From here, it was to follow the east coast via Catania,
linking up with the Seventh Army at Messina.

Much hard fighting was to precede fulfilment of this role, with an
overall casualty list for the Allies of 31,138, as against 167,000
amongst the Axis forces. The remnants of the two German divisions
made a successful withdrawal to Italy with much of their heavy
equipment.

Repercussions to the Sicilian campaign were immediate in Italy.
On the 25th July, Mussolini resigned, and Marshal Badoglio took
over the government. Mussolini was arrested next day, and remained
in custody till rescued by the Germans in a dramatic coup early in
September. But his fresh lease of freedom was short-lived, and
ended in tragedy soon after.

German divisions came pouring south over the passes into Italy,
until, by the 2nd September, when the Italians reluctantly accepted
the Allies' terms of unconditional surrender, thirteen fresh German
divisions had arrived in the country. Field-Marshal Rommel took
command of the forces in the north, while Field-Marshal Kesselring
remained in command of those to the south.

In western Europe, during May, came the courageous attack of the

1943

May — Royal Air Force on the Mohne Dam in the Ruhr. This successful operation—the fruits of many months of careful planning—won its leader a well-earned Victoria Cross.

Russia — In Russia, Hitler re-assumed the supreme military command during March. The previously critical position had been eased by Field-Marshal von Mannstein's well-calculated counter-offensive. For this operation, a force of twenty-five divisions had been collected. The twelve Panzer divisions included represented the greatest weight of armour yet employed in one battle.

21 Feb.
15 Mar. — Opening on the 21st February, a series of actions brought the Germans back into Kharkov by the 15th March, and won back additional points to the north and south of Kharkov before the thaw set in with a will, and put a stop to further operations.

Meanwhile, north and south of Kursk, lying about 120 miles north of Kharkov, the Russians had carved out for themselves a rectangular salient about 100 miles across. Hitler decided to try and pinch this salient out. He assembled a force of 7 Panzer divisions, 2 motorized divisions and 9 infantry divisions at Orel on the north flank of the salient. He collected a second force of 10 Panzer divisions, 1 motorized division and 7 infantry divisions at Byelgorod at the southern end. These forces, totalling about half-a-million men, were placed under command of Field-Marshal von Kluge, with the role of converging on Tim, 40 miles east of Kursk, and cutting off the Russian forces in the salient.

Bitter fighting followed. The first attacks were launched simultaneously

5 July — on the 5th July at 5.30 a.m., and initial successes were gained. The northern force made good about 10 miles, and the southern force between 30 and 40 miles. But losses were such in both men and

22 July — armour that by the 22nd July the operations had ended in failure and been abandoned. More—the Russians were so confident in their

15 July — strength that they had already, on the 15th July, launched a heavy counter-attack against the corresponding German salient that flanked their own in the north. They had attacked it from the north and from

4 Aug. — the south-east, and soon achieved striking success. By the 4th August, they had turned the Germans out of Orel, and on the same day recaptured Byelgorod at the south of their salient. For the Germans, this July offensive proved a major disaster, to which much of their subsequent difficulties were due. So large a proportion of German armour had in fact been lost that they could no longer maintain a lively and elastic defensive. That the defeat at Kursk was as fatal to the Germans as that at Stalingrad is no exaggeration.

The Russians now moved in against the Germans on a wide front towards the Dnieper river, west and south-west of Kursk. Kharkov again

	1943
changed hands on the 23rd August, and a general retreat of the German armies in the Donetz area followed. Further south, Taganrog on the north coast of the Sea of Azov was stormed by the Russians on the 30th.

23 Aug.

30 Aug.

The 1st Battalion was now doing advanced training with the 108th Indian Infantry Brigade of the 39th Indian Division at Lohadaga, near Ranchi, preparatory to moving back to a theatre of operations. Orders, however, hung fire.

1st Bn.

Mention has already been made in Chapter VII of the excessive time taken in bringing the 4th Battalion up to only 75 per cent of its strength. The dead hand of man-power shortage was everywhere being felt, and it was becoming apparent that India could not maintain as many divisions in the field as had been hoped. Hence the 39th Indian Division's move to Burma was first postponed and then cancelled; and in July it was told that it would be turned into a training division for the advanced preparation of troops and drafts destined for operational theatres, and would be moved back to the Dehra Dun area. Its units were all dispersed to other formations, but the 1st Battalion was kept for some weeks in a state of uncertainty. It was very generally felt in the Battalion that there was small scope for a Brigade Reconnaissance Battalion, and the soundness and practicability of the organization was doubted.

July.

Meanwhile individual and Company training went steadily on, and there can be no doubt that the Battalion profited much from these extra months preparation. Up to the break of the monsoon, training was carried out from jungle camps, and a good number of Battalion and Brigade exercises were worked through, before the rains brought the Battalion back into Lohadaga.

At last, in mid-August, the decision was made. The 7th Indian Division was in Ranchi, preparing for a move to the Arakan. A battalion of the Division dropped out, and it was decided to move the 1st Battalion in. It was moved to Kumthi, where it was rapidly stripped of its ponies and vehicles, but not so quickly fitted out with the normal war outfit of an infantry battalion. In fact, its outfit never was completed through respectable official sources, but through some valuable discoveries in the paddy-fields round Bawli, where equipment had been abandoned by formations which had departed after the first Arakan Campaign.

Aug.

But this is to anticipate.

For *the 2nd Battalion* the summer—in Cyprus—brought no particular excitements. Training of all types was carried out, starting with some strenuous work in the mountains during wintry weather in early

2nd Bn.

1943

Aug.
spring. Contrary to more normal Indian practice, the Battalion was moved down to the central plain for the summer, which was not to its liking, though it brought the doubtful amenities of the larger towns within reach. By the end of August, there seemed as little prospect of operational employment as in the spring, but the Battalion was fit and hard, and morale stood very high.

3rd Bn.

The 3rd Battalion pursued the even tenor of its way in Persia, extracting such interest and humour as might be found.

July-Aug.
In the spring, a large reconnaissance party travelled down to Bushire, 700 miles away. Later, during July and August, the Brigade went off to Shiraz to show the flag to the Bakhtiari and Kashgai hill tribes which had recently beaten up a Persian force, and were threatening the security of the Bushire-Teheran road. No opposition was met, and as most of the routes to be patrolled lay 5,000 feet above sea-level, days were pleasant and nights were cool, and the troops thoroughly enjoyed the change. The Brigade returned in early August, dropping the Battalion en route in Isfahan.

In Isfahan, business and pleasure were combined in a satisfactory way. The camping ground had been used for commando training by Brig. Fitzroy McLean for some months, before he left to join Gen. Tito in Serbia. There were good training facilities, for Isfahan lies, a green carpet, in a broad valley surrounded by grim rocky hills—somewhat in favour at an earlier time for the final disposal over the cliffs of political and civil offenders.

In Isfahan itself fruit gardens abounded, and peaches, grapes, melons and pomegranates were readily available. There was no entertainment in the accepted sense, but the Battalion made up its own drama party, which was a great success. Firm friends were made with the few European civilians, and particular kindness was met from Dr. Schaffter of the Church Missionary Society Hospital, who took many parties out sightseeing, after providing an excellent tea. He also arranged for the design and weaving of a carpet for the Gurdwara, in a pattern of blue, dark cream and a little red, with a Sikh quoit in the centre.

Meanwhile, however, other matters were afoot, and careful plans were maturing for the arrest of hostile agents known to be in the

31 Aug.
city. These plans matured at dawn on the 31st August, when the whole were arrested, and removed to the Battalion camp which lay about 12 miles away. The whole operation was over by 8 a.m., though some concern was felt at the possible reaction of the Persian Army, since some of those arrested were Persian officers. In the event, however, the only embarrassment proved to be the feeding of these guests. The only source from which meals could

be supplied was the officers' mess; and the officers' mess could at this time only muster one "chokra" cook who had to cook for the whole twenty-nine, which included some attached officers. As the chokra said, in rueful imitation of the Prime Minister: "Never had one man to cook for so many".

The 4th Battalion in Haifa continued training so far as its protective role allowed. Exercises against parachute troops were staged on the 5th, 6th and 7th March. In the middle of March, a demonstration showing the attack in mountain warfare was given for the Staff College. It was a comprehensive affair, carried through by two rifle companies and a proportion of "H.Q." Company. In this demonstration, Part I showed all the Battalion weapons, laid out for inspection. After they had been looked at, and their uses explained, they were shown in action. Part II showed an attack up a hill feature supported by all the available weapons within the Battalion. There was an attendance of about 200, and it caused much interest. There was a general demand from the Staff College that a demonstration should be given at every course; and it was asked that the demonstration should be staged early in the course instead of at the end, in order to give students a better appreciation of the types and capabilities of infantry weapons. A repeat was accordingly put on at the end of April for the next course. For the dress rehearsal, the Battalion invited Royal Navy, Royal Artillery and Royal Air Force units to send representatives, and a highly appreciative audience of some 200 ranks attended.

On the 15th May, the Battalion left Haifa by road and rail for the newly established Mountain Warfare Training Centre in the Lebanon Hills. The men were glad to leave Haifa after nine months of relative monotony. The new camp, which they reached on the 16th, was about 10 miles from the station and town, and lay in and about an olive grove 1,000 feet or so above the sea, which could be seen from the hills behind the camp. The summer climate proved quite bearable, and usually one blanket was needed at night. Inland at first the hills still had a certain amount of snow on them. The country was very fertile, and ample fruit was to be had. But even as compared with Egypt and Palestine, prices were very high.

Between the 16th and 26th May, the Battalion was busy taking over as demonstration battalion from the Gurkhas who preceded it. The normal programme provided for a week of demonstrations for a proportion of the officers and non-commissioned officers of the formation under training. During the following week, the demonstrations were repeated for another batch. The Battalion then provided an "enemy" for the formation for five collective exercises which lasted for

1943

anything from three to four weeks altogether. Much value was extracted by the Battalion itself from these exercises, since the men were able to see and use all the latest types of infantry weapons. Morale rose correspondingly; and as drafts slowly came in during the summer and autumn, its return to more nearly full strength gave it fresh hope of an approaching operational role.

14 June   Meanwhile on the 14th June there was a small interlude in the official Allied Nations Day celebrations. The Battalion provided a composite company 100 strong from its Sikhs and Punjabi-Mohammedans, as well as a Guard of Honour of twenty men under Capt. Mohammad Siddiq, M.C., for the inspecting officer. Special permission was given, for this one parade, to slope and order arms—a form of rifle exercise which had been abandoned early in the war and was not taught to recruits at the Training Battalion—and the Battalion's arms drill was the subject of much appreciative comment.

During June two more honours were awarded. Hav. Dhirta Singh received the MacGregor Memorial Medal and a grant of one hundred rupees for the valuable information brought in by him after his escape from Tobruk already recorded. L.-Naik Sohan Singh received the Indian Distinguished Service Medal for courage, fortitude and cheerfulness while escaping from Benghazi with a party of six Indian other ranks from other units. His party spent five weeks in the desert before finally contacting our advancing forces. It is a matter of regret that a detailed record of their adventures was not preserved.

It seems appropriate to mention here what the Battalion had meantime been doing for its men lost to the enemy during the previous operations. Since the day the first prisoner-of-war was lost to it, a fund had been running for provision of comforts for them. Every man in the Battalion contributed his mite, and the money was used to buy eatables, which were duly despatched. Later, an order was issued forbidding the despatch of food from the Middle East; and thereafter the money was sent to the English and Indian Red Cross Societies. No less than £400 had been sent to these societies by the end of 1943, and wonderful accounts were received from men in captivity of the excellent parcels they received. It is something that our western enemies did pay due regard in this matter to their responsibilities—a very different story from that current in prisoner-of-war camps in the Far East. A further contribution to the welfare of prisoners was made by Gen. Wilson Johnston in his scheme for "adopting" prisoners and writing to them.

6th Bn.   *The 6th Battalion* left Jhikergacha on the 18th March at a few
18 Mar.   hours notice, for the Arakan. The position at that time in this area

1943

was approaching a crisis with the British and Indian troops already there dispersed in scattered pockets down the Mayu Peninsula, where a sudden Japanese advance had put them at a serious disadvantage.

The 4th Indian Infantry Brigade of the 26th Indian Division, comprising the 6th/11th Sikh Regiment, the 3rd/9th Gurkha Rifles, and the 8th/8th Punjab Regiment, had now spent many months perfecting itself for mechanized warfare. Now that the crisis had come, however, its role was incontinently changed. Its motor vehicles were withdrawn, 28 mules, innocent of saddlery, were issued to each battalion, and the brigade was ordered off post-haste to the Arakan to thicken up our desperately weak forces there.

Under these not very happy auspices, the advance party had left under Maj. C. H. McVean, now second-in-command, on the 14th March for Maungdaw. The Battalion was relieved by the 15th Battalion of the Regiment—whose help and hospitality on the day the 6th Battalion left could not have been exceeded. And on the 18th, as already noted, the Battalion left, moving by sea to Maungdaw, a small port on the Arakan coast south of Chittagong.   14 Mar.

18 Mar.

On disembarking, the 3rd/9th Gurkha Rifles were sent off on an isolated mission to the east to hold up a Japanese infiltration, and so were temporarily lost to the brigade. The Sikhs also lost the services of a rifle company which was sent forward the same night to a small island in the Mayu river from which Japanese infiltration on that side might be blocked. A detachment of two companies of the 8th/8th Punjab Regiment was sent away for duties in the north, so that at the outset, the Brigade was left with a total of five rifle companies instead of the normal twelve. These circumstances more than any other, mark the prevailing conditions in the Arakan at that time.

The depleted 4th Indian Infantry Brigade moved inland the same night after disembarkation, to Buthidaung, along the road made famous later by the Battles of the Tunnels. A few days after its arrival in Buthidaung, the Brigade moved forward under Brig. Lowndes, who had taken over from Brig. Hungerford, evacuated sick.

The Battalion began to deploy in country and under conditions for which they had not trained, facing an enemy who was fighting a campaign for which he had made long and careful preparations. Our forces fought in the dark, and bought their experiences as they went along.

Information of the movements and whereabouts of our own troops was as spasmodic, and often misleading, as of the enemy. However, on the 30th March, the Brigade moved forward down the west side of the Mayu river to the assistance of hard-pressed troops under Brig. Wimberley. The Battalion—less "A" Company, which came   30 Mar.

1943	down-river to Hparabyin the same day—was the advanced guard. Approaching Theindaungpara, heavy enemy fire from both flanks was opened on "B" and "C" Companies, who suffered nineteen casualties. The enemy withdrew after a short sharp action leaving several dead. The Brigade spent the night, which was undisturbed, near the village.
31 Mar.	Little or nothing was known of the country through which the Brigade was moving, and a halt was called next day, and the Battalion dug in pending the results of Brigade reconnaissances. Intelligence reports indicated an enemy strength of about two companies in the
3 Apr.	vicinity, and on the 3rd April, Maj. M. Carter made a flanking reconnaissance on Prainagdaung, where he arrived about 6 p.m. and drew enemy fire. A defensive position was taken up, and next
4 Apr.	day Maj. Carter moved out westwards with a patrol of fifteen men on further reconnaissance of a high feature in the vicinity. No enemy was encountered this time, though many old camp sites, etc., were found.
	In the meantime, the 8th/8th Punjabis had moved forward and
3 Apr.	captured the Nawadaung area, and on the 3rd April, "B" Company of the Sikhs took over from them while the 8th/8th put in an attack, which was successful. Many casualties were inflicted on the Japanese at a cost of twenty to the 8th/8th. The Punjabis then withdrew to Hparabyin, "B" and "D" Companies of the Sikhs
6 Apr.	staying out till the 6th April, when they also withdrew on Hparabyin.
7 Apr.	On the 7th April, Sub. Mall Singh carried out a patrol with twenty men of "B" Company, but met no enemy.

Brig. Wimberley's Brigade meanwhile had broken out. After jettisoning all its heavy equipment, it had made its get-away across the Mayu Range and joined forces with another brigade. The immediate task of the 4th Indian Infantry Brigade had therefore lapsed.

At this time the main British force was deployed on the western side of the Mayu Range with its right flank on the sea. East of the Mayu Range was the 4th Indian Infantry Brigade, operating with its left flank on the Mayu river. The Japanese, with their usual skill at infiltration, had worked their way through the intricate jungle-clad terrain at the top of the range, and were threatening the inner flanks and rear-ward communications of both parts of the force, which was slowly pulling back.

17 Apr.	On the 17th April, "C" Company took up a position on rising
19 Apr.	ground at "35r." Two days later, on the 19th April, the Japanese threw in a determined attack in which the company commander, Capt. Haslop and seven other ranks were killed and nine men wounded. Lieut. Ujagar Singh, the company second-in-command, took over command, and held on for a day and a night against

frequent attacks by the enemy who were in considerable strength and fighting with determination. "D" Company coming to "C" Company's assistance, Lieut. Ujagar Singh was able to break off the action on the evening of the 20th. He was subsequently awarded the Military Cross for his admirable conduct of this action, whilst the Indian Distinguished Service Medal was awarded to Hav. Jota Singh, also of "C" Company, for his initiative, courage and devotion to duty in this and previous actions. *20 Apr.*

On the 23rd April, towards nightfall, a report was received of an enemy patrol infiltrating between two forward company areas. The commanding officer, Lieut.-Col. E. C. Johnson, decided to investigate the matter personally, and went forward through the scrub with a small light machine-gun detachment. Visibility, always bad in this enclosed country, was made more so by the darkness of the night, but the party reached and lay up at the edge of a narrow clearing. After remaining in position for some time without hearing or seeing anything of the enemy, the party was preparing to cross the clearing, when a heavy burst of light machine-gun fire was opened. Lieut.-Col. Johnson was severely wounded and had to be evacuated, command passing to Maj. McVean. *23 Apr.*

No further incidents marked the stay of the Battalion in the forward area. On the 7th May, it was withdrawn to Buthidaung, and on the 9th to Maungdaw. Four days later, a further withdrawal brought the Battalion back to Bawli Bazar, where it rejoined the 4th Indian Infantry Brigade, from which it had been detached for some time. On the 16th May, the Brigade moved back a few miles, before turning east over the hills by the Goppé Pass, to Goppé Bazar in the broad valley beyond. *7 May 9 May 13 May 16 May*

We shall hear more about Goppé Bazar and the passes over the hills in a later chapter, but the fighting for the most part was over in the current phase of the Arakan campaign. The Battalion stayed on in Goppé Bazar for about a fortnight reorganizing and training. As in so many other campaigns, climatic conditions contributed far more heavily to the casualty lists than the enemy. Here, in the depths of little developed tropical forest, with no mosquito-nets, quinine or preventive devices such as anti-mosquito oils, available to front-line units, it would be surprising if the troops had not suffered from serious depletion from disease. In point of fact, thanks mainly to these regrettable deficiencies, the Battalion strength now stood at no more than some 200 Viceroy's commissioned officers and other ranks. Of the British officers, four only remained at duty— Maj. McVean, Maj. M. W. H. Robinson, Maj. J. Tanner, and Maj. J. B. Smith. It seems altogether appalling that a fine Battalion could be brought so low in so short a time by causes altogether outside its

1943

control, but which, one feels, could have been much lessened with adequate foresight from above. It says much for those that remained that their spirit and morale remained at full pitch, and that they could have asked nothing better than to make contact again with the Japanese at the earliest moment.

A few days after reaching Goppé Bazar, the Battalion was joined by a draft of about 200 men under Lieuts. Nakai and Stephenson.

29 May Then on the 29th May it marched by stages to Rumkhapalong where it remained reorganizing and training for three weeks. During this time Lieut.-Col. I. H. McD. Latham, from the 4th Battalion, arrived to take over command.

The monsoon breaks early in the Arakan, and it soon became clear that the immediate threat to India in this area had passed. Most of the units of the 26th Indian Division were withdrawn to stations in India to re-equip and be brought up to strength. Among these went the 6th Battalion, which marched for Cox's Bazar on the

24 June coast on the 24th June. From Cox's Bazar the way led back full-circle to Jhikergacha Ghat where the Battalion arrived—one feels with dampened enthusiasm—to endure another insufferable Bengal summer

11 July —on the 11th July.

7th Bn. *The 7th Battalion*'s two-year tour in Razmak was drawing to an end, and everyone was glad that it should. The stay there had been a profitable one in every sense, but it was time the troops had a change. The mere fact of heavy duties, on a scale of one night in bed for the ordinary sepoy, caused no complaint; but it brought with it indirect penalties which included rather disappointing results in educational tests among other things.

However, to commemorate a stay in which all agreed that the Battalion had carved out a splendid reputation for itself, a Battalion

20 Mar. shield was as usual made and hung up in Razmak club on the 20th March by the commandant. The shield itself had been made by the Pioneer Sergeant of the Green Howards and a Peshawar jeweller had added the silver badge and scroll. This small ceremony was coupled with a party which well rounded off the two years spent in Razmak.

22 Mar. On the 22nd March, the Battalion left Razmak by M.T. convoy. Many old friends came to No. 1 Gate to see it off, and the Frontier Force pipe band played while the troops were forming up. That night was spent in Bannu.

The move to Shela Bagh at the Quetta end of the Khojak Pass was uneventful. Administrative arrangements went smoothly and all ranks enjoyed the journey. The Battalion arrived on the morning of

27 Mar. the 27th March and was met by Brig. Monier-Williams commanding the Khojak Brigade.

1943

Shela Bagh lies in a narrow glen running up into the Khojak Range, with rocky hills frowning down on it. Barracks for one company were built of concrete under the reconstruction scheme for the Quetta earthquake of nine or ten years before. The remaining barracks were kacha. The general state of the place was poor, and the next month was a busy one for everybody. Platoon and company training was got going immediately, and reconnaissances were made over all the ground within miles of Shela Bagh. During spare time the lines were overhauled, sports grounds and gardens put in order, company recreation rooms set up and games, etc., bought for them from the Amenities Fund.

A note on general military education as helped on in the Battalion at this time, will be of interest. War maps of all fronts were hung up in the Battalion information room, and flagged with brief details of all develpments. All current publications such as the *Fauji Akbbar, Jang ki Khabren, Current Affairs, Information Summaries*, etc., were made available. Photographs of aircraft, tanks, etc., were displayed in the information room, and it was hoped to supplement these with models as soon as available. Local training maps and important items of training to be carried out were also available to officers at any time. In addition, of course, to these, the usual subjects were taught as part of the soldier's normal educational training.

Tactical training started on an ambitious scale. Companies went out regularly on three- and four-day schemes. "D" Company made a new Battalion record. It marched 51½ miles in 47 hours— incorporating in the exercise several attack and defence schemes in addition.

On the 21st May, the Battalion celebrated "North Africa Victory Day". Not much could be done as "A", "B" and "H.Q." Companies were away on training exercises, but a commanding officer's parade was held during the morning, when both he and the subedar-major addressed the men and explained the significance of the victorious climax to the North African operations in Tunis. 21 May

In the afternoon a "water gymkhana" was held in the miniature swimming pool. A somewhat sombre note marred this otherwise enjoyable affair when some of the clerical staff announced their intention of demanding compensation for clothes spoilt in a rather ambitious obstacle race, but doubtless this was dealt with amicably in due course. The remainder of the Battalion which was carrying out its training exercises on the shores of Khushdil Khan lake—well known for its magnificent shooting at the proper season—celebrated the day in much the same way but with a good deal more water at their disposal.

On the 30th May, the Commander-in-Chief visited the Battalion and saw companies at normal training. He met all officers, and, before 30 May

1943

leaving, complimented the commanding officer on the general state of the Battalion.

Shooting competitions were now held every Saturday morning. On 12 June the 12th June, a mule competition was held to encourage the men in the care of mules and saddlery. Meanwhile, individual training had been re-started to admit of correcting the defects in elementary work which had come to light in the larger platoon and company schemes which have been described.

The Battalion was now definitely starting to grow up and find its feet. For this, its splendid start in Razmak had done much. However, the Khojak Brigade now contained many newly-raised battalions not yet fit for extensive training; and it was felt that the 7th Battalion should train alongside units of its own standard. Orders were accordingly received for a move to Fort Sandeman where these conditions could be met.

These orders were not, however, to be fulfilled without a false start. All preparations for the move were made, stores packed and vehicles overhauled. The advance party was due to leave Shela Bagh at midnight on the 19th/20th June, by road; but at 8 p.m. on the 19 June 19th, the Brigade commander raced into Shela Bagh in his car and informed the Battalion that the move had been postponed till the end of July.

It is to be hoped that the Battalion did not, on this, unpack a proportion of its stores to tide over the intervening six weeks. The probability is that it was sufficiently war-wise by this time to remain firmly and resolutely packed. At all events a message was 26 June received a week later, on the 26th June, ordering the immediate move of the Battalion to Fort Sandeman. The advance party moved 27 June off the next night by road, covering the 220 miles to Fort Sandeman in under 24 hours in spite of a number of minor breakdowns, which, 28 June says the record "showed that Bn. M.T. maintenance required to be put on a higher level", and the main body started off from Shela 30 June Bagh on the 30th.

The move arrangements merit some detailed description as a reminder that Frontier rail moves were not the simple matter they usually are in better organized surroundings.

Two troop specials were provided for the section of the journey between Shela Bagh and Bostan; but from Bostan no fewer than six specials were required to carry the Battalion up the narrow-gauge section from Bostan to Fort Sandeman. The first special left Shela Bagh on the 30th, and the first narrow-gauge special reached Fort Sandeman on the 2nd July. But the last troops 2 July were not in till three days later, on the 5th. What was involved 5 July in the change over of stores from one set of trucks to another at the break of gauge at Bostan is not mentioned, so presumably arrangements were adequate and the work went smoothly.

There was a good deal of congestion in Fort Sandeman at first, as the 6th/18th Garhwal Rifles who were being relieved, were not due to leave for several days. Companies were fitted in in odd corners all over the cantonment, and settling in had to be delayed.

The Zhob Brigade had its headquarters in Fort Sandeman, with three infantry battalions, a mule company, a company of sappers and miners and some smaller units. A fourth infantry battalion was located 120 miles away in Loralai.

Situated in the centre of a flat plain, training facilities were quite good. Many excellent camp sites were to be had within a dozen miles, and the field-firing area five miles away to the north was first-class. Small hills and ridges were available for mountain warfare training.

The summer climate was good, but malaria was rife, and great efforts were made to make all ranks "malaria-minded".

On the 19th July, the Battalion took over a six-weeks tour as Duty Battalion. Duties were very heavy, and were a great drag on normal training.

The 7th August was the third anniversary of the raising of the Battalion, and was observed with due form. In the morning an inter-company sports meeting was held—with average results but high enthusiasm. After the morning meal, the troops went to the cinema and saw an excellent film—*Taj Mahal*. Then, in the evening at 6.15 p.m., there was a hockey match between British officers and sepoys versus Viceroy's commissioned officers and non-commissioned officers—which went smoothly enough as hockey till somebody introduced a football, after which it became rugger and finally a free-for-all. Finally, after the evening meal, each company produced a twenty-minute playlet before a packed audience including the brigade commander and other officers from the station, and "B" Company won the Battalion prize for a good "security" play.

By the end of August, much training had been done in spite of heavy duties. Chief emphasis had been laid on individual training in which good progress had been made. Each company had also put in a week's camp, with field-firing, N.W.F. warfare and modern warfare training. A draft of fifty recruits had arrived from the Regimental Centre, and the Battalion was well set for its first appearance on a Zhob Column exercise in the first days of September.

The 14th Battalion, as already recorded, returned to Malakand from its two-month spell in the Khyber, in March. It was not,

1943

however, destined to remain much longer in an active role. For the reasons already noted in the references to the 1st Battalion earlier in the chapter, it had become necessary for the Indian Army to curb its offensive programme for lack of sufficient man-power to maintain it. Training divisions were being set up in India to give advanced instruction beyond the capabilities of normal training establishments, to officers and men awaiting despatch to units in the field; and units which were surplus to the numbers that could be maintained in the field were posted to the training divisions to provide the necessary instructional staff. Parallel with the 39th Division, which had been withdrawn, in this role, to the Dehra Dun area, the 14th Division was established in Chindwara. The 14th

July   Battalion of the Regiment was moved to Chindwara in July to become the training unit for the 11th Sikh Regiment in that division.

This, of course, was the end of the 14th Battalion as a service unit. It was reduced to a training cadre of about 200 ranks, and the remaining personnel were drafted to active battalions.

MG Bn.   *The Machine-Gun Battalion*, training in Chindwara, was now to pass through experiences not dissimilar from those which the 1st Battalion met while under training as a Brigade Reconnaissance Battalion in Lohadaga.

By this time, General Headquarters had approved a standard organization for a jungle-fighting division. The 7th Indian Division—and presumably with it the Machine-Gun Battalion—had directed its training accordingly. There was no doubt that training in general in the Machine-Gun Battalion under its commanding officer, Lieut.-Col. R. Gordon, was being pushed on with enthusiasm and vigour.

It is, of course, easy to be wise after the event, and condemn the shifts and manoeuvrings to which the authorities resorted in their effort to make the best use of the weapons and experience available. Planning risks had to be taken, and it was often impossible to foresee the consequences. It was a period of trial and error, of experiment and compromise, and of attempts to make the fullest use of what equipment was available, in the general interest. No doubt that was why, just before the Division completed its training, the decision was made to introduce the 4.2-inch mortar on a 50 per cent basis as a weapon for the Machine-Gun Battalion, and to withdraw the tracked vehicles.

This decision had one immediate consequence. The Battalion had to be completely re-organized and re-trained. The 7th Indian Division went off without it—to pick up later, it will be remembered—the 1st Battalion on its way to the Arakan.

Towards the end of the summer, the Machine-Gun Battalion was

1943

moved to Ranchi to train in its altered role, and to extract what comfort it could from the new weapons and methods allotted.

The 15th Battalion, as will have been seen in the 6th Battalion record, had been moved out to Jhikergacha Ghat in mid-March, to take over from the 6th Battalion, with additional responsibilities for aerodrome defence at Comilla and Agartala, a few miles from Comilla

15th Bn.

The 26th Battalion moved up from Bangalore to Poona in June, on relief by the 3rd Madras Battalion. During July and August, it was a continual round of escorts and guards, and one may suppose that the Jemadar Adjutant's life was a weary round of making-do on a minimum of nights in bed.

26th Bn.

India was getting well into its production-stride by this time, and many important war factories and depots were concentrated in the Poona neighbourhood. Guns, tanks, vehicles, and in fact consignments of every imaginable form of warlike store, were being continuously despatched to all parts of India, and a constant stream of escorts was being called for from the Battalion throughout these two busy months. At the end of August, the Battalion was transferred, less one company, to Santa Cruz near Bombay for a spell of not unwelcome coastal defence duties.

Chapter IX

SEPTEMBER 1943 TO FEBRUARY 1944

Backscreen

South Pacific In New Guinea, at the beginning of September 1943, the Allies
New Guinea were sapping up the north-east coast towards the Huon Peninsula, jutting boldly out to the east, and pointing a fat finger at New Britain Once the Peninsula was effectively occupied, the stage would be set for the decisive operation against Rabaul, 300 miles up the coast of New Britain and at its north-eastern end.

Certain steps had to be completed before the Huon Peninsula could be occupied. The first was the capture of Salamaua which had
July been attacked from the south at the beginning of July. To cut its communications northwards, an Australian force was landed east of Lae, a little up the coast, across the Markham river, on the
4 Sept. 4th September, and on the 5th, an American parachute regiment was
5 Sept. dropped 19 miles north-west of Lae to seize the air-field, at Nazdab. In this latter operation altogether 1,700 paratroops and 36 Australian gunners with guns were dropped by the Fifth Air-force. Describing it, Gen. Arnold in his report says, "In front forty-eight B-25's opened the fight by strafing Japanese positions and dropping fragmentation bombs. They were followed by six A-20's that laid the smoke-screen which covered the landing of our paratroops from the ninety-six C-47 Above these flew five B-17's carrying material, and three B-17's with Generals MacArthur and Kenney and their staffs. A fighter escort of 146 P-38's and P-47's covered the flight at various altitudes, while at Heath's Plantation, half-way between Nazdab and Lae, four B-17's and twenty-four B-24's bombed and strafed the Japanese positions."

11-16 Sept. Salamaua fell on the 11th September, and Australian troops were in Lae on the 16th.

Finschafen lies at the eastern tip of the Huon Peninsula. A force,
23 Sept. principally Australian, was landed north of the town on the 23rd
2 Oct. September, and had secured it by the 2nd October. From now till the
Jan. end of January, operations went steadily on till the whole of the Huon Peninsula had been secured.

Some time before possession of the Huon Peninsula was complete, active preparations for the next phase had been begun. At the near—or western—end of New Britain, the enemy had an air-field at Cape
15 Dec. Gloucester. This was neutralized by bombing on the 15th December

to cover the landing of troops at Arawe on the opposite—or southern—side. On the 26th December, the conquest of the western end of New Britain was completed by the occupation of Cape Gloucester air-field by American marines. This gave the Allies a reasonable foothold on New Britain together with an air-base substantially nearer Rabaul than heretofore.

New Britain offered no passable land approach to Rabaul from the west. In any case it was judged that there was no object in directly attacking it with troops if it could be neutralized by air action. A programme of incessant air assaults was prepared, including mast-height attacks on shipping and installations. The Tokyo wireless reacted gloomily to this, remarking on the 29th January that the Allies were directing attacks against Rabaul daily, with formations consisting on the average of 100 bomber and fighter aeroplanes, and that it could not hold out optimistic hopes.

Farther east, in the Solomons, operations were also in progress directed against Rabaul. New Georgia with its air-field had been captured during August, and a further jump of 125 miles north-west on the 9th October, brought the Americans to Vella Lavella Island. This operation had the effect of by-passing the strongly-held island of Kolombangara a few miles north of New Georgia.

The Treasury Islands lie just west of Vella Lavella, and two of the group were occupied on the 26th October. Next came the operation against the 150-mile long Bougainville Island at the north-west end of the Solomons, and some 250 miles east of Rabaul.

Diversionary landings were made on Choiseul Island, just to the south-east, and on the 1st November American marines landed on the west coast of Bougainville itself to secure an air-field at Empress Augusta Bay and bring fighter cover within reach of Rabaul. Ultimately a naval base and three air-fields were established here.

On the 5th November, a carrier task force delivered an air attack on Rabaul. The attack was repeated on the 12th. Meanwhile, preparations went busily on on Bougainville till on the 14th February an unopposed landing was made on Green Island, 150 miles east of Rabaul. This completed the Solomons campaign.

Preliminaries to the main operations in the Central Pacific had been completed during the summer and early autumn. These included the occupation of Baker Island in the Phoenix Group midway between Hawaii and the Solomons, and Muku Fetau and Nanumea in the Ellice Group half-way between the Phoenix Group and the Solomons. Soon after, on the 4th and 6th October, Wake Island, 2,000 miles north-west of these two groups, was heavily bombed.

Margin notes: 1943-44; 26 Dec.; 29 Jan.; South Pacific Solomons; 9 Oct.; 26 Oct.; 1 Nov.; 5 Nov.; 12 Nov.; 14 Feb.; Central Pacific; Sept.; 4-6 Oct.

1943-44

1 Nov.   The main operation opened on the 1st November, when three islands in the Gilberts—about 600 miles north of the Ellice Islands and the same distance west of the Phoenix Group—were invaded. On one of these, Tarawa, was fought one of the bloodiest of the smaller battles of the whole Pacific war. The fullest support was given to the landings, including the provision of amphibious tractors, launched beyond the range of shore batteries, and driven over the fringing reefs and up the beach, but when the opposing forces came to grips no quarter was shown. On Tarawa Island, the Americans lost 1,026 men killed and 2,556 wounded in eliminating a Japanese garrison of no more than 2,700 regular soldiers and 1,200 armed workmen. None the less all three islands were firmly in Allied hands
24 Nov.   by the 24th November.

This operation seemed an integral part of the New Guinea and Solomon Islands offensives towards Rabaul, in the south, and the Japanese seem to have been sufficiently convinced to commit their reserves in the Rabaul area accordingly. However, the next blow fell 500 miles north-west of the Gilberts. After a two-days intense bombardment, Majuro with its fine harbour, in the Marshall Islands,
1 Jan.   was captured without fighting on New Year's Day. Kwajanlein Atoll, attacked the same day, held out till the 8th February, on which day
8 Feb.   Namu and Roi Islands also fell after a resistance lasting six days.
19-22 Feb.   Between the 19th and 22nd February Eniwetok Atoll was captured.

These victories were only gained at a price. Both in weight of metal and in primitive savagery of fighting they rank with any comparable action of similar strengths. Describing the consequences of the air, sea and ground bombardment at Eniwetok, observers reckoned them not less absolute than those of the prolonged bombardments of the first war. "With the exception of rubble left by concrete structures, there were no buildings standing. All those which had been made of any other material except concrete had been completely burned or destroyed."

Rabaul in the south was matched as a Japanese base by Truk in the centre. Situated in the Carolines, west of the Marshalls and somewhat south of the direct line from the Marshalls to the Philippines, air bombardment was slowly built up against it till, by the end of
Jan.   January, it was virtually impotent. Attention was then transferred to other targets in the Carolines, pending the forthcoming extensive operations at the end of March.

Burma   In Burma, the fruits of the Quebec Conference in August began to mature early in 1944. At the conference, it had been decided, in China's interest, to step up the operations in Burma.
11 Jan.   On the 11th January, the XVth Corps in the Arakan on the eastern

272

1943-44

shores of the Bay of Bengal, moved south across the border into Burma, and re-took the small port of Maungdaw. However, much tribulation was to come before the Allied offensive in the Burma theatre came into its stride.

The XVth Corps advance was on a limited scale, and it was decisively checked at the beginning of February by a violent Japanese counter-offensive. However, the lesson of the Western Desert had not been lost on the troops in the Arakan. The system of self-contained boxes had been adopted in place of earlier methods, and was amply vindicated by the case of the 7th Divisional box. The box was completely cut off from all surface contact for some twenty-one anxious days during February. During this period, aircraft of the troop-carrier command, with British and American crews, dropped 1,500 tons of ammunition, food, petrol, oil and medical supplies on the box, at a cost of one Dakota. At the same time the ground communications of the Japanese forces were so disorganized by air bombing that they were worse supplied than the 7th Division itself. Feb.

Five hundred miles away, meanwhile, in North Assam, the first small beginnings were seen of Gen. Stilwell's movement down the Hukawng Valley on the new route to China. The Assam Railway, with its troublesome ferry-break across the Brahmaputra, brought supplies up from Bengal through Dimapur to Dibrugarh and beyond. From rail head, the Hukawng Valley winds away southwards. Its defence had been entrusted by the Japanese to their 1st Division which had played a prominent part in the Singapore campaign. Apart from this, the country was difficult in the extreme and progress at first very slow. Yet, by the end of February, the Allied forces had reached Maingkwan, some 80 miles south of Ledo where the road began. Here they were temporarily held up.

In the Mediterranean, the Allies had occupied Sicily, and by the 2nd September the Italians had accepted the demand for unconditional surrender. While this was going on, the Germans had stepped up their forces in Italy by another thirteen divisions, and were clearly resolved not to let Italy's domestic arrangements interfere with their own prosecution of the war on Italian territory. Italy
2 Sept.

An hour before dawn on the 3rd September, the Eighth Army under Gen. Montgomery crossed the Straits from Messina on the Sicilian side, to Reggio 10 miles or so to the east, and landed without difficulty. The combined British and American Fifth Army under Lieut.-Gen. Mark Clark was to land later, farther up the west coast of Italy, at Salerno, 160 miles to the north. It was supposed that the German forces would have been drawn down into the toe of Italy to oppose the Eighth Army landing, and that the Fifth Army would come in behind them. 3 Sept.

1943-44

The Germans, however, did exactly the opposite thing. They removed themselves out of the dangerously constricted area of the toe as fast as they could, and drew away north.

The Italian fleet had evacuated Taranto in the heel of Italy when
8 Sept. it steamed away to Malta on the 8th. The British 78th Division and
9 Sept. the 1st Airborne Division moved in next day. It was on this latter date that the Fifth Army began, at 4 a.m., to come ashore at Salerno, and a critical situation soon developed. Shipping shortages prejudiced the early arrival of heavy armour, and Allied fighters based on Sicily could only carry fuel enough to allow of fifteen minutes fighting over the beaches. The Luftwaffe was much better placed, and a
11 Sept. determined German attack launched on the 11th September, had powerful air support. Glider bombs made an unwelcome appearance in the form of radar-controlled rocket bombs launched from aircraft outside the anti-aircraft defence area. The battleship *Warspite* and the American cruisers *Philadelphia* and *Savannah* were hit by these bombs.

None the less, Gen. Eisenhower continued to base his hopes on
12-14 Sept. the air. Between the 12th and 14th September every possible form
15 Sept. of air support was turned on the enemy. Thanks to this, the crisis
16 Sept. was over by the 15th September, and on the 16th the Eighth Army linked up with the Fifth some 40 miles south-east of Salerno.

27 Sept. The advance now speeded up. On the 27th, Foggia near the east
1 Oct. coast, 120 miles up from Taranto, was captured. On the 1st October, Naples, 40 miles ahead from Salerno, also fell. Field-Marshal Kesselring then withdrew his army to the Volturno, about 15 miles north of Naples, but fell back thence to the Garigliano river, 40 miles to the north, in the middle of October. Between these two rivers he held intermediate delaying positions on the Trigno and Sangro, from each of which in turn he was methodically turned out.

From now operations slowed up. The terrain was difficult. The enemy's flanks were securely based on the coast-lines. These flanks could not be turned by sea for lack of landing craft. We were permanently committed to a policy of very heavy air and ground bombardments to cover every operation, with consequent demands on shipping space for which vessels were not readily available. Still further limiting the inflow of munitions, for the armies, the Fifteenth Strategic Air Force was being built up at Foggia, not under Gen. Eisenhower's command, but demanding some 300,000 tons of shipping during the most critical months of the Italian campaign.

The Gustav Line—the German position on the Garigliano—was too strong to be taken by frontal attack. It was decided hence that in this case, it must be turned from the sea. A strong holding attack
17-18 Jan. was launched on the Garigliano positions on the night of the 17th/18th

January. It failed to establish crossings over the river on the right, but on the left some successes were gained at Castelforte, at which point the attack was held up. By the 22nd the battle on this front was virtually over; but the same morning, at 2 a.m. the VIth Corps, with some 50,000 British and American troops, under Maj.-Gen. Lucas, landed practically unopposed on the Anzio beaches 60 miles west-north-west up the coast from the Garigliano, and 30 south of Rome. Unfortunately the initial success was not exploited. The pause to consolidate the beach-heads gave Kesselring the time and opportunity he needed. He kept the Allied forces on the defensive for several months, while a homeric struggle developed on the Garigliano on the lines of the bloodiest periods of the First World War.

22 Jan.

Meanwhile on the 24th December, Gen. Eisenhower, Gen. Montgomery and others had returned to the United Kingdom in connection with the maturing plans for the invasion of France. Gen. Sir Henry Maitland Wilson assumed Supreme Allied Command, from the 8th January, with Lieut.-Gen. Sir Oliver Leese as commander of the Eighth Army.

24 Dec.

8 Jan.

The chief problem for the Allied Command was now the reduction of the dominating key-point of Cassino, 20 miles from the west coast on the upper reaches of the Rapido, a tributary of the Garigliano. The small town clustered at the foot of Monastery Hill and the famous Abbey of St. Benedict. When the first battle, which raged from the 29th January to the 4th February, ended in failure, the Abbey was cited as mainly responsible, since it was supposed that the enemy were using if for observation, profiting from its immunity from our fire. Whether it was so used is at best doubtful, and in fact the monks later denied that it was ever so used. Monastery Hill itself provided all the observational facilities the enemy needed. However, it was decided that the Abbey must be destroyed to save unnecessary casualties in future operations, and on the 15th February, after twenty-four hours warning had expired, 453 tons of bombs were dropped on it by 229 bombers, and the Abbey, reduced to a heap of rubble, became by our own act, a far better strong point for a determined enemy than it could ever have been in its original shape.

29 Jan.-
4 Feb.

15 Feb.

Cassino was destined to draw the pick of the Fifth and Eighth Armies on to its rugged hill-sides in the weeks to come. Among these was the 4th Indian Division, which was now up to strength again. On the 1st February, we find it on its way there after a month's hard conditioning in the mud, sleet and slush of a wintry January in the Adriatic sector. It records that among the troops it relieved at Cassino, infantry brigades mustered barely 400 men and that one battalion was only fifty strong, and these in such a state of exhaustion that they were, in sober fact, taken out on relief in a state of collapse, on stretchers.

1 Feb.

1943-44

For the second battle of Cassino, the 4th Indian Division was allotted a sector on the right. To gain the selected start line, a preliminary forward move was involved. This was attempted on the
14 Feb. night of the 14th February, and the battle ebbed and flowed from
17 Feb. then on till the night of the 17th February when a fierce action developed which carried the attack well up the slopes of Monastery Hill, but at a pitiable loss in gallant lives. For two more days, the troops struggled to consolidate and extend their gains, but on the
19 Feb. 19th the battle was admitted a failure and was broken off.

At Sea   In the Atlantic and North Sea, bitter fighting accompanied the convoys moving to and fro. However, submarine pressure had slackened
9 Dec.   for the moment. On the 9th December, it was authoritatively announced that the number of merchant vessels sunk by U-boats in November was smaller than in any month since May 1940.
26 Dec. On Boxing night, on the Murmansk route, the 26,000-ton German battleship *Scharnhorst* was sent to the bottom.

W. Europe   In Western Europe, activity centred in an increasing degree round the new German secret weapons— the "V"s—on which great hopes of victory were built. Of these weapons, the "V1", or Vergeltungswaffe Ein, was, it will be remembered, a flying bomb. It was pilotless, jet-propelled, mechanically gyro-stabilised, but not radio-controlled. It was an aircraft with a wing-span of 16 feet and an overall length of 25 feet 4 inches. It was 2 feet 8½ inches wide. It carried 1,000 kilograms of explosive in its war-head. Its maximum speed lay between 350 and 400 miles per hour. It had a radius of 150 miles. Its motive power was derived from hydrogen peroxide, liquid oxygen and hydrazine hydrate.

The "V2" rocket, powered by the same fuel, had been under experiment since about 1927. It had a length of 47 feet, and a weight of 15 tons, which included about 1 ton (1,000 kilograms) of explosives. Its maximum velocity was supposedly 3,500 miles per hour. Its trajectory took it up to a height of some 70 miles in a maximum range of 200 miles. It was less accurate than the flying bomb, thanks partly to the complicated nature of its mechanism.

During August 1943 Allied bombing attacks began on V1 launching
17 Aug. sites and storage installations in France. On the 17th of that month, a notable raid was made by the Royal Air Force on Peenemunde, the German experimental V1 and V2 station in northern Germany. Whether or no it is the case, as has been said, that experimental work at Peenemunde was unaffected by this raid, it seems reasonably certain that actual production of V1's was put back nearly a year, which rates as a decisive reverse for the German strategy into which

1943

they were designed to fit. It was known in Germany that the V weapons were to bring a great change in their fortunes; but in the absence of any tangible production to back these hopes, the German Government had a difficult time nursing morale. V1 and V2 launching sites in the Pas de Calais were badly knocked about in the spring of 1944 by air action; and though the Germans gave it out that they were reserving these weapons for anti-invasion purposes, their first V1s did not, in fact, fall on London till seven days after the Allies had invaded Normandy in June. This, however, is to anticipate. Meanwhile, rocket projectiles were gradually replacing and reinforcing more orthodox forms of artillery fire both on land and in the air, and jet-propelled aircraft were coming to the fore.

In Russia, the Germans were unsuccessfully attempting to hold their own against the great counter-offensive that had been launched, while Hitler's own attack on the Kursk salient was still being pressed. Moving forward on a front of some 400 miles, the Russians were in Stalino on the 8th September. East of the Sea of Azov, in the rich agricultural area of the Kuban, Gen. von Kleist commanding the First Panzer and Seventeenth Armies—of some fourteen divisions—saw his foundations crumbling. He pulled out of his bridgehead with all speed, and crossed the Strait of Kerch into the Crimea. Novorossisk on the north coast of the Black Sea, 80 miles east of the Strait of Kerch, was occupied by Gen. Petrov's army group on the 15th September.

Russia

8 Sept.

15 Sept.

Similar successes rewarded Russian pressure in the centre. West of Kursk two lines of railway were cut, separating the German northern and southern groups of armies east of the Dnieper. On the 22nd September, the Russians took Poltava 70 miles south-west of Kharkov. On the 25th, they were in Smolensk, over 300 miles to the north-west. This is not to say that serious fighting was involved. The Germans were withdrawing very much in their own time, averaging between 1 and 3½ miles a day. They were very thoroughly "denying" the country's resources to the Russians as they went.

22 Sept.
25 Sept.

The Dnieper river follows a winding course to Kherson where it falls into the Black Sea. In its upper reaches, it flows over 200 miles west of Kursk, but the Germans were back to this line by the end of September. The momentum of the Russian advance was unexhausted, and on the 7th October they launched a general offensive over the whole front from the Volkhov river, below Leningrad, southwards to the Sea of Azov. Here in the south, a vast German salient followed the great Dnieper bend, and made a hazardous flank of it, and the Russians now shaped their operations to take advantage of it. By moving across the Dnieper above the bend, where it flows for about 250 miles on an almost east and west course between Dnepropetrovsk

7 Oct.

1943

and Kiev, they would be well placed to cut in behind the salient.
5-6 Oct. They crossed accordingly on the 5th and 6th October, and advancing rapidly south far in rear of the Zaporozhye-Melitopol area where furious fighting was now in progress, they were 80 miles due west
21 Oct. of the latter place, near Krivoi Rog, by the 21st. On the 23rd, the
23 Oct. Germans reacted to this move in their rear, and fell back from Melitopol.

This was not the end of the German dilemma in the south. They still had large forces in the Crimea, and these were liable to be cut off if the Russians made good their advance to Kherson at the mouth of the Dnieper. Possession of Kherson would place them across the sole line of retreat from the Crimea, via the Isthmus of Perekop
2 Nov. which lies south-east of Kherson. By the 2nd November, the threat was growing acute. The Russians were by then at Kahovka, less than 50 miles east of Kherson, and directly flanking the Perekop-Kherson road. However, the Germans staged a violent counter-attack on Krivoi Rog and checked them.
6 Nov. Elsewhere on the front, Russian pressure in the north-west meanwhile forced the Germans to abandon Kiev on the 6th November. By the
17 Nov. 17th, the Russians were in possession of Zhitomir, Ovruch and Korosten 80 miles west of Kiev on the vital Leningrad-Odessa railway. This placed the German forces about Krivoi Rog in an increasingly dangerous position since they now had large Russian forces far to their north-west directly threatening their communications with the German armies in the north. Von Mannstein reacted in his usual forceful style. He collected a force of about 150,000 men from six panzer and six infantry divisions, and directed it up the railway north-west from Krivoi Rog against Zhitomir and Korosten which were
19-20 Nov. re-taken on the 19th and 20th respectively. Thence, the advance wheeled east during early December to Radomsyl and Fastov, some
Dec. 50 miles wide of the Leningrad-Odessa railway.

Strategical values were changing with the changing fortunes of the war in Russia; and it was now becoming clear to the Russians that Vienna would be a goal of the first political and strategic consequence for the conquest from the Germans of Eastern Europe. Their movements were hence now directed in a more south-easterly direction towards the Balkans, as a necessary preliminary towards this end.

As regards the German dispositions, as they affected this intention, the position then was that they had three groups of armies in the theatre. The northern, under Field-Marshal Kuchler, stretched down from the Baltic to near Nevel, 250 miles south of Leningrad. The central, under Field-Marshal von Busch, carried on southwards to the vicinity of Ovruch, 350 miles north of Odessa. The southern, under Field-Marshal von Mannstein lay between Ovruch and the

1943-44

Black Sea. Owing to the blocking of the Leningrad-Odessa railway, inter-group communications were round-about and slow.

The northern and central fronts were strong. The southern, as we have seen, reached out forward south-easterly to Kherson, including the Dnieper bend, and was exposed to attack from the north. A resolute large-scale Russian offensive against the southern group might either completely cut it off, or might drive it away south-westwards, out of touch with the other two groups, into Rumania.

Before developing this plan, four large-scale operations, but limited in scope, were first attempted. An attack was made in the middle of the southern sector north and south of Zhitomir. The fighting went on from Christmas Eve till the 18th January, with the honours slightly in favour of the Russians. The second opened in the north on the 15th January and had driven the Germans on the front attacked back on an average of some 80 to 90 miles by the 23rd January. Switching back again to the southern sector, the third operation was directed towards Kanev, 70 miles down-stream of Kiev on the Dnieper, and Smela and Korsun a little farther south. Eight German divisions, forming the bulk of the German Eighth Army, were in this area. The operation started early in February and the eight divisions were cut off. Efforts to relieve them failed, though a large number of officers were evacuated by air. On the 17th, the remains of these divisions surrendered. Coupled with this operation came a sudden attack from Sarny on the south of the Pripet Marshes, 200 miles west-north-west of Kanev, and near the now open boundary between the central and southern groups. This offensive, which was pushed south and west for some 60 miles from Sarny, forced von Mannstein to hurry troops to the west to cover the approach to Galicia. The fourth limited offensive somewhat preceded the third initially. It opened on the 2nd February on a 40-mile front between Dnepropetrovsk, 150 miles north-east of Kherson on the Dnieper, and Sofievka, 60 miles to the west-south-west. Cutting the German forces in two on the 7th, Krivoi Rog was at long last captured by the Russians in the second half of February.

This completed the preliminaries to the great Russian offensive in the Dnieper bend, which opened on the 4th March, and which will be further referred to in the next chapter.

24 Dec.-
18 Jan.
15 Jan.-
23 Jan.

Feb.

17 Feb.

2 Feb.

7 Feb.

4 Mar.

The 1st Battalion, newly incorporated in the 7th Indian Division, was being fitted out with available war stores and equipment at Kumthi in the Ranchi neighbourhood. On the 30th September, it entrained at Ranchi for Madras. The long and tedious journey did not end till the 6th October, when the troops de-trained and went aboard the S.S. *Islami*, for Chittagong. Disembarking on the 11th, and straight into the waiting

1st Bn.

30 Sept.

6 Oct.
11 Oct.

1943

12 Oct. trains, the Battalion left for Dohazari where it arrived next day. De-training at Dohazari, the Battalion marched off at once to Tumbru, on the Burma border, 85 miles south. The march took five
17 Oct. days. At Tumbru, river craft were waiting, and the troops embarked in them next morning, and sailed down the Naf river to Bawli where the 7th Indian Division had its headquarters. Here the Battalion was given its role of divisional headquarters battalion, and was split up among the three brigades of the Division.

Before proceeding with a detailed account of the forthcoming campaign, it might prove convenient to explain very briefly the general situation at that time. During the monsoon both the British and the Japanese had been holding their forward positions very lightly, and the actual number of troops on the ground at this time was very small. A build-up was beginning to take place, on the British side at least—and the 7th Indian Division was the first of the fresh formations to arrive.

The intention was to advance as soon as preparations were complete, and make a combined land and sea attack on Akyab, some distance down the coast to the south. Akyab had been the objective of the earlier and unsuccessful Arakan campaign, in the closing stages of which the 6th Battalion had played some part; and it would prove a valuable acquisition as the only sea-port of any importance in the Arakan. For the current operation, the XVth Corps would be available, and it was intended to deploy it for the advance with the 5th Indian Division on the right and the 7th Indian Division on the left. Accordingly, when the 5th Indian Division arrived, it moved into the coastal sector north of Maungdaw, while the 7th Indian Division crossed the Mayu Range into the country to the east.

The latter area lay in a tangled mass of jungle-covered hills, intersected by stretches of flat rice fields, quite dry at this time of the year. The jungle was mostly thick bamboo. The hills were on the average between 100 and 200 feet in height, and were very steep. They lent themselves to defence, and were difficult to attack.

Initial operations in the early winter took the form of small unspectacular local advances with the intention of closing up on the Japanese forward positions north of the Maungdaw-Buthidaung road. The 7th Indian Division had in addition an administrative problem to solve.

There was no way available at first of carrying supplies for the Division across the Mayu Range by road. The only possibility lay in constructing a road over the 1,300-feet high Ngakyedauk Pass which wound its way through a mass of dense jungle and tangled ravines and spurs across the Range. This road was duly made by the divisional engineers. It was a fine engineering feat, and it opened the way for tanks, artillery and heavy transport to reach the division.

1944

The Pioneer Platoon of the 1st Battalion of the Regiment was attached to the divisional sappers for work on the road, and constructed some of the many bridges that had to be made. The finished road was to repay many times over, the labour put into its construction, during later operations.

Jan.

During January, the 7th Indian Division began to line up for the initial assault of the XVth Corps on the Japanese positions north of the Maungdaw-Buthidaung road.

About this time the Battalion suffered a heavy loss in its adjutant, Capt. P. J. Sheehan, who died of small-pox in Bawli Bazar. He was succeeded as adjutant by Capt. P. T. Cunningham, who remained in the appointment almost till the end of the war.

The Battalion story is an unavoidably complicated one during the early days of the operations by reason of being split up among the three different brigades.

Battalion headquarters, with "A" Company under Maj. G. Lerwill, was with the 114th Indian Infantry Brigade, east of the Kalapanzin river. Its task was to show strength in front of the strong Japanese position around Kyaukit while the Brigade itself was preparing for the offensive. Active night and day patrolling was therefore called for, together with frequent deep penetration into the Japanese defences. The success of these tactics is upheld by the official report that "it is a credit to this battalion that the Japs were sufficiently impressed with the exuberance of the Sikhs to put them down as a full battalion".

"D" Company, under Maj. J. G. Workman, was detached on a special protective and reconnaissance role in the Eastern Yomas overlooking the Division's left flank. This Company, known as "Workcol", isolated among densely forested hills, did excellent work and carried out many long-range patrols.

"B" Company, under Maj. J. R. B. Walker, was with the 33rd Indian Infantry Brigade, and "C" Company, under Maj. E. E. Spink, with the 89th Brigade. Both Companies were employed on patrolling and the collection of information for the coming offensive.

While the XVth Corps was perfecting its plans for an attack upon the Japanese, the Japanese were completing their preparations for attacking the XVth Corps, as part, many believed, of a comprehensive plan of invasion deep into India.

For this, two stages were developed, first the break-up of our forces in the Arakan, and then a drive, farther to the north, westwards through Manipur.

In the Arakan, the Japanese aimed at surrounding and destroying the 7th Indian Division in its somewhat exposed position east of the Mayu Range. Wheeling west towards the sea, they could then cut

1944

the main communications behind the 5th Indian Division in the coastal sector, and drive it into the Bay of Bengal. But of these intentions, the 1st Battalion of the Regiment was unaware, and it continued furthering to its utmost our own proposed offensive towards Akyab.

The Japanese were the first off the mark, but by the narrowest of margins. On the night of the 3rd February, the 33rd and 114th Indian Infantry Brigades were in the act of deploying for an attack on the enemy main positions covering Buthidaung, while a Japanese force of several thousand men commanded by Col. Tanabashi, and including artillery, engineers and ancillary units, was already actually on its way round the Division's left flank. The 89th Indian Infantry Brigade was in reserve, and bore the brunt of the heavy fighting that developed in the Linbabi area south of Taung Bazar.

3 Feb.

There was much confused fighting in the rear areas, but the Japanese advance was delayed. There was bitter fighting, in which "C" Company was engaged, during Japanese attacks on Brigade Headquarters. During this fighting, one of the Company's platoons, in particular, suffered very heavily, and it became a problem to get the wounded away. A party of the enemy was much harassing their evacuation until L.-Naik Karnail Singh, a non-commissioned officer of this platoon, charged out single-handed in the most gallant Frontier tradition, and drove the Japanese off. As a direct consequence, all the casualties were brought away—except Karnail Singh himself. His dead body was found some time later surrounded by dead Japanese. He was awarded a posthumous Indian Order of Merit for his outstanding gallantry and devotion.

The company commander, Maj. Spink, was wounded. He was being got away on a stretcher when the party with him was ambushed. Maj. Spink owed his life to the gallantry of his orderly No. 13070 Sep. Mehar Singh, who was awarded a Military Medal for his action.

Many other acts of gallantry distinguished this confused and bitter fighting, and a fair sample of the resolution and courage of the troops lies in the citation of No. 19900 L.-Naik Harchand Singh, second-in-command of a rifle section during an attack on a hill feature near Linbabi. The platoon swept up to a point only fifty yards from the top, when intense light machine-gun, grenade and rifle fire checked it, with serious loss. Harchand Singh was wounded under the right arm-pit. It was a bad wound, but he refused to go back; and when the platoon withdrew under the Company Commander's orders, L.-Naik Harchand Singh took up a position to cover the withdrawal of his section, moving slowly back with them, though meanwhile wounded in both ankles. He only consented to be removed to the Regimental Aid Post when all his section were safe. Such a standard of self-sacrifice and leadership was fittingly rewarded by the Indian Distinguished Service Medal.

1944

Enemy pressure on the 7th Indian Division steadily strengthened until, on the 6th February, Divisional Headquarters was over-run. After some very gallant fighting, Gen. Messervy with most of his headquarter personnel, withdrew to the divisional administrative area, which became known as the "Admin Box". Headquarters of brigades were contacted by wireless, and told to stand fast and form defensive boxes as well.

6 Feb.

"D" Company of the Battalion was called in from the Eastern Yomas in pursuance of this decision, and came in to Battalion Headquarters in the 114th Indian Infantry Brigade area. It was allotted a hill feature on the northern face of the box. Dispositions in the box remained much as before—i.e. the Kwazon area, with positions north of Kyaukit.

In the 33rd Indian Infantry Brigade area on the west bank of the Kalapanzin river, "B" Company was retained in a protective role with Brigade Headquarters just east of Point 182.

"C" Company, after its battle in the dark, formed a box with a company of the 7th/2nd Punjab Regiment, to protect a Field Regiment R.A. and some anti-aircraft gunners at Awlanbyin.

The Japanese captured the Ngakyedauk Pass on the 7th. With this the siege began. For three weeks, in a constant succession of large and small actions, the Japanese tried to hammer the Division into submission, but everywhere the troops stood firm, inflicting severe casualties on the enemy. Some of the fiercest fighting took place round the Admin Box, held by administrative and headquarters personnel. Present among these was Naik Kartar Singh, the Battalion Granthi, with the Granth Sahib. The Battalion M.T. was also there. All were employed in the defence of the box, but the only damage done to the Battalion seems to have been suffered by the Gurdwara harmonium, which was damaged by a bullet. Patched up, however, it continued to do duty in the Gurdwara till well after the war.

7 Feb.

The Japanese do not appear either to have expected this stubborn resistance, nor the development of an air-lift for the Division. The first Dakota came over on the 11th February, and the supply-drop went on daily till the siege was raised. All seriously wounded cases were evacuated from the overcrowded field-ambulances by light aircraft using rough improvised strips in brigade areas.

11 Feb.

These operations proved expensive for the Japanese. Our troops were full of fight, and the Japanese were split into small scattered parties which were methodically reduced by offensive action from the boxes, and by troops of the 26th Indian Division moved down from reserve in the north. During this period, "A" Company carried out several successful ambushes, and one platoon infiltrated into the Kyaukit defences and occupied a Japanese forward position. "B" Company

1943-44

20 Feb. had its share of fighting with the 33rd Indian Infantry Brigade; and on the 20th February carried out a particularly successful attack on a party of Japanese near Hill 182 overlooking Brigade Headquarters. The men went in with great dash under Sub. Gurcharan Singh, and threw the Japanese out with the bayonet.

23 Feb. On the 23rd February, in co-operation with troops of the 5th Indian Division who attacked from the west, the Ngakyedauk Pass was opened and the siege raised. By the end of February, the remnants of the defeated Japanese in the area had been mopped up.

It had been a complete and decisive victory, to which all had contributed. The victors did not, however, rest on their laurels.

2nd Bn. *The 2nd Battalion* was not to see action as early as the 1st. By the time it returned from Cyprus to Palestine and rejoined the 10th Indian Division, it had undergone intensive training in combined operations, and was a fighting-fit battalion—in all respects but one. The important exception was the matter of its strength.

The Battalion was to suffer much frustration from the man-power
Oct. shortage. In the first week of October, the 10th Indian Division was placed under orders for an immediate move to Italy; but as the 2nd Battalion was still about 100 men under strength, its orders were cancelled a few days later, and it was sent to Haifa instead to take over guard duties on the oil installations in the harbour area, from the 3rd/1st Punjab Regiment.

Here it remained for the rest of the winter, employed on a monotonous round of guards and duties. One company was sent to Jerusalem to provide a guard for the High Commissioner of Palestine; and the Battalion carried out many tactical demonstrations for the Staff College in Haifa. Otherwise, one day was very much like another, and nothing occurred worthy of record.

3rd Bn. *The 3rd Battalion* was in Isfahan at the end of the summer. At the end of October, it moved to Teheran, dropping detachments of one company each at Qum and Sultanabad. In Teheran, heavy duties were the rule; and the camp area, some miles down the Kazvin road, was stony and barren, while the road itself was always crowded with traffic and generally very dangerous.

History, however, was about to be made in Teheran, and the Battalion was to have some share in it.

25 Nov. On the 25th November, the word went round that an important personage was visiting Teheran, and that a British Battalion was expected in this connection, and would be accommodated in the British Embassy grounds. Guards over the front and back of the Embassy building would be provided by the Sikhs, who would also have their

1943

Carrier Platoon plus a party of fifty ranks standing by for escort
and patrol duty. An officer was to be provided in addition for permanent
liaison duty at the Embassy. The company detachments at Qum and
Sultanabad were ordered at the same time to be ready to take over
the railway stations at these two places.

On the 27th, it became generally known that the Rt. Hon. Mr. Winston   27 Nov.
Churchill, the Prime Minister, had arrived by air, and also that
Marshal Stalin and President Roosevelt were in Teheran and staying
at the Russian Legation. The Carrier Platoon was now constantly on
duty, and the Road Patrol party in frequent demand to clear roads
as one or other of these personages exchanged visits.

Next day, the 28th, Maj. G. C. Wilson, who was in officiating   28 Nov.
command of the Battalion, attended a conference at which Gen. Selby
announced the arrangements for the presentation of the Stalingrad
Sword by Mr. Churchill to Marshal Stalin. A Guard of Honour was to
be provided jointly by the British Battalion and the Sikhs in the
grounds of the Russian Legation. Ultimately, though preparations
for the Guard of Honour reached the point where Gen. Selby carried
out his own prior personal inspection of the troops, their part of the
programme had to be cancelled. Marshal Stalin was indisposed. The
ceremony was therefore held indoors. The troops were not entirely
disappointed, however. They were called upon to line the road, and
had a very good view of Mr. Churchill driving past in an open car.

It had not been generally realized that Mr. Churchill's sixty-ninth
birthday was at hand. However, units were somewhat belatedly
circularised on the 29th and asked if the idea of a birthday present   29 Nov.
would appeal to them. Naturally they were delighted with the idea-
but time was short, and the Battalion had only two hours in which
to consider what kind of locally available gift would be likely to
give Mr. Churchill most pleasure. However, there was a well-known
miniature painter, Imami, in Teheran. One of his works was acquired;
and, through the services of an old resident of the place, the miniature
was mounted and framed, and presented to the Prime Minister by a
party of three British officers, the Subedar-Major, and six other ranks
of the Embassy guard. The presentation was made by Hav. Kirpal
Singh, a son of the Battalion's old Granthi, on behalf of the Battalion
as a whole.

The Prime Minister left Teheran next day—the Sikhs and the British   30 Nov.
Battalion clearing the road to the aerodrome. Gen. Selby, at a special
parade, thanked the Battalion and complimented it on both turn-out
and drill, which he described as excellent.

A pleasant and not unreasonably cold winter followed, with skiing
and tobogganing on Sunday afternoons. An intimate sidelight is
shed on the off-duty distractions indoors, by the *Battalion Letter*

1943-44 which covers this period, and which refers briefly to the many cosmopolitan "dives" in Teheran where one could get a good meal, washed down with *vodka*, while attended by the more respectable ladies of the town. Teheran, it considered, was unique among places east of the Syrian desert. As it was the only place of civilization the Battalion reckoned that it had seen in three-and-a-half years, its judgement may have been biassed—but at all events it enjoyed itself, and was glad to see the winter out in these pleasant surroundings.

4th Bn. *The 4th Battalion* saw the year out in the Lebanon, spending an uncomfortable winter doing demonstrations in generally unpleasant weather at the Mountain Warfare School. A spirited description of the work carried out at the school is in the account which appears in a subsequent chapter under the 3rd Battalion record; for the 3rd Battalion paid a visit to the School the following autumn. The 4th Battalion meanwhile was housed rather unsatisfactorily in a tented camp where there was small comfort, and few recreational facilities.

Work, however, continued at its former high standard, and turn-out equally so. When the Commander-in-Chief, Middle-East Forces, Gen. Sir Bernard Paget, visited the School, a Guard of Honour, mounted under the adjutant, Capt. Hill, received many congratulatory notices.

Feb. With the end of February came the Jaipur Light Infantry to take over demonstration duties from the Battalion. The Sikhs were glad to see the end of this gruelling nine months in the Lebanon, but they freely admitted later on in Italy that the mountain training they had had, had been well worth it.

6th Bn. *The 6th Battalion* remained re-organizing and re-equipping in
24 Dec. Jhikergacha Ghat till Christmas Eve when it moved back to Ranchi. As will have been appreciated, Ranchi was looked on as the general training area for troops refitting for employment against the Japanese; and spirits rose higher as the men looked forward to the moment when they could get back and square the account for the previous spring's campaigning in the Arakan.

7th Bn. *The 7th Battalion*, in Fort Sandeman, had just received a draft of fifty men from the Regimental Centre, and described them as decidedly better, both physically and mentally, than the drafts which were received in 1942.

28 Aug. The Battalion advance party moved out the same day, the 28th August, on its first Zhob Column exercise. The column was to move to Dera Ghazi Khan and back; and "D" Company with attached troops left by M.T. on the 28th via Mekhtar to Khar, 150 miles away, below Fort Munro.

                                                                                  1943
The plan was for the column to concentrate, moving in hired M.T.,
at Khar, and then to move by march route to Dera Ghazi Khan,
another 50 miles on.

On the 2nd September, the Battalion less "D" Company, moved   2 Sept.
out 75 miles to Mekhtar, and spent the night in a perimeter camp.
This was the first time that the Battalion had moved in tactical
formation (modified somewhat by conditions in the Zhob), and generally
speaking the move went well. On account of rain and spates, many
of the nala crossings proved difficult, and a number of vehicles were
bogged. However, the men went to it with a will. The bogged vehicles
were all got out and the Battalion reached Mekhtar in good time.
The amenities of the excellent camp with its fine stream in which
the men all bathed, was a pleasant experience for all.

The same troubles were experienced next day on the way to Khar.   3 Sept.
The road was in bad condition almost throughout, and many of the
nalas barely passable owing to spate conditions. Considerable
delays occurred, but it was all good training, and most of the convoy
reached Khar safely that night.

Khar camp lies in a hollow with hills all round, and it was an
unexpected and pleasant change for the Battalion to be in such a
position with friendly tribesmen round instead of Mahsuds. As it was,
the Battalion was able to get in a useful spell of mountain warfare
training while the Brigade was gradually moving up. The country is
big, and on the Dera Ghazi Khan side, drops two or three thousand
feet down into the Rakhi Gorge, down which the road winds and zig-
zags on its way to Dera Ghazi Khan. All companies carried out training
in this area and profited by their toughening-up, a great deal, later.

By the 8th September, the 9th/9th Jats had arrived from Fort   8 Sept.
Sandeman and the 5th/9th Gurkha Rifles from Loralai, and the Brigade
was ready to proceed with the exercise.

On the 9th, the column moved down into the gorge, camping at   9 Sept.
Rakhi Gaj at the foot of the gorge, 15 miles from Fort Munro. The
7th Battalion was in the lead, and, by allotting company features, was
able to piquet the greater part of the gorge in good time. "C" Company
probably had the hardest time. Its furthermost piquet was on a feature
2,200 feet above the road. "48" W/T sets were used for the first time
and communication throughout the advance was decidedly good. When the
Battalion was deployed in this way, the 5th/9th Gurkha Rifles took
over, and piquetted the rest of the way into Rakhi Gaj, which lies
on the level ground at the foot of the drop from Fort Munro, and where
perimeter defence presented no difficulties.

Next day, the Battalion was rearguard for a long 16-mile move   10 Sept.
through broken country to Sakhi Sarwar camp. As rearguard, the Battalion
got away at 7 a.m., withdrew over twenty piquets on the way, and was

1943

into camp by 5.30 p.m. It was a hot, dusty day, but, though a number of fall-outs were collected by the way-side, no one fell out in the Battalion, and all were in good fettle when they reached Sakhi Sarwar, where they occupied a dispersed camp in the plain.

11 Sept. On the 11th, the Brigade covered 5 miles of desert country in box formation. From there to Dera Ghazi Khan, the country is a sandy waste, devoid of all interest except the beacon at Tombi, which was lit every night to prevent travellers straying into the desert and losing their lives there. For this long and tiring march, the Brigade closed on the road after the first 5 miles. It was fortunate in having a slight breeze to mitigate a little the heat and clouds of dust. After marching 17 miles, the column halted at Mitha Kuh for a short rest and some tea. Dera Ghazi Khan, 5 miles ahead, was reached in due course, and the column settled into a flat shadeless camp outside the town. With a shade temperature of 106, the troops were fortunate in having a canal with trees half-a-mile away. Soon after reaching camp most of the men were sent down there to bathe and rest. There had been no fall-outs in the Battalion during this trying march.

13 Sept. After a day's halt in Dera Ghazi Khan, the Brigade moved back by M.T. in three lifts to Rakhi Gaj. Next evening, the 14th, at 9 p.m.,
14 Sept., with the Sikhs as advance guard, the column marched back at speed, with close piquetting, to Khar. The Battalion moved on to Mekhtar next
15 Sept. day by M.T., and on again to Fort Sandeman on the 16th September.

The description of this fourteen-day training shows there was no relaxation in training in frontier areas during the war. Indeed, training in a sense was definitely harder, inasmuch as the incidence of other forms of fighting than hill warfare had to be incorporated, while yet maintaining full efficiency for operations in the hills against a tribal enemy. However, it has been well said that troops capable of fighting on the North-West Frontier are well-grounded to take their part in any form of warfare; and though this generalization can obviously not be taken too far without danger, yet there is a good deal of basic truth in it.

Meanwhile, the 7th Battalion was learning to excel elsewhere
6 Nov. than in an operational role. On the 6th November, it won the Baluchistan District Sports Meeting in Quetta.

9 Nov. On the 9th, with G.H.Q.'s blessing, a private recruiting party of Viceroy's commissioned officers and other ranks, with three British officers, went off with two of the Battalion vehicles on a recruiting-cum-liaison tour in the Sikh and Punjabi-Mohammedan areas of the Punjab and apparently scored excellent results.

15 Nov. A few days later, on the 15th, one of those grievous accidents occurred which mar the story of every unit from time to time. This was when No. 25687 Sep. Saidullah was driving his A. T. cart.

The mules bolted for some reason, but Saidullah hung on, trying to control them. Though he could have let go and saved himself, when the cart was obviously in danger of crashing into a wall, he would not—and so lost his life. Not a great matter in the war record of a whole battalion, but none the less one of those things that serve to remind one that the individual man is the basis of the whole.

We have already noticed that the 2nd Battalion was unable to leave with the 10th Indian Division for Italy in October, 1943, for lack of men. On the 17th January, we learn how some of the shortage was made good—and at what cost to others. A draft of seventy Sikhs for the 2nd Battalion was called for that day. To quote the 7th Battalion record: "This was a very serious problem as the Bn. was at that time 44 Sikhs below strength. Also the necessity of sending really good men was obvious. The draft was chosen finally from the large number of volunteers who came forward—a really good lot. We gave them a 'Bara Khana' before they went away the following day full of what they were going to do to the Germans when they met them. The next problem was to re-organize the Bn. to meet the new situation. We had been informed 'off the record' that we might be re-organized eventually on a half-Sikh and half-P.M. basis, therefore it was decided that a further P.M. company should be formed and that the present 'C' Company (Sikh) should be split up and transferred to H.Q. and the 2 Sikh rifle companies." It sounds fairly easy set out thus on paper, but the underlying problems are patent enough with a moment's thought. The re-organization was duly carried out, with effect from the 1st March.

The Machine-Gun Battalion had had the disappointment of losing its place in the 7th Indian Division, and had been sent from Chindwara to Ranchi to train with its new 4.2-inch mortars. Training went on all the winter—but it was time wasted so far as the Battalion was concerned. Six months of extensive trial convinced the authorities that the 4.2-inch mortar was impracticable as a weapon for Burma—or presumably any other available operational theatre—at that time owing to faulty ammunition and no guarantee of fresh supplies. To anticipate a little—the mortar was withdrawn, and, in the middle of 1944, the Battalion reverted to its former all medium machine-gun basis.

The 14th Battalion was with the 14th Training Division in Chindwara, where great and successful efforts were made to get down to a satisfactory organization for jungle warfare. In a short time, the Battalion had its instructors, training camps, and programme ready for drafts and then for recruits from the Regimental Centre.

During its stay with the 14th Division, the entire output of recruits

1944

17 Jan.

MG Bn.

14th Bn.

1944

from the Regimental Centre—which amounted to about 180 a month, including potential specialists such as M.T. drivers, signallers, pioneers, etc.—were posted, after attestation, to the 14th Battalion. In the same way all newly commissioned officers were sent to Chindwara after a month at the Regimental Centre, for further training before posting to active battalions. Jungle and specialist training were the principal responsibilities of the 14th Battalion, whose instructional and administrative staff was drawn from active battalions. The training given was severe, and of a high standard; and it may be assumed that the two months the average man in the ranks spent there, were of considerable value in fitting him for active operations.

15th Bn. Meanwhile, *the 15th Battalion* had been doubling its aerodrome defence role with hard training as an active battalion. In February, 1944, by which time it had been fully equipped with modem weapons,
Feb. it moved to Agetala, west of the hills between Imphal and Bengal, as army reserve troops.

26th Bn. *The 26th Battalion* left Santa Cruz for Poona in November, and took over internal defence duties, including the protection of strategic installations and sections of the railways.

Chapter X

MARCH TO AUGUST 1944

Backscreen

In the South Pacific, the fighting in New Britain was going well, and with it the neutralization of Rabaul at its eastern end. Policy was to progress by bounds within the tactical radius of land-based fighter aircraft; and in pursuance of this, an operation was begun on the 29th February against the Admiralty Islands which lie west of the Bismarck Archipelago and 250 miles north of New Guinea. Advance elements of the 1st Texas Cavalry Division were followed up by the remainder of the Division on the 6th March. Momote airfield was captured and a beach-head secured after a series of fanatical Japanese counter-attacks. Some of the Indian prisoners-of-war from Malaya, including details of the 5th Battalion, were found on the islands.

_{South Pacific}

_{29 Feb.}

_{6 Mar.}

On the 10th March a landing was made on the Willaumez Peninsula half-way up the northern coast of New Britain, and an air-strip at the village of Talasea secured. This brought American aircraft to within 160 miles of Rabaul, which the Japanese now realized was no longer tenable as a base.

_{10 Mar.}

West along the coast of New Guinea from the Vitiaz Strait which lies between New Guinea and New Britain, lay a succession of Japanese strongholds—Madang, Hansa Bay, and Wewak. Westward again from these came Hollandia, the great Japanese supply-base from which the enemy armies down the coast were fed and maintained.

Hollandia lay some 600 air-miles away from the nearest American fighter air-strip, and could not therefore be reached within the terms of the current fighter-support policy without a series of bloody contests for the intervening strongholds first. Under conditions of the strictest secrecy, however, a combined operation was now prepared with air-cover from naval carriers, to by-pass Madang, Hansa Bay, and Wewak, and capture Hollandia itself.

Hollandia lies just west of the boundary between Netherlands New Guinea and North-East New Guinea—the old Kaiser Wilhelm Land of pre-First World War days. Humboldt Bay bites into the coast-line just east of Hollandia, and Tanahmerah Bay makes another big dent some 30 miles along the coast to the west. Between these two bays runs the Cyclops Range, and just south of the Cyclops Range is a long irregular stretch of water, 15 or 20 miles long, running

1944

east and west parallel with the mountains, called Lake Sentani. Half-way along the northern edge of the lake, and not quite equidistant from Humboldt and Tanahmerah Bays, lay three Japanese air-fields.

The plan was to land the 41st Infantry Division in Humboldt Bay, near Hollandia town, to press inland westwards towards Cyclops Air-field, while the 24th Infantry Division landed at Tanahmerah Bay, and headed back east through the 7,000 feet Cyclops Mountains, towards Hollandia Air-field. In all, 37,500 fighting troops and 18,000 service troops were involved. The transports and naval craft, which made up the largest convoy hitherto assembled in the Pacific, sailed from Goodenough Island near the east end of Papua, on the

17 Apr. 17th April. Sailing west through Vitiaz Strait, it headed away north round the Admiralty Islands, as a final deception measure, and thence west and south-west towards its objectives, where it arrived
22 Apr. in the early hours of the 22nd April.

The previous day, the Japanese air-fields had been attacked from the air with a loss to the enemy of 245 aircraft, but on the 22nd, the enemy were completely surprised. The Japanese had been prepared at Wewak and Hansa Bay, but at Hollandia most of the beach defence troops took to their heels to escape the bombardment which preceded the landing, and opposition was either negligible or non-existent. There were the usual setbacks during the next few days, but by superhuman efforts, and the man-handling of almost everything forward from the beaches for lack of negotiable roads or
26 Apr. paths, the fighting troops joined hands on the 26th, and the organization of a base for the next advances westwards was hurried forward. At Hollandia, further batches of Indian prisoners-of-war from Malaya were recovered.

Of the Japanese Eighteenth Army, some 50,000 men were now cut off to the east. These troops slowly concentrated westwards,
12 July and on the 12th July, violently attacked Aitape, not far from
2 Aug. Hollandia. By the 2nd August, they had been finally checked.

This special operation against Hollandia was reckoned to have taken at least six months off the previous programme for operations along the New Guinea coast, but Gen. MacArthur was not the man
28 Apr. to let matters rest at that. Work began on the air-fields on the 28th April to strengthen and enlarge them for heavy transport aircraft, and next day the first C-47 landed safely. Road construction was started on a very large scale, and every effort made to turn Hollandia into a base fit for supporting future operations, with the minimum delay. This was achieved in between three and four weeks, and on the
17 May 17th May, the next operation was launched with an unopposed landing at Arare, 200 miles west of Hollandia. A few days later, Wakde Island

in the same neighbourhood was invaded, and its air-strip taken. And on the 27th May, another expedition was launched by the 41st Division—against Biak Island, 130 miles on from Wakde. The 8,000 Japanese troops on Biak Island put up the usual fanatical resistance, and the island with its three air-fields did not fall to the Americans till the 22nd June.

There was a pause in the operations now till the 30th July when a landing took place at Sansapur on the Vogelkop Peninsula at the western extremity of New Guinea. The place was strongly held, with a large garrison, but the Japanese were completely surprised and offered little resistance. The nearest reinforcements were at Manokwari, 120 miles to the east, where the headquarters of the Japanese Second Army was stationed, together with 15,000 troops, but extensive swamps and jungles lay across their path so that no early interference was expected. This important air- and naval-base thus passed without serious fighting into American hands, and brought the latter to a point only 600 miles from the South-East Philippines.

This concluded the New Guinea operations. The Allied forces had advanced 1,300 miles in just over twelve months, and had left behind them a total of 135,000 Japanese, cut off without hope of rescue. As Gen. Marshall wrote, the operation as a whole had been carried through in the face of adverse weather conditions and over formidable terrain which made troop movements and supply extraordinarily difficult. Malaria was a serious hazard, but with suppressive treatment and rigid mosquito control, it was no longer a serious limitation to tactical operations.

Admiral Nimitz in the Central Pacific had made good selected islands in the Marshalls, with a view to acquiring air and harbour facilities. From these islands he had been able to co-operate in the attack on the Japanese base at Truk in the Carolines, now under way from the Admiralty Islands. The Carolines lay to his west, and extended east and west over some 2,000 miles of sea. North of them lay the Marianas or Ladrone Islands, and these were to be the scene of Admiral Nimitz' next attack.

As a preliminary, a strong force including battleships and carriers, attacked the Pelew Islands on the 29th March. The Pelew Islands lie 500 miles beyond the western end of the Carolines. They were about the same distance or a little more, from Mindanao in the Philippines, and the western end of New Guinea lay about the same distance again to the south.

Two-and-a-half months later, after a heavy bombardment between the 10th and 12th June, a big operation was staged against Saipan Island in the Marianas. On the 15th June, the 2nd and 4th Marine

1944

9 July
Divisions went ashore, followed by the 27th Infantry Division. It was not until the 9th July that the violent Japanese resistance was broken down, and even then sporadic fighting still went on for several months. The losses in this bitter fighting were very heavy on both sides. Out of an estimated initial Japanese strength of 23,000, 21,036 dead were buried by the Americans. American losses numbered 2,359 killed, 11,481 wounded, and 1,213 missing—15,053 in all. But this Japanese defeat had more far-reaching consequences than the inconvenience of losing an important focal point on their communications, for it also brought about the fall of Gen. Tojo's government in Japan itself.

During the fighting for Saipan Island, a first-class naval action blew up. A strong Japanese fleet built up round aircraft-carriers appeared in the sea area between the Philippines and Marianas. Its role appeared to be to attack Admiral Spruance's American fleet from the air, and when he had been dealt with, to sail in against the Saipan beach-heads. Admiral Spruance was off Guam 200 miles south-west of Saipan, ready for such an eventuality. He successfully forestalled the Japanese commander by launching a violent air

19 June
attack against him on the 19th June; 353 Japanese aircraft were shot down in this encounter. This crippled the long-range effectiveness of the Japanese fleet, 300 miles to the north-west, and Admiral Spruance followed up his advantage by attacking again from the air

20 June
next day, and inflicting heavy loss. In this Battle of the Marianas, second only in importance to the Battle of Midway Island, and in the other actions in the expeditions against the Marianas, the Americans destroyed 848 aircraft, sank 30 ships, and damaged 51 others. The price paid by the Americans was 3 warships slightly damaged, and 151 aircraft and 98 airmen lost.

As soon as success in Saipan Island was sure, attention was

21 July
turned to Guam, 200 miles to the south-west. Here, on the 21st July, the 3rd Marine Division and 77th Infantry Division were put ashore.

10 Aug.
Organized resistance was broken by the 10th August. Tinian Island, just south of Saipan, was meanwhile invaded by the 2nd and 4th

24 July
Marine Divisions on the 24th July, and completely occupied by the

2 Aug.
2nd August.

Burma
4 Mar.
In North Burma, on the 4th March, Gen. Stilwell had reached Maingkwan in the Hukawng Valley, some 80 miles down the road from Ledo, on the new route to China. Pushing on a further 20 miles, he

20 Mar.
was in Jambubum on the 20th.

April
Crossing the divide, he moved into the Mogaung Valley at Shadazup, 30 miles ahead, during April, aiming for Kamaing, another 20 miles on. During this time Kachin Levies were active in the

1944

north, moving down the Malikha river to a point only 50 miles from Myitkyina. Eastwards, Marshal Wei Li Haung crossed the Salween, 250 miles away, and began closing in from that direction. By the 17th May, the United States Brig.-Gen. Merrill and his "Marauders" had captured the southern air-field in Myitkyina.   17 May

Gen. Stilwell's advance on Myitkyina was not the only influence affecting the Japanese in North Burma at this time. Co-ordinated with, and much assisting the Hukawng and Mogaung Valley operations, were the celebrated "Chindits"—Gen. Wingate's 3rd Division. The fly-in of the major part of this division was preceded only twelve hours before by an advance party of sappers, charged with the mission of preparing air-strips in a jungle clearing, of which only the most limited air-reconnaissance had previously been made, and in the depths of the thick forest country west of the Irrawaddy midway between Katha and Myitkyina. The success of this bold venture set a new standard in the experience of the forces in this theatre.

One brigade of the Division marched in. This was the 16th Infantry Brigade, made up of a battalion each of the Queen's and Leicesters. With them went a reconnaissance battalion and a gunner regiment—both organized as infantry—and detachments of Burma Rifles. Concentrating at Ledo, in the north of Assam, in detestable weather, soon after the turn of the year, the Brigade moved south some hundreds of miles through unreconnoitred mountains and forest, to a stronghold, named Aberdeen, a little north of Indaw. Indaw lies some miles west of the Irrawaddy, on the railway leading to Myitkyina, itself about 120 miles to the north-east. The other two brigades, including some African troops, flew in on the 5th March, to Broadway, where the sappers had made use of their twelve hours start to construct feasible landing strips. As soon as possible, the troops issued out south-westwards, one brigade establishing a block on the railway, at White City, north of Indaw and about east of Aberdeen. The other brigade operated in the general vicinity dominated by Indaw. The Japanese 18th Division, which was falling back in front of Gen. Stilwell, had its rear-ward communications effectively cut, but the Japanese offensive through Manipur and Imphal was not seriously embarrassed inasmuch as the enemy was looking forward to the British dumps rather than back to his own supply system, for maintenance. Coupled with other considerations, this Japanese offensive put paid to the hoped-for British offensive, and Gen. Wingate's division was withdrawn before the monsoon, flying out from Broadway. Gen. Wingate himself, meanwhile, had been killed on the 24th March in an air-crash, and had been succeeded   24 Mar. by Maj.-Gen. W. D. Lentaigne, previously commanding his 14th Infantry Brigade. However, Myitkyina, with its two remaining air-fields, fell on the 4th August, after a siege of eighty days, and Gen. Stilwell's   4 Aug. men had the victory at last.

1944

Brief thought these notes must be, they cannot possibly give anything like the true picture of these operations in North Burma without at least passing reference to the administrative problems and how they were solved. Operations were conducted through a mountainous and thickly forested country of great distances, poor communications and often severe climatic conditions. Gen. Marshall's view was that "the re-entry into Burma was the most ambitious campaign yet waged on the end of an air-borne supply line." The ration strength of Gen. Stilwell's forces varied between 25,000 and 100,000 men, and all mainly dependent on air-supplied food, equipment and ammunition. The Chindits had a less extended ration strength. But for both forces, C-46s and C-47s flew back and forth from a variety of points in the Brahmaputra Valley over formidable mountain barriers to delivery points in the jungle most difficult to identify. When the monsoon conditions of summer and early autumn are remembered, and it is realized that for three months during the most active part of the campaign, troop-carrier squadrons averaged 230 flying hours a month for each serviceable plane, the scale of the supply achievement is apparent.

The Japanese did not accept the challenge sitting down. With the failure of their offensive through the Arakan came the second stage of the operation somewhat to the north, coupled with a drive eastwards to push the Chinese back across the Salween.

The Japanese second offensive was aimed initially at Imphal, the headquarters of the IVth Indian Corps, in Manipur State in Assam. Of its attractions as an enemy objective, one must have been its extremely precarious supply line. This line followed the Assam Railway—with its inconvenient and vulnerable river-break and not very well equipped ferry service over the Brahmaputra—to Dimapur, which was supply railhead, for Imphal. Dimapur lies 80 air-miles— but more than twice that distance by the winding mountain road—north of Imphal. The nature of this road will be familiar enough to anyone who has followed the Banihal road into Kashmir. Following narrow, razor-backed ridges, or hanging precariously over deep ravines often many thousand feet below, and under frowning mountain peaks pushing up into the clouds, it demanded a high standard of driving skill and traffic control to maintain a steady flow of supplies, particularly during the long and heavy monsoon. Strategically, it had an even greater defect, running parallel to and never at a great distance from possible lines of attack. With this road blocked or denied, land communications with India could only pass over a second-class road running westward to the railway at Silchar, and not usable during the monsoon. Hence, if the Japanese could cut the Dimapur road north of Imphal, and again on its extension south on the way to Tiddim,

1944

100 air-miles south of Imphal, the troops there would be completely
cut off, and might be expected to be over-run comparatively quickly.
Operations against Dimapur and its air-fields, the denial of the
railway supply-line to Ledo, and interference with "Hump" traffic
to China would follow.

Accordingly, on the 15th March, the Japanese assaulted Tiddim,   15 Mar.
and forced the 17th Indian Division slowly back north. The next
attack was made on Tamu, across the formidable range of mountains
which closes in the Imphal Plain to the east. The 20th Indian Division
was forced to withdraw, and the Japanese occupied Tamu on the 22nd.   22 Mar.

Operations north of Imphal had been timed to coincide with those
just described, to the south and east. Sixty miles as the crow flies,
north of Imphal, and twenty miles south-east of Dimapur, is Kohima,
which is an important political and military point on the Dimapur
road. Kohima marks the point where the Dimapur road begins winding
down to lower levels northwards, after its long passage through the
mountains. Moving through the Somra hills, the Japanese advanced
on Kohima, cutting the Dimapur road on the 2nd April, and completely   2-7 Apr.
investing the defended post there on the 7th.

Reaction to the Japanese threat was instantaneous. The 5th Indian
Division was flown in to Imphal 400 miles from the Arakan, and
reinforcements were pushed up the railway to Dimapur, which was
not however attacked. One brigade of the 5th Indian Division was
moved north to the relief of Kohima, and the Royal West Kents, on
the 5th April, beat the enemy to it in the race for the last ridge, which   5 Apr.
served as a base for the Kohima "inner" garrison. They held this
ridge against overwhelming odds till the 18th, when Rajputs and   18 Apr.
Punjabis who had also been isolated on another height a mile to
the north fought through to their aid. The violence and ferocity of
this operation may be judged from the award of two posthumous
Victoria Crosses in the brigade—one to L.-Cpl. P. J. Harman, of the
Royal West Kents for gallantry in Kohima itself, and the other to
Jem. Abdul Hafiz, of the 9th Jat Regiment, for outstanding gallantry
near Imphal during the clearing of the road.

Though Kohima was relieved, the road could not be kept open.
And though Imphal was not surrounded, it was in state of siege till
the 7th June. In the meantime it was supplied by air, and reinforcements   7 June
totalling 2½ divisions complete with their artillery were flown in.
30,000 casualties were flown out in returning aircraft.

From captured diaries, it was clear enough that the Japanese had
started out on the road to Imphal with high hopes of a victorious
progress to Delhi. They were beaten by British air-power, coupled
with steadfastness in resistance and first-class generalship. Their
casualties were estimated at about 50 per cent of their strength; and

1944

their maintenance services were so dislocated by road conditions and the monsoon that—as, earlier, in Arakan—they were in far worse condition than our own troops. The "Death Valley" at Tamu, after their withdrawal, was a grim illustration of the perils of optimistic "G" planning unbacked by proper maintenance.

19 Aug. The Japanese withdrawal from Imphal was hotly pursued until, on the 19th August, they were driven back over the frontier into Burma, and new vistas were opened up for Allied operations.

Italy   In Italy, the Allies were still held on the Garigliano and Rapido rivers, with the Anzio beach-heads farther north in a state of siege. Much blood had been spilt and heroism displayed round Cassino which was still in enemy hands.

15 Mar. On the 15th March, a third great assault on Cassino was launched. Heavy air bombing preceded a two-hour artillery bombardment from 900 guns. The attack got away to an excellent start, but after eight
22 Mar. days of the most bitter fighting, in which the 4th Indian Division again took its share, the operation had to be called off and failure conceded.

11 May On the 11th May, after a programme of intensive bombing of the enemy's road and rail communications, a fresh attack was mounted. The Eighth Army had lengthened its front to the west. It had taken over the Cassino area from the Fifth Army, and was now called on to break through to the Liri Valley some 20 miles ahead, and advance astride Highway 6 on Valmontone, 22 miles short of Rome. The Fifth Army would follow a parallel line, between Highway 6 and the sea. The formations in the Anzio beach-head were to break out and move on Valmontone, 28 miles to their north-east. The 4th and 10th Indian Divisions had been incorporated in the Vth Corps with a defensive role on the Adriatic flank, but the 8th Indian Division was now in the XIIIth Corps of the Eighth Army, in the sector between Cassino and the right of the Fifth Army, and played a gallant part in the attack.

The attack was launched at 11 p.m. on the 11th May. There was severe initial opposition, but among the successes scored was the forcing of the Rapido, south of Cassino, by the 4th British and 8th Indian Divisions, who effected both bridge and ferry crossings against determined resistance.

During the next few days the battle surged back and forth with
13 May varying fortune. On the 13th May, the XIIIth Corps moved ahead from its bridge-head on the Rapido, and the 4th British and 8th Indian Divisions played a big part in the violent battles which raged through
14-16 May the 14th, 15th and 16th May. These assaults had the effect of much weakening the enemy hold on Cassino, and the IInd Polish Corps of

	1944
the Eighth Army co-operated in a second and more successful attack on the town. Fighting here continued against bitter opposition during the 17th and 18th, but by the afternoon of the latter day, both Cassino and Monastery Hill were in Allied hands.	17-18 May

Away to the left, in the Fifth Army, fighting continued over the whole front westwards to the sea. The enemy was forced gradually back, and by the 18th, our forward positions had advanced by some 9 or 10 miles.

Fierce, confused fighting continued between the 19th and 22nd.	19-22 May
The enemy was obviously not yet beaten. By the 23rd the battle had reached a critical stage, with the mounting of a second major thrust within the framework of the initial offensive. The results were	23 May
conclusive. By the 25th May, the enemy had been turned out of his positions in the "Hitler" Line and on the Liri River, and land	25 May
communications had been opened up with the Anzio beach-head, where a break-out had been effected on the 23rd. The steady advance continued over the whole front till the next organized German defensive line was reached, between Palestrina and the sea, some 20 miles from Rome. The enemy was given no respite here, and on	23 May
the 4th June, United States troops entered Rome.	4 June

The pursuit was carried on with vigour, but some re-grouping was made, with the 8th and 10th Indian Divisions joining the 2nd New Zealand Division in the Xth Corps, operating against Subiaco, 30 miles east of Rome.

On the 7th June, Civita-Vecchia, a large port 40 miles west-north-west of Rome was captured by United States formations. To	7 June
their right, British armour made a double-barrelled attack astride the Tiber towards Terni, an important centre of communications 45 miles due north. During the previous night, the enemy had begun to withdraw	6 June

on the Adriatic flank, and the Vth Corps, including the 4th Indian Division, moved forward to secure the lateral roads joining Pescara with Popoli and with Aquilla, a little north of an east and west line through Rome.

The Eighth Army was now directed on the general area around Florence, Bibbiena and Arezzo, 160 miles north of Rome. The Fifth Army was given an area about Pisa, Lucca and Pistoia—due west of Florence, and about 180 miles north-west of Rome. Progress was made all along the front, if somewhat unevenly. The Vth Corps on the Adriatic had difficulty in keeping touch with the enemy. It was in Pescara on the 10th June, by which day the New Zealanders and	10 June
8th Indian Division in the Xth Corps had occupied Avezzano and Licenza, 40 miles east of Rome. On their left, British formations were 20 miles north of Rome and progressing steadily.	
On the 11th June, the 10th Indian Division and 2nd New Zealand	11 June

1944

14-16 June	Division went into Eighth Army reserve. Progress was slowing up as enemy resistance grew stiffer. None the less, the Fifth Army had moved up 80 miles along the coast from Rome in the ten days up to the 14th June, and the Eighth Army 60 miles. By the 16th, the 8th Indian Division and 6th Armoured Division were north of Terni and on the way to Perugia over 100 miles north of Rome; formations to the right and left making comparable progress.
17 June	On the 17th morning, French troops invaded Elba, 18 miles off the west coast and in approximate alignment with the advance on land. A predominantly British naval force and a mainly American air component supported the operation, which was successfully completed
19 June	with relatively small loss, on the 19th.

By this time the troops were well ashore in Normandy—an amphibious operation was being planned against southern France—and important United States formations began to be withdrawn from the Fifth Army, together with four French divisions, for incorporation in the Seventh Army for the latter operation. The advance in Italy, however, went steadily on. By the end of June the 10th Indian Division was 9 miles north-east of Perugia in the Xth Corps sector. It relieved the 6th Armoured Division, and pushed on against stiff resistance towards Umbertide, 12 miles north of Perugia, capturing

6 July it on the 6th July. Moving steadily forward towards Citta di Castello, which lies a further 11 miles north, it was temporarily held up. The 4th Indian Division, now also under Xth Corps command, after a brief training interlude in Campobasso, was similarly held up. The enemy was now standing on the Ancona-Leghorn line, but violent

14-15 July attacks beginning on the night of the 14th/15th July secured both ports for the Allies by the 19th. The first Allied convoy sailed into

19-23 July Ancona on the 23rd.

Departures of ground and air formations for the pending operations in southern France now began to make themselves felt. However,

20 July on the 20th July, the Eighth Army was directed on Florence and instructed to gain contacts with the Pisa-Rimini line. The Fifth Army was to secure the line of the Arno river which runs into the sea just west of Pisa, 50 miles west of Florence, and develop operations against Pistoia and Lucca, 10 to 15 miles beyond. These operations brought small gains on the Fifth Army's front; but the Eighth Army scored important successes in all sectors against determined opposition

4-13 Aug. They had reached Florence and the Arno by the 4th August, and pushed the enemy back on to much of the Pisa-Rimini line. By the 13th, the forward troops were on approximately the line of the Cesano river, from the Adriatic to Frontone, thence through the mountains via Sansapolcri, 40 miles south-west of Rimini to the Arno near Pontassieve 8 miles east of Florence, and along its left bank to the sea.

1944

Enemy strength at this time was put at 26 German divisions, including 6 Panzer and Panzer Grenadier, together with 6 Italian Fascist divisions. Allied forces amounted to 21 divisions, including 4 armoured; but great air superiority off-set weakness on the ground.

On the 13th August, the 8th Indian Division crossed the Arno into Florence, but suffered no worse subsequent inconvenience than heavy German and Italian sniping during the next few days, and intermittent shelling. Other small advances were effected elsewhere, but nothing on a large scale was undertaken while re-grouping was carried out prior to an assault on the German main position—the "Gothic" line—on which the Germans were falling back. The 4th Indian Division was grouped with three British Divisions and an Armoured Division, in the Vth Corps. This corps was to bear the main burden of what was later described as some of the bloodiest fighting in the history of the British Army. The 8th Indian Division was under Fifth Army command, in the XIIIth Corps, in the Florence area. The 10th Indian Division, in the Xth Corps, with only the 9th Armoured Brigade to keep it company, was on the Eighth Army's defensive left flank.

It had been known for some time that the enemy intended to make a determined stand on the Gothic Line; but by the 25th August most   25 Aug.
of the strong outpost position covering it had been driven in. This was the line stretching from the Cesano river via Florence to the mouth of the Arno, some account of the early fighting for which has been given. The Gothic Line lay some 15 to 20 miles back, as a modified version of the former Pisa-Rimini line. Its total length from sea to sea was about 180 miles. Starting from Pesaro, 20 miles down the coast from Rimini, on the Adriatic, it ran a little south of west to Bibbiena in the upper Arno valley, and about the centre of the line. From here, it ran abruptly north-west for 25 miles. Thence, by turns west and north-west, it found its way to the Mediterranean 12 miles south of La Spezia, and 25 up the coast from the mouth of the Arno. Florence lay about 20 miles to its south.

The defences were not continuous, nor were they uniformly developed in depth. Much of the country was inaccessible to armour or mechanized formations, and the enemy took full advantage of this. Where the defences were built up, they consisted of the usual machine-gun and mortar emplacements, thickened up in vulnerable areas with concrete pill boxes on which anti-tank gun turrets could be mounted.

Air preparation began on the night of the 25th/26th August. On   25-26 Aug.
the 26th, the Eighth Army launched a general attack. The IInd Polish Corps attacked on the right, the Ist Canadian Corps in the centre, and the Vth British Corps on the left. By the 2nd September   2 Sept.

1944

the Poles had reached positions 8 miles up the coast from Pesaro. The Canadians, striking north level with the Poles who had attacked north-west, then pinched the latter out and took over their line, advancing to within 8 miles of Rimini. The Vth Corps came up against very heavy opposition, and, though the line was breached, little progress was made.

On the Fifth Army front, operations were confined to forcing the enemy slowly back from his outpost positions. This was still in progress at the beginning of September, by which time the enemy was almost back in his main positions.

Southern France   Plans for a landing on the south coast of France had been under preparation for many months. The operation should have been synchronized with the Normandy landings, but shortage of landing craft forbade. It was not till landing craft were released from Normandy that the invasion in the south could be carried out.

28 Apr.   Preparatory air operations for the landing began on the 28th April.
10 Aug.   They continued steadily till the 10th August, by which date 12,500 tons
11-15 Aug. of bombs had been dropped. Between the 11th and 15th August, emphasis was shifted to the Valence-Grenoble-Montmelian line, and to the Rhone bridges south of Valence.

15 Aug.   The invasion began with a violent air bombardment, opening at 2.15 a.m. on the 15th August. At 4.15 a.m., 396 troop-carrier aircraft dropped their loads. At 7.10 a.m., a heavy bombardment from sea and air was opened on the beaches, lying between Cavalaire and Agay, 28 and 56 miles along the coast east of Toulon. The aircraft of nine carriers took part in this bombardment.

Germans and Allies each disposed of ten divisions, but only three German divisions were on the coast. In the Allied Seventh Army—which had been ferried across by an aggregate of 2,110 ships of varying categories, mainly from Naples and Oran—the American VIth Corps was to lead the assault, with the 36th Division on the right, the 45th in the centre about St. Maxime, and the 3rd on the left. The two French Corps were to follow.

At 8 a.m., the first sea-borne wave came ashore. The enemy was caught napping and the landing went smoothly enough. Operations were directed westwards towards Toulon and Marseilles, both of which
22-28 Aug. were isolated by the 22nd August and occupied on the 28th. In the rapid advance which followed up the valley of the Rhone, the VIth Corps so far outran its ground maintenance that it had to be supplied with petrol and oil by a service of A-20 bombers, B-24 Liberators and C-47 transport planes. With this assistance, the 36th Division
2 Sept.   was about Lyons, 180 miles north of Marseilles, on the 2nd September.
8 Sept.   The 3rd Division cleared Besançon to the north-east on the 8th. The

French 1st Armoured Division took Dijon, 40 miles north of Lyons and 60 west of Besançon, on the 11th—and, near Sombernon, 18 miles west of Dijon, contacted Gen. Patton's Third Army, from Gen. Eisenhower's command. On the 15th September, Seventh Army operations became Gen. Eisenhower's responsibility—and it is on record that by the 20th, a total of 400,614 men, 65,480 vehicles, and 360,373 tons of cargo had been landed for this army.

1944

11 Sept.

15 Sept.

20 Sept.

Swinging north, a brief account must now be given of what was the consummation of the whole Allied strategy in the west—the invasion of Normandy.

Normandy

The basis of the plan was an initial landing by five divisions on a frontage of some 70 miles in the Bay of the Seine. The First (United States) Army, with the 82nd and 101st Airborne Divisions, was to operate on a front from a little short of Cherbourg to Port en Bessin. The Second (British) Army, which was part of the 21st Army Group, was responsible for the frontage eastwards to the estuary of the Orne river, a few miles south-west of Havre. Other formations in the 21st Army Group included the First (Canadian) Army, the 6th Airborne Division, and various Allied contingents.

The Germans had the Seventh Army in Normandy and Brittany, the Fifteenth Army in the Pas de Calais and Flanders, and the LXXXth and VIIIth Corps in Holland. These were organized into Army Group "B" under Field-Marshal Rommel, who was somewhat at odds with his superior, Field-Marshal von Rundstedt. There were definite misgivings as to the capacity of the German Armies generally to meet commitments in their current extended state, but Hitler would hear of no withdrawals. Von Rundstedt, accordingly, compromised. He preferred not to try and beat the invasion on the beaches, but to keep the bulk of his troops well back, and counter-attack when the Allies were committed but still off-balance. Rommel, on the other hand, wanted strong beach garrisons with reserves close up in rear. The compromise accordingly followed, and while the infantry were kept well forward, most of the armour was held back. As there was only the one chain of works along the coast, with little depth, and no secondary defensive line in rear, the position was not a really very happy one—particularly as the main landing, in von Rundstedt's view, was not expected in Normandy at all, but in the Pas de Calais, 150 miles or so to the east.

All told, von Rundstedt's command included Army Group "B"— already detailed—and Army Group "G", in which were the First and Nineteenth Armies under Field-Marshal von Blaskowitz stationed on the Biscay coast and in the Riviera. Of the total of 50 Infantry and 10 Panzer Divisions, 36 Infantry and 9 Panzer Divisions were between Holland and Lorient on the Bay of Biscay. Most were in the Pas de Calais. 9 Infantry and 1 Panzer Divisions were in Normandy.

1944

The actual landings have been too well publicized to need more than a comparatively brief note here; but a few figures and a short reference to some of the novel methods used may properly be included for comparison against the background of other theatres. Over 5,000 ships were used, plus a further 4,000 ship-to-shore craft. The five divisions making the initial assault were allotted 4,266 of this total. To protect the convoys and cover the landings, 702 naval craft and 25 flotillas of mine-sweepers were employed. For the actual landings, all motor vehicles and tanks were water-proofed to enable them to be driven through deep water, and amphibious tanks swam precariously in through the heavy seas, though not without some loss. As the landings were being made on open beaches, five shelter harbours were designed. These, under the code name "gooseberry", and consisting of a total of sixty block ships sunk in position, made less appeal to the popular mind than the "mulberries"—prefabricated ports, towed over in sections and fitted together on arrival. Finally "pluto", the submarine petrol supply line, made its bow.

In the air-cover programme for the assault, the fighter contribution reached the respectable total of 171 squadrons.

Preliminary air operations against railways and bridges effectively isolated the German Seventh Army. The high winds and rough seas that ushered in June caused a twenty-four-hour postponement of the invasion; and when at 4 a.m. on the 5th June, Gen. Eisenhower took the risk and decided to attack next day, he found an unexpected ally in the weather which was still such as to quieten what immediate fears the Germans had.

5 June

For the operation itself, airborne troops were to make their landing at 2 a.m. on the 6th. They were allotted 2,395 aircraft and 867 gliders. At 3.14 a.m., bombardment from the air was to be opened by a further 2,219 aircraft. Bombardment from the sea began at 5.50 a.m., and the first wave of troops came ashore at 6.30 a.m.

6 June

The airborne forces protected the flanks. The British 6th Airborne Division landed with precision on its objective at the mouth of the Orne. The American 82nd and 101st Airborne Divisions were less fortunate and were much scattered over the Carentan area at the base of the Cotentin Peninsula.

There was strong ground opposition in places, but a secure footing was gained within twenty-four hours. By the 10th June, the first air-field was in operation. By the 12th, 326,547 men, 54,186 vehicles, and 104,428 tons of stores had been landed. Air mastery was so complete that in Gen. Eisenhower's words—in fine weather, all enemy movement was brought to a standstill by day.

7-10 June

19-22 June

Fine weather, however, was not the rule. Between the 19th and 22nd June, severe gales raged. The American "mulberry" was completely

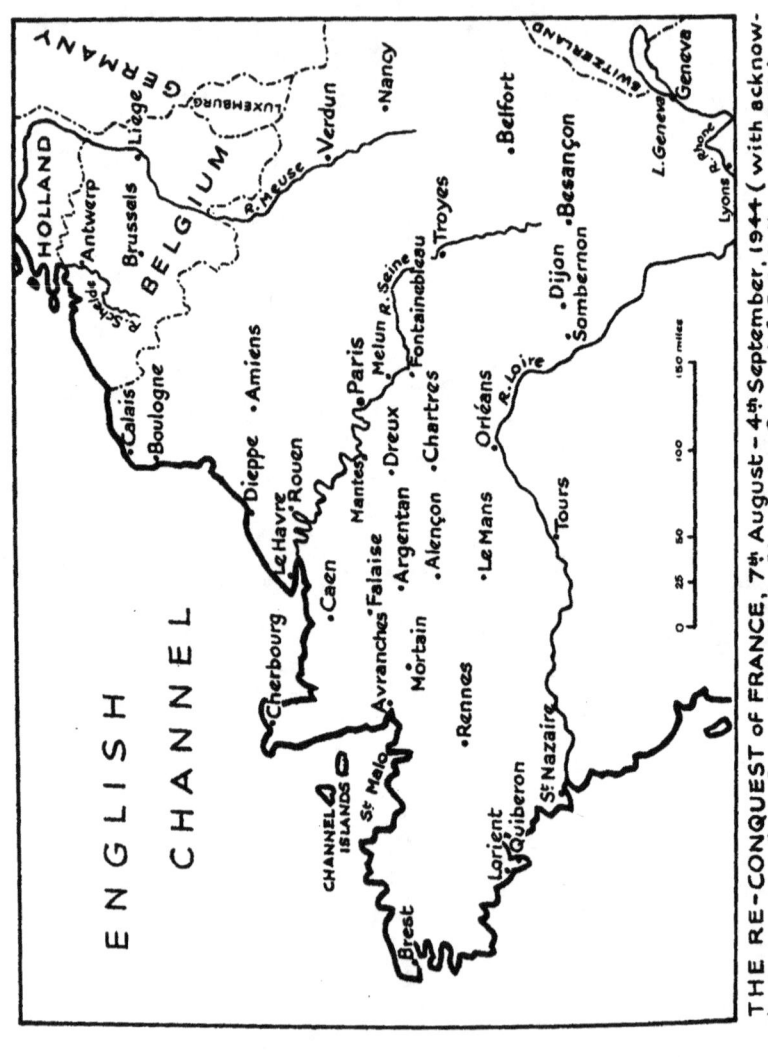

THE RE-CONQUEST of FRANCE, 7th August – 4th September, 1944 (with acknowledgements to "The Second World War" by Major-General J. F. C. Fuller, page 328.)

	1944
destroyed, and 415 ships wrecked or damaged. Cherbourg, however, fell on the 27th June, and by the end of July the port was in working order. | 27 June

Operations proceeded slowly enough till the night of the 16th/17th July, when the British Second Army made a feint by "artificial moonlight" to draw the enemy armour away west. "Artificial moonlight" was produced by focussing the beams of massed searchlights on the clouds, and the reflected light was a great help to the infantry. The crucial operation of the 18th July, when three armoured divisions were to take advantage of the hoped-for consequences of the feint, and attempt a break-through under what Gen. Eisenhower described as the heaviest and most concentrated air assault hitherto employed in support of ground operations, proved a disastrous failure, for the Germans had moved out of the area selected for bombing, and had organized their anti-tank defences behind it. The weather then took a hand and turned the country into a sea of mud, and so halted what offensive power the force still had.

16-17 July

18 July

The Americans began an offensive south of the Cotentin Peninsula on the 25th July. On the 29th, Gen. Patton's newly-constituted Third Army moved still farther south, crossed the Seine and created an open flank. Gen. Montgomery's command reached a point 20 miles in from the coast on the 4th August, and by the 10th had completed the isolation of Brittany, though not the capture of its ports.

25 July
29 July

4 Aug.
10 Aug.

The Germans had not been backward in bringing up reinforcements. On the 7th August, a powerful offensive was opened westwards against Gen. Patton's communications. This was directed towards Avranches which lies at the eastern extremity of the Gulf of St. Malo. Four hundred German tanks were employed, but for once the weather favoured the Allies, and enabled rocket-firing Typhoon aircraft to strike with effect and throw the attack into confusion. The Germans hung on to their positions for five critical days, but this was just so much too long, for the 21st Army Group were able to take advantage of the opportunity and strike with effect. The day the German offensive opened—the 7th August—the First Canadian Army, 33 miles south of the Orne river estuary and 50 east of Avranches, attacked towards Falaise. With great boldness, the infantry concerned were moved up for 2 miles to the German positions, and thence on for another 3 miles almost to the gun-line in "kangaroo" armoured transporters, before they debussed. On the 10th, they were ordered to press on towards Falaise while the American XVth Corps moved up north from Alençon towards Argentan, 25 miles south-east of Falaise. At the same time, the American First and British Second Armies came down behind Avranches towards Mortain, 25 miles east of Avranches and 40 south-west of Falaise.

7 Aug.

10 Aug.

1944

16 Aug. The Germans, with Panzer flank protection to keep the bottle-neck free for the infantry to pass, tried to make their way back, but it was too late. When Falaise fell to the Canadians on the 16th, the Panzer formations were pulled in, and the retreat became a *sauve*
19 Aug. *qui peut*. The pocket was finally closed on the 19th, by which date some 80,000 demoralized men had escaped, and were heading in disorder for the Seine. But the remaining 8 of the original 22 Infantry Divisions, and parts of 2 out of the 5 Panzer Divisions were
22 Aug. caught, and surrendered on the 22nd. About 2,000 vehicles were destroyed by air-action in spite of intense anti-aircraft fire and unfavourable weather.

Meanwhile events had been moving fast to the south where a rapid advance was made eastwards by the American Third Army on the north bank of the Loire, south-east of the Falaise fighting. The Seine was crossed both above and below Paris, and as a direct consequence the Germans withdrew from the city which the French Gen. Leclerc
25 Aug. entered on the 25th August. The British, Canadians and the American First Army had occupied the whole length of the Seine down-stream of Paris, and from here a fresh advance was made with the First Canadian Army along the coast, the Second British Army aiming for Central Belgium, the American First Army on the front Luxembourg-Liege, and the American Third Army already well on its way towards Nancy and Verdun, with a column directed on Belfort to link up with
3 Sept. the American Seventh Army from southern France. By the 3rd September, the southern flank of the Third Army was within 60 miles of the German frontier.

But the sands were running out, for thanks to the lack of sufficiently convenient and numerous ports, the supply position was growing daily more precarious, and the hopes of an immediate and decisive victory were growing dim.

Russia   In Russia, the German position was critical by early spring. An open flank had been created between the central and southern groups of armies. The southern group itself was stretched out far to the east in the huge salient of the Dnieper bend. Four limited Russian offensives—described in Chapter IX—had been launched with generally successful results, and the stage was set for an all-out Russian attack.

One hundred miles west of the Pripet Marshes, and 400 miles north-west of Odessa, lies the town of Kovel. From here, the opposing lines ran east-south-east for about 250 miles to Vinnitsa. On this part of the Russian front Marshal Zhukov was in command. From Vinnitsa east and then south-east, Marshal Koniev's 2nd Ukrainian Group held the line.
4 Mar. Marshal Zhukov opened the offensive on the 4th March, along a

60-mile front in the centre of his line. The attack followed a
southerly direction, and by the 6th had reached a point on the Odessa-
Lvov railway over 50 miles to the south. Exploitation westwards
along the railway brought the Russians to Tarnopol, 30 miles to the
west, by the 9th.

Marshal Koniev's offensive was launched on the 6th March from
a point near the northern end of the Dnieper bend. The attack faced
south-west, and by the 10th had surprised and captured the large
German base at Uman, 40 miles away; 500 tanks and 12,000 lorries
were seized. The Germans broke back in panic. They had already
lost a force of eight divisions in the Korsun neighbourhood a few
weeks before in one of the limited Russian offensives; and this
fresh disaster upset the strategic balance and left the Germans in
no state to resist. By the 15th March, Koniev's men were a further
80 miles south-west, astride the Odessa-Lvov railway, and drawing
very close to the Rumanian frontier.

Marshal Zhukov was pressing on to the south, and by the 30th
had captured Czernowitz, on the Pruth, 100 miles south of Tarnopol,
and 150 miles west of the point where Marshal Koniev had cut the
Odessa-Lvov railway 15 days before. Czernowitz was of great
strategic significance to the Russians. Its capture cut the last rail
link between the Germans in Poland and those in southern Russia.
Koniev established himself on the Pruth down-stream of Czernowitz,
so that by mid-April, the two groups were stabilized on a line
running from a little east of Kovel to the eastern extremity of Czecho-
Slovakia, thence to Jassy on the Pruth, and on east to Dubosari,
nearly 100 miles away on the Dniester.

South of these two Russian groups of armies lay Malinovsky's
Third Ukrainian Group. These armies had moved forward on the
13th March to the capture of Kherson at the mouth of the Dnieper.
Against very heavy opposition, they had made good an advance of
50 miles to the west by the 28th March and were in possession of
Nikolayev at the mouth of the Bug. On the 10th April, the Russians
entered the undefended port of Odessa, another 60 miles south-west.
Shortly after they reached the Dniester and linked up with Koniev's
left at Dubosari.

Fighting now spread to the Crimea where the German Seventeenth
Army of five German infantry divisions and seven weak Rumanian
divisions had fortified the more obvious approaches to the peninsula,
but had neglected the shallow, marshy lagoons, called Sivash,
which lie to the east of the Isthmus of Perekop which links the
Crimea to the mainland. The winter having been mild, these lagoons
did not freeze over. The Russians took a chance and decided to ford
them—and did so with surprising ease. The four Rumanian divisions

1944

responsible for guarding this part of the coast had reckoned on the unfrozen state of the water making their front reasonably secure, and had withdrawn to the centre of the Crimea.

8-9 Apr. When the attack came in on the 8th and 9th April, the Germans found themselves in difficulties not only along the north-east coast opposite the Sivash, but at the eastern tip at Kerch, and at the Isthmus of Perekop on the north-west. Gen. Tolbukhin's Fourth Ukrainian Group, which was responsible for the operation, then scattered the four Rumanian divisions in the centre by a fierce

11 Apr. assault on the 11th. The Germans then abandoned all their positions in a hurried withdrawal south to Simferopol, and were driven thence in great disorder to a rallying point at Sevastopol. The end was not long delayed. Russian bombardment of the fortress

6 May opened on the 6th May. A few days later the troops moved back to Cape Khersones at the south-west tip of the peninsula, and a few

12 May miles from Sevastopol. Here, on the 12th, the remainder of the Seventeenth Army, less three Rumanian divisions and some other troops shipped back beforehand, surrendered to the Russians.

The Germans were by now in an unenviable position. With few reserves, and with no lateral communications to facilitate tactical mobility, effective resistance became very difficult. No help could be expected from the home country, for every available man or weapon was earmarked for France, Italy and elsewhere. Their southern group of armies had been cut in two, with the left wing withdrawing north of the Carpathians, and the balance far away south in Rumania, and each part had now to be hurriedly organized as a separate formation. None the less, short of equipment and with progressively poorer drafts coming forward to maintain their much reduced strengths, they held on manfully, reinforcing their southern front in Rumania, where they thought the vitally important Ploesti oil-fields would be the next Russian objective.

The Russians, however, could afford to wait. They had at this time, spread over the front, some 300 divisions, of about 4,500,000 men. The Germans had only 200 divisions, and, with many at cadre strength, had probably not much more than one-third of the Russian strength in men. Russian communications and resources in the south were now much strained, and needed a little time to build up. On the Baltic and White Russian fronts, however, they were well organized as well as nearer home. The Russians therefore decided to let Ploesti wait, and switched their offensive north.

In this offensive, the Leningrad Group broke through the

10 June Mannerheim Line on the 10th June. Viborg fell on the 20th, and

20 June organized resistance in Finland thus came practically to an end.

Next came an offensive nearer the centre. This opened on the

                                                                    1944
23rd June on a 125-mile front between Vitebsk and Zhlobin; 100   23 June
Russian divisions were used, and by the 29th they had captured the 29 June
four hedgehogs on this front. By the 30th, they were threatening   30 June
Minsk, 100 miles in rear, and much of the German Ninth Army was
surrounded and annihilated. The Russians entered Minsk on the 3rd; 3 July
and next day, after the storming of Polotsk, 120 miles north-west of 4 July
Minsk, the 1939 Polish frontier was crossed. By the 10th, they had 10 July
surrounded Vilna another 100 miles north-west of Minsk. Vilna fell on the
13th, while three days later, with the capture of Grodno 100 miles 13 July
south-west of Vilna, a bridgehead was gained over the Niemen   16 July
between these two places, and the road opened into East Prussia.
  Troops on this front of attack having now out-run their communications, the Russians switched farther north to the Latvian front.
On the 12th July, an offensive was launched which took them, by   12 July
the 27th, nearly 200 miles to the west and resulted in the partial 27 July
envelopment of Riga. After the failure of a small counter-offensive
with three Panzer Divisions and one Infantry Division on the 16th   16 Aug.
August, the Germans decided to cut their losses, and began pulling
out of Estonia and Latvia while they could.
  Meanwhile, hostilities had broken out again a little to the south,
when the Russians launched extensive attacks in the Lvov area.
By the 30th July, the Germans were back in the eastern suburbs of   30 July
Warsaw. This terminated this series of Russian offensives in the
north, for the moment.
  In the south, fighting broke out again about the 20th August. Here, 20 Aug.
the Germans had the Eighth and Sixth Armies deployed across
Moldavia and Bessarabia. Their twenty-five divisions probably mustered
about 150,000 men, and they were supported by fifteen or sixteen
quite unreliable Rumanian divisions. They could not be reinforced.
Communications forbade.
  When the offensive opened, the Rumanians broke, and the Russians
surged forward north-west and south-west. By the 25th August, the   25 Aug.
bulk of the German Sixth Army was surrounded, and soon after
liquidated. On the 26th, Tolbukhin's left wing entered the fortress of 26 Aug.
Ismail on the Danube delta, and on the 27th was in Galatz. Other forces 27 Aug.
moving south occupied Ploesti on the 30th and Bucharest on the 31st. 30 Aug.
  Political events had contributed to the German debacle in the   31 Aug.
south. Rumanian resistance had ended on the 23rd August, and a   23 Aug.
few days later, King Michael had declared war on Germany. On the
26th August, Bulgaria had withdrawn from the war, and the Germans   26 Aug.
had begun hastily pulling out of Greece. To complete this brief
survey, the Russians occupied Sofia on the 16th September, and   16 Sept.
were in a position to initiate operations against Hungary and Austria
via the Danube Valley.

1944

Against this vast background of world events, how did the Regiment fare?

1st Bn.

March

The 1st Battalion was in the Arakan that spring, near the Ngakyedauk Pass, somewhat north of the Maungdaw-Buthidaung road, and serving in the role of divisional headquarters battalion in the 7th Indian Division. At the beginning of March when the Japanese offensive in that theatre fizzled out, it was relieved of its divisional headquarters role, and allotted to the 33rd Indian Infantry Brigade of the same division for the postponed offensive aimed at the eastern end of the Maungdaw-Buthidaung road.

The Battalion was in grand heart, full of confidence and with soaring morale. The weather was fine and sunny—not too hot by day, cool at night, but without the sharp chill of a month before. In these pleasant circumstances, the Battalion concentrated on the 29th February in Awlanbyin, and next day joined the 25th Dragoons just south of the Admin. Box for tank training prior to the operation.

29 Feb.
1 Mar.

The operation was to include the capture of Buthidaung, and the elimination of enemy garrisons in "Massive" and "Able", strong positions on the jungle-clad hills.

As a curtain-raiser to this, the Battalion was to capture a couple of hill features, "Poland" and "Rabbit", on the night of the 6th/7th March.

6-7 Mar.

Requisite reconnaissances were arranged, and on the evening of the 5th March, patrols went out to verify if Poland and Rabbit were in fact held. After confirmation received next morning, Lieut.-Col. Bamford decided to attack with "B" and "C" Companies up and "A" and "D" in reserve.

5 Mar.
6 Mar.

The same evening, at dusk, under a bright moon, the Battalion made its way through the rice-fields between the enemy-held positions on Massive and Able. The forming-up area lay just north of the main road and was reached in good time. For the attack on Poland, Maj. Brough led "C" Company forward across the road under a barrage from the corps and divisional artillery, which lifted as the leading platoon commenced the assault. The Company went up the hill with great dash, surprising a forward enemy post a little below the summit— the garrison withdrawing in haste as the charge came in. Over-running the post, the company swarmed up over the top and captured the Japanese main position there against slight opposition.

The leading section of the reserve platoon was held up as it moved along the ridge to deal with a second position in rear. A medium machine-gun in position there opened up on a second attack, which had gone in with fine enthusiasm, the men shouting their fatehs as they dashed forward, and held it up too, with some casualties. Sep. Sajjan Singh here displayed great gallantry in crawling forward

310

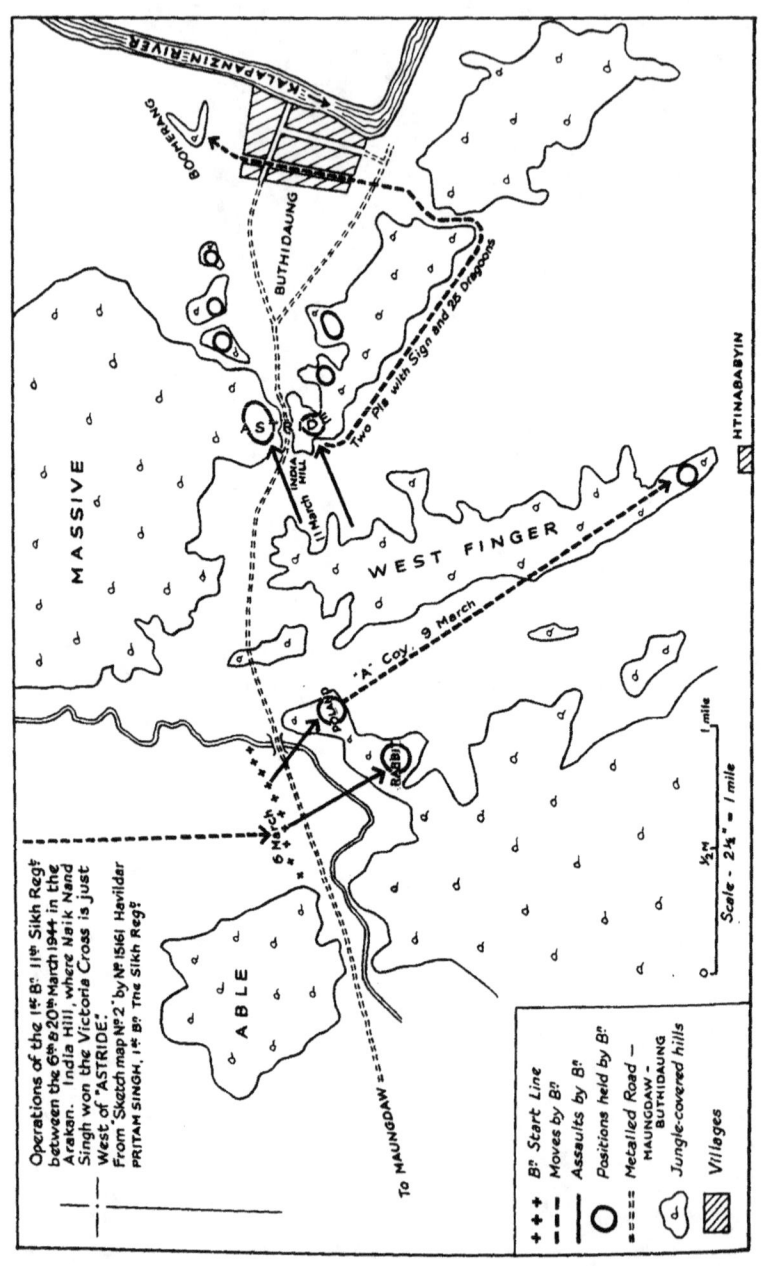

under extremely heavy enemy fire, and bringing back several
wounded men from within a few yards of the enemy machine-gun.
He was himself eventually wounded, but refused to leave his section
until the whole position was secured in the morning. For this he
was deservedly awarded a Military Medal.

At night, and in these circumstances, the machine-gun was not
easy to locate, and it was quite impossible to move down the steep
slopes to attack the position from a flank. The Company consolidated
till day-light, but the enemy meanwhile withdrew.

"B" Company, under Maj. Walker, had been attacking Rabbit on
"C" Company's right. Direction was hard to maintain, and the
leading platoon headed too far to the west and was held up by
impenetrable jungle. It took nearly an hour to find a way through, and
even then the men had great difficulty in climbing the steep hill-side,
and in several places had to cut a way through the undergrowth.
However, they met no opposition, and secured the position soon after
midnight, capturing two 47 m.m. anti-tank guns and much minor
equipment.

The remainder of the Battalion moved forward at once and dug in
against likely enemy counter-attacks. The Japanese command post
was discovered in the nala between Poland and Rabbit, the positions
on which were sited to cover it. The enemy was probably surprised
by the rapid advance up Poland, and, not suspecting the somewhat
later attack on Rabbit, failed to stand-to on the position there when
the artillery lifted. Whatever the circumstance, the positions on
Poland came under enemy shell-fire throughout the 7th, though early
completion of their trenches saved the Battalion all but a few
casualties.

7 Mar.

The enemy counter-attacks came in that night against both Poland
and Rabbit. It was a dramatic scene, amazingly still, with a full
moon high in the sky, as the Japanese were working their way forward
through the jungle to the attack. The Sikhs held their fire till the
Japanese were close up, and then gave a resounding "Jo bole so
nihal, sat siri akal", as they threw them back time after time. The
shouts rang clearly through the jungle and echoed round the hills,
while answering "fatehs" were periodically heard from men of the
4th/15th Punjab Regiment holding positions over on the left. The
self-confidence of the Sikhs was most inspiring, and the Japanese could
make no headway. Before dawn they withdrew back to their positions
farther south.

8 Mar.

A succession of further preliminaries still lay to the Battalion's
share before the attack on Buthidaung was to be mounted. "A"
Company, under command of Maj. Thomas, and supported by a squadron
of tanks of the 25th Dragoons, went forward on the 8th, and occupied

1944

a position west of Htinababyin. There was no opposition other than from marshy ground which held up the tanks about half-a-mile north of Dongyaung. The company took up a strong position on a ridge, while the tanks withdrew into reserve.

9 Mar. Next day, the 9th, the company moved forward to occupy the southern end of the ridge overlooking Htinababyin, while "D" Company, under Maj. Redding, raided enemy dumps in the Dongyaung area.

"A" Company's leading platoon met with very stiff resistance. A company attack was launched, and the leading platoon captured three enemy posts with fierce close-in fighting before being held up by light machine-guns firing at point-blank range. There had been many instances of gallantry displayed during the advance. The leading section commander, Naik Naranjan Singh, was wounded early on, but continued to lead his section, carrying the first two enemy trenches at the point of the bayonet in spite of heavy fire from several enemy light machine-guns. With all but two of his section killed or wounded, Naik Naranjan Singh assaulted the third trench up a precipitous slope, and killed its garrison with grenades. Of the two men with him, one was killed and the other wounded, but Naik Naranjan Singh continued to hold the enemy trench until the remainder of the company had consolidated and he was ordered to withdraw. For this example of high gallantry and self-devotion, he was awarded an Indian Distinguished Service Medal.

Sep. Mukhtiyar Singh was less fortunate, in losing his life. He was seen charging the remaining enemy post single-handed, firing his Bren gun from the hip and killing four or five of the enemy, but was not seen again. He was awarded a posthumous Indian Order of Merit for his example and courage.

A third award for gallantry in this hard-fought action was that of the Military Medal to No. 22356 Sep. Karam Singh, who was with Naik Naranjan Singh in his magnificent triple attack already described. Sep. Karam Singh went through with his section commander to the third line of trench, though already wounded, and contributed a full share towards the successful outcome. Thanks to this, all casualties were safely got away.

"D" Company, meantime, had gained complete surprise. It returned without loss the same evening, having moved up behind the enemy's forward positions, and destroyed three dumps without opposition.

Over and above these special actions, active patrolling had been carried on all along the front by the Battalion, and contacts achieved. One such patrol, consisting of four men, set off in bright moonlight on the night of the 8th/9th March. It had covered about a mile when it saw—and was seen by—a party of some forty Japanese

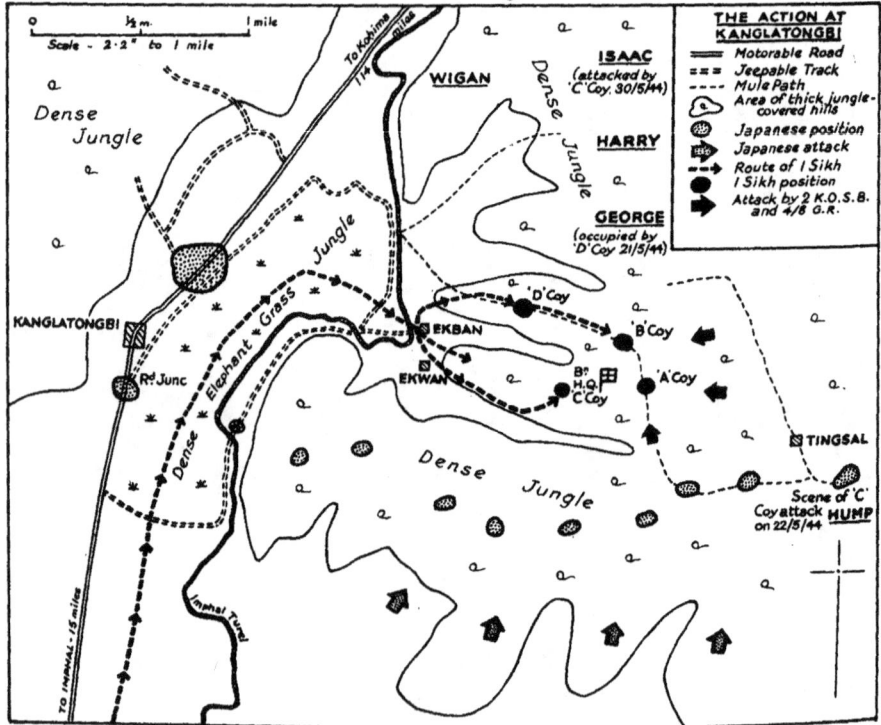

moving north towards Poland. The Sikh patrol took cover, but the Japanese, dropping a grenade-discharger party in a central position to cover their advance, moved round to out-flank the patrol. A member of the patrol, Sep. Charan Singh, began stalking the grenade-discharger party. Going forward alone, he crawled up to within a few yards of them, then jumped the Japanese soldier who had the discharger and killed him with one thrust of his bayonet. The other two Japanese gave a piercing shriek and fled. This bold move caused the immediate hurried withdrawal of the whole Japanese party, and won Sep. Charan Singh the Indian Distinguished Service Medal.

Covering the western approaches to Buthidaung was a Japanese position in the jungle-covered hills called "Astride". On the following night, the 9th/10th March, Hav. Bachan Singh took out a reconnaissance patrol to see what the Japanese were doing. The patrol moved close up to the position and brought back information of value to the higher command. Bunkers were being dug along the whole Astride position, and several posts had been constructed near the main road. 9-10 Mar.

As a result of this patrol report, the divisional commander, Gen. Messervy, himself came forward during the 10th afternoon to discuss the possibility of advancing the time of the Battalion's attack on Astride, which it had been intended to stage on or after the 12th. At the same time, harassing action by artillery and aircraft was arranged, in an effort to hamper and delay construction of the Japanese defences. The position was obviously critical—the alternative lying between attacking that night with tired and unprepared troops and inadequate reconnaissance, or attacking a better established enemy next morning. Lieut.-Col. Bamford accepted the latter. "A" and "D" Companies would be rested by then, and there was the additional prospect of support by some dive-bombers, together with all the corps artillery and a squadron of tanks. A company of the 4th/15th Punjab Regiment accordingly took over from "A" Company at Htinababyin, and the latter arrived back in the Battalion area at 8 p.m. for some well-earned sleep. 10 Mar.

Before light on the 11th March, the Battalion moved to a forming-up area behind West Finger, and Lieut.-Col. Bamford issued verbal orders for the attack from the lower slopes of this ridge at 6.30 a.m. 11 Mar.

For this attack, the forward troops were again "B" and "C" Companies. "B" Company, on the left, was to capture the hills north of the Maungdaw-Buthidaung road, while "C" Company took those on the south. "A" and "D" Companies were then to pass through and secure the eastern end of the Astride position. With the hills commanding the road in our hands, it would be possible to pass the 25th Dragoons and the 4th/8th Gurkha Rifles through to capture Buthidaung at first light on the 12th March.

At about 7 a.m., a squadron of Lee tanks reported from the 25th Dragoons.

As company commanders were finishing their orders to their platoon commanders, the bombers came over and gave a fine display of dive bombing, with all bombs in the target area. An hour later, fighters arrived, and straffed the whole area.

About 10 a.m., the enemy observed the Sikh mortars getting into position, and opened artillery and mortar fire on the ridge from behind the Astride position. At this time, both leading companies were moving forward to their assembly positions, and suffered some casualties. Immediate and accurate counter-battery fire was put down, and the enemy fire slackened considerably.

At 10.15 a.m., the artillery began laying smoke-screens on the left flank and in front of the objective, and mortars and medium machine-guns opened fire. The tanks moved forward at the same time, but without interference from enemy artillery fire, thanks to the smoke screen. By 10.30 a.m., tanks and assaulting companies were formed up on the start line ready for the attack.

The corps artillery now opened fire, putting down so concentrated a fire that the attacking infantry had to lie flat on their faces on the start line to avoid splinters from the barrage 500 yards ahead. Two or three were however hit. It must have been a weird and rather horrifying sight, with a background of smoke and dust from the original smoke screen, the furiously bursting shells, and the undergrowth on the objective now a mass of flame. The objective itself and the nearby fields were soon obliterated by drifting clouds of smoke. In all, over 7,000 shells were fired on a front of some 500 yards.

After ten minutes the barrage lifted and the leading companies and tanks advanced. The objective was invisible, but direction was easy to maintain. During the move across the open, the machine-gun overhead covering fire from tanks and machine-guns about West Finger was intense and continuous. The noise was deafening, completely obliterating the noise of the tanks, and even the artillery barrage now falling in rear of the Astride position. The moral effect of this overpowering support, on both our own troops and the enemy, was very great.

Cheering, and shouting "fatehs", the men charged into the enemy trenches, which were abandoned in disorder after slight resistance.

From its objective, "B" Company now saw large bodies of the enemy retreating south in front of Buthidaung. There was an artillery forward observation officer with the company, and he at once brought fire to bear, with good results. Buthidaung was set on fire by shelling, and some ground-straffing half-an-hour later by fighter aircraft was also successful.

By 11 a.m., the first objective was secure. "A" and "B" Companies passed through, and secured their objectives at the eastern end of the ridge unopposed. Ahead, no enemy were encountered and patrols entered Buthidaung without opposition.

The moment seemed ripe to exploit. After clearing a way through anti-tank mines, two platoons moved off at 2 p.m. south-east, to move round on Buthidaung from the south. They moved about 5 miles along the Kanbyin track and then wheeled north-east towards Buthidaung. The enemy, however, had pulled right back, and the Sikhs, riding on tanks, entered the town without seeing any enemy.

Apart from one tank damaged by a mine near Boomerang, a small hill on the northern outskirts of the town, there were no casualties in the move on Buthidaung. One platoon had to stay out to protect the tank during the night, and the remainder rejoined the Battalion, which was firmly established before dark on Astride. The tanks were safely back in Tank Valley.

Thanks to this unexpectedly decisive conclusion to the Sikhs' operation, the Gurkhas were sent forward at once, passing through Astride about 10.50 p.m., and taking up positions securing the southern exits from Buthidaung.

The general situation, however, was still confused. There was constant enemy activity all through the night, and "C" Company, south of the road, encountered numerous parties trying to find a way back through the jungle into their former positions. These attempts to recapture the hill features south of the road were quite unco-ordinated and were not pressed home. Unfortunately, however, Jem. Mehar Singh's platoon, guarding the disabled tank on Boomerang, left the garrison of Astride just too weak for it to be able to occupy India Hill, overlooking the road from the south. A Japanese platoon found its way onto India Hill unobserved, and it became necessary to evict it as soon as it was discovered, on the 12th March morning.

12 Mar.

The 25th Dragoons were passing through the position at the time, and it was essential to clear the enemy away before their transport arrived. "C" Company was ordered to get on with it without loss of time, and Maj. Brough promptly detailed Jem. Mehar Singh's platoon which he met returning from Boomerang as he left Battalion headquarters. India Hill was too close to "C" Company's position to allow artillery or mortars to support the attack, but a Lee tank from the 25th Dragoons was secured to cover the platoon forward.

India Hill is a knife-edged ridge with steep tree-clad slopes. The Japanese were holding deep trenches and fox-holes, well hidden and impossible to spot at any distance. The supporting tank therefore searched the whole area for several minutes while the platoon moved up to the assault, with Naik Nand Singh's section in the lead.

The only possible approach on to the hill followed a narrow track leading up to the enemy position. Along this track Naik Nand Singh led his section. Reaching the crest, the section came under heavy machine-gun and rifle fire, and every man was knocked over, either killed or wounded. None the less, Naik Nand Singh dashed forward alone under intense fire at point blank range. He was wounded by a grenade as he neared the first Japanese trench. Without hesitating he went on, captured the trench, and killed the two occupants with the bayonet.

Not far away was another trench. Under continuous heavy fire, Naik Nand Singh jumped up and charged it. He was again wounded by a grenade and knocked down, but he got up and hurled himself into the trench, again killing both occupants with the bayonet. He moved on again and captured a third trench, still single-handed.

With the capture of this third trench, enemy fire died away. Naik Nand Singh's encounter had taken little time, and the remainder of the platoon, checked for the moment by the sudden heavy fire opened on it as it reached the crest, now moved up and captured the remainder of the position, killing with bayonet and grenade thirty-seven out of the forty Japanese who were holding it.

Naik Nand Singh's part in this brilliant little action, his splendid resolution and utter disregard for his own life, were fittingly recognized by the award of the Victoria Cross.

As a sequel to this, and in recognition of his outstanding leadership and personal courage in the series of operations originating with the attack on Poland on the night of the 6th/7th March, an award of the Distinguished Service Order was made to Maj. John Brough. Further awards included the Indian Order of Merit to No. 23521-IO Jem. Mehar Singh who commanded the leading platoon in the attack on Poland where brilliant leadership and complete disregard for his own safety were largely responsible for its capture. Again, in the attack on India Hill, where Naik Nand Singh won his Victoria Cross, Jem. Mehar Singh, though wounded, led his platoon on with the same disregard for personal safety, with the consequences in enemy loss already described.

Others honoured were No. 20094 L.-Naik Dewa Singh and No. 19903 Sep. Hazara Singh, both awarded the Indian Distinguished Service Medal. L.-Naik Dewa Singh was wounded early in the attack on India Hill, being badly hit in both legs. However, he pulled himself forward on his stomach to a position from which he could give covering fire to his section. He covered them forward, but was then severely wounded by an enemy grenade that burst in front of him and hit him in the face. Nothing daunted, he continued supporting his section till the hill was captured.

Sep. Hazara Singh carried on something of a lone fight in the same action, throwing grenades and finally going in with the bayonet. He was credited with ten enemy killed, and undoubtedly did much to help his section forward to the capture of the remaining four trenches. His award, as with those of all, was typical of the courage and spirit that filled all ranks of the Battalion at all times during the war.

For the next few days the Battalion remained in and about the Buthidaung area. On the 20th March, it was withdrawn and given a protective role in the old Admin Box at the foot of the now famous Ngakyedauk Pass. 20 Mar.

Here nothing happened till the early morning of the 25th when a party of Japanese was reported in the hills overlooking the eastern entrance of the Admin Box. The Battalion was ordered to drive the enemy off, and two platoons of "A" Company and one of "B" were detailed for the task. 25 Mar.

Patrols moved out at 8 a.m. and reported the enemy to be about 100 strong and well dug-in in tunnelled positions. One tank and a few guns were available for support. Three separate attacks were put in and severe casualties inflicted on the enemy, but only two out of the three enemy localities were captured. Many instances of personal gallantry were again displayed. In the second attack for example, Jem. Didar Singh, leading his platoon forward under heavy machine-gun and grenade fire, could be seen time after time running forward and hurling grenades at a Japanese machine-gun post. He was killed in the action, but was awarded posthumously the Indian Order of Merit. Sep. Mohan Singh was with the leading section of the platoon. Light machine-gun fire pinned the section down, but Sep. Mohan Singh crawled forward alone close up to the enemy trenches and threw grenades at the machine-guns holding up his platoon. When his supply of grenades was exhausted he crawled back for a further supply which he took forward to continue his attack on the machine-guns. It was later learned that Sep. Mohan Singh had killed over ten of the enemy single-handed, and his subsequent award of a Military Medal was thoroughly deserved.

The action continued all day, but by night-fall the enemy were still clinging to a few of their bunkers. A platoon of "A" Company was left in occupation of the captured trenches alongside the enemy overnight, but by morning the enemy were gone, leaving some fifty bodies behind.

The next week passed relatively undisturbed, and on the 2nd April the Battalion moved out to the east bank of the Kalapanzin river 2 Apr.

1944

to hold the hill features round Kwazon Ridge, to assist the 114th Indian Infantry Brigade in that area. Maj. Thomas was unfortunately killed by enemy shell fire while taking over a position from the 4th/14th Punjab Regiment.

7-8 Apr. On the night of the 7th/8th April, the Battalion covered the withdrawal of the 114th Indian Infantry Brigade to Awlanbyin, and then itself withdrew northwards to a reserve area on the west bank of the Kalapanzin river opposite Taung Bazar. Here it joined its new formation, the 89th Indian Infantry Brigade.

"D" Company meanwhile had been operating on a detached role in the "Massive" jungle hills, north of the Maungdaw-Buthidaung road, to contain the remnants of the Japanese force still holding out there. There were one or two minor patrol encounters but nothing

10 Apr. more serious, and on the 10th April the Company rejoined the Battalion after handing over to troops of the 26th Indian Division.

In the Taung Bazar area, the Battalion was employed in digging defences and building bamboo huts in readiness for the approaching monsoon, but "B" and "C" Companies held defensive positions on the northern end of Long Ridge and Bogiyaung respectively to cover Taung Bazar itself. Both companies were spasmodically attacked by enemy raiding parties, and harassed by enemy artillery, but all attacks were beaten off with losses to the enemy, while casualties in the Battalion were negligible.

Orders were now issued for the Battalion to return to India to
26 Apr. rest and refit; but on the 26th April, the 89th Indian Infantry Brigade was hurriedly warned for a move to Imphal for temporary attachment to the 5th Indian Division, one of whose three brigades had been cut off in Kohima in the resumed Japanese offensive through Manipur, farther north.

27 Apr. Next day the Battalion moved out of Taung Bazar en route to Bawli Bazar, which was river-head for the forward areas in Arakan. The rifle companies marched over the Goppé Pass while the rest of the Battalion with the baggage, in lorries, went via the Ngakyedauk.

28 Apr. On the 28th, the Battalion, plus its mules, embarked on river craft and sailed up to Tumbru where it arrived in the afternoon. Disembarking and eating their evening meal, the troops left by lorry for Dohazari. After spending the whole night on the road, the convoy pulled into Dohazari at dawn, and the troops settled down in the transit camp, for a three-day rest and all the luxury of an organized camp—greatly welcomed after many months hard-lying. Drill parades were carried out each morning, and the men were in great heart.

2 May On the 2nd May, after holding an "Ardasa" thanksgiving service, the Battalion marched to Dohazari station with pipes playing, and
3 May entrained for Sylhet where it arrived early on the 3rd for the fly-in

to Imphal. The night was spent beside the air-strip, and all preparations made for the next morning's flight.

1944

Early in the morning on the 4th May, aircraft loads were laid out on the edge of the air-field, and the men paraded alongside their loads. The first aircraft took off about 11 a.m. on the uneventful hour's flight to Imphal; and the Battalion, complete with jeeps and baggage, was in its concentration area in a camp of bamboo huts some 12 miles north of Imphal, by 4 p.m. The mules arrived by air a few days later. The motor vehicles other than jeeps moved by road to Dimapur, where they remained until the Kohima-Imphal road was cleared many weeks later.

4 May

Imphal, at this time, was completely cut off otherwise than by air. Two enemy columns had effected this. One, moving up northwards from Burma, had been checked on the roads leading into the Imphal plain by the 20th and 23rd Indian Divisions. The other, which had swung north from the Chindwin, had been somewhat precariously held at Kohima and Kanglatongbi after seizing a considerable stretch of the road north to Kohima.

This, otherwise known as the Manipur road, debouches on to the Imphal plain at Kanglatongbi; and here exchanges its tangle of twists and turns, its hairpin bends and fantastic climbs and drops, for the smooth run-in down the valley of the, in many ways rather lovely, mountain torrent called the Imphal Turel. From here the hills on either side grow lower, and the valley opens out. After his exhausting drive from Dimapur, the driver feels that the worst is behind him, and he is nearly home.

The Japanese were holding the village of Kanglatongbi. Other positions lay along the ridge running away to the east on the other side of the Turel. From the hill-tops, the Japanese could see Imphal, and the goal of their immediate hopes, but, though unaware of it at the time, they had reached their limit, and would get no closer. They were beginning to out-run their supplies. They were getting hungry, for their plan to live on captured British supply dumps had not succeeded. But they were still in good fighting trim and full of determination.

This, then, was to be the scene of the Battalion's next fight.

Facing the enemy positions at Kanglatongbi were Saingmai Hill and Village. Both were held by our troops as forward defended localities—the village by a battalion of the West Yorkshire Regiment, and the hill by the 1st/3rd Gurkha Rifles. Except for the rice-fields on the Imphal plain, almost the whole area is thickly covered with jungle. From the air nothing can be seen of the ground which looks as though covered by a soft green coverlet, lovely to look at as it rolls away to the horizon like a great parsley bed.

6 May

1944

The hills are steep, and intersected by numerous deep nalas. Such few open stretches as occur in the valley are often covered with tall elephant grass studded with scattered trees. With visibility so limited, fighting by day had many of the characteristics of night fighting.

Under these conditions, the Battalion took over the forward positions on Saingmai Hill and in the village, on the 6th May.

The Japanese held Kanglatongbi in strength. Enemy positions had been located all along the ridge-top eastwards from the village, and any large outflanking movement was virtually impossible. It had therefore been decided by the 5th Indian Divisional commander, Maj.-Gen. Briggs, to stage a double-headed operation—clearing the western end of the dominating ridge while simultaneously forcing a way along the road. This would turn the flank of the positions farther to the east, and might force a withdrawal to the hills north of Ekban Ekwan.

The objective assigned to the 89th Indian Infantry Brigade in this attack was the western portion of the ridge, from its western extremity by the neighbouring Turel, as far as the tiny village of Tingsal, some 3 miles east of Kanglatongbi. The 4th/8th Gurkha Rifles would attack the right-half sector and the 2nd King's Own Scottish Borderers the left-half. "A" Company of the Sikhs had a special role, described below; and the Sikhs, less "A" Company,

11 May were in reserve. Orders were issued on the 11th May, but the attack was not timed to start till dawn on the 15th, in order that there might be ample time for full preparations.

"A" Company had a special role in the attack, and not a very easy one. Its task was to work its way through between the enemy forward localities, and seize the ridge between Tingsal and Ekwan behind the enemy's line. Ekwan lay between Kanglatongbi and Tingsal behind about the centre of the Brigade objective, and the operation would place the company astride the track along which all supplies to the enemy's units on the right had to go. Once there, the company had three tasks. The first was to divert Japanese attention from the main attack. The second was to discourage an enemy withdrawal. The third to contact the Gurkhas on the Japanese position. It was a most hazardous venture, for the Company would lie between the Japanese forward and reserve formations, and it would have an exceedingly precarious line of reinforcement or supply. However, this was considered more than outweighed by the advantages success would bring.

12 May Nothing was done till after dark on the 12th May when Sub. Naranjan Singh took out a patrol of three men to reconnoitre a route for "A" Company's advance. A good route was found, but it had the disadvantage

                                                                          1944
that the enemy were found to be holding the only accessible crossing
over the Turel. The patrol did its best to find a way round—but
tall, thick elephant grass is a most exhausting obstacle to force a
way through, especially at night, and it made little progress.

    The Company Commander, Maj. Adams, went out the following   13 May
night to try his luck, but again without success. The company
would have to go out next night, and time was getting short. Day
patrols on the 14th eventually solved the problem. There was an   14 May
enemy position at the road junction just south of Kanglatongbi, and
this, it was found, stretched for only 200 yards east of the road.
That implied a gap between the flank of the position, and the Turel
a little farther to the east. Through this gap it was decided that the
Company must go.

    As night fell the company set out. No mules were taken. Each
man carried two-days cooked food, 200 rounds of ammunition, 2 grenades,
and an entrenching tool. In addition all the Company Bren-guns
were carried, with 750 rounds of ammunition per gun, and 2-inch
mortars with 30 rounds per mortar. Thus, heavily laden and on a
pitch-black night over unreconnoitred country, they set out.

    The jungle was dense. The many small nalas proved formidable
obstacles. It rained hard from 10 p.m. till 2 a.m.—though this may
have been a blessing in some respects. Passing just east of the
Japanese defences at Kanglatongbi, it took the company five full
hours to cover 1,000 yards. It would have been difficult by daylight,
unladen, and with no enemy about. At night in pouring rain, heavily
loaded, and passing within 300 yards of an alert enemy, it was a
notable feat.

    Near Ekban Ekwan, the Company swung right to cross the river.
Here the country opened out and better going was made. At 5.30 a.m.
on the 15th, after a ten-hour march, the Company reached its   15 May
objective unopposed. By 6 a.m. Maj. Adams was talking to Battalion
headquarters on his wireless set, reporting that he was astride the
Japanese supply line and in a strong position.

    The security of the Company's tenure would obviously vary with
the success of the main attack. And this was not immediately
attained. While "A" Company's fighting patrol was making its way
south to distract the enemy and make contact with the Gurkhas,
the Gurkhas were failing to make their objective, and were held up.
The King's Own Scottish Borderers had slightly more success in
that one platoon reached the top of the ridge and seized and held
one of the peaks. But the Japanese forward garrisons were sufficiently
occupied for the moment, and the situation perhaps obscure enough
for them, for "A" Company to be left temporarily undisturbed.

    While the main attack was attempting to make good its objectives,

1944

"A" Company, less its fighting patrol, was feverishly digging itself in. There was no time for rest, for an enemy attack was expected any moment. No barbed wire was available, but the defences otherwise had just been finished at 4.30 p.m., when the first attack came in.

The Japanese came in from the north and east, clearly brought up from reserve formations. Attacks were delivered in furious succession from an infantry gun, several machine-guns and mortars, and many grenade dischargers. All attacks were repelled, but at about 5.30 p.m., the enemy knocked out a Bren-gun and a 2-inch mortar in one of the forward positions, and established themselves there.

Maj. Adams at once called up his reserve platoon and counter-attacked. A tremendous hand-to-hand struggle ensued, and the Japanese were thrown back in disorder, leaving thirty-one dead on the ground. Sikh casualties were thirteen killed and fourteen wounded.

In a struggle such as this, where every man was called on to fight with all the strength and power he could muster, there was neither time nor opportunity to assess every individual act of courage. One exception was No. 21026 Sep. Piara Singh, who rushed forward as soon as the enemy forced their way into the position, as already related, firing his light machine-gun from his hip, and, with Company Hav.-Maj. Sampuran Singh, inflicted serious casualties on the enemy after fierce hand-to-hand fighting. The effect of this onslaught eased matters, and did much towards the eviction of the Japanese from the captured position. Sep. Piara Singh was wounded in the neck by an enemy grenade, but remained at duty until reinforcements arrived next day. His action was worthily remembered in the award of a Military Medal. Company Hav.-Maj. Sampuran Singh was to achieve further distinction—and meet his death—three days later, as will be told in due course.

The counter-attack was over, and the report on it sent in, by 6.15 p.m.—but ammunition was now getting short, and there was no water. A relief party of twenty men, accordingly, under Lieut. Pritam Singh, set out from the Battalion, with ammunition, water, and food in packs, through the pouring wet night. It penetrated the enemy lines but could not get through to the Company. The Company itself had a quiet night.

16 May

Divisional Headquarters took the view that the best plan now would be to exploit the Sikh success. On the 16th morning the remainder of the Battalion prepared to move through the Japanese position, carrying the same scale of arms, ammunition and food as "A" Company had taken, together with additional supplies for that Company. The move was to be made in daylight, but the enemy's

1944

attention would be distracted by the attack of another brigade striking up the main road from the south.

The move began at 11.15 a.m. and was completed without incident just before dark. The Battalion passed at only 200 yards distance from the fighting on the road, but was unseen and unheard in the dense jungle. Even when it came out into the open west of Ekban, and crossed the Turel a few hundred yards from an enemy position, the Japanese took no action other than some ineffective shelling as the Companies pressed up the spurs to their positions.

All night long the Battalion dug itself in without enemy interference, and by morning was firmly entrenched, with patrols and snipers harassing the rear of the enemy forward positions. Maj. Lerwill, the second-in-command, brought up a convoy of mules which was met and escorted by a platoon. The attack up the road had forced the Japanese back for half-a-mile, and this enabled the mules to come farther up the road before taking to the jungle. Supplies of water, a day's cooked rations, additional ammunition, 3-inch mortars and medium machine-guns were all brought up, and "A" Company's wounded taken back. There was no enemy interference although by now a track had been worn through the jungle, and the Battalion's position was known.

17 May

At 7.30 p.m. an "A" Company patrol went south to harass the forward enemy positions, but was back an hour later with a report of sixty Japanese moving up. The Battalion stood to, and almost immediately heavy machine-gun and mortar fire was opened on the "A" Company positions. A few minutes later a determined attack came in from the north, east, and south, with wave after wave of infantry surging up through the trees under practically continuous close-range supporting fire. For more than five hours, from just before 9 p.m. until nearly 2.30 a.m., these attacks were thrown in on the "A" Company trenches, in thick darkness, and with most of the firing at ranges of 2 to 15 yards, but at no point did the Japanese penetrate the position till at 2.30 a.m., when torrential rain fell, a party of Japanese was able to creep up unheard, and over-run one section position, and consolidate. Attempts to enlarge its gains were stopped in a series of hand-to-hand struggles in the dark.

About 4 a.m. the commanding officer went forward to contact Maj. Adams. When he reached Company Headquarters, he found an enemy machine-gun established only 20 yards away, and Maj. Adams and Sub. Gurbachan Singh helping to throw back the Japanese. Though the Company was full of spirit, it was much weakened by casualties. The Japanese, on the other hand, had secured a good footing from which to launch further attacks. It was essential to throw them out before dawn.

18 May

1944

"B" and "C" Companies were entrenched on neighbouring spurs, and each was now ordered to send over a platoon to reinforce "A" Company. It was a most difficult operation, with the fight raging in the intense dark, and tracks made very slippery by the rain. Nevertheless, both platoons arrived safely, bringing reserve ammunition with them.

At 5.30 a.m., a little before dawn, Maj. Adams attacked. The Japanese were thrown off the position and driven down the hill in great disorder by the jubilant Sikhs. A red verey light soared up, and the enemy withdrew on all sides.

Dawn broke, revealing the scene. The stained, trampled undergrowth stank and steamed in the morning sun. The drips splashed monotonously from the trees. Before long, the wounded were being bandaged and hot tea issued, and the Japanese dead counted. There were thirty-seven inside the position, and very many more were afterwards found in the jungle farther down the hill. Quantities of rifles, several grenade dischargers, one light machine-gun and a mass of minor equipment was collected. Two wounded Japanese were captured, and from them and from a patrol which had spent the night out to the north, details of the enemy plan were pieced together. The attack had been made by a full battalion nearly 1,000 strong, from the reserve positions to the north. It had been ordered to take the position at any cost. Its casualties must have been well over 200, together with much irreplaceable ammunition, at a cost to the battalion of nine killed and sixty-six wounded.

In a confused action such as this, it was difficult to note the acts of individual gallantry and devotion that marked the whole operation. However, enough was known to secure an award of a posthumous Indian Order of Merit to Company Hav.-Maj. Sampuran Singh of "A" Company. This devoted non-commissioned officer led the counter-attack on the afternoon of the 15th May, when the Japanese were thrown out of the "A" Company position after a desperate hand-to-hand struggle. Then, throughout the furious battles of the night of the 17th/18th May, he had been continuously at close grips with the enemy in the effort to prevent their making further gains until the reinforcing platoons arrived. At dawn on the 18th, he led the victorious charge, losing his life just as the enemy were finally thrown off the position.

Coupled with Company Hav.-Maj. Sampuran Singh's award came a sheaf of Gallantry Certificates for individual acts of bravery and disregard of danger. These included Jem. Arjan Singh, No. 14391 Hav. Mukand Singh, No. 13659 Hav. Ralla Singh, No. 10914 Hav. Harchand Singh, and No. 16161 L.-Naik Sardara Singh.

Finally, we must record two other honours. It will have been noted

what a leading part was played by Maj. R. J. Adams in these bold
and hazardous operations. For his bravery, leadership, determination,
and coolness throughout, he was very properly awarded a Military
Cross; whilst for special courage in the night attack of the 17th/18th
May, an Indian Distinguished Service Medal was granted to
No. 26306 Sep. Bhag Singh. As Sep. Bhag Singh's part in the battle
must have been so typical of all who strove in the rain and darkness,
a more detailed description of his exploits follows.

Sep. Bhag Singh's section was one that bore the brunt of the
enemy's attacks. Bhag Singh himself was a very junior sepoy; but
when his section commander fell wounded, he took command of the
section on his own initiative, and commanded it with courage and
determination throughout the nine-hour battle. When the forward
section position was over-run, Sep. Bhag Singh at once adjusted
his own position to prevent further enemy inroads; and when
ammunition ran low, he got out into the open and moved about the
bullet-swept area to collect grenades and ammunition from wounded
men. On several occasions, he was seen to run out under heavy
machine-gun fire, from point blank range, and hurl grenades into
the enemy trenches. Then, in the final counter-attack which threw
the enemy out of the position, Sep. Bhag Singh charged out with
his men to close with the enemy. It is small wonder that the Japanese
were handled so roughly, in the face of determination and grit of
this order.

While the Battalion snatched a moment's breathing space, a mule
convoy came up, bringing wire. The wounded were sent down to
ambulances on the main road, and were in hospital near Imphal
soon after mid-day. No further attacks developed, though the
Japanese were still in their forward positions behind the Battalion;
but during the next two days Sikh patrols engaged parties of the
enemy on several occasions, moving behind their position on the
ridge.

On the evening of the 20th May, the Japanese were found to have   20 May
abandoned all their forward positions and withdrawn north of Ekban.
This was the turning point of the Burma campaign, and from this
time the Japanese were on the defensive.

Meanwhile, Gen. Savory, who had brought the news as far as
Brigade Headquarters, of the award of Naik Nand Singh's Victoria
Cross, wrote a few days later to say that Gen. Slim, commanding the
Fourteenth Army, had told him he looked upon the 1st/11th Sikh
Regiment, and the 1st/4th Gurkha Rifles as the two best battalions
under his command.

With the Kanglatongbi position behind it, the 89th Indian Infantry
Brigade now had in front a chain of hills running from south to north

1944

parallel with the road, which they flanked. These hills were named "George", "Harry" and "Isaac". From Isaac, a spur ran down towards the road. This was named "Wigan". The Brigade plan now calling for a northwards push along the road; "D" Company of the Battalion, under Maj. Workman, initiated the move by occupying

21 May George without opposition on the afternoon of the 21st May.

Away on the right flank, along the ridge, a little beyond Tingsal, was an important Japanese position called "Hump". The 9th

22 May Indian Infantry Brigade was to attack this position on the 22nd May. The 3rd/14th Punjab Regiment was detailed for the attack, and one rifle company of the Sikhs was required to co-operate.

The Hump position was exceedingly strong, with deep caves dug into the side of the hill, and it had withstood numerous well-supported attacks during the preceding three weeks. It was thought, however, that if the Sikh Company assaulted from the rear while the 9th Brigade attacked in front, there was a reasonable prospect of success.

"C" Company, under Maj. Spink, was detailed for the operation, but no time was allowed for prior reconnaissance, or even for a visit to the Headquarters of the 3rd/14th Punjab Regiment. The Company, however, was holding a position only a few hundred yards west of the Hump, and two assault platoons were duly detailed.

The morning broke in heavy rain. The steep slopes up towards the objective were very slippery, and the objective itself was obscured in low clouds. Lieut.-Col. Bamford tried to contact the 3rd/14th, but was unable to do so even by wireless. Conditions being so bad, and the plan of attack unco-ordinated, he called up the Headquarters of the 89th Indian Infantry Brigade to ask for a postponement. He was told that the operation was considered too urgent to admit of delay. The Commanding Officer then tried to contact the Commander of the 9th Indian Infantry Brigade, who was responsible for the attack, but was unsuccessful.

"C" Company therefore moved out under Maj. Spink at 9 a.m. and assaulted the position at 10.30 a.m. as ordered. There was no support either from artillery or the air, and the Sikhs as they crawled up the slippery slopes, suffered heavily from numerous machine-guns. One section reached the objective, but could not get at the enemy with the bayonet in their cave-type bunkers. It came under heavy mortar fire. Nearly every man was killed or wounded, and the section was forced to withdraw over the top towards the 9th Brigade.

Over twenty-five casualties were suffered by the Company in this small attack, which could never have been successful without good support even in good weather. What little chance it might have stood was ruled right out by the 9th Indian Infantry Brigade having cancelled the attack at the last moment owing to the state of the weather—a circumstance which was only learnt later on. The lessons of this small action are too obvious to need underlining.

Another regretted loss that day was the Battalion's signal officer, Lieut. Heaney, who had only just joined the Battalion. He was killed by a sniper on his way back from "D" Company, after checking signal communications.

The situation temporarily stabilized at this point, but a plan was under consideration for working wide round the flank of the main Japanese position. With this in view, the Battalion was concentrated in the Ekban area. However, the weather took a hand, and heavy rain which continued without ceasing from the evening of the 25th May till mid-day on the 27th, caused the cancellation of this plan. The next few days were spent patrolling to get more information about the enemy. Plans were then changed, and it was decided to attack the main Japanese position on Isaac with tank and artillery support from the front.

25 May
27 May

The weather cleared up, and by the 30th May it was possible to get the tanks up the slopes towards the enemy position. In the first phase of the attack, the 4th/8th Gurkha Rifles, supported by a troop of tanks of the 3rd Carabineers, assaulted the forward position on Harry. The enemy put up a strong resistance; and it was not until the tanks were right on top of the position that the enemy withdrew to the main position on Isaac.

30 May

By this time it was 2.30 p.m., but it was hoped to keep the Japanese on the run, and the Sikhs were ordered to send a rifle company through the Gurkhas to assault the main position.

Artillery support took some time to arrange, and it was not much short of 5 p.m. by the time this had been done, and the tanks in readiness, to help "C" Company in.

The attack went in and the Japanese were soon thrown back from the southern end of the objective which was captured by "C" Company. Though the attack was quickly over, there had been stiff opposition in which No. 21134 Sep. Sarwan Singh won a Military Medal for single-handed attack on a Japanese light machine-gun, during which he killed five Japanese; whilst a Gallantry Certificate was awarded to No. 24440 Sep. Kaka Singh for an action of similar order, but lesser only in degree. With these is coupled the award of a Military Cross to Maj. E. E. Spink for his outstanding gallantry and fine leadership in the operations on the 22nd and 30th May.

It was now getting dark and rain had begun falling again, and it was decided to hold hard till morning. However, artillery and tank support not ultimately being available, the Company withdrew under cover of darkness. Casualties, not otherwise serious, included Maj. Spink wounded in the attack, and Lieut. Pritam Singh wounded during the

1944 afternoon when the enemy shelled Wigan while the commanding officer was arranging mortar support for the attack. Lieut. Pritam Singh was subsequently awarded the Military Cross for his outstanding gallantry and leadership throughout these operations.

1 June On the 1st June, the 123rd Indian Infantry Brigade took over the forward positions on Wigan and Harry, and the Sikhs moved off on a detached role on the Division's eastern flank.

2 June After a night spent in Imphal, the Battalion started north-east next morning in pouring rain up the Iril valley. A 10-mile march through the mire and mud brought it up to the 3rd/9th Jat Regiment area in the afternoon, and the night was spent in bivouac in the valley south of Wakan.

3 June On the 3rd, positions were taken over from the Jats who were holding hill features on a 10,000 yard front in very mountainous country on the left flank of the Japanese main positions, and blocking the approaches down the Iril valley on Imphal. "A" and "D" Companies were deployed some 3 miles to the north on high hills round Point 4364, to contain the Japanese positions on "Everest", the dominating peak in this stretch of country, while the remainder of the Battalion took up positions round Wakan.

4 June On a visit he paid the Battalion on the 4th June, the Brigade Commander, Brig. Crowther, told the Battalion that it must do everything possible to infiltrate on to the Everest positions. These were exceptionally strong, and held by troops armed with a high proportion of machine-guns. They were beyond our artillery range and could not be taken by direct assault. The 9th Indian Infantry Brigade had several times attacked them with strong artillery support during May, and had paid a heavy price in casualties without any compensating success.

Day and night patrols set to work pin-pointing the Everest positions. All reported the positions strongly held and all confirmed that infiltration would be difficult and costly. However, on the 5th June, a patrol from behind the enemy lines returned with a report on the village of Nurathen, lying on the Japanese supply-line from the north. The village was occupied by enemy troops, and there was much movement there during the night.

Suspecting the presence of a Japanese headquarters in the village, it was decided to substitute a more profitable policy for that of infiltrating on Everest, and to send out a rifle company to raid Nurathen and then establish itself across the enemy supply-line.

6 June At 10 p.m. on the 6th June, "D" Company moved off from Point 4364 under an almost full moon down the steep track to the fields 1,500 feet below. Thence the way led for about 3 miles through marshy country to the village, away to the north.

1944

The move was uneventful till just south of the village when the forward platoon encountered an enemy post at the foot of a spur commanding the approaches to the village itself. The platoon over-ran the post, killing ten Japanese. It was a nicely-contrived little attack. No. 13075 Company Hav.-Maj. Arjan Singh, commanding the forward platoon, brought his men to within a few yards of the Japanese without attracting their attention; and No. 19100 L.-Naik Gurnam Singh with the leading section, pushed the attack home, though himself wounded at the outset. Arjan Singh was also hit, and wounded in the arm, but after the enemy had been driven out with loss, he successfully withdrew his command, under heavy fire from a nearby position, without loss. He was awarded a Military Medal, whilst Gurnam Singh received a Gallantry Certificate.

The enemy, of course, was now thoroughly on the alert, and a surprise raid on the village was no longer feasible. Maj. Workman, accordingly, moved up a hill overlooking the supply-line north of the village, prepared a strong position and sent out harassing patrols. No attack was made on the Company, but there was considerable patrol activity during the next few days, and enemy parties moving in the area were engaged, day and night.

On the 8th June, a patrol went north from "D" Company's position and discovered that the main enemy stronghold in the next line of defences, Point 5417, had been abandoned. It occupied the position and sent back immediate information to the Company. Meanwhile, the Japanese garrison which had gone back to a nearby village for food, without leaving a guard, began filtering back. The patrol was only four men strong—for the platoon which had been sent out by "D" Company on receipt of the news had not yet arrived—but it engaged the enemy, inflicted casualties, and made them withdraw. Several minutes later, it was attacked by about sixty Japanese, whom it held off for nearly twenty minutes. The leading troops of the reinforcing platoon were just too late, for the patrol had run out of ammunition and nearly been over-run, and was obliged to give way. The platoon tried to retake the position, but it had itself been re-inforced. Several casualties were sustained, including Maj. Workman and Sub. Bishan Singh, both wounded, and as it was found that the Sikhs were opposed by superior numbers, the troops were withdrawn to the Company position. However, the sobering effects on the enemy of this unexpected action together with the casualties inflicted were a compensating reflection to the company.

8 June

Needless to say, this rather frustrating little action had its highlights; and on this occasion it was No. 23842 Sep. Nazar Singh who achieved distinction.

1944

Nazar Singh, moving forward in the reinforcing platoon, saw that the patrol was surrounded, and without the least thought for the consequences dashed forward with his light machine-gun, under heavy fire, and engaged the enemy. He personally killed a considerable number of the enemy. More important still, the enemy were so disconcerted by this berserk charge that the patrol, which was now out of ammunition, was able to withdraw. In the alternative, it would almost certainly have been over-run, and the award of a Military Medal to Sep. Nazar Singh was a more than well-earned one.

While this action was proceeding, patrols had been into Nurathen village. No signs of a headquarters were found, but it was thought the village might have been being used as a staging point. This facility had been denied them by "D" Company; and as no attempts were made to eject the Company from its position, it was assumed that the enemy lacked reserves in this area.

11 June
12 June
On the 11th June, increased activity was noted in the enemy rear areas. On the 12th, a patrol reported that the Everest positions had been abandoned. "C" Company, under Maj. Redding, at once occupied them. This was the second time that the Japanese had pulled back out of strong positions after infiltration into their rear areas, since the Battalion reached the Imphal theatre.

The monsoon now began to take an increasing hand in the day-to-day administration of the troops. Heavy rain made the jeep tracks impassible, and the Battalion had become dependent on mule supply.

14 June
By the 14th June this, too, had had to be abandoned, and air-supply was substituted.

Patrol movement, however, continued unabated, and a practicable route round the enemy's left flank was found. To take advantage of this, Battalion Headquarters with "A" and "D" Companies, moved forward some 10 miles slightly east of north from Wakan, on the

22 June
22nd June, to Aishan. Aishan lay on the enemy supply-line between Kangpopki, on the Manipur road, and the main base at Ukhrul, about 30 miles due east of Kangpopki. The march was uneventful, and a period of a few fine days enabled the men to take up and prepare a strong position just east of Aishan village.

Lack of immediate Japanese reaction can be traced to their receding fortunes elsewhere. On the day the troops marched out to Aishan, troops from the 2nd British Division which had been fighting its way through appalling country south from Kohima, joined hands with the 5th Indian Division, and the siege of Imphal was at long last lifted.

23 June
Though no immediate interference was experienced, the Battalion did not dig its strong position at Aisham undisturbed. On the 23rd June, an "A" Company patrol encountered a strong enemy party moving east, and the patrol was forced to withdraw. The Japanese

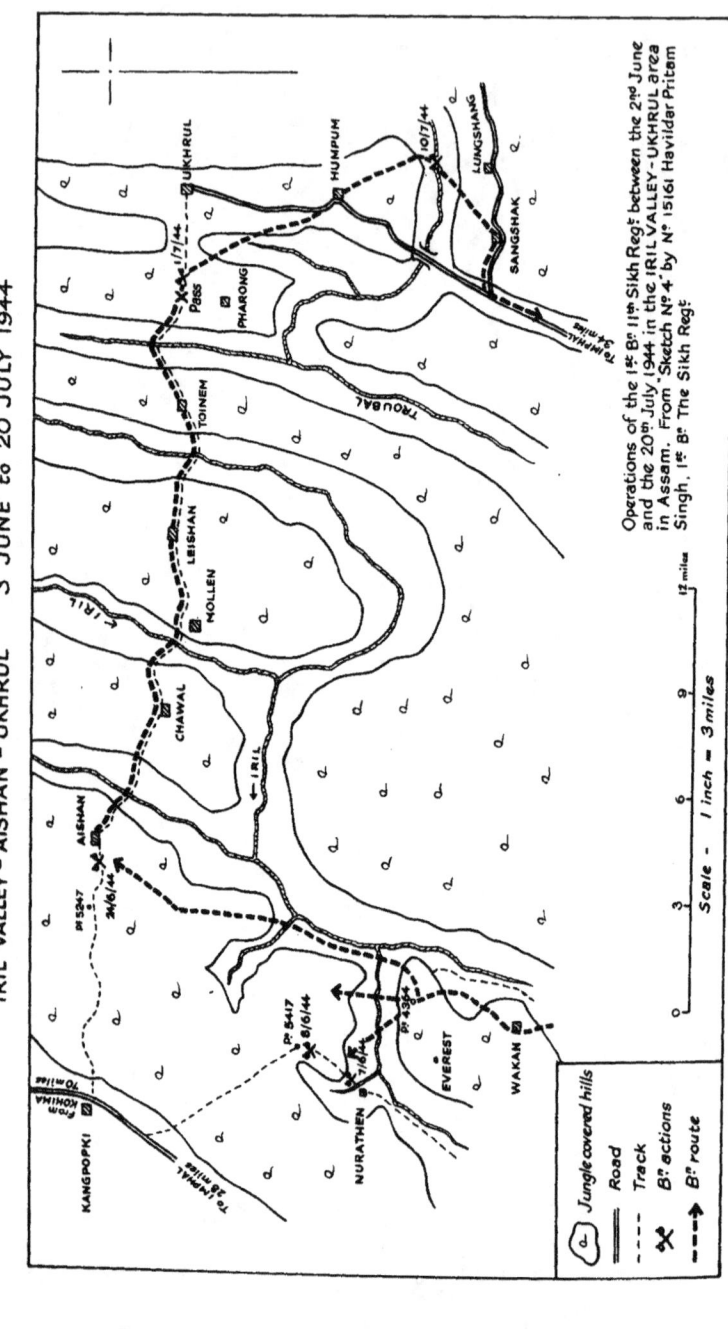

1944

were full of fight and followed up till they unexpectedly bumped into "D" Company's forward platoon. Several attempts were made to force the Sikhs back, but were repulsed each time with loss. The enemy then moved round to the high ground some 400 yards to the west, across the Sikhs' supply-line—thus cutting off the Sikhs who were themselves cutting off the Japanese. Next morning, "C" Company, moving forward to Aishan, was held up by them; and that night, the Japanese, now reckoned at about 300 strong with some guns and machine-guns, made a few half-hearted attempts to throw the Battalion back. These failing, with casualties to the Japanese, they broke up into small parties and made off to the north, where another, and much more difficult, line of withdrawal existed. The Battalion lost one man killed and four wounded in this action, but nine mules were killed by Japanese machine-gun fire during the night attack.

24 June

In a necessarily general record such as this, it is not possible to notice every little action; and yet, in the sum, these small affairs were productive of much that was inspiring and courageous.

It was for the less conspicuous actions of this kind that certain awards were made at this time. These included a Military Cross granted to No. 9019-IO Sub. Isher Singh, whose "steadfastness and leadership," so the citation runs, "have maintained the morale, determination and fighting spirit of his men throughout a long and arduous campaign...".

"He has been wounded," so the record goes on, "in four separate actions and each time he refused to go back to have his wounds dressed until the end of the action, and all other casualties had been evacuated to safety. On one occasion, during a Japanese attack on his company, Sub. Ishar Singh crawled round under heavy fire to each platoon to give them encouragement...".

Surely words like these should be written up in letters of brass.

Next comes No. 14011 L.-Naik Bachint Singh, who received a Military Medal, for consistently carrying out "excellent work in face of the enemy. His cheerfulness under trying conditions and his determination have been a constant inspiration to those around him. In particular, on the 18th June, L.-Naik Bachint Singh, on patrol, gained valuable information concerning an enemy post." A platoon was sent off to destroy the post, and "L.-Naik Bachint Singh led a section in this raid with great dash and drive and assisted in completely routing the enemy holding the post. Again, on 23 June, at Aishan, L.-Naik Bachint Singh displayed courage of a very high order when his platoon bore the brunt of a Japanese attack...".

Finally, No. 22699 L.-Naik Bhag Singh, awarded the Military Medal for a series of most hazardous patrols behind the enemy lines. All honour to L.-Naik Bhag Singh, and all good soldiers of his kind.

1944

By the end of June, the Japanese offensive had not only been effectively stopped; their main forces had been defeated on all sectors of the Imphal front, and were withdrawing back towards the Burma border.

The monsoon had set in and the troops in the forward areas were fighting in appalling conditions. In previous years, the break of the monsoon had automatically brought operations to a standstill, but not so in 1944.

The unmetalled roads and tracks became almost impassable for lorries and trucks. Jeep- or mule-supply at any distance from the main roads was out of the question. So air-supply became the accepted means of keeping operations mobile. This, in the monsoon, set the Royal Air Force some complex problems, but commitments were punctually fulfilled, except under dire difficulty.

In accordance then with the general policy of keeping mobile in despite of the weather, the 23rd Indian Division pressed on down the Tamu road across the hills south-east from Imphal, and the 5th Indian Division switched over to the southern front to pursue the retreating Japanese south down the road to Tiddim. The only Japanese still holding out were those facing the 20th Indian Division about 20 miles up the road leading from Imphal to Ukhrul. This enemy force held grimly to its positions to cover the withdrawal of the remaining Japanese forces in the north.

As soon as the Manipur road was open, the 89th Indian Infantry Brigade had reverted to command of the 7th Indian Division, which had been given the task of pursuing the Japanese retreating from the north through Ukhrul. The 33rd Indian Infantry Brigade was already on its way south towards Ukhrul. The 89th Indian Infantry Brigade was now directed cross-country on the same objective, and on to Sangshak. This move would, with luck, not only cut off the enemy bodies withdrawing from the Manipur road. It would also threaten the rear of those farther south facing the 20th Indian Division.

The 89th Indian Infantry Brigade was therefore to move, with animal transport and much reduced baggage, along a track from Kangpopki, which ran through Aishan, Chawal, Mollen, Leishan and Toinem. Two days' rations were to be carried, and an air-drop was being arranged for every second day.

1 July The first day's objective for the Battalion was to seize the pass 3 miles short of Ukhrul, and if possible push on to Ukhrul itself. Setting off at first light that morning, the 1st July, "B" Company, under Sub. Indar Singh, was in the lead. By mid-day the Company was in the ravine leading to the top of the pass, and had met no opposition. However, towards the far end of the ravine, the leading scouts were suddenly engaged by a Japanese post astride the track.

One small post, the Company surprised and over-ran, but the enemy holding the pass could not be dislodged. The jungle was very thick in this area and it was quite impossible to ascertain on the spot the extent of the enemy positions or the lie of the ground.

Time was passing, and the pass had, if possible, to be captured before dusk. High ground lay to the north and to the south of the Pass, and "A" Company was now directed against the former, and "D", under Sub. Hazara Singh, against the latter. Both companies experienced great difficulty in moving through the thick jungle and up the steep slopes in the pouring rain, but reached their objectives without opposition. Patrols moving inwards confirmed that some eighty of the enemy were holding a position covering a track junction on the pass. But as it was now nearly dark, positions held were consolidated while fighting patrols went out to cut the enemy line of withdrawal to Ukhrul.

Rain poured down, and the men spent a wretched enough night in the open. Patrols met no opposition at the eastern end of the pass, but they confirmed that the enemy were still in position covering the track junction at daylight. Arrangements were being made to move round and attack the position in rear—from the east—when a Japanese party from farther south attacked "D" Company, in order to cover the withdrawal of the party in the pass. The attack made no progress, but the enemy soon withdrew to Ukhrul. "C" Company followed up at once and seized the pass.

2 July

At 11 a.m., Brigade Headquarters and the 4th/8th Gurkha Rifles reached the top of the pass. A good view was to be had of Ukhrul and the country in between, and the Brigadier decided to form a base with the Sikhs, Brigade Headquarters and the mountain battery astride the pass, while the Gurkhas moved on to Ukhrul.

Meanwhile, the air-drop for the Brigade did not materialize. There was rain and heavy cloud in the Troubal valley so that the supply aircraft could not fly in low, up the valley.

At first light on the 3rd July, the Gurkhas moved forward, surprising the enemy and capturing the north-east corner of Ukhrul. The Japanese were strongly entrenched about the old fort in the southern part of the town, and at a track junction farther north, and the Gurkhas could make no progress.

3 July

Aircraft were unable again to drop supplies owing to cloud. Rations were almost exhausted and everyone was getting very hungry.

Next day, the King's Own Scottish Borderers edged their way round the southern outskirts of the town, but were held up by small posts in and around the fort. Two battalions were thus now committed in Ukhrul, while the Sikhs had to remain on the pass to protect Brigade Headquarters, the guns and the field ambulance. The

4 July

1944

need for a whole battalion to be retained for this was explained by a report from the 33rd Indian Infantry Brigade that 400 Japanese were on their way south from Ngainu, which lay a little north of the pass.

The weather remained appalling. No air-drop was possible, and rations were exhausted.

5 July On the 5th, the weather cleared at last, and, to the general relief, supplies came through in the afternoon.

During the next few days the Gurkhas and the King's Own Scottish Borderers made further efforts to find a way round the Japanese positions, but without success. Sikh patrols moving back north from the pass ambushed several small parties of Japanese making

6 July their way south. On the 6th July, the Japanese brought up some artillery south of Ukhrul and for two days intermittently shelled Brigade Headquarters and the Battalion, but inflicted very few casualties.

8 July On the 8th, the Japanese used an artillery screen against the Gurkhas to cover the withdrawal of their forces north of the town. The Gurkhas pushed ahead at once, and, about noon, contacted the 33rd Indian Infantry Brigade. During the afternoon, enemy rearguards withdrew from the fort area, covered by the artillery. The Gurkhas then took over the town.

9 July The Sikhs took over the lead next day, moving off before dawn cross-country. The first objective, Humpum village, 5 miles south of Ukhrul on the Imphal road was reported clear. The Battalion was then directed on a further 4 or 5 miles to Sangshak. A few Japanese stragglers were met but no organized resistance. However the Battalion did not reach Sangshak on the 9th. Moving cross-country east of the road, it bivouacked a few miles on from Humpum, and about an equal distance from Shagshak which now lay to the south-west.

10 July On the 10th, the Battalion was away early again, and ran into an enemy rearguard covering the river bridge in the valley south of Sangshak. "A" Company's leading platoon was held up, but a second platoon, crossing the river with some difficulty farther west, attacked the Japanese in rear, killed six, and obliged the rest to make off to the east. Pushing on, the way passed through a very strong Japanese position on the col between Sangshak and Semshang. The position had only recently been abandoned by the enemy, and six 105-m.m. guns, a 4-inch mortar, twelve lorries and much minor equipment were found there. A number of stragglers were picked up. The area took a long time to search, and the Battalion did not reach Sangshak till after dark. The leading company was engaged as it entered the village, but the Japanese withdrew after only slight resistance.

  1944

 At Sangshak a few months earlier, a parachute battalion had
borne the brunt of the Japanese offensive, and there had been bitter
fighting. The village had been burnt and was in ruins, and was in a
distressingly foul state, as the Japanese had made no attempt to
bury the dead or dispose of abandoned equipment. It was an
uncomfortable night for the Battalion among the ruins and filth, and
the men had their time well filled clearing the area next day.   11 July

 Patrols sent down the Imphal road reported the Japanese withdrawn, and the way to Imphal clear. Till the 19th July, however, the
Battalion was concentrated in Sangshak, patrolling far and wide but
encountering no formed body of the Japanese.

 On the 14th, Gen. Messervy opened an advanced Divisional   14 July
Headquarters in Sangshak, and spent three days there. This brought
a good deal of pleasure to the men, who fully appreciated his
presence in the forward area so soon after the road was cleared.
But there was a blow in store for the Battalion too. Scrub typhus,
one of the scourges of the Burma campaign, struck the Battalion in
Sangshak. Maj. Adams and twelve men contracted it; and though
they were taken straight to hospital in Imphal, and every effort made
by the doctors and special nurses, Maj. Adams and eight of the men
died. It is pleasant to know that Maj. Adams had the news a few
days before he died of the award of a Military Cross for his devotion
and courage in the Ekban battle.

 On the 19th July, troops from the 2nd British Division began to arrive, 19 July
taking over from the 89th Indian Infantry Brigade, which was to have a
rest. On the 20th, the Battalion did a 21-mile march, spending the night   20 July
at the 18th milestone from Imphal. The road was ankle-deep in mud, and
the men had a very tiring march. After resting a couple of days, the
Battalion moved off by motor transport to its rest area in Kohima.   23 July

 In Kohima, the Brigade settled down into a delightful area some
5 miles out of the town. The Battalion had a tented camp, and was
able to make itself comfortable for the first time for many months.
Morale was at its highest; but the prolonged and continuous operations,
often on short rations, had left many of the men physically debilitated
and there was much diarrhoea.

 Soon after reaching Kohima, two large parties went off on a
month's leave. About the same time a draft of 200 men arrived from
the 15th Battalion, which was being disbanded. The climate was
bracing, rations excellent, and new clothing and equipment were
speedily made available. On the 8th August, Gen. Sir George Giffard,   8 Aug.
commanding-in-chief the 11th Army Group, visited the Battalion and
congratulated the men on the fine part they had played in the recent
operations. All was now set for the resumption of battalion training,
tentatively fixed for the coming October.

1944

2nd Bn. *The 2nd Battalion*, in Haifa, was warned, at the end of April, to be ready to move over to Italy. The journey was made via Egypt;

May and, early in May, while being re-equipped, the Battalion had the distinction of a visit from the late Maharaj Kumar Amarjit Singh of Kapurthala.

9 June Nothing of event marked the journey to Italy; and by the 9th June, the Battalion had completed its concentration by road and rail at Lanciano on the east coast, where it joined the 4th Indian Division in the line.

16 June On the 16th June, the Division came out of the line and was withdrawn to Campo Basso, 50 miles north of Naples, to re-organize briefly after its bloody share in the battles for Cassino, and the subsequent pursuit, after the later break-through, up the Adriatic coast. Intensive training in mountain warfare on a M.T., mule and man-pack basis followed. During this period, the Battalion was

19 June posted on the 19th June to the 7th Indian Infantry Brigade in place of the 4th/16th Punjab Regiment. The circumstance that it was in the 7th Indian Infantry Brigade that the 4th Battalion of the Regiment had made such a name for itself in the Western Desert, was looked on as a happy omen.

During the first days of July, the Division moved forward; and on

4 July the 4th the Battalion was in action for the first time in Italy, against German troops, near Umbertide in the Mouro valley, some 120 miles NW of Lanciano. Stiff advanced guard fighting took place, and the Battalion was unfortunate in sustaining relatively heavy casualties before the end of the month. These included the loss, in circumstances of great gallantry, of No. 18667 Sep. Kartar Singh of "A" Company,

12 July who fell on the 12th July.

On that day, "A" Company attacked Mt. Pagliaiolo through a storm of artillery, machine-gun and mortar fire which bore especially heavily on the left platoon, to which Sep. Kartar Singh belonged.

When his section-commander fell severely wounded, Kartar Singh took over command of the section, and led it forward under heavy rifle and light machine-gun fire, with notable coolness and sang-froid. Coming under the fire of a German light machine-gun concealed in scrub thirty yards to his flank, Kartar Singh himself silenced the gun and killed two of its crew with hand grenades, while the section, on his orders, continued its advance.

Arriving on the crest of Mt. Pagliaiolo, the platoon now came under heavy and accurate small arms and mortar fire from the reverse slope. Kartar Singh, firing his tommy gun as he went, advanced straight towards the nearest enemy post, from which four of the enemy fled, leaving their light machine-gun on the ground. Though severely wounded at this stage, in the leg, Kartar Singh took charge of the

1944

abandoned light machine-gun, reloaded it, and moved straight ahead to a third enemy machine-gun post, which he silenced, killing three of the enemy as he charged down on it. He was killed a few minutes later while calling on his comrades to take over the ground he had gained.

For a sepoy in his first action against German troops, no greater leadership and courage could have been shewn. The posthumous award of the Indian Order of Merit testified the Battalion's acknowledgement of his heroism and self-sacrifice.

Sep. Kartar Singh was not alone in disregard of danger and its consequences. No. 13159 Hav. Dall Singh commanded the left flank section of the same platoon, and was held up by the fire of two enemy light machine-guns concealed in the scrub 150 to 200 yards to his left. He immediately organized a section attack, silenced and captured the two guns, and killed the five Germans manning them, at their posts, with the bayonet.

A few days later, on the 20th, Hav. Dall Singh achieved fresh laurels when leading a day patrol in the vicinity of Mt. Pirano. Here he located a party of enemy about twenty-five strong, armed with an 81 m.m. mortar mounted in a half-tracked carrier, and three light machine-guns, on the edge of a ravine. The nearest enemy elements were lying up in the scrub only twenty yards to his flank.

20 July

With his little party of five or six men, Hav. Dall Singh charged in at once, hurling grenades, and firing tommy guns and rifles, completely routing the whole enemy party, which out-numbered his by at least four to one, capturing the mortar and carrier, killing five of the enemy outright, and wounding others. The patrol suffered no casualties at all.

For this exploit, coupled with the action of the 12th, Hav. Dall Singh received the Indian Distinguished Service Medal.

Returning to the action against Mt. Pagliaiolo on the 12th—after "A" Company had captured the hill—"C" Company passed through it, with orders to attack and capture Mt. Favalto. In this operation, two sepoys—No. 19772 Sep. Harbans Singh, and No. 22306 Sep. Maghar Singh—both achieved Military Medals for outstanding gallantry and determination.

12 July

Sep. Harbans Singh was wounded severely in the shoulder by the very heavy mortar and small arms fire through which the Company had to pass, and both No. 1 and No. 2 of the Bren Group of his section—No. 7—were killed. Harbans Singh picked up the Bren-gun, collected magazines from his fallen comrades, and called on those around to continue their advance.

Three separate times thereafter, though in great pain from his wound, Harbans Singh accurately directed the fire of his gun onto enemy positions, and silenced them, enabling the advance to be continued.

1944

Though bleeding profusely from the wound in his shoulder, and pressed to do so, he refused to be evacuated to the Regimental Aid Post until his position on Mt. Favalto had been fully consolidated. He then set out unaccompanied for the Regimental Aid Post, collapsing on the way from weakness and loss of blood. One is glad to know that he survived to receive his well-deserved honour.

"C" Company, meanwhile, had attacked a feature from which enemy small arms and mortar fire were being directed against our main position on Mt. Pagliaiolo. After a severe struggle the enemy were driven off; but after some seven or eight casualties had been inflicted on the platoon which had carried out the actual operation, it was directed to withdraw on the main position. This it did—but on arrival it was found that one man, known to have been severely wounded, had been left on the forward feature.

No. 22306 Sep. Maghar Singh at once volunteered to get him in. Starting off on the return over the 800 yards of bullet-swept ground, under full enemy view, accurate fire was quickly opened on him from light machine-guns and mortars, the dust and smoke from which several times obscured him from view.

The wounded man was lying out in the open, and within enemy view, but Sep. Maghar Singh coolly re-adjusted his dressings, under fire, and returned the way he had gone, carrying the wounded man safely back. It is difficult to find words adequate to acts of heroism of this nature, but their cumulative effect on the already high spirit of the Battalion need no emphasis.

25 July On the 25th July, "B" Company was concerned in a gallant little action, when its commander, Maj. J. L. Key, who had only rejoined the previous day after recovering from a painful wound received on the 11th, led it forward from Mt. Variano to capture Le Ville village. Both the route to the village, and the village itself, were strongly held by the enemy, and the Company's advance was firmly resisted.

The Company, however, worked its way resolutely forward. Maj. Key himself led the attack on two separate houses on the route, entering them at the point of the revolver, and destroying by grenade and revolver fire the Spandau posts holding up the advance. In the first house, three of the enemy were killed out-right, and in the second a further five were killed and two light machine-guns captured.

In this and other actions, the Battalion gave a good account of itself, but it had suffered some seventy casualties by the time it went into rest in the last days of July at Arezzo in Central Italy. These casualties included one or two key men, and four experienced officers, three of whom were company commanders. Of these, Sandy Smith had run his jeep over a cliff-side in the dark. Keene, Masterton and Evans had been wounded—the latter two seriously.

1944
August

Early in August, the Division was in contact with strong enemy forces in the hills north of Arezzo. The country much favoured the defence, and gave the Germans excellent scope for observation, and good fields of fire to suit the high proportion of automatic weapons they usually carried. The hills were high and craggy, and the almost complete absence of roads in the area much cramped manoeuvre in the attack.

Defensive positions were generally screened by a net-work of light machine-guns—Spandaus. Manned as a rule by two men only, and with large dumps of reserve ammunition beside them, these proved extremely difficult to locate and knock out.

Behind this screen, vital areas were usually covered by exceptionally heavy artillery and mortar concentrations, often kept up for several days at a time. When leaving a position, the enemy always did so by night, and the withdrawal was carried well back to the next line.

On the 6th August, "B" Company, under Maj. Key, moved forward to protect the advance of two troops of tanks detailed to clear the road from Castiglion to Talla which was known to be held by the enemy.

6 Aug.

Maj. Key led his Company forward with great gallantry along the Bassagno ridge under heavy mortar and shell fire, to a point overlooking Talla. From here the Company came under closely observed and intense enemy mortar and machine-gun fire from several directions at once. When a little short of the village, a track of the leading tank was blown off by enemy mines laid on the road. The narrow approach was completely blocked for the remainder, and further advance was impossible. The Company dug in.

Though wounded in the arm by a shell splinter and bleeding profusely from his wound, Maj. Key refused to be attended to, and with great calmness located in turn enemy centres of resistance and directed the fire of his own mortars and machine-guns on them. For two hours he moved over exposed ground, encouraging his Company and showing complete contempt for enemy fire, much of which was directed against himself. When ordered to break off contact and move back, he withdrew his men without disorder or confusion, and was himself the last to walk from the enemy's view.

For his skilful and courageous handling of the Company, his presence of mind, and complete personal disregard of heavy enemy fire, this officer was awarded a well-earned Military Cross.

While this action was proceeding, "D" Company, under Maj. D. Farr, and "C" Company, under Maj. D. D. Pim, had come up to either side to extend the front. Here the Battalion was held for the next few days, but during this time valuable experience was obtained by active patrolling.

1944

10-11 Aug. During the night of the 10th/11th August, in heavy rain, the Brigade handed over to other troops, including Lovat's Scouts, whom the Battalion met for the first time. Operations were in prospect up the Adriatic coast against the Gothic Line, and re-grouping on a large scale was being carried out.

3-18 Aug. As part of this re-grouping, the 4th Indian Division concentrated between the 13th and 18th August forward of Ancona and not far from the Adriatic. The Eighth Army was to undertake an offensive against the Gothic Line from Rimini due west to Tavaletto, and the 4th Indian Division was located on the left flank of the offensive.

25 Aug. This large re-grouping was effected without the enemy's knowledge; and on the 25th August, the Battalion had the privilege of opening the innings for the Division.

It may not be out of place to quote here from the story of the 4th Indian Division, published under the title *Red Eagles*, under the authority of the Director of Public Relations, War Department, Government of India, shortly after the war. Describing the preliminary moves before the main operation, and the opening phases of the operation itself, it throws a light on the activities of the 2nd Battalion at this time. "On August 23rd," the account begins, "4 Ind Div began to move into position for that attack (i.e. on the Gothic Line) by concentrating behind a screen of Italian troops near Fossato, on the eastern slopes of the High Appenines. Here the enemy thinly covered his main Gothic Line position thirty miles ahead. 5th Brigade led a brilliant movement conducted at great speed, which in four days carried the Divisional front up to the hinge of the main Gothic Line position in front of Urpino and provided flank protection for the projected Eighth Army attack. In this advance 2/11th Sikhs marched 36 hours with only six hours halt, outdistancing their supplies and living on tomatoes and corn cobs from the fields. This rapid advance brought the Indian troops into the battle zone ahead of the German reserves, and enabled them to secure dominating ridges for their start line in the great Eighth Army assault, which began on the morning of August 31st."

It might be supposed from the above brief sketch that the advance to the start line for the main assault was conducted without enemy interference. This was not, however, the case where the Battalion was concerned.

When the Battalion led the way forward on the 25th August, it found the road had been blown-up and mined. Repairs to make it serviceable for units and formations in rear were taken in hand by the sappers, but the Battalion meanwhile moved out over the lofty hills to Cagli. Here all available jeeps were brigaded for a shuttle service up the rough mountain track, to speed up the Battalion's advan

1944

Cagli was secured unopposed. The road thence lay straight ahead for 5,000 metres—a little over 3 miles—to the large village of Aqualagna, understood to be held by an Italian irregular group operating under Allied Command.

Aqualagna lay in a bowl with lofty hills on three sides. It was known that these hills were held by German rearguards.

The advance to the village was carried out on a two-company front, astride the road. As the troops closed up to the outskirts, heavy artillery and mortar fire was opened from the German positions on the hills. At the same time, Italian small-arms fire broke out on the Battalion from the village itself.

Whether these so-called "loyal" Italians inflicted any loss on the Battalion is not shown, but they were firing with light automatics at about thirty yards range—maintaining, later, that they mistook our Sikhs for Germans.

The village had to be cleared, but for the 3½ hours still remaining before nightfall, very heavy shelling continued from the German positions, and serious casualties were caused. These included Maj. J. L. Key, commanding "B" Company, killed, together with all three platoon commanders, and Maj. D. Farr, commanding "D" Company wounded. In Key, the Battalion sustained the loss of a most gallant and capable officer; and the deeper sympathy was felt for his parents in that his father, Maj.-Gen. B. W. Key, who had already commanded the Battalion in the years immediately before the war, was a prisoner-of-war with the Japanese.

In the advance, the men had moved exceptionally well, and the speed of the Battalion's operations on this day undoubtedly caused the enemy to pull out prematurely from a strong position. The congratulations of the commander of the Vth Corps showed that the Battalion's sacrifices had not been in vain. Equally sincere congratulations were received from the divisional commander.

That night the Germans withdrew, and on the 26th August, the Battalion, still in the lead, moved on to the town of Fermignano, and secured the river crossing there. Other troops then passed through for the capture of the town itself.

25-26 Aug.

After a few days in reserve beneath the walls of the lovely university and cathedral town of Urbino, the Battalion moved on to play its part in the battle for the Gothic Line, an account of which will be found in the next chapter.

Meanwhile Lieut.-Col. A. E. Farwell, O.B.E., had handed over Command to Lieut.-Col. R. A. d'E. Ashe, in April, at Haifa, on appointment to command of the Jullundur Area; and Lieut.-Col. Ashe handed over to Lieut.-Col. P. S. Mitcheson, formerly of the 4th Battalion, at the beginning of August, on transfer to command of H.Q. Allied P.W. Repatriation Unit in Italy.

1944

3rd Bn.
March

May

The 3rd Battalion left Teheran early in March, and concentrated at Qum. From here, it moved on to a brigade camp at Tureh, about 120 miles away. The march to Tureh took seven days, and seems to have been pleasant enough after the first day which was hot. The troops reached Tureh well hardened and thoroughly fit, as well as pleased to be missing the blizzards and rain-storms which are the rule in the Persian uplands during March and April. Of the camp itself no special record remains except for the much welcomed visit of Lieut.-Col. Amarjit Singh, Maharaj Kumar of Kapurthala. Col. Amarjit Singh was paying visits to various fronts, and he had expressly travelled up to Persia in order to be able to report personally on the 3rd Battalion to His Highness the Maharajah of Kapurthala, its Honorary Colonel. A large guest-night was held in his honour in the mess, with two or three representatives from all units in the Brigade. A special foraging party had been sent to Teheran for delicacies to grace the table, and Blatchford and Forsyth returned well laden with caviar, strawberries, hams, nougat and other sweets, and wine, while James and Millachip went up into the nearby hills and collected snow and ice. The Workshops lent their portable hanger, which was lined with streamers of yellow, red and white made up from the mens' safas; and, with concealed lighting, the effect was, as the Battalion *News Letter* says, truly viceregal.

It is with regret that one must add that this was the last time the Battalion was to see this good friend, for he died soon after his return to India.

May drew on, and with it came the beginning of a move down to the torrid lowlands of Iraq. "C" Company went off first, leaving for Mosul by M.T., and taking with it a terminal of the Brigade signal section. A pack wireless set was carried, and good communication kept up over no less a distance ultimately than 500 miles. Arrived in Mosul, the detachment found itself alone, except for Col. Kinch, the Political Agent. It was a very different Mosul from the busy centre the Battalion had seen in 1941; and nowhere can the ebb of the war have been more apparent in 1944. Formerly, three infantry divisions had been spread over the countryside in a mass of camps, but now the whole vast area was under the plough. The literally hundreds of miles of anti-tank ditch which the Battalion had then helped to dig, now served a less passive purpose, in affording landholders a profitable source of compensation. Pill-boxes had created a market of their own. They were selling by the hundred at £10 each- but whether with an eye to the housing shortage or the more satisfactory conduct of family feuds, was uncertain.

Mosul had its pleasanter side in affording relaxation for the detachment, beating the islands of the Tigris and the Little Zab, for pig. On one unforgettable day, the detachment commander scored seven in rapid succession as they bolted across a stream in single file. What the Cawnpore Tent Club might have said to this is not in question; but that the detachment was catholic in its views on live-stock is shown by its possession of two brown bear cubs captured in the Kurdish hills.

In mid-June, the Battalion moved down by road for a six-weeks stay in Kirkuk. "D" Company took over a detachment post 5 miles out, guarding the oil installations of the Iraq Petroleum Company, where the oil underwent its first process of de-gassing and crude refinement before being pumped away on its 500-mile journey across the desert to Haifa and Tripoli. *(June, 1944 — margin)*

The anti-tank platoon took over another detachment some 20 miles away at Dibis, where a "Blondin-style" tight-rope ferry spans the river. Here, there was an old fort on a small hill overlooking the camp, and this the Battalion converted into a canteen and recreation room. A local leave camp was organized on the river bank, and small parties were sent here from the Battalion for a spell away from the heavy duties in Kirkuk.

Towards the end of June, three officers and twenty ranks enjoyed a pleasant busman's holiday in the mountain warfare school at Laq Louc, 6,000 feet up, in the Lebanon. Though it is on the record that the party entered into the strenuous training of the school with all a Sikh's normal hearty enthusiasm, the lighter side of life was not passed by, and the record contains a note of the burning of the hashish crop of the local bishop, and other divertissements.

At the beginning of August, the Battalion was under orders to return its guns to Ordnance, disband its anti-tank platoon and thereby rid itself of an exceptionally efficient body of specialists, and return to Baghdad. Here, heavy duties, with less than one night in bed, became its lot. There were, however, comfortable barracks. The days were roasting hot, but nights comparatively cool. Still better, there was a short but pleasant break in prospect, which will be dealt with in the next chapter. *(August — margin)*

The 4th Battalion had now left the Mountain Warfare School in Lebanon, and by April had moved to a hill station in Northern Syria, called Slenfe. Smuggling between Syria and Turkey was the local industry a little farther afield, and "C" Company was sent off for a tour of duty on the Turkish frontier to try and discourage it. This was effected by an unexciting but arduous programme of patrolling; but it is to be supposed from the evidence that the smugglers found the patrols too quick for them, and the Company evidently did what was required of it. *(4th Bn. April — margin)*

1944

During this period, the Battalion had the pleasure, like the 3rd, of a visit from the Maharaj Kumar of Kapurthala, who marked his appreciation by a generous gift to Battalion funds.

An extensive "flag march" through Northern Syria was now in the wind, and the Battalion was busy working out details when welcome counter-orders came through for a move to Haifa and thence overseas. Before proceeding to Haifa, the Battalion spent a few days in Tripoli. Arrived in Haifa, it had a busy time sorting out kit, handing over vehicles and generally preparing for service.

Early in July, the Battalion, under Lieut.-Col. D. M. Cornah, D.S.O.,
11 July moved down to Egypt, and, on the 11th, embarked at Alexandria.
17 July The ship arrived safely in Taranto on the 17th, after a crowded but uneventful passage.

More preparation, training and re-equipment followed, and on the
29 July 29th July, the Battalion moved up by road and rail to a concentration area in central Italy. From here, it went on forward, through Rome, to join the Eighth Army, and was posted to the 10th Indian Infantry
8 Aug. Brigade on the 8th August, at Montorchi.
9 Aug. On the 9th August, the Battalion took over a sector of front from the Durham Light Infantry, near Anghiari.

First contact with the enemy was quiet enough, and casualties for the present were light. The Battalion, however, did not stay
19 Aug. long in one place and on the 19th August, it was on its way to join its old formation, the 4th Indian Division, in which the 2nd Battalion had already made a name for itself.

The preliminary move of the 4th Indian Division forward to the Gothic Line has already been described in the 2nd Battalion record above. The 5th Indian Infantry Brigade to which the 4th Battalion was now posted, played its share equally with the 7th Indian Infantry Brigade; and during the long, hard marches through lofty, mountainous
23-27 Aug. country between the 23rd and 27th August, the troops gave of their best. Morale was high; and with a mountain scale of equipment which included mules, with jeeps to follow up where possible, the Battalion was in splendid trim.

These preliminary marches were carried out with the battalions stepping up one behind the other. They tested the fitness of the troops to the utmost, and the Cypriot mules, which had been issued to units of the Division, soon showed signs of exhaustion. On the 27th, after a march of fifteen hours, the Sikhs took over from the 1st/9th Gurkha Rifles on the heights of Monte Bello, then followed that Battalion through Fossombrone and over Monte Cesano, one of the steepest climbs met in Italy. Here the Battalion had a brush with the enemy, but, with a few casualties from shell fire, moved forward with tank support to within striking distance of the Gothic Line.

1944

The Gothic Line in this sector consisted of earth-works and minefields. All farm-houses and trees had been levelled to give clear fields of fire. The preparations were not in every respect complete; and the sudden appearance of the 4th Indian Division undoubtedly caught the enemy unawares, for the defences were not fully manned, and some of the minefields were found to be either dummy or not fully laid.

After a pause of two or three days, the Battalion carried out an attack on the Gothic Line on the 30th August, on the right of the 3rd/10th Baluchis, who had already made an initial breach in the defences. "A" Company of the Battalion, with a squadron of the 6th Royal Tank Regiment, was already in close contact, and difficulty was being experienced in getting orders through to it. However, at 4.45 p.m., "C" and "D" Companies shook rapidly out, and began to work forward down a long tree-covered slope, supported by artillery fire and excellent cover from the heavy machine-guns of the tank squadron. The objective consisted of a pair of fortified farm areas at the foot of the opposite slope, and these were quickly captured.

30 Aug.

As soon as the farm areas had been secured, "A" and "B" companies, moving very fast, passed through. Effectively surprising some small parties of the enemy, these Companies were established on their objective by dark. The advance was then continued up the farther slopes towards the fortified village of Monte Calvo. The troops moved with great dash, killed and wounded many of the enemy and took forty-two prisoners. The enemy were undoubtedly surprised by the speed of the attack—which indeed carried some of the men, in their keenness to close with the enemy, ahead of our own artillery support; and this was in part responsible for the Battalion's thirty casualties.

A night of confused fighting followed, with the enemy throwing in a succession of counter-attacks, mainly on "A" Company's front. Dawn saw the Battalion in position on the right of the 3rd/10th Baluchis, who were having a hard fight for Monte Calvo itself. It was now also possible to see the minefields through which the Battalion had passed the previous evening. One tank had run over a mine, but otherwise casualties had been light.

31 Aug.

During the morning, after a heavy concentration of bombing and shell fire, the Germans were forced out of Monte Calvo, and the Battalion moved forward, with the 1st/9th Gurkhas on its right. The enemy withdrew, leaving much equipment, with many mines there had been no time to lay.

The 6th Battalion was under training in Ranchi, looking forward

6th Bn.

1944

11 Apr. to the speedy return to an operational role against the Japanese. These hopes were not realized, however. On the 11th April, the Battalion moved north to Kohat, where a strenuous hot weather was passed, training in mountain warfare. Delightful as Kohat is as a winter station, the bare craggy hills that border it can make a purgatory of it in summer, and one's sympathies must lie with the 6th Battalion in its rather thankless and unglamorous role.

7th Bn. *The 7th Battalion* left Fort Sandeman on the 29th February for a column exercise up to Gulkach on the Waziristan border. It will interest many to follow the column in the mind's eye, and re-make acquaintance with some of these once well-known places, as well as again illustrating in a practical way one aspect of frontier activities during the war.

Marching out then to Zhob River Bridge, the column led off with a miserably cold night in an otherwise good camp. Next day, the

1 Mar. 1st March, with the Battalion as 2nd Echelon Piquetting Troops, it
2 Mar. moved on to Naweoba. On the 2nd, the Battalion, as Advance Guard, led the way through an immense Tangi with craggy rocks towering up on either side, very reminiscent of Rakhi Gaj on the way to Dera Ghazi Khan.

This march brought the column to Tora Darga, sited under an enormous crag on the top of which "B" Company had to put two camp piquets. Stores had to be hauled up, with much difficulty, by ropes, but the piquets were completed in good time.

3 Mar. The 3rd was a long tiring day with the Battalion as rearguard, moving up to the Zhob Militia post at Sambaza. There were over forty piquets to be withdrawn, so that it was nearly dark before the Battalion got in. On the other hand, the camp colour party had done its job well, and everything was ready for the troops when they did get in.

4 Mar. On the 4th March, the Battalion was second for piquetting, and in the 18 or 19 miles apparently over fifty piquets were put up—rather different, as the record remarks, from Waziristan conditions. Next

5 Mar. day, the Brigade rested, but not so the Battalion. Brigade Headquarters moved across the Waziristan border to contact Headquarters of the Wana Brigade, and the Sikhs, less "C" Company, went as escort. The operation went off well, the two headquarters meeting

6 Mar. on the Gulkach Narai. Next day, the column returned uneventfully home to Fort Sandeman.

Orders had been received during the column exercise for the Battalion to move to Loralai, 114 miles from Fort Sandeman, though still in the Zhob Brigade. Though a single-battalion station, the Sikhs reckoned that it promised better training facilities than Fort Sandeman, and were glad of the change.

	1944
The move was spread out over ten days from the 17th March, and on the 27th it was complete. No one who has served in Loralai will quarrel with the description given in the record; and particularly after Fort Sandeman it must have seemed a charming place with its well laid out gardens and avenues of tall trees. The promise of good training seemed likely to be fulfilled. There were several rifle ranges, and field-firing could be done anywhere. An innovation which will commend itself to past devotees of Ziarat, between Loralai and Quetta, was the determination to start a Jungle Warfare training camp there in July. The huge, twisted old junipers of the Ziarat hills may not bear the closest of resemblance to the Burma forests, as portrayed, for example, in the 1st Battalion narrative; but in any case, as we shall see, a better setting was ultimately enjoyed.	17-27 Mar.

Meanwhile, there was another long column exercise in April. Leaving "A" Company to look after the cantonment, the remainder went off on a six-day "Mechcol" on the 17th April. The first camp was at a small village called Rarkhan, about 75 miles from Dera Ghazi Khan. The 18th brought them to Barkhan, with the District Commander looking on at a scheme to clear an imaginary road-block. Though the 19th was spent in camp, each company did a "gasht" over the neighbouring hills which were pretty tough. On the 20th, the Battalion moved to Mekhtar, where the Zhob Column had camped in 1943; and next day it moved into dispersed camp with the Zhob Brigade, which was also out from Fort Sandeman on column. That evening the Battalion laid on some sports for the Brigade, and they seem to have gone with a swing. On the 22nd, the Battalion returned to Loralai.

17 Apr.
18 Apr.
19 Apr.
20 Apr.
21 Apr.
22 Apr.

On the 1st May, the new War Establishment (1-29C/3) was adopted. This involved the formation of the Administration Company, the introduction of two subedars per company, and elimination of havildar platoon commanders. News also came in that met a more mixed reception; for "we now learnt that we were to move to Risalpur early in May—this did not exactly please us as it looked as if we should forfeit our proposed training camp at Ziarat; and from a personal point of view we did not like the idea of moving into the heat of the plains, after 3 years in the hill climate." Well, perhaps that three-year spell was partly the reason for this change of locale. And perhaps it was not.

1 May

However that may be, on the 8th May, the move to Risalpur began. It took a week, and using all available transport, to move the Battalion and its stores to Harnai on the railway. Then, in Harnai—which is a most uninspiring dust-heap—there was another week's delay owing to a change in orders. However, after a train journey of two days and three nights, the Battalion arrived in Risalpur,

8 May

1944

where it was met by the Regimental Centre's Bugle and Fife Band sent over from Nowshera a few miles away, over the Kabul river, to play them up to their lines. Jacob and Birdwood Lines, which were allotted the Battalion, seem to have been in a shocking state of repair, but the Military Engineering Service then took a hand and made them habitable. Disappointing as all this may have seemed at first impact, there was infinitely better news to compensate it. In Risalpur, the Battalion found itself in the 155th Indian Infantry Brigade, a new formation, with a brigade staff drawn exclusively from the Burma theatre. However, nothing more than idle speculation was possible at the moment.

1 July   Meanwhile, five months individual training was prescribed as a start. On the domestic side, family quarters were made available on the 1st July, for the troops—one hundred quarters being allotted—the first time the troops had had their families with them since the

22 July   Battalion was raised. Battalion history was also made on the 22nd July, when the Drums and Bugles, which had begun training in February, played Retreat for the first time. This set the seal in the eyes of the rank and file to their now settled status as a "purani paltan"—in which they could take as high a pride as any of the old regular battalions. Finally, the published programme of courses, for the most part in jungle warfare, provided a grand incentive, and gave the men a reasonable certainty that they would soon find themselves in contact with a worth-while enemy.

MG Bn.   *The Machine-Gun Battalion* was still undergoing its abortive experimental training with 4.2-inch mortars; but this was given up and the mortars withdrawn by the middle of the summer. The Battalion

July   was re-issued with medium machine-guns in July, and soon after left Ranchi for Nasik, where, on a jeep and trailer basis, it joined the 19th Indian Division.

14th Bn.   *The 14th Battalion* carried on in its instructional role in Chindwara. One week followed another, with little to brighten the even flow of time. Draft followed draft, and the instructional staff was kept constantly busy providing young troops with the final polish to fit them for war.

15th Bn.   *The 15th Battalion* remained in Agertala as an army reserve unit, but was not called upon during the Japanese offensive in the Arakan.

April   In April, however, when the second offensive developed against Imphal—not very far from Agertala—the Battalion was flown in to Imphal at forty-eight hour's notice, and placed under command of the IVth Corps. It remained in Imphal on general duties throughout the siege.

1944

As has been noted elsewhere in this record, it had become apparent some time before that the Indian Army as a whole was over-extended, with more commitments than the available manpower could meet. The call on officers and men to maintain the many new units could not be met without prejudicing the supply of drafts for others. As soon as the siege of Imphal was raised, the 15th Battalion was ordered back to Nowshera for disbandment.

It is sad to think that the energy and care expended on bringing the Battalion to its final state of efficiency and morale could not have been rewarded in long service against the enemy; but the decision once taken had to be fulfilled, and the Battalion was broken up and its personnel dispersed.

The 26th Battalion remained on internal defence duties in Poona.   26th Bn.

Chapter XI

SEPTEMBER 1944 TO FEBRUARY 1945

Backscreen

South Pacific
The New Guinea campaign was over and Allied troops established 600 miles south-east of the Philippines. Mindanao is the southernmost of the Philippines, and about half-way to it is Morotai in the Spice Islands. Morotai is not the most important of the Spice Islands. That honour belongs to Halmahera, a little to the south. The Japanese reckoned on Halmahera as the next Allied objective, and garrisoned it with 30,000 men, leaving Morotai in charge of a detachment of three of four hundred men.

15 Sept.
On the 15th September, the Americans captured Morotai at a cost of five casualties, leaving the main enemy forces at Halmahera stranded without hope of rescue, or of active participation in the coming operations.

Gen. MacArthur was now well placed to play his part in a joint operation with the Central Pacific forces for the re-conquest of the Philippines.

Central Pacific
In the Central Pacific, American forces had occupied Guam, Tinian, and Saipan, approximately equidistant (about 1,500 miles) from the Philippines in the west, and the home islands of Japan lying only a little west of north. Any doubts the Japanese may have had on the direction the next advance would take were quickly dispelled. On

8 Sept.
the 8th September, the United States Third Amphibious Force appeared off the Pelew Islands, on the direct line to Mindanao. Then, on the

15 Sept.
15th September, simultaneously with the occupation of Morotai, 500 miles to the south-west, troops were landed on Pililu Island, about the same distance east of Mindanao.

Philippines
Just north of Mindanao in the Philippines are Leyte and Samar Islands. An attack on Mindanao was likely to be costly, and it was thought better policy to by-pass it in the expectation of a lesser scale of resistance on Leyte and Samar Islands.

There were certain risks in this decision inasmuch as the American forces would be operating beyond the range of land-based fighter cover. Carriers could supply this cover, as they had already done at Hollandia, but they would be exposed to considerably more risk from interference by the Japanese fleet.

1944

The Japanese garrison of the Philippines as a whole amounted to about 250,000 men. These were divided between Luzon Island in the north and Mindanao Island in the south. American occupation of Leyte Island would split these two detachments, and practically force naval action on the Japanese if they were to be re-united. This might give the United States Navy the chance they wanted to deal decisively with the enemy at sea.

In view of these considerations, the proposed attack on Leyte and Samar Islands was agreed to.

Carrier-borne air offensives against air installations on Formosa and Okinawa—mid-way between the Philippines and Japan—opened the operation on the 10th October. On the 13th and 15th, similar attacks were made on Luzon Island, doing much damage to Japanese aircraft. Finally, on the 18th and 19th, attacks were switched to airfields and shipping in the enclosed sea areas west of Leyte and Samar Islands, through which passes the shipping route both to Singapore and to Japan. 10-15 Oct. 18-19 Oct.

On the 19th October, the United States Sixth Army, on its way to Leyte Island, was observed by a Japanese reconnaissance aircraft. The Japanese immediately put into effect a preconceived naval plan involving a set-up for which no historical parallel can easily be found. 19 Oct.

What happened was briefly this. In the home islands was the Japanese Northern Force of 2 battleships, 3 cruisers and 10 destroyers. This was to steam south and along the east coast of Luzon Island to act as a decoy for the United States naval escort to the invading forces, and draw them away north. Meanwhile, the Japanese Central and Southern Forces from Singapore and the Pescadores (just west of Formosa and a little north of Luzon Island) were to pass through the Sulu Sea between Borneo and Mindanao, and strike at both flanks of the invaders. The plan was a bold one; and as the Central and Southern Forces totalled some 7 battleships, 16 cruisers and 23 destroyers, their intervention, if successful, might be decisive.

On the 22nd October, the very strong Singapore component was nearing Palawan Island at the western exits of the Sulu Sea. This meant that it was some 600 miles or more west of Leyte Island. By the 24th, it was in the neighbourhood of Sibuyan Island, well within the Philippines, 150 miles north-west of Leyte Island. A violent attack from the air sank one Japanese ship and damaged another, but there was nothing to justify the impression that got abroad that the Japanese fleet could be regarded as out of action for the present, and that it could be safely ignored. 22 Oct. 24 Oct.

Meanwhile, however, the Northern Force was on its way south, and was detected by reconnaissance aircraft during the operation off

351

1944

Sibuyan Island. The report told of a Japanese fleet with carriers 130 miles east of Cape Engano, at the northern tip of Luzon Island, and hence about 450 miles north of the Leyte-Samar area.

This report, coupled with the belief that the Singapore component was out of the running, as nearly as possible brought about the deployment the Japanese desired. The United States Third and Seventh Fleets were escorting the Sixth Army convoy, and Admiral Halsey now decided that he could safely leave unguarded the San Bernardino Channel, which gives access to the Pacific from the Philippine interisland waters, and sail north to deal with this new threat.

There are two main routes eastwards into the Pacific hereabouts. The San Bernardino Channel passes north of Samar Island. The Surigao Strait, 200 miles to the south, rounds the southern tip of Leyte Island. Admiral Kincaid with the Seventh Fleet was watching Surigao Strait, but apparently he was not made aware of the departure north of the naval forces guarding the San Bernardino Channel.

Part of the Southern Force from Singapore, under Vice-Admiral Nishimura, with 2 battleships, 1 cruiser and 4 destroyers, now attempted to force the Surigao Strait. It was sighted at midnight on

24-25 Oct. the 24th/25th October, and at 2.30 a.m. on the 25th, battle was
25 Oct. joined. The Japanese depended for fire-control on searchlights, whereas the American guns were radar-controlled. With the exception of one Japanese destroyer, the *Shigure*, the Japanese fleet had been annihilated by 3 a.m.

It was as well for the Americans that they disposed of the enemy's ships so quickly, for the main body of Admiral Kurita's Singapore fleet, comprising 5 battleships, 12 cruisers and 15 destroyers, was simultaneously steaming through the unguarded San Bernardino Channel, 200 miles to the north, and turning down the eastern coast of Samar Island. Carriers of the United States Seventh Fleet were cruising north-east of Leyte Gulf in the Pacific, 100 miles north of the main Seventh Fleet. At 6.53 a.m., these carriers came under fire.

Admiral Halsey, away up north, was steaming in the wrong direction, and he took some persuading, when news of the turn of events came through. It was not till mid-day that he accepted the situation, dropped a detachment to dispute the issue with the Japanese Northern Force, turned about and steamed back at high speed to Admiral Kincaid's assistance.

Admiral Kincaid had been badly caught. Evasive action was taken by his relatively defenceless carriers under a smokescreen laid down by their destroyer escort, but 2 carriers and 3 destroyers were sunk, and 7 escort carriers and 1 destroyer seriously damaged. The bulk of the Seventh Fleet was not only still far down in the Surigao Strait, but it was short of ammunition.

1944-5

What happened then is not wholly clear. With the issue apparently in their hands, the Japanese suddenly, at 9.25 a.m., turned about, headed for the San Bernardino Channel, and were away out of reach before the Third Fleet could intercept. It has been surmised that the Japanese destroyers were running short of fuel, and that may, of course, have influenced the unexpected withdrawal, which took place long before the Third Fleet put about.

Meanwhile, the Japanese Northern Force was routed, with the sinking of its 4 carriers, bringing the total Japanese loss to 3 battleships, 4 carriers, 10 cruisers and 9 destroyers. The American losses amounted to 3 carriers and 3 destroyers; and the Japanese never put to sea as a fleet again.

Operations on land had meanwhile been pursuing their course. The Sixth Army landed on Leyte Island on the 20th October, and made steady progress. By mid-November, the Japanese had been driven up into the north-west tip of the island. The constant Japanese efforts to reinforce the garrison were regularly stopped, and few extra troops were got ashore by them. On the 7th December, an American division was shipped round and landed half-way up the west coast. By the 11th, Japanese losses at sea had become so heavy that further attempts to reinforce the garrison were abandoned. Before the New Year, the island was completely occupied. 20 Oct.
November

7 Dec.

11 Dec.

Three hundred miles north-west of Leyte Island, and only seventy-five miles south of Manila Bay, is the island of Mindoro. With the fighting still in progress on Leyte Island, the Americans, true to their policy of bold leaps and calculated deception, invaded Mindoro. The operation was a complete success. By the 28th December, the island had been occupied and a fighter-base established there. 28 Dec.

Manila lies about half-way up the west coast of Luzon Island. As soon as Leyte was cleared, the offensive was carried forward against Luzon Island. Bold strategy was again employed. While demonstrations were being made towards the southern end of Luzon Island, the Sixth Army, in an armada of 850 ships, slipped through Surigao Strait into the Sulu Sea, and thence up north.

The selected beaches were far from where the Japanese expected them. They were 125 miles north of Manila itself, in the Lingayen Gulf, on the west coast of Luzon Island. On the 9th January, 68,000 troops were put on shore, and a beach-head organized 15 miles long and 3 miles in depth. The landing surprised the Japanese Higher Command, and within the week the Sixth Army was making rapid progress southwards towards Manila. A strong left flank-guard covered the open flank, and these held off attack, and enabled the main body to make straight for its objective. Some opposition was encountered 90 miles north-west of Manila, at Clark Field, the principal air-base on 9 Jan.

1945
25 Jan. the island, but this was broken down by the 25th. The XIth Corps,
29 Jan. landing a few days later, on the 29th, at Subic Bay at the west side of the Bataan Peninsular, about 60 miles south-west of Clark Field, turned the Japanese defences as well as denying them access into
31 Jan. the Bataan Peninsular. On the 31st, the United States 11th Airborne Division made an unopposed landing to the south of Manila Bay.

The Japanese had been out-manoeuvred, but fanatical resistance
23 Feb. followed till the fall of Manila on the 23rd February.

The fort of Corregidor guards the entrance to Manila Bay, and here, in the underground galleries that seamed it, desperate fighting
February followed. Finally, at the end of February, the Japanese fired the main magazine, bringing the galleries down in ruins and destroying themselves as well.

It was still many months before the Philippines were finally cleared, but this was not allowed to interrupt the energetic prosecution of the war northwards towards the Japanese home islands. The first requisite was the capture of air-bases nearer Japan. There seemed to be the choice of three, but Formosa was rejected for immediate invasion, partly by reason of its size, and the difficult nature of the country, and also thanks to the strength of its garrison. The second choice, Okinawa, tempting enough, was too exposed and distant for the moment. Iwo Jima, the third choice, was selected. It was relatively near, being about half-way between Honshu, the biggest of the Japanese home islands, and Saipan. It was not too large, measuring 5 miles in length and a little under 3 miles across its widest part, and covering some 8 square miles in all. It had two landing-beaches; and, though packed with troops (20,000), it had been frequently bombarded since July 1944. Now, from about the first week in December, it was subjected to a 70-day programme of continuous bombing.

In spite of the difficulty of effecting surprise, the landing, at
19 Feb. 9 a.m. on the 19th February, by the 4th and 5th Marine Divisions, was not seriously opposed. Progress at first was surprisingly fast.
20 Feb. By the 20th February, the Motoyama air-field in the north of the island, had been occupied. It was a different story, however, in the south, and desperate resistance was made. The 3rd Marine Division was
27 Feb. put ashore as reinforcement; but by the 27th February, still only half the island had been cleared. Conditions can be better imagined
28 Feb. than described, with a total of some 80,000 troops of both sides, crammed on this tiny pear-shaped island. On the 28th February, the summit of Suribachiyama in the southern tip of the island was cleared, but the fanatical resistance which had boiled up soon after the landings, continued unabated, with crippling casualties on both sides.

	1944-5
In Northern Burma, an air-supplied operation of great extent was being built up in the move south and east to Mandalay. The 36th Division, moving down the railway from Myitkyina, met the 19th Indian Division of the IVth Corps at Naba near Katha, about one-third of the way to Mandalay, on the 16th December. On the 2nd January, the Fourteenth Army occupied Ye-U, 60 miles north-west of Mandalay. On the 7th, it was at Shwebo, 20 miles nearer. Strong Chinese forces were moving south, to the east of the 36th Division, towards Bhamo on the Upper Irrawaddy, 60 miles south of Myitkyina, and the same distance east of Naba. These forces captured Bhamo on the 16th December. Other Chinese formations, farther afield on the west bank of the river Salween, joined up with those moving via Bhamo, and clearing the Burma road by the 27th January, enabled the first convoy for China to pass through on the 28th.	Burma 2 Jan. 7 Jan. 16 Dec. 27 Jan. 28 Jan.

It will be appreciated that to keep these sustained and mobile operations properly supplied by air, over a period of months, called for an aircraft deployment of great magnitude. Lord Mountbatten referred to it as the largest-scale air supply that has ever been seen. He notes that 96 per cent of our supplies to the Fourteenth Army went by air. Detailed figures include the total lift to the armies during the current campaign for the re-conquest of Burma—615,000 tons, three-fourths of which were carried by the United States Air Force, the remainder by the Royal Air Force. Reinforcements flown in—315,000, half by each air-force. Casualties flown out—110,000, three-fourths by the Royal Air Force, the balance by the Americans. The lift for the best month—March 1945,—94,300 tons. Lacking sufficient aircraft to carry out this programme, nearly double the hours were flown permissible as a rule for sustained operations.

The Fourteenth Army was still, as has been shown, west of the Irrawaddy at the beginning of January 1945. The IVth Corps was on its left, above Mandalay, but with some of its formations still away back in rear and fighting to clear the Myittha, behind the Chindwin. The XXXIIIrd Corps was on the right. Opposite lay the Japanese Fifteenth and Thirty-third Armies under Gen. Kimura. {January}

To cross the Irrawaddy north of Mandalay and turn south would be to meet the Japanese frontally and indulge in a slow and bloody slogging-match. But if the Japanese could be persuaded that this was in fact our intention, and that it was worth their while to bring their reserves to that area, the way might be opened for a paralysing stroke well downstream of Mandalay, towards the vital Japanese supply-line and air-base at Meiktila.

The 19th Indian Division of the IVth Corps lay at that corps' point of junction with the XXXIIIrd Corps. To commit troops from this Division to a river-crossing north of Mandalay might be taken as an

1945

14 Jan. indication that the IVth Corps was reinforcing the XXXIIIrd Corps, and that the main river crossing was to be staged there. On the 14th January, the river was crossed accordingly, and small bridge-heads established at Thabeikkyin and Singu, 60 miles and 30 miles north of Mandalay respectively. The Japanese fell into the trap and began moving their troops up towards these bridge-heads.

Under conditions of the closest possible secrecy, the IVth Corps, less the 19th Indian Division, was switched to Pakokku on the Irrawaddy, 80 miles south-west of Mandalay, and about 10 miles downstream of the confluence with the Chindwin. The actual move involved very long marches for some of the troops, but the Chindwin was pressed into service as an auxiliary line of communications. Large numbers of river craft were put together from local timber on the river bank, and everything possible done to ensure that the time-table was met. This was done.

11 Feb. On the 11th February, the 20th Indian Division crossed the
14 Feb. Irrawaddy at Sagaing, 25 miles below Mandalay. Then, on the 14th, troops of the 7th Indian Division crossed at Nyaungu 10 miles downstream from Pakokku. It was open to the Japanese to look upon this last crossing as a blind to distract their attention from more important matters farther north, if they so wished.

19 Feb. On the 19th February, the 19th Indian Division above Mandalay broke out from its bridge-heads southwards. Very bitter fighting lasted over the next two weeks as the Division slowly forced its way
7 Mar. south. On the 7th March, it captured Mandalay Hill. Mandalay fell
21 Mar. on the 21st.

During these weeks of savage fighting upstream, the 2nd British and 20th Indian Divisions had broken out of the Sagaing bridge-head, and moved up-river. Ava, half-way to Mandalay, was reached on the
19 Mar. 19th March, and junction effected with the 19th Indian Division at
21 Mar. Mandalay on the 21st.

These operations, fierce as they were, were only a cover to the
20 Feb. main operation farther south. On the 20th February, the 17th Indian Division advanced a little north of east and against inconsiderable
24 Feb. resistance, from the Nyaungu bridge-head, and, by the 24th February had covered the 30 miles to Taungtha, which lies something over 40 miles north-west of Meiktila.

Reaching Meiktila, the first of the eight air-fields was captured on
27 Feb. the 27th February and brought into use. Furious fighting for the
5 Mar. remaining air-fields followed, but on the 5th March the operation was completed by the 255th Indian Tank Brigade. Gen. Kimura therefore not only had had his communications cut, but the Fourteenth Army was in possession of ample air facilities to support the troops lying across them.

	1944
It Italy, fighting for the Gothic Line continued. The enemy recovered from his initial set-back on the Adriatic coast, and was full of fight. Allied strengths, on the other hand, had been weakened to provide troops for Southern France, and there was bad weather in the offing.	Italy
Heavy slogging marked the operations, but on the 21st September the 3rd Greek Mountain Brigade in the Eighth Army entered Rimini on the Adriatic. Slow progress was made on other Eighth Army sectors. The 4th Indian Division crossed the Rubicon at Cornacchiara, 10 miles west-south-west of Rimini, but could only maintain a slow advance there in face of severe opposition. On the 2nd October it was checked in an attack on a ridge near San Martino, a little to the south-west.	21 Sept. 2 Oct.
Meanwhile, the Fifth Army had opened the Battle of the Northern Apennines on the 13th September with an attack in great strength against the Gothic Line, in the central sector. The United States IInd Corps made the main effort, with the XIIIth British Corps protecting its right. The 8th Indian Division, in the latter corps, followed a line north-east from Vicchio, itself 15 miles north-east of Florence. The Division had a hard fight for the watershed north-east of Vicchio, but by capturing it it achieved distinction as having cracked the main Gothic Line defences there, though in terrain too difficult and on too narrow a front to admit of successful exploitation. However, this exploit on the 14th September was followed up on the night of the 16th/17th September, when United States troops or the left broke through elsewhere.	13 Sept. 14 Sept. 16-17 Sept.
Operations continued successfully for a while, and by the 22nd September, the United States IInd Corps and XIIIth British Corps were through the Gothic Line on a 30-mile front, and penetrations elsewhere had also been made. Furious fighting followed as the enemy tried to stop the breach, and prevent his forces on the Eighth Army front being cut off. It was very much a question whether he would be able to stabilize on a fresh defence-line in the Apennines, or would have to pull out north behind the river Po. But Gen. Alexander, quoted in the official despatch, put the situation in the starkest light. "The trouble is", he wrote, "that my forces are too weak relative to the enemy to force a break-through and so close the two pincers. The advance of both armies is too slow to achieve decisive results unless the Germans break and there is no sign of that."	22 Sept.
Meanwhile, further reductions had to be accepted. The 3rd Greek Mountain Brigade was required shortly for Greece, and orders for the transfer of the 4th Indian Division to the same country had to be issued on the 12th October. Now also the weather increasingly took a hand, with heavy rains everywhere, and movement for wheels	12 Oct.

1944

10 Oct. almost impossible off metalled roads. However, by the 10th October, the Eighth Army's interrupted new offensive in the Adriatic had swung into action. Within four days the Ist Canadian Corps had reached a point near Cesena, 18 miles north-west of Rimini; but weather and difficult going slowed up the Vth Corps, except on its left, where the 10th Indian Division captured Monte Farneto, 16 miles west of Rimini, after relieving the 4th Indian Division, which had already played more than its share, and which was due to move to Greece. The capture of Monte Farneto threatened the enemy's line of retreat from positions farther west, and assisted the advance of the Xth Corps.

Still, by the middle of October there was no sign yet that the enemy were preparing to pull out and withdraw behind the Po. German formations, it seemed, were also not only not being milked to reinforce the fronts in Eastern and Western Europe, but were being kept well up to strength. There were still the twenty-six German divisions, and a number of Italian Fascist divisions in the line.

27 Oct. Slow but steady advances continued till the 27th October, when the Fifth Army's offensive was suspended to allow the troops some respite. The weather had become bad and the fighting had been bitter throughout. Strengths were causing increasing anxiety—but the Eighth Army's offensive continued into November, and Forli, 30 miles north-west of Rimini, and the point where the highway from Florence

9 Nov. emerges from the Apennines, was captured on the 9th of that month.

The enemy had concentrated great strength about Faenza, about 8 miles north-west of Forli on Highway 9, at the expense of the formations nearer the Adriatic. To take advantage of this weakness, the Ist Canadian Corps of the Eighth Army advanced against heavy

2 Dec. opposition on the 2nd December, and by the 4th had captured Ravenna, 30 miles up from Rimini, and about 5 miles in from the Adriatic. Country to the west was over-run at the same time, though not in the same

4 Dec. degree, by the Vth Corps, attacking on the night of the 3rd/4th December towards Faenza, which had received still further reinforcements. The weather then broke again, rain pouring down and the shallow water-courses racing down in turbid torrents. When conditions improved, the offensive was resumed, and, with the 43rd Gurkha Lorried Brigade playing a leading part clearing the northern outskirts of Faenza, and the 10th Indian Division—to which the 4th Battalion of the Sikh Regiment had recently been posted—smashing through to their left with the New Zealanders, a crossing over the Senio was secured, and operations stabilized uneasily for the balance of the winter.

Western Europe
In Western Europe, the promising break-through from the Normandy beach-heads was outrunning its administrative tail, lacking necessary port facilities along the Channel to shorten its land communications.

The stage had been reached when a decision had to be made whether to continue the advance along the whole front at much reduced speed, or whether to turn the supply pipeline on to one or other of the two Army Groups, while accepting a standstill condition over a considerable part of the Allied front. Both Montgomery, with the 21st Army Group in the north, and Bradley with the 12th Army Group in the centre, put forward proposals for the latter alternative, but Gen. Eisenhower elected for a forward move along the whole front to the Rhine, establishing bridge-heads there where possible, and to wait there till the Port of Antwerp was open and in working trim. There were obviously two sides to the question—but much is held in some quarters to have been lost by this decision.

However, there was nothing in these orders to prevent commanders from keeping operations as mobile and decisive as possible, within the policy limit. And from this arose the epic of Arnhem.

A glance at the map will show Holland almost cut in two by the Zuyder Zee, shouldering down from the north into the very heart of the country. The more important part, industrially and commercially, lies to the west and south-west of the Zuyder Zee, and in this part of Holland at this time were very considerable German garrisons estimated at between 300,000 and 400,000 men.

The 65 to 70 air-miles between the southern extremity of the Zuyder Zee and the Escaut Canal, just south of the Belgian border where the British Second Army now was, carry a variety of land and water communications running east and west. The Rhine and the Meuse, running westwards to the sea, pass through the centre of this corridor. Railways are numerous, and find an especially important nodal point in Arnhem, a large city on the Neder Rijn, and some 7 miles north of the Rhine itself. South-west from Arnhem, looking towards the Second Army, were a succession of important tactical areas, with road and railway bridges of value to the enemy in western Holland. These included Nijmegen, 10 miles south-west of Arnhem, with two important bridges—one over the Maas-Waal Canal west of the town, the other the great road-bridge over the Waal (the southern branch of the Rhine, which divides just above Arnhem on its final stretch to the sea) at Nijmegen itself.

Eight miles south-west of Nijmegen is Grave, on the Meuse, or Maas, here a broad river, and spanned by an important bridge; 13 miles south-west of Grave is Veghel; thence another 11 miles brings one to Eindhoven, and a further 15 miles to the Second Army on the Escaut Canal.

Though the corridor between Arnhem and the Zuyder Zee, 30 miles to the north, has lines of communication running through it, these are infinitely less important than those to the south.

1944

The plan now was to fly in troops to three different areas between the Escaut Canal and Arnhem, and for these to establish a line of stepping-stones, which would be linked up at once into a serviceable corridor by ground troops of the Second Army. Formations detailed for the fly-in were the British 1st Airborne Division, the United States 82nd and 101st Airborne Divisions, and a Polish Parachute Brigade. Unfortunately, lack of transport aircraft made it impossible to complete the fly-in in less than four lifts, involving greater reliance on the kindness of the September weather than was justified.

17 Sept. On the 17th September, the first lift was flown in. The 101st Airborne Division landed between Eindhoven and Grave, and cleared that sector, to exclusive Grave which was captured by the 82nd Airborne Division, which also cleared the way to Nijmegen. The 1st Airborne Division was landed at Arnhem, where it made for the bridge over the Neder Rijn—the northern branch of the Rhine.

18 Sept. On the 18th, the second air-lift came in, but there was a good deal of resistance. However, the Guards Armoured Division made good
19 Sept. the corridor to a point south of Eindhoven. On the 19th, the Guards Armoured Division broke through over the Grave bridge, and joined hands with the 82nd Airborne Division, but the weather had gone to pieces, and no further air-lift was possible until after the operation was over.

20 Sept. On the 20th, with the weather still outrageous, the Guards crossed the Waal over the Nijmegen bridge which had been taken undamaged.
21 Sept. On the evening of the 21st, the 43rd Division reached the south bank of the Neder Rijn; but in spite of three days intense effort, it
25 Sept. was unable to link up with the 1st Airborne Division across the river. On the 25th, it was decided that the 1st Airborne Division must break out—and it did this under cover of darkness after a total loss of 7,000 men killed, wounded, and missing.

However, the corridor was held and caused great embarrassment to the enemy—and the operation, despite its sombre side, counts as one of the shining successes of the operations in Western Europe at this time, and indeed at any time.

Operations continued against the complicated defences of the
9 Nov. Scheldt Estuary and islands to seaward. These were cleared by the First Canadian Army by the 9th November. Antwerp received its first
26 Nov. Allied cargoes by the 26th.

The weather had been steadily deteriorating, and this still further checked the general speed of the advance. The Allies were still
16 Dec. far from being lined up along the Rhine, when the 16th December saw the sudden outbreak of the Battle of the Bulge.

Field-Marshal von Rundstedt was in command of this sudden offensive, planned and controlled by Hitler. It was directed in the first instance

against Liege, with subsequent exploitation towards Antwerp. Starting
in the Ardennes on a front of about 50 miles, between Monschau in
the north and Echternach in the south, a force of ten Panzer and
Panzer Grenadier divisions and fourteen or more motorized and infantry
divisions, with a very large air component, broke through on the
16th December and headed for the Meuse, some 50 miles to the west.
The attack came as a surprise. All Allied operations elsewhere had
to be dropped at once, while forces were rushed up to prevent the
widening of the gap. Gen. Patton's Third Army pressed up northwards
from Bastogne, 15 miles west of the original front line, while Montgomery
with the United States First and part of the Ninth Army took charge
in the north.

1944-5

Bastogne itself held firm. Though the enemy was prevented from
widening his base, either there or in the north, fog and the weather
generally told in his favour up till Christmas Eve. Then the weather
cleared, and the vast concentration of Allied aircraft standing ready,
came into action across the enemy supply lines. Vital supplies
such as fuel and oil for the German armour were cut off, and von
Rundstedt, with a penetration of some 50 miles to his credit, almost
to the Meuse, was obliged to pull back. Even so, it took till the
31st January to clear the salient completely.

24 Dec.

31 Jan.

The operation cost the Allies in the neighbourhood of 50,000
casualties. But the Germans lost nearer 70,000 in casualties, plus a
further 50,000 captured. Other losses included some 600 tanks,
1,600 aircraft and other weapons and equipment in proportion.

Gen. Eisenhower now returned to his original plan of advancing
on a broad front to the Rhine. The first stage opened on the 8th February
with the 21st Army Group and United States Ninth Army directed on
the long stretch of river line between Dusseldorf and the sea. Resistance
was bitter, but all objectives were in Allied hands by the 10th March.

8 Feb.

10 Mar.

In the 12th Army Group, the second stage brought the United States
First Army to Cologne by the 5th March, and on the 7th to a bridge-
head at Remagen some 20 miles downstream, where the footing gained
on the east bank was expanded by the 24th into a bridge-head 25 miles
long and 10 miles deep. The United States Third Army meanwhile
moved into the Saar Basin, and by the 22nd March completed the
occupation of the Rhine from Dusseldorf to Mainz, already begun to
the north by the United States First Army. A crossing was also
effected—at Oppenheim, south of Mainz.

5-7 Mar.

24 Mar.

22 Mar.

The 6th Army Group in the south completed the occupation of the
river line by the 25th March.

Rumania had given up the fight, and opened the way for the Southern
Group of armies from Russia, towards the Danube valley. Operations

Eastern
Europe

1944 continued on a vast scale through Bulgaria and Rumania, and can with difficulty be condensed down to more than a bare list of names—barely pronounceable to English tongues—and their dates of capture. Certain key dates, however, emerge.

19 Oct. Belgrade, the capital of Yugoslavia, fell to Marshal Malinovsky's
11 Nov. Second Ukrainian Group on the 19th October. By the 11th November, his forward troops were in the southern and eastern outskirts of Budapest, the Hungarian capital, also on the Danube, and 200 miles north of Belgrade, but paused there owing to German Panzer concentrations on their right. Further operations resulted in the occupation of all country downstream of Budapest as well as east of the city. Above, north of Budapest, as well as a small area bordering the city on the east, was a constricted patch of country in which the Germans had collected two Hungarian armies, and fifteen German divisions, with much armour. Marshal Malinovsky paused accordingly, while Marshal Tolbukhin's Third Ukrainian Group was ordered north to assist.

3 Dec. Here the situation rested, as from about the 3rd December.

In the north, a campaign was being fought to clear the way for an offensive against East Prussia. This preliminary campaign began
15 Sept. on the 15th September.

Once again the operations boil down to a list of difficult names
13 Oct. and dates, but, with the fall of Riga on the 13th October, Gen. Schörner, and the twenty or so German divisions garrisoning Courland, south of Riga, and western Lithuania generally, were cut off on their landward side.

Though land communications with East Prussia to the south were denied the German forces in this area, the Russians now started, on
16 Oct. the 16th October, an operation against the Insterburg Gap east of Königsberg, itself 200 miles south-south-west of Riga. After a measure of success, the Russians were finally so roughly treated that they went on the defensive, and there matters remained.

On the Polish front, meanwhile, nothing happened for the five months up till the middle of January.

However, it is time to return to the Danube front, where Marshal Malinovsky was awaiting aid from Marshal Tolbukhin in the south. Tolbukhin had left the neighbourhood of Mohács, on the Danube, about 110 miles south of Budapest near the frontier between Hungary
29 Nov. and Yugoslavia, on the 29th November. He kept his left well west of the Danube. Malinovsky, meanwhile, had worked his way upstream, past Vac, 20 miles above Budapest, where the river turns 90 degrees to the west, and was on his way towards Komarno, the main German base on this front, 50 miles west of Vac, and located on the Danube.

To protect Komarno, the Germans under Gen. Friesner, decided to hold their left, north of the Danube, and their right, from a point

1945

about 50 miles south of the Danube, defensively. A strong garrison was to be left in Budapest. A striking force was to be held behind the German centre, more or less west of Budapest. When the Russians assaulted the city, the striking force would be in a position to cause the maximum embarrassment to the Russians, and probably inflict a defeat on them.

In a sense, things turned out exactly as the Germans wished; and on the 2nd and 3rd January, Gen. Friesner was able to strike vigorously 2-3 Jan. in two sectors, northwards towards the Danube, and with considerable success. However, the Russians meanwhile attacked his unavoidably weak defences north of the Danube, broke through them, and by the 10th January, were within 2 miles of Komarno, possession of which 10 Jan. was vital to the Germans. The inevitable happened. Gen. Friesner had to cross over to the north bank to check this threat, and gave the Russians on the south of the river the opportunity to proceed with their operation against Budapest. Pest fell on the 18th January; 18 Jan. Buda, which Friesner no longer had the strength to relieve, held out gallantly for some weeks, but finally fell to overwhelming force on the 13th February. The road to Vienna, about 140 miles west-north- 13 Feb. west of Budapest, was open.

Gen. Friesner, however, was not himself beaten. His defensive lines were restored, and he launched a successful offensive from these lines in the third week in February. He was then reinforced by the Sixth Panzer Army, back from the Battle of the Bulge on the western front, and, on the 3rd March, opened a violent attack, with strong air 3 Mar. support, some 50 miles south of the Danube, on its east-west course upstream of Budapest, and something less west of the same river on its north-south course below the city. Advancing strongly eastwards, the Germans very nearly reached the Danube, but they ran out of fuel, and had to get their armour out as best they could. By the 15th March, the attack died away. 15 Mar.

Farther north, in Poland, in the sector running from south of Warsaw, southwards to the Carpathians, 150 miles away, furious Russian attacks were opened on the 12th and 14th January. Warsaw fell on 12-14 Jan. the 17th January. The German frontier was crossed to either side of 17 Jan. Breslau on the 20th January; and by the 15th February, the Russians 20 Jan. were 60 miles west of Breslau, and nearly half-way to Dresden, which 15 Feb. lies itself about 100 miles due south of Berlin.

Marshal Zhukov, on Marshal Koniev's right, reached the Oder at Lebus on the 10th February. Lebus is only about 60 miles east of 10 Feb. Berlin, but the Russians could not advance farther owing to the embarrassment caused to their communications by by-passed German strongholds in rear. Furthermore, Zhukov's open right flank was being increasingly threatened by German formations brought back by

1944-5	
23 Feb.	sea from East Prussia. Turning north, accordingly, he reduced the by-passed areas first, completing this phase by the 23rd February. He then moved north up to the Baltic coast, reaching the vicinity of Kolberg, 60 miles north-east of Stettin, on the 9th March, cutting the German forces in Pomerania in two.
14 Jan. 26 Jan.	Meanwhile, in East Prussia, operations had opened on the 14th January, and by the 26th, East Prussia was separated from Pomerania except by sea.

Thus, by the end of this period, the Germans were being forced back to the fortified line of the Oder, not much east of Berlin. The winter campaign had started with the Russians in a numerical superiority of the order of three-to-one, and with the Germans resisting as manfully as their weakness both in men and munitions allowed. But the end was clearly in sight.

1st Bn.	*The 1st Battalion* had spent some months at Kohima away north of Imphal. Meanwhile, the Fourteenth Army plan, briefly outlined in the Backscreen, was taking shape. The IVth Corps, it will be remembered, was to show itself on the Irrawaddy above Mandalay, and force a crossing, as the clearest possible indication to the Japanese that the IVth Corps was coming to the assistance of the XXXIIIrd Corps for the decisive operation in that area. In point of fact, it was being switched secretly away well south of Mandalay, to attempt to force its way in on the enemy's communications about Meiktila.
29 Dec.	The 7th Indian Division, to which the 1st Battalion belonged, was destined for Pakokku, 80 miles downstream of Mandalay. The Battalion accordingly left Kohima on the 29th December, moving by M.T. to Tamu in the Kabaw valley.

To lend colour to the circumstances in which the Battalion moved, some extracts follow from *Golden Arrow*—the story of the 7th Indian Division—published under authority of the Director of Public Relations, War Department, Government of India. The divisional sappers "had been the first to move and had constructed a new 'Ngakyedauk' over a range of hills bordering the Chindwin at Thaungdut. The 19th Indian Division used this pass later as part of the 'road to Mandalay'.

"But before Christmas came further orders for the sappers of the Golden Arrow Division. With part of 136 Field Regiment, they moved 250 miles south to engineer a new road from the Manipur river, crossing at Sinaung Myauk, below Kalemyo, down into the Myittha valley.

"While the sappers blasted and bulldozed their way through virgin jungle on a forty mile diversion which concealed our movements from the enemy remaining in the Myittha valley, the first guns of the 136 Field Regiment winched and hauled by 'quads' reached Gangaw and were deployed against the Jap stronghold.

"The sappers and gunners were the advance force of not only a divisional but a corps concentration which was the prelude to the decisive operation of the Burma war, the thrust into the heart of central Burma by the drive on Meiktila.

"The division was on the move, spread over three hundred miles of road from Kohima to Tamu and beyond. At this time the planning staff was fighting a battle with figures, for to provide road lift for an entire division including mule companies was no mean task.

"The first stage of the march was to take them to Gangaw. From Gangaw they were to move south 150 miles to the banks of the Irrawaddy. The move was secret. All Divisional signs were blacked out. The use of wireless was forbidden. This concentration of 7th Division, to be followed by 17th Indian Division at a later stage, was the master stroke of the 14th Army.

"The achievements of this trek to the banks of the Irrawaddy were phenomenal. All services played a distinguished part—for it was largely a service task. One mule company marched all the way from Kohima to Myitche, more than 400 miles—and arrived with all its animals in good condition after a trek which would have done credit to an explorer. The Divisional R.I.A.S.C. found itself faced with the lifting of men and mules and supplying at one time units spread over 8,000 square miles of country. In this they had the assistance of air-supply. Divisional signals laid over 800 miles of field cable in six weeks to maintain communication without wireless. The I.E.M.E. leapfrogged its workshop companies down the march route to keep the Division on the move.

"Operationally at this stage the Division's commitments were not great. Gangaw had fallen in the first week in January to men of the Chin Hills battalion of the Lushai Brigade after the biggest airstrike yet seen in the Burma war, which tore great rents in the enemy's jungle stronghold on the bank of the Myittha river.

"28 East African Brigade took over the advance down the Gangaw valley. This was a picked screen, for the intention of the 14th Army commander at this stage was to persuade the Japanese that the whole of 4th Corps had crossed the Chindwin and were headed for Mandalay. They were to assume that this East African brigade was part of the 11th East African Division which had chased them out of the Kabaw valley. Behind this deception screen the build-up of 4th Corps in the Myittha valley was to take place.

"While the East African brigade moved south on the general axis of the road in the direction of Pauk, General Evans deployed his forces behind them with the object of obtaining a quick grip on the north and west banks of the Irrawaddy at the point where the river turns south after its confluence with the Chindwin.

1944

"33 Brigade was still moving down the tenuous and rapidly deteriorating line of communication from Kohima to Kan—north of Gangaw—a distance of 350 miles.

"89 Brigade group on an all pack basis with Mountain Artillery in support was therefore sent off on a long left hook south of Gangaw between the Myittha and the Chindwin.

"On the extreme left flank moved the Divisional reconnaissance battalion of the 7/2nd Punjab, with the Lushai Scouts.

"Supplied entirely by air the 7/2nd Punjab moved through the rugged country on the east bank of the Myittha, marching 200 miles in four weeks to reach the Irrawaddy at Pakokku.

"89 Brigade group, consisting of the 1/11th Sikhs, the 2nd Battalion King's Own Scottish Borderers and the 4/8th Gurkha Rifles, moved south from Gangaw to cut the road from Tilin to Pauk, and to capture Pauk itself.

"114 Brigade moved behind the East Africans. At Lessaw the 4/14th Punjab broke an attempt by the Japs to capture the Tilin air strip. The brigade then moved east towards Pakokku.

"Here in the first week of February, stiff fighting for the possession of Pakokku took place, in which battalions of the 4/5th Royal Gurkha Rifles, and the 7/2nd and 4/14th Punjab were engaged against 214 Regt of the famous 33rd Japanese Division. Pakokku was strongly defended and the fighting on the outskirts and in the town lasted a week before the enemy garrison was subdued with the loss of some 350 men.

"While the southwards advance went on, 33 Brigade of the Division had been training at Gangaw for the crossing of the Irrawaddy.

"Assault boats, rafts and sapper equipment had been moved south down the line of communication...

"So far there was no indication that the enemy had any suspicion of our plan... But to make assurance doubly sure, the deception shadow play went on.

"The East African brigade, having reached Pauk, pushed on to Seikpyu on the west bank of the river opposite the oil town of Chauk with the object of making it appear that we were aiming a direct thrust at the oil-fields area. From the heavy counter-attacks which were thrown in this area it is apparent that the Jap swallowed the bait."

Thus *Golden Arrow*, and the frame into which the 1st Battalion story will now be placed.

29 Dec. The Battalion had moved down from Kohima to Tamu in the Kabaw valley by M.T. on the 29th December. The contrast since its first move along that road—but in the contrary direction—nearly three years before, was marked. Then, we had no planes and a slender supply-line by land. Now, tanks, guns and lorries were pouring down the road

in a steady stream in the opposite direction; the continuous roar of aeroplane engines was entirely ours; and air-supply was a proved and dependable source of maintenance. But on the debit side, only one of the original officers remained with the Battalion, and the ranks were equally charged with newcomers.

From Tamu, the Battalion moved to the Myittha valley where the 7th Indian Division was concentrating; and early in January the advance began.   *January*

At the outset the 89th Indian Infantry Brigade was in reserve, and the Battalion did not go into action. The fall of Gangaw about this time was followed by the advance of the East Africans southwards towards Pauk, and the 89th Brigade set off on its long left-hook.

The Brigade's primary mission was to cut the Japanese communications southwards from the Gangaw area; 50 miles south of Gangaw came the town of Tilin at the head-waters of the Myittha; 20 miles southeast of Tilin is Pauk, which itself lies 40 miles almost due west of Pakokku. The Japanese communications were to be cut between Tilin and Pauk, and Pauk itself captured.

The Brigade moved fast, and, starting on the 18th January, reached   *18 Jan.*
its objective at Yebo on the 25th, two days before the set date. Despite the comparatively short direct distance, the detour followed, between   *25 Jan.*
the Myittha and the Chindwin, involved a move of 180 miles over very difficult country. The completion of this in eight days on a pack basis was a most creditable performance.

Unfortunately, the threat to his rear had unsettled the enemy farther north. He pulled back quickly, and just beat the Brigade.

With the Battalion in the lead, the Brigade now pushed down the road. Contact was made with enemy rearguards, but these slipped away before they could be pinned.

Sinthe lies between Pakokku and Pauk, and was to be the IVth Corps air-head for the Irrawaddy crossing. By the 29th January, the Battalion   *29 Jan.*
had secured the village, while the Brigade seized Pauk and the high ground to the east. Pakokku, a few miles east of Sinthe was held in strength by the Japanese, till captured by the 114th Indian Infantry Brigade early on in February.

Some 18 miles downstream of Pakokku is the village of Myitche, opposite Pagan on the Irrawaddy east bank. The Sikhs were now ordered to patrol down the Yaw Chaung in that direction, and if possible occupy Myitche. The little-used track that led to it had been left uncovered by the Japanese, and Myitche undefended. There was hence no opposition, and, by occupying Myitche on the 5th February,   *5 Feb.*
the Battalion earned the distinction of being the first troops to reach the Irrawaddy south of Mandalay.

The assault-crossing of the Irrawaddy was to be effected by the

1945

33rd Indian Infantry Brigade at Nyaungu, a mile or two upstream of Pagan, and Myitche became a scene of feverish activity. The Sikhs themselves were by no means inactive, preparing a feint crossing some 6 miles downstream—one of the several deception measures up and down the river employed to mislead the enemy.

Very much the toads-under-the-harrow are troops employed in feints. They work with no hope of glory—or even of more than the unnoticed crumbs of such special equipment as may be allotted to the operation as a whole. So it was here. No assault craft were left over after the 33rd Indian Infantry Brigade's requirements had been met, and the Battalion was forced to rely on local country boats and understandably reluctant local country boatmen to carry out its hazardous task.

However, the Sikhs removed themselves from Myitche to a point farther down the river. Here they began vigorous patrolling with reconnaissances of both banks at the points selected for the feint. The local boatmen were won over, and took the first patrols across **11 Feb.** to the east bank on the 11th February. The bank was reconnoitred as far as the southern outskirts of Pagan, and found unoccupied. This in a sense was disappointing. It looked as if either the enemy had been too much occupied elsewhere to notice the feint preparations—or did not believe them.

However, the Divisional Commander saw no reason to let the opportunity slip. He decided to make the feint an actuality, and ordered the Battalion, with a battery of mountain artillery, to cross in force the following night.

The crossing was to be made in two phases.

12 Feb. In the first phase, that night, the 12th February, the force set out with the assistance of six country boats, to transport itself over 300 yards of swirling water, in pitchy darkness, to a large island. Arrived on this island, some twenty-five local bullock carts lent a hand to transport the stores for a distance of 2 miles to a selected concentration area. Curiously enough, these almost Heath Robinson preliminaries to what amounted to very nearly an *ad hoc* crossing, worked without a hitch; and by dawn on the 13th, the troops were safely tucked away, making active preparations for the final crossing.

This second phase, the final crossing, however, developed difficulties. During the first phase, a patrol with a wireless set had gone across **13 Feb.** to Pagan; but about 11 a.m. on the 13th, disturbing news was received. Pagan was now held. An alternative scheme had been prepared involving a landing farther downstream, but this was ruled out by the high wind and heavy swell which had sprung up, and which altogether prohibited the boats moving.

In the circumstances, it was decided to carry on with the original scheme. At 4 a.m., accordingly, on the 14th February, "B" Company, 14 Feb. under Maj. Merrick, set off in fifteen large unwieldy country craft. The first part of the crossing went off without interference, but when nearing the far bank, heavy machine-gun and rifle fire was opened with disastrous consequences. The local boatmen panicked, dropped their oars, and got down on the floor-boards, and the boats drifted off downstream out of control. The troops did their best but they were not accustomed to working in craft of that nature and in so strong a current. However, after drifting some time, Maj. Merrick got his boatmen working again, but it was naturally quite impossible to remount the assault, and he got his men as best he could back to the concentration area. Astonishingly enough, the only casualty was one man wounded.

However, the action was not without its uses, for, as afterwards appeared, it attracted a strong party of Japanese away from the main crossing, which was proceeding well. These Japanese went back to the main crossing when they saw the Sikhs draw off, but their services were lost to the enemy at a critical stage in the operations.

The night passed without incident, but early next morning there 15 Feb. was an interesting development. A white flag made its appearance on the enemy bank at Pagan, and two men crossed over with it. These were two ranks from the Indian National Army, a force of Indians fighting for the Japanese. They reported that the Japanese on their bank had moved off northwards, leaving one company of Indian National Army troops to hold Pagan, and said the company wished to surrender. Maj. Merrick at once volunteered to take his company across the river, but was unable to manage more than one platoon for lack of ferrying facilities. Only three country boats were available, and these the troops had to paddle as best they could themselves, with officers at the tiller. However, the little flotilla reached the far bank in safety, and as they did so, the company of Indians marched down the river and laid down its arms. More boats were hurriedly collected, and by evening Battalion Headquarters, with "A" and "B" Companies, were securely established in Pagan. The remainder of the Battalion, less "C" Company, which was protecting the southern flank of the Division west of the Irrawaddy, crossed with the mountain battery next morning, 16 Feb. and contact was established with the main bridge-head, for the right flank protection of which the Battalion was made responsible.

The Battalion had a satisfactory welcome from the Burmese in Pagan. The record speaks of their showing the troops round the ancient temples, of which many date back to the eleventh and twelve centuries, in this ancient capital of the Burmese kings with its countless beautiful pagodas. But they added with deep feeling that they could no longer display their more valued treasures, as these had been taken by the Japanese and removed, they said, to Tokyo.

1945

17 Feb. The Battalion did not linger in Pagan. Next day, the 17th, it shifted its ground 2 miles to the south and took up a position astride the road leading from Pagan to Chauk, 15 miles or so down-river. Patrols were directed southwards, and quickly contacted parties of the enemy moving north, presumably to the assistance of the Japanese troops opposing the main crossing at Nyaungu. "B" Company went
18 Feb. down the road next day to inflict what damage it could on these enemy parties, and brought on an action in which the Sikhs once more distinguished themselves.

The Company had not gone very far when the patrol working ahead contacted an enemy party in position near a ruined pagoda. Two men of the patrol were wounded, but the Company pushed on, and the enemy withdrew to a large red pagoda about half-a-mile farther south.

The ground here was very open, and Maj. Merrick considered that he could not advance without support. Lieut. Proudlock came back to Battalion Headquarters to explain how matters stood. On his report the commanding officer asked Brigade Headquarters for a troop of tanks, and added a section of 3-inch mortars from the Battalion, under Capt. Pritam Singh, to give further support. He then moved forward himself with a small headquarters to the ruined pagoda where the enemy had first been contacted.

The tanks arrived about 11 o'clock, and "B" Company advanced. The enemy were driven back to some high ground a little south. "B" Company and the tanks followed them up, keeping to the east of the road, while the commanding officer and mortars moved forward to the red pagoda.

The country to the west of the road, over across from "B" Company, was very broken. Something over a hundred Japanese were hiding in a village in this broken ground. The Company, however, never saw them, and passed them by unnoticed. Allowing the Company to go on its way, these Japanese closed in as soon as the coast was clear and attacked the red pagoda. Battalion Headquarters and the mortars were completely surprised. Capt. Pritam Singh was severely wounded almost at once. Maj. Webster and Lieut. Proudlock made every effort to get him away, but he was in an exposed position and they could not manage it. Headquarters and the mortars contrived to break away in a 15-cwt. truck just as the enemy closed in, and headed away after "B" Company. The Japanese then charged in, and an officer brandishing a sword rushed at Capt. Pritam Singh, but thinking he was dead, lowered his sword and moved on, leaving him where he lay.

"B" Company knew nothing at all of all this till the headquarter party caught it up. It being clearly necessary to clear away the Japanes in rear before they could consolidate, the Company turned about to attack the pagoda position at once.

It was the Japanese this time who were surprised. The tanks did great execution, blasting some out of their positions with their 75 m.m. guns, and catching others in the open with their machine-guns. After some confused and brisk fighting, the Japanese were thrown back, leaving some fifty killed on the ground. Casualties in the Company were less, but they suffered a grievous loss in their company commander, Maj. Merrick, mortally wounded leading his men in the latter part of the action.

Two platoons of "A" Company had been called forward by wireless and had taken up a covering position through which "B" Company withdrew. The whole force then moved back to the Battalion position.

Much credit for this successful withdrawal was due to No. 12773-IO Sub. Joginder Singh, "B" Company's second-in-command. He took over at once when Maj. Merrick fell, and, under very heavy mortar fire and machine-gun fire, with complete disregard for his personal safety, rapidly reorganized the Company, moving freely about between platoons. He next went over to the tanks, which had been singled out as a special target by the enemy, and coolly directed their fire on to enemy concentrations and strong-points. How valuable his contribution was at this critical juncture can only be guessed at, but it was probably decisive. He was slightly wounded, but paid no attention to it either then or later. It may be permissible to add here that when the night attack developed the same night, he displayed just such qualities of leadership again, and received a deservedly awarded Military Cross for his joint contribution in these two actions.

The action, it was learned, had broken up an enemy column moving north to the main bridge-head area, and had inflicted much loss on them.

To complete the story of this rather intricate little operation, it is worth following for a moment the fortunes of the Battalion Headquarters 15-cwt. truck, and its driver, Sep. Pertap Singh.

No. 12848 Sep. Pertap Singh's truck contained an "O" Group and a mortar section. When the Japanese charged in on the "O" Group, about 1 p.m., Pertap Singh drove quickly up to the mortar section, took the mortars on board, and, although a special target for the enemy, who were only about 60 yards away, coolly set off after "B" Company. The confused fighting that followed caused heavy casualties in the Company, but Pertap Singh and his truck seemed to bear charmed lives, in the thick of grenade discharger and mortar fire. The truck provided no cover, and Pertap Singh refused to leave it and look for some. Instead, he drove his truck from section to section, until he had himself personally loaded twelve wounded men into it. This self-imposed task relieved the troops from what might have been a

1945

difficult and costly business later. The award of a Military Medal was a well deserved one. Capt. Pritam Singh, meanwhile, lying out in the open, had been picked up and brought in by a tank.

18-19 Feb. Throughout the following night, that of the 18th/19th February, heavy attacks were made on "D" Company, under Maj. Dykes, holding a position some 2 miles east of the Battalion. The Company was heavily outnumbered, and held its position with difficulty, but the enemy was eventually beaten back with loss along the whole Company front. A vital point in the Company defences had been held by L.-Naik Maghar Singh, to whose courage and determination it was chiefly due that the enemy did not break in there. Constantly the target for enemy grenades, he was severely wounded on three separate occasions, but refused to leave his machine-gun, and threw the enemy back time after time till they finally withdrew. For this he received the award of a Military Medal, which he richly deserved.

During the attacks on "D" Company, subsidiary attacks were made on the Battalion position, but had no success.

A short lull now followed during which the 89th Indian Infantry

21 Feb. Brigade edged forward, moving on the 21st February a few miles south to Monakton. Here it took up a position in the dry, arid area north of Singu, which covered the approaches to Chauk and the oil-fields. The 4th/8th Gurkhas deployed astride the main road to Singu. The Sikhs took up a position 3 miles east of the Irrawaddy, with "D" Company in a detached position another 4 miles farther east in the village of Tetma. The King's Own Scottish Borderers were in reserve. Time was given for the troops to settle down and organize their defences;

23-24 Feb. but on the night of the 23rd/24th February a fierce assault was made and was repulsed with heavy loss to the enemy.

In this assault, L.-Naik Dilwara Singh showed his metal. His section was badly knocked about and his bren gun was put out of action. Seeing that his position was in danger of being over-run, L.-Naik Dilwara Singh jumped out of his trench under heavy enemy mortar and automatic fire, to get the Bren gun back into action. He was almost immediately wounded, but continued to fire his gun and hold the enemy in check. The Japanese redoubled their efforts to rush the post. L.-Naik Dilwara Singh was a second time wounded—this time in the left arm—but still refused to give in, keeping his gun in action and holding the enemy in check. For this example of courage and devotion he was awarded a Military Medal.

The enemy now abandoned further efforts to reinforce his troops at the main bridge-head from the south.

"Much gruelling work lay ahead", however, as the 7th Indian Division record *Golden Arrow* tells. "The bridgehead had to be held secure. South at Seikpyu on the western bank the Japs had reacted strongly to the East Africans advance. To the north, on the eastern side of the river, the Japs were in considerable strength and occupied the important river port of Myingyan, a railhead too for the metre gauge railway running east to Meiktila and beyond.

"The operations to clear the approaches to this town and to drive out the enemy garrison brought the Golden Arrow Division two more V.C.'s, both awarded to Sikhs from the same regiment—the 4/15th Punjab, making three Sikh V.C.'s in the Division".

This, however, is to anticipate. Meanwhile, the IVth Corps began rapidly concentrating east of the Irrawaddy, screened by the 17th Indian Division's mobile column, striking at Meiktila. By this move, not only were Gen. Kimura's communications back from Mandalay cut, but he was separated from the Japanese main forces farther south. Time, however, was required before either side was in a position to exploit the changed strategic position, and the Battalion was left in comparative peace in its positions for the remainder of the month.

The 2nd Battalion, in the van of the 4th Indian Division, had reached Urbino, 15 miles in from the Adriatic coast and nearly due east of Florence. This was on the 30th August. During the next few days it moved slowly north-westwards behind the enemy rearguards. On the 4th September, it watched the 4th Battalion advancing in great style with the 5th Indian Infantry Brigade of the 4th Indian Division to the capture of Tavaletto.

A few hours later the same day, the 2nd Battalion itself was in action, some 3,000 yards to the west, in an attack on the village of Poggio San Giovanni.

For this attack, "A" and "D" Companies, under Maj. Harwant Singh and Maj. J. W. Anson respectively, moved for some distance up the mined bed of the river Foglia, and then swung north into the hills in which Poggia San Giovanni lay. The village, on a commanding position in the enemy defence line, which here lay along a high razor-backed feature above the valley of the Conca, was strongly held. Late in the evening, concentrations from the divisional artillery were called for, and were effective in inflicting heavy casualties on the Germans. The village fell at last light after brisk fighting, and the establishment of our troops there did much to relieve pressure on the right flank of the Gurkhas, who were meeting strong enemy resistance in the hills.

The awards made to officers and men of "A" Company for the determination and valour with which this attack was carried through reflect the Battalion's fighting spirit at this time. Maj. Harwant Singh, commanding "A", the forward company, in the attack, accurately set the tone when his company was held up by three concealed machine-guns, which were sweeping the ridges and gullies across which his men were attacking. Moving about in the open among his forward troops, encouraging the men, locating the enemy machine-guns, and coolly making his plan to silence them, Maj. Harwant Singh drew heavy artillery and machine-gun fire; and in one burst of machine-gun fire, he was himself wounded in the chest, while every other member of his company headquarters was either killed or wounded.

However, having made his plan, and sent vital information back to Battalion Headquarters, Maj. Harwant Singh advanced with his right leading platoon, as soon as his left forward platoon which had moved higher up the ridge to turn the enemy right flank, had silenced the machine-guns, capturing a Spandau in addition, and killing its crew. During this phase of the attack Maj. Harwant Singh was wounded in the arm by shell-fire. Later, he was again hit, and wounded in the leg, but he continued to command his company with complete disregard for his own personal safety, for a total of 4½ hours after he was first hit. It was only when the position was firmly established, and a direct order had been given by Lieut.-Col. P. S. Mitcheson, commanding the Battalion, to hand over his company and come back for treatment that he consented to be removed to the Regimental Aid Post. For the fine and courageous example he set, Maj. Harwant Singh was very properly awarded a Military Cross.

It will have been observed that the continued advance of "A" Company's right leading platoon was made possible by an outflanking movement by the left leading platoon. This platoon was commanded by No. IC-42146 Jem. Kaka Singh.

When the Company was held up, at the time Maj. Harwant Singh received his first wound, Jem. Kaka Singh at once set about solving the impasse. He left one of his sections in position to engage the enemy's attention, and himself moved off to the left along a covered approach, with his other two sections, towards an outflanking position farther up the ridge. While on his way, he was suddenly engaged at 50 yards range by a Spandau, which had hitherto remained silent and which had not been located. Collecting his men, Jem. Kaka Singh promptly charged up the hill, throwing No. 65 grenades as he went, killed the German gunners, and captured the Spandau. He then brought his own Brens into action in an unavoidably exposed position, swept by German S.P. artillery fire, and silenced the three enemy machine-guns which had been holding up the Company advance. For this example of fine leadership, he was awarded a Military Cross.

Returning to the Company's right forward platoon—No. 7—No. 13103 Hav. Sham Singh, commanding its leading section, had been moving his section forward from ridge to ridge until he had worked his way apparently unobserved into a position close under an enemy machine-gun post. Collecting his men, he hurled in three grenades, and then charged in with the bayonet, bayoneting and killing the crew of four Germans manning the gun.

Moving forward again towards Poggio San Giovanni village, keeping well ahead of the Company, Hav. Sham Singh continued to set an example of courage and fearlessness which was the subject of general comment, and won him the award of a Military Medal.

Next day, the 5th September, patrols of "D" Company and the Gurkhas flushed an enemy observation post of twelve men. The "birds" obligingly broke both ways and the bag was equally shared with the Gurkhas.   5 Sept.

The troops were now pressing closely on the Gothic Line defences high up on the ridge, and from now on the enemy fought fiercely with heavy concentrations of artillery, and contested every yard of the ground.

The ground itself was mountainous and wooded, favouring delaying action. More careful integration of plans was required—a change not sufficiently realized in the first instance. Thus, on the 9th September, it was proposed to mount a somewhat complex night attack on a dominating ridge some distance away. It was first arranged that the 4th Battalion, from the 5th Indian Infantry Brigade, should secure the low-lying village of Onferno comparatively early in the night, as a preliminary. The 2nd Battalion would then pass through and carry out a night advance of 5,000 yards to attack the ridge.   9 Sept.

It was appreciated that there were risks, but pressure elsewhere on the front was causing embarrassment. It was thought that this pressure would be relieved if the attack was made, and it was just on the cards that if successful, a break-through might follow.

The omens were not very propitious, however. The Battalion's attempts at ground reconnaissance were strongly resisted, and movement drew artillery and mortar fire at once. The only officer to see the ground at all was the commanding officer, who was flown over it, and little was known from any source of the enemy's strength or dispositions. Further complications followed. The 4th Battalion was to be used elsewhere, and would not be available for the preliminary operation, which the 2nd Battalion would have to tackle itself.

By the 10th September, the Battalion had moved one ridge forward, and at 11.30 p.m. on the 11th, the advance began. Two companies were deployed forward, and two held back to exploit. As expected, the intervening ground was strongly held, and the left forward company which was advancing along a bare and narrow ridge, was held up. Much the same befell the right forward company. It was quickly in contact; but moving forward on ground not previously reconnoitred, and which was well mined, it made little progress.   10 Sept.

    11 Sept.

1944
12 Sept.

A third company was now interposed between the two forward companies, but it too was soon in difficulties. Daylight found the Battalion with its Battle Headquarters and "B" and "D" Companies, under Maj. J. W. Anson and Capt. A. W. Franklin respectively, digging in on a forward slope overlooked by the enemy, who held in great strength dominating ground in admirable artillery range of our troops' positions.

Bad enough as it was, the position was worsened when German snipers succeeded in setting fire to a haystack some 30 yards from the Battle Headquarters slit-trench. The column of flame and smoke that went up gave the enemy gunners an excellent aiming-mark for a 12-hour day of heavy and accurate shelling.

However, wireless orders were received at 5.30 p.m. to press on that night against the original objectives. How it can have been expected that the attack would succeed, unless information was available at the headquarters of higher formations which was not passed down to the Battalion, is not clear. Whatever the circumstances, one fresh company, together with one of those in action during the day, went in to the attack. Fierce close-quarter fighting brought no gains to the Battalion, and the position had subsequently to be turned by the Division on the right after a fierce struggle.

It is a truism that the more bitter the fighting the less fully can it be documented and described. But such light as is thrown on the operation in earlier paragraphs, is heightened by the record of individual gallantry given in the citations for decorations and awards. It may not be easy to link them with definite phases of the operation, but they testify in no uncertain manner to the endurance and gallantry of the Battalion as a whole.

Take the case, then, of No. IC-24425 Jem. Mewa Singh, commanding one of the platoons that made the night attack on Onferno on the night of the 11th/12th September. As already noted, the low-lying and closely scrub-covered ground was firmly held by the enemy. The attack was prematurely discovered, and Jem. Mewa Singh's platoon—in common with the Company as a whole—came under very heavy shell, mortar and small-arms fire. The platoon itself formed the right flank of the Company's advance, and was quickly engaged in close-quarter fighting, including not fewer than five enemy light machine-guns well dug in and concealed in the scrub-covered foothills ahead.

Further advance being impossible in the face of this opposition, Jem. Mewa Singh disposed his platoon so as to face the enemy on all fronts. While these positions were being taken up, and the men were digging in, the Jemadar moved fearlessly from section to section under heavy small-arms fire, encouraging all ranks, and creating a feeling of general confidence.

1944

Day breaking, heavy enemy mortar fire was directed on the platoon, and an immediate counter-attack was thrown in. Jem. Mewa Singh promptly moved to an exposed position from which he could watch the conduct of the fight, and the attack was driven off, seven enemy dead being accounted for, whilst at least as many more were known to have been carried away, dead or wounded.

Touch with the remainder of the company had been lost during the night, so Jem. Mewa Singh, having no instructions to the contrary, prepared to continue his advance alone towards the objective. This he did with considerable skill and coolness, reaching Onferno, which he found to be strongly held, and launching two attacks on it. Both attacks failed, and seeing no other course open to him, he withdrew his platoon with its nine casualties, safely back through the enemy lines.

Considering the extremely unpropitious start to the night's operations, and the daunting prospect that faced this isolated platoon when daylight came, it will be conceded that Jem. Mewa Singh showed resolution and resourcefulness of a very high order, and that his award of the Military Cross was a just one.

No. 11898 Hav. Pala Singh of "C" Company was engaged elsewhere during the night attack, his company being directed against Mt. Colemba.

Early on during the advance, the Company encountered strong enemy resistance from houses in Il Poggio village, where four Spandau posts had been sited. Hav. Pala Singh was told to take his platoon and overcome this resistance.

Posting two sections to support him forward by fire, he at once led the remaining section round by a flank onto the first of the Spandau posts.

Moving from house to house, armed with a machine carbine and grenades collected from the covering sections, Hav. Pala Singh himself knocked out two of the four posts, killing two enemy in each. Seeing the determination of the attack, the enemy hurriedly withdrew from the two remaining posts, thus opening the way for the Company's continued advance.

The following night, the 12th/13th September, when the Company was being withdrawn, a strong enemy counter-attack was thrown in. Hav. Pala Singh, entirely on his own initiative, moved off to a flank, where for 30 minutes, until the attack was beaten off, he was seen, single-handed, with a Bren gun and a pile of stick bombs, holding off a strong enemy threat with complete disregard for his own safety.

12-13 Sept.

These were the culminating examples of bravery and self-sacrifice to a series of courageous actions over the previous two months, and Hav. Pala Singh was awarded the Indian Distinguished Service Medal in recognition of them.

1944
11-12
Sept.

  Naik Atma Singh was in the same vicinity as Hav. Pala Singh during the night of the 11th/12th September; and, like Hav. Pala Singh, had been noted several times during the past two months when, as "C" Company patrol leader, he had led the way successfully through enemy-held positions.

  On the night of the 11th/12th September, Naik Atma Singh and his section were working their way ahead of the Company along a narrow and exposed ridge. On the way he surprised and captured two German soldiers, part of an enemy patrol, and killed with his own hand a third who attempted to give the alarm by shouting.

  Moving on again, the advance continued without further trouble for some 500 yards, when the section was held up by close-range light machine-gun fire from a post astride the track. Undeterred, Naik Atma Singh infiltrated through to the rear of the post, from where he launched a surprise attack, killing the enemy gunner.

  Reaching a position on an exposed forward slope, under close enemy view, the Company deployed as best it could, and spent the next twelve hours from dawn on the 12th September, under constant and very harassing fire from enemy sniper posts. Naik Atma Singh succeeded in locating one of these posts, and moved off on an individual stalk to try and destroy it. He was within only a few yards of it, when he was severely wounded. His award of a Military Medal it will be conceded, was very well earned.

  In the Onferno neighbourhood, meanwhile, No. 19371 Sep. Babu Singh had achieved an Indian Distinguished Service Medal in circumstances of great personal bravery and disregard for danger.

  The situation was that Sep. Babu Singh's section, which was leading its platoon's attack on Onferno village on the night of the 11th/12th September, ran into fierce resistance and was pinned to the ground. Babu Singh did not wait for any orders. He worked his Bren gun round to a flank, and, silencing two enemy machine-gun posts by fire, enabled his platoon to continue its advance. However, the situation proved to be more involved than had been expected, for fire was suddenly opened from well-sited light machine-gun posts in rear, and the platoon had to face about to counter it. In the ensuing confusion, Sep. Babu Singh was wounded in the left arm and thigh by light machine-gun fire and a shell-splinter but, handing over his gun to the No. 2, took over a sling of bombs and a tommy-gun, and telling the No. 2 to cover him, he made off alone for a machine-gun post which was much impeding the platoon's movements. He destroyed the post single-handed with the grenades he carried, killing the two German gunners at their gun.

  If one stops for an instant to consider in cold blood just what risks this gallant soldier took on behalf of his comrades, it will be clear enough that his Indian Distinguished Service Medal was the least award that could have been made him.

No. 12849 Hav. Chanan Singh was in this same general area during the fateful night of the 11th/12th September. This non-commissioned officer had only taken over command of his platoon less than three weeks before, when his platoon commander was killed in action, but he was noted as having led it with conspicuous gallantry on four separate occasions since.

On the night of the 11th/12th September his company was employed on a difficult night attack along a ridge which was believed to be strongly held by the enemy. Chanan Singh's platoon was selected to lead.

The platoon quickly made contact, and an extremely involved situation blew up. Small-arms fire was opened simultaneously from front and rear, and close fighting ensued.

There were three enemy light machine-gun posts on the platoon's front, and Hav. Chanan Singh decided to cope with these by taking his reserve section round to a flank under covering fire from the remainder of the platoon. The resistance, however, was too great for immediate success, but the platoon held on to ground which was vital to the Company, for the rest of the night.

Shortly before first light on the 12th September, the Company was ordered to withdraw, but was compelled to dig in hurriedly on a forward slope in full view of the enemy. A pause followed, and then orders came through to attempt an infiltration to the right towards the village of Onferno. The ground was complicated by low ridges which were firmly held by the enemy, and not much progress was possible. It was full daylight, and the enemy had good observation. However, Hav. Chanan Singh showed great personal initiative and determination to close with the enemy throughout the day under very heavy mortar and shell fire. He was severely wounded leading his platoon against light machine-gun posts strongly positioned in houses in the village of Ca Bernardo; but, though unable to walk, and suffering severely from loss of blood, he insisted on remaining with his platoon for the six hours till nightfall. For this example of fighting qualities, he received the Military Medal.

Last of the awards for this operation was the Indian Distinguished Service Medal granted to No. 13124 Hav. Jagir Singh of "A" Company.

During the second attack on Onferno on the night of the 12th/13th September, the leading Company—"B"—in this two-company operation secured the preliminary objective after fierce fighting. For the advance to the final objective, "A" Company was to pass through and continue the attack.

Jagir Singh was platoon havildar in "A" Company's leading platoon, which ran into trouble as soon as it passed the "B" Company position. The enemy mortar fire suddenly ceased, and a party of enemy of much the same strength counter-attacked without warning, in the dark, against the flank of Hav. Jagir Singh's platoon. The platoon commander was killed, and the "38" set which Hav. Jagir Singh was wearing at the time, received a hit from a shell-splinter, completely breaking the set, and wounding the havildar in the chest.

Jagir Singh immediately took charge. With a lusty "Wah Guru Ji", he led his platoon in onto the enemy, tommy-gunning three of the enemy where they stood. He then broke up the remaining enemy with the hand grenades he was carrying, and scattered them in the greatest disorder, leaving five of their dead on the ground.

However, under heavy and accurate shelling and mortaring, the Company could make little progress, and at the end of two hours fruitless endeavour, it was brought to a standstill. Hav. Jagir Singh, who by this time was suffering much from his wound, then occupied himself, while still under heavy fire, in organizing a platoon aid post, and in helping the two stretcher-bearers in their duties. Subsequently, when the platoon was withdrawn—which it carried out with parade-ground steadiness—Jagir Singh himself carried back over the 500 yards of difficult, fire-swept country, not only a wounded comrade, but the rifles of two of the platoon casualties in addition. He was awarded the Indian Distinguished Service Medal.

The total Battalion bill in casualties for the thirty-six hours of operations added about 150 to the previous losses, themselves not yet made good. Being too weak to sustain the normal establishment pending the arrival of reinforcements, the Battalion was temporarily reorganized on a three-company basis. To effect this while in close contact with an alert and active enemy was a grave decision; but fortunately at this moment, the enemy elected to stage one of his deep withdrawals, giving the Battalion a chance to shake down in its new form, while following up through the small independent state of San Marino, towering up above the surrounding countryside on its high rocky buttresses. Slight enemy interference only was experienced during this advance, the Brigade being for the time being in reserve.

The weather had been steadily deteriorating, and was now consistently bad. Rain was heavy and continuous, and made the going for guns and tanks slow and tedious. Aircraft were grounded by the muddy condition of the landing-strips and rivers were constantly flooding down in spate. It was almost impossible to keep the men dry, whether on the move or at rest. Few houses were left undestroyed, and nothing but gas capes was available to keep off the rain for those sleeping in the open, or while on the move. However, the advance went relentlessly on to the valley of the Rubicon; and on the high ground of this river, and on the line of the Marechio river, the Brigade was fiercely opposed.

1944
30 Sept.

For this operation, the Gurkhas made a preliminary attack and secured the right flank after heavy fighting. The Sikhs, with a composite British battalion (the amalgamated Camerons and Royal Sussex) on their right, then carried out a night attack on the 30th September on an objective north of the Rubicon.

The objective was part of a dominating ridge, with the village of Borghi at its western end. A night advance of about 4,500 yards had first to be carried out, and the Rubicon waded during the advance.

The attack was supported by exceptionally heavy concentrations from the corps artillery. The enemy defences on the ridge had already held up the advance for several days, and special artillery ammunition allotments had been made. The objective was something under half-a-mile in width, and during the four hours artillery programme for the attack, 24,600 shells of all types were fired. As a consequence, prisoners taken were in a dazed condition.

The attack was a complete success, at a cost to the Battalion of five casualties only. Three of the five were, unfortunately, officers. Lieut. E. W. Collins, commanding "A" Company, was wounded and taken prisoner during a German counter-attack. The fact of his capture, and that he was suffering from multiple wounds was announced over the German wireless not long after. Lieut. G. H. Mogford and Lieut. P. R. C. Heath—a son of Lieut.-Gen. Sir Lewis Heath, who had previously commanded the 1st Battalion, and was then a prisoner-of-war in Japanese hands—were caught in a burst of enemy artillery fire. The former died of his wounds, but Heath was more fortunate and made a good recovery. He had only joined the Battalion the previous day.

Rain now took charge once more. The Rubicon came down in heavy spate, preventing Battalion Headquarters and the tanks from moving forward onto the objective; and air reconnaissance and air supply had both to go by default.

Communication was kept up by wireless, and, at first light on the 1st October, the two forward companies were ordered to move westwards along the ridge to include features on their left. The movement was resisted, and was not successful.

1 Oct.

Soon after, on the night of the 3rd/4th October, units of the 10th Indian Division came up in relief, and the 4th Indian Division moved back for what proved a comparatively short period of rest and reorganization at the pretty Italian town of Perugia. There had been heavy battle casualties in the past three months—eleven British officers, twelve Viceroy's commissioned officers and over 400 other ranks—and an opportunity to reorganize was urgently needed.

During this short interlude, the Battalion had the pleasant duty of welcoming His Highness the Maharajah of Patiala, who was on a visit

1944-5

from Patiala to the Italian battle-fronts. His Highness, who held rank as an officer in the 2nd Battalion, was able to spend one night with it, and inspected and addressed the troops on parade next morning.

Unknown to the Battalion, however, its stay in Italy was now unexpectedly drawing to a close. The Germans were pulling fast out of Greece, leaving a disturbed and critical position behind them. Paradoxically, it was the communist underground element that had been most energetically carrying on the fight for liberation from the Germans, that contributed to the general ferment that immediately set in when liberation became a fact. Arms and ammunition had been dropped on these elements in considerable quantities from the air to enable them to carry on the struggle. Having succeeded in this, they now proceeded to use these arms to secure a minority communist regime, enforcing their aims on a scale of brutality far greater than any experienced by their unfortunate fellow-countrymen even under the Germans.

The 4th Indian Division had been selected, together with other reinforcements who were being shipped or flown in, to help establish the existing government for at least as long as was required to enable free elections to be held. This was made known to the Battalion
20 Oct. on the 20th October, and it moved south as soon as the Division concentrated, and embarked on the H.T. *Worcestershire*. Escorted
12 Nov. by the cruisers *Ajax* and *Sirius*, it arrived in Salonika in the first flight on the 12th November, and received a warm welcome from the Greek population.

The arrival of troops generally in Greece had been welcomed. Clashes could not be avoided in the first instance at some points, but these were largely confined to the Piraeus and Athens and did not spread elsewhere to any noticeable degree.

Still, with or without fighting, the position in both towns and countryside was explosive, and for two months—till the middle of
January January when a truce was declared and the E.L.A.S. (Communist) divisions were removed 20 miles from all towns—an outbreak of hostilities was always a close possibility.

Now, however, with the truce and the establishment of a semi-stable Greek government, the period of extreme tension ended. It had been a difficult time for the troops. Forbearance and commonsense had been called for from all, but under Brig. Lovett who commanded the troops in the Salonika area, the situation there remained under control till the truce (of Varkiza) was declared.

With the general easing that followed the truce, the troops moved out over a wider area, and the Battalion was posted to Komotini, the capital of Thrace. Here, with the general responsibility of backing

1944

up the troops of the Greek National Army, the Battalion found itself playing a variety of parts. Routine guards and duties alternated with executive organization and control of towns of thirty to forty thousand inhabitants. The Sikhs were well received wherever they went, and, with good opportunities for patrolling and other forms of training, they kept fit and in excellent spirits.

During the winter grand shooting was to be had, with geese and duck present in enormous numbers. Over and above these, and other game, the Battalion "guns" accounted for sixty brace of pheasants during this and the following winter. It was a first-rate break for the Battalion, and it is pleasant to realize that war can have its pleasanter as well as its grimmer side.

The 3rd Battalion had arrived in Baghdad in August, with a programme of duties that stretched its resources to the limit. One guard was forty strong. The others made up in numbers for what they lacked in strength, and the total left little chance for the average soldier to sleep more than one night in three in his bed.

3rd Bn.

August

It might have been supposed that under such conditions of discomfort and strain, during almost the hottest part of a Mesopotamian summer, the standard of turn-out and appearance might have relaxed. This was not so, and the Commander-in-Chief, Lieut.-Gen. Sir Arthur Smith, a soldier with all the high standards and ideals of a guardsman, confirmed this in a personal note of appreciation to the Battalion.

One pleasant duty which could now be fulfilled was the erection of a panel in Baghdad Church. Over an aggregate of nearly ten years in all during the First and Second World Wars, the Battalion had been closely associated with Mesopotamia and the later Iraq, and a long list of officers and men had laid down their lives there. A brief reference to the Church has already been made in the 4th Battalion's record in April 1942. In these latter days when the personal association of British officers with their Indian fellow-soldiers has ended, it is pleasant to reflect that this long and happy association has its memorials outside India as well as within it, and that the Church in Baghdad bears witness to those days of common devotion and glory. The 3rd Battalion's panel erected in honour of those of the Battalion who lost their lives during the years of the Battalion's stay in Mesopotamia and Iraq will, it is hoped, long stand to testify to it.

In early September, the 60th Indian Infantry Brigade, to which the 3rd Battalion belonged, moved off by road to the Lebanon for a course of intensive training in mountain warfare at the Mountain Warfare Training Centre of Mid-East Force. Moving in three M.T. echelons, with the Battalion in the first of these, the column passed through the deserted streets of Baghdad at an early hour, and out across the 500 miles

September

1944

of desert beyond. One big change had occurred since the Battalion last saw it. Then, the vehicles had stretched as far as the eye could see, each driver edging away to avoid the dust of the truck or lorry in front. Now the column rolled across mile after mile of tarmac road in orderly groups of ten to twelve vehicles in each; 18 miles per hour—100 miles a day—Wadi Mahommedi, Rutbah, H4, Mafraq, Damascus, Homs—all familiar names—were left behind as the trucks drove on across the desert. At last the rolling green hills of the Syrian coastal plain, and the blue strip of Mediterranean, first seen from a high pass on the Homs road, brought relief to tired eyes after the endless miles of yellow sand.

At Tripoli, the Rock School Squad had the camp ready among olive groves. Excellent training was provided in perfect country, rising 10,000 feet from sea-level to the cedars. The Battalion *News Letter* here paints a convincing picture of the country. First—the undulating olive groves, then tortuous mountain roads such as Beit Manzar where twenty-three successive hairpin bends are a fact and no figment of the imagination. Finally, the Jebel Aiton, overlooking a drop of 2,000 feet sheer into the Qousba Gorge. One can see it all, and imagine the tonic effect of training in such surroundings. The course concluded with a week's holiday, mainly taken up in exploiting the historical and scenic wonders of the country—some going down to Beirut, while others went up by companies to visit the Crusader Fort near Homs, and Baalbek with its great temple to Jupiter and immense red granite pillars from Asswan in Egypt—and other such places. Additional pleasure was occasioned by a visit from His Highness the Maharajah of Patiala, who was received by a Guard of Honour of Patiala men under Jem. Bhagat Singh, and who thereafter addressed the Battalion, visited the Gurdwara, and had tea in the Viceroy's commissioned officers' club.

November Meanwhile other employment was brewing for the Brigade. Early in November it left Tripoli on the first stage of a long 1,500-mile march through Baghdad and on to the Persian hills beyond. Travelling via Beirut and Damascus, thence to Baghdad and on through Khaniqin and Char Zebar, the long column wound its way up to Durud in Persia, 5,000 feet above sea-level, and under the shadow of a 14,000 foot peak of the Kuh-i-Ushtaran. Throughout this long journey the Battalion had no casualties either among vehicles or men; but, on arrival, Lieut.-Col. Squire, commanding the Battalion, found orders directing him straight back the way he had come for a course at the C.M.T.C. in Italy. He left accordingly after one day in Durud, back over the same 1,500 miles, and on by rail and ship to his destination—surely a fair record for individual movement of this nature.

Durud derived its importance from its position on the trans-Persian supply-route to Russia, and the Brigade was quickly deployed on railway protection duties. Contingents of both the United States and Russian Armies were similarly employed. The Brigade sector ran from Sultanabad in the north to Keshwar, a considerable distance south.

The railway was of first-class strategical importance, not on any account to be interrupted by either direct or incidental interference from any source. Tribal feuds somewhat complicated this duty in the Brigade sector, inasmuch as the railway ran for approximately 100 miles, along the dividing line between the Bakhtiaris, on the eastern side of the Ab-i-Diz river—the Ididi, or, more anciently, the Koprates—and their traditional enemies the Hurs, on the west. The Ab-i-Diz, through most of its turbulent course to Dizful in the foothills, follows a tortuous valley from which precipitous rocky mountains tower up thousands of feet to either side, much favouring the operations of raiding parties, and proportionately complicating defence. Following the railway line upstream, through the gap in the Tureh Range at Shahzand, not far from Durud, the route led north-east over the Central Persian Plateau to Sultanabad, 6,160 feet above sea-level—and here the Brigade's responsibility ended.

As will be seen, the principal problem lay in the protection of the southern sector. Here, following the Ab-i-Diz river, whose valley has much in common with the Chitral valley in northern India, tunnel followed tunnel in never-ending succession; 140 or more tunnels had been hacked or blasted through the constant sequence of bare rocky spurs falling steeply down into this hundred miles of valley below. It was a mountain wilderness where tribal enemies could pay good returns to active exploitation by German agents, with corresponding embarrassment to the Allies. The limited garrisons available were accordingly split up into posts of about a dozen men on average some 5 miles or so apart. Communication between posts was confined to the services of the American-operated railway, or to an occasional local sector road. Patrolling was hard, each man covering about twelve miles every day, and a further 5 miles each night. Meeting a train in the middle of an already too-small tunnel meant emerging like a chimney-sweep. When the Battalion took over the whole sector in February, there were some 200 miles of railway to be protected, though not all with such an extensive deployment as along the Ab-i-Diz.

With this background, we may return to some consideration of conditions in Durud, and hence, in its degree, in every outlying detachment and post. The winter was in sharp contrast to the sultry summer temperatures of Kirkuk, Mosul and Baghdad, and to the pleasant autumn interlude in Syria. Temperatures down to 30 degrees of frost were not uncommon. Tents were cold and dank. Heavy snowfalls were frequent; and during the occasional sunny intervals, the melting snow only further mired an already muddy camp. "D" Company, on detachment in Azna, experienced greater cold than at headquarters. There, breath froze on the pillows at night, in spite of twelve men and an oil stove in an 180-lb. tent.

However, there were pleasant compensations in Durud. The social side was helped out by the two large neighbouring camps, with their detachments of United States and Russian troops. An international rifle meeting was held, in which a representative Indian team took first place, with a British second and a Russian third. Sixty pairs of skis were sent to the Brigade during the winter, and excellent runs were enjoyed down a 3-mile slope from the 8,000 foot Razan pass nearby. The pass lying on the Aid-to-Russia route was kept open by snow-ploughs during the winter, thus enabling skiers to go up by truck and ski down.

Farther afield, a motor-cyclist trial was held in Khaniqin. A team of four despatch-riders went down from the Battalion, and was placed as the best competing Indian team among the 100 mixed entries for the gruelling 65-mile course.

Prodigies of shikar were achieved—duck and the like at Durud; pig, ibex, gazelle, oorial, bear, panther and chikor—down the Ab-i-Diz. The life may have been hard, but it was a happy one.

4th Bn.	*The 4th Battalion*, it will be remembered, had been sharing the fortunes of the 2nd in Italy, in the hard and gradually successful fighting for the Gothic Line. With the capture of Monte Calvo, the Battalion moved forward, with the 1st/9th Gurkha Rifles on its right.
3 Sept.	By the 3rd September it was a little short of Tavaletto.
4 Sept.	The attack on Tavaletto was carried out by the Camerons, the enemy reacting strongly, with heavy shelling and mortar fire all over the
8 Sept.	area. Many wooden schu mines were encountered. On 8th September, the Battalion had a day's rest before moving forward on the 9th to
9 Sept.	Castelnuovo, sustaining some twenty casualties from artillery fire during the move.
	At this stage, it will be remembered, it had been hoped that the 4th Battalion would co-operate with the 2nd in the latter battalion's rather desperate night attack to be launched on the late evening of the 11th. The 4th Battalion, however, had been earmarked for employment elsewhere, in a night attack of its own. This was carried out on the
11-12 Sept.	night of the 11th/12th September, also, in an attack which, starting down a steep descent, included objectives on the farther slopes, amongst them the heavily fortified village of Perrarese. A night of confused fighting ended with the forward companies short of their

objectives. Hostile fire had been heavy and continuous, and their S.P. guns gave the enemy infantry excellent close support. "D" Company succeeded in reaching the outskirts of Perrarese, but had subsequently to be drawn back, after heavy loss.

The 2nd and 4th Battalions spent equally unprofitable days on the 12th. As with the 2nd, so with the 4th—it lay pinned in extremely exposed positions the whole day through, on a forward slope, and unable to move till the onset of dark enabled it to withdraw and re-form behind the San Pietro ridge.   12 Sept.

The night of the 12th/13th September was a full one, spent sorting companies out, and preparing for the renewed, and again unsuccessful attack on the original objectives, on the 13th. All along the front, the enemy was resisting fiercely, and repelling all attacks. The Sikhs hung on, however, all that day, and the next, in positions much exposed to effective and damaging shell fire. A daylight patrol actually reached Perrarese, but came under heavy fire from machine-guns located about the minefield, and lost three men killed and two wounded.   12-13 Sept.
   13 Sept.
   14 Sept.

The Battalion was withdrawn that night for a short rest, but moved forward again on the 18th September in support of the 3rd/10th Baluchis and the 1st/9th Gurkha Rifles, who were forcing the German defences about San Marino state. The attack was successful and a good foothold secured. The Battalion was then moved across to the right flank, and during the evening carried out a highly successful night attack from behind the village of Albereto, completely surprising the enemy. Admirably planned, it was led in the first instance by "B" Company. Later, "A" Company passed through, and swung east to deal with an enemy-held village. "D" and "C" Companies then took over the advance, and reached the Battalion objectives beyond the Gurkhas' positions by 3 a.m. on the 19th. Enemy sappers were still busy laying mines when the two companies passed on to the objectives, but only one Battalion casualty was sustained. "B" Company had a few casualties from shell fire, but captured some prisoners en route in Valdragone. Here the Company had a heartfelt but somewhat embarrassing welcome from the villagers, who streamed forth from shelters as well as from the neighbouring railway tunnels, and somewhat interfered with the clearing up of snipers in the vicinity. Finally, the Camerons passed through to the capture of San Marino town, the Sikhs being well established astride the main road.   18 Sept.
   19 Sept.

The capture of San Marino ended the Battalion's operations for the time being, as shortly after the 4th Indian Division came out of the line, preparatory to its transfer to Greece. In his thanks to the Division for its hard-won successes, the Army Commander described the fighting as the bitterest since El Alamein and Cassino. During August and half September alone, the Battalion's casualties numbered just under 300 all ranks.

1944

October

The battalion went into rest at Tavernelle, enjoying visits to Rome and Florence. His Highness the Maharajah of Patiala paid the troops a welcome and appreciated visit. Orders for the move to Greece were meanwhile made known, and after a month in Tavernelle, the Battalion moved down to Taranto at the end of October with the rest of the 4th Indian Division. Here, at the end of the 500-mile journey south, the Battalion settled down to wait its turn to sail.

9 Nov.

However, on the 9th November, orders were suddenly received to return north again and join the 10th Indian Division. Moving back north by road and rail, the Battalion joined its new formation, the 25th Indian Infantry Brigade, not far north of San Marino. The winter rains had now set in in earnest, but most of the men were got under cover, and, in these conditions, a period of training followed, including some very cold assault-boat practice. After a week or two,

December early in December, the Battalion moved forward into a front-line sector near the Lamone river, about 40 miles forward of San Marino. Winter conditions were now at their worst—mud, cold and appalling tracks all conspiring to hamper operations.

A difficult period followed, plans being constantly changed. The enemy was extremely active, and there was much hostile shelling and mortar fire. Ultimately, however, not very long after the Battalion's arrival in the sector, an attack was mounted, with the King's Own and 3rd/1st Punjab Regiment forward, and the Sikhs (less "B" Company) in a dual role—in Brigade reserve and at the same time deployed in various holding tasks; "A" Company in particular coming in for a good deal of shelling while holding an important ridge.

"B" Company had been given a forward role in the attack, filling a gap between the King's Own and 3rd/1st. Its objective was the fortified Casseti farmhouse. The operation, preceded by a heavy barrage, took place after nightfall, and "B" Company, after a successful advance in the dark, rushed the objective, and after fierce fighting took it and began to dig in. Most unfortunately, the Company had got well ahead of the Battalions on either flank, which had not made sufficient headway to attract the enemy's reserves. A strong counter-attack presently developed against the Company. The enemy infantry brought up a gun, and casualties soon began to mount. After prolonged and bitter fighting, in which the Company lost over 50 per cent of its strength, including Sub. Falak Sher and almost all its non-commissioned officers, Maj. J. C. Hartley, commanding the Company, resolved to pull out. It says much for the discipline and good organization of the Company that in spite of the darkness and confusion the majority of the wounded were got away.

16 Dec.

Later, on the 16th December, when the enemy showed signs of loosening his hold, "C" Company moved forward over the scene of

"B" Company's late operation, passing on the way through a Schu minefield which caused casualties, and taking Casseti. A daylight view of the scene left no doubts at all of the very good fight "B" Company had put up, and it is pleasant to hear that the Divisional Commander congratulated the Company, and that Maj. Hartley received an immediate award of the Military Cross.

From then till the 21st December, a succession of costly and minor operations on the ridges overlooking the river Senio a mile or two to the north-west involved upwards of ninety casualties, mostly from artillery and mortar fire. All operations were much hampered by the bitter cold, wet and mud, which made all types of movement very difficult. And when, on the 21st, the Battalion was withdrawn to the rest area in Forli, 15 to 20 miles in rear, it was perishingly cold. However, the troops managed to clean up a little, and they were thankful to be away for a time from a muddy and uncomfortable sector and to enjoy Christmas out of the line. The Viceroy's commissioned officers held a party, and an issue of extra sweets and rum or cigarettes was made for the Sikh and Punjabi-Mohammedan rank-and-file. Further, a welcome draft arrived.

On the 3rd January, 1945, the Battalion took over defensive positions on the river Senio. Highway 9, which runs north-west from Rimini to Bologna and beyond, passes through Castel Bolognese, near the Senio crossing, a short 15 miles north-west from the rest area at Forli. The line now ran just south of Castel Bolognese and Highway 9. The sector seems to have been a lively one. Company positions were based on fortified houses, where all hands had to keep under cover by day. The enemy parachute formation opposite was much on the alert, and reacted at once to any signs of offensive activity. Mortaring and shelling were heavy.

Under-statement is supposed to be a peculiarly British trait. This was never better demonstrated than by the British Broadcasting Corporation, which told the troops there, as well as the world at large, that there was "only patrol activity on the river Senio". Actually, these heavy weeks were a severe test. The snow which fell soon after the Battalion took over remained on the ground, unmelted, till relief in February. Life was very hard. The men got little rest or comfort. Nights of patrolling were followed by cheerless days cooped up in cellars and dug-outs, snatching what rest they could, with only hurricane lamps to relieve the gloom. The cold, snow and damp made patrolling and outpost duty rigorous in the extreme. Nothing could be done by day, and for those not otherwise employed, the long shivering nights were spent in digging and wiring, the former often wasted, as trenches frequently filled rapidly with icy water. Rations came up at night by jeeps, mules and man-pack, and the steadily mounting casualties could only be got away under cover of the dark.

1945

In the early stages, "A" Company had a particularly uncomfortable time, with a succession of struggles for the farmstead of Columbarina. Here Hav. Ram Singh earned the Indian Distinguished Service Medal for his courage in holding the burning farmhouse. In due time, "C" Company relieved "A" Company, whereas "D" Company could not be relieved at all, and spent six wearing weeks in its positions. The Company had some tough times, with heavy shelling, and patrol encounters, and they suffered heavy casualties.

None-the-less, the men remained full of offensive spirit. Wearing though the constant night patrols must have been—twice casualties were suffered from schu mines laid by enemy patrols—yet parties of our men were constantly wading or rafting themselves across the Senio, and valuable information was brought in.

February Relief in early February was followed by a welcome week in rest, after which the Battalion found itself in a quieter sector. There was ample excitement, however. An enemy post on our side of the Senio gave constant trouble, but it was finally dealt with by Jem. Samundar Khan and a party of "B" Company men, who rushed the post, killed four paratroopers, captured four more, and put the rest to flight. Though wounded in the neck, Jem. Samundar Khan completed his task with great dash and determination.

Later in February, the Battalion was relieved by a Polish unit. It might have been supposed that a take-over of this sort would provide certain problems of speech, but the men rose to the occasion as usual, and found a common "lingua franca" in Italian, which both sides understood sufficiently well. Just before leaving, "A" Company stretcher-bearers had an unusual experience. While searching for a wounded man, they were captured and taken off. They got as far back as Milan before their Red Cross cards secured their release. They were sent back with a polite note to the corps commander requesting the return of a similar number of German stretcher-bearers.

The Battalion now went back for a month's rest in the Tiber valley where the weather was kind, and the men were housed in respectable buildings not in ruins. The promise of spring had its wonted effect on the good spirits of the Battalion—and here we may leave them for the present and turn to the activities of the remaining battalions of the Regiment.

6th Bn. *The 6th Battalion* had passed the summer under training in Kohat. It had been hoped that this period was a preliminary to a return to the eastern front, but these ambitions were dashed in the late autumn by orders for a move up the Tochi to Damdil.

23 Nov. On the 23rd November, the Battalion left Kohat by M.T. along the
24 Nov. Bannu road and up the Tochi, reaching Damdil on the 24th. First

1944

impressions were not very favourable—as anyone who knows Damdil will understand—but the Battalion quickly settled down into the Wana huts and confined space within the barbed wire.

For the next three months, the Battalion, as part of the Gardai Brigade, was responsible for road protection in the Asad Khel sector. During this monotonous period, it continued the activities common to all good battalions, in the improvement of the post defences and amenities. Among the latter came the rebuilding by the Pioneer Platoon of the officers' mess and Wana huts.

The 7th Battalion in Risalpur, carried out a 120-mile march to Tret on the Rawal Pindi-Murree road. The march was completed between the 2nd and 6th November. It stayed in Tret all through the winter, engaged in jungle warfare training. Hard as it was, the life was much to the men's liking, since they appreciated that it pointed the way to an operational role before very long.

7th Bn.

2-6 Nov.

The Machine-Gun Battalion was now on a jeep-and-trailer basis, and had joined the 19th Indian Division in Nasik. On the 1st November, it left by road and rail for Imphal, where it spent a few days at Mile 113. After this, it moved on to Moreh, the headquarters of the Division. From here, "A" Company was immediately sent off to join the 64th Indian Infantry Brigade which was concentrating at Sittaung on the west bank of the Chindwin. The Battalion, less "A" Company, was then attached to the 98th Indian Infantry Brigade, and moved on to Thanan, 30 miles north of Tamu.

MG Bn.

1 Nov.

From this point a road had to be constructed to carry neavy transport to the new Chindwin crossing at Tonhe. "D" Company was sent forward to Tonhe with the dual role of watching out for any Japanese crossing the river, and of constructing its own portion of the road. The remainder of the Battalion, i.e. less "A" and "D" Companies— was established at Mile 10.3 on the Tonhe road, and spent three hard weeks on serious digging.

East of the Chindwin, between Tonhe, which is well upstream of Sittaung, and Katha on the Irrawaddy, 100 miles to the east, bodies of Japanese troops were moving back eastwards. The 64th Indian Infantry Brigade, with "A" Company of the Machine-Gun Battalion attached, now spent a period of some three weeks scouring this area—or a great part of it—in a wide circle, endeavouring to pick these parties up. The country, although in no sense mountainous, is enclosed and difficult. A broad band of hills runs down from the north roughly mid-way between the Irrawaddy and the Chindwin. The broken and eroded nature of these hills is reflected in the flatter country to either side, which is intersected by innumerable chaungs and nalas. There are no proper

1944

roads, and the infrequent tracks are sandy and cut about.

The Brigade set off on its search, from Sittaung, about due east of Tamu, and on the Chindwin. The route led some distance to the east, and then wheeled north to Leu, about 40 miles east of the Chindwin. At Leu, the Brigade joined the direct track from Tonhe. Little detail is available about this sweep, other than that a few Japanese stragglers only were collected, and these all in very poor physical condition. But it established reasonably clearly that the Japanese were not active anywhere in this theatre, and that therefore the deployment of the 19th Indian Division eastwards towards the Irrawaddy well north of Mandalay, could probably be safely effected. It was essential to the Fourteenth Army plan that a formation of the IVth Corps should appear in this area to lend colour to the notion that the IVth Corps itself would be employed there. So, as soon as the sector of road terminating at Tonhe, and on which the Machine-Gun Battalion was, amongst others, busily employed, was completed, the Division would be able to cross there, and move via Leu and join the 36th Division moving south from Myitkyina.

7 Dec.   "A" Company remained a short time at Leu, and then, about the 7th December, sent back its twelve medium machine-guns, with twelve jeeps and trailers, over the 40 miles to Tonhe, to give anti-aircraft
12 Dec.   protection at the river crossing. About five days later, on the 12th, the guns were relieved by a detachment of Bofors, and rejoined "A" Company, which had moved on a little to Sinlamaung.

To follow the exact route of the Division is impossible without a very detailed large-scale map, but the stages are named below as a matter of record.

16-17 Dec.   The Battalion, less "A" Company, left Tonhe on the 16th December,
18-26 Dec.   crossing the Chindwin next day. It then pushed forward at 15 to 18 miles a day, halting at Sinlamaung, Pinbon, Manyu, Chaung, Katpanda, Kawya Chaung, Alezu near Pinlebu where Christmas was spent, and Myeni near Kawlin. The chase was getting close, and the troops were drawing up to the Japanese forces gradually being squeezed in between the 36th Division from the north and the 19th Division from the west. "D" Company was accordingly detached to Thityabin to block a possible escape route from the west. The Battalion, less "A"
27 Dec.   Company, still detached, followed in the same direction next day, the
28 Dec.   27th December, and reached Lobok on the 28th. Here transport was waiting to take it to an area just north of Leiktu, where its guns took over an area from the 2nd Battalion, the Royal Berkshire Regiment. The Japanese were holding a delaying position in Leiktu, which the 98th Indian Infantry Brigade was working round. In the event, the Battalion got no good M.M.G. tasks, but Japanese patrolling and sniping provided worth-while experience for the men at the cost of only minor casualties.

	1945
On the 2nd January, the Battalion, less "A" Company, pushed on ahead with the 98th Indian Infantry Brigade towards Kanbalu, on the Mandalay—Myitkyina railway, 75 miles south of Katha. Companies now had their first opportunity of supporting infantry actually in the attack. On the 5th January, immediately on the capture of Tantabin, the Battalion moved up to consolidate and form a firm base, into which Divisional Headquarters moved next day. On the 8th January, the Battalion again split, moving forward itself to Kin-U, but detaching "B" Company to Kongyi to support the southern crossing of the Irrawaddy, at Singu, 30 miles north of Mandalay. After two days at Kin-U crossroads, the Battalion was ordered, on the 10th January, to move on en route to Shwebo, on the Myitkyina railway, 40 miles north-north-west of Mandalay, and about 15 miles west of the Irrawaddy.	2 Jan. 5 Jan. 8 Jan. 10 Jan.

The campaign was moving fast, and at its first halt, the Battalion received fresh orders. Instead of Shwebo, it was now to make for Kabwet. Kabwet is a village on the bend of the Irrawaddy half-way between the two bridge-heads, Thabeikkyin and Singu—60 and 30 miles respectively north of Mandalay. Here, equidistant from the two bridge heads, it relieved a battalion of Gurkhas which had captured the village the previous day. It was a suspected crossing-place for Japanese stragglers coming in from the west, and the Battalion was to be deployed to head them off.   11 Jan.

There were plenty of Japanese in the vicinity, and the first small skirmish started at 8 a.m. while the Battalion was taking over from the Gurkhas. The defences were fired on from a patch of jungle to the east. A patrol was sent out, but no enemy were found. "A" and "B" Companies were still away on detachment. With the remaining companies, the Battalion deployed 8 M.M.G.s from "C" Company to cover the crossings on the river front. The remaining 16 M.M.G.s were posted to cover the flanks and rear with cross-fire. During the morning, another patrol sent out contacted a well-prepared Japanese position only 200 yards east of the perimeter, and had two men killed. Spasmodic firing from snipers and light machine-guns was directed into the perimeter during the afternoon and evening, but the night was undisturbed.   12 Jan.

Next morning, the 13th January, a report was received that some country boats had arrived at Yonbin, 2 miles from Kabwet, during the previous night. A platoon went out to investigate in the afternoon and found and destroyed eight well-built boats. No Japanese were seen. Whether or no by way of reprisal for this, the enemy started up a series of jitter attacks that evening, and kept them going all night. They were very sensitive to any movement east of Kabwet, and it was thought that they might have established a straggler collecting post in the chaung about half-a-mile away. Parties could be made up   13 Jan.

1945

there, and despatched round by night north of Kabwet to Yonbin, where a crossing could be made unseen and out of range.

As a result of the report on crossing facilities at Yonbin, Divisional Headquarters arranged for a company of the 1st Assam Regiment to be made available for offensive patrolling. At the same time, a "22" W.T. set was sent the Battalion. There had previously been no means of communicating with other troops except by road, and, in fact, there were no troops nearer than 15 miles away, at the two bridge-heads.

15 Jan. At 8 p.m. on the 15th January, five grenades from dischargers suddenly straddled Battalion Headquarters. Immediately after, light machine-gun fire opened onto the perimeter from the east. The Battalion M.M.G.s on that flank opened up, and the battle was on. After feeling for a soft spot, attacks were pressed in on the Battalion Headquarter sector and the west approaches to the village. Attacks came in under a shower of grenades from dischargers thickened up with mortars, but the ground was well covered by fire, and the repeated

16 Jan. attacks met with no success. Next morning, fifty-six Japanese dead were counted at a distance of between 10 and 20 yards from the perimeter.

The Battalion was not happy about its defences, however. It had no high-trajectory weapons as complement to the machine-guns, and the enemy had been able to work up close to the perimeter and dig in. Nearly all the Battalion's grenades had been used up during the night, so that the enemy had a freedom of movement denied to our own troops, provided only that they kept under cover from small-arms fire. They themselves, on the other hand, seemed well found in mortars and light machine-guns, and any movement by our men caused immediate reaction with these. A machine-gun battalion is not organized or equipped for detached action of the sort required in Kabwet, and it was decided in the circumstances to ask for assistance.

The 2nd Royal Berkshire Regiment was detailed by the 98th Indian Infantry Brigade to clear the area, which now obviously held something more than the disorganized stragglers previously suspected. It took time, however, for this help to develop.

After their abortive attacks of the previous night, the Japanese had been acting with energy. By 11 o'clock in the morning, they had sited a light machine-gun on a fixed line along the river bank, cutting off the Battalion from its water-supply. The perimeter was constantly under fire, as already implied above, and during the morning the Battalion had four killed and eleven wounded—the latter including Maj. Khushal Pal Singh, who was officiating in command. The wounded could no longer be evacuated.

At 5 p.m., the 2nd Royal Berkshire Regiment was contacted on the "22" set, but replied that they would be unable to reach Kabwet that night. During the night, the enemy again made determined but unnsuccessful attacks on the position, leaving more dead on the ground.

During the 17th morning, however, the enemy's attention was diverted by the 2nd Royal Berkshire Regiment attacking from the north with a 25-pounder in support. Fighting went on all day, but by nightfall one company of British troops had reached the position, contacted "D" Company, and thickened that part of the perimeter. 17 Jan.

Once again, night brought a renewal of fanatical attacks. Three times the enemy attacked, but all were held and the enemy eventually withdrew. At first light, patrols from the Battalion and from the company of the 1st Assam Regiment reconnoitred the enemy's forming-up position at the west end of Kabwet village, and found it clear. The bodies of six officers and sixty-two men were found there. Others had been buried, and it was thought that more still had been thrown into the Irrawaddy during the night. 18 Jan.

The immediate threat was past, but it was some time before the area was cleared. There was a village a mile north-east of Kabwet, near the chaung which had come under suspicion of being a straggler collecting centre. On the 19th January, the 2nd Royal Berkshire Regiment moved its headquarters there, and found the chaung to be a regular stronghold. A series of air-strikes, artillery concentrations and infantry attacks supported by armoured cars and machine-guns was organized, but it was not until the 2nd February that the area was properly cleared. During these operations the Battalion had some excellent M.M.G. shoots in support of the 2nd Royal Berkshire Regiment, but, unlucky again in its commanding officers, Maj. P. Parry-Evans who had rejoined from hospital and taken over command when Maj. Pal Singh was wounded, was himself killed on the 28th January by a burst of light machine-gun fire from a hidden bunker while on reconnaissance. 19 Jan.

2 Feb.

28 Jan.

On the 2nd February, with the Kabwet operations concluded, the Battalion, still less "A" and "B" Companies, moved to Onbauk, and thence to the southern of the 19th Indian Division bridge-heads, at Ngapyinin, near Singu. February

It is necessary now to look back and see how "A" Company had been faring.

"A" Company was last mentioned as despatching its M.M.G.s and jeeps and trailers back to Tonhe on the 7th December for anti-aircraft protection duties at the Chindwin crossing. The guns had been released on the 12th December, and had returned to Leu, to find that Company Headquarters had meanwhile gone on to Sinlamaung with the 64th Indian Infantry Brigade. The M.M.G.s caught up and on the 13th December, the re-united Company set off in the wake of the 2nd Worcestershire Regiment, which had left Sinlamaung three days before en route to Pinbon, 7 Dec.

12 Dec.

13 Dec.

1944-5.

50 road miles ahead. All possible kit had been left behind on the west bank of the Chindwin, so that with some overloading, Company transport was able to move everything in one lift. This is not to say that movement over the local tracks was easy. However, two days

15 Dec. strenuous work brought the company to Pinbon by the 15th December, where it came in support of the 2nd Worcestershire Regiment whom it accompanied on 10- to 15-mile daily marches to Nankan on the Myitkyina-Mandalay railway.

There was a skirmish at Nankan with a Japanese rearguard, and it looked as if the long monotonous days slogging along under a heavy pack were coming to an end. But the Japanese were not to be pinned, and nothing more serious than small daily skirmishes enlivened the continuing succession of marches from that time on.

From Nankan, the Brigade moved rapidly south roughly parallel with the railway. The Company marched with the leading battalion—by turns the 2nd Worcestershire Regiment, the 5th/10th Baluchis, and the 1st/6th Gurkha Rifles. The rough tracks prohibited the quick movement of M.T., so one platoon of the Company was detailed daily to go with the leading rifle company, carrying its guns and ammunition on man-pack.

With frequent skirmishes but no major action, the southward march
5 Jan. continued till the 5th January, on which date the Company found itself in a village some 8 miles east of Shwebo—itself about 40 miles north-north-west of Mandalay—and about 5 miles north of the metalled road linking Shwebo with the Irrawaddy.

From Shwebo to the Irrawaddy is some 15 miles, and the road linking them was of value to the Japanese. None-the-less, in spite of the threat to this line of communications, no Japanese had been encountered that day.

About 1 p.m., after the Company had been some two hours in the village, one platoon was detached and sent off with the 1st/6th Gurkha Rifles. Marching south, they reached the Shwebo-Irrawaddy road without interference. Up till that point, the track had run through jungle, but at the road-crossing, they left the jungle behind and found open country with paddy-fields.

Leaving the road, the little column now moved off cross-country
6 Jan. by the compass for the remainder of that day and part of the 6th. Arrived about 10 miles south of Shwebo—still with no interference by the Japanese—two road-blocks were quietly established. One was at a cross-roads on the main road to Mandalay. The other was about 6 miles east at a junction of the Old Mu Canal.

First blood fell to the block on the main road. A Japanese bullock-car
7 Jan. convoy came marching along it the same night and was badly shot up. Twenty-five dead were found lying there next morning, together

with several bullock carts containing such useful articles as soap, oil, and cloth.

That day, the 7th January, the 5/10th Baluchis, together with the Machine-Gun Company, less its platoon, attacked Shwebo from the east. There was a race for it with the 2nd British Division on the west, but the Baluchis beat them to it.

Three days later, on the 10th January, the Company concentrated near Shwebo air-field, but was ordered north at short notice to join the 98th Indian Infantry Brigade at Thabeikkyin on the Irrawaddy, the northern of the two impending crossings above Mandalay.

Arrived at Thabeikkyin, one platoon was put quietly across the river on the 12th January south of the proposed bridge-head in support of the 4th/4th Gurkha Rifles. Next day, the 13th, Company Headquarters followed, with a second platoon. The third platoon with the transport was left on the west bank. The west bank was high and the view over the river good. Ranges to likely targets were between 1,700 and 2,000 yards, which ensured a good beaten zone. The third platoon was hence well sited to provide harassing and defensive fire in front of the 4th/4th Gurkha Rifles perimeter.

Over on the east bank, Company Headquarters and the two platoons had a full time. Troops were very thin on the ground. There were excitements of one sort or another—from the activities of jitter parties to well-supported attacks in strength—every night. The M.M.G.s fired off a considerable amount of ammunition, but, contrary to text-book principles, most of the killing was done about 20 yards from the guns. Shelling, if spasmodic, was very accurate. Five or six shells would be fired in rapid succession at uncertain times. Then the enemy would move his guns out of action and lie quiet. But the men soon became inured to this. Hard and unrelenting as the life was, the weeks slipped quickly by, with little to mark one day from another.

One incident, however, did stand out. No very great matter in itself, it was remembered and talked about long after greater events had been forgotten.

One night, a Sikh havildar of the Company noticed a small Japanese patrol edging its way towards his position. It was about 50 yards away when he first saw it, so he quietly waited for it to come closer, meanwhile taking over the gun himself. When the patrol was within about 15 yards of him, he fired a long burst, killing five—as it was afterwards discovered—and wounding a sixth. He could hear the wounded man groaning. Meanwhile, the seventh—and last—member of the patrol, probably an officer, had slipped behind a fold in the ground, from where he presently called out in Urdu—"Please stop firing and let me get my wounded away. If you stop firing we will not harm you, for we are friends of the P.M.s". This to a Sikh havildar did not

1945

10 Jan.

12 Jan

13 Jan.

1945

strike at all the right note. Shouting out that he was no P.M. but a Sikh, the havildar let drive another burst. Insults in Urdu were then flung both ways for the next 15 minutes, and then the Japanese put his head out too far, and that was the end of him.

6 Feb. On the 6th February, the Company left the Thabeikkyin bridge-head, and rejoined the Battalion at Kyaukmyaung near the Singu crossing. This was the first time it had met the main body of the Battalion since leaving Moreh in early December. However, time for the picking up of threads and interchange of yarns was short, as the Company started crossing the river the same afternoon, and was all across by
7 Feb. the following day.

Looking back in time once more, we must see what had been happening to "B" Company. "B", it will be remembered, had been detached on
8 Jan. the 8th January, to move to Kongyi in support of the southern Irrawaddy crossing north of Mandalay, at Singu. The actual site of the crossing was Kyaukmyaung, just nearby, and "B" Company was with the first troops to cross. There was strong and obstinate opposition, including the heaviest artillery concentrations the enemy had ever put down in Burma. Of this, "B" Company, and later "C" Company, after the clearing up of the enemy positions at Kabwet, had a full share.

In the Singu bridge-head, a feature that saw as bloody fighting as any was Pear Hill. One platoon of "B" Company held its position there throughout, and added many enemy killed to its score. As at Thabeikkyin, the Japanese did their greatest violence at night; and men of "B", "C" and "D" Companies, at one time or another, helped in stemming the fierce attacks flung in every night against the main bridge-head. During this fighting no guns were put out of action although there was an unpleasantly high proportion of casualties amongst the experienced gun numbers.

Presently, as we have seen, the Battalion gradually concentrated at the Singu crossing, and for the first time since entering Burma was together in the same area. One detachment only was out—and this consisted of two platoons of "D" Company operating at Shwedaik, a village on the Irrawaddy west bank some 2 miles south of the Singu
3 Feb. crossing, and sent out on the 3rd February.

Operations now began to break out and extend the bridge-head
8 Feb. southwards. On the 8th February, "A" Company, less one platoon, was in support of the 2nd Worcestershire Regiment, attacking the long, straggling village of Kule. The village was captured just before nightfall, but only the northern portion was held, owing to its size. The Japanese put in a series of fierce, but unsuccessful counter-attacks during the night. Though the two machine-gun platoons only suffered a loss of two killed and four wounded, the Japanese paid heavily, judging by the dead left on the ground in the morning.

                                                                    1945
    That day, the 9th February, a heavy air-strike was put down on   9 Feb.
Kule, and the 3rd/6th Rajputana Rifles, with "A" Company's remaining
machine-gun platoon in support, moved in. Thence, they carried the
attack east across open country against three high, isolated hill
features, known as "A", "B", and "C". Following an air-strike,
the attack was put in on a three-company front, with the machine-gun
platoon supporting the right company. Japanese still lurking in the
southern end of Kule took a heavy toll of casualties from the right
company, but all objectives were taken, and Kule itself was completely
cleared later in the day.

    From the 13th February, operations were again intensified, and   13 Feb.
before the end of the month, Singu itself had been taken and built
up as a firm base. Supplies came in steadily by air throughout daylight
hours. The 98th and 64th Indian Infantry Brigades operated east and
west of Singu respectively, each with a machine-gun company in
support. Command of the Battalion had by this time been taken over
by Lieut.-Col. G. Lerwill, M.C., newly arrived from the 1st Battalion.

    Of the remainder of the Regiment, there is little to tell. *The 14th
Battalion* continued its steady round of routine in Chindwara. Of *the
26th Battalion* we hear a little more. It was still employed on dull   26th Bn.
routine duties in and about Poona, but it was doing its share with a
good heart. Much had been done to push ahead local development
schemes, and the livestock and vegetable farms which the Battalion
raised were the object of general comment. The Battalion stood
first in the whole area for the production of vegetables at this time.

Chapter XII

MARCH TO AUGUST 1945

Backscreen

Japan   Allied forces were closing in in the Pacific, but much blood was still to flow.

Fierce fighting was in progress on the little pear-shaped island of Iwo Jima, some 775 miles south of Tokyo. Troops had been poured in till there were 80,000 Americans and Japanese crammed into the 8 square miles of land. After three weeks of furious battling, Japanese

16 Mar. resistance began to slacken, but it was not till the 16th March, twenty-six days after the landing, that the island was clear of enemy. Fewer than 100 Japanese were taken alive. The remainder of the garrison of over 20,000 men, was killed. The cost to the Americans stood at 4,189 killed, 15,305 wounded, and 441 missing. In exchange a fighter base was acquired, and escort could now be given to the heavy bombers flying north against Japan from the Marianas, 800 miles to the south. On their return, lame ducks could find refuge and temporary repair instead of being in all probability lost on the journey home. The saving on this head alone is reckoned in hundreds of heavy aircraft.

About 1,000 miles west of Iwo Jima, running in a grand 800-mile curve from the southern tip of the Japanese home islands to Formosa, is a chain of islands variously known as the Liu-Kiu, the Riu Kiu or the Lu-Chu Islands. In the centre of this chain is a long, narrow, much indented island, with as many names as the chain itself—Great Liu-Kiu, Nawa Riu-Kiu and Okinawa Shima. History will know it best as Okinawa.

Lying 350 miles north-east of Formosa, and about the same distance south-west of the nearest Japanese home island, Kyushu, it was well placed equally for operations against North China or South-West Japan. It was well provided with harbours and air facilities. Its over-all length, on a north-east south-west axis, is about 140 miles. Its average width barely exceeds 15. Its garrison was estimated at between 65,000 and 70,000 men in the south end of the island. In the light of the subsequent casualty list, the total for the island as a whole must have been nearer 120,000 by the time it fell.

A little west of the south-west tip of Okinawa is the small island

26 Mar. of Kerama—occupied on the 26th March by the United States 77th Divisi as a preliminary to the assault on Okinawa itself.

1945

Meanwhile, an armada of impressive proportions had been assembled to carry the United States XXIVth Corps and IIIrd Marine Corps to Okinawa. Carried in 1,400 craft, and under escort of the United States Fifth Fleet, together with Vice-Admiral Sir Bernard Rawling's British Squadron, it represented the largest combined operation yet attempted in the Pacific.

Landings were to be made at Yontan and Kadena, a few miles from each other and about 40 miles up the west coast from the south end of the island. A strongly-supported feint landing was staged at Kiyan at the south end.

Going ashore on the 1st April under a very heavy naval bombardment, small initial resistance was met. However, moving down southwards on the 5th, the XXIVth Corps ran up against a strong defence system stretching from coast to coast right across the island. The relatively trivial resistance encountered by the IIIrd Marine Corps sweeping up north, confirmed that practically the whole garrison was facing the XXIVth Corps in the south.

1 Apr.

5 Apr.

The Japanese position had been carefully organized and was most formidable. With both flanks secure, it was based on a system of rocky cliffs, caves, and nalas, tunnelled and improved, and was fully manned.

Mounting Japanese resistance in the air lent added anxiety to the situation. Air assaults on Allied shipping were stepped up, and the by now familiar Kamikaze or Suicide attacks reached a new high pitch. It was now, too, that the Baka plane first appeared—a small, short-range rocket-accelerated aircraft with over a ton of explosives in its nose. Carried to the scene of attack attached to the under-side of a medium bomber, it was then released and directed on its target by its suicide pilot. Serious losses were caused, and much bomber effort had to be diverted from direct attacks on Japanese industrial and similar centres to striking Kamikaze air-fields in Kyushu. To give an idea of the impact of these Kamikaze aircraft, it was estimated that between October 1944 and June 1945, the Japanese sent out 2,550 Kamikaze missions, and that 475 were successful in securing hits or damaging near misses. Warship casualties included 45 craft sunk—mostly destroyers. Among the damaged, however, 12 aircraft carriers, 15 battleships and 16 escort and light carriers figured—some extremely seriously damaged, and with heavy losses in man-power.

On shore, the IIIrd Marine Corps cleared the northern part of Okinawa, and then returned to help the XXIVth Corps. On the 13th May, the Japanese defences were broken into at Naha on the west coast. The key to the defences, "Sugarloaf Hill", was captured on the 21st. The whole of Naha town was in American

13 May

21 May

1945

30 May / 21 June — hands by the 30th May, but the battle still dragged on with fanatical fury till the 21st June, when the island was finally cleared. By this time, American casualties had reached a total of about 50,000, over 10,000 of which were fleet casualties. Japanese losses totalled 109,629 killed and 7,871 captured. Aircraft losses cost the Japanese 3,400 planes shot down over the whole area extending up to Kyushu, and 800 destroyed on the ground. American aircraft losses exceeded 1,000.

In the Japanese home islands meanwhile, the Japanese higher command were growing increasingly anxious.

20 June — On the 20th June, just before Okinawa fell, the Emperor told his Supreme War Direction Council that the war must be closed on any terms short of unconditional surrender. The proposed conditions were rejected by the Allies, paving the way to two consequences of lasting importance. These were the dropping of the first atomic bombs, and the entry at the last possible moment, of Russia into the war against Japan. The first—test—

16 July — atom bomb had not yet been exploded. This was effected on the 16th July. But on the 6th August, the second bomb was dropped on Hiroshima.

6-10 Aug. — Russia declared war on Japan on the 8th. On the 9th the third atomic bomb was dropped—on Nagasaki; and next day, the 10th, cease-fire

14 Aug. — negotiations began with a broadcast from Tokyo. On the 14th, the Emperor accepted the provisions of the Potsdam Declaration. On the

2 Sept. — 2nd September, six years after the British Empire entered into war with Germany, the instrument of surrender was signed by Japanese envoys on the United States battleship *Missouri* in Tokyo Bay. Though much mopping up remained before distant Japanese detachments accepted the truth of the surrender, and blood inevitably flowed to some extent during the interval, the war was over and the era of reconstruction began.

Burma — In Burma, with our forces firmly established across the Japanese communications at Meiktila, the fighting for Mandalay went on with

21 Mar. — increasing bitterness till its fall on the 21st March.

Meanwhile, though chronologically it belongs to the previous chapter, a plan of operations had been carrying through in the Arakan with the object of ensuring the steady continuity of Fourteenth Army operations once these outran the air-supply line from Assam. The Fourteenth Army offensive could not be strictly speaking maintained by air from Assam once it passed south of Mandalay. But admirable alternative bases would be available in Akyab and Ramree Islands off the Arakan coast, once the Japanese were pushed out of them.

10 Dec. — Since the 10th December, accordingly, the XVth Corps in the Arakan had been working its way southwards down the Mayu Peninsula.

25 Dec.- 3 Jan. — Reaching the tip on Christmas Day, the already abandoned Akyab Island was occupied on the 3rd January.

1945

Inhospitable as the Arakan is above Akyab Island, it is infinitely more so below it. The formerly definite line of the coast merges into a maze of creeks, inlets and mangrove swamps as far as Sandoway, 160 miles to the south. On shore, the Arakan coast road, so-called, meanders with increasing vagueness and lack of definition through thick swampy jungles, where land operations could not be staged except at the last necessity.

To advance south by means of a series of leapfrog landings down the coast was the only practicable way out.

Looking south-east down the coast from Akyab Island, there is first, 30 miles away, the much enclosed Hunter's Bay and the Myebon Peninsula. On the 12th January, the 25th Indian Division successfully 12 Jan. landed there, and established itself with a view to pushing in east where strong Japanese positions were known to exist.

Meanwhile, 50 miles south of Myebon is Kyaukpyu at the northern tip of the 60-mile long Ramree Island. Kyaukpyu has an excellent harbour, and there are good air facilities. On the 21st January, the 21 Jan. 26th Indian Division went ashore near Kyaukpyu under a fierce naval bombardment by cruisers, destroyers and sloops, and a convincing air-strike by Liberators, Mitchells and Thunderbolts five minutes before the first wave of assault boats was due at the beach. Initial resistance was small, and by evening the Japanese were in full retreat.

Ramree is a large island. Its northern half shares to some degree the generally eroded appearance of the Arakan coast-line hereabouts, but the other half broadens out to a maximum of about 18 miles of relatively dry land. Lying about equidistant from Rangoon and Mandalay— 250 air-miles from each—it was well suited as a base for Dakota air-supply for the then impending Fourteenth Army operations.

By the 24th January, the 1st Lincolnshire Regiment was at Minbyin 24 Jan. on the west coast of the island and about one third of the way down. By the 28th, the northern half of the island was clear. Mines and 28 Jan. booby traps had been liberally sown by the retreating enemy, and the Indian sappers had a busy time, generally after night-fall, clearing them in the moonlight.

Ramree town lies on the east coast of the island, 40 miles southeast of Kyaukpyu. As troops of the 26th Indian Division entered the town, the Japanese doubled back towards the maze of mangrove swamps in the north-east, and thence by country-boat to the mainland. Here they fell in with the Royal Navy and the Arakan Coastal Force, posted there with this contingency in mind, and were almost annihilated. However, many scattered parties of the enemy were still at large on the island, and it was many months before they were accounted for.

Meanwhile, on the 24th January, the 25th Indian Division at Myebon 24 Jan.

1945

had staged an attack on enemy positions at Kangaw, 12 miles inland. After a fiercely-contested battle, the Japanese broke, and scattered back through the mountains towards An, leaving all their transport and heavy equipment behind. An, 50 miles south of Kangaw, has tactical significance as the temporary terminus of the track down the coast, and as the taking-off point for another track eastwards across the Arakan Yomas to the Irrawaddy Valley in the general latitude of Magwe and the oil-fields.

26 Jan. On the 26th January, the Royal Navy attacked and occupied Cheduba Island about 10 miles west of the southern half of Ramree Island, handing it over to the 26th Indian Division soon after.

The next landing down the coast was carried out by the 25th Indian Division. There is a small coastal village called Ru-Ywa, 40 miles south of Myebon, and about 15 miles south-west of An. Troops came 17 Feb. ashore here on the 17th February, and moved out north and east into the hills towards An and the track across into Burma.

The resuscitated Arakan coastal road, or track, makes its appearance again about here, and winds on southwards towards Taungup. At Taungup, a road forks east across the Yomas, 60 miles or so south of An. This road east from Taungup carried the Japanese communications westwards from Lower Burma.

On its way to Taungup, the coastal track crosses the Mai Chaung by ferry near Pyin Wan village. A point on the chaung, Letpan, was to be the scene of the next landing, by the 26th Indian Division. The operation involved a water approach through a tangle of inlets and mangrove swamps, and two preparatory landings had to be made on D minus 1 day before it was possible to commit the main body. These 19 Feb. preliminaries were effected on the previous night, the 19th February. In one, a battalion of the 13th Frontier Force Rifles landed at some distance from the intended beach, and made its way cross-country to seize Hill 1120, which dominated the landing place. In the other, a battalion of the 18th Garhwal Rifles landed with sappers to prepare for the rapid unloading of the artillery. It was essential to get the medium artillery ashore as early as possible in the landings, to give protection to landing-craft convoys as they made their way up the narrow inlet.

20 Feb. The Japanese were completely surprised, and the Division was quickly organized to make its way south along the track. By about 2 Mar. the 2nd March, it was 23 miles south of Letpan, and only 11 miles north of Taungup. Here, however, resistance stiffened, and every move forward was fiercely disputed. Gradually overcoming this resistance the troops reached the near neighbourhood of Taungup, 13-14 Apr. and on the night of the 13th/14th April a patrol found Taungup abandoned. According to one reasonably reliable account, there was

only one inhabitant still in the place—the Dak Bungalow chaukidar, who, when knocked up by the patrol at 4 o'clock in the morning, produced his visitor's book for the patrol leader to sign. There had been no entries in it since a British Officer had last been there—under one wonders what circumstances—in February 1942.

At Taungup, the Brigade of the 26th Indian Division by which this last advance had been carried out, was relieved by the 82nd West African Division, and rejoined the 26th on Ramree Island to prepare for the climax of the XVth Corps offensives—the capture of Rangoon from the sea.

A good deal of risk was involved in this operation. The Rangoon river is relatively shallow, and had been long left undredged. No supporting fire from heavy naval guns was therefore possible. The run-in for the assault craft, passing heavy batteries at Elephant Point and a selection of minefields laid by either side over the past three years, had a record length of 30 miles. The monsoon was due, and an early break might have disastrous consequences.

Elephant Point was to be silenced by Gurkha paratroops on D minus 1 day, but wireless silence would prevent the landing force knowing next day whether the attack had succeeded or no till it actually neared the point. In fact, it succeeded, but the Gurkhas, landing 1 May
there on the 1st May found only 37 Japanese troops in the position.
Next day, the 2nd, the landing force sailed up the river, sea-sick, 2 May
drenched and stiff and aching from the long six-hour trip in the assault boats. The troops crawled thankfully ashore 10 miles below Rangoon, on both banks of the river, but found the Japanese gone.
On the 3rd May, they climbed back into their boats, and sailed on 3 May
to Rangoon.

A few days later, contact was established with the Fourteenth Army not very far north of Rangoon.

Of the Fourteenth Army operations, more is generally known, and the account here will be correspondingly briefer.

Briefly, the Japanese, breaking south, fiercely attacked the Meiktila box, but without success. Meanwhile, the XXXIIIrd Corps was on its way down from Mandalay, while the 5th Indian Division and 2nd British Division closed in towards Meiktila. By the 5th April, the 5 Apr.
Japanese there were caught between two fires—from north and south.
On the 10th, abandoning guns and transport, they made away east 10 Apr.
into the Shan hills. The XXXIIIrd Corps then moved down the Irrawaddy via the oil-fields, to Prome. The IVth Corps, headed by the 5th and 17th Indian Divisions, behind a brigade of tanks, followed the main road via Toungoo and Pegu, to Rangoon. By-passed parties of Japanese were left to be dealt with by the 19th Indian Division in rear. 300 miles were covered in 16 days, and IVth Corps troops

1945

1 May · entered Pegu on the 1st May. The XXXIIIrd Corps, fighting its way through the oil-fields against considerable opposition, reached Prome
2 May · on the 2nd.

To close this brief account of a theatre in which the Indian Army was so uninterruptedly and so valiantly represented, it is proposed to quote Maj.-Gen. J. F. C. Fuller's summing-up on page 372 of *The Second World War*.

"Thus," he writes, "except for the clearing up of a considerable number of Japanese detachments, Burma was reconquered in one of the most remarkable campaigns of the entire war. Remarkable in that few other theatres of the war presented so many obstacles to organized fighting. Heat, rain, tropical diseases, mountains, rivers, swamps, and an all but total lack of roads seemed to have marked out Burma as one of the few regions in the world where powerful and highly equipped armies could not fight. Yet, in this last campaign half-a-million men were employed, and, as we have seen, armies of considerable size freely moved from north to south and west to east over high mountain ranges, broad rivers, and through dense forest and jungle at no mean speed. That this was possible was due to many factors, and, besides leadership and soldiership, the three outstanding were air-power, medical care and engineering.

"Of the first we have written fully; yet the other two were as important. Of the second it is astonishing to read that, whereas in 1943 'for every man who was admitted to hospital with wounds there had been one hundred and twenty who were casualties from tropical diseases... By 1945 the rate had dropped to ten men sick for every one battle casualty, and during the last six weeks of the war these ten had been reduced to six'. And of the third, that to keep the Fourteenth Army and XVth Corps on the move, 72,000 engineers and 130,000 labourers were needed, and mainly for the construction of roads and air-fields—the maintenance of mobility."

The subsequent mopping-up operations are described in the stories of the 1st and the Machine-Gun Battalion later, and nothing more need be said here.

Italy · In Italy an uneasy stability persisted through the winter, punctuated by ceaseless offensive patrolling and short, fierce clashes on either side. In the bigger sense, it was uneventful—but for the man in the ranks, it was a restless, uncomfortable, but not a wasted period of time.

On the eastern half of the front, the troops were now well down the northern face of the Apennines, which here bear away north-west. Though by no means clear of the foot-hills, the lines ran through flatter country, but country much favouring the defence.

1945

This part of Italy is one of those regions where the river beds tend to rise with the passage of time, from the accumulation of silt brought down in times of flood. To keep the rivers within their channels, built-up banks are made—and from these banks, standing relatively high above the countryside, admirable command of the approaches could be exercised.

The Germans had made full use of the river-lines, fortifying both the inner and the outer faces of both banks, burrowing through them, and constructing carefully sited trenches and defended localities. At selected points, the banks had been cut through to facilitate flooding the approaches, and the approaches themselves were sown with minefields and covered with wire entanglements. The rivers themselves were impassible tank obstacles, prohibiting any easy exploitation following capture of the near bank.

Allied tactics were varied to suit these novel conditions. Artillery was pushed forward wherever possible early in an action, for enfilade fire on the reverse slopes of the river banks. Tunnels and fox-holes were dealt with by flame-throwing equipment. To ensure maximum surprise in an attack, troops were encouraged to lean forward, pushing small inconspicuous parties forward to dig in and then gradually strengthening their positions, and repeating the manoeuvre. By this means, forward posts in many places were established within ten or a dozen yards of the enemy, and the problem of a long approach in the attack was to an extent avoided.

Ahead of the Allied line, along the Senio, and thence some way south of Bologna, there were certain broad tactical features. An advance up the coast was barred by Lake Comacchio, just north of the Senio, and extending to within a mile or two of the Adriatic. The lake was nearly 20 miles long on a roughly east-west axis, and averaged about 7 miles in width. 30 miles west of the west end of Lake Comacchio is Bologna, on the retention of which the Germans set great store. Bologna is on the plain at the foot of the Apennines, on the great Highway 9, which runs north-west from Rimini right up into the industrial north-west, skirting the northern edge of the Apennines the whole way. In a very general way parellel with Highway 9, and 30 miles north of it at Bologna, is the river Po which falls into the Adriatic through a large swampy delta 20 miles north of Lake Comacchio. It was on the Po that the enemy had been expected to withdraw ever since the first Allied footing in the Gothic Line, and it presented a formidable obstacle.

On the 11th April, the Eighth Army, in a massive assault, finally smashed the defences on the river Senio, and on the Santerno, running parallel with it and 5 or 6 miles north-west. Pursuit groups were pushed ahead, moving north-west between Lake Comacchio and

11 Apr.

1945

Bologna. German reserve formations attempted to take up rallying positions at various points, among others at Medecina, 15 miles east of Bologna. Here an encounter battle took place in which Gurkhas from armoured troop carriers, and tanks of the 14th/20th King's Hussars indulged in a 10-minutes wild-west mêlée in the half-light of dusk, inflicting heavy casualties in hand-to-hand fighting, and driving the scattered remnants out in panic. The 10th Indian Division played a leading part in the initial stages, but later, with the British Armoured Division on right and the New Zealanders on the left squeezing inwards as the pursuit turned northwards from above Bologna, the Division was held back and briefed for the expected mountain fighting in the Euganean Hills, west of Padua.

21 Apr. Bologna fell on the 21st April, the Po was crossed on the 26th,
26 Apr. and the Adige soon after; and before the enemy could collect and stand again, the German armies in Italy unconditionally surrendered,
29 Apr. with nearly 1,000,000 men, on the 29th.

Meanwhile, on the 28th, Mussolini was assassinated by Italian
28 Apr. partisans in circumstances of some squalor at Donga near Lake Como.

Germany In Western Europe, the Allies had completely occupied the Rhine
25 Mar. west bank by the 25th March.
23 Mar. Two days before, on the 23rd, the Rhine had been crossed, as a major, water-borne operation, north and south of Wesel, some 50 miles north of Cologne. Under Field-Marshal Montgomery, with the United States Ninth Army on the right, and the British Second Army on the left, and with air-borne co-operation by the United States 17th and British 6th Airborne Divisions just north of Wesel, the crossing, launched at 8 a.m., was a complete success. The existing bridge-heads farther up-stream on the 12th Army Group front were extended, and the German positions broken. Other crossings followed, and by
1 Apr. the 1st April the German Rhine defences had disintegrated. The Ruhr had also been surrounded by the 1st, and with it a force which,
18 Apr. after stiff fighting, surrendered on the 18th April with 30 generals and 325,000 men.

Leaving Berlin 100 miles to the north, Eisenhower moved his main effort southwards from Leipzig towards the Czechoslovak border which was reached on the 18th April. Limited offensives more in the Berlin direction brought American troops to Magdeburg on the Elbe, 80 miles west of Berlin, also on the 18th.

Farther north, the 21st Army Group reached the Elbe south of
29 Apr. Hamburg on the 29th April.

There had been no delay this time from supply problems. The armoured columns were throughout supplied by air; 60,000 tons of freight, including 10,255,509 gallons of petrol, were flown forward during April.

408

	1945
Meanwhile, east of Berlin, the Russians were on the line of the Oder, opposite Berlin, by mid-February. In the south, by the beginning of March, they were poised for the resumed advance on Vienna, which was occupied on the 13th April.	February 13 Apr.
To cover Berlin, the Germans had collected the Third Tank Army, and the Ninth, Twelfth and Twenty-first Armies. These held the line of the Oder from Stettin in the north, to Frankfurt-on-Oder, and thence south along the Niesse river.	
On the 17th April, the Russians on the Niesse, under Koniev, broke forward, and wheeling right-handed, with their left on the Elbe, scattered the German Ninth Army, and moved northwards towards Berlin some 80 miles away.	17 Apr.
Simultaneously, Zhukov, in the centre, advanced from about Kustrin, 60 miles east of Berlin, smashing through the German Twelfth Army, and passing round the northern outskirts of Berlin by the 22nd, while Koniev joined up from the south. By the 25th, Berlin was completely cut off, and forces moving into the city against fierce opposition. Violent street fighting gradually drove the defenders back point by point till only the centre was left, and that under artillery fire. The end came quickly. On the 30th April, Hitler committed suicide, and on the 2nd May, the Berlin garrison surrendered.	22 Apr. 25 Apr. 30 Apr. 2 May
Eisenhower, meanwhile, had called a halt on the Elbe and in the Erz Gebirge on the Czechoslovak frontier. The 21st Army Group was directed on Lubeck, 40 miles north-east of Hamburg. In the south, the objective was Linz on the Danube, nearly 100 miles west of Vienna. These moves were under way when on the 3rd May representations were made to Field-Marshal Montgomery to accept the surrender of three of the armies recently opposing the Russians on the Oder. This being refused, unconditional surrender of all German armed forces in northern Germany, Holland, Schleswig-Holstein and Denmark was offered on the 4th to Field-Marshal Montgomery, who accepted it as a local tactical measure. At 8 a.m. on the 5th, hostilities ceased on the front of the 21st Army Group. On the 7th, the instrument of surrender was signed again at Supreme Allied Headquarters in Rheims, and was finally ratified in Berlin on the 9th.	 3 May 4 May 5 May 7 May 9 May
Thus, while hostilities went on with unremitting violence in the east, the war in Europe was over.	
The 1st Battalion was in position north of Singu, some 3 miles east of the Irrawaddy, downstream from Pakokku, with "D" Company on detachment in Tetna, a further 4 miles east Of the remainder of the 89th Indian Infantry Brigade, the 4th/8th Gurkha Rifles were astride the main road to Singu, and the King's Own Scottish Borderers in reserve. It was a dry dusty area; but beyond Singu, which was a suburb of Chauk, lay the oil-fields.	1st Bn.

1945

It was soon apparent that the enemy was beginning to concentrate strong forces on the Brigade front preparatory to an attempted breakthrough against the Irrawaddy bridge-head north of Pagan.

6 Mar. The Battalion was kept busy patrolling; and on the 6th March a fighting patrol of sixteen men went out to destroy a Japanese post in Taungbi Ywathit village. The village had been half-cleared when the leading section ran into an unlocated enemy light machine-gun post. The section commander was seriously wounded in the neck, while three other members of the section were also hit. Among these was No. 15868 Sep. Bhola Singh, whose subsequent actions now followed a familiar pattern. Regardless of his wound, he took over command of the section, reorganized it under covering fire from other members of the section, then crawled forward to the exposed position where his section commander was lying, and dragged him back to cover, complete with his equipment and tommy-gun. He kept his section in action till ordered to withdraw, then sent the rest back, staying on alone to give them covering fire. He then followed, bringing back the body of his section commander, who had died of his wounds. The award of a Gallantry Certificate followed.

The main concentration was on the front of the 4th/8th Gurkhas who forestalled the enemy attack, breaking into the concentration area, with tank support. A second enemy force established itself astride a track about 600 yards south of Tetna. Nothing was known

11 Mar. of this force till the 11th March when two "D" Company patrols were moving about in the vicinity, though without encountering the enemy. Meeting by arrangement at a pre-determined rendezvous, the two patrols, numbering fifteen men in all, now had the enemy between them and home. Moving back in company along the track and suspecting nothing out of the ordinary, the patrols in due course ran into the enemy, and charged in with fixed bayonets under the mistaken impression that it was a Japanese ambush lying up for them. Such was the determination of this charge that it carried them right through the Japanese position, which was found later to be held by about 150 men. Not a single man came through unhurt; eight Sikhs were killed and seven seriously wounded, among the latter No. 25233 Sep. Kapur Singh, who was awarded a Military Medal for outstanding steadfastness and courage, covering the withdrawal of his fellow-wounded with a Bren-gun, under a hail of fire, which shot the last magazine off his gun, and inflicted a second wound. With both arms hit, he none the less carried his gun out of action. In this wild charge they had killed twice their number and so shattered the morale of the Japanese that they evacuated the position and withdrew south.

This did not end the nuisance in the Tetna area, however. On the
15 Mar. evening of the 15th March, a determined and sustained attack by strong

1945

forces of Japanese was launched on the position, now held by "A"
Company, which had since relieved "D". With Maj. Webster in
command and a section of the Battalion mortars in support, the
company beat off the continuous attacks, which went on all night,
with, as the only casualty, Sub. Naranjan Singh slightly wounded.
Twenty enemy dead were picked up on or near the wire next morning. 16 Mar.

On the 22nd March, the Battalion was relieved by the King's Own 22 Mar.
Scottish Borderers, and came into reserve on the Irrawaddy bank.
It was a well-deserved rest. The past month had spelt hard living—
it had been too hot for comfort; water had been very scarce; and the
continuous long-range patrolling over soft sand had brought small
tangible reward. The rest, however, did not last long.

Since the Gurkhas' successful attack earlier in the month, the
enemy had moved back to Singu, 5 miles south. On the 27th March, 27 Mar.
the Sikhs taking over from the Gurkhas, obtained permission to
establish a patrol base on a hill called "Fantasia", just north of Singu.

Fantasia was well-named, and at first looked like proving an
unhealthy choice. It was over-looked by enemy observation posts;
and, as it boasted little natural cover, it attracted a good deal of
artillery fire at first. Later, however, the enemy gave up concentrating
on Fantasia, and resumed his earlier spells of intermittent harassing
fire spread over the whole Battalion position.

These intermittent shellings cost the Battalion one regretted
loss in Maj. J. Frith, R.A., commanding No. 347 Battery. Maj. Frith
was an old friend of the Battalion, and had lived with it for a long
time. Unfailing and invaluable artillery support had always been
forthcoming both in the Arakan and in the present campaign. What
this co-operation had meant to the Battalion in terms of fighting strength
and reduction in casualties cannot be assessed; but it was generally
felt that John Frith's influence had done much to further the splendid
spirit which existed between the Sikh jawans and the British ranks
of the Battery, and his loss was a personal one to all.

By the beginning of April, the IVth Corps had passed through the
bridge-head, linked up with the 19th Indian Division from Mandalay,
and freed the 7th Indian Division to assume the offensive southwards
down the Irrawaddy. In the third week of April, however, the Japanese,
outflanked from the east, vacated the oil-fields, and on the 19th April, 19 Apr.
the Battalion entered Chauk unopposed.

Meanwhile, on the 16th April, Lieut.-Col. Spink took over command 16 Apr.
of the Battalion from Lieut.-Col. Hamilton.

The Irrawaddy line had been allotted to the XXXIIIrd Corps and
the 7th Indian Division was now accordingly transferred to that Corps.
The advance southwards was vigorously pursued, with the 33rd Indian
Infantry Brigade which had been already responsible for manoeuvring

1945

21 Apr.   the Japanese out of Chauk by the threat from the flank, advancing and occupying Yenangyaung in the face of stubborn opposition, on the 21st.

The Japanese garrisons of Chauk and Yenangyaung now crossed over to the Irrawaddy west bank. The 89th Indian Infantry Brigade was directed to follow them over, seize Salin, and cut off as many of the enemy as possible.

For this operation, the crossing was to be made and the bridge-head secured by the 1st Battalion. "A" Company, under Maj. Webster led the way—in craft more suited to the task than the earlier crossing—at

23 Apr.   8.30 p.m. on the 23rd April. Though the crossing was in fact not opposed, great credit was due to the Company for the speed and smoothness of the operation. The troops had had no previous experience of paddling these craft, but they put them across with silence and despatch, and the Battalion was firmly established on the opposite bank by midnight.

24 Apr.   The Brigade passed through astride the main road and occupied Salin, without, however, bringing the enemy to action. The Japanese had moved off south as fast as they could to avoid interception, and were re-crossing back to the eastern bank again. However, other objectives were in sight for the Division.

We have seen in the introductory backscreen to this chapter that the 25th Indian Division of the XVth Corps had been engaged in severe fighting during February in the Arakan Yomas where the track from An crosses over into Burma in the general latitude of the oil-fields. Troops of the Japanese 54th Division had been falling back along this track and approaching Thayetmyo some distance south down the Irrawaddy. The 89th Indian Infantry Brigade was ordered off at short notice to intercept them.

25 Apr.   The Brigade moved off on the 25th April with the Battalion in the lead. Little opposition was encountered as the enemy were using
30 Apr.   tracks farther to the west. On the 30th April, the Battalion entered Minbu, about half-way to Thayetmyo without opposition. Minbu, which is a pleasant little town, proved almost undamaged, and full of abandoned dumps of ammunition and other enemy equipment.

2 May   Pausing at Minbu till the 2nd May, the Battalion led the Brigade in a series of forced marches over deep muddy tracks, which the pre-monsoon rains had already made almost impassible. Despite these difficulties, the column covered over 50 miles in three days, and by
6 May   the 6th May had cut the first Japanese escape route at Yenema. It was a close thing, and there was a touch of drama about the arrival at this remote hamlet, for the Japanese advance party reached it at the same moment as "A" Company, intent on laying out a camp site for the night for the main Japanese column, half-an-hour in rear.

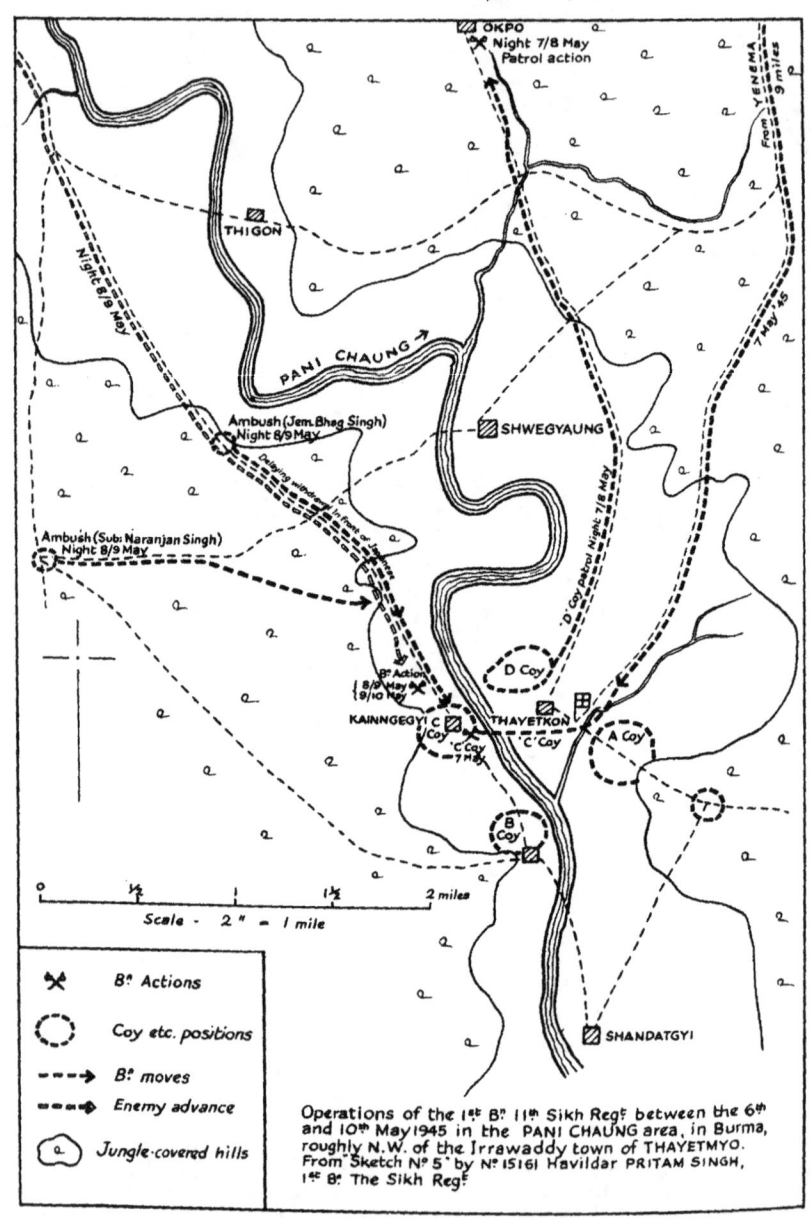

"A" Company took charge of the situation with its usual spirit, No. 27730 Sep. Bawa Singh distinguishing himself by literally throwing his Bren-gun into action, and killing fifteen Japanese with three long bursts, and cleared matters up for the time being. A Gallantry Certificate was subsequently awarded to Bawa Singh in recognition of his action.

The 4th/8th Gurkha Rifles were being pressed forward at speed to take over from the Battalion at Yenema, and enable the latter to move on south-west and cut the next possible Japanese line of withdrawal, which lay along a track following the Pani Chaung in the next valley to the west. "C" Company, accordingly, under Maj. Heath, moved off about midnight, while the remainder of the Battalion followed, on relief by the 4th/8th Gurkha Rifles, at 7 o'clock the next morning.   7 May

"C" Company safely reached the Pani Chaung, 15 miles from Yenema, and then bore off south-east over a small range of hills to Shandatgyi, close to the Chaung. While the forward platoon was moving over these hills and down to Shandatgyi, Maj. Heath sent a small patrol off to his right to the village of Kainngegyi, about half-a-mile away, and a little upstream. The patrol reported the village occupied, and added that it had seen a large party of Japanese bathing there.

With a section of 3-inch mortars in support, the Company changed front and attacked the village with two platoons under Sub. Bachan Singh. The enemy had sufficient warning to put up a very stiff opposition at the edge of the village. About eighty Japanese were in position there in well-sited bunkers, with five machine-guns in support. "A" Company's leading platoon suffered a number of casualties and was held up close to the enemy's defences which were located behind a strong bamboo stockade just inside the village.

The casualties included a number of wounded lying out much exposed and so near the enemy that it would have been hazardous either to put down further supporting fire, or to set fire to the village, until they had been collected. This was a long, tedious and costly business, in which Sub. Bachan Singh set a sterling example of personal devotion and leadership. With supreme disregard for his own safety, he went forward with three other men to try and silence an enemy post which was preventing the collection of these casualties. Under very heavy fire, and at point blank-range, the party crawled forward to within a few yards of the enemy trench, but was there held up by the six-foot bamboo stockade. Being unable to force a way through the stockade, Sub. Bachan Singh set about bombarding the enemy post with grenades. His three companions being almost immediately killed, the Sub. crawled back and collected another party which he led round to a flank to assault the post from another direction. The stockade still proving an insuperable obstacle, and further casualties having been suffered, Sub. Bachan Singh arranged for two of his men to give him covering fire while he crawled forward and dragged six men to safety. For this and his subsequent acts of gallantry and devotion, Sub. Bachan Singh received an award of the Military Cross.

No. 13750 Naik Hukma Singh was one of Sub. Bachan Singh's supporters in this hazardous action. It was his section that went forward with Sub. Bachan Singh in the second attempt to rescue the wounded. Naik Hukma Singh, with his section, crawled forward to within fifteen yards of the enemy trench, as already related; and by that time, many men of his section had been hit, and he himself had been twice severely wounded in the head. Despite his wounds, alone, Naik Hukma Singh continued to try and force a way through a small gap in the stockade, and to throw grenades into the enemy post; but when Sub. Bachan Singh gave the signal to withdraw, Hukma Singh immediately took over the Bren-gun from a wounded sepoy, and in a very exposed position under very heavy fire, continued to give covering fire until Sub. Bachan Singh completed the rescue—and thereafter, till he collapsed from loss of blood and lapsed into unconsciousness. An Indian Distinguished Service Medal commemorated this act of selfless heroism and self-sacrifice.

While these events were enacting at Kainngegyi, the Company's leading platoon had been called back from Shandatgyi. The Battalion mortars arrived just in time to cover in a full-scale Company attack, but artillery support was not at that time available.

Closing up on the village, the Company set fire to it with smoke grenades, but there was bitter fighting before the enemy were driven out. Sub. Bachan Singh again displayed great gallantry in this attack, personally leading forward the leading troops and inspiring all by his example. Much credit rests with this devoted officer for the successful termination of this affair, at the close of which thirty-three Japanese dead were counted and a mass of equipment collected.

It had been a tiring and a relatively expensive day for the Company. There had been about twenty casualties, but the men were in high spirits, and immensely pleased with the booty which included a large number of binoculars. swords and other trophies, and five bottles of the Imperial Japanese Saki.

The commanding officer had arrived on the scene at the start of "C" Company's first attack, and had appreciated that the spot was admirably adapted for blocking the Pani Chaung valley. The remainder of the Battalion was accordingly ordered forward as quickly as possible and deployed in suitable positions while "C" Company was still engaged. From the number of Japanese officers killed and the nature of the equipment captured, the village was clearly some sort of enemy headquarters. Villagers further said that parties of enemy troops had been moving south down this track, and added that a large body of the

enemy was then resting at Okpo village some 5 miles to the north.
To deal with these, a fighting patrol of twenty men of "D" Company was detailed under Jem. Mehar Singh to raid Okpo village that night. This meant another 5 miles of most difficult country for the platoon over and above the 15 miles already covered, but the advance was carefully and successfully carried out, and the platoon reached its destination unchecked about midnight.

Jem. Mehar Singh first posted stops all round the village, and the latter was then set on fire. The Japanese were taken completely by surprise and ran out in disorder. In the glare of the flames good targets were had, and twenty-five Japanese were killed before sheer weight of enemy numbers forced the platoon to withdraw. Returning at dawn with this remarkable report, the commanding officer decided to check up, and a small officer's patrol made its way to Okpo to see. The report proved to have been perfectly correct, and the twenty-five Japanese bodies were still lying there. All in all, it was an outstanding achievement for the platoon had covered 25 miles in twenty-two hours, and had successfully ambushed a large party of enemy by night in previously unreconnoitred country.

8 May

Throughout the 8th May patrols scoured the valley of the Pani Chaung, and located a body of troops some 12 miles to the north. At the same time, Brigade Headquarters reported—at 5 p.m.—that the enemy main body had pulled back from Yenema and turned west, and that it might be expected down the Pani Chaung that night.

Four miles north of the Battalion position, the main track from the north divided in three. One track led to a valley 5 miles west of the Pani Chaung. A second turned east and crossed the Yenema track about 5 miles north-east of Shandatgyi. The main track led down direct to Shandatgyi through the Battalion position.

It was judged likely that the enemy would use either the main route, or the track which led round to the west. Accordingly, two platoons were sent off to lie up. One, under Jem. Bhag Singh, was to watch the main route. The other, under Sub. Naranjan Singh, was posted on the western track. The latter position was about a mile south-west of Jem. Bhag Singh's, and both were about 2 miles roughly north of the Battalion.

Jem. Bhag Singh's operated of necessity more as a covering detachment than an old-fashioned ambush. About 9 p.m., a very large enemy column, which proved to have been about 2,500 strong, with seventy-five lorries and some sixty bullock carts, ran into it. Jem. Bhag Singh, though he had no idea at the moment just what the column consisted of, appreciated that it was out of his class, as a platoon ambush, and adopted skilful delaying tactics with a view to causing the enemy to expend his strength and lose time. Falling back from

1945

9 May

successive positions, each held till the enemy deployed, the platoon imposed a delay of some seven hours on the Japanese. By that time, somewhere about three in the morning of the 9th May, when within about half-a-mile of the Battalion position, the platoon slipped away back into "C" Company's area athwart the track on the west bank of the Chaung. A few minutes later, about 3.30 a.m., the leading elements of the enemy contacted the Company position.

It is to be supposed that the enemy mistook this new collision for another phase of Jem. Bhag Singh's delaying tactics, for the column allowed its transport to move up close behind the forward troops within only a few hundred yards of the Company. But the din that now broke out, supplemented by the very accurate artillery and mortar fire directed by the artillery forward observation officer and the mortar observation post, soon undeceived them. Undeterred, however, an attack was rapidly built up by the Japanese under cover of a 75-m.m. gun and an anti-tank gun.

Sub. Naranjan Singh, meanwhile, had been following the course of the action as the noise of the fighting drew level, and then slowly receded towards the Battalion. Correctly appreciating what was going on, he decided to move off east and co-operate against the enemy's right flank. Moving cautiously through the dark towards the sound of the firing, he struck the centre of the enemy column just as it came up against "C" Company. Sub. Naranjan Singh and his platoon were in no very enviable position with stuff coming over from both sides. None-the-less, the attack was pushed gallantly home, causing considerable casualties and damage to the enemy, including the destruction of two 3-ton lorry-loads of hostile troops with anti-tank rifle grenades.

Profiting by the general state of confusion in the enemy ranks, a platoon of "D" Company was now sent out from its forward position on the east bank of the Chaung to move up that bank. Orders were for it to attack the enemy's left flank and if possible silence and capture the 75-m.m. gun.

The enemy were indeed in an unenviable situation. The track was a milling mass of troops and transport, and there was nothing for the Japanese but to extricate themselves as best they could. About 7.30 a.m., they began to withdraw, followed up by "B" Company under Maj. Redding. This brought them to a stand, whereupon "A" Company moved up into "C" Company's area ready to circle round west through the jungle and strike at their flank and rear.

At bay, now, desperately trying to cover the congested mass of transport which was vainly trying to turn about and get sorted out, the enemy turned on "B" Company, about 8 a.m., when that Company's pressure began to make itself felt, some 400 yards along the track from "C" Company's front, and counter-attacked with fanatical fury. The Company suffered heavy casualties, and seemed in danger of being over-run by sheer weight of numbers, and "A" Company had to be diverted and sent to its assistance.

Fighting went on for some time, and it was not until nearly 2 o'clock in the afternoon that the situation in "B" Company had been fully restored. The enemy had managed to organize a strong rearguard position covering his disordered column, and it was thought best to defer further action till nightfall, other than maintaining touch with patrols.

About 8 p.m., however, soon after dark, the enemy began probing the "C" and "B" Company areas, and about midnight he attacked, though without great determination. More probably, the attack was a feint to cover the withdrawal of the transport which "D" Company heard revving up about this time. Harassing fire was accordingly opened on the track by the artillery.

Enemy pressure did not relax, however, until about 4 a.m. on the 10th. When light came, "D" Company moved forward to the track junction 4 miles north. Six Japanese stragglers were killed, but the main body—of which the Battalion had accounted for over 250 men—had slipped away and was withdrawing west with all the speed it could muster. It did not escape, however. While the Sikhs were holding the enemy in the Pani Chaung valley, the Gurkhas, who had followed the Sikhs to Shandatgyi, on relief themselves by the King's Own Scottish Borderers, had sent two companies to Taungdaw in the next valley to the west, and only 15 miles due east of An, and effectively blocked the last escape route. These two companies were subjected to desperate attacks over a three-day period before the Japanese finally abandoned their transport and slipped away in small parties into the jungle. The total enemy loss amounted to between five and six hundred killed, and the whole of the transport taken or destroyed.

For the part his Company had played during the night of the 9th/10th May, and for the admirable and inspired leading which had contributed towards it, Maj. D. W. J. Redding, commanding "B" Company, was awarded the Military Cross. Though no other decorations were awarded for this confused but gallant action, in which it would have been almost impossible to single out one brave man from another, it is proposed to refer briefly to two isolated deeds, not so much for the recognition accorded, as to demonstrate once more the astounding sense of self-sacrifice and devotion to duty that signalized this fine battalion.

The first case was that of No. 21303 Sep. Ranjit Singh, awarded a posthumous Mention in Despatches. Ranjit Singh was a forward scout who moved out with others after the Japanese attack had come to a standstill, to probe their strength and dispositions. The jungle was very thick, and visibility poor. An enemy light machine-gun post was in position only some 30 yards from the track which the Company was following, but Ranjit Singh never saw it till he had passed by it. The light machine-gun was trained on the track, and covering the section and platoon advancing behind the forward scouts.

That was the position. Ranjit Singh on the wrong side of the light machine-gun, and his unsuspecting mates liable to be shot down at any moment. Nothing could be done to warn the oncoming troops unless he paid the price himself.

It cannot have taken this gallant man two seconds to decide on his course of action. He unhesitatingly charged the enemy post, which immediately swung round and opened fire on him. He was seen to stagger twice in his wild charge, but he reached the post, and the gun almost at once stopped firing. Savage and bitter fighting ensued for some time, and the Company, which was heavily out-numbered, was finally forced to withdraw.

The following morning after the enemy had been finally driven back, Ranjit Singh's body, riddled with bullets, was found lying on top of the bodies of two Japanese and the light machine-gun which he had thus silenced. Truly, of so many deeds of these grand troops it can be said: "Greater love hath no man...".

Among the Sikh casualties, one of the most regretted was Lieut. Amar Singh, a most gallant officer, who was first wounded at the head of his men, and seen lying in the open about 50 yards from the enemy. One of his men, No. 23916 Sep. Sawan Singh, immediately dashed forward under heavy machine-gun fire, and brought him in. It was all to no purpose, though, for Amar Singh had been mortally wounded, and died soon after. Sep. Sarwan Singh was awarded a Gallantry Certificate for his courageous action.

In company with the King's Own Scottish Borderers, the Battalion now temporarily severed its connection with the 89th Indian Infantry Brigade, which had been directed on Thayetmyo to take up monsoon quarters, reorganize and refit for the autumn campaign. The two detached battalions were placed temporarily under command of the 268th Indian Infantry Brigade with the role of working independently down two tracks leading to Kama, an Irrawaddy town some 10 miles or so upstream of Prome. Here the 268th Brigade had been located to prevent the escape of some parts of the shattered Japanese 54th Division from the Arakan, and parties left behind by the 5th and 17th Indian Divisions in their rapid move down the main road to Rangoon.

These orders arrived when the 89th Brigade was at Mindon; and the Battalion marched away south on its special mission, just as

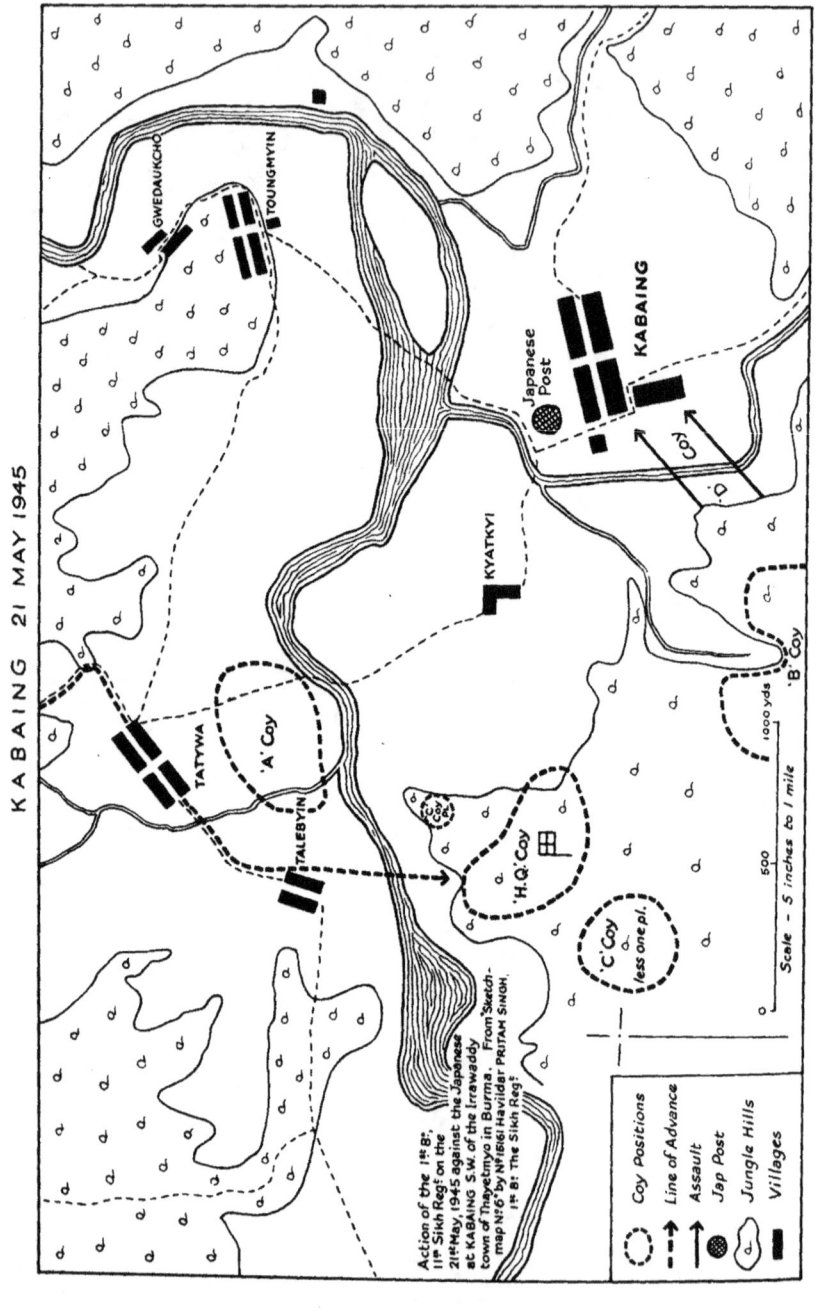

                                                                    1945
dawn was breaking, on the 21st May. The operation was expected   21 May
to take five days. The first march was the longest, and it was to take
the Battalion to Kabaing, 15 miles south of Mindon. The monsoon
proper was just breaking. There had been several days of heavy rain.
The track was deep in mud, and the various streams which had to be
crossed had become raging torrents, waist-deep, and a problem to
cross for both man and mule. Sun and rain followed each other intermittently. The atmosphere was steamy and oppressive. The track
wound up and down over the hills and the heavy mud which clung
tenaciously to the boots, the stifling humidity and the constant ups
and downs, made the march most arduous. It was a very weary battalion
that eventually began to close on Kabaing.

To reduce the time on the road as much as possible for the main
body, "B" Company, under Maj. Redding, had been despatched from
Mindon some four hours ahead of the Battalion. With protective commitments
to meet, the company moved slower than the main body, so that by
3 o'clock in the afternoon, when "B" Company was half-a-mile or so
from Kabaing, the main body was only about half-an-hour behind.

At this moment, 3 p.m., Maj. Redding wirelessed back that according
to a village report there were about 100 Japanese in Kabaing, with
two or more guns.

Patrols went forward to investigate while the Battalion moved up.
Lieut.-Col. Spink joined Maj. Redding and the two went forward to
the leading platoon to make a field-glass reconnaissance. A patrol
now came in and reported the village to be in fact held. It also
reported a sentry post with a light machine-gun ahead of the village
covering the crossing where the track passed through the stream just
north of the village.

This was not welcome news just then. The men were tired, it was
getting late, an air-drop of supplies was expected at any moment,
and the Battalion had to get into position and dig in quickly since
more parties of Japanese were expected to be passing through Kabaing
that night.

Across the stream, and overlooking Kabaing from the south-west,
was some high ground which clearly must be held. A villager agreed
to lead the Battalion there by a covered route. To lessen the risk,
it was decided to send up "C" Company alone in the first instance.
This was safely carried through, and the Company occupied the hill
seemingly unobserved.

Leaving "A" Company to lay out a dropping zone for supplies,
and to cover the approaches on the north side of the stream, the
rest of the Battalion now moved forward after "C" Company.

By 4.30 p.m., "B" Company was established on a high hill directly
overlooking Kabaing. All dominating ground round the village was

in the Battalion's hands, but the enemy was still apparently unaware of it.

"D" Company had been detailed to attack the village, and now came forward into "B" Company's area. Maj. Brough, the Company Commander, came forward for a reconnaissance. What he saw was an open stretch of rice-fields, 500 yards across, with a tributary of the main stream beyond it. Behind the tributary lay the village—but in the tributary was a large party of Japanese quietly having a bathe.

The attack had been timed for 5 p.m. Mortar covering fire was to be provided, and it is very much to the mortar officer's credit that it was provided. Without prior registration, accurate mortar fire was a problem since maps were inaccurate and the jungle dense. However, Capt. Proudlock successfully solved that problem for when it came down, the mortar fire was absolutely accurate.

The commanding officer had gone forward with a wireless set to "B" Company's area to watch progress. "D" Company had closed up to the edge of the jungle ready for the assault. The rest of the battalion was busy digging itself in, when three minutes before 5 o'clock, a burst of firing broke out in "A" Company's area across the main stream. "Everyone's heart sank," the record reads. "The adjutant, Captain Cunningham, immediately came up on the wireless-set from battalion headquarters (just south of the main stream), and reported that an enemy foraging party had come across to the village held by "A" Company (a little north of the main stream), who had been forced to open fire; they had killed four Japanese. He was at once followed by Major Brough who asked, with a furious voice what was happening. He reported that the Japanese who were bathing, had all scuttled back into the village, that all chance of surprise was lost and that the attack across the rice-fields must now be a costly business."

Thus Maj. Brough, for whose views one must have every sympathy.

It was arguable, however, that the situation could still be saved. Obviously it was from the north that the enemy would expect attack, though as only a few shots had been fired, the enemy might be suspicious. However, the Battalion's presence in the enemy rear was still apparently undiscovered, and Maj. Brough was instructed to proceed with his attack.

For the mortar concentration, 100 rounds had been allotted, and at 5.5 p.m., the first were lobbed over, and "D" Company began its dash across the open. The Japanese had manned their positions covering the track across the stream to the north, and they were completely and overwhelmingly surprised by the attack from the south.

Back they accordingly rushed to man alternative dispositions covering the open rice-fields, only to be caught with absolute precision in the open by the mortar concentration. "D" Company crossed the open with a dash and speed hardly to be expected after the long and tiring day that had passed, and charged in with the bayonet before the enemy recovered. Under the inspired leadership of Maj. Brough and Sub. Gurcharan Singh, they completely over-ran the Japanese, and by 6.30 p.m., the last strong-point had been taken. 15 to 20 enemy escaped to the south-west. Of the 73 dead, over 50 had been killed with the bayonet. 3 guns and 5 heavy machine-guns were taken as well as a mass of other equipment. The cost to the Battalion was 3 killed and 9 wounded.

Maj. Brough had already been awarded the Distinguished Service Order for the earlier fighting in the Arakan during March, 1944. For his leadership and gallantry at Kabaing, he was given the Military Cross. Sub. Gurcharan Singh, who had obtained the Military Cross in the Arakan in February, 1944, received a bar to it.

Meanwhile, as the mortar fire opened, the first Dakota arrived, with supplies and ammunition, and the air-drop began.

Such decisive results could not have been achieved without individual examples of resolution and courage. One such case was that of L.-Naik Bhag Singh. This non-commissioned officer led his section with great dash to the capture of the first trench, where he personally killed three of the enemy with his bayonet. Leading his section on to the next line of trenches, he was held up by light machine-gun fire, and was wounded. However, with complete disregard for his wound, he charged the enemy post single-handed. He was hit in the chest, but charged on undeterred and killed the two Japanese manning the gun. He then led his section on and captured his final objective. He was awarded the Indian Distinguished Service Medal.

Casualties could be evacuated only by air, and the Battalion had to halt on the 22nd May at Kabaing to construct a strip on which aircraft could land to pick the casualties up. This was unfortunate, as the Japanese were able to make good their get-away, and could not again be brought to action. On the 23rd, the march was resumed. Japanese stragglers were picked up at intervals, and the track south was found littered with abandoned equipment. Otherwise the journey was uneventful, and the Battalion reached Kama safely on the 26th, and halted there briefly before moving on.

Meanwhile, the remainder of the 7th Indian Division, with some extra battalions from the 20th Indian Division attached, had been engaged in furious fighting at Zalon on the Irrawaddy east bank, 8 miles north of Prome and not very far from Kama. At Zalon, the Japanese had established a bridge-head to keep open an escape route to the east. Ringing round the bridge-head, the 33rd Indian

1945

Infantry Brigade threw in a succession of fierce attacks on the northern face, with an enemy loss of some 1,500 killed and seventy prisoners. Only a depleted and shaken remnant of the escaping forces found their way through into the thickly wooded belt of hills to the east called the Pegu Yomas.

The monsoon was now a fact, but Burma had been nearly enough cleared for the forces to be able to take up the question of re-fitting and training preparatory to post-monsoon operations which were expected to open about the 15th October. The intervening months were not to be quite the well-ordered training period expected, but that was not to be known at the time. Thayetmyo, about 200 miles north of Rangoon and on the west bank of the Irrawaddy, had been selected as the monsoon headquarters of the 89th Indian Infantry Brigade, and here the Battalion duly arrived on the 2nd June.

2 June

The first consideration was to get as large a body of men as possible away on leave, and the first few days were spent settling in, cleaning up, and preparing for this. In the event, only forty men were able to get away at this time, as the expected air-lift did not materialize. Another disappointment was the loss, on relief, of the Battalion's much-loved medical officer, Capt. Sarkar. He had served through two long and arduous campaigns with the 1st Battalion, and had been decorated with the Military Cross for courage and devotion in tending the wounded several times under fire in the Arakan.

8 June

Celebrations for the Burma victory were now being arranged, and on the 8th June, Lieut.-Col. Spink, who had been selected to command the composite battalion made up of contingents from all battalions of the 7th Indian Division, left by road for Rangoon. With him went the thirty men detailed from the 1st Battalion. The main Prome road had only just been cleared of the Japanese, and the party noted with interest the various positions the Battalion had held in 1942, much as the 4th Battalion had done when moving back to Kassala en route to the Western Desert in April 1941. The Japanese had not done much work on the road, but it was still in reasonable condition. After the tortuous jungle tracks to which the Battalion had become painfully accustomed, it was a pleasant change to drive over a macadam surface. Rangoon proved to be less damaged than expected. Stores, vehicles and personnel were pouring in through the port, and the place was a hive of activity.

15 June

The Rangoon Victory Parade took place on the 15th June. Though marred by rain it was a most impressive function. Admiral Lord Louis Mountbatten, the Supreme Allied Commander, took the salute, and the forces marching past included representatives of not only the British and Indian divisions which had fought in the Burma campaign but also of the American, Dutch, French, Chinese and local Burma

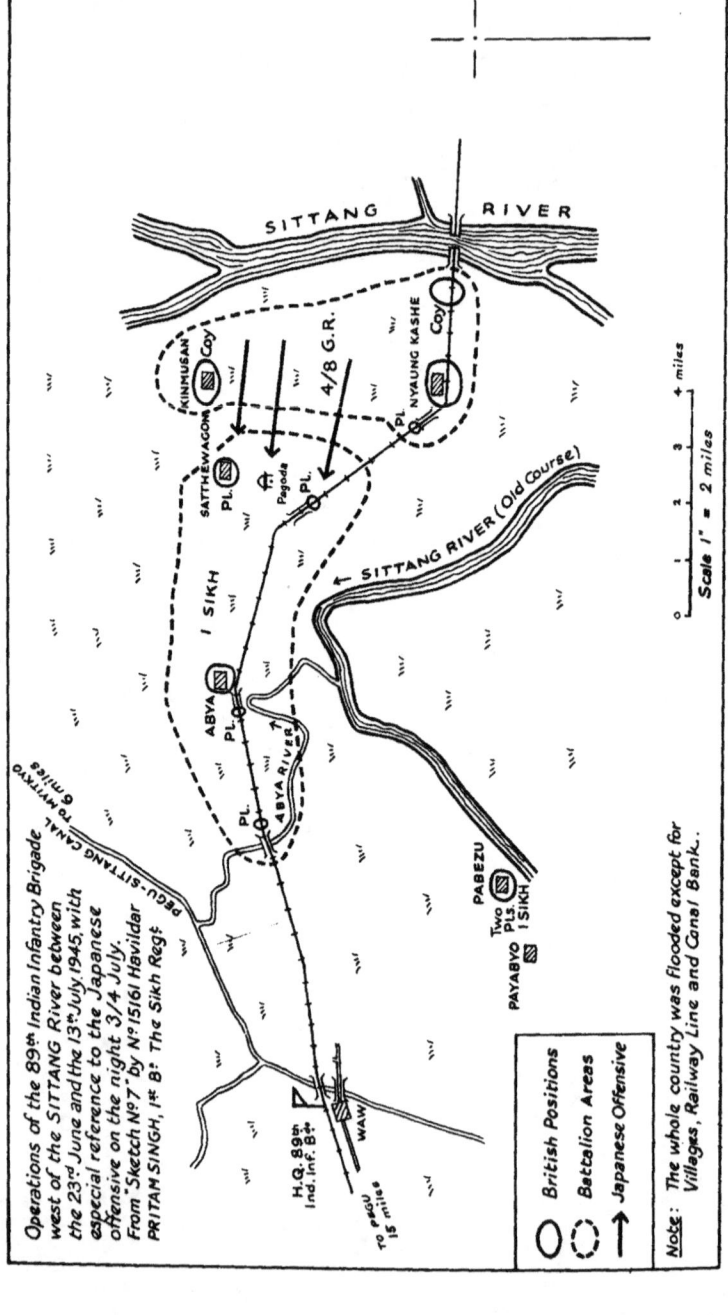

                                                                    1945
Patriot forces in addition. However, trouble was again in the offing,
and the Battalion, amongst others, was soon on the move once more.

Much work had been done in Thayetmyo in the lines, and on
construction of ranges and parade grounds. However, difficulties had
been cropping up with the Japanese parties trickling eastwards
through the Pegu Yomas to join up with the remnants of their forces
moving out. The 5th Indian Division had been coping with this in
the Pegu area, and the 7th Indian Division was ordered to move
across and take over.

The 89th Indian Infantry Brigade, less the King's Own Scottish
Borderers, crossed the Irrawaddy to Allanmyo on the 17th June. On   17 June
the 19th, the Battalion moved in M.T. to Okpu, continuing the journey   19 June
next day to the Brigade concentration area at Hmawbi, where it
arrived about noon. Hmawbi lies on the Rangoon-Prome road about   20 June
30 miles north of Rangoon, and just 3 miles from the scene of one
of the Battalion's early battles in 1942.

The Pegu Yomas lie between the Irrawaddy on the west and the
Sittang river on the east, and, as already noted, various parties of
Japanese, who may have amounted to a considerable force in the
aggregate, were working their way through the Yomas on their way
east. The main Japanese forces were east of the Sittang, and it was
thought more than likely that they would mount an offensive across
the Sittang westwards to extricate their men in the Pegu Yomas, and
do as much harm as they could.

With this general background, the Brigade was now deployed west
of the Sittang river. The sector allotted included part of the Rangoon-
Moulmein railway. There had been a bridge over the Sittang at
Nyaungkashe, but this had been destroyed during the withdrawal in
1942. The Brigade's task was to prevent the Japanese crossing over
the river from the east.

On the Rangoon-Moulmein railway, and in the Brigade sector, are   23 June
three points which are worth fixing straight away. First comes Waw,
13 miles short of the Sittang. Next Abya, 7 miles from the Sittang.
Finally Nyaungkashe, a mile or so from the bank on which the Japanese
had small detachments holding out in bridge-head positions on the
west bank, itself. Off the railway were one or two other points;
10 miles north of Nyaungkashe, on the Sittang west bank, lay Myithkyo,
approached by a canal. Then, a mile north of the railway, between
Abya and Nyaungkashe, is Satthewagon. 5 or 6 miles south-east of
Waw is Payabyo. The coming operations may be easier to follow if
these points are collected in this way for easier reference, at the start.

On the 23rd June, the Battalion moved east to Waw. On the 24th,   23 June
it moved on to Abya in relief of the 3rd/2nd Punjab Regiment. Next   24 June
day, the 25th June, he 4th/8th Gurkha Rifles passed through Abya, to   25 June

423

1945

take over from the Burma Regiment at Nyaungkashe. The same day, the 3rd/6th Gurkha Rifles moved up the canal to Myithkyo. To complete the Brigade, the 7th York and Lancaster Regiment came temporarily under command, and was located in the Waw area.

The Brigade was thus dispersed over a wide area, the whole of which, however, was under water, thanks to the monsoon rains, except for the villages, the railway and the canal banks. It was a somewhat dismal prospect—tactically, as well as to the eye, for the railway, which was the only line of supply, was exposed to attack by the Japanese, who could move in boats up the old Sittang channel which swung in westwards, flanking the railway, south of Nyaungkashe. In artillery positions, the advantage lay decidedly with the Japanese. The country across the Sittang was wooded and hilly, and provided ample gun positions with excellent observation. West of the river, guns had to be located in sectors of the railway, which much restricted the artillery that could be employed. This was to have some influence on the operations.

However, for several days nothing happened. Jeeps were converted to "locomotives" to haul supplies along the railway. Defences were built up—there was no question of digging down in that flooded countryside. Active patrolling went on in and about the villages in the area so far as the floods allowed. No signs of Japanese activity were found in the Sikh sector, though the 4th/8th Gurkha Rifles at Nyaungkash had several clashes with the Japanese bridge-head detachments, and were fairly constantly shelled.

2 July On the 2nd July, one platoon of "C" Company was ordered up to Satthewagon to protect the supply-route forward to a company of the 4th/8th Gurkha Rifles lying north of the railway.

On the 2nd also, a party of no fewer than 300 officers and men was sent on leave. This seems an astonishing circumstance at this juncture, and quite indefensible. Of course, it was desired to get as many men rested as possible before the October campaign began, but it pulled the Battalion down gravely below strength, and left it, as will be seen, with commitments it was ill-fitted, with only about 500 ranks, to fulfill.

3 July Next day, the 3rd July, "C" Company, less its platoon at Satthewagon was detached to Payabyo, to take over from part of the York and Lancaster Regiment which had been withdrawn from the Brigade. As one company was already employed guarding the numerous bridges along the railway, this left Battalion Headquarters and two very weak rifle companies for active duties. This gave some cause for anxiety as there were indications that the Japanese were reinforcing their bridge-head garrisons on the Sittang west bank, and were also reported to be showing increased activity near Myithkyo. During the

3rd, the "B" Company platoon guarding the forward-most bridge in the Battalion area, was heavily shelled.

That night, there was a good deal of noise up the line—firing on the railway, and shelling in the 4th/8th Gurkha Rifles area. A report came in from Hav. Didar Singh in the "B" Company platoon which had been shelled during the day, to account for some of the firing. Jem. Bhag Singh's detached "C" Company platoon near Satthewagon was being engaged, but not heavily. Both telephone lines to the platoon had been cut, and now most unfortunately the wireless was out of order. Brigade Headquarters supplied further disquieting news. The 4th/8th Gurkha Rifles had been surrounded, and a strongly pressed attack had been put in under cover of heavy shell-fire.

3-4 July

Nothing further could be discovered at the moment, but just as dawn broke another report came in from Hav. Didar Singh. Two parties of Japanese were dug in on his front. One had worked its way in between Hav. Didar Singh and a bridge just west of Nyaungkashe, held by the Gurkhas. The second party was located near a pagoda, about midway between his platoon and Jem. Bhag Singh's platoon, a couple of miles away at Satthewagon.

4 July

Jem. Bhag Singh, meanwhile, felt that the position was getting out of hand, and decided that he must try to get news through while he could, to say that his platoon had been surrounded, had been very heavily attacked all night, and was running short of ammunition. No. 24075 Sep. Babu Singh undertook to bring the message, and his adventures in doing so have the authentic ring of a boy's thriller. He stripped off his uniform, put on a loin-cloth, and crawled along a flooded chaung to where he had noticed a collection of villagers, whom the Japanese were clearing out of their village. Mingling with these, and passing within a yard of a Japanese sentry, Sep. Babu Singh brought the message back, and earned the award of a Military Medal. There was no doubt that the platoon had put up a splendid fight. Jem. Bhag Singh with his twenty-two men had held off determined attacks for a period of over eight hours by forces of Japanese estimated at about 150, and they finally forced them to withdraw to the farther end of the village leaving thirty-three dead on the barbed wire.

Obviously the situation had to be cleared up, and at once. "A" Company under Maj. Webster was sent off to push the enemy out of Satthewagon village. He was to drive them out of their position at the pagoda, and then establish himself at Satthewagon. The country being in the condition it was, rapid movement was a problem, and it was 11 o'clock before the village was cleared.

Re-organizing, and moving on towards the pagoda, a strong reconnaissance patrol went ahead to find out what it could about the

1945

enemy's dispositions. The enemy was full of fight and at once opened heavy and continuous automatic and mortar fire from an isolated mound by the pagoda. All around were flooded rice-fields with water often waist-deep in the frequent depressions. The honours of the reconnaissance fell to Sep. Gurdial Singh, the leading man of a section which had been detailed to try and discover the enemy's strength. He was within 30 yards of the enemy when he was wounded. He signalled to his section for covering fire, and when this came, crawled still closer, being again wounded. Nothing daunted, he worked his way up to within a few feet of an enemy machine-gun post, lobbed a grenade in, killed three Japanese, and silenced the post. The subsequent award of a Military Medal was well-earned.

One thing the reconnaissance made abundantly clear was that adequate artillery or air support was needed if the position was to be taken. It was too late for this to be arranged at once, and it was decided to postpone the attack till next day when it was hoped air support could be arranged.

5 July However, on the 5th other orders were received. The Gurkha company east of Satthewagon had been cut off and had to be extricated. "A" Company successfully effected this, but it was a difficult operation and took all day. The attack on the pagoda position had hence to be again postponed.

Later on the 5th evening, the Battalion received a welcome reinforcement in the return of "C" Company from Payabyo.

The situation in Nyaungkashe, meanwhile, was growing most unsatisfactory. The Gurkhas were under constant and heavy shellfire. Though supplies were being flown in regularly, casualties were piling up, and could not be got away. The Sikhs were accordingly ordered to re-open the railway to Nyaungkashe.

It was really a hopeless prospect from the start. The planned air support did not materialize on account of bad weather, and what limited artillery support was available was made still less by ammunition shortage. However, the Battalion did what it could. It kept up heavy

6 July pressure on the enemy throughout the 6th, and the following night, and displayed gallantry and resolution against overwhelming odds, of which all too few cases came to light.

In certain instances, however, particulars were recorded. One such was that of Sep. Ujagar Singh of "A" Company. In a gallant but hopeless Company attack, Maj. Webster was seriously wounded, and Lieut. Joginder Singh killed leading one of the forward platoons, and his body left out. Sep. Ujagar Singh volunteered to bring the body in, although it meant crossing 200 yards of flooded rice-fields swept by enemy artillery and small-arms fire. Sep. Ujagar Singh was untouched till just after reaching Lieut. Joginder Singh's body. He had raised the body, and was trying to hoist it on his shoulder when he was hit and his leg broken. Though unable to walk, he dragged the body back into cover, where he lost consciousness through exhaustion and pain. He died later of his wound, but his devotion was remembered through a posthumous mention in despatches.

When Maj. Webster, commanding "A" Company, was wounded, Sub. Gurbachan Singh, I.D.S.M., took over command. The Company had been brought to a stand by overwhelming fire, only a few yards from the enemy position. In spite of the general noise and confusion, and the incessant fire, Sub. Gurbachan Singh freely exposed himself regardless of personal danger, cheering and encouraging his men; and it was chiefly due to his initiative and able leadership that all the wounded were brought away, and the Company successfully withdrawn. For this example of initiative and soldierly skill, he was given the award of a Military Cross.

Company Hav.-Maj. Jaswant Singh was another of this gallant band. He dragged two wounded men into cover from a very exposed position close under the enemy position, then swam with one across a flooded stream to a place of safety, returning to repeat the performance, under heavy fire, with the second. He, like L.-Naik Bakhshi Singh, whose record follows, was mentioned in despatches for his gallant conduct.

L.-Naik Bakhshi Singh, though young and very junior as a non-commissioned officer, found himself the only non-commissioned officer left in his platoon. Shouldering his responsibility in manly fashion, he led his men against impossible odds time after time till ordered to withdraw. It was reckoned as due to his courage and initiative alone that the platoon with all its wounded was got safely away.

Finally, Sep. Ralla Singh, who was also mentioned in despatches, had been pinned with his section to the ground near the enemy position. Every man in the section was killed except himself. He grabbed the Bren-gun and opened covering fire for the other two sections of his platoon which had been ordered to withdraw. He then saw his platoon commander lying wounded close by. He dragged him back, bound by bound, only stopping to engage the enemy with his Bren-gun. He brought both his platoon commander and his gun back through 250 yards of flooded rice-fields under continuous enemy fire, to safety.

Three gallant but unsuccessful attacks were put in against the various strong-points along the railway. By the early hours of the 7th July, the Battalion was reduced to two weak composite companies. Two British officers, and five Viceroy's commissioned officers had been either killed or wounded, and the proportion of non-commissioned officers casualties was heavy. Lieut.-Col. Spink then informed the

Brigadier that, failing air support in sufficient strength to neutralize the enemy strong-points, he felt that further assaults would be valueless.

There was no means of knowing what the enemy's reaction had been to the tenacious resistance of the 4th/8th Gurkha Rifles, and the resolution and courage of the Sikhs, and the situation, meanwhile, did not commend itself as very satisfactory. Nyaungkashe, as already noted, does not lie on the Sittang river bank, but a mile or two back. The enemy had all along been well established on the west bank of the river, and there was no reason to regard possession of Nyaungkashe itself as vital. The vagaries of the monsoon made it difficult to promise air support for any given moment, and so it was decided to pull the 4th/8th Gurkha Rifles back, and establish a new forward area at Abya where the Sikhs had their headquarters. To free the Sikhs to co-operate in the Gurkha withdrawal, the 4th/15th Punjab Regiment was to move over from the 33rd Indian Infantry Brigade and take over at Abya. On this, the Sikhs proposed to concentrate forward on their leading company at Satthewagon that same day, the 7th. Satthewagon itself is only about 4 miles north-north-west of Nyaungkashe.

By a curious turn of fate, the weather immediately cleared, and Royal Air Force support was overwhelming. Just what happened is hard to say, but it looks as if the Japanese had felt no happier

7-8 July about the prospects than had the Brigade. At all events, both sides began pulling out simultaneously. The Sikhs at once occupied the pagoda position and later reinforced the forward position on the railway, now held by a composite "C"-"D" Company, under Maj. Brough.

8 July The 4th/8th Gurkha Rifles made a successful withdrawal, but, as soon as the Japanese discovered it, they tried to re-occupy their vacated advanced positions. This, they were unable to do, being

8-9 July thrown back with considerable loss during the night of the 8th/9th July by Maj. Brough and his composite company.

11 July The 33rd Indian Infantry Brigade now relieved the 89th. On the
13 July 11th July, the Battalion was withdrawn to Waw. On the 13th, it moved
15 July to Hlegu about 30 miles east of Rangoon, and on the 15th, to Dabein, a few miles from Hlegu.

So ended, somewhat unsatisfactorily, the Sikhs' last battle—against impossible odds and under arduous and trying conditions. But glory is not always to be sought in victory and success. There is the greater need of resolution and constancy when success is denied, and no one who has read this record can deny that the men of the 1st Battalion had displayed these qualities to the full. Constantly cheerful, accepting great odds with gallantry and resolution, the men of the Battalion had, in fact, achieved a major success, little apparent though that was at the time. From captured orders it was later established that the

1945

Japanese had planned to break through and capture Waw, and extricate their forces from the Pegu Yomas. The battles that have been described, however, had so damped their resolve that they made no further attempt to advance after their attacks on the night of the 8th/9th July.

It was a fitting postscript to these operations that Sub. Gurbachan Singh, of whose gallantry the record bears witness, should have represented the Battalion at the surrender ceremony at Rangoon on the 19th September.

19 Sept.

With this we come to the end of the Battalion's fighting services in the Second World War. Much, however, was to happen before these fine troops were to see the Punjab again; and of this a brief account will be found where we take leave of the Battalion in the Epilogue.

The 2nd Battalion was at Komotini, the capital of Thrace, in early spring, actively assisting in the restoration of normal conditions in Greece. Duties included many unusual functions—among them the distribution of large numbers of Red Cross food parcels to distant villages in the mountains of northern Greece the previous autumn before the snows isolated them. Currency proved a problem, for the rate of exchange altered with bewildering and usually unfavourable irregularity, and proved wholly baffling to most ranks. Prices soared, as was the case with most European countries during the period of re-organization. Butter rose to £3 the pound, while a suit of clothes, irrespective of quality, ran up to £200. It was quite fantastic—but, with all its problems, this tour in Greece was a great tonic after the blood and sweat and drudgery of the years before.

2nd Bn.

During May, the Battalion was inspected on parade by Gen. Sir Claude Auchinleck, Commander-in-Chief in India. He complimented the men highly on their turn-out and drill. During June, Divisional sports were held, and the Battalion came out the winners by a large margin. The same team went on to represent the Brigade at the All-Greece Military Sports meeting in Athens, and was beaten by a few points only by a British Armoured Brigade, which could call on five units at full strength, and whose team contained several professional athletes.

May

June

In contact with the Greeks, the Sikhs aroused much interest, as they were looked on as having originated from early Greek stock. Special interest was taken in the Battalion's guards, and guard-mounting drew a large attendance of onlookers. However, invited to give more practical proof of their interest by rolling their beards in the Sikh manner, they seemingly demurred.

So, in light-hearted style which none can grudge them, the men of the 2nd Royal Battalion saw the war out. Six months were to pass before the Battalion returned to India, as the post-script will show;

1945

but the time was well spent, morale was kept high, and training and turn-out remained throughout at the traditional high level. The Battalion was specially selected to provide for a two-months tour at Athens the first Indian guard at the G.O.C.'s (Gen. Sir Ronald Scobie's) headquarters and residence, and at that of the Ambassador; and these detachments earned most favourable comment for their bearing, turn-out and discipline.

3rd Bn. *The 3rd Battalion* was still on the "Aid-to-Russia" railway in the spring of 1945, watching with envy one regular battalion after another fade away to an operational role on one or other of the fighting fronts. However, interest presently was focussed on Scheme "Longhop".

It would have been too much to expect law and order in Persia to survive the indirect strains and stresses of the war without some falling off. At best, the Persian tribes have strong traditions of independence from governmental control. Matters had gradually been approaching a climax, and Persian officials and police in the remoter regions of the oil-fields were finding increasing difficulty in carrying out their duties. Some were beaten up or otherwise maltreated by the tribesmen. Morale was on the down-grade, and this, it was felt, might have a serious effect on the efficient prosecution of the war if allowed to go on. Accordingly, it was decided to try the effect of a flag march through the oil-fields to bolster up their prestige.

Flag marches are not usually particularly complicated matters, but Scheme "Longhop" was an exception on the administrative side. The Battalion had for a good many years been on a mechanized transport basis. For this incursion into the oil-fields, however, mule transport would have to be used.

This brought many previously familiar but now forgotten problems in its train. Apart from this, there could be no daily supply system. The column would have to carry with it supplies for a considerable period, and this raised the question of the incremental factor—the provision of supplies for the mules that carried the supplies, and the provision of still more supplies for these. It is freely admitted that Battalion H.Q. suffered many headaches before this problem was satisfactorily solved. But solved it was, and the loading tables were ready in good time before the Battalion was due to march out.

To carry out Scheme "Longhop", the Battalion had first to gather in its detachments scattered over 200 miles of railway, and bring them down to the plains. For this a giant omnibus train was arranged **March** at the end of March to pick them up and carry them down to Andimishk at the foot of the mountains. Battalion Headquarters made its way down by road—over the Razan Pass, where so many pleasant ski-ing days had been spent, and down the unending series of twists and bends on the southern side, to the bottom. Concentrated at Andimishk, the

1945

Battalion was ready to receive its transport and set out for the oil-fields.

That, however, was as far as it went. Orders arrived for the Battalion to prepare instead for the much longed-for move into an operational theatre. Meanwhile, it was to leave Andimishk on the 1st April, and move to Abadan, pending relief by a battalion from India. 1 Apr.

After a brief stay in Abadan, the Battalion moved up to Zobeir transit camp to hand in its stores. On the 20th April, the first half of the Battalion went on to Baghdad. From Baghdad, the anti-tank platoon, which had been re-formed in Abadan, went on to Cairo to join the R.A. Base Depot for training (and the Battalion rifle team later joined it there). But the remainder had again to face disappointment and a change of orders. The commanding officer had been warned by the General Staff at General Headquarters that the Battalion's destination was likely to be changed; and he was told soon after that the Battalion was to go back to India. In spite of their long absence from their homes, this came as a blow to the men, who saw their hopes of service in Italy finally shattered. The Battalion's short stay in Syria, and contact with troops with much honourable service on a fighting front to their credit, had whetted the men's appetite for similar chances of showing their metal. 20 Apr.

So the troops in Baghdad climbed back into the train, and travelled back to Zobeir. Here the Battalion was inspected by the Commander-in-Chief, Lieut.-Gen. Sir Arthur Smith, who came down especially by air for the purpose. He gave an inspiring address and received a Fateh which woke the echoes.

On the night of the 29/30th April, the Battalion embarked at Maqil. No better description of the scene can be given than that provided in the Battalion *News Letter* covering the move. "After some alteration", it reads, "we had been allotted accommodation on all decks at the stem of the ship. Eleven o'clock at night found the whole Battalion seated on the quayside alongside the ship, in closely-packed squares of two hundred to two hundred and fifty men, each with his big pack and light kit. Without previous warning we were visited by the C.-in-C. India. The visit could not have been at a more auspicious time. The entire embarkation went without a single hitch and in complete silence. A striking contrast to the 1,200 leave details occupying the remainder of the boat. Accommodation on the ship was 'tang' and the heat below decks oppressive. We were fortunate in a smooth trip but nevertheless glad to reach our destination, Karachi, where we found a train waiting to take us to Risalpur across the river from the Regimental Training Centre. All thoughts were centred on leave, and after taking over the barracks we settled down to getting 29-30 Apr.

the men back to their homes." The *Letter* goes on to add that most of the men who sailed with the Battalion for Iraq in 1941, came back with it. Over 600 men had been continuously at duty for two years, and over 500 for four. With little glamour to relieve the day-to-day monotony since 1941, the long years without leave must have borne heavily on some.

The welcome back to India had been austere, and there was some natural disappointment at the intelligence "security" which had prevented so many of the Battalion's friends knowing about it. "It is true", the *Letter* notes, "that officers and men of the Training Centre gave us a warm welcome but all up the line from the port of disembarkation disappointed jawans scanned the crowds at railway stations without seeing one familiar face. Security couldn't have been better; as a welcome home it couldn't have been worse. Nevertheless, fatehs rang out on leaving every station however small."

A postscript must be added before saying good-bye to this much-tried and little-rewarded battalion. Its anti-tank platoon at least, arrived in an operational theatre, if no nearer than the R.A. Base Camp in Cairo. The two British officers, Maj. H. J. A. Millachip and Capt. G. E. Challenor, had gone ahead by air from Baghdad, and were followed by the men some weeks later. The platoon was fitted into spacious quarters at Almaza just outside Cairo, and the men, who had not seen a six-pounder for two years, were soon handling the guns like old hands. Their range performance with live ammunition was first-class; and when the night-shoot was staged at the end of the course, the Americans from a nearby air-field came roaring up on jeeps and ambulances to see what the noise was about.

The course ended just before V.E. Day. Meanwhile the Battalion rifle team had arrived in Cairo to attend the Mid-East Rifle Meeting at Maadi. The team did well. All members qualified for monetary prizes and the Subedar-Major secured second place in the individual pistol competition.

After V.E. Day, the platoon was given a week's leave, which was spent at the Star of India Hotel in Cairo. This leave hostel for Indian other ranks had all the comforts of a first-class hotel, and amusements of all sorts available, including trips to places of interest.

It was not only in India that secrecy about the Battalion's movements was preserved. It was kept secret from the anti-tank platoon as well. It seems almost incredible that one day, after the Battalion had settled down in Risalpur, the anti-tank platoon—after providing a guard of honour for Gen. Paget at Meena—should have travelled solemnly down to meet it at Suez. But so it was—one of the unsolved mysteries of the war. However, with the passage of time, the position was reversed, and the platoon shipped back under Capt. Challenor to Bombay, whence it made its way back to the Battalion, instead.

1945
4th Bn.

It will be remembered that *the 4th Battalion*, after its winter of bitter cold and wet, had been transferred for a month's rest to a pleasant little village in the Tiber valley.

After this, it went back to the mountains, 15 miles from the outskirts of Bologna. There was a hill-top sector here, Monte Grande, which the 10th Indian Division was taking over from an American division. *Teheran to Trieste*, the story of the 10th Indian Division, published under the authority of the Director of Public Relations, War Department, Government of India, describes the locale. "It was a place of ill-omen, which had seen much heavy fighting. The Germans set great store by it. The country was deer-stalker's landscape, with high look-outs and deep scours. Everyone could see a good deal of everyone else, so a smokescreen, supplied in the first instance by the 85th U.S. Division, and afterwards by "ack-ack" gunners, served to cloak maintenance movements in the Sillaro valley.

"For two months 10 Ind. Div. pinned down the enemy in this important sector. Strong offensive patrols constantly penetrated the defences...".

Arrived in this sector, and in and about the ruined village of Frassineto, the Battalion found itself in a bleak and desolate area of steep slopes and barren hill-tops. Opposite lay its old rivals the 1st German Para Division. Though the weather was dry on the whole, there was little other comfort. Movement was not generally possible except by night. Snipers on both sides were active, shelling and mortar fire were heavy after dark, patrolling was constant at all times throughout the twenty-four hours, and the forward companies got little rest.

3-4 Apr.

On the night of the 3rd/4th April, after an intense concentration of artillery and mortar fire, German paratroops put in a heavy attack on Frassineto. They over-ran an outpost section in spite of stout resistance, and got close up to "D" Company's position, under Maj. C. F. Pow in Frassineto village. After a fire fight in which our mountain artillery took part, they were driven off. A later attack was equally unsuccessful. Frassineto was a vital area in the defence system, and the results of this action, which it was later discovered cost the enemy some fifty casualties or more than double those sustained by the Battalion, were the more satisfactory for this reason.

Inevitably, however, under constant shelling and mortaring, and with active and offensive patrolling, there was much wastage from battle casualties. One, especially regretted, was Capt. J. U. Knox, whose father, Col. E. F. Knox, D.S.O., had commanded the Battalion during and after the First World War. In his short period of service, Jimmy Knox had made a fine name for himself, and he was sadly missed. Capt. V. Gledhill, who was wounded, and Jem. Kishan Singh, who was killed, were others whose loss was felt. Jem. Kishan Singh

1945	was a young Viceroy's commissioned officer who might well have gone far. He had made a name for himself as carrier-havildar in the early days, and had already been awarded the Indian Distinguished Service Medal.
11 Apr.	On the 11th April, the overwhelming assault of the Eighth Army broke through the Senio and Santerno defences, but the 25th Indian Infantry Brigade remained in its positions till the advance of the Poles manoeuvred the Germans out. Though the 10th and 20th Indian Infantry Brigades of the Division played a gallant part in the pursuit, the 25th Indian Infantry Brigade had little part before the Division was stopped and briefed for mountain operations near Padua. The enemy surrendered before anything came of this, so that the Battalion was still on the Reno river north of Bologna when the "cease-fire"
29 Apr.	went, on the 29th.

A Victory Parade was held in the Division, with sports and general festivities; and there was a welcome "stand easy", with games, and visits for leave parties to Florence, Venice, and Rome.

Rumour was not idle, however. The fighting was over in the west, but it was mounting in intensity in the east, and it was believed that the 10th Indian Division would be sent there. In readiness for this, seven British officers were sent off at various times, for short leave in the United Kingdom.

20 May About the 20th May, the Battalion moved up into the disputed territory near the Morgan Line, and took over the not very palatable duty of keeping the peace between Yugoslavs and Italians. No very serious incidents took place, though the Yugoslavs, here, in the rocky ridges between Gorizia and the sea, were not easy to make friends with. This was hardly surprising with the troops of the 10th Indian Division billeted in the same village with the Yugoslav troops who had seized Venetia Guilia. Much forbearance and patience had to be exercised before these Yugoslavs, including well-armed Amazons, were persuaded to accept the terms of the temporary treaty.

Gen. Sir Claude Auchinleck, Commander-in-Chief, India, spent a short while with the Battalion while engaged in these duties.

June Mid-June brought a further advance, the Battalion moving forward to the hills near Daniele. Difficulties at once recurred, from resentment due to the advance. Quoting from the record—"After considerable talking, and a rather peculiar football match (in which the Battalion appeared to be taking on the Yugoslav Army side at a game we don't profess to play), new positions were agreed to in an atmosphere of friendship."

July July passed quietly, and much more time was available for sports. Visits also were paid by all ranks to various places of interest, including Venice and parts of Austria. Several leave parties went to the United Kingdom. Meanwhile, the Division staged a very successful show about 30 miles from Trieste. The programme included a tattoo with scenes of village life in India, Indian dances, and sports. The Battalion was represented in them by two Punjabi-Mohammedan sepoys.

Early in August, the Battalion moved to Merna near Trieste, finding pleasant billets in spite of the many destroyed houses in the area. The inhabitants were far from friendly, but it was an enjoyable stay except insofar as the river was out of bounds for bathing owing to some infection that had been traced to it. The news of the end of the war with Japan was fittingly celebrated, and Capt. R. V. Webb took a contingent of 200 Sikhs to take part in the XIIIth Corps tattoo in Trieste. This was a mammoth show. All arms were represented, and in addition there was a detachment from the United States forces, as well as contingents from the Italian and Yugoslav armies. A good proportion of the Battalion managed to see the show, and were agreed that the Battalion's detachment looked very well, led by the imposing figure of Bob Webb.

The final moves in the Battalion's stay in Italy, and the manner of its return to India, will be dealt with in the Epilogue.

Back on the North-West Frontier of India, *the 6th Battalion* had its headquarters in Damdil. For the three months to February, it had been responsible for road protection duties in the Asad Khel sector. In March, it took over a three-months tour of the same duties in the Dizh sector. Tal Fort (Tochi) now lay in its area, and was garrisoned by one company, changed monthly. Though the previous battalion had had many casualties, the 6th Battalion had one only during the current three months. Sixteen tribesmen carried out a well-planned ambush in Dizh Narai, and one Punjabi-Mohammedan sepoy was killed. In the action that ensued, Jem. Hakam Khan with fine presence of mind and disregard for his personal safety, successfully dispersed the enemy without further loss, and was awarded a certificate of commendation from the Commander-in-Chief.

On the 12th May, the Battalion moved up in M. T. to Gardai. The local tribesmen showed their appreciation at its departure with a volley of ineffective rifle fire as the column passed Asad Khel. For all its bleakness and trying heat, Gardai went down well with the Battalion. As in Damdil, improvements in camp amenities were effected, and the Battalion soon settled down. Only one occurrence of note relieved the otherwise uneventful hot weather. This was when that stormy petrel, the Faqir of Ipi, brought down his ancient 3.7-inch howitzers and shelled the post in early summer. Beyond starting some cheerful chatter in the lines, the bombardment was ineffective.

1945
7th Bn.

	The 7th Battalion had spent some pleasant cold weather weeks undergoing strenuous training in jungle warfare in Tret, at the foot of the Murree hills. On completion of the course, it moved back on
11 Apr.	the 11th April, to Risalpur. Mobilization orders came in immediately
1 May	after, and on the 1st May the Battalion was moved to Nowshera, 4 miles away on the south bank of the Kabul.

A few busy weeks passed in Nowshera before leaving, on the 27th,
27 May   for Bombay, where "B" Company rejoined from a spell of duty in Belgaum. Embarking on the H.T. *Mooltan*, the Battalion sailed on
2 June   the 2nd June for Port Tewfik, leaving behind the M.T.O. and the twelve best drivers, with the six-wheeled carriers, to follow in another ship.

An uneventful journey brought the Battalion to Port Tewfik, on
13 June   the 13th June. Disembarking the same day, it moved 65 miles to a desert camp at Qassassin, where it halted to await orders.

When these arrived a few days later, the Battalion learnt that it was destined for employment on internal security duties in Syria.

Up to five weeks before, the Battalion had only had eight motor vehicles on charge. Now, it was suddenly faced with an immediate issue of eighty, and the need for providing them with drivers, in the absence of the M.T.O. and the pick of the M.T. personnel. Last-minute arrangements proved effective, however, and the road party, under Maj. J. Tredinnick, successfully brought its vehicles over the aggregate of about 1,000 miles to its destination. Right-of-the-road driving caused small embarrassment, and the convoy arrived with only 4 per cent casualties to vehicles. Considering that only two days notice was given for the vehicles to be drawn and manned, and for the column to get away, this must be called a creditable effort.

20 June   On the 20th June, the Battalion, less its road party, left Qassassin by rail on a rather dull and uneventful journey. Arrived up in Syria, "D" Company, under Maj. J. D. M. Watson, was dropped at Hama. The rest of the Battalion went on to the Casernes Turques, 10 miles north of Aleppo.

In Aleppo, as a temporary measure, Lieut. A. Pickett of Hodson's Horse was attached as M.T.O. to organize the Battalion's transport, keep it on the road, and train drivers. As a result of his excellent arrangements, a first-class organization was in being by the time the Battalion's own M.T.O., Lieut. R. V. Tuck, arrived with his drivers three weeks later.

Casernes Turques had been a French fort—rather surprisingly—and the Battalion settled down here to a round of varied and not always very pleasant duties. Disturbances were constantly breaking out, and Maj. E. C. W. Fowler, temporarily commanding the Battalion, had, as Military Commander of Aleppo, to do his best to iron out these clashes between the different parties.

1945

Consequential calls on the Battalion involved guards for V.P.'s in the city, desert patrols beyond it, escort duties to French convoys of refugees, and assistance to French troops stationed in the city. Casernes Turques had been chosen as a clearing centre for all French families in Syria, and their protection was one of the Battalion's responsibilities.

In Hama, "D" Company had moved into the French barracks imposingly known as Reduit Rosse La ba Place d'Hama, where it relieved a company of the Bombay Grenadiers. The Company was the only effective military detachment in Hama, where there was still much tension.

As in Aleppo, there were actually French troops still in Hama, in the Reduit Rosse. But, as equally in Aleppo, these troops were in need of protection, a duty which devolved on our Company. The French had previously bombed Hama stirring up the Syrian patriots, and the French troops had been in an awkward position till the Indian Army detachment arrived.

Over and above assistance to the French troops, "D" Company was charged with escorting through the town convoys of French refugees leaving northern Syria. It also had to provide guards over a large French bomb dump, covering an area of about 2 square miles north of Hama, and littered with bombs, shells and detonators.

This dump was the scene of the only real excitement of the Battalion's stay in Syria. The platoon finding the duties there was a detachment, linked to Company Headquarters by wireless. It was an extensive area for a single platoon, and could only be adequately watched by a system of numerous small patrols. One night, a party of fifteen Arabs, armed with rifles, pistols and knives, set on one of these two-man patrols, but was fortunately spotted before it could close. The patrol kept its head, waited till the charging Arabs were within 20 yards, and then opened fire, killing one and wounding several others at the cost of only eleven rounds.

Generally, the Company carried out its difficult task with efficiency and despatch, and there seems to be no doubt that much of the credit was due to it for easing and finally ending what had been a critical situation.

By the end of July, the situation in Aleppo and North Syria generally was quiet. People were once more walking freely in the streets at night. At this stage, on the 22nd July, the Battalion was relieved by the 4th/8th Punjab Regiment, and next day moved back by road and rail into Palestine. On the 25th July, it arrived at Ar Rama, 20 miles east of Acre. Here it took over duties as Demonstration Battalion to the Middle East School of Infantry from the 3rd/7th Rajput Regiment. As always, these duties proved of much value to the Battalion, enabling the troops to absorb many new ideas on the employment of infantry and other arms.

22 July
23 July
25 July

1945

MG Bn. Casting back east to Burma, it will be remembered that *the Machine-Gun Battalion* was heavily involved in the break across the Irrawaddy river just prior to the move down south against Mandalay.

1 Mar. Once again, the Battalion had been split up among the brigades of the 19th Indian Division, and its distribution on the 1st March was as follows.

"A" Company was with the 98th Indian Infantry Brigade; "B" Company with the 62nd; and "C" with the 64th. "D" Company was placed with the Divisional base area, on three hours notice to move. Battalion Headquarters continued its movement south through Chaungna, Sethi and Mheintha.

Mandalay lay about 40 miles to the south.

The Division now organized a mobile column to push on to Mandalay. Lieut.-Col. Gardiner of the 1st/15th Punjab Regiment was in command, and "D" Company of the Machine-Gun Battalion, under Maj. Daly, was

5 Mar. sent up on the 5th March from the Divisional base area to join it. On the
7 Mar. 7th March, the troops reached Sinywagale, and next day had a successful
8 Mar. shoot in support of an attack on a pagoda area north of Mandalay.

On the same day, the 8th March, Battalion Headquarters moved to Madaya, about 8 miles north of Mandalay. Here it was joined by "B" Company, which had been unable to accompany the 62nd Indian Infantry Brigade to Maymyo, in the hills, east of Mandalay, as the Brigade was moving on a pack basis, for which the necessary equipment was not available for its attached machine-gun company. However, the Company was not deprived of its chances, for it was sent up with the Royal Berkshire Regiment in relief of "D" Company, for the attack on Mandalay Hill, which was captured after a stiff fight. In the action, Hav. Anokh Singh exhibited great gallantry, dashing ahead of the attacking infantry with an armful of grenades to kill seven Japanese in an underground passage who were holding up the advance. Just after he had thrown his last grenade, and accomplished his object, he was shot through the heart. Shortly afterwards, No. 23861 Sep. Naranjan Singh earned a gallantry certificate for a fine example of initiative and resolution. He was the No. 3 of a gun which was helping the infantry forward. Nos. 1 and 2 were killed by snipers, silencing the gun. Sep. Naranjan Singh was 20 yards behind at the time, but he dashed forward to the gun, pushed the dead bodies aside, and continued to fight his gun until our infantry, under his covering fire, had taken their objective.

9 Mar. On the 9th March, Battalion Headquarters moved to Taungbyon, south from Madaya, and on the 10th to Kabaing railway station. Here "D" Company rejoined on release from duty with the mobile column.

Mandalay was drawing very close, and the 98th Indian Infantry Brigade, with "A" Company under command, was deploying for the final assault. This took some days to organize as the position was a

438

strong one, and the Japanese garrison clearly determined to hold out
to the last. To thicken up the machine-gun support, "B" Company
was posted to the Brigade to join "A" Company, on the 12th March. 12 Mar.
Next day, the 13th, "D" Company was posted too, and was
established on Mandalay Hill, with the task of preventing movement 13 Mar.
in Fort Dufferin by day, and of providing harassing fire by night.
From the machine-gunner's point of view, conditions were perfect
for these tasks. Obervation was excellent, and for the twenty-five
and more targets registered, any gun could be brought to bear on any
of these targets within 45 seconds.

Meanwhile many small actions were being fought by detachments
from the Battalion. All cannot be described, but some stand out.
An attack, for example, was made in the southern streets of Mandalay.
Two "B" Company guns were employed. Being unable to get a good
enough view, the section commander crawled forward to a better
O.P., but was seriously wounded while on the way. No. 21992 Sep.
Sajjan Singh, in charge of one of the guns, at once handed it over,
while arranging for covering fire to be opened. He then set out
forward after his section commander, brought him in, dressed his
wound, and took command of the section. During the subsequent
withdrawal of our infantry through the section position, Sep. Sajjan
Singh covered three wounded British soldiers left behind, enabling
them to be evacuated, and remained covering the withdrawal alone
till directly ordered by his company commander to come out of action.
For this example of coolness and courage, he received an immediate
award of the Military Medal.

On another occasion, Maj. M. W. S. Hogg, commanding "B" Company,
took an opportunity rarely offered to company commanders. The
No. 1 of a gun was wounded, and Maj. Hogg took over the gun. Almost
immediately, a Japanese anti-tank gun concealed in shrubbery 70 yards
away, fired two quick shots. Maj. Hogg saw the flashes, and at once
fired a burst, riddling the four Japanese behind the gun with bullets.

With the thirty-six guns of "A", "B" and "D" Companies all under
command of the 98th Indian Infantry Brigade, a concentration of
potential machine-gun fire power was effected greater than any the
Battalion had previously provided. Overhead fire was arranged from
Mandalay Hill, and from the east and west along the tops of the walls.
A lavish allocation of ammunition was made by the division for the
attack—10,000 rounds per gun, a genuine tonic after the strict ammunition
economy that had been the rule. The prospect of a set-piece attack
set every man on his toes, and tails were up.

"C" Company was now brought into the plan of attack, so that
from the 14th to the 20th March, all four companies were deployed 14-20 Mar.
round Fort Dufferin, with "D" Company, as before, on Mandalay Hill.

1945

However, nothing came of it, for the fort was taken—to the Battalion's qualified disappointment—after the air-strike and artillery bombardment, and without the need for machine-gun support. "A" Company, however, had the privilege of moving straight into the fort, and occupying positions on the four corners of the walls.

21 Mar. Next day, the 21st March, the Battalion lined the route inside Fort Dufferin, and provided part of the guard of honour during the flag-hoisting ceremony under Gen. Slim.

Meanwhile, the movement south had cleared the road part of the way to Meiktila, and the 19th Indian Division now moved down it at speed. Though movement was easier on the main Rangoon road than had been the rule farther north, considerable distances had to be covered, and transport was in short supply. Jeeps that had constantly crossed the Chin Hills, generally with big overloads, were beginning to show signs of wear.

29 Mar. Moving steadily south, "A" Company came under command of the 64th Indian Infantry Brigade at Wundwin for operations against Thazi, a few miles east of Meiktila on the Taunggyi-Loilem road. On the

31 Mar. 31st, the remainder of the Battalion was ordered down to Wundwin too. No attached transport could be provided, and the move hence

5 Apr. took some days, the Battalion arriving on the 5th April. Next day,

6 Apr. the 6th, Battalion Headquarters moved on into Meiktila, but the remaining companies, "B", "C" and "D", were detached to the 98th Indian Infantry Brigade. The position was that parties of Japanese were moving out into the hills east of the road, and the 98th Indian Infantry Brigade was deployed in the Yozon area to deal with them. Nothing much came of these operations, but a "C" Company platoon successfully ambushed a party of Japanese, including two officers. Led by No. 14766 Hav. Sher Khan, the platoon then went on to capture bullock carts containing a quantity of useful equipment.

16 Apr. By the 16th April, "A", "C" and "D" Companies were back with Battalion Headquarters in Meiktila, and the men were enjoying the bathing in the lake. "B" Company, still under command of the 98th Indian Infantry Brigade, was in the Thazi area; and one platoon of "C" Company was in support of a brigade of the 36th Division for a few days about this time.

The 19th Indian Division was soon on the move again, mopping up Japanese parties, more especially those in the hills to the east, as it followed up after the 5th and 17th Indian Divisions on the way to Rangoon. Arrived in Toungoo, about 130 miles south of Meiktila,

29 Apr. on the 29th April, the Machine-Gun Battalion found a confused situation. Large numbers of by-passed Japanese had collected on a road running east through Mawchi, and Toungoo itself was under sporadic artillery fire from them. For the protection of Toungoo the Battalion was sited

1945

in positions round the town, together with certain gun positions across on the far bank of the Sittang river, near which Toungoo lies. Lieut.-Col. G. Lerwill, M.C., commanding the Battalion, was placed in charge of the defences.

In addition to the apparently formidable Japanese force on the Mawchi road to the east, the Division had also problems to solve on the west, where stragglers from the Irrawaddy valley had been trickling into the Pegu Yomas in the hope of finding their way across to their compatriots east of the Sittang. The monsoon would shortly break and bring added complications.

The active threat, however, was definitely on the Mawchi road, and the Battalion was kept well on its toes coping with a steady succession of targets. A fair bag of Japanese was recorded, mostly at very short range at night. On several occasions, close support fire was opened by day, and once or twice there were indirect shoots from the map.

One small action brought No. 15036 Naik Puran Singh, "A" Company, an immediate award of the Military Medal. Naik Puran Singh was in command of a small fighting patrol sent out to silence a Japanese medium machine-gun. Showing fine dash and spirit in this hazardous mission, he killed four Japanese and wounded two others before being himself wounded by a sniper in another bunker.

During early May, more troops began arriving in Toungoo on their way forward. Having no immediate task, they were incorporated in the Toungoo defences, which now included the Battalion, less "B" Company, two companies of the 2nd Welch Regiment, one troop 8th Cavalry and one battery 33rd Anti-Tank Regiment, known as a whole by the code-name "Mute". The enemy, however, remained pretty quiet. Artillery fire was kept up from the Mawchi road, but the few Japanese stragglers that got into the Toungoo area from the west were mostly captured.

May

By the 10th May, news had arrived of the successful operations of the 7th Indian Division, some angles of which have been noted in the record of the 1st Battalion above, and it was known that the remaining Japanese forces on the Irrawaddy were definitely on the way across the Pegu Yomas enroute for the Salween, east of the Sittang.

10 May

To assist in intercepting these along the line of the Rangoon road, Battalion Headquarters with "A" and "C" Companies was moved south. One platoon was dropped at Oktwin in support of the 8th/12th Frontier Force Regiment. A second platoon was sent farther down the road to the 2nd Royal Berkshire Regiment at Nyaungchidauk. Headquarters and the remaining troops were established at Kywebwe, between the two.

The immediate occupation during the next few days was the posting

1945

of ambushes up and down the main road and railway line. Nothing
16 May came of it, however, and on the 16th May, the Battalion returned to Toungoo.

17 May On the 17th, the Battalion sent "C" Company east from Toungoo—this time to take part in operations along the Mawchi road. "A" Company at the same time took over dispersed positions in three villages east of the Sittang.

The position on the Mawchi road had been comparatively inactive, with the Japanese stubbornly resisting the slow advance of our
19 May troops. However, by about the 19th May, they had been pushed back to Mile 10, and something more ambitious had been planned for the 20th, when it was hoped to stage a "right-hook" with the object of cutting the road at Mile 15, and sealing off any Japanese remaining in Thandaung.

The Mawchi road runs through very thick jungle, presenting considerable difficulties to forces moving off the road. To enable "C" Company (less one platoon operating against Kalaw, in the Shan Hills, farther north) to cope, it was issued on the 19th May with sixty-five mules. In spite of the short notice, and the improvizations which had to be made to fit the equipment to the mules, everything was ready by due time.

The troops taking part in the operation were the 3rd/6th Rajputana Rifles, the 8th/12th Frontier Force Regiment less two companies, and "C" Company under Maj. R. Schlaefli. The force, under code-name "Cracker" was commanded by Brig. Beyts.

20 May The force marched off from Mile 9 at first light on the 20th May. Working its way round through the jungle, it was in the vicinity of the objective by the evening. Unfortunately, the enemy was on the alert, and surprise failed. The force spent the night where it was, and
21 May attacked next morning, the 21st, but could not force its way nearer than 500 yards from Mile 15. As the country was hopeless from an air-drop angle, it was decided to withdraw.

The withdrawal was skilfully carried out—"C" Company's guns being used in the lay-backs, and being lucky to escape with only two killed and three wounded in return for about twenty Japanese casualties. The enemy twice got round and cut the track, but were each time by-passed by fresh tracks cut through the jungle by the withdrawing forces. In spite of this awkward scramble through the jungle, and the five days in all taken up by the operation, the Company got back with mules and equipment intact. The Battalion medical officer, Capt. J. M. Pinto, who had accompanied the force, and did excellent work for the force under difficult conditions, was awarded a mention in despatches for his services.

In the thickly forested country flanking the Mawchi road, it was

impossible to deploy large forces. One company of machine-guns
was adjudged sufficient to support such forces as could be used,
and companies went out for three weeks at a time turn and turn about.
There was no slackening in operations, but the troops were fighting
under great difficulties, apart from the discomfort, and a number of
valuable men were lost. The object of cutting off Thandaung was
gradually achieved, and by the 28th May a platoon of "A" Company
was established just beyond Mile 13.4 where the road forks, and with
Thandaung and its Japanese garrison well in rear.

By the 1st June, the Battalion was deployed as under. Battalion
Headquarters was with the 62nd Indian Infantry Brigade at Pyonchaung.
"A" Company was under the 98th Indian Infantry Brigade at Mile 15
on the Mawchi road. "B" Company, less one platoon, was with the
8th Cavalry at Mile 211 on the Rangoon road. One platoon of "B"
Company was at Toungoo railway station, under the 33rd Anti-Tank
Regiment. "C" Company, less one platoon, was under the 62nd
Indian Infantry Brigade at Mile 10 on the Mawchi road. One platoon
"C" Company was with the 64th Indian Infantry Brigade in the
Kalaw area. "D" Company was under the 62nd Indian Infantry Brigade
at Mawchi road L. of C., and by the 18th June, was at Mile 22 on
the Mawchi road, having taken over from "A" Company.

We have already noted in the 1st Battalion record that efforts
were to be made during the monsoon to give troops some rest and
training, and enable them to re-organize and re-fit in readiness for
the autumn campaign, expected to open in the middle of October.
In the 1st Battalion, these proposals had little effect other than
sending the battalion into action at not much over half-strength thanks
to the despatch of leave men to India on the very eve of battle. In
the Machine-Gun Battalion, the consequences of this policy were
less clear-cut if equally paradoxical.

On the 19th June, the Battalion, less "D" Company, began moving
into monsoon quarters in the rice-mill at Kywebwe, some way south
of Toungoo, on the Rangoon road for a period of rest and training,
sandwiched in between operations against the Japanese. Training
was carried out faithfully, and by the 25th June, three cadres had
begun, and the freshening-up of work with the medium machine-gun,
driving, maintenance and signals was in full swing.

On the operational side, the Battalion carried out two roles. It
kept its Company in action on the Mawchi road; and at the same
time, it maintained detachments distributed north and south of
Kywebwe along the Rangoon road, to watch the exits in the neighbourhood from the Pegu Yomas which were still thought to harbour
numerous parties of Japanese.

That the Battalion was able to fill these operational functions

1945

28 May

1 June

18 June

19 June

1945

and still get in useful training, and presumably enjoy some relaxation in moderate comfort at Kywebwe, is to its credit, but the opportunity only lasted till the 23rd July.

1 July Meanwhile, on the 1st July, "D" Company, on the Mawchi road, was involved in a sticky little action which might have had serious consequences.

It will be understood that the fighting there was very unpleasant and that the monsoon made movement—and in fact all phases of operations—difficult. It was probably at least partly due to this that the machine-gun company, when supporting the forward infantry company on a feature known as "Nevis" at Mile 24, was left temporarily unprotected during inter-battalion reliefs.

How far it is correct to say that the troops generally had begun to take it for granted that the Japanese would remain inactive during the middle of the day, it is impossible to say. In fact, there was never much hostile activity at this time of day, and perhaps that is partly why a company of the 3rd/6th Rajputana Rifles was carrying out the relief of a company of the 2nd Welch Regiment at that time on the 1st July. Two only of "D" Company's guns were in position on the spot, but without infantry protection, when a scurry of some forty Japanese suddenly broke upon them. One machine-gun was rushed, and the No. 1 killed. Thanks, however, to the effective supporting fire of the other, the enemy failed either to capture the gun or take the position, and retired in disorder. Two gun numbers were wounded.

That the gun crews behaved in traditional manner, with resolution and courage, is borne out by the immediate award for this action of the Military Medal to two of their number. These were No. 21076 Sep. Sultan Mahmood, and No. 21743 Sep. Dadu Khan.

23 July On the 23rd July, the Battalion was ordered to take over the Zeyawadi area south of Toungoo. Apparently no direct immediate information could be had about the area. Two other sources were accordingly tapped, with satisfactory results. These were Force 136, and a battalion of the Burma National Army (then known as the Patriotic Burma Force).

From the information provided, ambushes were set—though nothing fell into them. But, with four guns mounted on the A.P.V.s of the 8th Cavalry, a few Japanese were bagged. Later two platoons of medium machine-guns were each placed under command of the 4th/4th and 1st/6th Gurkha Rifles, and these put in some successful shooting. Enemy targets were good, and heavy casualties inflicted, including large numbers killed. "B" Company was out with the 5th/10th Baluchis between Oktwin on the Rangoon road, and the Sittang, and also did well, accounting for about fifty Japanese from a party commanded by Gen. Koba. But, satisfactory as these small actions were, it was felt that the Battalion might have done better still if only more mules had been available. As the record puts it—"Jeeps and flooded paddy fields just didn't mix".

1945

About the 20th August, "D" Company was sent out with a company of the 1st/6th Gurkha Rifles to Shwegyin, east of the Sittang Bend, about 60 miles south of Toungoo. Though the Japanese surrender had been officially notified several days before, the news either had not reached the Japanese in this sector, or else was dis-credited by them, for they were still showing vigorous resistance. However, in place of the operations anticipated at Shwegyin, the Company had instead the privilege of receiving the first of the surrendered personnel from the Japanese forces in this part of the front. The Company Commander, Maj. Phillipps, was placed in charge of the Shwegyin civil jail, a protective cordon of machine-guns was sited in and around it, and the prisoners were collected there with due ceremony.

20 Aug.

Thus ended the Machine-Gun Battalion's first and last campaign. It had only been engaged in active operations for nine or ten months, but it had played a gallant part and acquitted itself well. Though, as we have seen, there had been much close-quarter fighting, none of its forty-eight guns had ever passed into enemy hands, nor had any been destroyed otherwise than by enemy shell-fire. For a young battalion, it had an impressive list of honours and mentions in despatches, and the youngsters that made it up had filled their specialized role in a manner for which no praise can be too high.

The 26th Battalion carried on faithfully with its routine duties in Poona, and continued to uphold the good name of the Regiment wherever its men were met.

26th Bn.

EPILOGUE

The war was over. During the years since it began, the battalions of the Regiment had left their home stations in orderly succession as the needs of the day demanded. Now it is time to gather up the threads and show the manner of their return.

Wishful thinking being the persuasive thing it is, many had believed that as soon as the "cease-fire" went, release and repatriation would almost immediately follow.

The war was certainly over so far as warlike operations against Japanese and Germans were concerned. But the tumult of reconstruction was to come. We have seen some angles of this in the experiences of the 2nd Battalion in Greece and of the 4th in Yugoslavia. Liberated peoples, grown accustomed to the habit of non-co-operation with enemy governments, needed time to adjust themselves to the change. Restless elements supplied with arms during the war for internal sabotage of enemy projects, now felt the urge to use them against the more law-abiding of their fellow-citizens to seize what power they could while the chance offered. There were peoples that desired their independence from former rulers, and could not wait till some semblance of sanity and order returned to the world.

Then, there were the more prosaic difficulties. Shipping had sustained much damage in the war, and there was too little left to meet all needs at once. Priority had, in common humanity, to be given to the relief and rehabilitation of disorganized and starving countries, and there was little left for many months for the repatriation of troops. So, one way or another, the Battalions of the Regiment overseas drifted back haphazard and at long intervals.

1st Bn. *The 1st Battalion* was at Dabein not far from Rangoon when the "cease-fire" went. For a while, it took over railway guard duties on the Rangoon-Pegu line. There seemed no reason to expect an early move, and the troops settled down to training and games, and to feeling their way back to the half-forgotten routine of peacetime life. However, they were not left there long. Japanese forces were still at large in Siam, and the 7th Indian Division was put under short notice to move east, occupy the country, round up and disarm the Japanese, and assist in the repatriation of the large numbers of prisoners-of-war confined there.

Little things bulk large in the life of a battalion. One of the factors on which success in action had often depended was the Battalion's first-line mules. Faithful service had been given by them throughout the Burma Campaign, particularly in the Manipur battles of 1944 when they had brought food and ammunition to the troops, passing through the enemy's forward positions, often without adequate protection. They had often been worked almost to dropping-point in all kinds of weather, and seldom had adequate rest. Now they were withdrawn, to the genuine grief of their drivers.

The Division was moving to Bangkok by air from Mingaladon, a few miles out of Rangoon. The Battalion moved to Mingaladon, which was the Divisional concentration area, on the 22nd September, but did not immediately move on. A month passed before aircraft were forthcoming, and the pause was a welcome one, as it enabled the troops to smarten themselves up and prepare for their new role. Also, the opportunity was taken to carry out two small ceremonies, with the presentation of Japanese swords captured by the Battalion in action. One of these was presented to Maj.-Gen. Crowther, then commanding the 17th Indian Division, but under whom the Battalion had served so long in the 89th Indian Infantry Brigade. The other was presented to No. 347 Battery of the 136th Field Regiment, R.A., which had given the Sikhs staunch support ever since the fighting round Buthidaung in the Arakan in March, 1944. In its turn, the Battalion received an inscribed shell-case—the last which No. 347 Battery had fired against the Japanese.

Ultimately, the Battalion emplaned at Hmawbi air-field near Rangoon on the 22nd October, landing the same day at Danmaung near Bangkok. From the air-field, it was moved in M.T. to Bangkok city, and billeted on the outskirts in buildings in the Watana College area.

Guards and duties proved very heavy in Bangkok, and training was virtually excluded. One interesting assignment was the demonstration platoon sent down to the 1st Dutch Battalion (all ex-prisoners-of-war) at Chaulburi on the sea-coast 30 miles south-east of Bangkok. Maj. Jones was made responsible for their training for operations in the Netherlands East Indies, and the picked platoon from "B" Company, under Sub. Pritam Singh, which gave the demonstrations, earned a deservedly high reputation.

Another platoon, under Jem. Harnek Singh, was permanently attached to the Military Police to assist with police duties in the city.

Busy as the troops were, there was less scope temporarily for employment for the officers, who were able to see a good deal of the gayer and more amusing side of Bangkok social life. They were housed in comfortable, modern, well-furnished houses, very different from the style of accommodation they had grown accustomed to. Games received a good deal of attention, and though sports grounds

1945-46

were very limited, hockey was taken up with enthusiasm, and many games played with the 4th/15th Punjab Regiment and with the Dutch forces.

November — Early in November, 1945, the large leave-party re-joined, which had left in May. With it was Sub.-Maj. and Hon. Lieut. Budh Singh, O.B.I., I.D.S.M. Shortly after, "A" Company, under Maj. Farrow, left for Son Suk, on the coast about 40 miles south-east of Bangkok. It had a busy time supervising the unloading of sea-going ships in the outer anchorage with cargoes for Bangkok, and escorting the lighters up the shallow Bangkok river to the docks.

About the same time, Lieut.-Col. E. E. Spink, D.S.O., M.C., the commanding officer, left for leave in England. As the only one of its British officers who had been able to fight with the Battalion throughout the war, it is pleasant to read of his presentation, before leaving, with a captured Japanese sword, inscribed "in appreciation", from the officers and men of the Battalion. He was temporarily succeeded in command by Maj. E. R. Jones.

December — Early in December, the Battalion provided a guard of honour at Danmaung aerodrome for Gen. Sir Miles Dempsey, K.C.B., K.B.E., D.S.O., M.C., Commander-in-Chief Allied Land Forces, South-East Asia, and received his congratulations on its turn-out and smartness.

7 Dec. On the 7th December, unexpected orders came in for a move overseas in an operational role to Java. About this time, Lieut.-Col. P. G. Bamford, D.S.O., who had been away for a year on staff duties in the United States and later in Australia and the Pacific, arrived to take over command.

After hurried preparations, the Battalion embarked for Batavia
10 Dec. on the 10th December in the United States transport *Georgetown Victo* in company with the 4th/8th Gurkha Rifles. However, orders were changed just before sailing, and the Battalion was diverted to Malaya
19 Dec. arriving at Port Dickson on the west coast on the 19th.

From Port Dickson, the Battalion moved up by rail and lorry to Bahau, a rubber-planting district in pleasant country 60 miles from the coast and about 200 miles from Singapore. Conditions had been steadily deteriorating in this area, with numerous armed Chinese bands roaming the countryside and creating communal tension between Chinese and Malays. Three companies of the Battalion were distributed among rubber estates within a radius of a few miles from Battalion Headquarters. They occupied estate buildings, and their presence had a steadying effect. No incidents occurred after the troops' arrival and the time passed peacefully.

The Battalion's pipes-and-drums had meantime been re-formed in
Jan., 1946 Nowshera, and put under training. In January, they joined the Battalion and ceremonial parades and guard-mounting were re-instituted. Training

athletics and hockey all played their part, and the time till the end of February passed uneventfully by.

In March, the Battalion left for a coal-mining district, Batu Arang, about 30 miles from Kuala Lumpur, on internal security duty. The stay here was a short one, and at the end of the month, the scene had changed to a tented camp outside Kuala Lumpur, where preparations were put in hand for the Trooping of the Colour and the Centenary Celebrations to be held in May.

The Malaya Command athletic meeting was held on the 26th and 27th April. Fifteen teams on a Brigade level took part. With the Sikhs winning three events and scoring second place in five, the 98th Indian Infantry Brigade won easily over a strong Royal Air Force team.

About this time, the brass band arrived from Nowshera, and by the 1st May, arrangements for the Trooping of the Colour and Centenary Celebrations were complete.

Gen. Messervy, an old friend of the Battalion in his 7th Indian Divisional days, and now Commander-in-Chief in Malaya, gave the Battalion the use of his personal aircraft to bring a limited number of spectators from India. These included Gen. Savory, then Adjutant-General in India, His Highness the Rajah of Faridkot, Maj. Webster and Capt. Pritam Singh who had just recovered from severe wounds, and five pensioners—Honorary Capt. Thakur Singh Sardar Bahadur, O.B.I., Honorary Lieut. Sampuran Singh Sardar Bahadur, O.B.I., Sub. Man Singh, Sub. Bhagat Singh, and Sub. Hardit Singh.

Admiral the Lord Louis Mountbatten, Supreme Allied Commander, honoured the Battalion by agreeing to take the salute.

The parade was held on the grass playing-fields of the Selangor Club in Kuala Lumpur on the 4th May. The parade was witnessed by some 15,000 people including the late Sir Edward Gent, Governor of the Malaya Union, Gen. Stopford, Commander-in-Chief, Allied Land Forces, South-East Asia, His Highness the Rajah of Faridkot, His Highness the Sultan of Selangor together with the ruling Sultans of four other Malay States, Air Vice-Marshal J. D. Breakey, Air Officer Commanding, Malaya, Maj.-Gen. Lovett, commanding the 7th Indian Division, and representatives from all formations and units in Malaya.

The Regimental Colour, still borne on the pike which was shattered by a bullet during the Lucknow battles in 1857, was initially in charge of Hav. Nand Singh, V.C. The two sentries were L.-Naik Dewa Singh, I.D.S.M., and L.-Naik Karam Singh, M.M. The Battalion was marched onto the parade ground by Battalion Hav.-Maj. Sarwan Singh, with the pipes-and-drums playing "Gully Ravine", a march specially composed to commemorate the battle of the 4th June 1915 in Gallipoli.

Admiral Mountbatten inspected the Battalion and then gave a stirring address. The Regimental Colour, borne by Jem. Bhag Singh, M.C.,

1946

March

26-27 Apr.

1 May

4 May

1946

was then trooped in traditional manner. History was, in one sense, made by this Trooping—being the first time a Colour had been Trooped by any Regiment since the beginning of the war, and it was the first time the "guards" had paraded in three ranks. Though it had been possible to fit out only the band and drums with the ceremonial red safas and white gaiters, the Battalion looked both smart and workmanlike in olive green uniforms, with yellow pags and large chakkars, and made an admirable background to the splash of colour provided by the pipes-and-drums and the Regimental brass band.

Later, Admiral Mountbatten, sending a signed portrait for the officers' mess, wrote in the warmest terms of the Battalion's turn-out and drill. Meanwhile, the parade itself finished with a "Jo Bole So Nihal, Sat Siri Akal" for the King-Emperor and Admiral Mountbatten.

5 May Next day, the 5th May, a centenary commemoration service was held in the Gurdwara. On the 8th, there was another ceremonial
8 May parade, when Japanese swords captured in action were presented to Lieut.-Gen. Savory, His Highness the Rajah of Faridkot, Sub.-Maj. Budh Singh, and Hav. Nand Singh, V.C.

8 June A month later, on the 8th June, the Colours, pipes-and-drums and seventy men, including Hav. Nand Singh, V.C., and seventeen others with gallantry decorations, marched in under Maj. Harwant Singh for the big Victory Parade in Kuala Lumpur. The Battalion's were the only Colours carried, and this was the first time two Colours had been taken on parade together since the beginning of the war. A large and representative parade was held, including men of all units in the area, and contingents from the Royal Navy, the Royal Air Force, and the Malaya Military Police.

After this, a temporary move to Bentong in the centre of Malaya was followed by a transfer to Kota Bharu on the east coast, near the Siamese border. Kota Bharu is no name to conjure with—being as it was, for so many thousands of brave men, the starting-point on the long, painful journey to Singapore at the end of 1941. Now, however, the prospects were changed, and the Battalion spent four pleasant months here, in the capital of Kelantan, with training and games and a deal of ceremonial to pass the time. Numerous guards of honour had to be found, and the men earned a high reputation for their drill, bearing, turn-out and discipline.

September In September, "B" Company was sent to Bangkok on a two-months tour, guarding Japanese war criminals. In October, the Battalion
October left Kota Bharu for the west coast of Malaya in preparation for the return to India.

Meanwhile, throughout their stay in Malaya, the pipes-and-drums had been kept very busy. They beat Retreat at one time or another in almost all the larger towns, and earned high praise for their playing and drill. All-in-all, it was with regret that Malaya saw the Battalion go. Gen. Lovett, commanding the 7th Indian Division, writing to Lieut.-Col. Bamford, commanding the Battalion, told him that the "battalion was and is quite outstanding in the division, and I told the Chief so the other day when I saw him."

The sands were running out On the 12th November, the Battalion sailed for India from Port Swettenham in the Dutch Transport *Boisevain*, arriving in Bombay on the 19th. The 2nd Royal Battalion was then in Santa Cruz, a few miles north of Bombay, and gave it a great welcome at the docks. Entraining for Delhi, the Battalion was assigned an internal security role, but large parties of the men were able to get away on well-earned leave.

Thus ends the record of the Ferozepur Regiment's service in the Second World War. True to the traditions of its hundred years of loyalty and devotion, it is safe to say that the Battalion's name and good repute never stood higher than now. The cost had been heavy: 195 of all ranks had lost their lives, and 665 had been wounded. But the memory of duty done will live on.

The 2nd Battalion, still in Greece when the "cease-fire" went, had been earning a great reputation for the bearing, smartness and discipline of its men—both in general, and in particular during the two months when two of its companies were providing ceremonial guards in Athens.

Time soon passed away in the pleasant land of Greece, and in due course, the Battalion embarked for India at the end of January, 1946. It was nearly five years since the Battalion had sailed away from Karachi to Iraq. Since then, it had travelled far, and seen much—Iraq, Syria, Persia, Palestine, North Africa, Cyprus, Italy and Greece. Now the troops were glad India was to be added to the list.

On the 8th February, the Battalion came ashore at Karachi, to an impressive welcome home. Moving north by rail, the journey was something in the nature of a "progress". At Hyderabad, Sind, the civil authorities and the Women's Voluntary Service provided a feast for the men which roused their lively appreciation. At Lahore, Maj.-Gen. A. B. Blaxland, commanding the District. Brig. Holworthy, who had previously commanded the 4th Indian Division, and Brig. A. E. Farwell, who had held command of the Battalion, all came to meet them.

On the 11th February, the Battalion detrained in Nowshera. The troops settled down in the Garrison Company lines. A "bara khana" was provided for all ranks by the Regimental Centre that evening, and the troops felt they were really home at last.

Till the end of April, when the men came back from leave, life was something in the nature of a continuous Regimental reunion, for the

1946

12 Nov.

19 Nov.

2nd Bn.

Jan., 1946

8 Feb.

11 Feb.

April

1945-46

               3rd Battalion was in Risalpur, the 4th in Campbellpur, and the Machine-Gun Battalion passed through during this period to Peshawar.

23 June   However, all good things have their endings. On the 23rd June, the Battalion advance party left Nowshera for Santa Cruz, just

2 July   north of Bombay, and on the 2nd July, the Battalion followed. Once again the journey was a "progress", with the train losing time all the way under stress of the crowds of well-wishers that thronged the stations at every stop through the Punjab. At Campbellpur, the 4th Battalion laid on a splendid party. At Rawal Pindi Maj.-Gen. B. W. Key, D.S.O., M.C., commanding the Rawal Pindi Area, and who had commanded the Battalion between 1936 and 1939, met the train and went down it, talking to the men. At Bhatinda, Brig. Jaswant Singh, representing His Highness the Maharajah of Patiala, who was away from the State and could not attend, did the honours with a sumptuous "khana" for the men, and dinner for the British and Viceroy's commissioned officers. This was the more appreciated as Brig. Jaswant Singh and his staff had come a long way for the purpose. Finally, on

6 July   the night of the 6th July, back in the 7th Infantry Brigade of the 4th Indian Division, the Battalion detrained in Santa Cruz, thankful for a fine spell in the early monsoon.

               And here, in Santa Cruz, we must take our leave of this grand battalion and leave them to deal jointly with the Bombay disturbances, and the preparations for the Centenary Celebrations, successfully carried out with a Troop, and a presentation of medals by the Commander-in-Chief, Gen. Sir Claude Auchinleck, and a spate of

14-19 Dec.   associated revellings between the 14th and 19th December, 1946. May the fine old Regiment of Ludhiana long flourish.

3rd Bn.   *The 3rd Battalion* had returned to India before the war ended, and settled down in Risalpur. It was not, however, to be supposed that with hostilities still in full swing with Japan, the Battalion was intended for a long spell of ordinary cantonment life. After the men had come back from leave, news came in that it was cast for the role of Reconnaissance Battalion in the 8th Indian Division—with a presumptive role in Burma or beyond.

               Before anything could come of this, however, the Japanese accepted the demand for unconditional surrender, and the Battalion was almost immediately warned for service in Waziristan.

Sept., 1945   September saw them on their way, after a wonderful send-off by the Regimental Centre, en route to Mir Ali, taking a short cut to by-pass Peshawar, and thence via Kohat, Bannu and Saidgi. But it was a tour of a few months only. Restless to the end, they were back in

Apr., 1946   Nowshera in April 1946, and thence finally to Thal, Kurram, in October, where we must take leave of them.

If the enemy saw nothing of the 3rd Battalion on the fighting fronts, that was the enemy's gain. That it maintained its high traditions under trying and thankless conditions over so many long years, merits the highest praise. The war must have brought many disappointments to it, but it never failed to give its best. Long may the name of Rattray's Sikhs be heard in the Indian Army.

The 4th Battalion was at Merna near Trieste when the war ended in August 1945. As was to be expected, rumours of an early return to India soon began to circulate, and in fact at the end of September, the Battalion moved back to Pavia. This pleasant town just south of Milan was comparatively free from war damage, and the Battalion found excellent quarters in barracks, with space available for playing-fields. Shooting and fishing whiled away the time for some. For others, Milan had many attractions to offer. The Italian population in Pavia could not have shown more kindness and hospitality. The troops were well catered for in games, Baluchi rugger being the most popular. Preparations for the winter were put in hand, but in October, orders came in indicating that the Division was for India.

Plans were made to hold a leave-taking Divisional Parade in Milan, but were cancelled owing to rain. There were other entertainments, however, including a most successful farewell lunch for all the officers of the Division. Formal farewell was taken of the British units of the Division by the Divisional commander at this lunch, as none were coming back east with the Division to India. The Battalion lost many good friends in the King's Own, in the 25th Indian Infantry Brigade, and the 97th Field Regiment, R.A. In all theatres of the war, the infantry had shown high appreciation of the services of their affiliated gunners, and the 4th Battalion felt the loss of such excellent friends as Col. Mullins, commanding the Field Regiment, and Maj. Buckmaster, whose battery had given the Battalion valued support in many difficult corners.

On the 9th November, 1945, the Battalion entrained at Pavia in a collection of covered goods wagons, and set off for Taranto. The wagons were not uncomfortable, and the men took pleasure in noting the various landmarks where they had fought, and the progress being made in bringing the countryside back to normal. The villages were still in ruins, but roads and bridges were being quickly restored.

The Taranto Transit Camps were notoriously squalid areas, and heavy rain did little to cheer people up while waiting for a boat. However, with packing up, games and general preparations, the time passed quickly enough. On the 23rd November, the Battalion embarked

1945-46

by lighter on H.M.T. *Ormonde*, together with Divisional Headquarters, all Brigade Headquarters, and the 4th/10th Baluchis. A few details were left behind—a small number of sick in hospital and the driver of the one jeep which the Battalion was to be allowed to bring
24 Nov. home to India. Otherwise, the Battalion saw the last of Italy on the 24th.

"Most of us", the Battalion record states, "were sorry to leave a pleasant country (except in winter) and we had received many kindnesses from Italians of all classes. Many of the men learnt to speak Italian and all certainly found much of interest in the farms and cattle of the country districts. Florence, Rome, Venice, Austria were among the places visited, and the post-war period in Italy is one which we all enjoyed. Naturally the men were delighted at the idea of seeing home again, and our voyage in H.M.T. *Ormonde* was a very pleasant one, in good weather with no rough seas. The Battalion received an 'unsolicited testimonial' from the ship's captain for their behaviour and for the way they kept the troop decks."

"After a quick voyage", the account goes on, "we landed at
5 Dec. Karachi on the 5th December, and after a civic welcome and an address by His Excellency, the Governor of Sind, the bulk of the Battalion left by train for Nowshera the same evening. We had a pleasant journey with the troops in great form, and reached Nowshera on the
8 Dec. 8th December. Here, all was ready for us, and the Training Centre did all they could to help us and entertain us, while we sorted out things and got the men away on leave."

"The men went off in batches of 200, all in great heart, leaving a few officers and a small depot here. We, the depot, have been sorting things out and gradually getting ourselves organized for service in India. The Battalion will reform at Nowshera, and then
Mar., 1946 in March, we move to Campbellpur, together with the 3rd/1st Punjabis, and 3rd/18th Royal Garhwal Rifles of the 25th Indian Infantry Brigade. We are glad to be staying as members of the 10th Indian Division."

Campbellpur proved to be no bed-of-roses. The troops were fitted into a hutted camp, which had been unoccupied for a very long time. All water had to be pumped from the Haro river, and the pumps available when the troops first arrived were so old and worn out that they could not supply enough water for drinking, cooking and washing. Some old disused wells were looked over, but proved to have been so silted up with drifting sand as not to be worth opening up. Later, however, new pumps arrived and more taps were put in, and sanction was belatedly received for the Battalion to construct married quarters for itself on a no-expense basis.

So, bit by bit, the 36th settled down to peacetime soldiering under the somewhat rigorous conditions of post-war life. Here, then, we must bid them good-bye and God-speed.

1945-46

As already indicated earlier on, it had been decided not to re-raise the *5th Battalion* after its capture in Malaya. This decision, to the general regret, was confirmed after the war, so that this, the youngest of the Regiment's pre-war battalions, which had earned an unrivalled name for itself in the First World War, and maintained the highest level of soldierly efficiency in all its subsequent transactions, disappeared finally from the rolls of the Regiment.

5th Bn.

The 6th Battalion moved up from Gardai to Razmak on the 10th September, 1945, and settled in to Megiddo Lines, occupied in former years by the 3rd and 5th Battalions. Within the first week of its arrival it had taken the first and second prizes for the best saddled pair of mules in Waziristan District, and was presented with the same challenge cup which the 5th Battalion had won in 1939.

6th Bn.
10 Sept.

In a sense it was appropriate that the Battalion should be in Razmak, which was so soon to cease to be a military station, for it was the 6th Battalion's last station, too. Disbandment orders came through in July 1946. Leaving Razmak in M.T. on the 31st July, with halts at Bannu and Kohat, the Battalion arrived in Nowshera on the 2nd August. Two "bara khanas" were held to celebrate the Battalion's sixth anniversary, and a small sports meeting was held. Then, on the 5th August, 1946, the disbandment parade was held in West Wilcox Lines. Maj.-Gen. B. W. Key, D.S.O., M.C., the Colonel of the Sikh Regiment, took the salute, and presented the Military Cross to Capt. Ujagar Singh.

July, 1946

2 Aug.

5 Aug.

So ends the chronicle of a faithful battalion which saw little of the warmth of battle, but bore the long years of steady, dull routine with cheerfulness and good courage.

The 7th Battalion remained at Ar Rama, east of Acre till September, 1945, when it moved over to Camp 253A, on the Haifa-Beirut road some 3 miles north of Acre. Over and above its demonstration duties in the Mid-East School of Infantry, the Battalion temporarily filled an internal security role. Lieut.-Col. J. G. B. Walker, commanding the Battalion, was appointed to command the North Sector, Palestine, when he arrived back from sixty-one days leave in the United Kingdom on the 16th November, in connection with the Palestine Disturbances at the end of 1945.

7th Bn.

Sept., 1945

16 Nov.

During these months in Acre, the Battalion went well ahead in sport, winning by a large margin the Area Sports Meeting in Haifa in September. Then, in November, it entered a team of seven men for "The Mile of the Middle-East" in the 31st Indian Armoured Division's annual sports at Beirut, and secured 1st, 2nd and 4th places.

Its Punjabi-Mohammedan personnel, meanwhile, made good use of their opportunities, spending Mohurrum in Jerusalem—where most of the British officers also went to visit the Holy Sepulchre—and Maulvi Khan Mohd made the pilgrimage to Mecca.

Dec., 1945
22-27 Dec.

In December, 1945, the Battalion handed over at the School to the 1st Duke of Cornwall's Light Infantry, and between the 22nd and 27th December moved to Damascus for Internal Security duty. A rather grim Christmas was spent in a very temporary wayside camp in Palestine. Duties in Damascus were taken over from the 2nd Kashmir Battalion. Maj. J. D. M. Watson, with "B" Company, was detached to Palmyra, about 150 miles from Damascus, and Maj. N. Egan took H.Q. Company to Qatana, 20 miles from Damascus. A platoon detachment was located in the Bekaa Valley in Lebanon, 70 miles away. The remainder stayed in Damascus.

In Damascus, the Battalion was largely responsible for the provision of escorts for French personnel and goods under evacuation from Syria. Guards were found over a number of French buildings. A mobile column was organized to cope with possible clashes between French and Syrian nationals. Life, hence, was fairly strenuous. Guard duty took up most of the men's time, and very little training was possible. Off duty, the Punjabi-Mohammedans were able to visit the many Ziarats in the vicinity. Living conditions were not very satisfactory, however, and at the end of a few weeks permission was obtained to station two rifle companies in Qatana, where the conditions on the whole were much better.

To relieve the monotony of never-ending guards, patrols were sent out two or three times a month, and covered a good deal of interesting country, including Soueida in the Jebel Druse, Homs and Hama on the Orontes, and Baalbek in the Bekaa Valley. They were always well received by the local inhabitants, who invariably insisted on providing entertainment of some sort in the way of food or drink.

In Palmyra, life was quite different. Though the amenities could not compare with Damascus, the troops found the place to their liking. Duties were reasonably light, and a fair amount of training was done. Patrols kept constant touch with the movements of the Bedouin tribes, and many friends were made among the sheikhs who came in to visit the Company in Palmyra, and take tea or coffee there. In February, 1946, Maj. Gurdev Singh, with "D" Company, relieved "B" and had the added pleasure of excellent shooting when the weather warmed up a little, as quantities of game moved into the area.

Feb., 1946

Athletics as usual absorbed much of what spare time could be found. Shortly after arrival in Syria, a much-advertised long-distance relay race was held over the 54 miles between Tripoli and Beirut. Teams were to consist of fifteen runners, and forty men of the Battalion went into training under Maj. N. Egan with a view to providing two teams.

1946

Ultimately, thirty-four teams entered from units all over the Middle East.

The race was magnificently organized. It was started by the British Broadcasting Corporation in London, and broadcasts were made at regular intervals during the day. The results were all the Regiment could have wished. The Battalion's "A" team came in first, the "B" team second—and both teams beat the existing record.

Over and above this notable success, the Battalion ran away with both the other sporting events held during its short stay in Palestine—the triangular sports meeting at Beirut, and the Palestine cross-country championships.

In March, 1946, orders were received for the withdrawal of British and French troops from Syria. The withdrawal was to be carried out by stages. First to go was the Palmyra detachment. Thereafter, the Battalion gradually concentrated in Mezze, on the outskirts of Damascus, and in Qatana.   March

On the 23rd March, Lieut.-Col. J. G. B. Walker handed over temporary command to Maj. E. C. W. Fowler. There was still some time before the Battalion was due to leave Damascus, and to celebrate this final departure of our troops, a special party was held. The Prime Minister and all heads of Syrian Government Departments were invited in addition to the Battalion's personal British friends. The occasion went off extremely well, and was felt to have done its share towards cementing the existing good-fellowship with the Syrians.   23 Mar.

On the 13th April, 1946, the Battalion marched out, reaching Baghdad by road on the 18th. The journey was uneventful, but good bags of sand-grouse helped out the rations. In Baghdad, trains were ready waiting, and the Battalion arrived in Shaiba Transit Camp next day. Here, the troops remained till the 8th May, pending vacation of their allotted barracks in Maqil.   13 Apr.
18 Apr.
19 Apr.
8 May

Under command of British Troops, Iraq, the Battalion became part of the permanent garrison. Guards and escorts made heavy demands, and few men were left for training. For two months, however, in the summer, the Battalion was struck off all duties for range and field-firing classification.

Conditions may have seemed trying. No one who knows Lower Iraq in the summer can have any illusions about that. Nights in bed may have been few. But the men maintained their high level both at work and games. In April, 1946, Sub. Hazara Singh won the Open Pistol Competition at the Mid-East Rifle Meeting, and the Battalion's grand record for athletics never faltered. Between June 1945 and January 1947, it won every athletic contest it was able to enter.

At the end of 1946, we find the Battalion strength given as 16 British officers, 22 Viceroy's commissioned officers and 751 other ranks.

457

1945-47

Mar., 1947   In March, 1947, the Commander British Troops, Iraq, awarded Sub. Sher Khan and No. 25756 L.-Naik Feroze Khan his Commendation for good work done during a raid on the Ordnance Depot.

    In late summer, orders at last arrived for the Battalion's homecoming and all preparations were made for embarkation at Busra on the

17 Sept. 22nd September. On the 17th, however, orders were received to split the Battalion before leaving Iraq to conform with the re-deployment of the old Indian Army, consequent on the partition between India and Pakistan.

    This meant the parting of many good friends, but the work was put through faithfully and with good feeling. The two Punjabi-Mohammedan

22 Sept. Companies embarked on the 22nd, to join the 3rd/13th Frontier Force
7 Oct. Rifles in Lahore. The Sikhs took ship on the 7th October for Bombay, moving thence to Deolali. Here, they were brought up to strength as an all-Sikh battalion with one company each from the 3rd/15th and 4th/15th Punjab Regiment. The fusion was expected to be complete

20 Oct. by about the 20th October, 1947, and here, with all its personnel returned to their native country, we take our leave of this fine battalion which had done so much during its seven years of service to uphold the name and traditions of the Regiment.

MG Bn.   *The Machine-Gun Battalion*, in July 1945, had taken over the
20 Aug. Zeyawadi area, south of Toungoo in Burma. On the 20th August, "D" Company had been sent to Shwegyin, 58 miles or a little more south of Toungoo. Though sent out on an operational role, it arrived in Shwegyin in time to take over the first surrendered personnel of the Japanese forces.

20 Sept. On the 20th September, the Battalion found itself together in Toungoo. The troops were quartered under canvas and in the remains of the old market buildings. This was a notable moment, being the first time the entire Battalion had been together since leaving Imphal at the start of the campaign.

    As elsewhere, sports meetings were started in Toungoo, and the Battalion walked away with the Divisional Dusehra Sports Meeting.

Oct., 1945   In October, 1945, Lieut.-Gen. Sir Montagu Stopford, K.B.E., C.B., D.S.O., M.C., commanding the Twelfth Army, visited the Battalion, walked round the parade, and saw "D" Company at drill.

Dec., 1945   Between the 6th and 10th December, a big Divisional tattoo was held in Toungoo fort. For this, the Battalion provided a drill display by a party of eighty men under Capt. A. F. Ellison, the adjutant. Pre-war drill movements were worked to, unfamiliar as they were, and the display, from many points of view proved the highlight of the tattoo. Capt. Ellison was admirably backed up by Sub. Abdul Ilahi and Sub. Indar Singh, I.D.S.M., and the only anxious moment

1945-46

in the display occurred when an enthusiastic young Punjabi-Mohammedan slapped the small of the butt of his rifle so hard in the second movement of the slope, that he broke it. But this went undetected by the spectators.

Another display in which the Battalion had a less direct part was the combined gymnastic team formed from Divisional personnel. Jem. Assa Singh of the Machine-Gun Battalion was put in charge of this entry, and produced a most polished display from men who had scarcely so much as seen a "horse" for four or five years. Altogether, the Battalion came very well out of a tattoo which was remarkable amongst other things, for the number of races taking part. To name only a few, there were Sikhs, Punjabi-Mohammedans, Pathans—and most other Indian classes— Lushais, Nagas, Karens, Burmese, East and Central Africans, all in addition to Welsh and English.

Christmas Eve was enlivened by a mess party for fifty children from the local convent school. Lieut Collins came over with the Pipe Band of the 1st Battalion, and, disguised in scarlet safa cloth and a cotton wool beard, rounded off a party where, as the record puts it "a most impressive and satisfactory quantity of food was eaten by the children".   24 Dec., 1945

Over the New Year, the Battalion moved up to Kalaw, the lovely, pine-clad hill station in the Southern Shan States, eastwards from Meiktila. With vistas of green hills and deep valleys full of almond blossom, the troops settled down in cheerful contemplation of the big vocational training scheme planned to include all forms of farming and a number of crafts, in Kalaw. Unfortunately, the Battalion was not left long in Kalaw to profit by it. On the 4th February, Maj. Bagshawe took the advance party down to Toungoo again, and on the 10th, the Battalion handed over its camp and area to the Royal Berkshire Regiment, and followed him.   Jan., 1946   4 Feb.   10 Feb.

Toungoo, this time, proved the complete antithesis of Kalaw. The Battalion was allotted as camping area a waterless, shadeless, dusty expanse, formerly the emergency landing-ground, and later the Tattoo staging area. Here, a long list of guards and duties fell to the men. One of these held the elements of interest, however. This was the guard of two non-commissioned officers and eight men detailed for the daily train between Toungoo and Rangoon.

This train was composed on an average of seventy covered wagons and flats. In length it was not far short of half-a-mile. It stopped everywhere. Between stations, when it did not actually stop it frequently slowed down to a crawl. Hence, it was a god-send to civilian train-jumpers who had been all too long without the means of getting about. Keeping these gentry off the train was a big enough problem as it was, quite apart from checking the pilfering which had become a feature of railway traffic.

1946

As regards the pilfering, automatic weapons were barred, which placed the escort at a disadvantage in the case of armed dacoities. In dealing with train-jumpers, persuasion only could be used to induce the offenders to leave the train. What construction was placed on "persuasion" by train escorts is not on record, but the use of fire-arms was rightly banned. Still, the journeys to and from Rangoon must have been a trying experience for the escorts.

17 Feb. On the 17th February, 1946, the Regimental brass band arrived on tour through Burma. Accompanying it came Capt. P. R. Wills, and Sub. Gurdial Singh of the 4th Battalion, lately returned from a prisoner-of-war camp in Germany, in addition to Jem. Ajaib Singh, the bandmaster. Their playing gave much pleasure, and it was with regret that they were seen off on their way to Meiktila, Kalaw and Taunggyi—accompanied by Maj. K. H. Whately.

Meanwhile, a good hockey ground had been made, and a tennis court as well. India was in the offing, and morale was very high.

With April, 1946, the Battalion found itself saying good-bye to the 19th Indian Division, and setting sail from Rangoon. Early in

May, May, 1946, after a brief stay at Alipur Rest Camp in Calcutta, the Battalion entrained for Nowshera. In common with trains generally in India at that time, the journey north was well behind schedule. Gen. Key was down on Rawal Pindi station both on the night the Battalion was due, and again early next morning. But the train was 14½ hours late, and the men were sorry to miss him. Arrived in Nowshera, the Battalion was met with the disappointing news that it would be disbanded on or before the 1st April, 1947. The machine-guns were put away, the Light Aid Detachment which had served the Battalion so well under its old friend, Conductor F. C. D. Tinkhan joined the 3rd Armoured Brigade in Risalpur, and station duties were taken over from four disbanding garrison companies.

10 Nov. One pleasant ceremony, however, remained. On the 10th November, 1946, Maj.-Gen. Key attended a ceremonial parade of the Battalion in Nowshera on the polo ground, the scene of so many impressive ceremonies over the years since the Regiment had taken root in Nowshera. Many distinguished visitors and old friends came to see the parade, at which Gen. Key, after taking the General Salute and inspecting the Battalion, presented decorations and captured Japanese swords. In its olive-green uniforms, the Battalion looked smart and workmanlike, and its drill was up to the best standards of the Regime After the march-past, a happy reunion took place at the excellent luncheon party that followed.

Though one must view with regret the passing of this fine battalion, traditions must survive. Its record of gallantry and devotion is of the highest, and the story of its deeds will stir the heart of many a young soldier in the years to come.

The 26th Battalion saw the war out in Poona. Victory celebrations were held at a searchlight tattoo, for which the Battalion provided one company for what proved to be a first-rate exhibition of arms drill, for which the Area Commander gave high praise. In the Victory Parade march-past, the full Battalion paraded in the Indian Infantry section, and again gave a good account of itself.

1946
26th Bn.

In April 1946, the Battalion packed up ready to leave for the Regimental Centre for disbandment. It was finally disbanded there on the 16th May, 1946.

Apr., 1946

16 May

In its four years service, this battalion, manned by troops who for one reason or another could not be sent to operational duty, had shouldered heavy responsibilities in India, and had freed younger and more active troops for the fighting fronts. With quiet competence and willing cheerfulness, it had foregone the rewards reaped by the men overseas. To the end, it was known for dependability and smartness everywhere it served.

CONCLUSION

The time has come to ring down the curtain on the record of this brief passage in the Regiment's life. Domestic details have jostled in these pages with events of world importance. Gaps in some parts of the narrative have rung the changes with perhaps excessive abundance elsewhere, and it may be found that the tale told does not in all cases square with the official histories yet to come.

However this may be, the record shows in some sort the sepoy's daily life in a world-wide war of the pre-atomic age. For though it was undeniably the atom bomb that brought the war to its final conclusion, it played no part in the day-to-day employment of any battalion of the Regiment. It has been the compiler's object, wherever possible, to lend light and colour to the bare bones of impersonal fact, to bring out the cheerful irrelevancies which so often testify to high resolution, to divest the war in some degree of its austerity and bring the warmth of personal relationships into their proper place in a story of great endurance and loyalty.

It has not always been possible to achieve these ideals—whether for lack of suitable openings, or for the plain want of material to draw upon. But it is believed that a reader may find much inspiration in these tales of war against odds, and that some may be tempted to seek out fresh material to gild and enrich this record of simple faith, enduring courage, good-fellowship, and trust.

The following is the list of Honours and Awards granted to officers and men of the Regiment during the war:

Victoria Cross	1
Distinguished Service Order	7
Bar to Distinguished Service Order	1
Military Cross	31
Bar to Military Cross	2
Indian Order of Merit	12
Indian Distinguished Service Medal	36
Military Medal	34
Mentions in Despatches	103
Gallantry Certificates	15
Commendation Cards	14
Macgregor Memorial Medal	1

In addition, one O.B.E. was awarded, and two M.B.E.s.

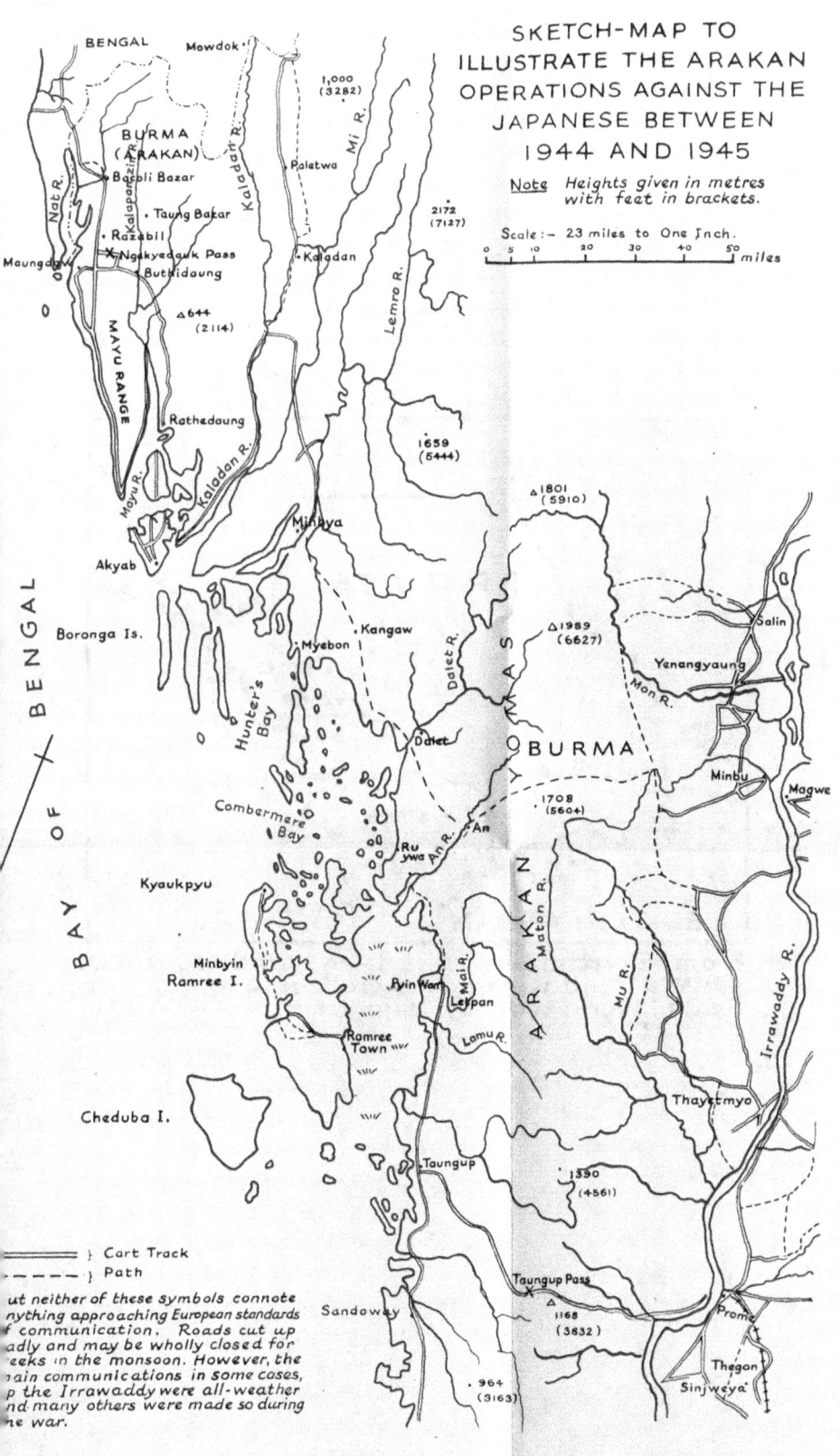

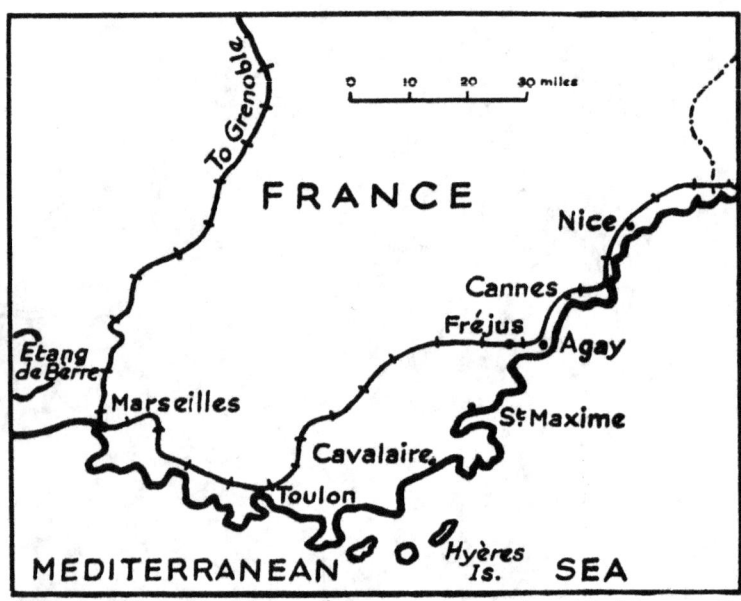

From Sketch Map - "THE INVASION OF SOUTHERN FRANCE" (and with acknowledgements to "The Second World War" by Major General J.F.C. Fuller, page 323.)

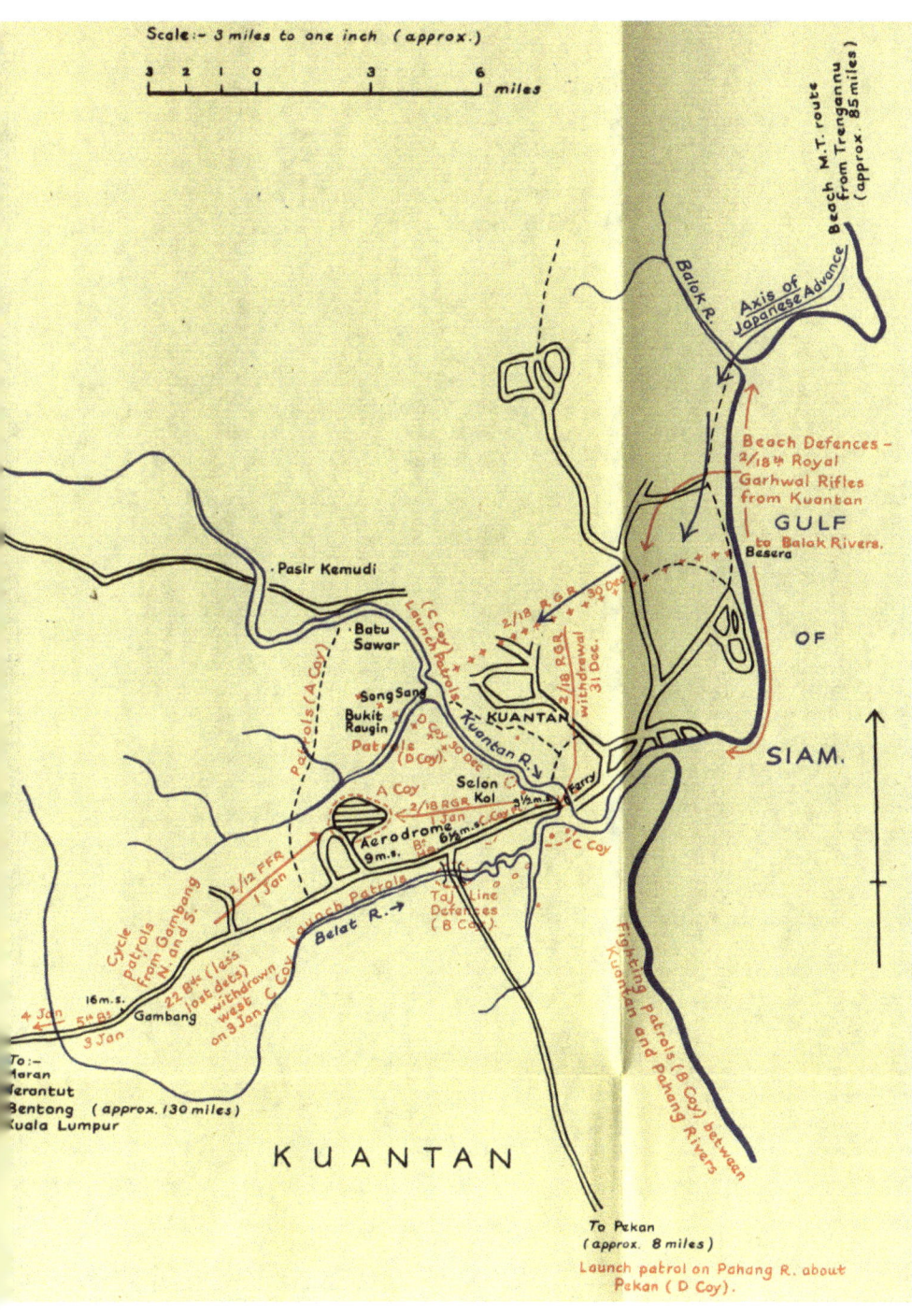

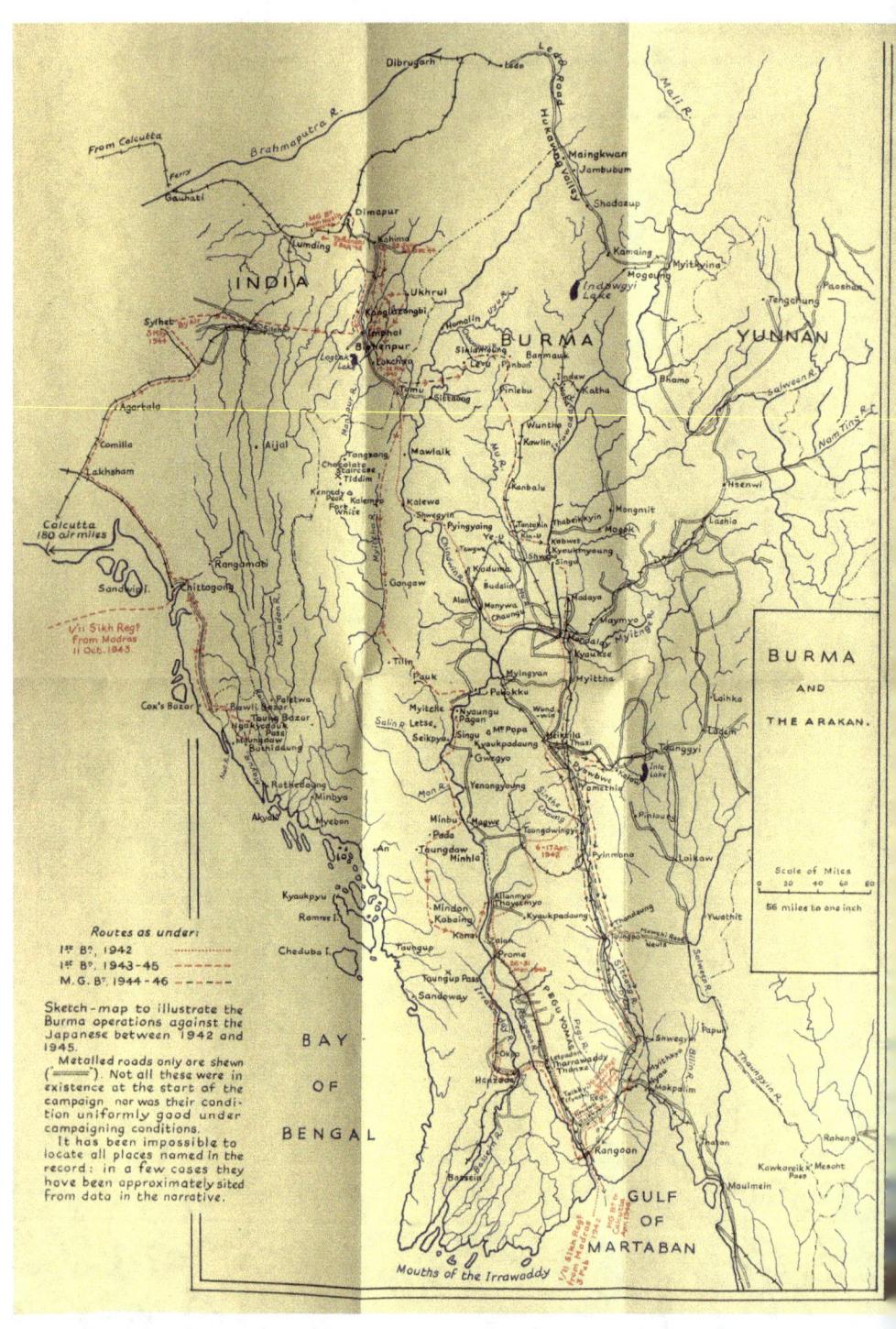

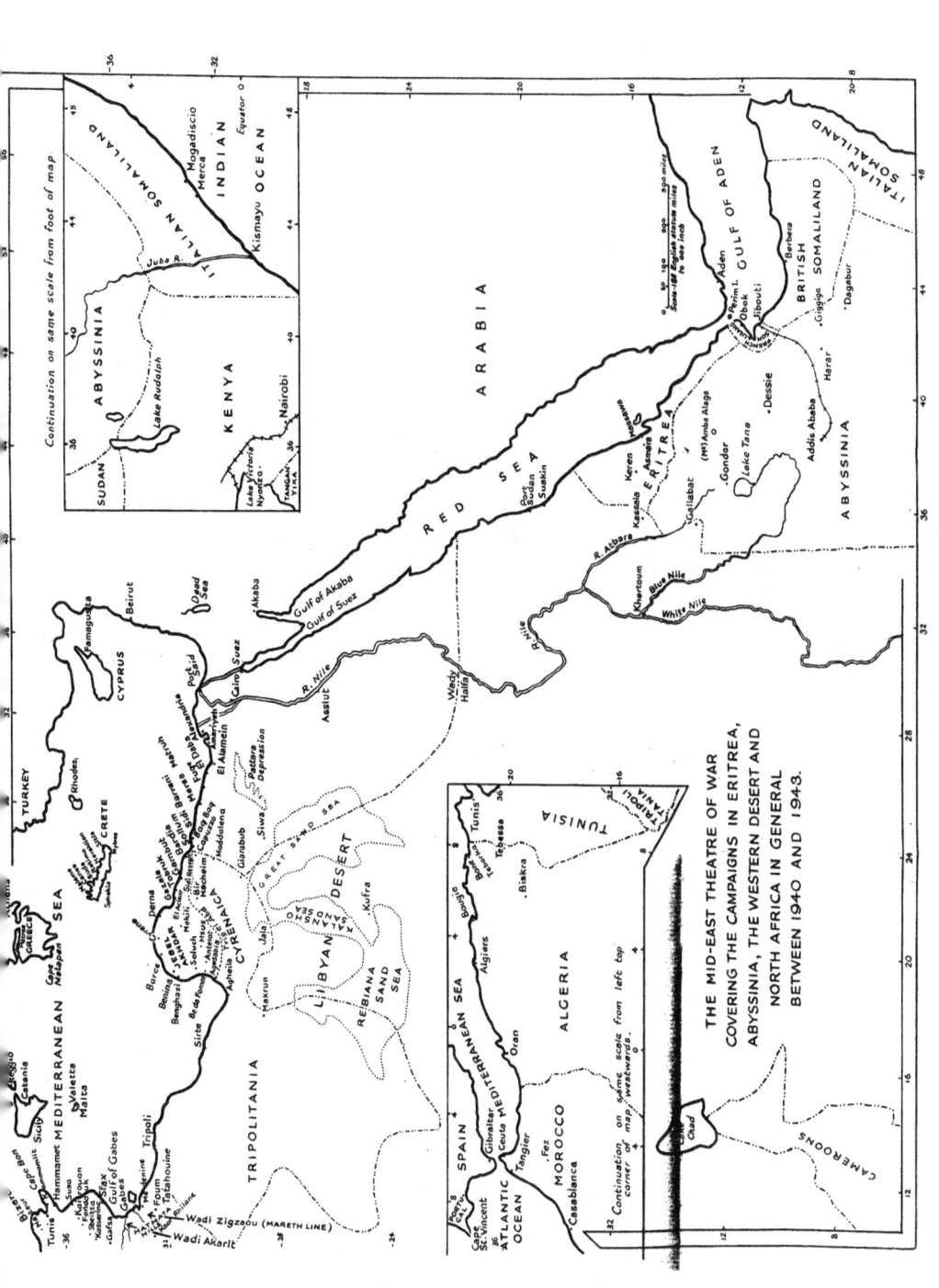

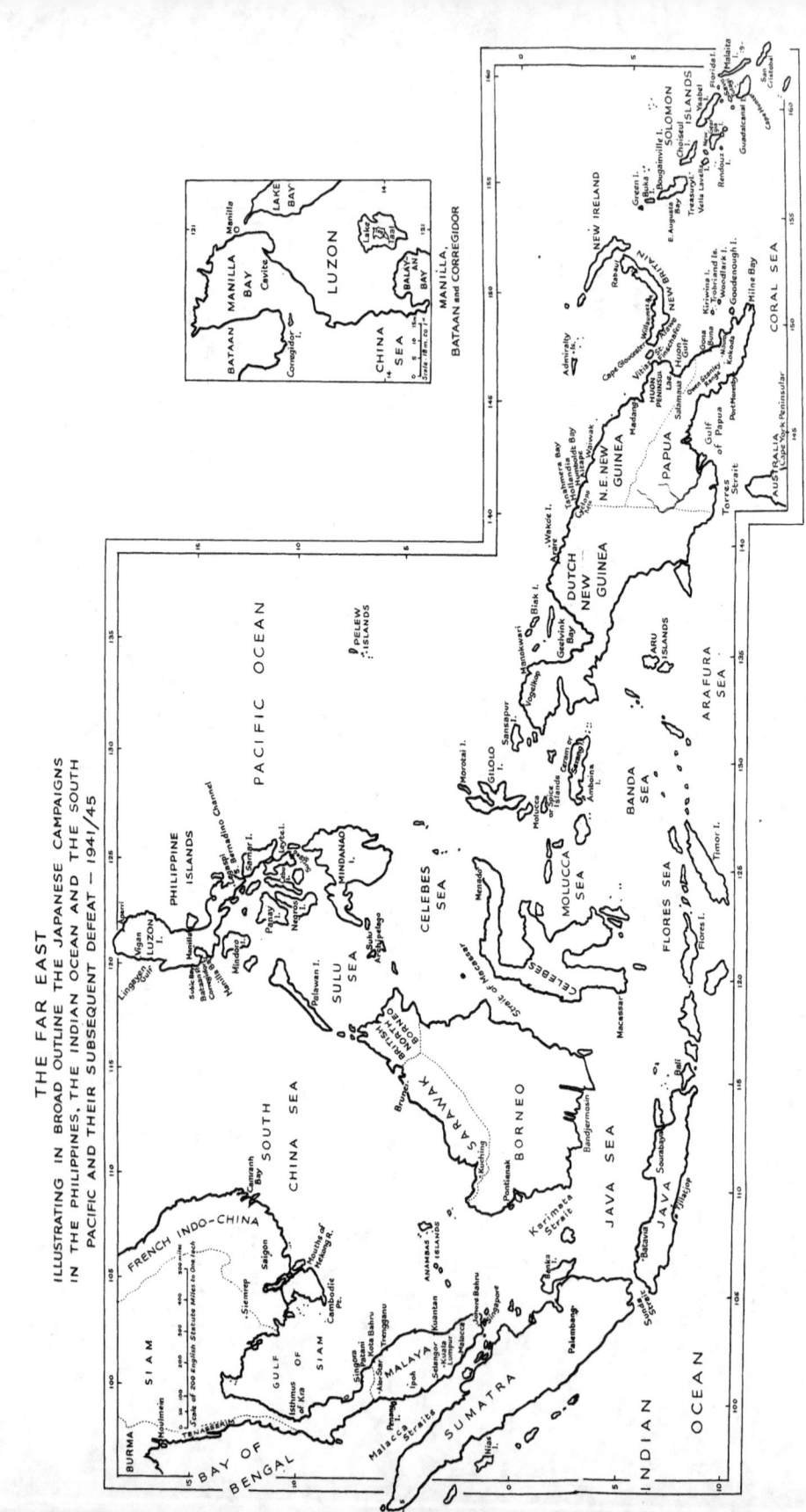

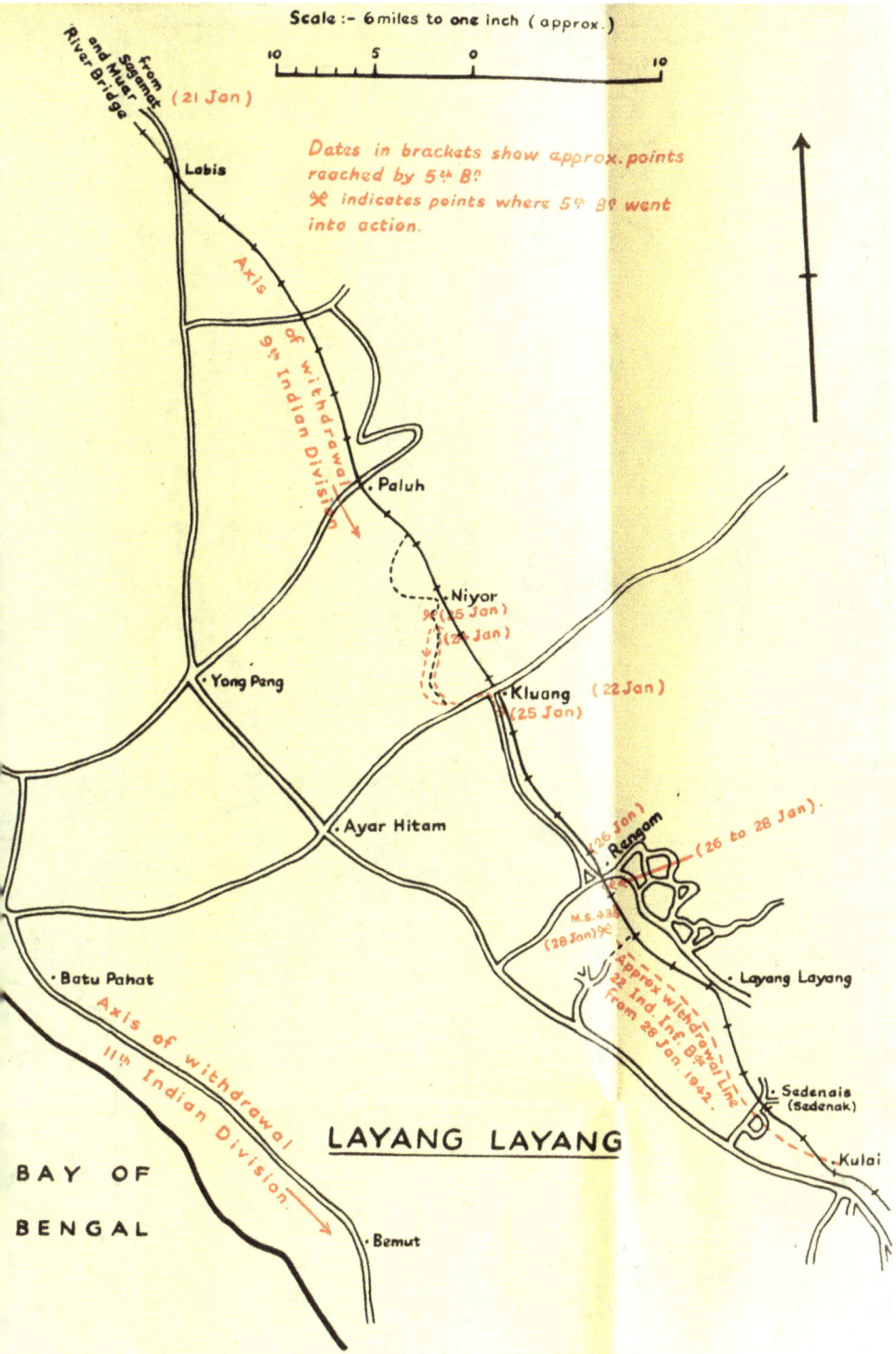

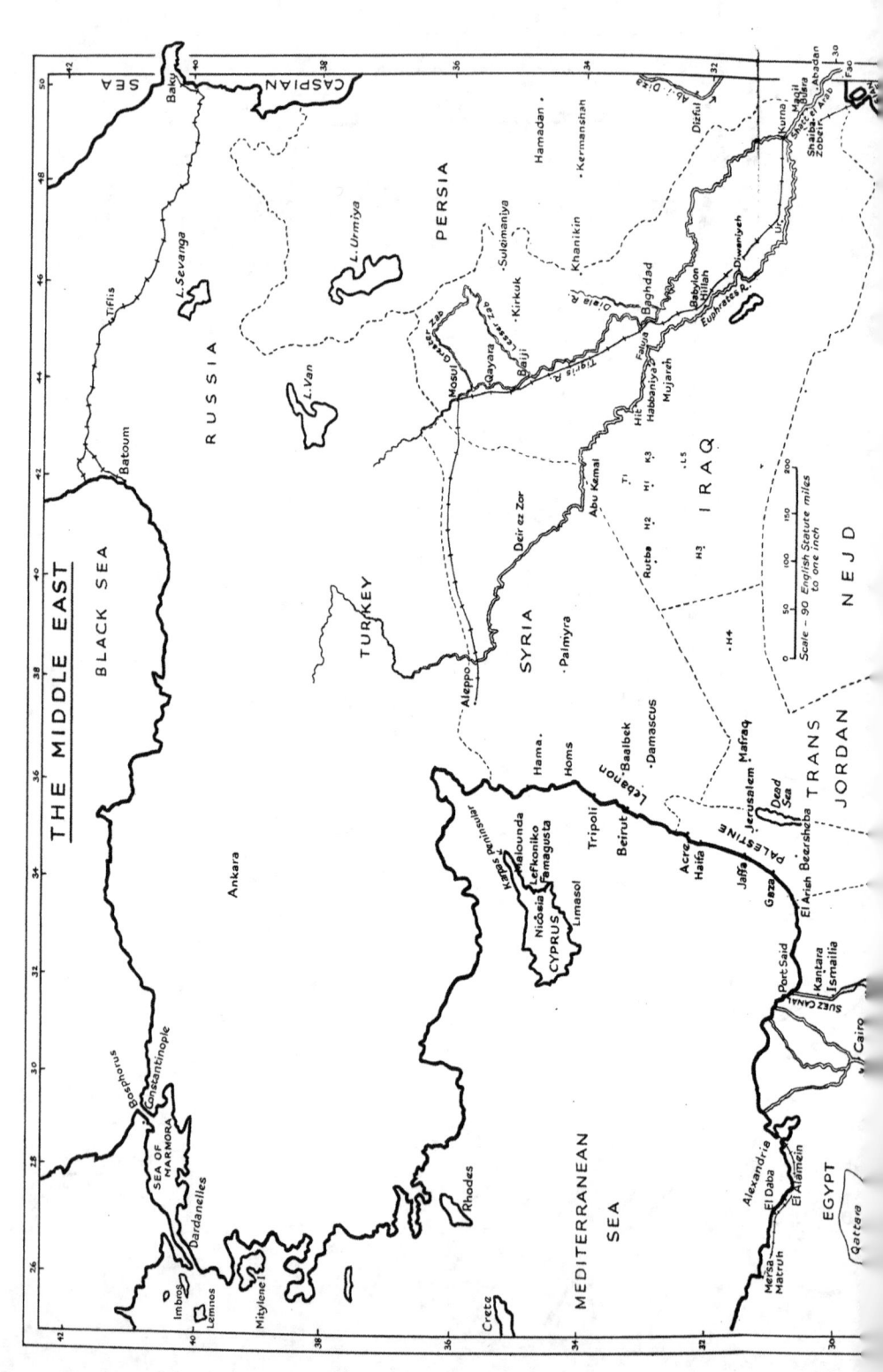

www.ingramcontent.com/pod-product-compliance
Lightning Source LLC
Chambersburg PA
CBHW050300010526
44108CB00040B/1906